YEARBOOK OF AMERICAN & CANADIAN CHURCHES 1996

Sixty-fourth issue Annual

YEARBOOK OF AMERICAN & CANADIAN CHURCHES 1996

Edited by Kenneth B. Bedell

Prepared and edited for the Education, Communication and Discipleship Unit of the National Council of the Churches of Christ in the U.S.A., 475 Riverside Drive, New York, NY 10115-0050

Published and Distributed by Abingdon Press Nashville

Yearbook of American
and Canadian Churches
1996

Joan Brown Campbell
Publisher

Michael A. Maus
Editorial Director

Kenneth B. Bedell
Editor

Mary Jane Griffith
Cam Linton
Production Assistants

Printed in the United States of America

ISBN 0-687-05589-X

ISSN 0195-9034

Library of Congress catalog card number: 16-5726

Preparation of this Yearbook is an annual project of the National Council of Churches of Christ in the United States of America.

This is the sixty-fourth edition of a yearbook that was first published in 1916. Previous editions have been entitled, Federal Council Yearbook (1916-1917), Yearbook of the Churches (1918-1925), The Handbook of the Churches (1927), The New Handbook of the Churches (1928), Yearbook of American Churches (1933-1972), and Yearbook of American and Canadian Churches (1973-present).

CONTENTS

I. Church in the '90s: Trends and Developments

II. Directories

III. Statistical Section

IV. A Calendar of Religious Dates

Indexes

I
THE CHURCH IN THE '90s: TRENDS AND DEVELOPMENTS

A Closer Look at the Numbers

This year 99 denominations in the United States and 49 denominations in Canada reported statistical data to the Yearbook. While the statistics reported here are not a complete census of denominations in the United States and Canada, they represent a summary of membership in denominations which is as complete as possible.

Four generalities can be made about the statistics reported this year.

1. Religious organizations are diverse
2. A few denominations dominate the religious scene
3. The trend of declining mainline denominations continues
4. Financial contributions to denominations continue to increase

Religious organizations are diverse

As Table 1 indicates, Christians dominate the religious scene in the United States, but there are still large numbers of people who identify with other religions.

Table 1 Religions in the United States

Religion	Estimated Adult Pop.	Est. Percentage of Adult Pop.
Christian	151,225,000	86.2
Jewish	3,137,000	1.8 (2.2)*
Muslim/Islamic	527,000	0.3 (0.5)+
Unitarian Universalist	502,000	0.3
Buddhist	401,000	0.2 (0.4)+
Hindu	227,000	0.1 (0.2)+
Native American	47,000	
Scientologist	45,000	
Baha'i	28,000	
Taoist	23,000	
New Age	20,000	
Ekankar	18,000	
Rastafarian	14,000	
Sikh	13,000	
Wiccan	8,000	
Shintoist	6,000	
Deity	6,000	
Other Unclassified	831,000	

* "Core" Jewish population including ethnic-cultural Jews. +Adjusted for possible undercount.

Table 1 from *One Nation Under God: Religion in Contemporary American Society*, by Barry A. Kosmin and Seymour P. Lachman. New York: Harmony Books, 1993. Pages 16-17. Used with persmission.

Religious organizations in the United States and Canada are diverse in their size. They range from small Hutterian Brethren groups where children attend German school after public school to the large Roman Catholic Church with over 60 million members in the United States and more than 12 million members in Canada. Four of the largest ten denominations have predominately African-American membership.

The diversity includes participation in all the major religions of the world.

A few denominations dominate the religious scene

Table 2 shows the thirty-five largest denominations in the United States.

While North Americans have a great deal of choice of religious organizations, the vast majority choose one of the larger groups. For example, in the United States, denominations report a total membership of 158,426,003 people to the Yearbook. Over half of this total is in three denominations: The Roman Catholic Church, the Southern

Table 2 United States Denominational Ranking

Denomination	Inclusive Membership	Percent of total reported	Cumulative percentage
The Roman Catholic Church	60,190,605	37.99	37.99
Southern Baptist Convention	15,614,060	9.86	47.85
The United Methodist Church	8,584,125	5.42	53.27
National Baptist Convention USA, Inc.	8,200,000	5.18	58.44
The Church of God in Christ	5,499,875	3.47	61.91
Evangelical Lutheran Church in America	5,199,048	3.28	65.20
The Church of Jesus Christ of Latter-Day Saints	4,613,000	2.91	68.11
Presbyterian Church (U.S.A.)	3,698,136	2.33	70.44
National Baptist Convention of America Inc.	3,500,000	2.21	72.65
African Methodist Episcopal Church	3,500,000	2.21	74.86
The Lutheran Church- Missouri Synod	2,596,927	1.64	76.50
Episcopal Church	2,504,682	1.58	78.08
National Missionary Baptist Convention of America	2,500,000	1.58	79.66
Progressive National Baptist Convention Inc.	2,500,000	1.58	81.24
Assemblies of God	2,324,615	1.47	82.70
The Orthodox Church in America	2,000,000	1.26	83.97
Greek Orthodox Archdiocese of North & South America	1,950,000	1.23	85.20
Churches of Christ	1,651,103	1.04	86.24
American Baptist Churches in the U.S.A.	1,507,934	0.95	87.19
United Church of Christ	1,501,310	0.95	88.14
Baptist Bible Fellowship International	1,500,000	0.95	89.09
African Methodist Episcopal Zion Church	1,230,842	0.78	89.86
Christian Churches and Churches of Christ	1,070,616	0.68	90.54
Pentecostal Assemblies of the World	1,000,000	0.63	91.17
Jehovah's Witnesses	945,990	0.60	91.77
Christian Church (Disciples of Christ)	937,644	0.59	92.36
Seventh-day Adventist Church	775,349	0.49	92.85
Church of God (Cleveland, Tenn.)	722,541	0.46	93.30
Christian Methodist Episcopal Church	718,922	0.45	93.76
Church of the Nazarene	597,841	0.38	94.14
United Pentecostal Church International	550,000	0.35	94.48
International Council of Community Churches	500,000	0.32	94.80
The Salvation Army	443,246	0.28	95.08
Wisconson Evangelical Lutheran Synod	414,874	0.26	95.34
Diocese of the Armenian Church of America	414,000	0.26	95.60

Baptist Convention and the United Methodist Church. The thirty-five denominations with memberships greater than 400,000 account for more than 95 percent of the total membership.

The pattern of a small number of denominations accounting for the vast majority of church members is also true in Canada. There are seven denominations with memberships greater than 200,000. These denominations account for over ninety percent of all the members reported to the Yearbook.

Table 3 Canada Denominational Ranking

Denomination	Inclusive Membership	Percent of total reported	Cumulative percentage
The Roman Catholic Church in Canada	12,584,789	66.59	66.59
The United Church of Canada	1,903,394	10.07	76.66
Orthodox Church in America (Canada Section)	1,000,000	5.29	81.95
The Anglican Church of Canada	848,256	4.49	86.44
The Presbyterian Church in Canada	236,822	1.25	87.69
Greek Orthodox Diocese of Toronto (Canada)	230,000	1.22	88.91
The Pentecostal Assemblies of Canada	226,678	1.20	90.10

Declining membership

Membership decline in the mainline denominations has been noted for several decades. This decline continues. Although both the American Baptist Church in the U.S.A. and the United Church of Christ reported membership declines, the decline in the United Church of Christ was great enough for membership in the American Baptist Church in the U.S.A. to surpass membership in the United Church of Christ. Also, for the first time the membership in the Jehovah's Witnesses is greater than the membership of the Christian Church (Disciples of Christ).

The decline of membership in the mainline denominations does not indicate that people are turning away from organized religion in general. Fifty-nine denominations in the United States reported statistics for both the 1995 and 1996 editions of the Yearbook. All together these denominations gained almost half a million new members. Together the Roman Catholic Church and the Southern Baptist Convention gained more than half a million members.

Table 4 lists denominations according to their membership. It shows the actual annual increase or decrease and the percentage increase or decrease that this represents. Because a number of larger denominations do not report statistics annually, this table does not give a complete picture of the changes in denominational membership.

Table 4 United States Membership Changes

Denomination	Membership Change	Percentage Change
The Roman Catholic Church	332,563	0.56
Southern Baptist Convention	215,418	1.40
The United Methodist Church	-62,470	-0.72
Evangelical Lutheran Church in America	-13,737	-0.26
The Church of Jesus Christ of Latter-Day Saints	93,000	2.06
Presbyterian Church (U.S.A.)	-98,630	-2.60
The Lutheran Church- Missouri Synod	-2,008	-0.08
Assemblies of God	52,897	2.33
American Baptist Churches in the U.S.A.	-8,571	-0.57

Denomination	Membership Change	Percentage Change
United Church of Christ	-28,868	-1.89
Jehovah's Witnesses	19,376	2.09
Christian Church (Disciples of Christ)	-20,373	-2.13
Seventh-day Adventist Church	13,646	1.79
Church of God (Cleveland, Tenn.)	22,024	3.14
Church of the Nazarene	6,707	1.13
Wisconson Evangelical Lutheran Synod	-2,012	-0.48
Reformed Church in America	-7,094	-2.24
Antiochian Orthodox Christian Archdiocese of North America	-50,000	-14.29
Baptist Missionary Association of America	-576	-0.25
The Evangelical Free Church of America	899	0.40
International Church of the Foursquare Gospel	5,143	2.36
Christian Reformed Church in North America	-3,391	-1.58
National Association of Free Will Baptists	-7,001	-3.26
Church of the Brethren	-2,431	-1.66
General Association of Regular Baptist Churches	-18,563	-11.98
The Wesleyan Church	1,395	1.21
Pentecostal Church of God, Inc.	10,640	10.35
Mennonite Church	-43	-0.04
Cumberland Presbyterian Church	-1,364	-1.49
Church of God of Prophecy	-1,800	-2.49
Evangelical Presbyterian Church	78	0.14
North American Baptist Conference	191	0.44
Grace Brethren Churches, Fellowship of	-2,473	-7.13
Churches of God, General Conference	-626	-1.93
The Missionary Church	413	1.45
Moravian Church in America, Northern Province	-926	-3.23
Evangelical Lutheran Synod	3,886	18.08
United Brethren in Christ	55	0.22
The Evangelical Congregational Church	-385	-1.61
American Carpatho-Russian Orthodox Greek Catholic Church	220	1.15
Brethren in Christ Church	166	0.92
Brethren Church (Ashland, Ohio), The	-89	-0.68
The Latvian Evangelical Lutheran Church in America	-934	-6.98
Apostolic Overcoming Holy Church of God, Inc.	1,095	9.71
Apostolic Faith Mission Church of God	-4,400	-28.57
Church of God in Christ (Mennonite)	242	2.30
Church of the Lutheran Confession	146	1.67
The Southern Methodist Church	-15	-0.19
Primitive Methodist Church in the U.S.A.	-62	-0.84
Church of God, Mountain Assembly, Inc.	1,057	20.79
The Church of God (Seventh Day), Denver, Colo.	200	3.64
Old German Baptist Brethren	87	1.57
The International Pentecostal Church of Christ	349	7.36
Reformed Church in the United States	-32	-0.76
The Estonian Evangelical Lutheran Church	-90	-2.21
The Schwenkfelder Church	156	6.44
Allegheny Wesleyan Methodist Connection (Original Allegheny Conf.)	13	0.64
Albanian Orthodox Diocese of America	-10	-0.53

Financial contributions to denominations continue to increase

Almost all denominations that report financial information to the Yearbook show an increase in receipts. This is true even for denominations with decreasing membership. Examples of total receipts and percent change from the previous year are given below.

Because many denominations report membership but not financial statistics to the Yearbook, this list is very incomplete. Yet, it is significant that even denominations that are loosing members are increasing their income.

Table 5 Total Contribution Changes in the United States

Denomination	Total Contributions	Percentage Change
Southern Baptist Convention	6,078,782,460	12.94
The United Methodist Church	3,430,351,778	3.85
Evangelical Lutheran Church in America	1,689,892,487	3.02
Presbyterian Church (U.S.A.)	2,107,167,041	4.77
The Lutheran Church- Missouri Synod	946,937,471	2.86
American Baptist Churches in the U.S.A.	370,230,512	-7.04
United Church of Christ	623,810,484	0.31
Christian Church (Disciples of Christ)	385,517,365	3.35
Seventh-day Adventist Church	732,944,260	7.27
Church of the Nazarene	477,106,894	12.34
Wisconson Evangelical Lutheran Synod	166,850,854	3.14
Reformed Church in America	181,014,238	13.79
Baptist Missionary Association of America	61,565,974	7.24
National Association of Free Will Baptists	68,300,000	13.27
Church of the Brethren	81,366,277	1.58

II
DIRECTORIES

1. UNITED STATES COOPERATIVE ORGANIZATIONS, NATIONAL

The organizations listed in this section are cooperative religious organizations that are national in scope.

All organizations are listed alphabetically including the National Council of the Churches of Christ in the USA.

The Alban Institute, Inc.

Founded in 1974, the Alban Institute, Inc., is a non-profit, non-denominational membership organization. Its mission is to work to encourage local congregations to be vigorous and faithful so that they may equip the people of God to minister within their faith communities and in the world. Through its publications, education programs, consulting and training services and research, The Alban Institute provides resources and services to congregations and judicatories of all denominations and their lay and ordained leaders. The Institute has long been a pioneer in identifying, researching and publishing information about key issues in the religious world such as conflict management, clergy transition, involuntary termination of clergy and lay leadership. The Institute's resources include over 100 book titles, over 40 courses offered nationally each year, and a staff of senior consultants located across the country ready to assist local congregations. Individuals, congregations, and institutions may support Alban's work as well as maintain their cutting-edge skills for ministry through membership in The Institute.

HEADQUARTERS

4550 Montgomery Ave., Ste. 433N, Bethesda, MD 20814-3341 Tel. (800)486-1318

Media Contact, David Sharpe

OFFICERS

Pres., The Rev. James P. Wind, Ph.D.

Exec. Vice-Pres., Ms. Leslie L. Buhler

American Bible Society

In 1816, pastors and laymen representing a variety of Christian denominations gathered in New York City to establish an organization "to disseminate the Gospel of Christ throughout the habitable world." Since that time the American Bible Society (ABS) has continued to provide God's Word, without doctrinal note or comment, wherever it is needed and in the language and format the reader can most easily use and understand. The ABS is the servant of the denominations and local churches. It provides Scriptures at exceptionally low costs in various attractive formats for their use in outreach ministries here in the United States and all across the world.

Today the ABS serves more than 100 denominations and agencies, and its board of trustees is composed of distinguished laity and clergy drawn from these Christian groups.

Forty nine years ago the American Bible Society played a leading role in the founding of the United Bible Societies, a federation of 120 national Bible societies around the world that enables global cooperation in Scripture translation, publication and distribution in more than 200 countries and territories around the world. The ABS contributes approximately 45 percent of the support provided by the UBS to those national Bible Societies requesting support to meet the total Scripture needs of people in their own countries.

The work of the ABS is supported through gifts from individuals, local churches, denominations and cooperating agencies. Their generosity helped make the distribution of 287.2 million copies of the Scriptures during 1994, out of a total of 608 millon copies of the Scriptures distributed by all member societies of the UBS.

HEADQUARTERS

National Service Center, 1865 Broadway, New York, NY 10023 Tel. (212)408-1200

Media Contact, Int. Pub. Rel., Rev. Thomas May, Tel. (212)408-1432 Fax (212)408-1456

OFFICERS

Chpsn., James Wood

Vice-Chpsn., Mrs. Sally Shoemaker Robinson

Pres. & CEO, Dr. Eugene B. Habecker

Vice-Pres. for Scripture Publications, Maria I. Martinez

Vice-Pres. for Dev., Arthur Caccese

Vice-Pres. for Admin./CFO, Patrick English

Departmental Heads: Church Relations & ABS Chaplain, Asst. to Pres., Rev. Fred A. Allen; Scripture Publications, Assoc. Vice-Pres., Rev. Dr. David G. Burke; Volunteer Activities & Field Services, Dir., Dr. Haviland C. Houston; National Program Promotions, Dir., Jeanette Russo; Public Relations, Int. Dir., Rev. Thomas May; Human Resources, Dir., Robert P. Fichtel; Scripture Production Services, Dir., Gary R. Ruth

American Council of Christian Churches

Founded in 1941, The American Council of Christian Churches (ACCC) is a multi-denominational agency for fellowship and cooperation among Bible-believing churches in various denominations/fellowships: Bible Presbyterian Church, Evangelical Methodist Church, Fellowship of Fundamental Bible Churches (formerly Bible Protestant), Free Presbyterian Church of North America, Fundamental Methodist Church, General Association of Regular Baptist Churches, Independent Baptist Fellowship of North America, Independent Churches Affiliated, along with hundreds of independent churches. The total membership nears 2 million. Each denomination retains its identity and full autonomy, but cannot be associated with the World Council of Churches, National Council of Churches or National Association of Evangelicals.

The ACCC was formed to be a voice of Biblical Fundamentalism and to encourage and strenthen believers in their stand for the Truth. No church or individual can be a part of the ACCC and at the same time be connected in any way with the National Council of Churches (NCC), World Council of Churches (WCC), or the National Association of Evangelicals (NAE).

The ACCC is a council and not an association. It is issues-oriented. The ACCC comes together as a multi-denominational group to deal with issues that affect all Fundamentalists. Member churches believe in the inspiration and inerrancy of Scripture; the triune God; the virgin birth; substitutionary death and resurrection of Christ and His second coming; total depravity of man; salvation by grace through faith; and the necessity of maintaining the purity of the church in doctrine and life.

HEADQUARTERS

P.O. Box 19, Wallingford, PA 19086 Tel. (610)-566-8154 Fax (610)892-0992
Media Contact, Exec. Dir., Dr. Ralph Colas

OFFICERS

Pres., Dr. Richard A. Harris
Vice-Pres., Rev. Mark Franklin
Exec. Sec., Dr. Ralph Colas
Sec., Rev. Ron Fieker
Treas., Mr. William H. Worrilow, Jr.
Commissions: Chaplaincy; Education; Laymen; Literature; Missions; Radio & Audio Visual; Relief; Youth

American Friends Service Committee

Founded by and related to the Religious Society of Friends (Quakers), but supported and staffed by individuals sharing basic values, regardless of religious affiliation. Attempts to relieve human suffering and find new approaches to world peace and social justice through nonviolence. Work in 25 countries includes development and refugee relief, peace education, and community organizing. Sponsors off-the-record seminars around the world to build better international understanding. Conducts programs with U.S. communities on the problems of minority groups such as housing, employment and denial of legal rights. Maintains Washington, D.C. office to present AFSC experience and perspectives to policymakers. Seeks to build informed public resistance to militarism and the military-industrial complex. A co-recipient of the Noble Peace Prize. Programs are multiracial, non-denominational, and international.

Divisions: Community Relations; International, Peace Education.

HEADQUARTERS

1501 Cherry St., Philadelphia, PA 19102 Tel. (215)241-7000 Fax (215)864-0104
Dir. of Media Relations, Ron Byler

OFFICERS

Chpsn., Donald Gann
Treas., Kate Nicklin
Exec. Dir., Kara Newell

The American Theological Library Association, Inc.

The American Theological Library Association, Inc. (ATLA) is a special library association that works to improve theological and religious libraries and librarianship by providing continuing education, developing standards, promoting research and experimental projects, encouraging cooperative programs and publishing and disseminating research tools and aids. Founded in 1947, ATLA currently has a membership of over 200 institutions and 600 individuals.

HEADQUARTERS

820 Church St., Ste. 300, Evanston, IL 60201 Tel. (708)869-7788 Fax (708)869-8513
Media Contact, Dir. of Member Services

OFFICERS

Pres., Linda Corman, Trinity College Library, 6 Hoskin Ave., Toronto, ON M5S 1H8
Vice-Pres., M. Patrick Graham, Pitts Theology Library, Emory University, Atlanta, GA 30322
Sec., Marti Alt, Ohio State University Libraries, 1858 Neil Ave. Mall, Columbus, OH 43210-1286
Exec. Dir. & CEO, Albert E. Hurd

American Tract Society

The American Tract Society is a nonprofit, nonsectarian, interdenominational organization instituted in 1825 through the merger of most of the then-existing tract societies. As one of the earliest religious publishing bodies in the United States, ATS has pioneered in the publishing of Christian books, booklets and leaflets. The volume of distribution has risen to more than 22 million pieces of literature annually.

HEADQUARTERS

P.O. Box 462008, Garland, TX 75046 Tel. (214)-276-9408 Fax (214)272-9642
Media Contact, Dir. of Marketing, Perry Brown

OFFICERS

Chpsn., Edith Luft

The American Waldensian Society

The American Waldensian Society (AWS) promotes ministry linkages, broadly ecumenical, between U.S. churches and Waldensian (Reformed) -Methodist constituencies in Italy and Waldensian constituencies in Argentina-Uruguay. Founded in 1906, AWS aims to enlarge mission discovery and partnership among overseas Waldensian-Methodist forces and denominational forces in the U.S.

AWS is governed by a national ecumenical board, although it consults and collaborates closely with the three overseas Waldensian-Methodist boards.

The Waldensian experience is the earliest continuing Protestant experience.

HEADQUARTERS

475 Riverside Dr., Rm. 1850, New York, NY 10115 Tel. (212)870-2671 Fax (212)870-2499

Media Contact, Exec. Dir., Frank G. Gibson, Jr.

OFFICERS

Pres., Rev. Laura R. Jervis
Vice-Pres., Rev. James O'Dell
Sec., Rev. Kent Jackson
Treas., Lon Haines
Exec. Dir., Rev. Frank G. Gibson, Jr.

Appalachian Ministries Educational Resource Center (AMERC)

The Appalachian Ministries Educational Resource Center (AMERC) is the largest ecumenical consortial effort in the history of theological education in the U.S. Forty-six seminaries comprise the consortium with 37 other theological institutions sending their students for AMERC training programs. Forty-seven denominations are represented in its students.

The goal of AMERC is to train persons for the Christian ministry in small towns and rural communities in Appalachia and beyond. In order to fulfill this goal, AMERC has the following objectives: (1) to provide participants with the highest quality of training in relating to Christian Theology and ministry to the people, cultures and political economies of Appalachia; (2) to provide direct experiences of Appalachian life both religious and secular and to help participants reflect theologically these experiences; (3) to recruit, support and encourage persons considering ministry in Appalachia and similar settings; (4) to provide and promote research of Appalachia and its churches; (5) to cooperate with religious bodies in the region in planning and implementing educational programs; (6) to provide training for theological faculty and denominational leaders; and (7) to seek and find spiritual, personal, financial, and administrative resources to suppport AMERC programs.

HEADQUARTERS

300 Harrison Rd., Berea, KY 40403 Tel. (606)986-8789 Fax (606)986-2576

Media Contact, Network Adm., Kathy Williams

OFFICERS

Co-Exec. Dir., Rev. Dr. Mary Lee Daugherty
Co-Exec. Dir., Rev. Dr. J. Stephen Rhodes
Chpsn. of Board, Dr. Douglass Lewis

The Associated Church Press

The Associated Church Press was organized in 1916. Its member publications include major Protestant, Catholic, and Orthodox groups in the U.S. and Canada. Some major ecumenical journals are also members. It is a professional Christian journalistic association seeking to promote excellence among editors, recognize achievements, and represent the interests of the religious press. It sponsors seminars, conventions, awards programs, and workshops for editors, staff people, and business managers.

HEADQUARTERS

Media Contact, Exec. Dir., Dr. John Stapert, P.O. Box 30215, Phoenix, AZ 85046-0215 Tel. (602)-569-6371 Fax (602)569-6180

OFFICERS

Pres., Joe Roos, 2401 15th St. NW, Washington, DC 20009

Exec. Dir., Dr. John Stapert, P.O. Box 30215, Phoenix, AZ 85046-0215 Tel. (602)569-6371

Treas., Nena Asquith, P.O. Box 1245, Bethlehem, PA 18016-1245

The Associated Gospel Churches

Organized in 1939, The Associated Gospel Churches (AGC) endorses chaplains primarily for Fundamental Independent Baptist Churches to the U.S. Armed Forces. The AGC has been recognized by the U.S. Department of Defense for 55 years as an Endorsing Agency, and it supports a strong national defense. The AGC also endorses VA chaplains, police, prison and civil air patrol chaplains.

The AGC provides support for its associated constituent churches, (Fundamental Independent Churches), seminaries, Bible colleges and missionaries.

The AGC believes in the sovereignty of the local church, the historic doctrines of the Christian faith and the infallibility of the Bible.

HEADQUARTERS

Media Contact, Pres., George W. Baugham, D.D., National Hdqt., 1 Chick Springs Rd. Ste.115, Greenville, SC 29609 Tel. (803)467-1970 Fax (803)467-1976

OFFICERS

Commission on Chaplains, Pres. and Chmn., George W. Baugham, D.D.
Vice-Pres., Rev. Chuck Flesher
Sec.-Treas., Mrs. Eva Baugham
Natl. Field Sec., Rev. Bob Ellis

Association for the Development of Religious Information Systems

The Association for the Development of Religious Information Systems (or Services) was established in 1971 to facilitate coordination and cooperation among information services that pertain to religion. Its goal is a worldwide network that is interdisciplinary, inter-faith and interdenominational to serve both administrative and research applications.

HEADQUARTERS

P.O. Box 210735, Nashville, TN 37221-0735 Tel. (615)662-5189

Media Contact, Coord., David O. Moberg, 7120 W. Dove Ct., Milwaukee, WI 53223-2766 Tel. (414)357-7247

Association of Catholic Diocesan Archivists

The Association of Catholic Diocesan Archivists, which began in 1979, has been committed to the active promotion of professionalism in the management of diocesan archives. The Association meets annually: in the even years it has its own summer conference, in the odd years it meets in conjunction with the Society of American Archivists. Publications include *Standards for Diocesan Archives*, *Access Policy for Diocesan Archives* and the quarterly *Bulletin*.

HEADQUARTERS

Archives & Records Center, 5150 Northwest Hwy., Chicago, IL 60630 Tel. (312)736-5150 Fax (312)736-0488

Media Contact, Ms. Nancy Sandleback

OFFICERS

Episcopal Mod., Archbishop of Chicago, Joseph Cardinal Bernardin

Pres., Msgr. Francis J. Weber, 15151 San Fernando Mission Blvd., Mission Hills, CA 91345 Tel. (818)365-1501

Vice-Pres., Dr. Charles Nolan, 1100 Chartres St., New Orleans, LA 70116 Tel. (504)529-2651 Fax (504)529-2001

Sec.-Treas., Sr. Catherine Louise LaCoste, C.S.J., P.O. Box 85728, San Diego, CA 92186-5728 Tel. (619)574-6309

Bd. Members: Kinga Perzynska, P.O. Box 13327, Capital Station, Austin, TX 78711 Tel. (512)-476-4888 Fax (512)476-3715; Timothy Cary, P.O. Box 07912, Milwaukee, WI 19807 Tel. (414)769-3407 Fax (414)769-3408; Ms. Lisa May, P.O. Box 907, 1700 San Jacinto, Houston, TX 77001 Tel. (713)659-5461 Fax (713)759-9151; John J. Treanor, 5150 Northwest Hwy., Chicago, IL 60630 Tel. (312)736-5150 Fax (312)736-0488; Mrs. Bernice Mooney, 27 C St., Salt Lake City, UT 84103-2397 Tel. (801)328-8641 Fax (801)328-9680

Newsletter Editor, Nancy Sandleback

Association of Statisticians of American Religious Bodies

This Association was organized in 1934 and grew out of personal consultations held by representatives from *The Yearbook of American Churches, The National* (now *Official) Catholic Directory*, the Jewish Statistical Bureau, The Methodist (now The United Methodist), the Lutheran and the Presbyterian churches.

ASARB has a variety of purposes: to bring together those officially and professionally responsible for gathering, compiling and publishing denominational statistics; to provide a forum for the exchange of ideas and sharing of problems in statistical methods and procedure; and to seek such standardization as may be possible in religious statistical data.

HEADQUARTERS

c\o Evangelical Lutheran Church in America, 8765 W. Higgins Rd., Chicago, IL 60631-4198 Tel. (312)380-2803 Fax (610)380-1465

Media Contact, Sec.-Treas., Rev. David L. Alderfer, Jr.

OFFICERS

Pres., Greta Lauria, Presbyterian Church USA, 100 Witherspoon, #4420, Louisville, KY 40202-1396 Tel. (502)569-5360 Fax (502)569-8005

1st Vice-Pres., Dr. Paul R. Gilchrist, Presbyterian Church USA, 1852 Century Pl. #190, Atlanta, GA 30345 Tel. (404)320-3366 Fax (404)320-7219

2nd Vice-Pres., Rev. Richard H. Taylor, United Church of Christ, 292 Bellview, Benton Harbor, MI 49022 Tel. (616)925-0695

Sec.-Treas., Rev. David L. Alderfer, Evangelical Church in America, 8765 W. Higgins Rd., Chicago, IL 60631-4198 Tel. (312)380-2803 Fax (312)380-1465

The Association of Theological Schools in the United States and Canada

The Association of Theological Schools is the accrediting agency for graduate theological education in North America. Its member schools offer graduate professional and academic degrees for church-related professions. For information about enrollment in member schools see "Trends in Seminary Education" in the statistical section of this book in sections 8 and 9.

HEADQUARTERS

10 Summit Park Drive, Pittsburgh, PA 15275-1103 Tel. (412)788-6505 Fax (412)788-6510

Media Contact, Dir. of Comm., Nancy Merrill, Tel. (412)788-6505

OFFICERS

Pres., James H. Costen, Interdenominational Theological Center, Atlanta, GA

Vice-Pres., Diane Kennedy, Aquinas Institute of Theology, St. Louis, MO

Secretary, Samuel T. Logan, Westminster Theo. Seminary, Philadelphia, PA

Treasurer, Anthony T. Ruger, Consultant, Oak Park, IL

STAFF

Executive Director, James L. Waits

Associate Director: Daniel O. Aleshire

Blanton-Peale Institute

Blanton-Peale Institute is dedicated to helping people overcome emotional obstacles by joining mental health expertise with religious faith and values. The Blanton-Peale Graduate Institute provides advanced training in marriage and family therapy, psychotherapy and pastoral care for ministers, rabbis, sisters, priests and other counselors. The Blanton-Peale Counselor Centers provide counseling for individuals, couples, families and groups. Blanton-Peale also offers a nationwide telephone support service for clergy, social service agencies and other employers and promotes interdisciplinary communication among theology, medicine and the behavioral sciences. Blanton-Peale was founded in 1937 by Dr. Norman Vincent Peale and psychiatrist Smiley Blanton, M.D.

HEADQUARTERS

3 W. 29th St., New York, NY 10001 Tel. (212)725-7850 Fax (212)689-3212

Media Contact, Anne E. Impellizzeri

OFFICERS

Chpsn., John Allen

Vice-Chpsn., Arthur Caliandro

Sec., E. Virgil Conway

Treas., Bruce Gregory

Pres. & CEO, Anne E. Impellizzeri

Bread For The World

Bread for the World is a non-profit, nondenominational Christian citizen's movement of 45,000 members that advocates specific hunger policy changes and seeks justice for hungry people at home and abroad. Founded in 1974, Bread for the World is supported by more than 45 Protestant, Catholic and Evangelical denominations and church agencies. Rooted in the gospel of God's love in Jesus Christ, its 45,000 members write, call and visit their members of Congress to win specific legislative changes that help hungry people, and place the issue of hunger on the nation's policy agenda.

Bread for the World works closely with Bread for the World Institute. The Institute seeks to inform, educate, nurture and motivate concerned citizens for action on policies that affect hungry people.

HEADQUARTERS

1100 Wayne Ave., Suite 1000, Silver Spring, MD 20910 Tel. (301)608-2400 Fax (301)608-2401

Media Contact, Michele Tapp, 1100 Wayne Ave., Suite 1000, Silver Spring, MD 20910 Tel. (301)-608-2400 Fax (301)608-2401

OFFICERS

Pres., Rev. David Beckmann
Vice-Pres., Phoebe de Reynier
Bd. Chpsn., Maria Otero
Bd. Vice-Chpsn., Fr. Clarence Williams, CPPS

Campus Crusade for Christ International

Campus Crusade for Christ International is an interdenominational, evangelistic and discipleship ministry dedicated to helping fulfill the Great Commission through the multiplication strategy of "win-build-send." Formed in 1951 on the campus of UCLA, the organization now includes 43 separate ministries reaching out to almost every segment of society. There are more than 113,991 full-time, trained associate and volunteer staff in 161 countries, with the numbers expanding almost daily. The NewLife 2000 (Reg) strategy to give every person on earth an opportunity to say "yes" to Jesus Christ by the year 2000 includes thousands of churches of all denominations and 350 mission groups.

HEADQUARTERS

100 Sunport La., Orlando, FL 32809 Tel. (407)-826-2000 Fax (407)826-2120

Media Contact, Sid Wright

OFFICERS

Pres., William R. Bright
Exec. Vice-Pres., Stephen B. Douglass
Vice-Pres. of Admn. & Chief Fin. Officer, Kenneth P. Heckmann
Vice-Pres. of Intl. Ministries, Bailey E. Marks

CARA--Center for Applied Research in the Apostolate

CARA--the Center for Applied Research in the Apostolate is a not-for-profit research organization of the Roman Catholic Church. It operates on the premise that not only theological principles but also the findings of secular sciences, especially sociology and psychology, must be the basis for pastoral care.

CARA performs a wide range of studies and services including church management, religious life research and planning, church personnel, education, and parish development. Since its roots are Roman Catholic, many of its studies are done for dioceses, religious orders, educational institutions and social service agencies. Interdenominational studies are also performed.

HEADQUARTERS

Georgetown University, Washington, DC 20057-1033 Tel. (202)687-8080 Fax (202)687-8083

Media Contact, Gerald H. Early

Center for Parish Development

The Center for Parish Development is an ecumenical, non-profit research and development agency whose mission is to help church bodies learn to become faithful expressions of God's mission in today's post-modern, post-Christendom world. Founded in 1968, the Center brings to its client-partners a strong theological orientation, a missional ecclesial paradigm with faithful Christian communities as the focus of mission, research-based theory and practice of major change, a systems approach, and years of experience working with national, regional, and local church bodies.

The Center staff provides research, consulting and training support for church organizations engaging in major change. The Center is governed by a 12-member Board of Directors.

HEADQUARTERS

5407 S. University Ave., Chicago, IL 60615 Tel. (312)752-1596

Media Contact, Exec. Dir., Paul M. Dietterich

OFFICERS

Chpsn., Eugene L. Delves, 9142 S. Winchester Ave., Chicago, IL 60620
Vice-Chpsn., Pastor Gordon Nusz, United Methodist Church, 111 E. Ridge St., Marquette, MI 49855
Sec., Lea Woll, SLW, 1000 E. Maple, Mundelein, IL 60060
Exec. Dir., Paul M. Dietterich

Chaplaincy of Full Gospel Churches

The Chaplaincy of Full Gospel Churches (CFGC) is a unique coalition of nondenominational churches and networks of churches united for the purpose of being represented in military and civilian chaplaincies. Since its inception in 1984, CFGC has grown rapidly -presently representing over 6.4 million American Christians.

Churches, fellowships and networks of churches which affirm the CFGC statement of faith that "Jesus is Savior, Lord and Baptizer in the Holy Spirit today, with signs, wonders and gifts following" may join the endorsing agency. CFGC represents its 112 member-networks of churches and numerous independent churches before the Pentagon's Armed Forces Chaplains Board, the National Conference of Ministry to the Armed Forces, Endorsers Conference for Veterans Affairs Chaplaincy, Federal Bureau of Prisons, College of Chaplains, and other groups requiring professional chaplaincy endorsement. The organization also ecclesiastically credentials professional counselors.

HEADQUARTERS

2721 Whitewood Dr., Dallas, TX 75233-2713 Tel. (214)331-4373 Fax (214)333-4401

Media Contact, David B. Plummer

OFFICERS

Pres. & Dir., Rev. Dr. E. H. Jim Ammerman
Deputy Dir., Rev. Dr. Charlene Ammerman
Assoc. Dir., Rev. David B. Plummer
Vice-Pres., Ed Leach

MEMBER BODIES

American Evangelistic Association
Apostolic Brethren Inc.

Apostolic Christian Churches International
Apostolic Faith Missions of Portland Oregon
Apostolic Ministers Conference of Philadelphia
Ascension Fellowship International
Assemblies of God International Fellowship
Assemblies of the Lord Jesus Christ
Associated Brotherhood of Christians
Associated Evangelical Gospel Assemblies
Association of Evangelical Congregations
Association of Faith Churches and Ministries
Association of Vineyard Churches
Azusa Fellowship
Beth Messiah Congregation
Bethel Fellowship International
Bible Way of Our Lord Jesus Christ Worldwide
Calvary Chapels
Calvary Ministries International, Inc.
Christ Gospel Church International
Christ's Church Fellowship
Christian Church of North America
Christian Evangelistic Assemblies
Church of God Apostolic
Church of God (Jerusalem Acres)
Church of God (Mountain Assembly)
Church of God in Christ International
Church on the Rock International
Congregational Holiness Church
Convenant Ministries International
Defenders of the Christian Faith, Inc.
Evangel Fellowship International
Evangelistic Messengers' Association
Evangelistic Missionary Fellowship
Faith Christian Fellowship
Faith Fellowship Ministries
Faith Tabernacle Corporation of Churches
Faith Tech Ministries
Fellowship of Charismatic Churches and Ministers Intl.
Fellowship of Christian Assemblies
Fellowship of Vineyard Harvester Churches
Foundation of Praise
Free Gospel Church, Inc.
Free Gospel Church of Christ
Freedom Church
Full Counsel Christian Fellowship
Full Faith Churches of Love
Full Gospel Assemblies, International
Full Gospel Church in Christ
Full Gospel Evangelistic Association
Full Gospel Fellowship of Churches
Full Gospel Ministers' Association
Fundamental Assembly of God International
Gate Fellowship of Churches
Global Christian Ministries
Gospel Crusade Ministers Fellowship
Gospel Ministers and Churches International
Grace Fellowship
Greater Emmanuel International Fellowship
Holy Temple Church of Christ, Inc.
House of God
Independent Assemblies of God International
Interdenominational Ministries,Inc.
International Apostolic Fellowship
International Christian Churches
International Conference of Word Ministries
Intl. Convention of Faith Churches and Ministers
International Evangelical Churches
International Evangelism Crusades
International Fellowship
International Gospel Assemblies
International Ministerial Association
International Ministerial Fellowship
International Ministers Forum
Jacksonville Theo. Seminary Fellowship, Intl.
Kingsway Fellowship International
Lester Sumrall Evangelistic Association
Liberty Fellowship Churches
Life Ministerial Fellowship, Intl.
Lighthouse Gospel Fellowship
Living Witness of the Apostolic Faith
Men and Women Ministry Intl.
Ministerial Fellowship of the USA
Ministers Fellowship International
Missionary Gospel Church International
Mount Sinai Holy Church of North America
Network of Kingdom Churches
Original Glorious Church of God in Christ
Overcoming Faith Fellowship International
Overseas Student Christian Fellowship
Pentecostal Assemblies /Churches of Jesus Christ
Pentecostal Assemblies of Jesus Christ
Pentecostal Churches of the Apostolic Faith
Pentecostal Minsterial Association
Philadelphia Pentecostal Church of the Firstborn
Resurrection Churches nad Ministries
Revival Fellowship Group
Revival For Christ
Revival Time USA
Rhema Fellowship of Churches and Ministers
United Christian Church Ministerial Association
United Church of Jesus Christ (Apostolic)
United Crusade Fellowship Missions Conference International
United Evangelical Churches
United Full Gospel Church
United Gospel Fellowship of Covenant Ministries
United Network of Christian Ministers and Churches
Victory Fellowship of Ministries
World Bible Way Fellowship
World Evangelism Fellowship
World Ministries Fellowship
World Salt

Christian Endeavor International

Christian Endeavor is a Christ-centered, youth-oriented ministry which assists the local church in reaching young people with the gospel of Jesus Christ, discipling them in the Christian faith and equipping them for Christian ministry and service in their local church, community and world. It reaches across denominational, cultural, racial and geographical boundaries.

Christian Endeavor International produces materials for program enrichment, provides seminars for equipping youth leaders for effective ministry and holds conferences and conventions for Christian inspiration, spiritual growth and fellowship.

Organized in Portland, Me., in February 1881, there now are active Christian Endeavor groups in approximately 78 nations and island groups, totaling over 3 million members.

HEADQUARTERS

3575 Valley Rd., P.O. Box 820, Liberty Corner, NJ 07938-0820 Tel. (908)604-9440 Fax (908)604-6075
Exec. Dir., Rev. David G. Jackson

OFFICERS

Pres., Rev. Richard Cattermole
Exec. Dir., Rev. David G. Jackson

Christian Holiness Association

The Association is a coordinating agency of those religious bodies that hold the Wesleyan-Arminian theological view. It was organized in 1867.

HEADQUARTERS

CHA Center, P.O. Box 100, Wilmore, KY 40390 Tel. (606)858-4091 Fax (606)858-4096
Media Contact, Ofc. Mgr., Patricia Walls

OFFICERS

Pres., Dr. John A. Byers, West Milton, OH
Exec. Dir., Rev. Steven J. Schellin, Lancaster, OH

AFFILIATED ORGANIZATIONS

The American Rescue Workers
Association of Evangelical Churches
Association of Independent Methodists
Bible Holiness Movement
Brethren in Christ Church
Church of God, Anderson, IN
The Church of the Nazarene
Churches of Christ in Christian Union
Congregrational Methodist Church
Evangelical Christian Church
Evangelical Church of North America
Evangelical Friends Alliance
Evangelical Methodist Church
Free Methodist Church in North America
Japan Immanuel Church
Missionary Church (North Central Dist.)
OMS, International, Inc.
The Salvation Army
The Salvation Army in Canada
United Brethren in Christ Church (Sandusky Conference)
The Wesleyan Church
World Gospel Mission

Christian Management Association

Christian Management Association is an association devoted to educating, equipping and encouraging its members to improve their management skills. There are 23 local chapters and more than 2,300 members in North America participating in strengthening, encouraging and challenging one another to perform the Lord's work with excellence and integrity.

CMA has resources and services to help with church management, planning, leading, fund raising, administration, data processing, finance, accounting and law.

CMA's mission is to help CEOs and managers in leading and managing Christian organizations and churches.

HEADQUARTERS

P.O. Box 4638, Diamond Bar, CA 91765 Tel. (909)861-8861 Fax (909)860-8247
Media Contact, CEO, John Pearson

OFFICERS

Chpsn. of the Bd., Patrick L. Clements, Church Extension Plan, P.O. Box 12629, Salem, OR 97309
Treas., C. E. Crouse, Jr., Capin, Crouse & Company, 720 Executive Park Dr., Greenwood, IN 46143
CEO, John Pearson

A Christian Ministry in the National Parks

The Ministry is an independent ecumenical movement providing interdenominational religious services in 65 National Parks, Monuments and Recreation Areas. For 20 years it was administered by the National Council of Churches. On Jan. 1, 1972, it became an independent movement representing more than 40 denominations, 60 local park committees, more than 300 theological seminaries and 16 separate religious organizations. The program recruits and staffs 300 positions, winter and summer, in 65 areas.

HEADQUARTERS

222 1/2 E. 49th St., New York, NY 10017 Tel. (212) 758-3450

OFFICER

Dir., Dr. Warren W. Ost

Church Growth Center

The Church Growth Center is an interfaith, nonprofit, professional organization of men and women who have the responsibility for promoting, planning and/or managing meetings, workshops, conferences and consultation services for churches, assemblies and other religious organizations.

Founded in 1978, the Church Growth Center ministry strives toward bringing about the transformational change of the Christian Church toward the effective implementation of the Lord's Great Commission to make disciples of all peoples.

With focus on the Great Commission, today the Church Growth Center provides resources in the form of books, workshop materials and services which are used both nationally and internationally. Also included under the arm of the Church Growth Center are the departments of creative Consultation Services, The Church Doctor Radio ministry, HarvestSearch, Great Commission Bookstore, MissionTeams International, Nehemiah Guest House, *Strategies for Today's Leader* magazine, and The American Society for Church Growth.

The Church Growth Center conducts conferences and meetings in Africa, Cambodia, Japan, Korea, Russia and other locations.

HEADQUARTERS

1230 U. S. Highway Six, P.O. Box 145, Corunna, IN 46730 Tel. (219)281-2452 Fax (219)281-2167
Media Contact, Office Mgr., Cheryl A. Kroemer

OFFICERS

Pres., Dr. Kent R. Hunter, D. Min. S., T.D.
Vice-Pres., Rev. Paul Griebel, 312 S. Oak St., Kendallville, IN 46755
Sec.-Treas., Mr. Roger Miller, 1060 Park Dr., Turkey Lake, Lagrange, IN 46761

Church Women United in the U.S.A.

Church Women United in the U.S.A. is an ecumenical lay movement providing Protestant, Orthodox, Roman Catholic and other Christian women with programs and channels of involvement in church, civic and national affairs. CWU has 1,600 units formally organized in communities in all 50 states, greater Washington, D.C. and Puerto Rico.

HEADQUARTERS

475 Riverside Dr., Rm. 812, New York, NY 10115 Tel. (212)870-2347 Fax (212)870-2338

CWU Washington Ofc., 110 Maryland Ave. NE, Rm. 108, Washington, DC 20002 Tel. (202)544-8747

Media Contact, Martha M. Cruz, Tel. (212)870-2344

OFFICERS

Pres., Ann B. Garvin, New York, NY

1st Vice-Pres., Van Lynch, Trimble, TN

2nd Vice-Pres., Shirley Nilsson, Albuquerque, NM

Sec.-Treas., Rhoda Akiko Iyoya, Pasadena, CA

Regional Coordinators: Central, Miriam Cline, Urbandale, IA; East Central, Catherine Childs, Columbus, OH; Mid-Atlantic, Annette Jones, Washington, DC; Northeast, Carolyn Hill-Jones, Ossining, NY; Northwest, Louise Smith-Woods, Seattle, WA; South Central, Kitty Polk; Southeast, Gloria B. Montalvo, Cabo Rojo, PR; Southwest, Nancy Warner, Acampo, CA

Consultation on Church Union

Officially constituted in 1962, the Consultation on Church Union is a venture in reconciliation of nine American communions. It has been authorized to explore the formation of a united church, truly catholic, truly evangelical and truly reformed. In 1992 the participating churches were African Methodist Episcopal Church, African Methodist Episcopal Zion Church, Christian Church (Disciples of Christ), Christian Methodist Episcopal Church, The Episcopal Church, International Council of Community Churches, Presbyterian Church (U.S.A.), United Church of Christ and The United Methodist Church.

The Plenary Assembly, which normally meets every four or five years, is composed of 10 delegates and 10 associate delegates from each of the participating churches. Included also are observer-consultants from more than 20 other churches, other union negotiations and conciliar bodies. The Executive Committee has set the date of the 1998 Plenary as December 9-13, 1998; the location will be the Hyatt Regency Hotel in St. Louis. The Executive Committee will recommend to the Plenary that the Inaugural Liturgy for the Church of Christ Uniting take place on the First Sunday in Advent (December 3), in 2000. Location will be St. Louis.

The Executive Committee is composed of the president, two representatives from each of the participating churches and the secretariat. The secretariat consists of the full-time executive staff of the Consultation, all of whom are based at the national office in Princeton, N.J. Various task groups are convened to fulfill certain assignments. In 1990 there were four task groups: Communications; Unity & Justice; Theology and Special Gifts. In addition there was an Editorial Board for the annual Lenten Booklet of devotional meditations.

HEADQUARTERS

151 Wall St., Princeton, NJ 08540 Tel. (609)921-7866 Fax (609)921-0471

Media Contact, Gen. Sec., Dr. Daniell C. Hamby

OFFICERS

Gen. Sec., Dr. Daniell C. Hamby

Treas./Bus. Mgr., Christine V. Bilarczyk

Pres., Dr. Vivian U. Robinson, 125 Hernlen St., Augusta, GA 30901

Vice-Pres.: Bishop Vinton R. Anderson, P.O. Box 6416, St. Louis, MO 63108; Rev. Alice C. Cowan, Trinity Episcopal Church, Oxford, OH 45656

Sec., Mr. Abraham Wright, 1912-3 Rosemary Hills Dr., Silver Springs, MD 20910

REP. FROM PARTICIPATING CHURCHES

African Methodist Episcopal Church: Bishop Vinton R. Anderson, 4144 Lindell Blvd., Ste. 222, St. Louis, MO 63108; Bishop H. Hartford Brookins, 3015 El Video Dr., Bel Air, CA 90049

African Methodist Episcopal Zion Church: Bishop Marshall H. Strickland, 2000 Cedar Circle Dr., Baltimore, MD 21228; Bishop Cecil Bishop, 2663 Oakmeade Dr., Charlotte, NC 28270

Christian Church (Disciples of Christ): Rev. Dr. Paul A. Crow, Jr., P.O. Box 1986, Indianapolis, IN 46206; Rev. Mildred Slack, Five Church Assoc., 2149 South Grand, St. Louis, MO 63104

Christian Methodist Episcopal Church: Bishop Marshall Gilmore, 2323 W. Illinois Ave., Dallas, TX 75224; Dr. Vivian U. Robinson, 8th Episcopal Dist. Hdqt., 1256 Hernlen St., Augusta, GA 30901

The Episcopal Church: Rt. Rev. William G. Burrill, 935 East Ave., Rochester, NY 14607; Rev. Dr. Rena Karefa-Smart, 4601 North Park Ave., Chevy Chase, MD 20815

Intl. Council of Community Churches: Rev. Dr. Jeffrey R. Newhall, 19715 S. LaGrange Rd. Ste. C, Mokena., IL 60448; Mr. Abraham Wright, 1612-3 Rosemary Hills Dr., Silver Springs, MD 20910

Presbyterian Church (U.S.A.): Rev. Michael E. Livingston, CN-821, Princeton, NJ 08542; Mrs. Dorothy G. Barnard, 2410 Fairoyal Dr., St. Louis, MO 63131

United Church of Christ: Rev. Clyde H. Miller, Jr., 950 28th St., Boulder, CO 80303; Rev. Dr. Thomas E. Dipko, Exec. V.P. 1st. Christian Church, 700 Prospect Ave., Cleveland, OH 44115; Rev. Diane C. Kessler, Mass. Council of Churches, 14 Beacon St., Boston, MA 02108

The United Methodist Church: Bishop William B. Grove, 234 Lark St., Albany, NY 12210; Rev. Dr. Larry D. Pickens, 5600 S. Indiana Ave., Chicago, IL 60649

Ecumenics International

Ecumenics International, the only senior-level Orthodox Christian research delegation on ecumenics, is a multireligious, interdisciplinary not-for-profit academic service provider incorporated under the NY State Department of Education and the State University of NY. EI is an NGO affiliate of the UN, associated with the UN University for Peace in Costa Rica, a consultant to the Ecumenical Patriarchate of Constantinople, and a member of the UN's NGO Committee on the Freedom of Religion or Belief. EI works with global organizations and with national agencies developing educational curricula ranging from grassroots seminars to university programs with members and affiliates in 52 countries in all regions of the world cooperating with higher ranked religious and spiritual representatives.

The General Secretariat and Board of Trustees oversee the EI University Project which addresses the practical needs of educational institutions by assisting schools, colleges, and universities to resolve the emerging social liabilities of multireligious intolerance. The University Project offers professional training on interactive preventative diplomacy and conflict resolution. The University Project Apprenticeship Opportunity Program invites people to study ecumenics through long-term, comprehensive internships.

EI Press includes the *Ecumenics International Trajectory Quarterly*, the *Empowering Women and Men Through* series, *Ediciónes Ecuménica*, multireligious texts and peace-education documents. EI Press' book *Transforming Hard-Talk into Heart-Speak: An Interactive Conflict Resolution Manual & Ecumenical Workbook for Interreligious Encounter & Dialogue*, a leading peace-education text based on UN processes of preventative diplomacy and UN documents, was inaugurated through an accredited program at the US Military Academy at West Point.

HEADQUARTERS

P.O. Box 144, Sloatsburg, NY 10974-0144 Tel. (914)398-2133 Fax (914)398-2133

Media Contact, Communications Sec., Mary Gibson Dunne

OFFICERS

Sec.-Gen., Anastasios Zavales
Assoc. Sec.-Gen., Patrick John Farrell
Gen. Sec. Intern, Christopher James Maresca
Research Foundation Sec., Joseph Brian MacMenamin
Representation Endowment Sec., George Enrique Bedoya
Senior Board Member, Robert Muller, Chancellor, UN University for Peace

Evangelical Council for Financial Accountability

Founded in 1979, the Evangelical Council for Financial Accountability has the purpose of helping Christ-centered, evangelical, nonprofit organizations earn the public's trust through their ethical practices and financial accountability. ECFA assists its over 800 member organizations in making appropriate public disclosure of their financial practices and accomplishments, thus materially enhancing their credibility and support potential among present and prospective donors.

HEADQUARTERS

P.O. Box 17456, Washington, DC 20041-0456 Tel. (703)713-1414 Fax (703)713-1133

Media Contact, Pres., Paul D. Nelson

OFFICERS

Pres., Paul D. Nelson
Deputy Exec. Officer, Martha James
Dir. of Member Services, Lucinda Repass
V.P. Member Review, Clarence Reimer

Evangelical Press Association

The Evangelical Press Association is an organization of editors and publishers of Christian periodicals which seeks to promote the cause of Evangelical Christianity and enhance the influence of Christian journalism.

HEADQUARTERS

485 Panorama Rd., Earlysville, VA 22936 Tel. (804)973-5941 Fax (804)973-2710

Media Contact, Exec. Dir., Ronald Wilson

OFFICERS

Pres., Joel Belz, World Magazine, P.O. Box 2330, Asheville, NC 28802
Sec., Diane McDougal, Worldwide Challenge, 100 Sunport Ln., Orlando, FL 32822
Treas., Mike Umlandt, Luis Bulau Evang. Assoc., P.O. Box 1173, Portland, OR 97207
Exec. Dir., Ronald Wilson

Fellowship of Reconcilliation

The Fellowship of Reconciliation is an interfaith pacifist organization that has been working for peace and justice since 1915. The FOR has programs in the areas of international peace, social justice and nonviolence education in an effort to respond creatively and compassionately to issues of violence and injustice.

HEADQUARTERS

Box 271, Nyack, NY 10960 Tel. (914)358-4601 Fax (914)358-4924

Media Contact, Ed. and Communications Dir., Richard Deats

OFFICERS

Chpsn., Natl. Council, Rev. James Lawson, Holman United Methodist Church, 3320 W. Adams Blvd., Los Angeles, CA 90018
Vice-Chpsn., Natl. Council, Lou Ann Ha'aheo Guanson, P.O. Box 62305, Honolulu, HI 96839-2305
Exec. Dir., Jo Becker

PEACE FELLOWSHIPS & AFFILIATED GROUPS

Baptist Peace Fellowship
Brethren Peace Fellowship
Buddhist Peace Fellowship
Catholic Peace Fellowship
Church of God Peace Fellowship
Disciples Peace Fellowship
Episcopal Peace Fellowship
Jewish Peace Fellowship
Lutheran Peace Fellowship
Muslim Peace Fellowship
New Call to Peacemaking
Orthodox Peace Fellowship
Presbyterian Peace Fellowship
Unitarian Universalist Peace Fellowship
United Church of Christ FOR
United Methodist Peace Fellowship

Glenmary Research Center

The Research Center is a department of the Glenmary Home Missioners, a Catholic society of priests and brothers. The Center was established in 1966 to serve the rural research needs of the Catholic Church in the United States. Its research has led it to serve ecumenically a wide variety of church bodies. Local case studies as well as quantitative research is done to understand better the diversity of contexts in the rural sections of the country. The Center's statistical profiles of the nation's counties cover both urban and rural counties.

HEADQUARTERS

235 E. Ponce De Leon Ave., Ste. 226, Decatur, GA 30030 Tel. (404)377-7010

Media Contact, Lesilie Montelongo

OFFICERS

Pres., Rev. Gerald Dorn, P.O. Box 465618, Cincinnati, OH 45246-5618

1st Vice-Pres., Rev. Wilfred Steinbacher, P.O. Box 465618, Cincinnati, OH 45246-5618
2nd Vice-Pres., Bro. Jack Henn, P.O. Box 465618, Cincinnati, OH 45246-5618
Treas., Mr. Robert Knueven, P.O. Box 465618, Cincinnati, OH 45246-5618
Dir., Sr. Mary Priniski

Interfaith Impact for Justice and Peace

Interfaith Impact for Justice and Peace is the religious community's united voice in Washington. It helps Protestant, Jewish, Muslim and Catholic national organizations have clout on Capitol Hill and brings grassroots groups and individual and congregational members to Washington and shows them how to turn their values into votes for justice and peace.

Interfaith Impact for Justice and Peace has established the following Advocacy Networks to advance the cause of justice and peace: Justice for Women; Health Care; Hunger and Poverty; International Justice and Peace; Civil and Human Rights. The Interfaith Impact Foundation provides an annual Legislative Briefing for their members.

Members receive the periodic Action alerts on initiatives, voting records, etc., and a free subscription to the Advocacy Networks of their choice.

HEADQUARTERS

110 Maryland Ave. N.E., Ste. 203, Washington, DC 20002 Tel. (202)543-2800 Fax (202)547-8107
Media Contact, Legislative Dir., Fr. Paul Ojibway, S.A.

OFFICERS

Legislative Dir., Fr. Paul Ojibway, S.A.
Chpsn. of Bd., Jane Hull Harvey, United Methodist Church

MEMBERS

African Methodist Episcopal Church
African Methodist Episcopal Zion Church
Alliance of Baptists
American Baptist Churches, USA: Washington Office; World Relief Office
American Ethical Union
American Muslim Council
Center of Concern
Christian Methodist Episcopal (CME) Church
Christian Church (Disciples of Christ)
Church of the Brethren
Church Women United
Commission on Religion in Appalachia
Episcopal Church
Episcopal Urban Caucus
Evangelical Lutheran Church in America
Federation of Southern Cooperatives/LAF
Federation for Rural Empowerment
Graymoor Ecumenical and Interreligious Institute
Jesuit Social Ministries
Maryknoll Fathers and Brothers
Moravian Church in America
National Council of Churches of Christ: Church World Service; Washington Office
National Council of Jewish Women
NETWORK
Peoria Citizens Committee
Presbyterian Church (USA)
Progressive National Baptist Convention
Presbyterian Hunger Fund
Reformed Church in America
Rural Advancement Fund
Society of African Missions
Southwest Organizing Project
Southwest Voter Registration/Education Project
Toledo Metropolitan Ministries
Union of American Hebrew Congregations
Unitarian Universalist Association
Unitarian Universalist Service Committee
United Church of Christ: Bd. for Homeland Ministries; Bd. for World Ministries; Hunger Action Ofc.; Ofc. of Church in Society
United Methodist Church: Gen. Bd. of Church & Society; Gen. Bd. of Global Ministries Natl. Div.; Gen. Bd. of Global Ministries Women's Div.; Gen. Bd. of Global Ministries World Div.
Virginia Council of Churches
Western Organization of Resource Councils

International Union of Gospel Missions

The International Union of Gospel Missions (IUGM) is an association of almost 250 rescue missions and other ministries that serve more than 7 million homeless and needy people in the inner cities of the U.S., Canada and overseas each year. Since 1913, IUGM member ministries have offered emergency food and shelter, youth and family services, prison and jail outreach, rehabilitation and specialized programs for the mentally ill, the elderly, the urban poor and street youth.

HEADQUARTERS

1045 Swift, N. Kansas City, MO 64116-4127 Tel. (816)471-8020 Fax (816)471-3718
Media Contact, Exec. Dir., Rev. Stephen E. Burger

OFFICERS

Exec. Dir., Rev. Stephen E. Burger
Pres., Richard McMillen, 10 S. Prince St., Lancaster, PA 17603 Tel. (717)393-7709 Fax (717)393-4966
Vice-Pres., Dr. Malcolm C. Lee, P.O. Box 1112, Richmond, CA 94802 Tel. (510)215-4888 Fax (510)215-0178
Sec.-Treas., Mr. Rick Alvis, 245 N. Delaware St., Indianapolis, IN 46204 Tel. (317)635-3575 Fax (317)687-3629

NATIONAL PROGRAM UNITS AND STAFF

Education, Rev. Michael Liimatta
Research, Alice Young
Membership Services, Debbie McClendon
Newsletter and Magazine: Stephen E. Burger; Debra Palmer
Convention, Stephen E. Burger
Business Admn., Len Conner
Historian, Delores Burger
Exec. Sec., Madeleine Wooley
Communications & Development, Phil Rydman

Interreligious Foundation for Community Organization (IFCO)

IFCO is a national ecumenical agency created in 1966 by several Protestant, Roman Catholic and Jewish organizations, to be an interreligious, interracial agency for support of community organization and education in pursuit of social justice. Through IFCO, national and regional religious bodies collaborate in development of social justice strategies and provide financial support and technical assistance to local, national and international social-justice projects.

IFCO serves as a bridge between the churches

and communities and acts as a resource for ministers and congregations wishing to better understand and do more to advance the struggles of the poor and oppressed. IFCO conducts training workshops for community organizers and uses its vast national and international network of organizers, clergy and other professionals to act in the interest of justice.

HEADQUARTERS

402 W. 145th St., New York, NY 10031 Tel. (212)926-5757 Fax (212)926-5842

Media Contact, Dir. of Communications, Gail Walker

OFFICERS

Pres. & Dir., Community Dev., Natl. Min., Dr. Benjamin Greene, Jr., American Baptist Churches in the U.S.A.

Inter-Varsity Christian Fellowship of the U.S.A.

Inter-Varsity Christian Fellowship is a non-profit, interdenominational student movement that ministers to college and university students and faculty in the United States. Inter-Varsity began in the United States when students at the University of Michigan invited C. Stacey Woods, then General Secretary of the Canadian movement, to help establish an Inter-Varsity chapter on their campus. Inter-Varsity Christian Fellowship-USA was incorporated two years later, in 1941.

Inter-Varsity's uniqueness as a campus ministry lies in the fact that it is student-initiated and student-led. Inter-Varsity strives to build collegiate fellowships that engage their campus with the gospel of Jesus Christ and develop disciples who live out biblical values. Inter-Varsity students and faculty are encouraged in evangelism, spiritual discipleship, serving the church, human relationships, righteousness, vocational stewardship and world evangelization. A triennial missions conference held in Urbana, Illinois, jointly sponsored with Inter-Varsity-Canada, has long been a launching point for missionary service.

HEADQUARTERS

6400 Schroeder Rd., P.O. Box 7895, Madison, WI 53707 Tel. (608)274-9001 Fax (608)274-7882

Media Contact, Dir. of Development Services, Carole Sharkey, P.O. Box 7895, Madison, WI 53707 Tel. (608)274-9001 Fax (608)274-7882

OFFICERS

Pres. & CEO, Stephen A. Hayner
Vice-Pres.: C. Barney Ford; Robert A. Fryling; Samuel Barkat; Dan Harrison
Sec., H. Yvonne Vinkemulder
Treas., Thomas H. Witte
Bd. Chpsn., Thomas Boyle
Bd. Vice-Chpsn., Virginia Viola

Laymen's National Bible Association, Inc.

The Laymen's National Bible Association, Inc. (LNBA) is an autonomous, interfaith organization of lay people who advocate regular Bible reading. LNBA sponsors National Bible Week (Thanksgiving week) each November. Program activities include public service advertising, distribution of nonsectarian literature and thousands of local Bible Week observances by secular and religious organizations. LNBA also urges constitutionally acceptable use of the Bible in public school classrooms. All support comes from individuals, corporations and foundations.

LNBA was founded in 1940 by a group of business and professional people. It publishes a quarterly newsletter and has the IRS nonprofit status of a 501(c)(3) educational association.

HEADQUARTERS

1865 Broadway, 12th floor, New York, NY 10023 Tel. (212)408-1390 Fax (212)408-1448

Media Contact, Exec. Dir., Thomas R. May, 1865 Broadway, 12th Floor, New York, NY 10023 Tel. (212)408-1390 Fax (212)408-1448

OFFICERS

Pres., Stewart S. Furlong
Chpsn., Victor W. Eimicke
Chpsn. Emeritus, Kenneth S Giniger, Esq.
Vice-Pres., Max Chopnick, Esq.
Vice-Pres., Ron Anderson
Vice-Pres., George Q. Nichols
Treas., Irvin J. Borowsky
Sec., J. Marshall Gage

The Liturgical Conference

Founded in 1940 by a group of Benedictines, the Liturgical Conference is an independent, ecumenical, international association of persons concerned about liturgical renewal and meaningful worship. The Liturgical Conference is known chiefly for its periodicals, books, materials and sponsorship of regional and local workshops on worship-related concerns in cooperation with various church groups.

HEADQUARTERS

8750 Georgia Ave., Ste. 123, Silver Spring, MD 20910-3621 Tel. (301)495-0885

Media Contact, Exec. Dir., ----

OFFICERS

Pres., Frank Senn
Vice-Pres., Eleanor Bernstein
Sec., Mark Bangert
Treas., Fred Anderson
Exec. Dir., ----

The Lord's Day Alliance of the United States

The Lord's Day Alliance of the United States, founded in 1888 in Washington, D.C., is the only national organization whose sole purpose is the preservation and cultivation of Sunday, the Lord's Day, as a day of rest and worship. The Alliance also seeks to safeguard a Day of Common Rest for all people regardless of their faith. Its Board of Managers is composed of representatives from 25 denominations.

It serves as an information bureau, publishes a magazine, Sunday, and furnishes speakers and a variety of materials such as pamphlets, a book, *The Lord's Day,* videos, posters, radio spot announcements, decals, cassettes, news releases, articles for magazines and television programs.

HEADQUARTERS

2930 Flowers Rd. S., Ste. 16, Atlanta, GA 30341 Tel. (770)936-5376 Fax (770)454-6081

Media Contact, Exec. Dir. & Ed., Dr. Jack P. Lowndes

OFFICERS

Exec. Dir. & Ed., Dr. Jack P. Lowndes

Pres., Dr. Paul Craven, Jr.
Vice-Pres.: Charles Holland; Roger A. Kvam; Timothy E. Bird; John H. Schaal; William B. Shea; W. David Sapp
Sec., Rev. Donald Pepper
Treas., Mr. E. Larry Eidson

Lutheran World Relief

Lutheran World Relief (LWR) is an overseas development and relief agency based in New York City which responds quickly to natural and man-made disasters and supports more than 160 long-range development projects in countries throughout Africa, Asia, the Middle East and Latin America.

Founded in 1945 to act in behalf of Lutherans in the United States, LWR has as its mission "to support the poor and oppressed of less-developed countries in their efforts to meet basic human needs and to participate with dignity and equity in the life of their communities; and to alleviate human suffering resulting from natural disaster, war, social conflict or poverty."

HEADQUARTERS

390 Park Ave. S., New York, NY 10016 Tel. (212)532-6350 Fax (212)213-6081
Media Contact, Jonathan C. Frerichs

OFFICERS

Exec. Dir., Kathryn F. Wolford

The Mennonite Central Committee

The Mennonite Central Committee is the relief and service agency of North American Mennonite and Brethren in Christ Churches. Representatives from Mennonite and Brethren in Christ groups make up the MCC, which meets annually in February to review its program and to approve policies and budget. Founded in 1920, MCC administers and participates in programs of agricultural and economic development, education, health, self-help, relief, peace and disaster service. MCC has about 950 workers serving in 50 countries in Africa, Asia, Europe, Middle East and South, Central and North America.

MCC has service programs in North America that focus both on urban and rural poverty areas. Additionally there are North American programs focusing on such diverse matters as community conciliation, employment creation and criminal justice issues. These programs are administered by two national bodies--MCC U.S. and MCC Canada.

Contributions from North American Mennonite and Brethren in Christ churches provide the largest part of MCC's support. Other sources of financial support include the contributed earnings of volunteers, grants from private and government agencies and contributions from Mennonite churches abroad. The total income in 1994, including material aid contributions, amounted to $38,768,514.

MCC tries to strengthen local communities by working in cooperation with local churches or other community groups. Many personnel are placed with other agencies, including missions. Programs are planned with sensitivity to locally felt needs.

HEADQUARTERS

Box 500, 21 S. 12th St., Akron, PA 17501 Tel. (717)859-1151 Fax (717)859-2171
Canadian Office, 134 Plaza Dr., Winnipeg, MB R3T 5K9 Tel. (204)261-6381 Fax (204)269-9875
Media Contact, Exec. Sec., John A. Lapp, P.O. Box 500, Akron, PA 17501 Tel. (717)859-1151 Fax (717)859-2171

OFFICERS

Exec. Secs.: Intl., John A. Lapp; Canada, Marv Frey; U.S.A., Lynette Meck

National Association of Ecumenical Staff

This is the successor organization to the Association of Council Secretaries which was founded in 1940. The name change was made in 1971.

NAES is an association of professional staff in ecumenical and interreligious work. It was established to provide creative relationships among them and to encourage mutual support and personal and professional growth. This is accomplished through training programs, through exchange and discussion of common concerns at conferences, and through the publication of the *Corletter,* in collaboration with NCCC Ecumenical Networks.

HEADQUARTERS

National Council of Churches, 475 Riverside Dr.,Rm. 677, New York, NY 10115-0050 Tel. (212)870-2155 Fax (212)870-2690
Media Contact, Dir., Ecumenical Networks:NCCC USA, Dr. Kathleen S. Hurty

OFFICERS

Pres., Rev. Thomas H. Van Leer, Gtr. Mpls. Council of Churches, 14300 County Hwy. 62, Minnetonka, MN 55345 Tel. (612)949-4540 Fax (612)949-4510
Vice-Pres., Rev. Peg Chemberlin, MN Council of Churches, 122 W. Franklin Ave., Minneapolis, MN 55404 Tel. (612)870-3600 Fax (612)870-3622
1996 Program Chpsn., Rev. Dr. Carol Worthing, IL Conference of Churches, 615 S. 5th St., Springfield, IL 62703 Tel. (217)544-3423 Fax (217)544-9307
Sec., Rev. David Baak, Grand Rapids Area Ctr. for Ecumenism, 38 Fulton W., Grand Rapids, MI 49503 Tel. (616)774-2042 Fax (616)774-2883
Treas., Ms. Alice M. Woldt, Church Coun. of Gtr. Seattle, 4759 15th Ave. NE, Seattle, WA 98105-4404 Tel. (206)525-1213 Fax (206)525-1218
Registrar, Rev. N. J. L'Heureux, Queens Fed. of Churches, 86-17 105th St., Richmond Hill, NY 11418 Tel. (718)847-6764

The National Association of Evangelicals

The National Association of Evangelicals (NAE) is a voluntary fellowship of evangelical denominations, churches, organizations and individuals demonstrating unity in the body of Christ by standing for biblical truth, speaking with a representative voice, and serving the evangelical community through united action, cooperative ministry, and strategic planning.

NAE is comprised of approximately 42,500 congregations nationwide from 47-member denominations and individual congregations from an additional 26 denominations, as well as several hundred independent churches. The membership of the association also includes approximately 250 parachurch ministries and educational institutions. Through these organizations NAE directly and indirectly benefits over 27 million people. These ministries represent a broad range of theological traditions, but all subscribe to the distinctly evangelical NAE Statement of Faith. The association is a nationally recognized entity by the public sector with a reputation for integrity and effective service. The Cooperative ministries of the National Association of Evangelicals demonstrate the association's intentional desire to promote cooperation without compromise.

HEADQUARTERS

450 Gundersen Dr., Carol Stream, IL 60188 Tel. (708)665-0500 Fax (708)665-8575

Office of Public Affairs, 1023 15th St. N.W., Ste. 500, Washington, DC 20005 Tel. (202)789-1011 Fax (202)842-0392

Media Contact, Dir., Ofc. of Information, David L. Melvin, P.O. Box 28, Wheaton, IL 60189 Tel. (708)665-0500 Fax (708)665-8575

OFFICERS

Pres., Dr. David Rambo, P.O. Box 35000, Colorado Springs, CO 80935

1st Vice-Pres., Rev. Leonard J. Hofman, 2237 Radcliffe Circle Dr., Grand Rapids, MI 49546

2nd Vice-Pres., Dr. R. Lamar Vest, P.O. Box 2430, Cleveland, TN 37320-2430

Sec., Dr. Jack Estep, P.O. Box 828, Wheaton, IL 60189

Treas., Dr. Joseph E. Jackson, P.O. Box 2430, Cleveland, TN 37322-2430

STAFF

Pres., Don Argue, Ed.D.
Vice-Pres., Rev. David L. Melvin
Finance & Management: Vice-Pres., Darrell L. Fulton
Office of Public Affairs, Vice-Pres., Dr. Robert P. Dugan, Jr.
Policy Analyst, Rev. Richard Cizik
Counsel, Dr. Billy A. Melvin
Special Representative, Timothy D. Crater
Vice-Pres.-At-Large, Forest Montgomery

MEMBER DENOMINATIONS

Advent Christian General Conference
Assemblies of God
Baptist General Conference
Brethren Church, The (Ashland, Ohio)
Christian & Missionary Alliance
Christian Catholic Church(Evan. Protestant)
Christian Church of North America
Christian Reformed Church in Noth America
Christian Union
Church of God of the Mountain Assembly
Church of the Nazarene
Church of the United Brethren in Christ
Churches of Christ in Christian Union
Conservative Baptist Assoc. of America
Conservative Congregational Christian Conf.
Conservative Lutheran Association
Elim Fellowship
Evangelical Church of North America
Evangelical Congregational Church
Evangelical Free Church of America
Evangelical Friends Intl./North America
Evangelical Mennonite Church
Evangelical Methodist Church
Evangelical Presbyterian Church
Evangelistic Missionary Fellowship
Fellowship of Evangelical Bible Churches
Fire-Baptized Holiness Church of God of the Americas
Free Methodist Church of North America
General Association of General Baptists
Intl. Church of the Foursquare Gospel
Intl. Pentecostal Church of Christ
Intl. Pentecostal Holiness Church
Mennonite Brethren Churches, USA
Midwest Congregational Christian Fellowship
Missionary Church
Open Bible Standard Churches
Pentecostal Church of God
Pentecostal Free Will Baptist Church
Presbyterian Church in America
Primitive Methodist Church, USA
Reformed Church in America (Mid America)
Reformed Episcopal Church
Reformed Presbyterian Church of N.A.
Salvation Army
Wesleyan Church

The National Conference

The National Conference, founded in 1927 as the National Conference of Christians and Jews is a human relations organization dedicated to fighting bias, bigotry and racism in America. The National Conference promotes understanding and respect among all races, religions and cultures through advocacy, conflict resolution and education.

Primary program areas include interfaith and interracial dialogue, youth intercultural communications, training for the administration of justice and the building of community coalitions. The NCCJ has 61 regional offices staffed by approximately 240 people. Nearly 200 members comprise the National Board of Trustees and members from that group form the 22-member Executive Board. Each regional office has its own local board of trustees with a total of about 2,800. The National Board of Trustees meets once annually, the Executive Board at least three times annually.

HEADQUARTERS

71 Fifth Ave., New York, NY 10003 Tel. (212)206-0006 Fax (212)255-6177

Media Contact, Dir. of Communications, Christopher Bugbee

OFFICER

Pres., Sanford Cloud, Jr.

National Conference on Ministry to the Armed Forces

The Conference is an incorporated civilian agency. Representation in the Conference with all privileges of the same is open to all endorsing or certifying agencies or groups authorized to provide chaplains for any branch of the Armed Forces.

The purpose of this organization is to provide a means of dialogue to discuss concerns and objectives and, when agreed upon, to take action with the appropriate authority to support the spiritual ministry to and the moral welfare of Armed Forces personnel.

HEADQUARTERS

4141 N. Henderson Rd., Ste. 13, Arlington, VA 22203 Tel. (703)276-7905 Fax (703)276-7906

Media Contact, Clifford T. Weathers

STAFF

Coord., Clifford T. Weathers
Admn. Asst., Maureen Francis

OFFICERS

Chpsn., K. A. Schwendiman
Chpsn.-elect, Vincent McMenamy
Sec., Ronald Miller
Treas., William B. Leonard, Jr.
Committee Members: Catholic Rep., Msgr. John J. Glynn; Protestant Rep., Rev. W. Robert Johnson, III; Jewish Rep., Rabbi David Lapp; Orthodox Rep., Gregory Havrilak; Member-at-Large, Donald A. Njaa

National Council of the Churches of Christ in the U.S.A.

The National Council of the Churches of Christ in the U.S.A. is the preeminent expression in the United States of the movement toward Christian unity. The NCC's 32 member communions, including Protestant, Orthodox and Anglican church bodies, work together on a wide range of activities that further Christian unity, that witness to the faith and that serve people throughout the world. More than 48 million U.S. Christians belong to churches that hold Council membership. The Council was formed in 1950 in Cleveland, Ohio, by the action of representatives of the member churches and by the merger of 12 previously existing ecumenical agencies, each of which had a different program focus. The roots of some of these agencies go back to the 19th century.

HEADQUARTERS

475 Riverside Dr., New York, NY 10115. Tel. (212)870-2511
Media Contact, Dir. of News Services, Carol J. Fouke, 475 Riverside Dr., Rm. 850, New York, NY 10015, Tel. (212)870-2252, Fax (212)870-2030

GENERAL OFFICERS

Pres., Bishop Melvin G. Talbert
Gen. Sec., Rev. Dr. Joan B. Campbell
Pres.-Elect, Rt. Rev. Craig Anderson
Immediate Past Pres., Rev. Dr. Gordon L. Sommers
Sec., Bishop Cecil Bishop
Treas., Rev. Dr. Margaret J. Thomas
Vice-Pres., World Service and Witness, Rev. Dr. Will L. Herzfeld
Vice-Pres.,National Ministries, Rev. Dr. Richard Hamm
Vice-Pres at Large: Rev. Joan Parrott; Archbishop Khajag Barsamian

ELECTED STAFF

THE GENERAL SECRETARIAT

Tel. (212)870-2141 Fax (212)870-2817
Gen. Sec., Rev. Dr. Joan B. Campbell
Operations Manager, Barbara J. George
Assoc. for Ecumenical Relations, Rev. Eileen W. Lindner
Assoc. for Racial Justice, Dr. Mac Charles Jones
Washington Office: 110 Maryland Ave. NE Washington, D.C. 20002. Tel. (202)544-2350. Fax (202)543-1297. Assoc. Dir., Mary Anderson Cooper

Inter-Faith Relations

Co-directors: Dr. Jay T. Rock, Tel. (212)870-2560 and Rev. Dr. Bert Breiner. Tel. (212)870-2156

Faith and Order

Interim Dir., Rev. Norman A. Hjelm. Tel. (212)870-2569

Communication Commission

Dir., Mike Maus
Dir., News Services, Carol J. Fouke
Dir., Electronic Media, Rev. David W. Pomeroy
Dir., Interpretation Resources, Sarah Vilankulu
Assoc. Dir., Electronic Media, Rev. Roy T. Lloyd

CHURCH WORLD SERVICE AND WITNESS

Tel. (212)870-2257 Fax (212)870-2055
Unit Dir./Deputy Gen. Sec., Rodney I. Page
Dir. of Operations, Mary Ida Gardner
Dir., Constituency Information and Development, Mel Lehman
Dir., Agricultural Missions, Jun Atienza
Dir., World Community, elmira Nazombe
Dir., Global Educ., Loretta Whalen, 2115 N. Charles St., Baltimore, MD 21218. Tel. (410)727-6106 Fax (410)727-6108
Dir., CWS/LWR Ofc. on Development Policy, Carol Capps, 110 Maryland Ave., NE, Suite 108, Washington, DC 20002. Tel. (202)543-6336 Fax (202)543-1297
Dir., Emergency Response, Jerry Bilton
Dir., Immigration & Refugee Program, Beth Ferris
Dir., Leadership Development, John W. Backer
Dir., Overseas Personnel, Esdras Rodriguez-Dias
Dir., Intl. Congregations & Lay Ministry, Arthur O. Bauer
Dir., Africa, Willis H. Logan
Dir., Caribbean & Latin America, Oscar Bolioli Fax: (212)870-3220
Dir., East Asia & the Pacific, Victor W. C. Hsu
Dir./Dir. China Program, Jean Woo
Dir., Japan North America Commission (JNAC), Patricia Patterson
Dir., Europe/USSR, Paul Wilson
Dir., Middle East, David Weaver
Dir., Southern Asia, Larry Tankersley
Community Education and Fund Raising
Tel. (219)264-3102 Fax (219)262-0966
Dir., Community Educ. & Fund Raising, Rev. Mel H. Luetchens, P.O. Box 968, Elkhart, IN 46515

NATIONAL MINISTRIES UNIT

Tel (212)870-2491
Deputy Gen. Sec./Dir. National Ministries Unit, Rev. Dr. Robert L. Polk
Dir., Bible Translation and Utilization, Rev. Dr. Arthur O. Van Eck
Dir., Economic and Environmental Justice, Dr. Jean Sindab
Dir., Ecumenical Networks, Dr. Kathleen Hurty
Dir./Education for Mission/Publisher, Friendship Press. ---
Editors, Friendship Press, Rev. Barbara Withers, Ms. Susan Winslow
Art Production Manager, Sean Grandits
Dir., Evangelization, Rev. George Handley
Dir., Justice for Women, Ms. Karen Hessel
Dir., Ministries in Christian Education, Ms. Dorothy Savage
Associate Director, Ministries in Christian Education, Dr. Joe Leonard
Staff Assoc. for Professional Church Leadership, Peggy Shriver
Assoc. for Racial Justice, Ms. Sammy Toineeta
Coordinator, Urban Programs, Rev. Charles Rawlings
Executive Director, Ecumenical Programs for Urban Service, Ms. Jan Schrock
National Coordinator for the Educational Awards Program, Mrs. Nell B. Gibson
Chair, Worship and the Arts, Dr. Fred Graham

Related Movements

Interfaith Center for Corporate Responsibility, Timothy Smith. Tel. (212)870-2293

Natl. Farm Worker Ministry, Acting Executive Director, Olgha Sierra Sandman

FINANCE AND ADMINISTRATION

Tel. (212)870-2094 Fax (212)870-3112
Asst. Gen. Sec., Rev. Dr. Clifford Droke
Financial Management
Dir. of Treasury Operations, Howard Jost
Controller, Leo Lamb
Deputy Controller, Simon Lai
Asst. Controller, William B. Price

Business Information Services

Co-dir., Rev. Nelson R. Murphy
Co-dir., Phyllis Sharpe
Dir. Governance/ Administrative Ser., Melrose B. Corley

Office of Human Resources

Senior Manager, Michael W. Mazoki
Manager, Recruitment and Employee Relations, Laura Williams
Manager, Training and Staff Development, Aklilu Tadesse

CONSTITUENT BODIES OF THE NATIONAL COUNCIL (with membership dates)

African Methodist Episcopal Church (1950)
African Methodist Episcopal Zion Church (1950)
American Baptist Churches in the U.S.A. (1950)
The Antiochian Orthodox Christian Archdiocese of North America (1966)
Armenian Church of America, Diocese of the (1957)
Christian Church (Disciples of Christ) (1950)
Christian Methodist Episcopal Church (1950)
Church of the Brethren (1950)
Coptic Orthodox Church (1978)
The Episcopal Church (1950)
Evangelical Lutheran Church in America (1950)
Friends United Meeting (1950)
Greek Orthodox Archdiocese of North & South America (1952)
Hungarian Reformed Church in America (1957)
Intl. Council of Community Churches (1977)
Korean Presbyterian Church in America, Gen. Assembly of the (1986)
Moravian Church in America, Northern Province, Southern Province (1950)
Natl. Baptist Convention of America (1950)
Natl. Baptist Convention, U.S.A., Inc. (1950)
Orthodox Church in America (1950)
Philadelphia Yearly Meeting of the Religious Society of Friends (1950)
Polish Natl. Catholic Church of America (1957)
Presbyterian Church (U.S.A.) (1950)
Progressive Natl. Baptist Convention, Inc. (1966)

Reformed Church in America (1950)
Russian Orthodox Church in the U.S.A., Patriarchal Parishes of the (1966)
Serbian Orthodox Church in the U.S.A. & Canada (1957)
The Swedenborgian Church (1966)
Syrian Orthodox Church of Antioch(Archdiocese of the U.S. and Canada) (1960)
Ukrainian Orthodox Church in America (1950)
United Church of Christ (1950)
The United Methodist Church (1950)

National Institute of Business and Industrial Chaplains

NIBIC is an interfaith organization that includes members from a wide variety of denominations and work settings, including corporations, manufacturing plants, air and sea ports, labor unions and pastoral counseling centers. NIBIC has six membership categories, including Clinical, Professional, Affiliates and Organizational.

NIBIC works to establish professional standards for education and practice; promotes and conducts training programs; provides mentoring, networking and chaplaincy information; encourages research and public information dissemination; communicates with business leaders and conducts professional meetings. NIBIC publishes a quarterly newsletter and co-sponsors The Journal of Pastoral Care. A public membership meeting and training conference is held annually.

HEADQUARTERS

2650 Fountainview, Ste. 444, Houston, TX 77057 Tel. (713)266-2456 Fax (713)266-0845

Media Contact, Rev. Diana C. Dale, 2650 Fountainview, Ste. 444, Houston, TX 77057 Tel. (713)266-2456 Fax (713)266-0845

OFFICERS

Pres., Rev. Diana C. Dale
Vice-Pres., Rev. David Plummer
Sec., Rev. Alan Tyson
Treas., Rev. Robert Palmer

National Interfaith Coalition on Aging

The National Interfaith Coalition on Aging (NICA), a constituent unit of the National Council on Aging, is composed of Protestant, Roman Catholic, Jewish and Orthodox national and regional organizations and individuals concerned about the needs of older people and the religious community's response to problems facing the aging population in the United States. NICA was organized in 1972 to address spiritual concerns of older adults through religious sector action.

Primary objectives of NICA are: to enable religious organizations to serve older adults; to encourage religious communities to promote ministry by and with older adults; to support religious workers in aging in their many roles; to be a forum for religious dialogue about aging; and to be an advocate for older adults' concerns.

NICA supports development of programs and services for older people by religious organizations, agencies, judicatories and congregations; develops and distributes resources that help churches and synagogues develop services that improve the quality of life of older people; convenes national and regional training conferences for those who work with older adults; assists its members in advocacy efforts on behalf of quality of life for older people; and maintains dialogue with the Administration on Aging.

HEADQUARTERS

c/o NCOA, 409 Third St., SW, 2nd Floor, Washington, DC 20024 Tel. (202)479-6689 Fax (202)479-0735

Media Contact, NCOA Dir. of Communications, Louise Cleveland

OFFICERS

Chpsn., Elaine Tiller
Chpsn.-Elect, Josselyn Bennett
Past Chpsn., Dr. Carol S. Pierskalla
Sec., ----
Prog. Mgr., Rev. John F. Evans

National Interfaith Hospitality Networks

The National Interfaith Hospitality Networks is a non-profit organization which works with congregations to form Networks which provide shelter, meals and assistance to homeless families. The program mobilizes existing community resources: churches and synagogues for overnight lodging, congregations for volunteers, social service agencies for referrals and day programs. The Network also employs a director who provides assistance and advocacy to Network families as they seek housing and jobs.

NIHN provides technical assistance as well as videotapes, guides and manuals for successful programs.

HEADQUARTERS

120 Morris Ave., Summit, NJ 07901 Tel. (908)-273-1100
Media Contact, Pres., Karen Olson

National Interreligious Service Board for Conscientious Objectors

NISBCO, formed in 1940, is a nonprofit service organization supported by individual contributions and relating to more than thirty religious organizations. Its purpose is to defend and extend the rights of conscientious objectors to war and organized violence. NISBCO provides information on how to register for the draft and to document one's convictions and qualify as a conscientious objector, how to cope with penalties if one does not cooperate, and how to qualify as a conscientious objector while in the Armed Forces. It also provides more general information and training for counselors and the public about conscientious objection, military service and the operation of the draft and possible programs for national service. It operates an international advocacy program for conscientious objectors focusing on Latin America.

As a national resource center it also assists research in its area of interest including the peace witness of religious bodies. Its staff provides referral to local counselors and attorneys and professional support for them. Through publications and speaking, NISBCO encourages people to decide for themselves what they believe about participation in war and to act on the basis of the dictates of their own informed consciences.

HEADQUARTERS

1612 K St. NW, Ste. 1400, Washington, DC 20006-2802 Tel. (202)293-3220 Fax (202)293-3218
Media Contact, Exec. Dir., L. William Yolton

OFFICERS

Exec. Dir., L. William Yolton
Chpsn., David A. Robinson
Vice-Chpsn., Mary H. Miller
Sec., Titus M. Peachey
Treas., Olive M. Tiller

National Religious Broadcasters

National Religious Broadcasters is an association of more than 800 organizations which produce religious programs for radio and television or operate stations carrying predominately religious programs. NRB member organizations are responsible for more than 75 percent of all religious radio and television in the United States, reaching an average weekly audience of millions by radio and television.

Dedicated to the communication of the Gospel, NRB was founded in 1944 to safeguard free and complete access to the broadcast media. By encouraging the development of Christian programs and stations, NRB helps make it possible for millions to hear the good news of Jesus Christ through the electronic media.

HEADQUARTERS

7839 Ashton Ave., Manassas, VA 22110 Tel. (703)330-7000 Fax (703)330-7100
Media Contact, Pres., Brandt Gustavson

OFFICERS

Chmn., Robert Straton, Walter Bennett Communications, Ft. Washington, PA
1st Vice Chmn., Stu Epperson, Salem Communications, Winston-Salem, NC
2nd Vice Chmn., Sue Bahner, WDCW, Syracuse, NY
Sec., Tom Rogeberg, In Touch Ministries, Atlanta, GA
Treas., Richard Mason, Focus on the Family, Colorado Springs, CO
Dir. of PR, Ron Kopczick, NRB, 7839 Ashton Ave., Manassas, VA 22110 Tel. (703)330-7000 Fax (703)330-7100

National Woman's Christian Temperance Union

The National WCTU is a not-for-profit, nonpartisan, interdenominational organization dedicated to the education of our nation's citizens, especially children and teens, on the harmful effects of alcoholic beverages, other drugs and tobacco on the human body and the society in which we live. The WCTU believes in a strong family unit and, through legislation, education and prayer, works to strengthen the home and family.

WCTU, which began in 1874 with the motto, "For God and Home and Every Land," is organized in 58 countries.

HEADQUARTERS

1730 Chicago Ave., Evanston, IL 60201 Tel. (708)864-1396
Media Contact, Michael C. Vitucci, Tel. (813)394-1343

OFFICERS

Pres., Rachel Kelly
Vice-Pres., Rita Wert, 2250 Creek Hill Rd., Lancaster, PA 17601
Promotion Dir., Nancy Zabel
Treas., Joan Van Loh
Rec. Sec., Mildred Burks, 3924 Penniman Ave., Oakland, CA 94619

MEMBER ORGANIZATIONS

Loyal Temperance Legion (LTL), for boys and girls ages 6-12
Youth Temperance Council (YTC), for teens through college age

North American Baptist Fellowship

Organized in 1964, the North American Baptist Fellowship is a voluntary organization of Baptist Conventions in Canada and the United States, functioning as a regional body within the Baptist World Alliance. Its objectives are: (a) to promote fellowship and cooperation among Baptists in North America and (b) to further the aims and objectives of the Baptist World Alliance so far as these affect the life of the Baptist churches in North America. Its membership, however, is not identical with the North American membership of the Baptist World Alliance.

Church membership of the Fellowship bodies is more than 28 million.

The NABF assembles representatives of the member bodies once a year for exchange of information and views in such fields as evangelism and education, missions, stewardship promotion, lay activities and theological education. It conducts occasional consultations for denominational leaders on such subjects as church extension. It encourages cooperation at the city and county level where churches of more than one member group are located.

HEADQUARTERS

Baptist World Alliance Bldg., 6733 Curran St., McLean, VA 22101
Media Contact, Dr. Denton Lotz

OFFICERS

Pres., Dr. Harold Bennett, 202 Long Valley Rd., Brentwood, TN 37027
Vice-Pres., Dr. Robert Roberts, Box 851, Valley Forge, PA 19482-0851

MEMBER BODIES

American Baptist Churches in the USA
Baptist General Conference
Canadian Baptist Federation
General Association of General Baptists
National Baptist Convention of America
National Baptist Convention, USA, Inc.
North American Baptist Conference
Progressive National Baptist Convention, Inc.
Seventh Day Baptist General Conference
Southern Baptist Convention

North American Broadcast Section, World Association for Christian Communication

This group was created in 1970 to bring together those persons in Canada and the United States who have an interest in broadcasting from a Christian perspective.

An annual conference is held during the week after Thanksgiving in the United States that draws more than 200 persons from at least 25 communions.

HEADQUARTERS

1300 Mutual Building, Detroit, MI 48226 Tel. (313)962-0340 Fax (313)962-9044

OFFICERS

Bus. Mgr., Rev. Edward Willingham

Parish Resource Center, Inc.

Parish Resource Center, Inc. promotes, establishes, nurtures and accredits local Affiliate Parish Resource Centers. Affiliate centers educate, equip and strengthen subscribing congregations of all faiths by providing professional consultants, resource materials and workshops. The Parish Resource Center was founded in 1976. In 1995, there were six free-standing affiliates located in Lancaster, PA; Long Island, NY; South Bend, IN.; Denver, CO.; Dayton, OH and New York City. These centers serve congregations from 41 faith traditions.

HEADQUARTERS

633 Community Way, Lancaster, PA 17603 Tel. (717)299-2223 Fax (717)299-7229
Media Contact, Pres., Dr. D. Douglas Whiting

OFFICERS

Chair, Richard J. Ashby, Jr.
Vice-Chair, Dr. James D. Glasse
Sec., Dr. Robert Webber
Treas., R. Leslie Ellis
Pres., Dr. D. Douglas Whiting

Pentecostal/Charismatic Churches of North America

The Pentecostal/Charismatic Churches of North America (PCCNA) was organized October 19, 1994, in Memphis TN. This organizational meeting came the day after the Pentecostal Fellowship of North America (PFNA) voted itself out of existence in order to make way for the new fellowship.

The PFNA had been formed in October 1948 in Des Moines, IA. It was composed of white Pentecostal denominations. The move to develop a multiracial fellowship began when the PFNA Board of Administration initiated a series of discussions with African American Pentecostal leaders. The first meeting was held July 10-11, 1992, in Dallas, TX. A second meeting convened in Phoenix, AZ, January 4-5, 1993. On January 10-11, 1994, 20 representatives from each of the two movements met in Memphis to make final plans for a Dialogue which was held in Memphis, October 1994.

This racial reconciliation meeting has been called "The Memphis Miracle." During this meeting the PFNA was disbanded, and the PCCNA was organized.

HEADQUARTERS

1001 E. Washington St., Greensboro, NC 27301 Tel. (910)272-6564
Media Contact, Bishop Ithiel Clemmons

EXECUTIVE COMMITTEE

Chpsn., Bishop Ithiel Clemmons
1st. Vice-Chpsn., Bishop B. E. Underwood, P.O. Box 12609, Oklahoma City, OK 73157
2nd Vice-Chpsn., Rev. Thomas E. Trask, 1445 Booneville Ave., Springfield, MO 65802
Sec., Bishop Charles Blake, 3045 S. Crenshaw Blvd., Los Angeles, CA 90026
Treas., Dr. John R. Holland, 1910 Sunset Blvd., Los Angeles, CA 90016
Members: Bishop Barbara Amos, 1010 E. 26th, Norfolk, VA 23504; Rev. Billy Joe Daugherty, 7700 S. Lewis, Tulsa, OK 74136; Rev. Robert Harrison, 4308 Golden Hill Dr., Pittsburg, CA 94565; Dr. Jack Hayford, 14300 Sherman Way, Van Nuys, CA 91405-2499; Bishop Gilbert Patterson, 547 Mississippi Blvd., Memphis, TN 38126; Dr. Paul Walker, 2055 Mt. Paran N.W., Atlanta, GA 30327; Bishop Oswill Williams, P.O. Box 2910, Cleveland, TN 37320

Project Equality, Inc.

Project Equality is a non-profit national interfaith program for affirmative action and equal employment opportunity.

Project Equality serves as a central agency to receive and validate the equal employment commitment of suppliers of goods and services to sponsoring organizations and participating institutions, congregations and individuals. Employers filing an accepted Annual Participation Report are included in the Project Equality "Buyer's Guide."

Workshops, training events and consultant services in affirmative action and equal employment practices in recruitment, selection, placement, transfer, promotion, discipline and discharge are also available to sponsors and participants.

HEADQUARTERS

Pres., 6301 Rockhill Dr., Ste. 315, Kansas City, MO 64131 Tel. (816)361-9222 Fax (816)361-8997

Media Contact, Pres., Rev. Maurice E. Culver

OFFICERS

Chpsn., Emilio F. Carrillo
Vice-Chpsn., Sister Christine Matthews
Sec., John Colon
Treas., Rev. Kirk Perucca
Pres., Rev. Maurice E. Culver

SPONSORS/ENDORSING ORGANIZATIONS

American Baptist Churches in the U.S.A.
American Friends Service Committee
American Jewish Committee
Assoc. Of Junior Leagues, Intl.
Central Conference of American Rabbis
Church of the Brethren
Church Women United
Consultation on Church Union
The Episcopal Church
Evangelical Lutheran Church in America
National Association of Church Personnel Administration
National Council of Churches of Christ in the U.S.A.
National Education Association
Presbyterian Church (USA)
Reformed Church in America
Roman Catholic Dioceses & Religious Orders
The United Methodist Church
Unitarian Universalist Association
Union of American Hebrew Congregations
United Church of Christ
United Methodist Assoc. of Health & Welfare Ministries
YWCA of the USA

Protestant Radio and Television Center, Inc.

The Protestant Radio and Television Center, Inc. (PRTVC) is an interdenominational organization dedicated to the purpose of creating, producing, marketing and distributing audio-visual products for the non-profit sector. Its primary constituency is religious, educational and service-oriented groups.

Chartered in 1949, PRTVC provides a state-of-the-art studio facility, professional staff and a talent pool for radio, TV, cassettes and other forms of media production.

Affiliate members include the Episcopal Church, Evangelical Lutheran Church in America, Presbyterian Church (U.S.A.), Agnes Scott College, Candler School of Theology, Emory University and Columbia Theological Seminary.

HEADQUARTERS

1727 Clifton Rd., NE, Atlanta, GA 30329 Tel. (404)634-3324 Fax (404)634-3326

Media Contact, Sandra Rogers

OFFICERS

Bd. Chpsn., Dr. Gerald Troutman
Vice-Chpsn., Dale VanCantfort
Treas., William W. Horlock
Pres., William W. Horlock
Sec., Betty Chilton

Religion In American Life, Inc.

Religion In American Life (RIAL) is a unique cooperative program of some 50 major national religious groups (Catholic, Eastern Orthodox, Jewish, Protestant, Muslim, etc.). It provides services for denominationally-supported, congregation-based outreach and growth projects such as the current *Invite a Friend* program. These projects are promoted through national advertising campaigns reaching the American public by the use of all media. The ad campaigns are produced by a volunteer agency with production/distribution and administration costs funded by denominations and business groups, as well as by individuals. Since 1949, RIAL ad campaign projects have been among the much coveted major campaigns of The Advertising Council. This results in as much as $20 million worth of time and space in a single year, contributed by media as a public service. Through RIAL, religious groups demonstrate respect for other traditions and the value of religious freedom. The RIAL program also includes seminars and symposia, research, leadership awards programs and the placement of worship directories in hotels, motels and public places throughout the nation.

HEADQUARTERS

2 Queenston Pl., Rm. 200, Princeton, NJ 08540 Tel. (609)921-3639 Fax (609)921-0551

Exec. Asst., Sharon E. Lloyd, 2 Queenston Pl., Princeton, NJ 08540 Tel. (609)921-3039 Fax (609)921-0551

EXECUTIVE COMMITTEE

Natl. Chpsn., O. Milton Gossett, Saatchi & Saatchi Worldwide
Chpsn. of Bd., Rev. Dr. Edwin G. Mulder
Vice-Chpsns.: Bishop Khajag Barsamian, Primate (Armenian Church of America); Most Rev. William H. Keeler, (Archbishop of Baltimore); Rabbi Ronald B. Sobel, (Cong. Emanu-El of the City of N.Y.)
Sec., Beverly Campbell, (Church of Jesus Christ of LDS)
Treas., Robertson H. Bennett

STAFF

Pres., Dr. Nicholas B. van Dvck
Exec. Asst., Sharon E. Lloyd
Worship Directory Mgr., Jane Kelly

Religion News Service

Religion News Service (RNS) has provided news and information to the media for more than 60 years. Purchased August 1, 1994 by the Newhouse News Service, it is staffed by veteran jounalists who cover stories on all of the world religions as well as trends in ethics, morality and spirituality.

RNS provides a daily news service, a weekly

news report, and photo and graphic services. The daily service is available via the AP Data Features wire, fax, Ecunet, or e-mail. The weekly report is available electronically or by mail. Photos and graphics are supplied electronically.

HEADQUARTERS

1101 Connecticut Ave. NW, Ste. 350, Washington, DC 20036 Tel. (202)463-8777 Fax (202)463-0033
Media Contact, Dale Hanson Bourke

OFFICERS

Publisher, Dale Hanson Bourke
Editor, Joan Connell
News Editor, Tom Billitteri

Religion Newswriters Association

Founded in 1949, the RNA is a professional association of religion news editors and reporters on secular daily and weekly newspapers, news services and news magazines. It sponsors five annual contests for excellence in religion news coverage in the secular press. Annual meetings are held during a major religious convocation.

HEADQUARTERS

Media Contact, Newsletter Ed., Charles Austin, 634 Johnson Ct., Teaneck, NJ 07666 Tel. (201)-641-6636 Fax (201)836-3497

OFFICERS

Pres., Richard Dujardin, Providence Journal-Bulletin, Providence, RI 02902
1st Vice-Pres., Cecile Holmes White, Houston Chronicle, Houston, TX 77210
2nd Vice-Pres., Gustav Niebuhr, New York Times
Sec., David Briggs, Associated Press
Treas., Gayle White, Atlanta Constitution, 72 Marietta St. NW, Atlanta, GA 30303

Religious Conference Management Association, Inc.

The Religious Conference Management Association, Inc. (RCMA) is an interfaith, nonprofit, professional organization of men and women who have responsibility for planning and/or managing meetings, seminars, conferences, conventions, assemblies or other gatherings for religious organizations.

Founded in 1972, RCMA is dedicated to promoting the highest professional performance by its members and associate members through the mutual exchange of ideas, techniques and methods.

Today RCMA has more than 2,300 members and associate members.

The association conducts an annual conference and exposition which provide a forum for its membership to gain increased knowledge in the arts and sciences of religious meeting planning and management.

HEADQUARTERS

One RCA Dome, Ste. 120, Indianapolis, IN 46225 Tel. (317)632-1888
Media Contact, Exec. Dir., DeWayne S. Woodring

OFFICERS

Pres., Rainer B. Wilson, Sr., Church of Christ Holiness, U.S.A., 819 Hampton, Newport News, VA 23607
Vice-Pres., Rudy Becton, United Pentecostal Church Intl., 8855 Dunn Rd., Hazelwood, MO 63042
Sec.-Treas., Jack Stone, Church of the Nazarene, 6401 The Paseo, Kansas City, MO 64131
Exec. Dir., DeWayne S. Woodring, Religious Conf. Mgt. Assoc., One RCA Dome, Ste. 120, Indianapolis, IN 46225

The Religious Public Relations Council, Inc.

RPRC is an international, interfaith, interdisciplinary association of professional communicators who work for religious groups and causes. It was founded in 1929 and is the oldest non-profit professional public relations organization in the world. RPRC's 500 members include those who work in communications and related fields for church-related institutions, denominational agencies, non- and interdenominational organizations and communications firms who primarily serve religious organizations.

Members represent a wide range of faiths, including Presbyterian, Baptist, Methodist, Lutheran, Episcopalian, Mennonite, Roman Catholic, Seventh-day Adventist, Jewish, Salvation Army, Brethren, Bahá'í, Disciples, Latter-Day Saints and others.

On the national level, RPRC sponsors an annual three-day convention, and has published five editions of a *Religious Public Relations Handbook* for churches and church organizations, and a videostrip, *The Church at Jackrabbit Junction.* Members receive a quarterly newsletter (*Counselor*), and a quarterly digest of professional articles (*MediaKit*). RPRC also co-sponsors an annual national teleconference. There are 14 regional chapters.

RPRC administers the annual Wilbur Awards competition to recognize high quality coverage of religious values and issues in the public media. Wilbur winners include producers, reporters, editors and broadcasters nationwide. To recognize communications excellence within church communities, RPRC also sponsors the annual DeRose-Hinkhouse Awards for its own members.

In 1970, 1980 and 1990, RPRC initiated a global Religious Communications Congress bringing together thousands of persons from western, eastern and third-world nations who are involved in communicating religious faith. Another Congress is planned for 2000.

HEADQUARTERS

475 Riverside Dr. #1948A, New York, NY 10115-1948 Tel. (212)870-2985 Fax (212)870-3578
Media Contact, Lois J. Anderson

OFFICERS

Pres., Daniel R. Gangler, United Methodist Reporter, P.O. Box 660275, Dallas, TX 75226 Tel. (214)630-6495 Fax (214)630-0079
Vice-Pres., Shirley Whipple Struchen, United Methodist Comm., 475 Riverside Dr. #1948A, New York, NY 10115
National Coord., Lois J. Anderson

Standing Conference of Canonical Orthodox Bishops in the Americas

This body was established in 1960 to achieve cooperation among the various Eastern Orthodox

Churches in the United States. The Conference is "a voluntary association of the Bishops in the Americas established to serve as an agency to centralize and coordinate the mission of the Church. It acts as a clearing house to focus the efforts of the Church on common concerns and to avoid duplication and overlapping of services and agencies. Special departments are devoted to campus work, Christian education, military and other chaplaincies, regional clergy fellowships, and ecumenical relations."

HEADQUARTERS

8-10 East 79th St., New York, NY 10021 Tel. (212)570-3500 Fax (212)861-2183

Media Contact, Ecumenical Officer, Rev. Dr. Milton B. Efthimiou, 10 E. 79th St., New York, NY 10021

OFFICERS

Chpsn., His Eminence Iakovos

Vice Chpsn., Most Rev. Metropolitan Silas

MEMBER CHURCHES

Albanian Orthodox Diocese of America

American Carpatho-Russian Orthodox Greek Catholic Ch.

Antiochian Orthodox Christian Archdiocese of All N.A.

Bulgarian Eastern Orthodox Church

Greek Orthodox Archdiocese of North & South America

Orthodox Church in America

Romanian Orthodox Church in America

Serbian Orthodox Church for the U.S.A. & Canada

Ukrainian Orthodox Church of America

Ukrainian Orthodox Church of Canada

T.H.E.O.S. International

T.H.E.O.S. is a nonprofit, nondenominational self-help support network of men and women who provide emotional assistance to the widowed. Established in 1962, T.H.E.O.S. chapters hold monthly group meetings so that bereaved people can help themselves and others through the process of grieving. The organization also publishes a magazine called *Survivor's Outreach*, the brochure "What Do You Say to a Widowed Person?" and a grief bibliography. In addition, T.H.E.O.S. hosts an international annual conference.

T.H.E.O.S. is comprised of more than 500 volunteers throughout the United States and Canada. There are 75 T.H.E.O.S. chapters in North America.

HEADQUARTERS

322 Boulevard of the Allies, Ste. 105, Pittsburgh, PA 15222-1919 Tel. (412)471-7779 Fax (412)-471-7782

Media Contact, Will Burgunder

United Ministries in Higher Education

United Ministries in Higher Education is a cooperative effort to provide religious programs and services on campuses of higher education.

HEADQUARTERS

Media Contact, Res. Sec., Linda Danby Freeman, 7407 Steele Creek Rd., Charlotte, NC 28217 Tel. (704)588-2182 Fax (704)588-3652

OFFICERS

Admn. Coord., Clyde O. Robinson, Jr., 7407 Steele Creek Rd., Charlotte, NC 28217 Tel. (704)588-2182 Fax (704)588-3652

Treas., Gary Harke, P. O. Box 386, Sun Prairie, WI 53590 Tel. (608)837-0537 Fax (608)825-6610

Personnel Service, Kathy Carson, 11780 Borman Dr., Ste. 100, St.Louis, MO 63146 Tel. (314)-991-3000 Fax (314)993-9018

Resource Center, Linda Danby Freeman, 7407 Steele Creek Rd., Charlotte, NC 28217 Tel. (704)588-2182 Fax (704)588-3652

PARTICIPATING DENOMINATIONS

Christian Church (Disciples of Christ)

Church of the Brethren

Moravian Church (Northern Province)

Presbyterian Church (U.S.A.)

United Church of Christ

Vellore Christian Medical College Board (USA), Inc.

The Vellore Christian Medical College Board has been linked since 1900 to the vision of the young American medical doctor, Ida S. Scudder. Dr. Ida's dream initially was to ensure quality health care for women and children in India.

American women and men representing several church denominations wanted to be a part of Dr. Ida's dream and in 1916 recommended Vellore as the site for the proposed Missionary Medical College for Women. Since 1947 the Christian Medical College has admitted women and men. The hospital has a commitment to serve all regardless of ability to pay. The partnership between Vellore India and Vellore USA has continued uninterrupted to the present time.

HEADQUARTERS

475 Riverside Dr., Rm. 243, New York, NY 10115 Tel. (212)870-2640 Fax (212)870-2173

Media Contact, Exec. Dir., Dr. Robert H. Carman

OFFICERS

Pres., Alfred E. Berthold, 2452 Club Rd., Columbus, OH 43221

Vice-Pres., Miriam Ballert, 7104 Olde Oak Ct., Prospect, KY 40059

Sec., Sarla Lall, 475 Riverside Dr., Rm. 1540, New York, NY 10115

Treas., Anish Mathai, 235 W. 56th St., Apt. 25M, New York, NY 10119

The World Conference on Religion and Peace (WCRP/USA)

The World Conference on Religion and Peace in the United States (WCRP/USA) provides a forum for the nation's religious bodies based upon respect for religious differences and the recognition that in today's world cooperation among religions offers an important opportunity to mobilize and coordinate their great moral and sociological capacities for constructive action inherent in religious communities.

WCRP/USA provides American religious bodies with opportunities for the following: to clarify their respective orientation to both national and international social concerns; to coordinate their efforts with other religious groups on behalf of widely-shared concerns; to design, undertake and evaluate joint action projects and to communicate and collaborate with similar national religious forums organized by WCRP around the world.

HEADQUARTERS

WCRP/USA OFFICE, 777 United Nations Plaza, New York, NY 10017 Tel. (212)687-2163 Fax (212)983-0566

Media Contact, Sec. Gen., Dr. William F. Vendley

OFFICERS

Pres., Ms. Mary Jane Patterson

Sec. Gen., Dr. William F. Vendley

Vice-Pres.: Dr. Viqar A. Hamdani; Ms. Judith M. Hertz; Rev. Malcolm R. Sutherland; Rev. Robert Smylie

Sec., Ms. Edna McCallion

Treas., Rev. Robert McClean

Officers *Ex Officio*: Intl. Pres., Mrs. Norma U. Levitt

Exec. Comm. Officers: Dr. John Borelli; Edward Doty; Dr. Jane Evans; Ms. Betty Golumb; Dr. Anand Mohan; Rev. Katsuji Suzuki

World Day of Prayer

World Day of Prayer is an ecumenical movement initiated and carried out by Christian women in 170 countries who conduct a common day of prayer on the first Friday of March to which all people are welcome. There is an annual theme for the order of worship which has been prepared by women in a different country each year. In 1996 the women of Haiti have prepared the theme, "God Calls Us To Respond." The WDP motto is informed prayer and prayful action. The offering at this service is gathered by the WDP National Committee and given to help people who are in need.

HEADQUARTERS

World Day of Prayer International Comm., 475 Riverside Dr., Rm. 824, New York, NY 10115 Tel. (212)870-3049 Fax (212)870-3049

Exec. Dir., Eileen King

World Methodist Council-North American Section

The World Methodist Council, one of the 30 or so "Christian World Communions," shares a general tradition which is common to all Christians.

The world organization of Methodists and related United Churches is comprised of 71 churches with roots in the Methodist tradition. These churches found in 107 countries have a membership of more than 29 million.

The Council's North American Section, comprised of nine Methodist and United Church denominations, provides a regional focus for the Council in Canada, the United States and Mexico. The North American Section meets at the time of the quinquennial World Conference and Council, and separately as Section between world meetings. The Section will meet in Rio de Janeiro, Brazil in August 1996 during the 17th World Methodist Conference.

North American Churches related to the World Methodist Council have a membership of over 15 million and a church community of more than 31 million.

Headquarters

P.O. Box 518, Lake Junaluska, NC 28745 Tel. (704)456-9432 Fax (704)456-9433

Media Contact, Gen. Sec., Joe Hale

OFFICERS

Pres., Bishop L. Bevel Jones, III, P.O. Box 18750, Charlotte, NC 28218

Vice-Pres.: Mr. Horacio Aguilar Madrid; Bishop Richard O. Bass, Sr.; Bishop John Bryant; Dr. David L. McKenna; Dr. Brian D. Thorpe; Dr. Earle L. Wilson

Treas., Dr. James W. Holsinger, Jr.

Asst. Treas., Mrs. Edna Alsdurf

Sec., Dr. Joe Hale

Presidium Members from North America: Bishop Nathaniel L. Linsey; Mrs. Frances Alguire; Bishop Raul Ruiz

YMCA of the USA

The YMCA is one of the largest private voluntary organizations in the world, serving about 30 million people in more than 100 countries. In the United States, about 2,000 local branches, units, camps and centers annually serve almost 13 million people of all ages, races and abilities. About half of those served are female. No one is turned away because of an inability to pay.

The YMCA is best known for health and fitness. The Y teaches youngsters to swim, organizes youth basketball games and offers adult aerobics. But the Y represents more than fitness--it works to strengthen families and help people develop values and behavior that are consistent with Christian principles.

The Y offers hundreds of programs including day camp for children, child care, exercise for people with disabilities, teen clubs, environmental programs, substance abuse prevention, family nights, job training and many more programs from infant mortality prevention to overnight camping for seniors.

The kind of programs offered at a YMCA will vary; each is controlled by volunteer board members who make their own program, policy, and financial decisions based on the special needs of their community. In its own way, every Y promotes good health, strong families, confident youth, solid communities and a better world.

The YMCA was founded in London, England, in 1844 by George Williams and friends who lived and worked together as clerks. Their goal was to save other live-in clerks from the wicked life of the London streets. The first members were evangelical Protestants who prayed and studied the Bible as an alternative to vice. The Y has always been nonsectarian and today accepts those of all faiths at all levels of the organization.

HEADQUARTERS

101 N. Wacker Dr., Chicago, IL 60606 Tel. (312)-977-0031 Fax (312)977-9063

Media Contact, Public Relations Assoc., Jan McCormick

OFFICERS

Board Chpsn., Daniel E. Emerson

Exec. Dir., David R. Mercer

Public Relations Assoc., Jan McCormick

Young Women's Christian Association of the United States

The YWCA of the U.S.A. is comprised of 374 affiliates in communities and on college campuses across the United States. It serves one million members and program participants. It seeks to empower women and girls to enable them, coming together across lines of age, race, religious belief, economic and occupational status to make a significant contribution to the elimination of racism and the achievement of peace, justice, freedom and dignity for all people. Its leadership is vested in a National Board, whose functions are to unite into an effective continuing organization the autonomous member Associations for furthering the purposes of the National Association and to participate in the work of the World YWCA.

HEADQUARTERS

726 Broadway, New York, NY 10003 Tel. (212)-614-2700 Fax (212)677-9716
Chief of Staff, Cynthia Sutliff

OFFICERS

Pres., Ann Stallard
Sec., Nancy Obermeyer
Exec. Dir., Prema Mathai-Davis

Youth for Christ/USA

Founded in 1944, the mission of YFC is to communicate the life-changing message of Jesus Christ to every young person.

There are 231 locally controlled YFC programs serving in cities and metropolitan areas of the United States.

YFC's Campus Life Club program involves teens who attend approximately 1,433 high schools in the United States. YFC's staff now numbers approximately 900. In addition, nearly 10,000 part-time and volunteer staff supplement the full-time staff. Youth Guidance, a ministry for nonschool-oriented youth includes group homes, court referrals, institutional services and neighborhood ministries. The year-round conference and camping program involves approximately 35,000 young people each year. A family-oriented ministry designed to enrich individuals and church family education programs is carried on through Family Forum, a daily five-minute radio program on more than 300 stations. Independent, indigenous YFC organizations also work in 127 countries overseas.

HEADQUARTERS

U.S. Headquarters, P.O. Box 228822, Denver, CO 80222 Tel. (303)843-9000 Fax (303)843-9002
Canadian Organization, 822-167 Lombard Ave., Winnipeg, MB R3B 0T6
Media Contact, Pres., Roger Cross, Box 228822, Denver, CO 80222 Tel. (303)843-9000 Fax (303)843-9002

OFFICERS

United States, Pres., Roger Cross
Canada, Pres., ----
Intl. Organization: Pres., Dr. Gerry Gallimore

US COOPERATIVE ORGANIZATIONS

2. CANADIAN COOPERATIVE ORGANIZATIONS, NATIONAL

In most cases the organizations listed here work on a national level and cooperate across denominational lines. Regional cooperative organizations in Canada are listed in section 7.

Aboriginal Rights Coalition (Project North)

ARC is a coalition for education and action on issues of Aboriginal justice in Canada. It works in partnership with native organizations and local network groups. The major focus is on the just settlement of Aboriginal land rights, impact of major resource development, self-determination, and related military and environmental concerns.

HEADQUARTERS

151 Laurier E., Ottawa, ON K1N 6N8 Tel. (613)-235-9956 Fax (613)235-1302
Media Contact, Natl. Coord., Ed Bianchi

OFFICERS

Co-Chpsns.: Lorraine Land; Brian George
Natl. Coord., Ed Bianchi

MEMBER ORGANIZATIONS

Anglican Church of Canada
Canadian Conference of Catholic Bishops
Council of Christian Reformed Churches in Canada
Evangelical Lutheran Church in Canada
Mennonite Central Committee
Oblate Conference of Canada
Presbyterian Church of Canada
Religious Society of Friends (Quakers)
Society of Jesus (Jesuits)
United Church of Canada

Alliance For Life—Alliance Pour La Vie

Alliance For Life was incorporated in 1972 to promote the right to life from conception to natural death. A registered charity for the purpose of education, Alliance conducts research on all life issues: abortion, infanticide, euthanasia and more. Alliance publishes materials to disseminate the information gained through that research. Alliance has prepared a one-hour documentary on untimely pregnancy and maintains a toll-free line to counsel women with inconveniently timed pregnancies and to help others suffering from post-abortion syndrome.

Alliance is the umbrella organization for 245 pro-life organizations in Canada. Governed by a Board of Directors composed of representatives from all provinces, it holds annual conferences in alternating provinces. Conferences are open to the public.

In 1992, Alliance For Life was split to permit the establishment of Alliance Action, Inc., a non-profit, non-charitable entity which is mandated to do advocacy work which Alliance For Life cannot do as a charity. It is located at the same address and publishes *Pro Life News*, a monthly news magazine.

HEADQUARTERS

B1-90 Garry St., Winnipeg, MB R3C 4H1 Tel. (204)942-4772 Fax (204)943-9283
Media Contact, Exec. Dir., Anna M. Desilets

ALLIANCE FOR LIFE OFFICERS

Pres., Chuck Smith
1st Vice-Pres., Kim Dewar
2nd Vice-Pres., Rachel Murray
Treas., Jim Arsenault
Sec., Betty Smith

ALLIANCE ACTION OFFICERS

Pres., Rachel Murray
Media Contact, Exec. Dir., Ingrid Krueger, Tel. (204)943-5273 Fax (204)943-9283
1st Vice-Pres., Chuck Smith
2nd Vice-Pres., Kim Dewar
Treas., Jim Arsenault
Sec., Betty Smith
Medical Advisor, Dr. J. L. Reynolds

Association of Canadian Bible Colleges

The Association brings into cooperative association Bible colleges in Canada that are evangelical in doctrine and whose objectives are similar. Services are provided to improve the quality of Bible college education in Canada and to further the interests of the Association by means of conferences, seminars, cooperative undertakings, information services, research, publications and other projects.

HEADQUARTERS

Box 4000, Three Hills, AB T0M 2N0 Tel. (403)-443-5511 Fax (403)443-5540
Media Contact, Sec./Treas., Peter Doell

OFFICERS

Pres., Larry McKinney, Tel. (204)433-7488 Fax (204)433-7158
Vice-Pres., James Cianca, Tel. (519)434-6801 Fax (519)434-4998
Sec./Treas., Peter Doell, Tel. (403)443-5511 Fax (403)443-5540
Members-at-Large: Virginia Sherman, Tel. (403)-284-5100 Fax (403)220-9567; David Boyd, Tel. (705)748-9111 Fax (705)748-3931; Walter Unger, Tel. (604)853-3358 Fax (604)853-3063

Canadian Bible Society

As early as 1804, the British and Foreign Bible Society was at work in Canada. The oldest Bible Society branch is at Truro, Nova Scotia, and has been functioning continually since 1810. In 1904, the various auxiliaries of the British and Foreign Bible Society joined to form the Canadian Bible Society.

The Canadian Bible Society has 16 district offices across Canada, each managed by a District Secretary. The Society holds an annual meeting consisting of one representative from each district, plus an Executive Committee whose members are appointed by the General Board.

Each year contributions, bequests and annuity

income of $11 million come from Canadian supporters. Through the Canadian Bible Society's membership in the United Bible Societies' fellowship, over 64 million Bibles, Testaments and Portions were distributed globally in 1994. At least one book of the Bible is now available in over 2,090 languages.

The Canadian Bible Society is nondenominational. Its mandate is to translate, publish and distribute the Scriptures, without doctrinal note or comment, in languages that can be easily read and understood.

HEADQUARTERS

10 Carnforth Rd., Toronto, ON M4A 2S4 Tel. (416)757-4171 Fax (416)757-3376
Media Contact, Dir., Ministry Funding, Barbara Walkden

OFFICER

Gen. Sec., Dr. Floyd C. Babcock

Canadian Centre for Ecumenism

The Centre was founded in 1963 for the promotion of interdenominational dialogue in Montreal. It grew by stages to become a national, bilingual, ecumenical resource centre for the promotion of Christian unity and interfaith understanding. The centre established an interchurch board of directors in 1976 and obtained a federal charter. Collaborating with the Canadian Council of Churches in work for Christian Unity, the Centre is an office related to the Canadian Conference of Catholic Bishops and offers its services to other churches as well as other religions.

The Centre has three major areas of activity: education, dialogue and prayer/sharing of spiritual riches. Its quarterly magazine Ecumenism/Oecuménism is published in English and French and goes out to 44 countries. A specialized library is open to the public M-F, 9-5.

HEADQUARTERS

2065 Sherbrooke St. W, Montreal, QC H3H 1G6 Tel. (514)937-9176 Fax (514)937-2684
Media Contact, Bernice Baranowski

OFFICERS

Pres., Richard Bowie, Ogilvie-Renault, 1981 Mcgill College Ave. 12th Floor, Montréal, QC H3A 3C1
Vice-Pres., Richard Bowie, 181 Morrison Ave., Mont Royal, QC H3R 1K5
Treas., Gaudry Delisle, 11450 Filion St., Montréal, QC H4J 1T1
Exec. Dir., Rev. Philippe Thebodeau

The Canadian Council of Churches

The Canadian Council of Churches was organized in 1944. Its basic purpose is to provide the churches with an agency for conference and consultation and for such common planning and common action as they desire to undertake. It encourages ecumenical understanding and action throughout Canada through local councils of churches. It also relates to the World Council of Churches and other agencies serving the worldwide ecumenical movement.

The Council has a Triennial Assembly, a Governing Board which meets semiannually and an Executive Committee. Program is administered through two commissions--Faith and Witness, Justice and Peace.

HEADQUARTERS

40 St. Clair Ave. E, Ste. 201, Toronto, ON M4T 1M9 Tel. (416)921-4152 Fax (416)921-7478
Media Contact, Gen. Sec. Rev. Robert H. Mills, Tel. (416)921-7759

OFFICERS AND STAFF

Pres., Dr. Alexandra Johnston
Vice-Pres.: Archbishop Gilles Ouellet; Archbishop Hovnan Derderian; Major Helen Hastie
Treas., Mr. John Hart
Int. Gen. Sec., Rev. Robert H. Mills
Assoc. Sec., Rev. Douglas duCharme
Faith & Witness, Dr. Eileen Scully

AFFILIATED INSTITUTION

Canadian Churches' Forum for Global Min.: Co-Dirs. Robert Faris; Kevin Anderson, 11 Madison Ave., Toronto, ON M5R 2S2 Tel. (416)924-9351

MEMBERS

The Anglican Church of Canada
The Armenian Orthodox Church - Diocese of Canada
Baptist Convention of Ontario and Quebec
British Methodist Episcopal Church*
Canadian Conference of Catholic Bishops*
Christian Church (Disciples of Christ)
Coptic Orthodox Church of Canada
Ethiopian Orthodox Church in Canada
Evangelical Lutheran Church in Canada
Greek Orthodox Diocese of Toronto (Canada)
Orthodox Church in America, Diocese of Canada
Polish National Catholic Church
Presbyterian Church in Canada
Reformed Church in Canada
Religious Society of Friends--Canada Yearly Meeting
Salvation Army--Canada and Bermuda
The Ukrainian Orthodox Church
The United Church of Canada
*Associate Member

Canadian Evangelical Theological Association

In May 1990, about 60 scholars, pastors and other interested persons met together in Toronto to form a new theological society. Arising out of the Canadian chapter of the Evangelical Theological Society, the new association established itself as a distinctly Canadian group with a new name. It sponsored its first conference as CETA in Kingston, Ontario, in May 1991.

CETA provides a forum for scholarly contributions to the renewal of theology and church in Canada. CETA seeks to promote theological work which is loyal to Christ and his Gospel, faithful to the primacy and authority of Scripture and responsive to the guiding force of the historic creeds and Protestant confessions of the Christian Church. In its newsletters and conferences, CETA seeks presentations that will speak to a general theologically-educated audience, rather than to specialists.

CETA has special interest in evangelical points of view upon and contributions to the wider conversations regarding religious studies and church life. Members therefore include pastors, students and other interested persons as well as professional academicians. CETA currently includes about 100 members, many of whom attend its annual conference in the early summer.

HEADQUARTERS

c/o Glen G. Scorgie, N. American Baptist College, 11525 23rd Ave., Edmonton, AB T6J 4T3 Tel. (403)437-1960 Fax (403)436-9416
Media Contact, Glen G. Scorgie

OFFICERS

Pres., Dr. Glen G. Scorgie
Sec./Treas., Dr. W. David Buschart
Publications Coord., Dr. John G. Stackhouse, Jr.
Executive Members: Dr. Edith Humphrey; Mr. Alan Bulley; Dr. Terry Tiessen

Canadian Society of Biblical Studies/Société des Études Bibliques

The society was founded in 1933 to stimulate the critical investigation of classical biblical literature and related areas of research by exchange of scholarly research in publications and in public forum.

The CSBS/SCEB has 283 members and meets annually in conjunction with the Learned Societies of Canada. Every year the Society publishes a Bulletin and is a member of the Canadian Corporation for the Study of Religion/Corporation Canadienne des Sciences Religieuses, which publishes Studies in Religion/Sciences religieuses quarterly.

HEADQUARTERS

Dept. of Religious Studies, Memorial University of Newfoundland, St. John's, NF A1C 5S7 Tel. (709)737-8166 Fax (709)737-4569
Media Contact, Exec. Sec., Dr. David J. Hawkin

OFFICERS

Pres., Jack Lightstone, 1455 deMaisonneuve Blvd. W., Concordia University, Montreal, PQ H3G 1M8 Tel. (514)848-4892
Vice-Pres., Wayne McCready, Univ. of Calgary, Dept. of Religious Studies, Calgary, AB T2N 1N4 Tel. (403)220-5886
Sec., Dr. David J. Hawkin, Tel. (709)737-8173
Treas., Kim Ian Parker, Tel. (709)737-8594
Publications Coord., Tom Robinson, Univ. of Lethbridge, Dept of Religion, 4401 University Dr., Lethbridge, AB T1K 3M4
Programme Coord., Adele Reinhartz, Dept. of Religious Studies, McMaster Univ., Hamilton, ON L8S 4K1 Tel. (905)525-9140
Member-at-Large, John L. McLaughlin, 316 Washington Ave., Wheeling Jesuit College, Wheeling, WV 26003 Tel. (304)243-2380

Canadian Tract Society

The Canadian Tract Society was organized in 1970 as an independent distributor of Gospel leaflets to provide Canadian churches and individual Christians with quality materials proclaiming the Gospel through the printed page. It is affiliated with the American Tract Society, which encouraged its formation and assisted in its founding, and for whom it serves as an exclusive Canadian distributor. The CTS is a nonprofit international service ministry.

HEADQUARTERS

26 Hale Rd., P.O. Box 2156, Brampton, ON L6T 3S4 Tel. (905)457-4559 Fax (905)457-4559
Media Contact, Mgr., Donna Croft

OFFICERS

Pres., Stanley D. Mackey
Sec., Robert J. Burns

The Church Army in Canada

The Church Army in Canada has been involved in evangelism and Christian social service since 1929.

HEADQUARTERS

397 Brunswick Ave., Toronto, ON M5R 2Z2 Tel. (416)924-9279
Media Contact, National Dir., Capt. Walter W. Marshall

OFFICERS

National Dir., Capt. Walter W. Marshall
Asst. Dir., Capt. R. Bruce Smith
Dir. of Training, Capt. Roy E. Dickson
Field Sec., Capt. Reed S. Fleming
Bd. Chmn., Ivor S. Joshua, C.A.

The Churches' Council on Theological Education in Canada: An Ecumenical Foundation

The Churches' Council (CCTE:EF) maintains an overview of theological education in Canada on behalf of its constituent churches and functions as a bridge between the schools of theology and the churches which they serve.

Founded in 1970 with a national and ecumenical mandate, the CCTE:EF provides resources for research into matters pertaining to theological education, opportunities for consultation and cooperation and a limited amount of funding in the form of grants for the furtherance of ecumenical theological education.

HEADQUARTERS

60 St. Clair Avenue E, Ste. 302, Toronto, ON M4T 1N5 Tel. (416)928-3223 Fax (416)928-3563
Media Contact, Exec. Dir., Dr. Thomas Harding

OFFICERS

Bd. of Dir., Chpsn., Dr. Richard Crossman, Waterloo Lutheran Seminary, 75 University Ave. W., Waterloo, ON N2L 3C5
Bd. of Dir., Vice-Chpsn., Sr. Ellen Leonard, CSJ, Univ. of St. Michaels's College, 81 St. Mary St., Toronto, ON M5S 1J4
Treas., Donald Hall, 80 Strathallan Blvd., Toronto, ON M5N 1S7
Exec. Dir., Dr. Thomas Harding

MEMBER ORGANIZATIONS

The General Synod of the Anglican Church of Canada
Canadian Baptist Ministries
The Evangelical Lutheran Church in Canada
The Presbyterian Church in Canada
The Canadian Conference of Catholic Bishops
The United Church of Canada

Concerns, Canada: a corporate division of Alcohol & Drug Concerns, Inc.

Concerns, Canada is a registered, non-profit, charitable organization that has been closely associated with the Christian Church throughout its long history. The organization's mandate is "to promote and encourage a positive lifestyle free from dependence upon alcohol, tobacco and other drugs."

The organization was granted a national charter in 1987, moving from an Ontario charter dating back to 1934. Among its services are: Toc Alpha (its youth wing for 14-to-24 year olds; PLUS (Positive Life-Using Skills), a teacher curriculum for grades 4 to 8; two Institutes on Addiction Studies; courses for clients of the Ontario Ministry of Corrections; and educational materials for target groups.

HEADQUARTERS

4500 Sheppard Ave. E, Ste. 112H, Agincourt, ON M1S 3R6 Tel. (416)293-3400
Media Contact, Exec. Dir., Rev. Karl N. Burden

OFFICERS

Pres., Keith Farraway, Douglas Dr. R.R. 2, Bracebridge, ON P1l 1W9
Vice-Pres.: Rev. Larry Gillians, 11 Dundas St. W., Napanee, ON K7R 1Z3; Scot Lougheed, 97 Dean Ave., Guelph, ON N1G 1L7
Treas., Jean Desgagne, Union Bank Of Switzerland, 154 Univeristy Ave., Toronto, ON M5H 3Z4
Exec. Dir., Rev. Karl N. Burden

Ecumenical Coalition for Economic Justice (ECEJ)

Ecumenical Coalition for Economic Justice (ECEJ) is a national project of five Canadian churches (Anglican Church in Canada, Roman Catholic Church, Lutheran Church, Presbyterian Church and United Church of Canada) mandated to assist popular groups and progressive church organizations struggling for economic justice in Canada and the Third World. ECEJ pursues these objectives through research, popular education and political action. ECEJ is guided by an administrative committee composed of representatives from each of the sponsoring churches.

Research priorities for the next year includes global economics, women and economic justice, coalition building and social policy.

HEADQUARTERS

77 Charles St. W, Ste. 402, Toronto, ON M5S 1K5 Tel. (416)921-4615 Fax (416)922-1419
Media Contact, Educ. & Communications, Jennifer Wershler-Henry

OFFICERS

Co-Chpsn., Jim Marshall
Co-Chpsn., Doryne Kirby

STAFF

Researcher, John Dillon
Women & Economic Justice, Programme Coord., Lorraine Michael
Education Programme Coord., Jennifer Wershler-Henry
Admn. Coord., Diana Gibbs Bravo

Evangelical Fellowship of Canada

The Fellowship was formed in 1964. There are 28 denominations, 115 organizations, 1,025 local churches and 15,000 individual members.

Its purposes are: "Fellowship in the gospel" (Phil. 1:5), "the defence and confirmation of the gospel" (Phil. 1:7) and "the furtherance of the gospel" (Phil. 1:12). The Fellowship believes the Holy Scriptures, as originally given, are infallible and that salvation through the Lord Jesus Christ is by faith apart from works.

In national and regional conventions the Fellowship urges Christians to live exemplary lives and to openly challenge the evils and injustices of society. It encourages cooperation with various agencies in Canada and overseas that are sensitive to social and spiritual needs.

HEADQUARTERS

Office: 175 Riviera Dr., Markham, ON L3R 5J6 Tel. (416)479-5885 Fax (416)479-4742
Mailing Address: P.O. Box 8800, Stn. B, Willowdale, ON M2K 2R6
Media Contact, Exec. Dir., Dr. Brian C. Stiller, 175 Riviera Dr., #1, Markham, ON L3R 5J6 Tel. (416)479-5885 Fax (416)479-4742

OFFICERS

Exec. Dir., Dr. Brian C. Stiller
Pres., Rev. Ken Birch
Vice-Pres., Rev. Abe Funk
Treas., Mrs. Marjorie Osborne
Sec., Rev. Grover Crosby
Past Pres., Dr. Donald Jost
Committee Members-at-Large: Dr. Arnold Cook; Dr. W. Harold Fuller; Mr. Donald Simmonds; Rev. Andrew Wong; Rev. Gillis Killam; Dr. Paul Magnus; Dr. Rick Penner; Capt. Sandra Rice; Mrs. Lynn Smith; Mr. Geoff Tunnicliffe
Task Force on Evangelism, Chpsn., Dr. William McRae
Social Action Commission, Chpsn., Mrs. Janet Epp Buckingham
Task Force on Education, Chpsn., Dr. Glenn Smith
Women in Ministry Task Force, Chpsn., Mrs. Rae Ann Thorsteinson

Interchurch Communications

Interchurch Communications is made up of the communication units of the Anglican Church of Canada, the Evangelical Lutheran Church in Canada, the Presbyterian Church in Canada, the Canadian Conference of Catholic Bishops (English Sector), and the United Church of Canada. ICC members collaborate on occasional video or print coproductions and on addressing public policy issues affecting religious communications.

HEADQUARTERS

3250 Bloor St. W., Etobicoke, ON M8X 2Y4
Media Contact, Chpsn., Douglas Tindal, Anglican Church of Canada, 600 Jarvis St., Toronto, ON M4Y 2J6 Tel. (416)924-9199 Fax (416)968-7983

OFFICERS

Chpsn., Mr. Douglas Tindal, Anglican Church of Canada, 600 Jarvis St., Toronto, ON M4Y 2J6 Tel. (416)924-9199 Fax (416)968-7983
Vice-Chpsn., Rev. Randolph L. Naylor, United Church of Canada, 3250 Bloor St. W., Etobicoke, ON M8X 2Y4 Tel. (416)231-7680 Fax (416)232-6004

MEMBERS

Mr. Merv Campone, Evangelical Lutheran Church in Canada, 21415-76th Ave., RR #11, Langley, BC V3A 6Y3 Tel. (604)888-4562 Fax (604)888-3162
Rev. Glenn Cooper, Presbyterian Church in Canada, Box 1840, Pictou, NS B0K 1H0 Tel. (902)-485-1561 Fax (902)485-1562
Rev. Rod Booth, United Church of Canada, 3250 Bloor St. W., Etobicoke, ON M8X 2Y4 Tel. (416)231-7680 Fax (416)232-6004

Inter-Varsity Christian Fellowship of Canada

Inter-Varsity Christian Fellowship is a non-profit, interdenominational student movement centering on the witness to Jesus Christ in campus communities: universities, colleges and high schools and through a Canada-wide Pioneer Camping program. It also ministers to professionals and teachers through Nurses and Teachers' Christian Fellowship.

IVCF was officially formed in 1928-29 by the late Dr. Howard Guinness, whose arrival from Britain challenged students to follow the example of the British Inter-Varsity Fellowship by organizing themselves into prayer and Bible study fellowship groups. Inter-Varsity has always been a student-initiated movement, emphasizing and developing leadership on the campus to call Christians to outreach, challenging other students to a personal faith in Jesus Christ and studying the Bible as God's revealed truth within a fellowship of believers. A strong stress has been placed on missionary activity, and the triennial conference held at Urbana, IL (jointly sponsored by U.S. and Canadian IVCF) has been a means of challenging many young people to service in Christian vocation. Inter-Varsity works closely with and is a strong believer in the work of local and national churches.

HEADQUARTERS

Unit 17, 40 Vogell Rd., Richmond Hill, ON L4B 3N6 Tel. (905)884-6880 Fax (905)884-6550
Media Contact, Gen. Dir., Rob Regier

OFFICERS

Gen. Dir., Rob Regier

John Howard Society of Ontario

The John Howard Society of Ontario is a registered non-profit charitable organization providing services to individuals, families and groups at all stages in the youth and criminal justice system. The Society also provides community education on critical issues in the justice system and advocacy for reform of the justice system. The mandate of the Society is the prevention of crime through service, community education, advocacy and reform.

Founded in 1929, the Society has grown from a one-office service in Toronto to 17 local branches providing direct services in the major cities of Ontario and a provincial office providing justice policy analysis, advocacy for reform and support to branches.

HEADQUARTERS

6 Jackson Pl., Toronto, ON M6P 1T6 Tel. (416)-604-8412 Fax (416)604-8948
Media Contact, Exec. Dir., Graham Stewart

OFFICERS

Pres., Gerry Treble, 595 Trafalgar St., London, ON N5Z 1E6
Vice-Pres., Susan Reid-MacNevin, Dept.of Sociology, Univ. of Guelph, Guelph, ON N1G 2W1
Treas., Hugh Peacock, Ontario Labour Relations Board, 400 University Ave., 4th Fl., Toronto, ON M7A 1V4
Sec., Richard Beaupe, 4165 Fernand St., Hamner, ON B3A 1X4
Exec. Dir., Graham Stewart

LOCAL SOCIETIES

Oshawa
Hamilton
Kingston
London
Toronto
Collins Bay
St. Catherines
Ottawa
Brampton
Peterborough
Sarnia
Sault Ste. Marie
Sudbury
Thunder Bay
Lindsay
Waterloo
Windsor

John Milton Society for the Blind in Canada

The John Milton Society for the Blind in Canada is an interdenominational Christian charity whose mandate is producing Christian publications for Canadian adults or young people who are visually impaired or blind. As such, it produces *Insight*, a large-print magazine, *Insound*, a cassette magazine and *In Touch*, a braille magazine. The John Milton Society also features an audio cassette library called the *Library in Sound*, which contains Christian music, sermons, seasonal materials and workshops.

Founded in 1970, the Society is committed to seeing that visually-impaired people receive accessible Christian materials by mail.

HEADQUARTERS

40 St. Clair Ave. E., Ste. 202, Toronto, ON M4T 1M9 Tel. (416)960-3953
Media Contact, John V. Miller

OFFICERS

Pres., James MacMillan
Vice-Pres., Robert Bettson
2nd Vice-Pres., Henry Finlayson
Exec. Dir., John V. Miller

Lutheran Council in Canada

The Lutheran Council in Canada was organized in 1967 and is a cooperative agency of the Evangelical Lutheran Church in Canada and Lutheran Church-Canada.

The Council's activities include communications, coordinative service and national liaison in social ministry, chaplaincy and scout activity.

HEADQUARTERS

1512 St. James St., Winnipeg, MB R3H 0L2 Tel. (204)786-6707 Fax (204)783-7548
Media Contact, Pres., Bishop Telmor Sartison

OFFICERS

Pres., Rev. Telmor Sartison
Sec., Rev. William Huras
Treas., Mr. Stephen Klinck

Mennonite Central Committee Canada (MCCC)

Mennonite Central Committee Canada was organized in 1964 to continue the work which several regional Canadian inter-Mennonite agencies had been doing in relief, service, immigration and peace. All but a few of the smaller Mennonite groups in Canada belong to MCC Canada.

MCCC is part of the binational Mennonite Central Committee (MCC) which has its headquarters in Akron, Pa. from where the overseas development and relief projects are administered. In 1993-94 MCCC's budget was $18,300,000, about 40 percent of the total MCC budget. There were 430 Canadians of a total of 908 MCC workers serving in North America and abroad during the same time period.

The MCC office in Winnipeg administers projects located in Canada. Domestic programs of Voluntary Service, Native Concerns, Peace and Social Concerns, Food Program, Employment Concerns, Ottawa Office, Victim/Offender Ministries, Mental Health and immigration are all part of MCC's Canadian ministry. Whenever it undertakes a project, MCCC attempts to relate to the church or churches in the area.

HEADQUARTERS

134 Plaza Dr., Winnipeg, MB R3T 5K9 Tel. (204)-261-6381 Fax (204)269-9875

Communications, John Longhurst, 134 Plaza Dr., Winnipeg, MT R3T 5K9 Tel. (204)261-6381 Fax (204)269-9875

OFFICER

Exec. Dir., Marvin Frey

Project Ploughshares

The founding of Project Ploughshares in 1976 was premised on the biblical vision of transforming the material and human wealth consumed by military preparations into resources for human development. An internationally recognized Canadian peace and justice organization, the Project undertakes research, education, advocacy programs on common security, demilitarization, security alternatives, arms transfer controls, demobilization and peacebuilding. Project Ploughshare is a project of the Canadian Council of Churches and is supported by national churches, civic agencies, affiliated community groups and more than 10,000 individuals.

Publications: the Ploughshares *Monitor*(quarterly), the Armed Conflicts Report(annual), Briefings and Working Papers(occasional).

HEADQUARTERS

Institute of Peace and Conflict Studies, Conrad Grebel College, Waterloo, ON N2L 3G6 Tel. (519)888-6541 Fax (519)885-0014

Media Contact, Program Coord., Grant Birks

OFFICERS

Chpsn., Ron Mathies

Treas., Philip Creighton

SPONSORING ORGANIZATIONS

Anglican Church of Canada

Canadian Catholic Organization for Development & Peace

Canadian Unitarian Council

Canadian Friends Service Committee

Christian Church (Disciples of Christ) in Canada

Conrad Grebel College

Inter-Pares

Evangelical Lutheran Church in Canada

Mennonite Central Committee Canada

Mennonite Conference of Eastern Canada

Oxfam Canada

Presbyterian Church in Canada

Union of Spiritual Communities in Christ (Doukhobors)

United Church of Canada

Voice of Women

Religious Television Associates

Religious Television Associates was formed in the early 1960s for the production units of the Anglican, Baptist, Presbyterian, Roman Catholic Churches and the United Church of Canada. In the intervening years, the Baptists have withdrawn and the Lutherans have come in. RTA provides an ecumenical umbrella for joint productions in broadcasting and development education. The directors are the heads of the Communications Departments participating in Interchurch Communications.

HEADQUARTERS

3250 Bloor St. W., Etobicoke, ON M8X 2Y4 Tel. (416)366-9221 Fax (416)366-8204

Media Contact, Exec. Dir., Rod Booth

OFFICERS

Chpsn., Douglas Tindal, 600 Jarvis St., Toronto, ON M4Y 2J6

Vice-Pres., Rev. Randolph L. Naylor, Tel. (416)-231-7680 Fax (416)232-6004

MEMBER ORGANIZATIONS

The Anglican Church of Canada

Canadian Conference of Catholic Bishops

The Canadian Council of Churches

The Evangelical Lutheran Church in Canada

The Presbyterian Church in Canada

The United Church of Canada

Scripture Union

Scripture Union is an international interdenominational missionary movement working in over 110 countries.

Scripture Union aims to work with the churches to make God's Good News known to children, young people and families and to encourage people of all ages to meet God daily through the Bible and prayer.

In Canada, a range of daily devotional booklets are offered to individuals, churches, and bookstores from age four through adult. Sunday School curriculum and various evangelism and discipling materials are also offered for sale.

A program of youth and family evangelism, including beach missions and community-based evangelistic holiday clubs, is also undertaken.

HEADQUARTERS

1885 Clements Rd., Unit 226, Pickering, ON L1W 3V4 Tel. (905)427-4947 Fax (905)427-0334

Media Contact, Gen. Dir., Rob Cornish

DIRECTORS

Mr. Harold Murray, 216 McKinnon Pl. NE, Calgary, AB T2E 7B9

Alan Cairnie, R.R. #6, Renfrew, ON K7V 3Z9

Dr. Paul Pitt, 5 Bendale Blvd., Scarborough, ON M1J 2B1

Ruth Russell, 14 Caronridge Cres., Agincourt, ON M1W 1L2

L. Claude Simmonds, Windfield Terr. E, Ste. 301, 1200 Don Mills Rd., Don Mills, ON M3B 3N8

Michael White, 251 Jefferson Sideroad, R.R. #1, Richmond Hill, ON L4C 4X7

Nancy Smail, 1510 Dundas St. W., Whitby, ON L1N 5R4
Rev. George Sinclair, 125 Victoria St., Eganville, ON K0J 1T0
Dr. Paul White, 21 Berkham Rd., Scarborough, ON M1H 2T1
Mr. John McAuley, 6 Jallan Dr., Ajax, ON L1S 6J2
Mrs. June Wynne, 2639 Mill Bay Rd., Mill Bay, BC V0R 2P0
Dr. T. V. Thomas, 2146 Robinson St., Ste. 1B, Regina, SK S4T 2P7

Student Christian Movement of Canada

The Student Christian Movement of Canada was formed in 1921 from the student arm of the YMCA. It has its roots in the Social Gospel movements of the late 19th and early 20th centuries. Throughout its intellectual history, the SCM in Canada has sought to relate the Christian faith to the living realities of the social and political context of each student generation.

The present priorities are built around the need to form more and stronger critical Christian communities on Canadian campuses within which individuals may develop their social and political analyses, experience spiritual growth and fellowship and bring Christian ecumenical witness to the university.

The Student Christian Movement of Canada is affiliated with the World Student Christian Federation.

HEADQUARTERS

310 Danforth Ave., Ste. C3, Toronto, ON M4K 1N6 Tel. (416)463-4312
Media Contact, Gen. Sec., Rick Garland

OFFICER

Gen. Sec., Rick Garland

Taskforce on the Churches and Corporate Responsibility

The Taskforce on the Churches and Corporate Responsibility is a national ecumenical coalition of the major Christian churches in Canada founded in 1975 to assist its members in implementing policies adopted by them in the area of corporate social responsibility. Areas of special concern include human rights and aboriginal rights, environment, military exports and corporate governance. The Taskforce facilitates communication on these and other issues between church shareholders and other shareholders and corporate managers.

HEADQUARTERS

129 St. Clair Ave., W., Toronto, ON M4V 1N5 Tel. (416)923-1758 Fax (416)927-7554
Media Contact, Coord., Daniel Gennarelli, Tel. (416)923-1758 Fax (416)927-7554

OFFICERS

Coord., Daniel Gennarelli
Bd. Co-Chpsns.: Anne Denomy; Tim Ryan
Treas., Mike Kelly
Chpsn., Corp. Governance Comm., Milton Barlow
Chpsn. Inter-Church Comm. on Ecology, David Hallman

MEMBERS

Anglican Church of Canada
Basilians
Canadian Conference of Catholic Bishops
Canadian University Service Overseas
Catholic Church Extension Society of Canada
Congregation of Notre Dame
Evangelical Lutheran Church in Canada
Grey Sisters of the Immaculate Conception
Jesuit Fathers of Upper Canada
Les Soeurs de Sainte-Anne
Oblate Conference of Canada
Presbyterian Church in Canada
Redemptorist Fathers
Religious Hospitallers of St. Joseph
School Sisters of Notre Dame
Scarboro Foreign Mission Society
Sisterhood of St. John the Divine
Sisters of Charity--Mount St. Vincent
Sisters of Charity of the Immaculate Conception
Sisters of Mercy Generalate
Sisters of St. Joseph--Diocese of London
Sisters of St. Joseph--Sault Ste. Marie
Sisters of St. Joseph--Toronto
Sisters of the Holy Names of Jesus & Mary Windsor, ON
Sisters of Holy Names of Jesus and Mary, Longueil, P.Q.
Sisters of Providence of St. Vincent dePaul
Sisters of St. Martha
United Church of Canada
Ursulines of Chatham Union
Young Women's Christian Association

Ten Days for World Development

Supported by five of Canada's major Christian denominations. Ten Days is dedicated to helping people discover, examine and reflect on the ways global and domestic structures and policies promote and perpetuate poverty and injustice for the majority of the world's people. Ten Days is an education and action program that attempts to influence the policies and practice of Canadian churches, government, business, labour, education and the media.

HEADQUARTERS

77 Charles St. W. Ste. 401, Toronto, ON M5S 1K5 Tel. (416)922-0591 Fax (416)922-1419
Media Contact, Natl. Coord., Dennis Howlett

STAFF

Natl. Coord., Dennis Howlett
Coord. for Leadership Dev. & Regional Communication, David Reid
Resource Coord., ----
Admn. Asst., Ramya Hemachandra

MEMBER ORGANIZATIONS

Anglican Church of Canada
Canadian Cath. Orgn. for Dev. & Peace
Evangelical Lutheran Church in Canada
Presbyterian Church in Canada
United Church of Canada

Women's Interchurch Council of Canada

Women's Inter-Church Council of Canada is a national Christian women's council that encourages women to grow in ecumenism, to share their spirituality and prayer and to engage in dialogue about women's concerns. The Council calls women to respond to national and international issues affecting women and to take action together for justice. WICC sponsors the World Day of

Prayer and Fellowship of the Least Coin in Canada. Human rights projects are supported and a quarterly newsletter distributed.

HEADQUARTERS

815 Danforth Ave., Ste 402, Toronto, ON M4J 1L2 Tel. (416)462-2528

Media Contact, Exec. Dir., Vivian Harrower, Fax (416)462-3915

OFFICERS

Pres., Ann Austin Cardwell

Exec. Dir., Vivian Harrower

World Vision Canada

World Vision Canada is a Christian humanitarian relief and development organization. Although its main international commitment is to translate child sponsorship into holistic, sustainable community development, World Vision also allocates resources to help Canada's poor and complement the mission of the church.

World Vision's Reception Centre assists government-sponsored refugees entering Canada. The NeighbourLink program mobilizes church volunteers to respond locally to people's needs. A quarterly publication, Context, provides data on the Canadian family to help churches effectively reach their communities. The development education program provides resources on development issues. During the annual 30-Hour Famine, people fast for 30 hours while discussing poverty and raising funds to support aid programs.

HEADQUARTERS

6630 Turner Valley Rd., Mississauga, ON L5N 2S4 Tel. (905)821-3030 Fax (905)821-1356

Media Contact, Senior Information Officer, Mr. Philip Maher, Tel. (905)567-2726

OFFICERS

Pres., J. Don Scott

Exec. Vice Pres., Dave Toycen

Vice-Pres.: Intl. & Govt. Relations, Linda Tripp; Natl. Programs, Don Posterski; Fin. & Admin., Charlie Fluit

Young Men's Christian Association in Canada

The YMCA began as a Christian association to help young men find healthy recreation and meditation, as well as opportunities for education, in the industrial slums of 19th century England. It came to Canada in 1851 with the same mission in mind for young men working in camps and on the railways.

Today, the YMCA maintains its original mission□helping individuals to grow and develop in spirit, mind and body□but attends to those needs for men and women of all ages and religious beliefs. The YMCA registers almost 1.3 million participants and 300,000 annual members in 64 autonomous associations representative of their communities.

The program of each association differs according to the needs of the community, but most offer one or more programs in each of the following categories: community support, housing and shelters, guidance and counselling, camping and outdoor education, leadership development, refugee and immigrant services, international development and education.

The YMCA encourages people of all ages, races, abilities, income and beliefs to mix in an environment which promotes balance in life, breaking down barriers and helping to create healthier communities.

HEADQUARTERS

2160 Yonge St., Toronto, ON M4S 2A9 Tel. (416)-485-9447 Fax (416)485-8228

Media Contact, Dir., Communications, Dianne LeBreton

OFFICERS

Chpsn., Betty Black

CEO, Sol Kasimer

Young Women's Christian Association of/du Canada

The YWCA of/du Canada is a national voluntary organization serving 44 YWCAs and YM-YWCAs across Canada. Dedicated to the development and improved status of women and their families, the YWCA is committed to service delivery and to being a source of public education on women's issues and an advocate of social change. Services provided by YWCAs and YM-YWCAs include adult education programs, residences and shelters, child care, fitness activities, wellness programs and international development education. As a member of the World YWCA, the YWCA of/du Canada is part of the largest women's organization in the world.

HEADQUARTERS

80 Gerrard St. E., Toronto, ON M5B 1G6 Tel. (416)593-9886 Fax (416)971-8084

Media Contact, CEO, Judith Wiley

OFFICERS

CEO, Judith Wiley

Pres., Ann Mowatt

Youth for Christ/Canada

Youth For Christ is an interdenominational organization founded in 1944 by Torrey Johnson. Under the leadership of YFC's 11 national board of directors, Youth For Christ/Canada cooperates with churches and serves as a mission agency reaching out to young people and their families through a variety of ministries.

YFC seeks to have maximum influence in a world of youth through high-interest activities and personal involvement. Individual attention is given to each teenager through small group involvement and counselling. These activities and relationships become vehicles for communicating the message of the Gospel.

HEADQUARTERS

822-167 Lombard Ave., Winnipeg, MB R3B 0V3 Tel. (204)989-0056 Fax (204)989-0067

OFFICER

Natl. Dir., Dr. Arnold K. Friesen

3. RELIGIOUS BODIES IN THE UNITED STATES

The following lists were supplied by the denominations. They are printed in alphabetical order by the official name of the organization. A list of religious bodies by family group is found at the end of this section.

Information found in other places in this yearbook is not repeated. The denominational listing points you to additional information. Specifically, addresses and editor's names for periodicals are found in the listing of United States Periodicals. Also, statistical information is found in the statistical section.

When an organization supplied a headquarters address it is listed immediately following the description of the organization. This address, telephone number and fax number is not reprinted for entries that have exactly the same address and numbers. An address or telephone number is only printed when it is known to be different from the headquarters'. Individuals listed without an address can be contacted through the headquarters.

Denominations were asked to provide the name of a media contact. Many responded with a specific person that newspaper or other reporters can contact for official information. These people are listed with the headquarters address.

The organizations listed here represent the denominations to which the vast majority of church members in the United States belong. It does not include all religious bodies functioning in the United States. *The Encyclopedia of American Religions* (Gale Research Inc., P.O. Box 33477, Detroit MI 48232-5477) contains names and addresses of additional religious bodies.

Advent Christian Church

The Advent Christian Church is a conservative, evangelical denomination which grew out of the Millerite movement of the 1830s and 1840s. The members stress the authority of Scripture, justification by faith in Jesus Christ alone, the importance of evangelism and world missions and the soon visible return of Jesus Christ.

Organized in 1860, the Advent Christian Church maintains headquarters in Charlotte, N.C., with regional offices in Rochester, N. H., Princeton, N.C., Fort Worth, Tex., Lewiston, Idaho, and Lenoir, N.C. Missions are maintained in India, Nigeria, Japan, Liberia, New Zealand, Malaysia, the Philippines, Mexico and Memphis, Tenn.

The Advent Christian Church maintains doctrinal distinctives in three areas: conditional immortality, the sleep of the dead until the return of Christ and belief that the kingdom of God will be established on earth made new by Jesus Christ.

HEADQUARTERS

P.O. Box 23152, Charlotte, NC 28227 Tel. (704)-545-6161 Fax (704)573-0712

Media Contact, Exec. Vice-Pres., David E. Ross

OFFICERS

Pres., Rev. Glennon Balser

Exec. Vice-Pres., David E. Ross

Sec., Rev. John Gallagher, P.O. Box 551, Presque Isle, ME 04769

Appalachian Vice-Pres., Rev. James Lee, 1338 Delwood Dr. SW, Lenoir, NC 28645

Central Vice-Pres., Rev. Clarence DuBois, 1401 Illinois Ave., Mendota, IL 61342

Eastern Vice-Pres., Rev. Glenn Rice, 130 Leighton St., Bangor, ME 04401

Southern Vice-Pres., Rev. Brent Ross, 3635 Andrea Lee Ct., Snellville, GA 30278-4941

Western Vice-Pres., Mr. Larry McIntyre, 1629 Jamie Cr., West Linn, OR 97068

The Woman's Home & Foreign Mission Soc., Pres., Mrs. Bea Moore, Rt. 8, Box 274, Loudon, NH 03301

PERIODICALS

Advent Christian News; The Advent Christian Witness; Insight; Maranatha

African Methodist Episcopal Church

This church began in 1787 in Philadelphia when persons in St. George's Methodist Episcopal Church withdrew as a protest against color segregation. In 1816 the denomination was started, led by Rev. Richard Allen who had been ordained deacon by Bishop Francis Asbury and was subsequently ordained elder and elected and consecrated bishop.

HEADQUARTERS

1134 11th St., NW, Washington, DC 20001 Tel. (202)371-8700

Media Contact, Bishop, Eighth District, Donald Ming, 2138 St. Bernard Ave., New Orleans, LA 70119 Tel. (504)948-4251

PERIODICALS

The Christian Recorder; A.M.E. Review; Journal of Christian Education; Secret Chamber; Women's Missionary Magazine; Voice of Missions

African Methodist Episcopal Zion Church

The A.M.E. Zion Church is an independent body, having withdrawn from the John Street Methodist Church of New York City in 1796. The first bishop was James Varick.

HEADQUARTERS

Dept. of Records & Research, P.O. Box 32843, Charlotte, NC 28232 Tel. (704)332-3851 Fax (704)333-1769

Media Contact, Gen. Sec.-Aud., Dr. W. Robert Johnson, III

OFFICERS

President, Bishop George E. Battle, Jr., 8233 Charles Crawford Ln., Charlotte, NC 28213 Tel. (704)598-7419 Fax (704)343-3745

Sec., Bishop Marshall H. Strickland, 2000 Cedar Circle Dr., Baltimore, MD 28213 Tel. (704)598-7419

Asst. Sec., Bishop Clarence Carr, 2600 Normandy Dr., Greendale, MO 63121 Tel. (314)727-2940 Fax (314)727-0663
Treas., George W. C. Walker, Sr., 3654 Poplar Rd., Flossmoor, IL 60422 Tel. (708)799-5599
Member of Board of Bishops, Bishop Clinton R. Coleman, 3513 Ellamont Rd., Baltimore, MD 21215 Tel. (410)466-2220
Member of Board of Bishops, Bishop Charles H. Foggie, 1200 Windermere Dr., Pittburgh, PA 15218 Tel. (704)846-9370 Fax (704)846-9371
Member of Board of Bishops, Bishop William Alexander Hilliard, 690 Chicago Blvd., Detroit, MI 48202
Member of Board of Bishops, Bishop J. Clinton Hoggard, 4515 Willard Ave., Apt 203, S.Chevy Chase, MD 20815 Tel. (301)652-9010
Member of Board of Bishops, Bishop John H. Miller, Sr., Springdale Estates, 8605 Caswell Ct., Raleigh, NC 27612 Tel. (919)848-6915

GENERAL OFFICERS AND DEPARTMENTS

Gen. Sec.- Auditor, Rev. W. Robert Johnson, III
Dept. of Finance, Sec., Miss Madie L. Simpson, P.O. Box 31005, Charlotte, NC 28230 Tel. (704)-333-4847 Fax (704)333-6517
A.M.E. Zion Publishing House: Gen. Mgr., Anthony Brown, P.O. Box 30714, Charlotte, NC 28230 Tel. (704)334-9596
Dept. of Overseas Missions: Sec.-Ed., Rev. Dr. Kermit J. DeGraffenreidt, 475 Riverside Dr., Rm. 1935, New York, NY 10115 Tel. (212)870-2952 Fax (212)870-2055
Dept. Brotherhood Pensions & Min. Relief: Sec.-Treas., Rev. David Miller, P.O. Box 34454, Charlotte, NC 28234-4454 Tel. (704)333-3779 Fax (704)333-3867
Christian Education Dept.: Sec., Rev. Raymon Hunt, P.O. Box 32305, Charlotte, NC 28232-2305 Tel. (704)332-9323 Fax (704)332-9332
Dept. of Church School Literature: Ed., Ms. Mary A. Love, P.O. Box 31005, Charlotte, NC 28231 Tel. (704)332-1034 Fax (704)333-1769
Dept. of Church Extension & Home Mission: Dr. Lem Long, Jr., P.O. Box 31005, Charlotte, NC 28231 Tel. (704)334-2519 Fax (704)334-3806
Dept. of Evangelism: Dir., Dr. Norman H. Hicklin, P.O. Box 33623, Charlotte, NC 28231 Tel. (704)-342-3070 Fax (704)537-9247
Dir. of Public Affairs, Dr. Thaddeus Garrett, Jr., 1730 M St., NW, Ste. 808, Washington, DC 20036 Tel. (202)332-0200 Fax (202)872-0444
Dept. of Health & Social Concerns: Dir., Dr. James E. Milton, 101 Bay St., Tuskegee, AL 36083

JUDICIAL COUNCIL

Pres., Judge Adele M. Riley, 625 Ellsworth Dr., Dayton, OH 45426 Tel. (513)837-2514 Fax (513)496-7236
Vice.-Pres., Rev. John E. Watts, 709 Keats Dr., Vallejo, CA 94590 Tel. (707)552-1139
Mrs. Alean Rush, 22 Parkview Dr., Rochester, NY 14625
Rev. James A. Crumlin, Atty., 4306 Winrose, Louisville, KY 40211
Dr. Mozella G. Mitchell, P.O. Box 1855, Brandon, FL 33509
Mr. Robert E. Richardson, 1511 K St. NW, Ste.1026, Washington, DC 20005
Mr. J. R. Broughton, 3449 Rollingreen Ridge SW, Atlanta, GA 30331
Rev. Walter L. Leigh, Rte. 4, Box 868, Hertford, NC 27944

BISHOPS

Piedmont: Bishop Ruben L. Speaks, 1238 Maxwell St., P.O. Box 986, Salisbury, NC 28144 Tel. (704)637-1471; Office, 217 W. Salisbury, Salisbury, NC 28144 Tel. (704)637-6018 Fax (704)-639-0059
Mid-Atlantic I: Bishop Cecil Bishop, 2663 Oakmead Dr., Charlotte, NC 28270 Tel. (704)846-9371 Fax (704)846-9371
North Eastern Region: Bishop George W. C. Walker, Sr., 3654 Poplar Rd., Flossmoor, IL 60422 Tel. (708)799-5599
Mid-Atlantic II: Bishop Milton A. Williams, 12904 Canoe Ct., Ft. Washington, MD 20744 Tel. (301)292-0002 Fax (301)292-6655
Eastern West Africa: Bishop S. Chuka Ekemam, Sr., 680 Akwakuma Lay Out, Owerri, Nigeria, W. Africa, Tel. 234-83-231303
South Atlantic: Bishop George E. Battle, Jr., 8233 Charles Crawford La., Charlotte, NC 28213 Tel. (704)547-7405 Fax (704)343-3745
Southwestern Delta: Bishop Joseph Johnson, 4 Russwood Cove, Little Rock, AK 72211 Tel. (501)228-2759 Fax (501)228-9069
Cahaba: Bishop Richard K. Thompson, 1420 Missouri Ave., Washington, DC 20011 Tel. (202)-723-8993
Mid-West: Bishop Enoch B. Rochester, 32 Trebling Ln., Willingboro, NJ 08046 Tel. (609)871-2759 Fax (800)243-LOVE
Western West Africa: Bishop Marshall H. Strickland, II, 2000 Cedar Circle Dr., Baltimore, MD 21228 Tel. (410)744-7330 Fax (410)788-5510
Eastern North Carolina: ----, 7013 Toby Ct., Charlotte, NC 28213 Tel. (704)598-7419
Western: Bishop Clarence Carr, 2600 Normandy Dr., Greendale, MO 63121 Tel. (314)727-2931 Fax (314)727-0663

CONNECTIONAL LAY COUNCIL

Pres., Mrs. Mary E. Taylor, 604 Almond Ave., Dayton, OH 45417 Tel. (513)263-9090
Sec., Ms. Frances J. Glenn, 221 Emmett St., Rock HIll, SC 29730 Tel. (803)329-2271

WOMANS HOME & OVERSEAS MISSIONARY SOC.

Pres., Dr. Adlise Ivey Porter, 1991 Thornhill Pl., Detroit, MI 48207 Tel. (313)393-3972
Exec. Sec., Mrs. Alice Steele-Robinson, 3735 Rock Hill Church Rd., Concord, NC 28027 Tel. (704)795-1506

PERIODICALS

Star of Zion; Quarterly Review; Missionary Seer; Church School Herald

Albanian Orthodox Archdiocese in America

The Albanian Orthodox Church in America traces its origins to the groups of Albanian immigrants which first arrived in the United States in 1886, seeking religious, cultural and economic freedoms denied them in the homeland.

In 1908 in Boston, the Rev. Fan Stylian Noli (later Archbishop) served the first liturgy in the Albanian language in 500 years, to which Orthodox Albanians rallied, forming their own diocese in 1919. Parishes began to spring up throughout New England and the Mid-Atlantic and Great Lakes states. In 1922, clergy from the United States traveled to Albania to proclaim the self-governance of the Orthodox Church in the homeland at the Congress of Berat.

In 1971 the Albanian Archdiocese sought and gained union with the Orthodox Church in America, expressing the desire to expand the Orthodox witness to America at large, giving it an indigenous character. The Albanian Archdiocese remains vigilant for its brothers and sisters in the homeland and serves as an important resource for human rights issues and Albanian affairs, in addition to its programs for youth, theological education, vocational interest programs and retreats for young adults and women.

HEADQUARTERS

523 E. Broadway, S. Boston, MA 02127
Media Contact, Sec., Ms. Dorothy Adams, Tel. (617)268-1275 Fax (617)268-3184

OFFICERS

Metropolitan Theodosius, Tel. (617)268-1275
Chancellor, V. Rev. Arthur E. Liolin, 60 Antwerp St., East Milton, MA 02186 Tel. (617)698-3366
Lay Chpsn., Gregory Costa, 727 Righters Mill Rd., Narberth, PA 19103 Tel. (610)664-8550
Treas., Ronald Nasson, 26 Enfield St., Jamaica Plains, MA 02130 Tel. (617)522-7715

PERIODICAL

The Vineyard/Update

Albanian Orthodox Dicoese of America

This Diocese was organized in 1950 as a canonical body administering to the Albanian faithful. It is under the ecclesiastical jurisdiction of the Ecumenical Patriarchate of Constantinople (Istanbul).

HEADQUARTERS

6455 Silver Dawn Lane, Las Vegas, NV 89118 Tel. (702)221-8245 Fax (702)221-9167
Media Contact, The Rev. Ik. Ilia Katre

OFFICER

Vicar General, The Rev. Ik. Ilia Katre

Allegheny Wesleyan Methodist Connection (Original Allegheny Conference)

This body was formed in 1968 by members of the Allegheny Conference (located in eastern Ohio and western Pennsylvania) of the Wesleyan Methodist Church, which merged in 1966 with the Pilgrim Holiness Church to form The Wesleyan Church.

The Allegheny Wesleyan Methodist Connection is composed of persons "having the form and seeking the power of godliness, united in order to pray together, to receive the word of exhortation, and to watch over one another in love, that they may help each other to work out their salvation." There is a strong commitment to congregational government and to holiness of heart and life. There is a strong thrust in church extension within the United States and in missions worldwide.

HEADQUARTERS

1827 Allen Dr., Salem, OH 44460 Tel. (216)337-9376
Media Contact, Pres., Rev. John Englant

OFFICERS

Pres., Rev. John Englant
Vice-Pres., Rev. William Cope, 1231 Conser Dr., Salem, OH 44460
Sec., Rev. W. H. Cornell, 960 Lafayette Ave., Niles, OH 44446
Treas., Mr. James Kunselman, 2161 Woodsdale Rd., Salem, OH 44460

PERIODICAL

The Allegheny Wesleyan Methodist

The American Association of Lutheran Churches

This church body was constituted on Nov. 7, 1987. The AALC was formed by laity and pastors of the former American Lutheran Church in America who held to a high view of Scripture (inerrancy and infallibility). This church body also emphasizes the primacy of evangelism and world missions and the authority and autonomy of the local congregation.

Congregations of the AALC are distributed throughout the continental United States from Long Island, N.Y., to Los Angeles. The primary decision-making body is the General Convention, to which each congregation has proportionate representation.

HEADQUARTERS

The AALC National Office, 10800 Lyndale Ave. S., Ste. 120, Minneapolis, MN 55420 Tel. (612)-884-7784
The AALC Regional Office, 2211 Maynard St., Waterloo, IA 50701 Tel. (319)232-3971
Media Contact, Admn. Coord., Rev. Dick Day, P.O. Box 416, Waterloo, IA 50704 Tel. (319)-232-3971

OFFICERS

Presiding Pastor, Dr. Duane R. Lindberg, P.O. Box 416, Waterloo, IA 50701 Tel. (319)232-3971
Asst. Presiding Pastor, Rev. Kevin McClure, P.O. Box 211, Manvel, ND 58256 Tel. (701)696-8213
Sec., Rev. Dick Hueter, N9945 Highway 180, Wausaukee, WI 54177 Tel. (715)732-0327
Treas., Rev. Harley Johnson, 107 E. Liberty, Newark, IL 60541 Tel. (815)695-5039
Admn. Coord., Pastor Dick Day, P.O. Box 416, Waterloo, IA 50704 Tel. (319)232-3971

PERIODICAL

The Evangel

The American Baptist Association

The American Baptist Association (ABA) is an international fellowship of independent Baptist churches voluntarily cooperating in missionary, evangelistic, benevolent and Christian education activities throughout the world. Its beginnings can be traced to the landmark movement of the 1850s. Led by James R. Graves and J. M. Pendleton, a significant number of Baptist churches in the South, claiming a New Testament heritage, rejected as extrascriptural the policies of the newly formed Southern Baptist Convention (SBC). Because they strongly advocated church equality, many of these churches continued doing mission and benevolent work apart from the SBC, electing to work through local associations. Meeting in Texarkana, Tex., in 1924, messengers from the various churches effectively merged two of these major associations, the Baptist Missionary Association of Texas and the General Association, forming the American Baptist Association.

Since 1924, mission efforts have been supported in Canada, Mexico, Central and South America, Australia, Africa, Europe, Asia, India, New Zealand, Korea and Japan. An even more successful domestic mission effort has changed the ABA from a predominantly rural southern organization to one with churches in 45 states.

Through its publishing arm in Texarkana, the ABA publishes literature and books numbering into the thousands. Major seminaries include the Missionary Baptist Seminary, founded by Dr. Ben M. Bogard in Little Rock, Ark., Texas Baptist Seminary, Henderson, Tex., Oklahoma Missionary Baptist College in Marlow, Okla., and Florida Baptist Schools in Lakeland, Fla.

While no person may speak for the churches of the ABA, all accept the Bible as the inerrant Word of God. They believe Christ was the virgin-born Son of God, that God is a triune God, that the only church is the local congregation of scripturally baptized believers and that the work of the church is to spread the gospel.

HEADQUARTERS

4605 N. State Line Ave., Texarkana, TX 75503 Tel. (903)792-2783

Media Contact, Public Rel. Dir., Gene Smith

OFFICERS

Pres., James F. Holmes, 109 Tanglewood Dr., North Little Rock, AR 72118

Vice-Pres.: G. F. Crumley, 2602 Alice Dr., Hattiesburg, MS 39402; Art Richardson, 457 Mark Ave., Shafter, CA 93263; Marlin Gipson, 1526 N. Mulberry Ave., Panama City, FL 32405

Rec. Clks.: Larry Clements, P.O. Box 234, Monticello, AR 71655; Gene Smith, 5602 Deer Creek Dr., Texarkana, TX 75503

Publications: Ed.-in-Chief, Bill Johnson, P.O. Box 502, Texarkana, AR 75504; Bus. Mgr., Tom Sannes

Meeting Arrangements, Dir., Edgar N. Sutton, P.O. Box 240, Alexandria, AR 72002

Sec.-Treas., D. S. Madden, P.O. Box 1050, Texarkana, TX 75504

American Baptist Churches in the U.S.A.

Originally known as the Northern Baptist Convention, this body of Baptist churches changed the name to American Baptist Convention in 1950 with a commitment to "hold the name in trust for all Christians of like faith and mind who desire to bear witness to the historical Baptist convictions in a framework of cooperative Protestantism."

In 1972 American Baptist Churches in the U.S.A. was adopted as the new name. Although national missionary organizational developments began in 1814 with the establishment of the American Baptist Foreign Mission Society and continued with the organization of the American Baptist Publication Society in 1824 and the American Baptist Home Mission Society in 1832, the general denominational body was not formed until 1907. American Baptist work at the local level dates back to the organization by Roger Williams of the First Baptist Church in Providence, R. I. in 1638.

HEADQUARTERS

P.O. Box 851, Valley Forge, PA 19482 Tel. (610)-768-2000 Fax (610)768-2275

Media Contact, Dir., ABC News Service, Richard W. Schramm, Tel. (610)768-2077 Fax (610)768-2320

OFFICERS

Pres., G. Elaine Smith

Vice-Pres., Randy J. Gauger

Budget Review Officer, Anne J. Mills

Gen. Sec., Daniel E. Weiss

Assoc. Gen. Sec.-Treas., Cheryl H. Wade

REGIONAL ORGANIZATIONS

Central Region, ABC of, ----, 5833 SW 29th St., Topeka, KS 66614-2499

Chicago, ABC of Metro, Millie B. Myren, 28 E. Jackson Blvd., Ste. 210, Chicago, IL 60604-2207

Cleveland Baptist Assoc., Dennis E. Norris, 1836 Euclid Ave., Ste. 603, Cleveland, OH 44115-2234

Connecticut, ABC of, Lowell H. Fewster, 100 Bloomfield Ave., Hartford, CT 06105-1097

Dakotas, ABC of, Ronald E. Cowles, 1524 S. Summit Ave., Sioux Falls, SD 57105-1697

District of Columbia Bapt. Conv., W. Jere Allen, 1628 16th St., NW, Washington, DC 20009-3099

Great Rivers Region, ABC of the, Malcolm G. Shotwell, P.O. Box 3786, Springfield, IL 62708-3786

Indiana, ABC of, ----, 1350 N. Delaware St., Indianapolis, IN 46202-2493

Indianapolis, ABC of Greater, Larry D. Sayre, 1350 N. Delaware St., Indianapolis, IN 46202-2493

Los Angeles Bapt. City Mission Soc., ----, 1212 Wilshire Blvd., Ste. 201, Los Angeles, CA 90017-1902

Maine, ABC of, Gary G. Johnson, P.O. Box 667, Augusta, ME 04332-0667

Massachusetts, ABC of, Linda C. Spoolstra, 20 Milton St., Dedham, MA 02026-2967

Metropolitan New York, ABC of, James D. Stallings, 475 Riverside Dr., Rm. 432, New York, NY 10115-0432

Michigan, ABC of, Robert E. Shaw, 4578 S. Hagadorn Rd., East Lansing, MI 48823-5355

Mid-America Baptist Churches, Gary L. Grogan, Ste. 15, 2400 86th St., Des Moines, IA 50322-4380

Nebraska, ABC of, J. David Mallgren, 6404 Maple St., Omaha, NE 68104-4079

New Jersey, ABC of, A. Roy Medley, 3752 Nottingham Way, Ste. 101, Trenton, NJ 08690

New York State, ABC of, William A. Carlson, 5842 Heritage Landing Dr., East Syracuse, NY 13057-9359

Northwest, ABC of, Paul D. Aita, 13838 First Ave. S., Seattle, WA 98168-3438

Ohio, ABC of, ----, P.O. Box 376, Granville, OH 43023-0376

Oregon, ABC of, W. Wayne Brown, 0245 SW Bancroft St., Ste. G, Portland, OR 97201-4270

Pacific Southwest, ABC of the, John J. Jackson, 970 Village Oaks Dr., Covina, CA 91724-3679

Pennsylvania & Delaware, ABC of, ----, P.O. Box 851, Valley Forge, PA 19482-0851

Philadelphia Baptist Assoc., Larry K. Waltz, 100 N. 17th St., Philadelphia, PA 19103-2736

Pittsburgh Baptist Assoc., Clayton R. Woodbury, 1620 Allegheny Bldg., 429 Forbes Ave., Pittsburgh, PA 15219-1627

Puerto Rico, Baptist Churches of, E. Yamina Apolinaris, Mayaguez #21, Hato Rey, PR 00917

Rhode Island, ABC of, Donald H. Crosby, 734 Hope St., Providence, RI 02906-3535
Rochester/Genessee Region, ABC of, W. Kenneth Williams, 151 Brooks Ave., Rochester, NY 14619-2454
Rocky Mountains, ABC of, Louise B. Barger, 1344 Pennsylvania St., Denver, CO 80203-2499
South, ABC of the, Walter L. Parrish, II, 525 Main St., Ste. 105, Laurel, MD 20707-4995
Vermont/New Hampshire, ABC of, Louis A. George, P.O. Box 796, Concord, NH 03302-0796
West, ABC of the, Robert D. Rasmussen, P.O. Box 23204, Oakland, CA 94623-0204
West Virginia Baptist Convention, Lloyd D. Hamblin, Jr., P.O. Box 1019, Parkersburg, WV 26102-1019
Wisconsin, ABC of, George E. Daniels, 15330 W. Watertown Plank Rd., Elm Grove, WI 53122-2391

BOARDS

Bd. of Educational Ministries: Exec. Dir., Jean B. Kim; Pres., Trinette V. McCray
American Baptist Assembly: Green Lake, WI 54941; Pres., Kenneth P. Giacoletto; Chpsn., Beverly Dunston Scott
American Baptist Historical Society: 1106 S. Goodman St., Rochester, NY 14620; or P.O. Box 851, Valley Forge, PA 19482-0851; Admn./Archivist, Beverly C. Carlson; Pres., Loyd M. Starrett
American Baptist Men: Exec. Dir., Z. Allen Abbott, Jr.; Pres., John O. Ford
American Baptist Women's Ministries: Exec. Dir., Carol Franklin Sutton; Pres., Evon Laubenstein
Ministerial Leadership Commission: Exec. Dir., Craig A. Collemer
Bd. of Intl. Ministries: Exec. Dir., John A. Sundquist; Pres., Esther M.R. Irish
Bd. of Natl. Ministries: Exec. Dir., Aidsand F. Wright-Riggins; Pres., Lena M. Nelson
Ministers & Missionaries Benefit Bd.: Exec. Dir., Gordon E. Smith; Pres., Mary H. Purcell, 475 Riverside Dr., New York, NY 10115
Minister Council: Dir., Carole (Kate) H. Penfield; Pres., Milton P. Ryder

PERIODICALS

Baptist Leader; The Secret Place; American Baptist Quarterly; American Baptists In Mission

The American Carpatho-Russian Orthodox Greek Catholic Church

The American Carpatho-Russian Orthodox Greek Catholic Church is a self-governing diocese that is in communion with the Ecumenical Partriarchate of Constantinople. The late Patriarch Benjamin I, in an official Patriarchal Document dated Sept. 19, 1938, canonized the Diocese in the name of the Orthodox Church of Christ.

HEADQUARTERS

312 Garfield St., Johnstown, PA 15906 Tel. (814)-536-4207
Media Contact, Chancellor, V. Rev. Msgr. Frank P. Miloro, Tel. (814)539-8086 Fax (814)536-4699

OFFICERS

Bishop, Rt. Rev. Bishop Nicholas Smisko
Vicar General, V. Rev. Msgr. John Yurcisin, 249 Butler Ave., Johnstown, PA 15906
Chancellor, V. Rev. Msgr. Frank P. Miloro
Treas., V. Rev. Msgr. Ronald A. Hazuda, 115 East Ave., Erie, PA 16503

PERIODICAL

Cerkovnyj Vistnik--The Church Messenger

American Evangelical Christian Churches

Founded in 1944, the AECC is composed of individual ministers and churches who are united in accepting "Seven Articles of Faith." These seven articles are: the Bible as the written word of God; the Virgin birth; the deity of Jesus Christ; Salvation through the atonement; guidance of our life through prayer; the return of the Saviour; the establishment of the Millenial Kingdom.

The organization offers credentials (licenses and ordinations) to those who accept the Seven Articles and who put unity in Christ above individual interpretations and are approved by A.E.C.C.

A.E.C.C. seeks to promote the gospel through its ministers, churches and missionary activities.

Churches operate independently with all decisions concerning local government left to the individual churches.

The organization also has ministers in Canada, England, Bolivia, Philippines and Thailand.

HEADQUARTERS

P.O. Box 47312, Indianapolis, IN 46227 Tel. (317)784-9726
Media Contact, Natl. Mod., Dr. Otis O. Osborne, 1421 Roseland Ave., Sebring, FL 33870 Tel. (941)382-4462

INTERNATIONAL OFFICERS

Mod., Dr. Otis O. Osborne, 1421 Roseland Ave., Sebring, FL 33870 Tel. (941)382-4462
Sec., Dr. Charles Wasielewski, Box 51, Barton, NY 13734 Tel. (607)565-4074
Treas., Dr. S. Omar Overly, 2481 Red Rock Blvd., Grove City, OH 43123-1154 Tel. (614)871-0710

REGIONAL MODERATORS

Far West: Rev. Richard Cuthbert, 1195 Via Seville, Cathedral City, CA 92234 Tel. (619)321-6682
Carolinas-Georgia: Rev. Larry Walker, P.O. Box 1165, Lillington, NC 27546 Tel. (919)893-9529
Chesapeake: ----
Florida: Rev. James Fullwood, 19123 2nd St. NE, Lutz, FL 33549 Tel. (813)949-6624
Indiana: Rev. Gene McClain, Box 337, Morgantown, IN 46160 Tel. (812)597-5021
Maryland: Dr. Kenneth White, 701 Spruce St., Hagerstown, MD 21740 Tel. (301)790-3923
Michigan: Rev. Arthur Mirck, Box 361, Hazel Park, MI 48030 Tel. (313)754-8838
Mid-West: Rev. Charles Clark, P.O. Box 121, Pleasant Hill, IL 62366 Tel. (217)734-9431
New England: Rev. Paul Gilbert, 190 Warwick Rd., Melrose, MA 02176 Tel. (617)979-0056
New York: Rev. John Merrill, 75 Sam Brown Rd., Lockwood, NY 14859 Tel. (607)598-2761
Ohio: Dr. S. Omar Overly, 2481 Red Rock Blvd., Grove City, OH 43123-1154 Tel. (614)871-0710
Pennsylvania: Rev. Wesley Kuntz, 34 Catherine Ave., Latrobe, PA 15650 Tel. (412)537-5630; Rev. Charles Jennings, P.O. Box 679, Clark Summit, PA 18841 Tel. (717)941-3503
Texas: Rev. Roy Roberts, 11436 Bristle Oak Tr., Austin, TX 78750 Tel. (512)335-9262
Montana: Rev. Alvin House, P.O. Box 393, Darby, MT 59829 Tel. (406)821-3141

American Rescue Workers

Major Thomas E. Moore, was National Commander of Booth's Salvation Army when a dispute flared between Booth and Moore. Moore resigned from Booth's Army and due to the fact that Booth's Army was not incorporated at the time, Moore was able to incorporate under said name, name changed in 1890 to American Salvation Army. In 1913 the current name American Rescue Workers was adopted.

It is a national religious social service agency which operates on a quasimilitary basis. Membership includes officers (clergy), soldiers/adherents (laity), members of various activity groups and volunteers who serve as advisors, associates and committed participants in ARW service functions.

The motivation of the organization is the love of God. Its message is based on the Bible. This is expressed by its spiritual Ministry, the purposes of which are to preach the gospel of Jesus Christ and to meet human needs in his name without discrimination and is a branch of the Christian Church.

HEADQUARTERS

2827 Frankford Ave., P.O. Box 4766, Philadelphia, PA 19134 Tel. (215)739-6524

Washington DC Capital Area Office, 716 Ritchie Rd., Capitol Heights, MD 20743 Tel. (301)336-6200

National Field Office, 1209 Hamilton Blvd., Hagerstown, MD 21742 Tel. (301)797-0061

Media Contact, Natl. Communication Sec., Col. Robert N. Coles, Natl. Field Ofc., Fax (301)797-1480

OFFICERS

Commander-In-Chief & Pres. of Corp., General Paul E. Martin, Rev.

Chief of Staff, Col. Claude S. Astin, Jr., Rev.

Natl. Bd. Pres., Col. George B. Gossett, Rev.

Special Services/Aide-de-Camp, Col. Robert N. Coles, Rev., Natl. Field Ofc.

Ordination Committee, Chpsn., Col. Robert N. Coles, Rev.

Natl. Chief Sec., Col. Joyce Gossett

PERIODICAL

The Rescue Herald

The Anglican Orthodox Church

This body was founded on Nov. 16, 1963 in Statesville, N. C., by the Most Rev. James P. Dees. The church holds to the Thirty-Nine Articles of Religion, the 1928 Book of Common Prayer, the King James Version of the Bible and basic Anglican traditions and church government. It upholds biblical morality and emphasizes the fundamental doctrines of the virgin birth, the incarnation, the atoning sacrifice of the cross, the Trinity, the resurrection, the second coming, salvation by faith alone and the divinity of Christ.

Branches of the worldwide Orthodox Anglican Communion are located in South India, Madagascar, Pakistan, Liberia, Nigeria, the Philippines, the Fiji Islands, South Africa, Kenya, the Central African Republic, Colombia and Japan.

The entire membership totals over 300,000.

An active program of Christian education is promoted both in the United States and on a worldwide basis. This includes but is not limited to weekly Sunday School Bible study classes and weekday youth clubs.

The Anglican Orthodox Church operates Cranmer Seminary in Statesville, North Carolina, to train men for holy orders.

HEADQUARTERS

P.O. Box 128, Statesville, NC 28687 Tel. (704)-873-8365 Fax (704)873-8948

Media Contact, Admn. Asst., Mrs. Betty Hoffman

OFFICER

Presiding Bishop, The Most Rev. Robert J. Godfrey, 323 Walnut St., P.O. Box 128, Statesville, NC 28687 Tel. (704)873-8365

PERIODICAL

The News

The Antiochian Orthodox Christian Archdiocese of North America

The spiritual needs of Antiochian faithful in North America were first served through the Syro-Arabian Mission of the Russian Orthodox Church in 1895. In 1895, the Syrian Orthodox Benevolent Society was organized by Antiochian immigrants in New York City. Raphael Hawaweeny, a young Damascene clergyman serving as professor of Arabic language at the Orthodox theological academy in Kazan, Russia, came to New York to organize the first Arabic- language parish in North America in 1896, after being canonically received under the omophorion of the head of the Russian Church in North America. Saint Nicholas Cathedral, now located at 355 State St. in Brooklyn, is considered the "mother parish" of the Archdiocese.

On March 12, 1904, Hawaweeny became the first Orthodox bishop to be consecrated in North America. He traveled throughout the continent and established new parishes. The unity of Orthodoxy in the New World, including the Syrian Greek Orthodox community, was ruptured after the death of Bishop Raphael in 1915 and by the Bolshevik revolution in Russia and the First World War. Unity returned in 1975 when Metropolitan Philip Saliba, of the Antiochian Archdiocese of New York, and Metropolitan Michael Shaheen of the Antiochian Archdiocese of Toledo, Ohio, signed the Articles of Reunification, ratified by the Holy Synod of the Patriarchate. Saliba was recognized as the Metropolitan Primate and Shaheen as Auxiliary Archbishop. A second auxiliary to the Metropolitan, Bishop Antoun Khouri, was consecrated at Brooklyn's Saint Nicholas Cathedral, in 1983. A third auxiliary, Bishop Basil Essey, was consecrated at Wichita's St. George Cathedral, in 1992. Two additional bishops were added in 1994: Bishop Joseph Zehlaoui and Bishop Demetri Khoury.

The Archdiocesan Board of Trustees (consisting of 60 elected and appointed clergy and lay members) and the Metropolitan's Advisory Council (consisting of clergy and lay representatives from each parish and mission) meet regularly to assist the Primate in the administration of the Archdiocese.

HEADQUARTERS

358 Mountain Rd., Englewood, NJ 07631 Tel. (201)871-1355 Fax (201)871-7954

Media Contact, Vicar, The V. Rev. George S. Corey, 52 78th St., Brooklyn, NY 11209 Tel. (718)748-7940 Fax (718)855-3608

OFFICERS

Primate, Metropolitan Philip Saliba

Auxiliary, Bishop Antoun Khouri
Auxiliary, Bishop Joseph Zehlaoui
Auxiliary, Bishop Demetri Khoury
Auxiliary, Bishop Basil Essey

PERIODICALS

The Word; Again Magazine

Apostolic Catholic Assyrian Church of the East, North American Dioceses

The Holy Apostolic Catholic Assyrian Church of the East is the ancient Christian church that developed within the Persian Empire from the day of Pentecost. The Apostolic traditions testify that the Church of the East was established by Sts. Peter, Thomas, Thaddaeus and Bartholomew from among the Twelve and by the labors of Mar Mari and Aggai of the Seventy. The Church grew and developed carrying the Christian gospel into the whole of Asia and islands of the Pacific. Prior to the Great Persecution at the hands of Tamer'leng the Mongol, it is said to have been the largest Christian church in the world.

The doctrinal identity of the church is that of the Apostles. The church stresses two natures and two Qnume in the One Person, Perfect God-Perfect man. The church gives witness to the original Nicene Creed, the Ecumenical Councils of Nicea and Constantinople and the church fathers of that era. Since God is revealed as Trinity, the appellation "Mother of God" is rejected for the Ever Virgin Blessed Mary Mother of Christ, we declare that she is Mother of Emmanuel, God with us!

The church has maintained a line of Catholicos Patriarchs from the time of the Holy Apostles until this present time. Today the present occupant of the Apostolic Throne is His Holiness Mar Dinkha IV, 120th successor to the See of Selucia Ctestiphon.

HEADQUARTERS

Catholicos Patriarch, His Holiness Mar Dinkha, IV, Metropolitanate Residence, The Assyrian Church of the East, Baghdad, Iraq
Media Contact, Chancellor to the Bishop, The Rev. Chancellor C. H. Klutz, 7201 N. Ashland, Chicago, IL 60626 Tel. (312)465-4777 Fax (312)-465-0776

BISHOPS-NORTH AMERICA

Diocese Eastern USA: His Grace Bishop Mar Aprim Khamis, 8908 Birch Ave., Morton Grove, IL 60053 Tel. (847)966-0617 Fax (847)966-0012
Diocese Western USA: His Grace Bishop Mar Bawai Soro, St. Joseph Cathedral, 680 Minnesota Ave., San Jose, CA 95125 Tel. (408)286-7377 Fax (408)286-1236
Diocese of Canada: His Grace Bishop Mar Emmanuel Joseph, St. Mary Cathedral, 57 Apted Ave., Weston, ON M9L 2P2 Tel. (416)744-9311

PERIODICAL

Qala min M'Dinkha (Voice from the East)

Apostolic Christian Church (Nazarene)

This body was formed in America by an immigration from various European nations, from a movement begun by Rev. S. H. Froehlich, a Swiss pastor, whose followers are still found in Switzerland and Central Europe.

HEADQUARTERS

Apostolic Christian Church Foundation, 1135 Sholey Rd., Richmond, VA 23231 Tel. (804)-222-1943 Fax (804)236-0642
Media Contact, Exec. Dir., James Hodges

OFFICERS

Exec. Dir., James Hodges

Apostolic Christian Churches of America

The Apostolic Christian Church of America was founded in the early 1830s in Switzerland by Samuel Froehlich, a young divinity student who had experienced a religious conversion based on the pattern found in the New Testament. The church, known then as Evangelical Baptist, spread to surrounding countries. A Froehlich associate, Elder Benedict Weyeneth, established the church's first American congregation in 1847 in upstate New York. In America, where the highest concentration today is in the Midwest farm belt, the church became known as Apostolic Christian.

Church doctrine is based on a literal interpretation of the Bible, the infallible Word of God. The church believes that a true faith in Christ's redemptive work at Calvary is manifested by a sincere repentance and conversion. Members strive for sanctification and separation from worldliness as a consequence of salvation, not as a means to obtain it. Security in Christ is believed to be conditional based on faithfulness. Uniform observance of scriptural standards of holiness are stressed. Holy Communion is confined to members of the church. Male members are willing to serve in the military, but do not bear arms. The holy kiss is practiced and women wear head coverings during prayer and worship.

Doctrinal authority rests with a council of elders, each of whom serves as a local elder (bishop). Both elders and ministers are chosen from local congregations, do not attend seminary and serve without compensation. Sermons are delivered extemporaneously as led by the Holy Spirit, using the Bible as a text.

HEADQUARTERS

3420 N. Sheridan Rd., Peoria, IL 61604
Media Contact, Sec., Dale R. Eisenmann, 6913 Wilmette, Darien, IL 60561 Tel. (708)969-7021

OFFICERS

Sec., Elder (Bishop) Dale R. Eisenmann, 6913 Wilmette, Darien, IL 60561 Tel. (708)969-7021

PERIODICAL

The Silver Lining

Apostolic Faith Mission Church of God

The Apostolic Faith Mission Church of God was founded and organized July 10, 1906, by Bishop F. W. Williams in Mobile, Ala.

Bishop Williams was saved and filled with the Holy Ghost at a revival in Los Angeles under Elder W. J. Seymour of The Divine Apostolic Faith Movement. After being called into the ministry, Bishop Williams went out to preach the gospel in Mississippi, then moved on to Mobile.

On Oct. 9, 1915, the Apostolic Faith Mission Church of God was incorporated in Mobile under Bishop Williams, who was also the general overseer of this church.

HEADQUARTERS

Ward's Temple, 806 Muscogee Rd., Cantonment, FL 32533

Media Contact, Natl. Sunday School Supt., Elder Thomas Brooks, 3298 Toney Dr., Decatur, GA 30032 Tel. (404)284-7596

OFFICERS

Bd. of Bishops: Presiding Bishop, Donice Brown, 2265 Welcome Cir., Cantonement, FL 32535 Tel. (904)968-5225; Billy Carter; J. L. Smiley; T. L. Frye; D. Brown; T. C. Tolbert; James Truss

NATIONAL DEPARTMENTS

Missionary Dept., Pres., Sarah Ward, Cantonment, FL

Youth Dept., Pres., W. J. Wills, Lincoln, AL

Sunday School Dept., Supt., Thomas Brooks, Decatur, GA

Mother Dept., Pres., Mother Juanita Phillips, Birmingham, AL

INTERNATIONAL DEPARTMENTS

Morobia, Liberia, Bishop Beter T. Nelson, Box 3646, Bush Rhode Islane, Morobia, Liberia

Apostolic Faith Mission of Portland, Oregon

The Apostolic Faith Mission of Portland, Oregon, was founded in 1907. It had its beginning in the Latter Rain outpouring on Azusa Street in Los Angeles in 1906.

Some of the main doctrines are justification by faith; spiritual new birth, as Jesus told Nicodemus and as Martin Luther proclaimed in the Great Reformation; sanctification, a second definite work of grace; the Wesleyan teaching of holiness; the baptism of the Holy Ghost as experienced on the Day of Pentecost and again poured out at the beginning of the Latter Rain revival in Los Angeles.

Mrs. Florence L. Crawford, who had received the baptism of the Holy Ghost in Los Angeles, brought this Latter Rain message to Portland on Christmas Day 1906. It has spread to the world by means of literature which is still published and mailed everywhere without a subscription price. Collections are never taken in the meetings and the public is not asked for money.

Camp meetings have been held annually in Portland, Ore., since 1907, with delegations coming from around the world.

Missionaries from the Portland headquarters have established churches in Korea, Japan, the Philippines and many countries in Africa.

HEADQUARTERS

6615 SE 52nd Ave., Portland, OR 97206 Tel. (503)777-1741 Fax (503)777-1743

Media Contact, Gen. Overseer, Dwight L. Baltzell

OFFICER

Gen. Overseer, Rev. Dwight L. Baltzell

PERIODICAL

Higher Way

Apostolic Lutheran Church of America

Organized in 1872 as the Solomon Korteniemi Lutheran Society, this Finnish body was incorporated in 1929 as the Finnish Apostolic Lutheran Church in America and changed its name to Apostolic Lutheran Church of America in 1962.

This body stresses preaching the Word of God. There is an absence of liturgy and formalism in worship. A seminary education is not required of pastors. Being called by God to preach the Word is the chief requirement for clergy and laity. The church stresses personal absolution and forgiveness of sins, as practiced by Martin Luther, and the importance of bringing converts into God's kingdom.

HEADQUARTERS

Rt. 1 Box 462, Houghton, MI 49931 Tel. (906)482-8269

Media Contact, Sec., James Johnson

OFFICERS

Pres., Earl Kaurala, 119 Penny Way, Marquette, MI 49855

Sec., James Johnson

Treas., Ben Johnson, Rt. 2, Box 566, Astoria, OR 97103

PERIODICAL

Christian Monthly

Apostolic Overcoming Holy Church of God, Inc.

The Right Reverend William Thomas Phillips (1893-1973) was thoroughly convinced in 1912 that Holiness was a system through which God wanted him to serve. In 1916 he was led to Mobile, Ala., where he organized the Ethiopian Overcoming Holy Church of God. In April 1941 the church was incorporated in Alabama under its present title.

Each congregation manages its own affairs, united under districts governed by overseers and diocesan bishops and assisted by an executive board comprised of bishops, ministers, laymen and the National Secretary. The General Assembly convenes annually.

The church's chief objective is to enlighten people of God's holy Word and to be a blessing to every nation. The main purpose of this church is to ordain elders, appoint pastors and send out divinely called missionaries and teachers. This church enforces all ordinances enacted by Jesus Christ. The church believes in water baptism (Acts 2:38, 8:12, and 10:47), administers the Lord's Supper, observes the washing of feet (John 13:4-7), believes that Jesus Christ shed his blood to sanctify the people and cleanse them from all sin and believes in the resurrection of the dead and the second coming of Christ.

HEADQUARTERS

1120 N. 24th St., Birmingham, AL 35234

Media Contact, Natl. Exec. Sec., Juanita R. Arrington, Tel. (205)324-2202

OFFICERS

Senior Bishop & Exec. Head, Rt. Rev. Jasper Roby

National Treas., Elder W. T. Parker

Exec. Sec., Mrs. Juanita R. Arrington

PERIODICAL

The People's Mouthpiece

Armenian Apostolic Church of America

Widespread movement of the Armenian people over the centuries caused the development of two seats of religious jurisdiction of the Armenian Apostolic Church in the World: the See of Etchmiadzin, in Armenia, and the See of Cilicia, in Lebanon.

In America, the Armenian Church functioned under the jurisdiction of the Etchmiadzin See from 1887 to 1933, when a division occurred within the American diocese over the condition of the church in Soviet Armenia. One group chose to remain independent until 1957, when the Holy See of Cilicia agreed to accept them under its jurisdiction.

Despite the existence of two dioceses in North America, the Armenian Church has always functioned as one church in dogma and liturgy.

HEADQUARTERS

Eastern Prelacy, 138 E. 39th St., New York, NY 10016 Tel. (212)689-7810 Fax (212)689-7168

Western Prelacy, 4401 Russel Ave., Los Angeles, CA 90027 Tel. (213)663-8273 Fax (213)663-0438

Media Contact, Vasken Ghougassian

OFFICERS

Eastern Prelacy, Prelate, Archbishop Mesrob Ashjian

Eastern Prelacy, Chpsn., Onnig Marashian

Western Prelacy, Prelate, Archbishop Datev Sarkissian, 4401 Russell Ave., Los Angeles, CA 90027 Fax (213)663-0428

Western Prelacy, Chpsn., Khajag Dikidjian

DEPARTMENTS

AREC, Armenian Religious Educ. Council, Exec. Coord., Deacon Shant Kazanjian

ANEC, Armenian Natl. Educ. Council, Exec. Coord., Gilda Kupelian

PERIODICAL

Outreach

Assemblies of God

From a few hundred delegates at its founding convention in 1914 at Hot Springs, Ark., the Assemblies of God has become one of the largest church groups in the modern Pentecostal movement worldwide. Throughout its existence it has emphasized the power of the Holy Spirit to change lives and the participation of all members in the work of the church.

The revival that led to the formation of the Assemblies of God and numerous other church groups early in the 20th century began during times of intense prayer and Bible study. Believers in the United States and around the world received spiritual experiences like those described in the Book of Acts. Accompanied by baptism in the Holy Spirit and its initial physical evidence of "speaking in tongues," or a language unknown to the person, their experiences were associated with the coming of the Holy Spirit at Pentecost (Acts 2), so participants were called Pentecostals.

The church also believes that the Bible is God's infallible Word to man, that salvation is available only through Jesus Christ, that divine healing is made possible through Christ's suffering and that Christ will return again for those who love him. In recent years, this Pentecostal revival has spilled over into almost every denomination in a new wave of revival sometimes called the charismatic renewal.

Assemblies of God leaders credit their church's rapid and continuing growth to its acceptance of the New Testament as a model for the present-day church. Evangelism and missionary zeal at home and abroad characterize the denomination.

Assemblies of God believers observe two ordinances--water baptism by immersion and the Lord's Supper, or Holy Communion. The church is trinitarian, holding that God exists in three persons: Father, Son and Holy Spirit.

HEADQUARTERS

1445 Boonville Ave., Springfield, MO 65802 Tel. (417)862-2781 Fax (417)862-8558

Media Contact, Sec. of Public Relations, Juleen Turnage, Fax (417)862-5554

EXECUTIVE PRESBYTERY

Gen. Supt., Thomas E. Trask

Asst. Supt., Charles T. Crabtree

Gen. Sec., George O. Wood

Gen. Treas., James E. Bridges

Foreign Missions, Exec. Dir., Loren O. Triplett

Home Missions, Exec. Dir., Charles Hackett

Great Lakes, Robert K. Schmidgall, P.O. Box 296-1155, Aurora Ave., Naperville, IL 60540

Gulf, Phillip Wannenmacher, 1301 N. Boonville, Springfield, MO 65802

North Central, David Argue, P.O. Box 22178, Lincoln, NE 68542

Northeast, Almon Bartholomew, P.O. Box 39, Liverpool, NY 13088

Northwest, R. L. Brandt, 1702 Colton Blvd., Billings, MT 59102

South Central, Armon Newburn, P.O. Box 13179, Oklahoma City, OK 73113

Southeast, Dan Betzer, 1550 Colonial Blvd., Ft. Myers, FL 33907

Southwest, Tommy Barnett, 13613 N. Cave Creek Rd., Phoenix, AZ 85022

Language Area, Jesse Miranda, 3527 Thaxton, Hacienda Heights, CA 91745

INTERNATIONAL HEADQUARTERS

Chief Operational Officer, Michael Messner

Division of the Treasury, Gen. Treas., James E. Bridges

Division of Christian Education, Natl. Dir., ----

Division of Church Ministries, Natl. Dir., Terry Raburn

Division of Foreign Missions, Exec. Dir., Loren O. Triplett

Division of Home Missions, Exec. Dir., Charles Hackett

Div. of Publication, Gospel Publishing House, Natl. Dir., Joseph Kilpatrick

PERIODICALS

Enrichment: A Journal for Pentecostal Ministry; At Ease; Caring; High Adventure; Memos: A Magazine for Missionettes Leaders; Mountain Movers; Pentecostal Evangel; Christian Education Counselor; Woman's Touch; Heritage; On Course

Assemblies of God International Fellowship (Independent/Not affiliated)

April 9, 1906 is the date commonly accepted by Pentecostals as the 20th-century outpouring of God's spirit in America, which began in a humble gospel mission at 312 Azusa Street in Los Angeles.

This spirit movement spread across the United States and gave birth to the Independent Assemblies of God (Scandinavian). Early pioneers instrumental in guiding and shaping the fellowship of ministers and churches into a nucleus of independent churches included Pastor B. M. Johnson, founder of Lakeview Gospel Church in 1911; Rev. A. A. Holmgren, a Baptist minister who received his baptism of the Holy Spirit in the early Chicago outpourings, was publisher of *Sanningens Vittne*, a voice of the Scandinavian Independent Assemblies of God and also served as secretary of the fellowship for many years; Gunnar Wingren, missionary pioneer in Brazil; and Arthur F. Johnson, who served for many years as chairman of the Scandinavian Assemblies.

In 1935, the Scandinavian group dissolved its incorporation and united with the Independent Assemblies of God of the U.S. and Canada which by majority vote of members formed a new corporation in 1986, Assemblies of God International Fellowship (Independent/Not Affiliated).

HEADQUARTERS

5284 Eastgate Mall, San Diego, CA 92121 Tel. (619)677-9701 Fax (619)677-0038

Media Contact, Exec. Dir. & Ed., Rev. T. A. Lanes

OFFICERS

Exec. Dir., Rev. T. A. Lanes

Vice-Pres., Rev. Winston Mattsson-Boze

Sec., Rev. George E. Ekeroth

Treas., Dr. Joseph Bohac

Canada, Sec., Harry Nunn, Sr., 15 White Crest Ct., St. Catherines, ON 62N 6Y1

PERIODICAL

The Fellowship Magazine

Associate Reformed Presbyterian Church (General Synod)

The Associate Reformed Presbyterian Church (General Synod) stems from the 1782 merger of Associate Presbyterians and Reformed Presbyterians. In 1822, the Synod of the Carolinas broke with the Associate Reformed Church (which eventually became part of the United Presbyterian Church of North America).

The story of the Synod of the Carolinas began with the Seceder Church, formed in Scotland in 1733 and representing a break from the established Church of Scotland. Seceders, in America called Associate Presbyterians, settled in South Carolina following the Revolutionary War. They were joined by a few Covenanter congregations which, along with the Seceders, had protested Scotland's established church. The Covenanters took their name from the Solemn League and Covenant of 1643, the guiding document of Scotch Presbyterians. In 1790, some Seceders and Covenanters formed the Presbytery of the Carolinas and Georgia at Long Cane, S.C. Thomas Clark and John Boyse led in the formation of this presbytery, a unit within the Associate Reformed Presbyterian Church. The presbytery represented the southern segment of that church.

In 1822 the southern church became independent of the northern Associate Reformed Presbyterian Church and formed the Associate Reformed Presbyterian Church of the South. "Of the South" was dropped in 1858 when the northern group joined the United Presbyterian Church and "General Synod" was added in 1935. The General Synod is the denomination's highest court; it is composed of all the teaching elders and at least one ruling elder from each congregation.

Doctrinally, the church holds to the Westminster Confession of Faith. Liturgically, the synod has been distinguished by its exclusive use of psalmody; in 1946 this practice became optional.

HEADQUARTERS

Associate Reformed Presbyterian Center, One Cleveland St., Greenville, SC 29601 Tel. (864)-232-8297

Media Contact, Principal Clk., Rev. C. Ronald Beard, D.D., 3132 Grace Hill Rd., Columbia, SC 29204 Tel. (803)787-6370

OFFICERS

Mod., Rev. J. Allen Derrick, D.D., P.O. Box 88, Richburg, SC 29729

Mod.-Elect, Mr. John H. Doudoukjian, 231 Chippewa Dr., Columbia, SC 29210-6508 Tel. (803)-772-2469

Principal Clk., Rev. C. Ronald Beard, D.D., 3132 Grace Hill Rd., Columbia, SC 29204

AGENCIES AND INSTITUTIONS

Ofc. of Admn. Services, Dir., Mr. Ed Hogan

Assoc. Reformed Presb. Foundation, Inc.

Assoc. Reformed Presb. Retirement Plan

Ofc. of Christian Education, Dir., David Vickery

Ofc. of Church Extension, Dir., Rev. James T. Corbitt

Ofc. of Synod's Treasurer, Mr. Guy H. Smith, III

Ofc. of Secretary of World Witness, Exec. Sec., John E. Mariner, Tel. (864)233-5226

Bonclarken Assembly, Dir., Mr. James T. Brice, 500 Pine St., Flat Rock, NC 28731 Tel. (704)692-2223

Erskine College, Pres., James W. Strobel, Ph.D., Due West, SC 29639 Tel. (864)379-8759

Erskine Theological Seminary, Dean, Rev. Randall R. Ruble, Ph.D., Due West, SC 26939 Tel. (864)379-8885

PERIODICALS

The Associate Reformed Presbyterian; The Adult Quarterly

The Association of Free Lutheran Congregations

The Association of Free Lutheran Congregations, rooted in the Scandinavian revival movements, was organized in 1962 by a Lutheran Free Church remnant which rejected merger with The American Lutheran Church. The original 42 congregations were joined by other like-minded conservative Lutherans, especially from the former Evangelical Lutheran Church and the Suomi Synod. There has been more than a fivefold increase in the number of congregations. Congregations subscribe to the Apostles', Nicene and Athanasian creeds; Luther's Small Catechism; and the Unaltered Augsburg Confession. The Fundamental Principles and Rules for Work (1897) declare that the local congregation is the right form of the kingdom of God on earth, subject to no authority but the Word and the Spirit of God.

Distinctive emphases are: (1) the infallibility and inerrancy of Holy Scriptures as the Word of God; (2) congregational polity; (3) the spiritual unity of all believers, resulting in fellowship and cooperation transcending denominational lines; (4) evangelical outreach, calling all to enter a personal relationship with Jesus Christ; (5) a wholesome Lutheran pietism that proclaims the Lordship of Jesus Christ in all areas of life and results in believers becoming the salt and light in their communities; (6) a conservative stance on current social issues.

A two-year Bible school and a theological seminary are in Minneapolis. Support is channeled to churches in Brazil, Mexico, Canada and India.

HEADQUARTERS

3110 E. Medicine Lake Blvd., Minneapolis, MN 55441 Tel. (612)545-5631 Fax (612)545-0079

Media Contact, Pres., Rev. Robert L. Lee

OFFICERS

Pres., Rev. Robert L. Lee

Vice-Pres., Rev. Elden K. Nelson, 1633 Co. Rd. 8 SE, Kandiyohi, MN 56251

Sec., Rev. Bruce Dalager, 2708 Olive, Grand Forks, ND 58201

PERIODICAL

The Lutheran Ambassador

Baptist Bible Fellowship International

Organized on May 24, 1950 in Fort Worth, Tex., the Baptist Bible Fellowship was founded by about 100 pastors and lay people who had grown disenchanted with the policies and leadership of the World Fundamental Baptist Missionary Fellowship, an outgrowth of the Baptist Bible Union formed in Kansas City in 1923 by fundamentalist leaders from the Southern Baptist, Northern Baptist and Canadian Baptist Conventions. The BBF elected W. E. Dowell as its first president and established offices and a three-year (now four-year with a graduate school) Baptist Bible College.

The BBF statement of faith was essentially that of the Baptist Bible Union, adopted in 1923, a variation of the New Hampshire Confession of Faith. It presents an infallible Bible, belief in the substitutionary death of Christ, his physical resurrection and his premillennial return to earth. It advocates local church autonomy and strong pastoral leadership and maintains that the fundamental basis of fellowship is a missionary outreach. The BBF vigorously stresses evangelism and the international missions office reports 797 adult missionaries working on 94 fields throughout the world in 1995.

There are BBF-related churches in every state of the United States, with special strength in the upper South, the Great Lakes region, southern states west of the Mississippi, Kansas and California. There are six related colleges and one graduate school or seminary.

A Committee of Forty-Five, elected by pastors and churches within the states, sits as a representative body, meeting in three subcommittees, each chaired by one of the principal officers: an administration committee chaired by the president, a missions committee chaired by a vice president and an education committee chaired by a vice-president.

HEADQUARTERS

Baptist Bible Fellowship Missions Bldg., 720 E. Kearney St., Springfield, MO 65803 Tel. (417)-862-5001 Fax (417)865-0794

Mailing Address, P.O. Box 191, Springfield, MO 65801

Media Contact, Mission Dir., Dr. Bob Baird, P.O. Box 191, Springfield, MO 65801

OFFICERS

Pres., Sam Davison, Southwest Baptist Church, 1300 SW 54th St., Tulsa, OK 73119

First Vice-Pres., Dave Hardy, Eastland Baptist Church, 1835 S. 129th E Ave., Tulsa, OK 74108

Second Vice-Pres., Don Elmore, Temple Baptist Church, P.O. Box 292, Springdale, AR 72764

Sec., K. B. Murray, Millington Street Baptist Church, Box 524, Winfield, KS 67156

Treas., Ken Adrian, Thomas Rd. Baptist Church, 5735 W. Thomas Rd., Phoenix, AZ 85031

Mission Dir., Dr. Bob Baird, P.O. Box 191, Springfield, MO 65801

PERIODICALS

The Baptist Bible Tribune; The Preacher

Baptist General Conference

The Baptist General Conference, rooted in the pietistic movement of Sweden during the 19th century, traces its history to Aug. 13, 1852. On that day a small group of believers at Rock Island, Ill., under the leadership of Gustaf Palmquist, organized the first Swedish Baptist Church in America. Swedish Baptist churches flourished in the upper Midwest and Northeast, and by 1879, when the first annual meeting was held in Village Creek, Iowa, 65 churches had been organized, stretching from Maine to the Dakotas and south to Kansas and Missouri.

By 1871, John Alexis Edgren, an immigrant sea captain and pastor in Chicago, had begun the first publication and a theological seminary. The Conference grew to 324 churches and nearly 26,000 members by 1902. There were 40,000 members in 1945 and 135,000 in 1993.

Many churches began as Sunday schools. The seminary evolved into Bethel, a four-year liberal arts college with 1,800 students, and theological seminaries in Arden Hills, Minn. and San Diego, California.

Missions and the planting of churches have been main objectives both in America and overseas. Today churches have been established in the United States, Canada and Mexico, as well as a dozen countries overseas. In 1985 the churches of Canada founded an autonomous denomination, The Baptist General Conference of Canada.

The Baptist General Conference is a member of the Baptist World Alliance, the Baptist Joint Committee on Public Affairs and the National Association of Evangelicals. It is characterized by the balancing of a conservative doctrine with an irenic and cooperative spirit. Its basic objective is to seek the fulfillment of the Great Commission and the Great Commandment.

HEADQUARTERS

2002 S. Arlington Heights Rd., Arlington Heights, IL 60005 Tel. (708)228-0200 Fax (708)228-5376

Media Contact, Pres., Dr. Robert S. Ricker

OFFICERS

Pres. & Chief Exec. Officer, Dr. Robert S. Ricker

Exec, Vice-Pres., Ray Swatkowski

OTHER ORGANIZATIONS

Business, CFO, Stephen R. Schultz

Bd. of Home Missions, Exec. Dir., Dr. John C. Dickau

Bd. of World Missions, Exec. Dir., Rev. Ronald Larson

Bd. of Regents: Bethel College & Seminary, Pres., Dr. George K. Brushaber, 3900 Bethel Dr., St. Paul, MN 55112

PERIODICAL

The Standard

Baptist Missionary Association of America

A group of regular Baptist churches organized in associational capacity in May, 1950, in Little Rock, Ark., as the North American Baptist Association. The name changed in 1969 to Baptist Missionary Association of America. There are several state and numerous local associations of cooperating churches. In theology, these churches are evangelical, missionary, fundamental and for the most part premillennial.

HEADQUARTERS

9219 Sibly Hole Rd., Little Rock, AR Tel. (501)-455-4977 Fax (501)455-3636

Mailing Address, P.O. Box 193920, Little Rock, AR 72219-3920

Media Contact, Dir. of Baptist News Service, James C. Blaylock, P.O. Box 97, Jacksonville, TX 75766 Tel. (903)586-2501 Fax (903)586-0378

OFFICERS

Pres., Grady L. Higgs, P.O. Box 34, Jacksonville, TX 75766

Vice-Pres.: Leon L. Carmical, 930 N. 10th Ave., Laurel, MS 39440; Roy L. McLaughlin, 6299 Miller Rd., Swartz Creek, MI 48473

Rec. Sec.: Rev. Ralph Cottrell, P.O. Box 1203, Van, TX 75790; Don J. Brown, P.O. Box 8181, Laruel, MS 39441; James Ray Raines, 5609 N. Locust, N. Little Rock, AR 72116

DEPARTMENTS

Missions: Gen. Sec., Rev. F. Donald Collins, P.O. Box 193920, Little Rock, AR 72219-3920

Publications: Ed.-in-Chief, Rev. James L. Silvey, 311 Main St., P.O. Box 7270, Texarkana, TX 75505

Christian Education: Bapt. Missionary Assoc. Theological Sem., Pres., Dr. Philip R. Bryan, Seminary Heights, 1530 E. Pine St., Jacksonville, TX 75766

Baptist News Service: Dir., Rev. James C. Blaylock, P.O. Box 97, Jacksonville, TX 75766

Life Word Broadcast Ministries: Dir., Rev. George Reddin, P.O. Box 6, Conway, AR 72032

Armed Forces Chaplaincy: Exec. Dir., Bobby C. Thornton, P.O. Box 240, Flint, TX 75762

BMAA Dept. of Church Ministries: Bobby Tucker, P.O. Box 3376, Texarkana, TX 75504

Daniel Springs Encampment: James Speer, P.O. Box 310, Gary, TX 75643

Ministers Benefit Dept.: Craig Branham, 4001 Jefferson St., Texarkana, AR 75501

OTHER ORGANIZATIONS

Baptist Missionary Assoc. Brotherhood: Pres., Arthur Smith, R.R. 7, Box 1370, Laurel, MS 39440

National Women's Missionary Auxiliary: Pres., Mrs. Ray Thompson, R.R. 7, Box 540, Gilmer, TX 75644

PERIODICAL

The Gleaner

Beachy Amish Mennonite Churches

The Beachy Amish Mennonite Church was established in 1927 in Somerset County, Pa. following a division in the Amish Mennonite Church in that area. As congregations in other locations joined the movement, they were identified by the same name. There are currently 88 churches in the United States, 8 in Canada and 25 in other countries. Total membership is 7,678, according to the 1993 Mennonite Yearbook.

Beachy Churches believe in one God eternally existent in three persons (Father, Son and Holy Spirit); that Jesus Christ is the one and only way to salvation; that the Bible is God's infallible Word to us, by which all will be judged; that heaven is the eternal abode of the redeemed in Christ; and that the wicked and unbelieving will endure hell eternally.

Evangelical mission boards sponsor missions in Central and South America and in Kenya, Africa.

The Mission Interests Committee, founded in 1953 for evangelism and other Christian services, sponsors homes for handicapped youth and elderly people, mission outreaches among the Indians in Canada and a mission outreach in Europe.

HEADQUARTERS

Media Contact, Ervin N. Hershberger, Rt. 1, Box 176, Meyersdale, PA 15552 Tel. (814)662-2483

ORGANIZATIONS

Amish Mennonite Aid: Sec.-Treas., Vernon Miller, 2675 U.S. 42 NE, London, OH 43140 Tel. (614)879-8616

Mission Interests Committee: Sec.-Treas., Melvin Gingerich, 42555 900W, Topeka, IN 46571 Tel. (219)593-9090

Choice Books of Northern Virginia: Supervisor, Simon Schrock, 4614 Holly Ave., Fairfax, VA 22030 Tel. (703)830-2800

Calvary Bible School: HC 61, Box 202, Calico Rock, AR 72519 Tel. (501)297-8658; Sec.-Treas., Elmer Gingerich, HC 74, Box 282, Mountain View, AR 72560 Tel. (501)296-8764

Penn Valley Christian Retreat, Bd. Chmn., Jacob K. Stoltzfus, RR 2, Box 165, McVeytown, PA 17015 Tel. (717)529-2935

PERIODICAL

The Calvary Messenger

Berean Fundamental Church

Founded 1932 in North Platte, Neb., this body emphasizes conservative Protestant doctrines.

HEADQUARTERS

Box 6103, Lincoln, NE 68506 Tel. (402)483-6512 Fax (402)483-6642

Media Contact, Pres., Pastor Doug Shada

OFFICERS

Pres., Doug Shada

Vice-Pres., Rev. Richard Crocker, 419 Lafayette Blvd., Cheyenne, WY 82009 Tel. (307)635-5914

Sec., Rev. Roger Daum, R.R.2, Box 155, Cozad, NE 69130 Tel. (308)784-3675

Treas., Virgil Wiebe, P.O. Box 6103, Lincoln, NE 68506

Exec. Advisor, Curt Lehman, Tel. (402)483-4840

Exec. Advisor, Rev. Carl M. Goltz, P.O. Box 397, North Platte, NE 69103 Tel. (308)532-6723

The Bible Church of Christ, Inc.

The Bible Church of Christ was founded on March 1, 1961 by Bishop Roy Bryant, Sr. Since that time, the Church has grown to include congregations in the United States, Africa and India. The church is trinitarian and accepts the Bible as the divinely inspired Word of God. Its doctrine includes miracles of healing, deliverance and the baptism of the Holy Ghost.

HEADQUARTERS

1358 Morris Ave., Bronx, NY 10456 Tel. (718)-588-2284

Media Contact, Pres., Bishop Roy Bryant, Sr.

OFFICERS

Pres., Bishop Roy Bryant, Sr., 3033 Gunther Ave., Bronx, NY 10469 Tel. (718)379-8080

V. Pres., Asst. Bishop Derek G. Owens

Sec., Sissieretta Bryant

Treas., Elder Artie Burney

EXECUTIVE TRUSTEE BOARD

Chpsns.: Elder Alberto L. Hope; Bishop Derek G. Owens, 100 W. 2nd St., Mount Vernon, NY 10550 Tel. (914)664-4602

OTHER ORGANIZATIONS

Foreign Missions: Pres., Elder Autholene Smith

Home Missions: Pres., Evangelist Eleanor Samuel

Sunday Schools: Gen. Supt., Elder Alice Jones

Evangelism: Natl. Pres., Evangelist Gloria Gray

Youth: Pres., Deacon Tommy Robinson

Minister of Music: Ray Brown

Minister of Education, Gloria Pratt

Prison Ministry Team: Pres., Evangelist Marvin Lowe

Presiding Elders: Delaware, Elder Roland Miflin, Diamond Acre, Dagsboro, DE 19939; North Carolina, Elder George Houston; Adm., Elder Larry Bryant, West Johnson Rd., Clinton, NC 28328; Monticello, Elder Jesse Alston, 104 Waverly Ave., Monticello, NY 12701; Mount Vernon, Elder Artie Burney, Sr., 100 W. 2nd St., Mount Vernon, NY 10550; Bronx, Elder Anita Robinson; Annex, Elder Reginald Gullette, 1069 Morris Ave., Bronx, NY 10456

Bible School: Pres., Dr. Roy Bryant, Sr.

Bookstore: Mgr., Evangelist Beryl C. Foster, Tel. (718)293-1928

Project Angel, Pres., Deacon Anthony Robinson

PERIODICALS

The Voice; The Gospel Light; The Messenger; The Challenge

Bible Fellowship Church

The Bible Fellowship Church grew out divisions in the Mennonite community in Pennsylvania in the 1850s. Traditional church leadership resisted the freedom of expression and prayer meetings initiated by several preachers and church leaders. These evanglical Mennonites formed the Evangleical Mennonite Society. Over the next two decades various like minded groups in Canada, Ohio and Pennsylvania joined the Society.

The group continues to follow Mennonite doctrine with the addition to their articles of faith of an emphasis on the Wesleyan "Second Blessing."

In 1959 the Conference became the Bible Fellowship Church and new articles of faith were ratified.

HEADQUARTERS

Media Contact, Sec. of Corp., Greater Bible Fellowship Church, 693 Church Rd., Graterford, PA 19426 Tel. (610)489-9389

Media Contact, David J. Watkins

OFFICERS

Chmn., James A. Bell

Vice-Chmn., Carl C. Cassel

Sec., Randall A. Grossman

Asst Sec., Robert W. Smock

BOARDS AND COMMITTEES

Bd. of Dir., Bible Fellowship Church

Bd. of Christian Education

Board of Extension

Bible Fellowship Church Homes, Inc.

Board of Pensions

Board of Pinebrook Bible Conference

Board of Missions

Board of Publication and Printing

Bd. of Victory Valley Camp

Board of Higher Education

PERIODICAL

Fellowship News

Bible Holiness Church

This church came into being about 1890 as the result of definite preaching on the doctrine of holiness in some Methodist churches in southeastern Kansas. It became known as The Southeast Kansas Fire Baptized Holiness Association. The name was changed in 1945 to The Fire Baptized Holiness Church and in 1995 to Bible Holiness Church. It is entirely Wesleyan in doctrine, episcopal in church organization and intensive in evangelistic zeal.

HEADQUARTERS

600 College Ave., Independence, KS 67301 Tel. (316)331-3049

Media Contact, Gen. Supt., Gerald Broadaway

OFFICERS

Gen. Supt., Gerald Broadaway

Gen. Sec., Wayne Knipmeyer, Box 457, South Pekin, IL 61564

Gen. Treas., Dale Cauthon, R.R. 1, Box 8B, Independence, KS 67301

PERIODICALS

The Flaming Sword; John Three Sixteen

Bible Way Church of Our Lord Jesus Christ World Wide, Inc.

This body was organized in 1957 in the Pentecostal tradition for the purpose of accelerating evangelistic and foreign missionary commitment and to effect a greater degree of collective leadership than leaders found in the body in which they had previously participated.

The doctrine is the same as that of the Church of Our Lord Jesus Christ of the Apostolic Faith, Inc., of which some of the churches and clergy were formerly members.

This organization has churches and missions in Africa, England, Guyana, Trinidad and Jamaica, and churches in 25 states in America. The Bible Way Church is involved in humanitarian as well as evangelical outreach with concerns for urban housing and education and economic development.

HEADQUARTERS

4949 Two-Notch Rd., Columbia, SC 29204 Tel. (800)432-5612 Fax (803)691-0583

Media Contact, Chief Apostle, Presiding Bishop Huie Rogers

OFFICERS

Presiding Bishop, Bishop Huie Rogers, 4949 Two Notch Rd., Columbia, SC 29204 Tel. (800)432-5612 Fax (803)691-0583

Gen. Sec., Bishop Edward Williams, 5118 Clarendon Rd., Brooklyn, NY 11226 Tel. (718)451-1238

Brethren Church (Ashland, Ohio)

The Brethren Church (Ashland, Ohio) was organized by progressive-minded German Baptist Brethren in 1883. They reaffirmed the teaching of the original founder of the Brethren movement, Alexander Mack, and returned to congregational government.

HEADQUARTERS

524 College Ave., Ashland, OH 44805 Tel. (419)-289-1708 Fax (419)281-0450

Media Contact, Dir. of Brethren Church Ministries, Ronald W. Waters

GENERAL ORGANIZATION

Dir. of Pastoral Ministries, Rev. David Cooksey

Dir. of Brethren Church Ministries, Rev. Ronald W. Waters

Ed. of Publications, Rev. Richard C. Winfield

Conf. Mod. (1996-1997), Dr. John Shultz

BOARD

The Missionary Bd., Exec. Dir., Rev. Reilly Smith

PERIODICAL

The Brethren Evangelist

Brethren in Christ Church

The Brethren in Christ Church was founded in Lancaster County, Pa. in about the year 1778 and was an outgrowth of the religious awakening which occurred in that area during the latter part of the 18th century. This group became known as "River Brethren" because of their original location near the Susquehanna River. The name "Brethren in Christ" was officially adopted in 1863. In theology they have accents of the Pietist, Anabaptist, Wesleyan and Evangelical movements.

HEADQUARTERS

General Church Office, P.O. Box 290, Grantham, PA 17027-0290 Tel. (717)697-2634 Fax (717)-697-7714

Media Contact, Mod., Harvey R. Sider, Tel. (717)-697-2634 Fax (717)697-7714

OFFICERS

Mod., Rev. Harvey R. Sider, P.O. Box 290, Grantham, PA 17027 Tel. (717)697-2634 Fax (717)-697-7714

Gen. Sec., Dr. R. Donald Shafer

Treasurer, Allen Carr

OTHER ORGANIZATIONS

General Conference Board: Mod., Rev. Harvey R. Sider

Bd. of Directors: Chpsn., Harold Albrecht, RR 2, Petersburg, ON N0B 2H0

Bd. for Media Ministries: Chpsn., John Yeatts, Messiah College, Grantham, PA 17027; Exec. Dir., Roger Williams, P.O. Box 189, Nappanee, IN 46550

Bd. for World Missions: Chpsn., Lowell D. Mann, 8 W. Bainbridge St., Elizabethtown, PA 17022 Fax 1; Exec. Dir., Rev. Jack McClane, P.O. Box 390, Grantham, PA 17027-0390

Jacob Engle Foundation Bd. of Dir.: CEO, Dr. Donald R. Zook

Pension Fund Trustees: Chpsn., Donald R. Zook

Bd. for Stewardship Services: Chpsn., Marlin Thomas, 100 Willow Valley Lakes Dr., Willow, PA 17584-9456

Publishing House: Exec. Dir., Roger Williams, Evangel Press, P.O. Box 189, Nappannee, IN 46550

PERIODICAL

Evangelical Visitor

Christ Catholic Church

The church is a catholic communion established in 1968 to minister to the growing number of people who seek an experiential relationship with God and who desire to make a total commitment of their lives to God. The church is catholic in faith and tradition and its orders are recognized as valid by catholics of every tradition. Participating cathedrals, churches and missions are located in several states and Canadian provinces.

HEADQUARTERS

5165 Palmer Ave., Niagara Falls, ON L2G 1Y4 Tel. (416)354-2329 Fax (416)354-9934

Media Contact, Suffragen Bishop, The Most Rev. Karl Pruter, P.O. Box 98, Highlandville, MO 65669 Tel. (417)587-3951

OFFICERS

Archbishop, The Most Rev. Donald W. Mullan

PERIODICAL

St. Willibrord Journal

Christadelphians

The Christadelphians are a body of people who believe the Bible to be the divinely inspired word of God, written by "Holy men who spoke as they were moved by the Holy Spirit" (II Peter 1:21). They also believe in the return of Christ to earth to establish the Kingdom of God; in the resurrection of those dead, at the return of Christ, who come into relation to Christ in conformity with his instructions, to be judged as to worthiness for eternal life; in opposition to war; in spiritual rebirth requiring belief and immersion in the name of Jesus; and in a godly walk in this life.

The denomination was organized in 1844 by a medical doctor, John Thomas, who came to the United States from England in 1832, having survived a near shipwreck in a violent storm. This experience affected him profoundly, and he vowed to devote his life to a search for the truth of God and a future hope from the Bible.

HEADQUARTERS

Media Contact, Trustee, Norman D. Zilmer, Christadelphian Action Society, 1000 Mohawk Dr., Elgin, IL 60120-3148 Tel. (708)741-5253

LEADERS

Co-Ministers: Norman Fadelle, 815 Chippewa Dr., Elgin, IL 60120-4016; Norman D. Zilmer, 1000 Mohawk Dr., Elgin, IL 60120-3148

PERIODICALS

Christadelphian Tidings; Christadelphian Watchman; Christadelphian Advocate

The Christian and Missionary Alliance

The Christian and Missionary Alliance was formed in 1897 by the merger of two organizations begun in 1887 by Dr. Albert B. Simpson, The

Christian Alliance and the Evangelical Missionary Alliance. The Christian and Missionary Alliance is an evangelical church which stresses the sufficiency of Jesus--Savior, Sanctifier, Healer and Coming King--and has earned a worldwide reputation for its missionary accomplishments. The Canadian districts became autonomous in 1981 and formed The Christian and Missionary Alliance in Canada.

HEADQUARTERS

P.O. Box 35000, Colorado Springs, CO 80935-3500 Tel. (719)599-5999 Fax (719)593-8692
Media Contact, Rev. Robert L. Niklaus

OFFICERS

Pres., Rev. David Rambo, PhD
Vice-Pres., Rev. P. F. Bubna, DD
Sec., Rev. F. W. Grubbs, DD
Vice-Pres. for Fin./Treas., Mr. L. L. McCooey, CPA
Vice-Pres. for Church Ministries, Rev. R. H. Mangham, DO
Vice-Pres. for Overseas Ministries, Rev. P. N. Nanfelt
Vice-Pres. for Gen. Services, Mr. D. A. Wheeland

BOARD OF MANAGERS

Chpsn., Rev. Paul L. Alford, LLD, DD
Vice-Chpsn., Rev. James M. Grant

DISTRICT SUPERINTENDENTS

Central: Rev. Howard D. Bowers, 1218 High St., Wadsworth, OH 44281 Tel. (216)336-2911 Fax (216)334-3702
Central Pacific: Rev. D. Duane Adamson, 3824 Buell St., Ste. A, Oakland, CA 94619 Tel. (510)-530-5410 Fax (510)530-1369
Eastern: Rev. Randall B. Corbin, DMin., 1200 Spring Garden Dr., Middletown, PA 17051 Tel. (717)766-0261 Fax (717)766-0486
Great Lakes: Rev. Dahl B. Seckinger, 2250 Huron Pkwy, Ann Arbor, MI 48104 Tel. (313)677-8555 Fax (313)677-0087
Metropolitan: Rev. Paul B. Hazlett, 349 Watchung Ave., N. Plainfield, NJ 07060 Tel. (908)668-8421 Fax (908)757-6299
Mid-Atlantic: Rev. C. E. Mock, 7100 Roslyn Ave., Rockville, MD 20855 Tel. (301)258-0035 Fax (301)258-1021
Midwest: Rev. Gerald R. Mapstone, 260 Glen Ellyn Rd., Bloomingdale, IL 60108 Tel. (708)-893-1355 Fax (708)893-1027
New England: Rev. Cornelius W. Clarke, P.O. Box 288, S. Easton, MA 02375 Tel. (508)238-3820 Fax (508)238-2361
Northeastern: Rev. David J. Phillips, Jr., 6275 Pillmore Dr., Rome, NY 13440 Tel. (315)336-4720 Fax (315)336-4720
Northwestern: Rev. Gary M. Benedict, 1813 Lexington Ave. N., Roseville, MN 55113-6127 Tel. (612)489-1391 Fax (612)489-8535
Ohio Valley: Rev. David F. Presher, 4050 Executive Park Dr., Ste. 402, Cincinnati, OH 45241 Tel. (513)733-4833
Pacific Northwest: Rev. Richard W. Colenso, DD, P.O. Box 1030, Canby, OR 97013 Tel. (503)226-2238 Fax (503)263-8052
Puerto Rico: Rev. Julio Aponte, P.O. Box 51394, Levittown, PR 00950 Tel. (809)261-0101 Fax (809)261-0107
Rocky Mountain: Rev. Harvey A. Town, 2545 Saint Johns Ave., Billings, MT 59102-4652 Tel. (406)656-4233 Fax (406)656-5502
South Atlantic: Rev. Gordon G. Copeland, 10801 Johnston Rd., Ste. 125, Charlotte, NC 28226 Tel. (704)543-0470 Fax (704)543-0215
South Pacific: Rev. Bill J. Vaughn, 4130 Adams St., Ste. A, Riverside, CA 92504-3009 Tel. (909)351-0111 Fax (909)351-0146
Southeastern: Rev. Mark T. O'Farrell, P.O. Box 720430, Orlando, FL 32872-0430 Tel. (407)-823-9662 Fax (407)823-9668
Southern: Rev. A. Eugene Hall, 8420 Division Ave., Birmingham, AL 35206-2752 Tel. (205)-836-7048 Fax (205)836-7168
Southwestern: Rev. Daniel R. Wetzel, 5600 E. Loop 820 S., Fort Worth, TX 76119 Tel. (817)-561-0879 Fax (817)572-4131
Western: Rev. Fred G. King, 1301 S. 119th St., Omaha, NE 68144 Tel. (402)330-1888 Fax (402)330-7213
Western Great Lakes: Rev. John W. Fogal, W6107 Aerotech Dr., Appleton, WI 54915 Tel. (414)-734-1123 Fax (414)734-1143
Western Pennsylvania: Rev. D. Paul McGarvey, P.O. Box 429, Punxsutawney, PA 15767 Tel. (814)938-6920 Fax (814)938-7528

INTERCULTURAL MINISTRIES DISTRICTS

Cambodian: Supt., Rev. Joseph S. Kong, 1616 S. Palmetto Ave., Ontario, CA 91762 Tel. (909)-988-9434 Fax (909)395-0572
Dega: c/o Rev. Edward A. Cline, P.O. Box 35000, Colorado Springs, CO 80935
Haitian: Dir., Rev. Paul V. Lehman, 21 College Ave., Nyack, NY 10960 Tel. (914)353-7305
Hmong: Supt., Rev. Timothy Teng Vang, P.O. Box 219, Brighton, CO 80601 Tel. (303)659-1538 Fax (303)659-2171
Jewish: Missionary, Rev. Abraham Sandler, 9820 Woodfern Rd., Philadelphia, PA 19115 Tel. (215)676-9089
Korean: Supt., Rev. Gil Kim, 2175 Lemoine Ave., Rm. 304, Fort Lee, NJ 07024 Tel. (201)461-5755 Fax (201)461-5756
Lao: Dir., Mr. Sisouphanh Ratthahao, 260 Glen Ellyn Rd., Bloomingdale, IL 60108 Tel. (708)-741-3879
Native American: Dir., Mr. John C. Cranford, 1618 NW 19th St., Gresham, OR 97030 Tel. (503)492-1313
Spanish Central: Supt., Rev. Kenneth N. Brisco, 260 Glen Ellyn Rd., Bloomingdale, IL 60108 Tel. (708)924-7171 Fax (708)924-7172
Spanish Eastern: Supt., Rev. Marcelo Realpe, 313 6th Ave., Paterson, NJ 07524-2022
Spanish Western: Dir., Rev. Angel V. Ortiz, 334 Springtree Pl., Escondido, CA 92026-1417 Tel. (619)489-4835 Fax (619)747-9887
Vietnamese: Supt., Rev. Tai Anh Nguyen, 1681 W. Broadway, Anaheim, CA 92802 Tel. (714)491-8007

NATIONAL ASSOCIATIONS

African American Pastors Assoc.: Pres., Rev. Gary Hughes, 465 Ridgeway, White Plains, NY 10605-4207 Tel. (914)949-3714
Chinese Association of the C&MA: c/o Rev. Peter Chu, 14209 Secluded La., Gaithersburg, MD 20878 Tel. (301)294-8067
Filipino Association of the C&MA: c/o Rev. Angelino B. Apelar, 11033 Old River School Rd. #3, Downey, CA 90241 Tel. (310)928-4336

PERIODICAL

Alliance Life

Christian Brethren (also known as Plymouth Brethren)

The Christian Brethren began in the 1820s as an orthodox and evangelical movement in the British Isles and is now worldwide. The name Plymouth Brethren was given by others because the group in Plymouth, England, was a large congregation. In recent years the term Christian Brethren has replaced Plymouth Brethren for the "open" branch of the movement in Canada and British Commonwealth countries and to some extent in the United States.

The unwillingness to establish a denominational structure makes the autonomy of local congregations an important feature of the movement. Other features are weekly observance of the Lord's Supper and adherence to the doctrinal position of conservative, evangelical Christianity.

In the 1840s the movement divided. The "exclusive" branch, led by John Darby, stressed the interdependency of congregations. Since disciplinary decisions were held to be binding on all assemblies, exclusives had subdivided into seven or eight main groups by the end of the century. Since 1925 a trend toward reunification has reduced that number to three or four. United States congregations number approximately 300, with an estimated 19,000 members.

The "open" branch of the movement, stressing evangelism and foreign missions, now has about 850 U.S. congregations, with an estimated 79,000 members.

HEADQUARTERS

Media Contact, Editor, Kenneth Botton, P.O. Box 190, Wheaton, IL 60189 Tel. (708)653-6573 Fax (708)653-6595

CORRESPONDENT

Interest Ministries, Pres., Jim Hislop, P.O. Box 190, Wheaton, IL 60189 Tel. (708)653-6573 Fax (708)653-6595

OTHER ORGANIZATIONS

Christian Missions in Many Lands, Box 13, Spring Lake, NJ 07762

Stewards Foundation, 218 W. Willow, Wheaton, IL 60187

International Teams, Box 203, Prospect Heights, IL 60070

Emmaus Bible College, 2570 Asbury Rd., Dubuque, IA 52001

Stewards Canada, 9 Horner Ct., Richmond Hill, ON L4C 4Y8

Stewards Ministries, 1655 N. Arlington Hts. Rd., Arlington Hts., IL 60004

Vision Ontario, P.O. Box 28032, Waterloo, ON N2L 6J8

PERIODICAL

Interest

Christian Catholic Church (Evangelical-Protestant)

This church was founded by the Rev. John Alexander Dowie on Feb. 22, 1896 at Chicago, Ill. In 1901 the church opened its headquarters in Zion, Ill. Theologically, the church is rooted in evangelical orthodoxy. The Scriptures are accepted as the rule of faith and practice. Other doctrines call for belief in the necessity of repentance for sin and personal trust in Christ for salvation, baptism by trine immersion and tithing as a practical method of Christian stewardship. The church teaches the Second Coming of Christ and all the basic evangelical doctrines.

The Christian Catholic Church is a denominational member of The National Association of Evangelicals. It has work in 8 other nations in addition to the United States. Branch ministries are found in Michigan City, Ind., Phoenix, Ariz., Tonalea, Ariz. and Lindenhurst, Ill.

HEADQUARTERS

2500 Dowie Memorial Dr., Zion, IL 60099 Tel. (708)746-1411 Fax (708)746-1452

PERIODICAL

Leaves of Healing

Christian Church (Disciples of Christ)

Born on the American frontier in the early 1800s as a movement to unify Christians, this body drew its major inspiration from Thomas and Alexander Campbell in western Pennsylvania and Barton W. Stone in Kentucky. Developing separately, the "Disciples," under Alexander Campbell, and the "Christians," led by Stone, united in 1832 in Lexington, Ky.

The Christian Church (Disciples of Christ) is marked by informality, openness, individualism and diversity. The Disciples claim no official doctrine or dogma. Membership is granted after a simple statement of belief in Jesus Christ and baptism by immersion--although most congregations accept transfers baptized by other forms in other denominations. The Lord's Supper--generally called Communion--is open to Christians of all persuasions. The practice is weekly Communion, although no church law insists upon it.

Thoroughly ecumenical, the Disciples helped organize the National and World Councils of Churches. The church is a member of the Consultation on Church Union. The Disciples and the United Church of Christ have declared themselves to be in "full communion" through the General Assembly and General Synod of the two churches. Official theological conversations have been going on since 1967 directly with the Roman Catholic Church, and since 1987 with the Russian Orthodox Church.

Disciples have vigorously supported world and national programs of education, agricultural assistance, urban reconciliation, care of persons with retardation, family planning and aid to victims of war and calamity. Operating ecumenically, Disciples personnel or funds work in more than 100 countries outside North America.

Three manifestations of church polity (general, regional and congregational) operate as equals, with strong but voluntary convenantal ties to one another. Entities in each manifestation manage their own finances, own their own property, and conduct their own programs. A General Assembly meets every two years and has voting representation from each congregation.

HEADQUARTERS

130 E. Washington St., P.O. Box 1986, Indianapolis, IN 46206-1986 Tel. (317)635-3100 Fax (317)635-3700

Media Contact, Dir. of News & Information, Cliff Willis

OFFICERS

Gen. Minister & Pres., Richard L. Hamm

Mod., Janet A. Long, Washington Ave. Christian Church, 301 Washington Ave., Elyria, OH 44035

1st Vice-Mod., Saundra Bryant, All Peoples Center, 822 E. 20th St., Los Angeles, CA 90011

2nd Vice-Mod., Paul D. Rivera, 850 Oxford Ct., Valley Stream, NY 11580

GENERAL OFFICERS

Gen. Minister & Pres., Richard L. Hamm

Dep. Gen. Min./Vice-Pres. for Admn., Donald B. Manworren

Dep. Gen. Min./Vice-Pres. for Inclusive Ministries, John R. Foulkes

ADMINISTRATIVE UNITS

Bd. of Church Extension: Pres., James L. Powell, 130 E. Washington St., P.O. Box 7030, Indianapolis, IN 46207-7030 Tel. (317)635-6500 Fax (317)635-6534

Christian Bd. of Pub. (Chalice Press): Pres., James C. Suggs, 1316 Convention Plaza Dr., P.O. Box 179, St. Louis, MO 63166-0179 Tel. (314)231-8500 Fax (314)231-8524

Christian Church Foundation, Inc.: Pres., James P. Johnson, Fax (317)800-1991

Church Finance Council, Inc.: Pres., Robert K. Welsh

Council on Christian Unity, Inc.: Pres., Paul A. Crow, Jr.

Disciples of Christ Historical Society: Pres., Peter M. Morgan, 1101 19th Ave. S., Nashville, TN 37212-2196 Tel. (615)327-1444 Fax (615)327-1445

Division of Higher Education: Pres., G. Curtis Jones, Jr., 11780 Borman Dr., Ste. 100, St. Louis, MO 63146-4159 Tel. (314)991-3000 Fax (314)-991-2957

Division of Homeland Ministries: Pres., Ann Updegraff Spleth, Fax (317)635-4426

Division of Overseas Ministries: Pres., Patricia Tucker Spier, Fax (317)635-4323

National Benevolent Association: Pres., Richard R. Lance, 11780 Borman Dr., Ste. 200, St. Louis, MO 63146-4157 Tel. (314)993-9000 Fax (314)-993-9018

Pension Fund: Pres., Lester D. Palmer, 130 E. Washington St., Indianapolis, IN 46204-3645 Tel. (317)634-4504 Fax (317)634-4071

REGIONAL UNITS OF THE CHURCH

Alabama-Northwest Florida: Int. Regional Minister, Bronson Netterville, 1336 Montgomery Hwy. S., Birmingham, AL 35216-2799 Tel. (205)823-5647 Fax (205)823-5673

Arizona: Regional Minister, Gail F. Davis, 4423 N. 24th St., Ste 700, Phoenix, AZ 85016-5544 Tel. (602)468-3815 Fax (602)468-3816

Arkansas: Exec. Minister, Barbara E. Jones, 6100 Queensboro Dr., P.O. Box 191057, Little Rock, AR 72219-1057 Tel. (501)562-6053 Fax (501)-562-7089

California North-Nevada: Int. Regional Minister/Pres., Susan O. Bowman, 111-A Fairmount Ave., Oakland, CA 94611-5918 Tel. (510)839-3550 Fax (510)839-3553

Canada: Exec. Minister, Robert W. Steffer, 128 Woolwich St., Ste. 202, P.O. Box 64, Guelph, ON N1H 6J6 Tel. (519)823-5190 Fax (519)823-5190

Capital Area: Regional Minister, Wm. Chris Hobgood, 8901 Connecticut Ave., Chevy Chase, MD 20815-6700 Tel. (301)654-7794 Fax (301)654-8372

Central Rocky Mountain Region: Exec. Regional Minister, William E. Crowl, 2080 Kline St., Lakewood, CO 80215-1411 Tel. (303)274-8567 Fax (303)274-2212

Florida: Regional Minister, Jimmie L. Gentle, 924 N. Magnolia, Ste. 200, Orlando, FL 32803 Tel. (407)843-4652 Fax (407)246-0019

Georgia: Regional Minister, David L. Alexander, 2370 Vineville Ave., Macon, GA 31204-3163 Tel. (912)743-8649 Fax (912)741-1508

Idaho-South: Regional Minister, Larry Crist, 4900 No. Five Mile Rd., Boise, ID 83713-1826 Tel. (208)322-0538 Fax (208)375-5442

Illinois-Wisconsin: Regional Minister/Pres., Nathan S. Smith, 1011 N. Main St., Bloomington, IL 61701-1797 Tel. (309)828-6293 Fax (309)829-4612

Indiana: Regional Minister, C. Edward Weisheimer, 1100 W. 42nd St., Indianapolis, IN 46208-3375 Tel. (317)926-6051 Fax (317)923-3658

Kansas: Regional Minister/Pres., Ralph L. Smith, 2914 S.W. MacVicar Ave., Topeka, KS 66611-1787 Tel. (913)266-2914 Fax (913)266-0174

Kansas City (Greater): Int. Regional Minister/Pres., Richard E. Butler, 5700 Broadmoor, Ste. 205, Mission, KS 66202-2405 Tel. (913)-432-1414 Fax (913)432-3598

Kentucky: Gen. Minister, A. Guy Waldrop, 1125 Red Mile Rd., Lexington, KY 40504-2660 Tel. (606)233-1391 Fax (606)233-2079

Louisiana: Regional Minister, Bill R. Boswell, 3524 Holloway Prairie Rd., Pineville, LA 71360-5816 Tel. (318)443-0304 Fax (318)449-1367

Michigan: Regional Minister, Morris Finch, Jr., 2820 Covington Ct., Lansing, MI 48912-4830 Tel. (517)372-3220 Fax (517)372-2705

Mid-America Region: Regional Minister, Stephen V. Cranford, Hwy. 54 W., P. O. Box 104298, Jefferson City, MO 65110-4298 Tel. (314)636-8149 Fax (314)636-2889

Mississippi: Regional Minister, William E. McKnight, 1619 N. West St., P.O. Box 4832, Jackson, MS 39296-4832 Tel. (601)352-6774

Montana: Regional Minister, Karen Frank-Plumlee, 1019 Central Ave., Great Falls, MT 59401-3784 Tel. (406)452-7404

Nebraska: Regional Minister, N. Dwain Acker, 1268 S. 20th St., Lincoln, NE 68502-1699 Tel. (402)476-0359 Fax (402)476-0350

North Carolina: Regional Minister, Rexford L. Horne, 509 N.E. Lee St., P.O. Box 1568, Wilson, NC 27894 Tel. (919)291-4047 Fax (919)291-3338

Northeastern Region: Regional Minister, Charles F. Lamb, 1272 Delaware Ave., Buffalo, NY 14209-1531 Tel. (716)882-3735 Fax (716)882-7671

Northwest Region: Regional Minister/Pres., Robert Clarke Brock, 6558-35th Ave. SW, Seattle, WA 98126-2899 Tel. (206)938-1008 Fax (206)933-1163

Ohio: Regional Pastor/Pres., Howard M. Ratcliff, 38007 Butternut Ridge Rd., P.O. Box 299, Elyria, OH 44036-0299 Tel. (216)458-5112 Fax (216)458-5114

Oklahoma: Regional Pastor, Thomas R. Jewell, 301 N.W. 36th St., Oklahoma City, OK 73118-8661 Tel. (405)528-3577 Fax (405)528-3584

Oregon: Regional Minister, Mark K. Reid, 0245 S.W. Bancroft St., Ste. F, Portland, OR 97201-4267 Tel. (503)226-7648 Fax (503)228-6983

Pacific Southwest Region: Regional Minister, Don W. Shelton, 1755 N. Park Ave., Pomona, CA 91768-1893 Tel. (909)620-5503 Fax (909)620-4825

Pennsylvania: Regional Minister, W. Darwin Collins, 670 Rodi Rd., Pittsburgh, PA 15235-4524 Tel. (412)731-7000 Fax (412)731-4515

South Carolina: Regional Minister, David L. Alexander, 1098 E. Montague Ave., North Charleston, SC 29405 Tel. (803)554-6886 Fax (803)554-6886

Southwest Region: Int. Regional Minister, Harold E. Cline, 3209 S. University Dr., Fort Worth, TX 76109-2239 Tel. (817)926-4687 Fax (817)926-5121

Tennessee: Regional Minister/Pres., Glen J. Stewart, 3700 Richland Ave., Nashville, TN 37205-2499 Tel. (615)269-3409 Fax (615)269-3400

Upper Midwest Region: Regional Minister/Pres., Richard L. Guentert, 3300 University Ave., P.O. Box 1024, Des Moines, IA 50311-1024 Tel. (515)255-3168 Fax (515)255-2625

Utah: Exec. Regional Minister, William E. Crowl, 2080 Kline St., Lakewood, CO 80215-1411 Tel. (303)274-8567 Fax (303)274-2212

Virginia: Regional Minister, R. Woods Kent, 518 Brevard St., Lynchburg, VA 24501 Tel. (804)-846-3400

West Virginia: Regional Minister, William B. Allen, Rt. 5, Box 167, Parkersburg, WV 26101-9576 Tel. (304)428-1681 Fax (304)428-1684

PERIODICALS

The Disciple; Vanguard; Mid-Stream: An Ecumenical Journal

Christian Church of North America, General Council

Originally known as the Italian Christian Church, its first General Council was held in 1927 at Niagara Falls, N.Y. This body was incorporated in 1948 at Pittsburgh, Pa., and is described as Pentecostal but does not engage in the "the excesses tolerated or practiced among some churches using the same name."

The movement recognizes two ordinances--baptism and the Lord's Supper. Its moral code is conservative and its teaching is orthodox. Members are exhorted to pursue a life of personal holiness, setting an example to others. A conservative position is held in regard to marriage and divorce. The governmental form is, by and large, congregational. District and National officiaries, however, are referred to as Presbyteries led by Overseers.

The group functions in cooperative fellowship with the Italian Pentecostal Church of Canada and the Evangelical Christian Churches--Assemblies of God in Italy. It is an affiliate member of the Pentecostal Fellowship of North America and of the National Association of Evangelicals.

HEADQUARTERS

1294 Rutledge Rd., Transfer, PA 16154-9005 Tel. (412)962-3501 Fax (412)962-1766

Media Contact, Exec. Sec., Mrs. Lynn Brest

OFFICERS

Executive Bd., Gen. Overseer, Rev. John DelTurco, P.O. Box 1198, Hermitage, PA 16148

Exec. Vice-Pres., Rev. Andrew Farina, 3 Alhambra Pl., Greenville, PA 16125

Asst. Gen. Overseers: Rev. James Demola, P.O. Box 157, Mullica Hill, NJ 08062; Rev. Vincent Prestigiacomo, 21 Tyler Hill Rd., Jaffrey, NH 03452; Rev. Charles Gay, 26 Delafield Dr., Albany, NY 12205; Rev. Michael Trotta, 224 W. Winter Ave., New Castle, PA 16101; Rev. William Nash, 8 Belleview Blvd. #402, Clearwater, FL 34616

DEPARTMENTS

Benevolence, Rev. Eugene DeMarco, 155 Scott St., New Brighton, PA 15066

Church Growth & Media Ministries, Rev. John Ferguson, 78C Kaphank Ave., Yaphank, NY 11980

Faith, Order & Credentials, Rev. Andrew Farina, 3 Alhambra Pl., Greenville, PA 16125

Missions, Rev. John DelTurco, P.O. Box 1198, Hermitage, PA 16148

Publications & Promotion, Rev. John Tedesco, 1188 Heron Rd., Cherry Hill, NJ 08003

Youth, Education & Sunday School, Rev. Lours Fortunato, Jr., 248 Curry Pl., Youngstown, OH 44504

PERIODICAL

Vista

Christian Churches and Churches of Christ

The fellowship, whose churches were always strictly congregational in polity, has its origin in the American movement to "restore the New Testament church in doctrine, ordinances and life" initiated by Thomas and Alexander Campbell, Walter Scott and Barton W. Stone in the early 19th century.

HEADQUARTERS

Media Contact, No. American Christian Convention Dir., Rod Huron, 4210 Bridgetown Rd., Box 11326, Cincinnati, OH 45211 Tel. (513)598-6222 Fax (513)598-6471

CONVENTIONS

North American Christian Convention: Dir., Rod Huron, 4210 Bridgetown Rd., Box 11326, Cincinnati, OH 45211 Tel. (513)598-6222; NACC Mailing Address, Box 39456, Cincinnati, OH 45239

National Missionary Convention, Coord., Walter Birney, Box 11, Copeland, KS 67837 Tel. (316)-668-5250

Eastern Christian Convention, Kenneth Meade, 5300 Norbeck Rd., Rockville, MD 20853 Tel. (301)460-3550

PERIODICALS

Christian Standard; Restoration Herald; Horizons; The Lookout

The Christian Congregation, Inc.

The Christian Congregation is a denominational evangelistic association that originated in 1798 and was active on the frontier in areas adjacent to the Ohio River. The church was an unincorporated organization until 1887. At that time a group of ministers who desired closer cooperation formally constituted the church. The charter was revised in 1898 and again in 1970.

Governmental polity basically is congregational. Local units are semi-autonomous. Doctrinal positions, strongly biblical, are essentially universalist in the sense that ethical principles, which motivate us to creative activism, transcend national boundaries and racial barriers. A central tenet, John 13:34-35, translates to such respect for sanctity of life that abortions on demand, capital punishment and all warfare are vigorously opposed. All wars are considered unjust and obsolete as a means of resolving disputes.

Early leaders were John Chapman, John L. Puckett and Isaac V. Smith. Bishop O. J. Read was chief administrative and ecclesiastic officer for 40 years until 1961. Rev. Dr. Ora Wilbert Eads has been general superintendent since 1961. Ministerial affiliation for independent clergymen is provided.

HEADQUARTERS

804 W. Hemlock St., LaFollette, TN 37766
Media Contact, Gen. Supt., Rev. Ora W. Eads, D.D., Tel. (423)562-8511

OFFICER

Gen. Supt., Rev. Ora W. Eads, D.D.

Christian Methodist Episcopal Church

In 1870 the General Conference of the Methodist Episcopal Church, South, approved the request of its colored membership for the formation of their conferences into a separate ecclesiastical body, which became the Colored Methodist Episcopal Church.

At its General Conference in Memphis, Tenn., May 1954, it was overwhelmingly voted to change the name of the Colored Methodist Episcopal Church to the Christian Methodist Episcopal Church. This became the official name on Jan. 3, 1956.

HEADQUARTERS

First Memphis Plaza, 4466 Elvis Presley Blvd., Memphis, TN 38116
Media Contact, Exec. Sec., Dr. W. Clyde Williams, 201 Ashby St., N.W., Ste. 212, Atlanta, GA 30314 Tel. (404)522-2736 Fax (404)522-2736

OFFICERS

Exec. Sec., Dr. W. Clyde Williams, 201 Ashby St., NW, Suite 212, Atlanta, GA 30314 Tel. (404)-522-2736
Sec. Gen. Conf., Rev. John Gilmore, Mt. Olive CME Church, 538 Linden Ave., Memphis, TN 38126

OTHER ORGANIZATIONS

Christian Education: Gen. Sec., Dr. Ronald M. Cunningham, 4466 Elvis Presley Blvd., Ste. 214, Box 193, Memphis, TN 38116-7100 Tel. (901)-345-0580
Lay Ministry: Gen. Sec., Dr. I. Carlton Faulk, 1222 Rose St., Berkeley, CA 94702 Tel. (415)655-4106
Evangelism, Missions & Human Concerns: Gen. Sec., Rev. Raymond F. Williams, 14244 Avenida Munoz, Riverside, CA 92508 Tel. (909)656-9716
Finance: Sec., Mr. Joseph C. Neal, Jr., P.O. Box 75085, Los Angeles, CA 90075 Tel. (213)233-5050
Publications: Gen. Sec., Rev. William George, 4466 Elvis Presley Blvd., Memphis, TN 38116 Tel. (901)345-0580
Personnel Services: Gen. Sec., Dr. N. Charles Thomas, P.O. Box 9, Memphis, TN 38101 Tel. (901)345-0580
Women's Missionary Council: Pres., Ms. Judith E. Grant, 723 E. Upsal St., Philadelphia, PA 19119 Tel. (215)843-7742

BISHOPS

First District: Bishop William H. Graves, 4466 Elvis Presley Blvd., Ste. 222, Memphis, TN 38116 Tel. (901)345-0580
Second District: Bishop Nathaniel L. Linsey, 6322 Elwynne Dr., Cincinnati, OH 45236 Tel. (513)-861-0655
Third District: Bishop Dotcy I. Isom, Jr., 5925 W. Florissant Ave., St. Louis, MO 63136 Tel. (314)-381-3111
Fourth District: Bishop Thomas L. Hoyt, Jr., 109 Holcomb Dr., Shreveport, LA 71103 Tel. (318)-222-6284
Fifth District: Bishop Richard O. Bass, 310 18th St. N., Ste. 400, Birmingham, AL 35203 Tel. (205)-252-2587
Sixth District: Bishop Othal H. Lakey, 2001 M.L. King, Jr. Dr. SW, Ste. 423, Atlanta, GA 30310 Tel. (404)752-7800
Seventh District: Bishop Oree Broomfield, Sr., 6524 16th St., N.W., Washington, DC 20012 Tel. (202)829-8070
Eighth District: Bishop Marshall Gilmore, Sr., 1616 E. Illinois, Dallas, TX 75216 Tel. (214)-372-9073
Ninth District: Bishop E. Lynn Brown, 3844 W. Slauson Ave., Ste. 1, Los Angeles, CA 90043 Tel. (213)294-3830
Tenth District: Bishop Charles Helton, 5937 Ruth Dr., Charlotte, NC 28215 Tel. (704)567-6092
Retired: Bishop Henry C. Bunton, 853 East Dempster Ave., Memphis, TN 38106; Bishop Chester A. Kirkendoll, 10 Hurtland, Jackson, TN 38305; Bishop C. D. Coleman, Sr., 1000 Longmeadow Ln., DeSoto, TX 75115; Bishop Joseph C. Coles, Jr., P.O. Box 172, South Boston, VA 24592

PERIODICALS

The Christian Index; The Missionary Messenger

Christian Reformed Church in North America

The Christian Reformed Church represents the historic faith of Protestantism. Founded in the United States in 1857 and active in Canada since 1908, it asserts its belief in the Bible as the inspired Word of God, and is creedally united in the Belgic Confession (1561), the Heidelberg Catechism (1563), and the Canons of Dort (1618-19).

HEADQUARTERS

2850 Kalamazoo Ave., SE, Grand Rapids, MI 49560 Tel. (616)246-0744 Fax (616)247-5895
Media Contact, Gen. Sec., Dr. David H. Engelhard

OFFICERS

Gen. Sec., Dr. David H. Engelhard
Exec. Dir. of Ministries, Dr. Peter Borgdorff
Financial Coord., Mr. Robert Van Stright

OTHER ORGANIZATIONS

The Back to God Hour: Dir. of Ministries, Dr. Calvin L. Bremer, International Headquarters, 6555 W. College Dr., Palos Heights, IL 60463
Christian Reformed Home Missions: Dir., Rev. John A. Rozeboom

Christian Reformed World Missions, US: Dir., Rev. William Van Tol
Christian Ref. World Missions, Canada: Dir., Mr. Albert Karsten, 3475 Mainway, P.O. Box 5070, Burlington, ON L7R 3Y8
Christian Reformed World Relief, US: Dir., Mr. John De Haan
Christian Reformed World Relief, Canada: Dir., Mr. Ray Elgersma, 3475 Mainway, P.O. Box 5070, Burlington, ON L7R 3Y8
CRC Publications: Dir., Mr. Gary Mulder
Ministers' Pension Fund: Admn., Mr. Robert Van Stright
CRC Pastoral Ministries, Adm. Dir., Ms. Beth Swagman

PERIODICAL

The Banner

Christian Union

Organized in 1864 in Columbus, Ohio, the Christian Union stresses the oneness of the Church with Christ as its only head. The Bible is the only rule of faith and practice and good fruits the only condition of fellowship. Each local church governs itself.

HEADQUARTERS

c/o Christian Union Bible College, P.O. Box 27, Greenfield, OH 45123 Tel. (513)981-2897
Media Contact, Pres., Dr. Joseph Harr, 3025 Converse-Roselm Rd., Grover Hill, OH 45849 Tel. (419)587-3226

OFFICERS

Pres., Dr. Joseph Harr
Vice-Pres., Rev. Harold McElwee, P.O. Box 132, Milo, IA 50166 Tel. (419)822-4261
Sec., Rev. Joseph Cunningham, 1005 N. 5th St., Greenfield, OH 45123 Tel. (513)981-3476
Asst. Sec., Rev. Earl Mitchell, 17500 Hidden Valley Rd., Independence, MO 64057 Tel. (816)-373-3416
Treas., Rev. Lawrence Rhoads, 902 N.E. Main St., West Union, OH 45693 Tel. (513)544-2950

Church of Christ

Joseph Smith and five others organized the Church of Christ on April 6, 1830 at Fayette, N.Y. In 1864 this body was directed by revelation through Granville Hedrick to return in 1867 to Independence, Mo. to the "consecrated land" dedicated by Joseph Smith. They did so and purchased the temple lot dedicated in 1831.

HEADQUARTERS

Temple Lot, P.O. Box 472, Independence, MO 64051 Tel. (816)833-3995
Media Contact, Gen. Church Rep., William A. Sheldon

OFFICERS

Council of Apostles, Secy., Apostle Smith N. Brickhouse
Gen. Bus. Mgr., Bishop Alvin Harris
Gen. Recorder, Isaac Brockman

PERIODICAL

Zion's Advocate

Church of Christ, Scientist

The Christian Science Church was founded by New England religious leader Mary Baker Eddy in 1879 "to commemorate the word and works of our Master (Christ Jesus), which should reinstate primitive Christianity and its lost element of healing." In 1892 the church was reorganized and established as The First Church of Christ, Scientist, in Boston, also called The Mother Church, with local branch churches around the world, of which there are nearly 2,400 in 63 countries today.

The church is administered by a five-member board of directors in Boston. Local churches govern themselves democratically. Since the church has no clergy, services are conducted by laypersons elected to serve as Readers. There are also about 2,500 Christian Science practitioners who devote their full time to healing through prayer.

Organizations within the church include the Board of Education, the Board of Lectureship, the Committee on Publication and the Christian Science Publishing Society.

HEADQUARTERS

The First Church of Christ, Scientist, 175 Huntington Ave., Boston, MA 01945
Media Contact, Mgr., Comm. on Publication, M. Victor Westberg, Tel. (617)450-3301 Fax (617)-450-3325

OFFICERS

Bd. of Dirs.: Chpsn., Virginia S. Harris; William H. Hill; Olga M. Chaffee; J. Anthony Periton; John Lewis Selover
Pres., David C. Driver
Treas., John Lewis Selover
Clk., Olga M. Chaffee
First Reader, David L. Degler
Second Reader, Mary Ridgeway

PERIODICALS

The Christian Science Monitor; The Christian Science Journal; Christian Science Sentinel; The Herald of Christian Science; Christian Science Quarterly

The Church of God

The Church of God, from which many groups of the Pentecostal and Holiness Movement stemmed, was inaugurated by Bishop A. J. Tomlinson, who served as General Overseer from 1903 to 1943. The church is episcopal in administration and evangelical in doctrines of justification by faith, sanctification as a second work of grace and baptism of the Holy Ghost. Believers speak with other tongues and participate in miracles of healing. Bishop Homer A. Tomlinson served as General Overseer from 1943 to 1968 and Bishop Voy M. Bullen has been the General Overseer since 1968.

HEADQUARTERS

Box 13036, 1207 Willow Brook, Apt. #2, Huntsville, AL 35802 Tel. (205)881-9629
Media Contact, Gen. Overseer, Voy M. Bullen

OFFICERS

Gen. Overseer & Bishop, Voy M. Bullen
Gen. Sec.-Treas., Marie Powell

CHURCH AUXILIARIES

Assembly Band Movement, Gen. Sec., Bishop Bill Kinslaw
Women's Missionary Band, Gen. Sec., Maxine McKenzie
Theocratic Bands, Gen. Sec., Rev. Ted Carr
Victory Leader's Band, Youth, Gen. Sec., Ellen Abshire
Admn. for Highway & Hedge Campaign, Earnest Hoover

Sunday School, Gen. Sec., Judy Foskey

PERIODICAL

The Church of God Quarterly; COG Newsletter

Church of God (Anderson, Ind.)

The Church of God (Anderson, Ind.) began in 1881 when Daniel S. Warner and several associates felt constrained to forsake all denominational hierarchies and formal creeds, trusting solely in the Holy Spirit as their overseer and the Bible as their statement of belief. These people saw themselves at the forefront of a movement to restore unity and holiness to the church, not to establish another denomination, but to promote primary allegiance to Jesus Christ so as to transcend denominational loyalties.

Deeply influenced by Wesleyan theology and Pietism, the Church of God has emphasized conversion, holiness and attention to the Bible. Worship services tend to be informal, accentuating expository preaching and robust singing.

There is no formal membership. Persons are assumed to be members on the basis of witness to a conversion experience and evidence that supports such witness. The absence of formal membership is also consistent with the church's understanding of how Christian unity is to be achieved--that is, by preferring the label Christian before all others.

The Church of God is congregational in its government. Each local congregation is autonomous and may call any recognized Church of God minister to be its pastor and may retain him or her as long as is mutually pleasing. Ministers are ordained and disciplined by state or provincial assemblies made up predominantly of ministers. National program boards serve the church through coordinated ministries and resource materials.

There are Church of God congregations in 85 foreign countries, most of which are resourced by one or more missionaries. There are slightly more Church of God adherents overseas than in North America. The heaviest concentration is in the nation of Kenya.

GENERAL OFFICES

Box 2420, Anderson, IN 46018 Tel. (317)642-0256 Fax (317)642-5652

Media Contact, Gen. Sec., Leadership Council, Edward L. Foggs

LEADERSHIP COUNCIL

Gen. Sec., Edward L. Foggs

Assoc. Gen. Sec., David L. Lawson

Church and Ministry Service, Dir., Jeannette R. Flynn

World Service, Exec. Dir., James E. Williams

OTHER ORGANIZATIONS

Bd. of Christian Education, Exec. Dir., Sherrill D. Hayes, Box 2458, Anderson, IN 46018

Bd. of Church Extension & Home Missions, Pres., J. Perry Grubbs, Box 2069, Anderson, IN 46018

Missionary Bd., Pres., Norman S. Patton, Box 2498, Anderson, IN 46018

Women of the Church of God, Exec. Sec.-Treas., Doris J. Dale, Box 2328, Anderson, IN 46018

Bd. of Pensions, Exec. Sec.-Treas., Jeffrey A. Jenness, Box 2299, Anderson, IN 46018

Mass Communications Bd., Exec. Sec.-Treas., James R. Martin, Box 2007, Anderson, IN 46018

Warner Press, Inc., Pres., Robert G. Rist, Box 2499, Anderson, IN 46018

PERIODICALS

Vital Christianity; Church of God Missions; The Shining Light

Church of God by Faith, Inc.

Founded 1914, in Jacksonville Heights, Fla., by Elder John Bright, this church believes the word of God as interpreted by Jesus Christ to be the only hope of salvation and Jesus Christ the only mediator for people.

HEADQUARTERS

3220 Haines St., P.O. Box 3746, Jacksonville, FL 32206 Tel. (904)353-5111 Fax (904)355-8582

Media Contact, Ofc. Mgr., Sarah E. Lundy

OFFICERS

Bishop Emeritus, W. W. Matthews, P.O. Box 907, Ozark, AL 36360

Presiding Bishop, James E. McKnight, P.O. Box 121, Gainesville, FL 32601

Treas., Elder Theodore Brown, 93 Girard Pl., Newark, NJ 07108

Ruling Elders: Elder John Robinson, 300 Essex Dr., Ft. Pierce, FL 33450; Elder D. C. Rourk, 207 Chestnut Hill Dr., Rochester, NY 14617

Exec. Sec., Elder George Matthews, 8834 Camphor Dr., Jacksonville, FL 32208

Church of God (Cleveland, Tenn.)

America's oldest Pentecostal Church began in 1886 as an outgrowth of the holiness revival under the name Christian Union. Reorganized in 1902 as the Holiness Church, in 1907 the church adopted the name Church of God. Its doctrine is fundamental and Pentecostal; it maintains a centralized form of government and an evangelistic and missionary program.

HEADQUARTERS

P.O. Box 2430, Cleveland, TN 37320 Tel. (615)-472-3361 Fax (615)478-7066

Media Contact, Dir. of Publ. Relations, Michael L. Baker, Tel. (615)478-7112 Fax (615)478-7066

EXECUTIVES

Gen. Overseer, Robert White

Asst. Gen Overseers: Ray H. Hughes

Asst. Gen. Overseers: G. Dennis McGuire; Robert E. Fisher

Gen. Sec.-Treas., Walter P. Atkinson

DEPARTMENTS

Benefits Board, CEO, O. Wayne Chambers

Benevolence, Dir., John D. Nichols

Black Evangelism, Dir., Joseph E. Jackson

Business & Records, Dir., Julian B. Robinson

Chaplains Commission, Dir., Robert D. Crick

Computer Services, Dir., Timothy D. O'Neal

Cross-Cultural Min., Dir., Billy J. Rayburn

East Coast Bible College, Pres., Lawrence Leonhardt

European Bible Seminary, Dir., Philip Morris

Evangelism & Home Missions, Dir., James C. Fulbright

Hispanic Institute of Ministry, Dir., Isaias Robles

Hispanic Ministry, Dir., Esdras Betancourt

International Bible College, Pres., Alex Allan

Ladies Ministries, Dir., Mrs. Rebecca Jenkins

Lay Ministries, Dir., Leonard Albert

Lee College, Pres., C. Paul Conn
Legal Services, Dir., Dennis W. Watkins
Media Ministries, Dir., R. Lamar Vest
Men of Action, Dir., Robert Pace
Ministerial Care, Dir., Paul F. Henson
Ministerial Development, Dir., Larry G. Hess
Ministry to the Military, Dir., G. Dennis McGuire
Music Ministries, Dir., Delton Alford
Publications, Dir., Kenneth T. Harvell
Public Relations, Dir., Michael L. Baker
Puerto Rico Bible School, Dir., Ernesto L. Rodriguez
School of Theology, Pres., Cecil B. Knight
Southwest Indian Ministries, Dir., Douglas M. Cline
Stewardship, Dir., Al Taylor
Western School of Christian Ministry, Dir., W. A. Davis
World Missions, Dir., Roland Vaughan
Youth & Christian Education, Dir., T. David Sustar

PERIODICALS

Church of God Evangel; Unique Ladies Ministries

Church of God General Conference (Oregon, IL and Morrow, GA)

This church is the outgrowth of several independent local groups of similar faith. Some were in existence as early as 1800, and others date their beginnings to the arrival of British immigrants around 1847. Many local churches carried the name Church of God of the Abrahamic Faith.

State and district conferences of these groups were formed as an expression of mutual cooperation. A national organization was instituted at Philadelphia in 1888. Because of strong convictions on the questions of congregational rights and authority, however, it ceased to function until 1921, when the present General Conference was formed at Waterloo, Iowa.

The Bible is accepted as the supreme standard of faith. Adventist in viewpoint, the second (premillenial) coming of Christ is strongly emphasized. The church teaches that the kingdom of God will be literal, beginning in Jerusalem at the time of the return of Christ and extending to all nations. Emphasis is placed on the oneness of God and the Sonship of Christ, that Jesus did not pre-exist prior to his birth in Bethlehem and that the Holy Spirit is the power and influence of God. Membership is dependent on faith, repentance and baptism by immersion.

The work of the General Conference is carried on under the direction of the board of directors. With a congregational church government, the General Conference exists primarily as a means of mutual cooperation and for the development of yearly projects and enterprises.

The headquarters and Bible College were moved to Morrow, Ga. in 1991.

HEADQUARTERS

P.O. Box 100,000, Morrow, GA 30260 Tel. (404)-362-0052 Fax (404)362-9307
Media Contact, Pres., David Krogh

OFFICERS

Chpsn., Pastor Stephen Bolhous, 9 Pancake La., Fonthill, ON L0S 1E2
Vice-Chpsn., Pastor Billie Kennedy, 29120 Church of God Rd., Springfield, LA 70462
Pres., David Krogh, Georgia Ofc.
Sec., Pastor Dale Swartz, 6375 S. Kessler-Frederick Rd., Tipp City, OH 45371
Treas., Frank Johnson, Rt. 2, Box 211, Hector, MN 55342

OTHER ORGANIZATIONS

Bus. Admn., Controller, Gary Burnham, Georgia Ofc.
Atlanta Bible College, Pres., David Krogh, Georgia Ofc.

PERIODICALS

The Restitution Herald; A Journal From the Radical Reformation; Church of God Progress Journal

The Church Of God In Christ

The Church of God in Christ was founded in 1907 in Memphis, Tenn., and was organized by Bishop Charles Harrison Mason, a former Baptist minister who pioneered the embryonic stages of the Holiness movement beginning in 1895 in Mississippi.

Its founder organized four major departments between 1910-1916: the Women's Department, the Sunday School, Young Peoples Willing Workers and Home and Foreign Mission.

The Church is trinitarian and teaches the infallibility of scripture, the need for regeneration and subsequent baptism of the Holy Ghost. It emphasizes holiness as God's standard for Christian conduct. It recognizes as ordinances Holy Communion, Water Baptism and Feet Washing. Its governmental structure is basically episcopal with the General Assembly being the Legislative body.

HEADQUARTERS

Mason Temple, 939 Mason St., Memphis, TN 38126
World Headquarters, 272 S. Main St., Memphis, TN 38103 Tel. (901)578-3800
Mailing Address, P.O. Box 320, Memphis, TN 38101
The Mother Church, Pentecostal Institutional, 229 S. Danny Thomas Blvd., Memphis, TN 38126 Tel. (901)527-9202
Media Contact, Dr. David Hall, Tel. (901)578-3814

PERIODICALS

Whole Truth; The Voice of Missions

Church of God in Christ, International

The Church of God in Christ, International was organized in 1969 in Kansas City, Mo., by 14 bishops of the Church of God in Christ of Memphis, Tenn. The doctrine is the same, but the separation came because of disagreement over polity and governmental authority. The Church is Wesleyan in theology (two works of grace) but stresses the experience of full baptism of the Holy Ghost with the initial evidence of speaking with other tongues as the spirit gives utterance.

HEADQUARTERS

170 Adelphi St., Brooklyn, NY 11205 Tel. (718)-625-9175
Media Contact, Natl. Sec., Rev. Sis. Sharon R. Dunn

Church of God in Christ, Mennonite

The Church of God in Christ, Mennonite was organized in Ohio in 1859 by the evangelist-reformer John Holdeman. The church unites with the faith of the Waldenses, Anabaptists and other such groups. Emphasis is placed on obedience to the teachings of the Bible, including the doctrine of the new birth and spiritual life, noninvolvement in government or the military, head-coverings for the women, beards for the men and separation from the world shown by simplicity in clothing, homes, possessions and life-style. The church has a world-wide membership of about 15,000, most of them in the United States and Canada.

HEADQUARTERS

P.O. Box 313, 420 N. Wedel Ave., Moundridge, KS 67107 Tel. (316)345-2532 Fax (316)345-2582

Media Contact, Dale Koehn, P.O. Box 230, Moundridge, KS 67107 Tel. (316)345-2532 Fax (316)-345-2582

PERIODICAL

Messenger of Truth

Church of God, Mountain Assembly, Inc.

The church was formed in 1895 and organized in 1906 by J. H. Parks, S. N. Bryant, Tom Moses and William Douglas.

HEADQUARTERS

110 S. Florence Ave., P.O. Box 157, Jellico, TN 37762 Tel. (423)784-8260 Fax (423)784-3258

Media Contact, Gen. Sec.-Treas., Rev. James Kilgore

OFFICERS

Gen. Overseer, Rev. Cecil Johnson

Asst. Gen. Overseer/World Missions Dir., Rev. Lonnie Lyke

Gen. Sec.-Treas., Rev. James Kilgore, Box 157, Jellico, TN 37762

Youth Ministries & Camp Dir., Rev. Ken Ellis

PERIODICAL

The Gospel Herald

Church of God of Prophecy

The Church of God of Prophecy is one of the churches that grew out of the work of A. J. Tomlinson in the first half of this century. It was named in 1952, but historically shares the traditions of the holiness classical pentecostal church, the Church of God (Cleveland, TN).

At the death of A. J. Tomlinson in 1943, M. A. Tomlinson was named overseer and served until 1990. He emphasized unity and fellowship that is not limited socially, racially or nationally. The present general overseer, Billy D. Murray, Sr. is committed to promoting Christian unity and moving forward with world-wide evangelism.

The official teachings include special emphasis on sanctification, the doctrine of Spirit-baptism and belief that tongues-speech is an initial evidence. The church teaches an imminence-oriented eschatology that involves a premillennial return of the risen Jesus which itself will be preceded by a series of events; a call for the sanctity of the home which includes denial of a multiple marriage; practice of water baptism by immersion, the Lord's Supper and washing of the saints' feet; total abstinence from intoxicating beverages and tobacco; a concern for moderation in all dimensions of life; and an appreciation for various gifts of the Holy Spirit.

The Church is racially integrated on all levels and various leadership positions are occupied by women. The Church's history includes a strong emphasis on youth ministries, national and international missions and various parochial educational ministries.

INTERNATIONAL OFFICES

P.O. Box 2910, Cleveland, TN 37320-2910

Media Contact, Perry Gillum, Tel. (423)559-5336 Fax (423)559-5338

OFFICERS

Gen. Overseer, Bishop Billy D. Murray, Sr.

Admn. Asst.: Perry Gillum; Adrian Varlack; Jose A. Reyes, Sr.

Admn. Committee: Billy D. Murray; Perry Gillum; Oswill Williams; John Pace; Jose A. Reyes, Sr.; Jerlena Riley; Adrian Varlack

GENERAL STAFF

Center for Biblical Leadership, Educ. Dept., Oswill Williams

Communications Bus. Mgr., Thomas Duncan

Communications Min. (English), William M. Wilson

Communications Min. (Spanish), Jose A. Reyes, Sr.

Evangelism Dir., William M. Wilson

Fin. Dir., Jerlena Riley

Genl. Ofc. Mgr./Personnel Dir., Perry Gillum

Ministerial Services Dir., Adrian Varlack

Women's Ministries, Cathy Payne

World Language Dir., John Pace

World Missions Dir., Randy Howard

Youth & Children's Ministries, H. E. Cardin

PERIODICALS

White Wing Messenger; Victory (Youth Magazine)

The Church of God (Seventh Day), Denver, Colo.

The Church of God (Seventh Day) began in southwestern Michigan in 1858, when a group of Sabbath-keepers led by Gilbert Cranmer refused to give endorsement to the visions and writings of Ellen G. White, a principal in the formation of the Seventh-Day Adventist Church. Another branch of Sabbath-keepers, which developed near Cedar Rapids, Iowa, in 1860, joined the Michigan church in 1863 to publish a paper called *The Hope of Israel*, the predecessor to the Bible *Advocate*, the church's present publication. As membership grew and spread into Missouri and Nebraska, it organized the General Conference of the Church of God in 1884. The words "Seventh Day" were added to its name in 1923. The headquarters of the church was in Stanberry, Mo., from 1888 until 1950, when it moved to Denver.

The church observes the seventh day as the Sabbath. It believes in the imminent, personal and visible return of Jesus; that the dead are in an unconscious state awaiting to be resurrected, the righteous to immortality and the wicked to extinction by fire; and that the earth will be the eternal abode of the righteous. It observes two ordinances: baptism by immersion and an annual Communion service accompanied by foot washing.

HEADQUARTERS

330 W. 152nd Ave., P.O. Box 33677, Denver, CO 80233 Tel. (303)452-7973 Fax (303)452-0657

Media Contact, Pres., Calvin Burrell

OFFICERS

Board Chpsn., Whaid Rose
Conference Pres., Calvin Burrell
Dir. of Admin., John Crisp
Dir. of Finance, Jayne Kurycuk
Spring Vale Academy, Dir., Richard Weidenheft
Youth Agency, Dir., John & Ruth Tivald
Bible Advocate Press, Dir., Roy Marrs
Women's Assoc., Pres., Mrs. Emogene Coulter
Missions Abroad, Dir., Victor Burford
Summit School of Theology, Dir., Jerry Griffin

PERIODICAL

The Bible Advocate

The Church of Illumination

The Church of Illumination was organized in 1908 for the express purpose of establishing congregations at large, offering a spiritual, esoteric, philosophic interpretation of the vital biblical teachings, thereby satisfying the inner spiritual needs of those seeking spiritual truth, yet permitting them to remain in, or return to, their former church membership.

HEADQUARTERS

Beverly Hall, 5966 Clymer Rd., Quakertown, PA 18951 Tel. (800)779-3796

Media Contact, Dir. General, Gerald E. Poesnecker, P.O. Box 220, Quakertown, PA 18951 Tel. (215)536-7048 Fax (215)529-9034

OFFICER

Dir.-General, Gerald E. Poesnecker, P.O. Box 220, Quakertown, PA 18951

The Church of Jesus Christ (Bickertonites)

This church was organized in 1862 at Green Oak, Pa., by William Bickerton, who obeyed the Restored Gospel under Sidney Rigdon's following in 1845.

HEADQUARTERS

Sixth & Lincoln Sts., Monongahela, PA 15063 Tel. (412)258-3066

Media Contact, Exec. Sec., John Manes, 2007 Cutter Dr., McKees Rocks, PA 15136 Tel. (412)-771-4513

OFFICERS

Pres., Dominic Thomas, 6010 Barrie, Dearborn, MI 48126
First Counselor, Paul Palmieri, 319 Pine Dr., Aliquippa, PA 15001
Second Counselor, Robert Watson, Star Rt. 5, Box 36, Gallup, NM 87301
Exec. Sec., John Manes, 2007 Cutter Dr., McKees Rocks, PA 15136 Tel. (412)771-4513

PERIODICAL

The Gospel News

The Church of Jesus Christ of Latter-day Saints

This church was organized April 6, 1830, at Fayette, N.Y., by Joseph Smith. Members believe Joseph Smith was divinely directed to restore the gospel to the earth, and that through him the keys to the Aaronic and Melchizedek priesthoods and temple work also were restored. Members believe that both the Bible and the Book of Mormon (a record of the Lord's dealings with His people on the American continent 600 B.C. - 421 A.D.) are scripture. Membership is surpassing nine million in 1994.

In addition to the First Presidency, the governing bodies of the church include the Quorum of the Twelve Apostles, the Presidency of the Seventy, the First Quorum of the Seventy, the Second Quorum of the Seventy and the Presiding Bishopric.

HEADQUARTERS

50 East North Temple St., Salt Lake City, UT 84150 Tel. (801)240-1000 Fax (801)240-1167

Media Contact, Dir., Media Relations, Don LeFevre, Tel. (801)240-4377 Fax (801)240-1167

OFFICERS

Pres., Gordon B. Hinckley
1st Counselor, Thomas S. Monson
2nd Counselor, James E. Faust
Council of the Twelve Apostles: Pres., Boyd K. Packer; Robert D. Hales; Jeffrey R. Holland; L. Tom Perry; David B. Haight; Henry B. Eyring; Neal A. Maxwell; Russell M. Nelson; Dallin H. Oaks; M. Russell Ballard; Joseph B. Wirthlin; Richard G. Scott

AUXILIARY ORGANIZATIONS

Sunday Schools, Gen. Pres., Harold G. Hillam
Relief Society, Gen. Pres., Elaine Jack
Young Women, Gen. Pres., Janette Hales Beckham
Young Men, Gen. Pres., Jack H. Goaslind
Primary, Gen. Pres., Patricia P. Pinegar

PERIODICALS

The Ensign; Liahona Magazine; The New Era; Friend Magazine

Church of Our Lord Jesus Christ of the Apostolic Faith, Inc.

This church body was founded by Bishop R.C. Lawson in Columbus, Ohio, and moved to New York City in 1919. It is founded upon the teachings of the apostles and prophets, Jesus Christ being its chief cornerstone.

HEADQUARTERS

2081 Adam Clayton Powell Jr. Blvd., New York, NY 10027 Tel. (212)866-1700

Media Contact, Exec. Sec., Bishop T. E. Woolfolk, P.O. Box 119, Oxford, NC 27565 Tel. (919)693-9449 Fax (919)693-6115

OFFICERS

Board of Apostles: Chief Apostle, Bishop William L. Bonner; Presiding Chief Apostle, Bishop Gentle L. Groover; Bishop Frank S. Solomon; Bishop Henry A. Ross, Sr.; Bishop Matthew A. Norwood; Bishop James I. Clark, Jr.; Bishop Wilbur L. Jones; Bishop J. P. Steadman
Bd. of Bishops, Chmn., Bishop Ronald H. Carter
Bd. of Presbyters, Pres., Elder Michael A. Dixon
Exec. Secretariat, Sec., Bishop T. E. Woolfolk
Natl. Rec. Sec., Bishop Fred Rubin, Sr. (J.B.)
Natl. Fin. Sec., Bishop Clarence Groover
Natl. Corr. Sec., Bishop Raymond J. Keith, Jr. (J.B.)
Natl Treas., Elder Richard D. Williams

Church of the Brethren

German pietists-anabaptists founded the Church of the Brethren in 1708 under Alexander Mack in Schwarzenau, Germany. They entered the colonies in 1719 and settled at Germantown, Pa. They have no other creed than the New Testament, hold to principles of nonviolence, temperance and volunteerism and emphasize religion in daily life.

HEADQUARTERS

Church of the Brethren General Offices, 1451 Dundee Ave., Elgin, IL 60120 Tel. (708)742-5100 Fax (708)742-6103

New Windsor Service Center, P.O. Box 188, New Windsor, MD 21776 Tel. (301)635-6464 Fax (301)635-8789

Washington Office, 110 Maryland Ave. NE, Box 50, Washington, DC 20002 Tel. (202)546-3202 Fax (202)544-5852

Media Contact, Dir. of Interpretation, Howard Royer, Elgin Ofc.

OFFICERS

Mod., H. Fred Bernhard
Mod.-Elect, David M. Wine
Sec., Anne M. Myers

GENERAL BOARD STAFF

Ofc. of Gen. Sec.: Gen. Sec., Donald E. Miller

ADMINISTRATIVE COUNCIL

Treasurer's Ofc.: Treas., Judy Keyser

General Services Commission: Assoc. Gen. Sec./Exec. of Comm., Dale E. Minnich

Parish Ministries Commission: Assoc. Gen. Sec./Exec. of Comm., Glenn F. Timmons

World Ministries Commission: Assoc. Gen. Sec./Exec. of Comm., Joan G. Deeter

Annual Conference: Mgr., Duane Steiner; Treas., Judy Keyser

Brethren Benefit Trust: Pres., Wilfred E. Nolen

PERIODICAL

Messenger

Church of the Living God (Motto: Christian Workers for Fellowship)

The Church of the Living God was founded by William Christian in April 1889 at Caine Creek, Ark. It was the first black church in America without Anglo-Saxon roots and not begun by white missionaries.

Christian was born a slave in Mississippi on Nov. 10, 1856 and grew up uneducated. In 1875 he united with the Missionary Baptist Church and began to preach. In 1888 he left the Baptist Church and began what was known as Christian Friendship Work. Believing himself to have been inspired by the Spirit of God through divine revelation and close study of the Scriptures, he was led to the truth that the Bible refers to the church as The Church of the Living God (I Tim. 3:15).

The church believes in the infallibility of the Scriptures, is Trinitarian and believes there are three sacraments ordained by Christ: baptism (by immersion), the Lord's Supper (unleavened bread and water) and foot washing.

The Church of the Living God, C.W.F.F., believes in holiness as a gift of God subsequent to the New Birth and manifested only by a changed life acceptable to the Lord.

HEADQUARTERS

430 Forest Ave., Cincinnati, OH 45229 Tel. (513)-569-5660

Media Contact, Chief Bishop, W. E. Crumes

OFFICERS

Executive Board: Chief Bishop, W. E. Crumes; Vice-Chief Bishop, Alonza Ponder, 5609 N. Terry, Oklahoma City, OK 73111; Exec. Sec., Bishop C. A. Lewis, 1360 N. Boston, Tulsa, OK 73111; Gen. Sec., Mrs. Gwendolyn Robinson, 8611 S. University, Chicago, IL 60619; Gen. Treas., Elder Harry Hendricks, Milwaukee, WI; Bishop E. L. Bowie, 2037 N.E. 18th St., Oklahoma City, OK 73111; Chaplain, Bishop E. A. Morgan, 735 S. Oakland Dr., Decatur, IL 62525; Bishop Robert D. Tyler, 3802 Bedford, Omaha, NE 68110; Bishop Luke C. Nichols, Louisville, KY; Bishop Jeff Ruffin, Phoenix, AZ; Bishop R. S. Morgan, 4508 N. Indiana, Oklahoma City, OK 73118; Bishop S. E. Shannon, 1034 S. King Hwy., St. Louis, MO 63110; Bishop J. C. Hawkins, 3804 N. Temple, Indianapolis, IN 46205; Overseer, Elbert Jones, 4522 Melwood, Memphis, TN 38109

NATIONAL DEPARTMENTS

Convention Planning Committee
Young People's Progressive Union
Christian Education Dept.
Sunday School Dept.
Natl. Evangelist Bd.
Natl. Nurses Guild
Natl. Women's Work Dept.
Natl. Music Dept.
Gen. Sec. Ofc.

PERIODICAL

The Gospel Truth

Church of the Lutheran Brethren of America

The Church of the Lutheran Brethren of America was organized in December 1900. Five independent Lutheran congregations met together in Milwaukee, Wisc., and adopted a constitution patterned very closely on that of the Lutheran Free Church of Norway.

The spiritual awakening in the Midwest during the 1890s crystallized into convictions that led to the formation of a new church body. Chief among the concerns were church membership practices, observance of Holy Communion, confirmation practices and local church government.

The Church of the Lutheran Brethren practices a simple order of worship with the sermon as the primary part of the worship service. It believes that personal profession of faith is the primary criterion for membership in the congregation. The Communion service is reserved for those who profess faith in Christ as savior. Each congregation is autonomous and the synod serves the congregations in advisory and cooperative capacities.

The synod supports a world mission program in Cameroon, Chad, Japan and Taiwan. Approximately 40 percent of the synodical budget is earmarked for world missions. A growing home mission ministry is planting new congregations in the United States and Canada. Affiliate organizations operate several retirement/nursing homes, conference and retreat centers.

HEADQUARTERS

1007 Westside Dr., Box 655, Fergus Falls, MN 56538 Tel. (218)739-3336 Fax (218)739-5514

Media Contact, Pres., Rev. Robert M. Overgaard

OFFICERS

Pres., Rev. Robert M. Overgaard, Sr.
Vice-Pres., Rev. David Rinden
Sec., Rev. Richard Vettrus, 707 Crestview Dr., West Union, IA 52175
Exec. Dir. of Finance, Mr. Bradley Martinson
Lutheran Brethren Schools, Pres., Rev. Joel Egge, Lutheran Brethren Schools, Box 317, Fergus Falls, MN 56538
World Missions, Exec. Dir., Rev. Matthew Rogness
Home Missions, Exec. Dir., Rev. Armin Jahr
Church Services, Exec. Dir., Rev. David Rinden
Youth Ministries, Exec. Dir., Mr. Nathan Lee

PERIODICAL

Faith & Fellowship

Church of the Lutheran Confession

The Church of the Lutheran Confession held its constituting convention in Watertown, S.D., in August of 1960. The Church of the Lutheran Confession was begun by people and congregations who withdrew from church bodies that made up what was then known as the Synodical Conference over the issue of unionism. Following such passages as I Corinthians 1:10 and Romans 16:17-18, the Church of the Lutheran Confession holds the conviction that mutual agreement with the doctrines of Scripture is essential and necessary before exercise of church fellowship is appropriate.

Members of the Church of the Lutheran Confession uncompromisingly believe the Holy Scriptures to be divinely inspired and therefore inerrant. They subscribe to the historic Lutheran Confessions as found in the Book of Concord of 1580 because they are a correct exposition of Scripture.

The Church of the Lutheran Confession exists to proclaim, preserve and spread the saving truth of the gospel of Jesus Christ, so that the redeemed of God may learn to know Jesus Christ as their Lord and Savior and follow him through this life to the life to come.

HEADQUARTERS

460 75th Ave., NE, Minneapolis, MN 55432 Tel. (612)784-8784

Media Contact, Pres., Daniel Fleischer

OFFICERS

Pres., Rev. Daniel Fleischer
Vice-Pres., Rev. Elton Hallauer, 608 1st St., Hancock, MN 56244
Mod., Prof. Ronald Roehl, 515 Ingram Dr. W., Eau Claire, WI 54701
Sec., Rev. Paul Nolting, 626 N. Landing Rd., Rochester, NY 14625
Treas., Lowell Moen, 3455 Jill Ave., Eau Claire, WI 54701
Archivist-Historian, John Lau
Statistician, Harvey Callies

PERIODICALS

The Lutheran Spokesman; Journal of Theology

Church of the Nazarene

The Church of the Nazarene resulted from the merger of three independent holiness groups. The Association of Pentecostal Churches in America, located principally in New York and New England, joined at Chicago in 1907 with a largely West Coast body called the Church of the Nazarene and formed the the Pentecostal Church of the Nazarene. A southern group, the Holiness Church of Christ, united with the Pentecostal Church of the Nazarene at Pilot Point, Texas, in 1908. In 1919 the word "Pentecostal" was dropped from the name. Principal leaders in the organization were Phineas Bresee, William Howard Hoople, H. F. Reynolds and C. B. Jernigan. The first congregation in Canada was organized in November 1902 by Dr. H. F. Reynolds in Oxford, Nova Scotia.

The Church of the Nazarene emphasizes the doctrine of entire sanctification or Christian Holiness. It stresses the importance of a devout and holy life and a positive witness before the world by the power of the Holy Spirit. Nazarenes express their faith through evangelism, compassionate ministries, and education.

Nazarene government is representative, a studied compromise between episcopacy and congregationalism. Quadrennially, the various districts elect delegates to a general assembly at which six general superintendents are elected.

The international denomination has 10 liberal arts colleges, two graduate seminaries, 37 Bible colleges, three schools of nursing, a teacher's training college, and a junior college. The church maintains over 600 missionaries in 110 world areas. World services include medical, educational and religious ministries. Books, periodicals and other Christian literature are published at the Nazarene Publishing House.

The church is a member of the Christian Holiness Association and the National Association of Evangelicals.

HEADQUARTERS

6401 The Paseo, Kansas City, MO 64131 Tel. (816)333-7000 Fax (816)361-4983

Media Contact, Gen. Sec./Headquarters Operations Officer (HOO), Dr. Jack Stone, Tel. (816)333-7000, Ext. 2366

OFFICERS

Gen. Supts.: Jerald D. Johnson; John A. Knight; William J. Prince; Donald D. Owens; James H. Diehl; Paul G. Cunningham
Gen. Sec. (HOO), Jack Stone
Gen. Treas. (HFO), Robert Foster

OTHER ORGANIZATIONS

General Bd.: Sec., Jack Stone
General Bd.: Treas., Robert Foster
Church Growth Div., Dir., Bill Sullivan
Chaplaincy Min., Dir., Curt Bowers
Evangelism Min., Dir., Bill Sullivan
Pastoral Min., Dir., Wilbur Brannon
Communications Div., Dir., Michael Estep
Media International, Dir., David Anderson
Publications Intl., Dir., Ray Hendrix
Planned Giving, Dir., Steve Weber
Int. Bd. of Educ.,, Ed. Commissioner, Jerry Lambert
Pensions & Benefits Services USA & Intl., Don Walter
Stewardship Services, Dir., Steve Weber
Sunday School Min. Div., Dir., Talmadge Johnson
Adult Min., Dir., Randy Cloud
Children's Min., Dir., Miriam Hall
NYI Min., Dir., Fred Fullerton
World Mission Div., Dir., Louie Bustle

Nazarene World Missionary Soc., Dir., Nina Gunter
Multi-Cultural Ministries, Dir., Tom Nees

PERIODICALS

Herald of Holiness; World Mission; Preacher's Magazine; Crosswalk; Grow Magazine

Churches of Christ

Churches of Christ are autonomous congregations whose members appeal to the Bible alone to determine matters of faith and practice. There are no central offices or officers. Publications and institutions related to the churches are either under local congregational control or independent of any one congregation.

Churches of Christ shared a common fellowship in the 19th century with the Christian Churches/Churches of Christ and the Christian Church (Disciples of Christ). Fellowship was gradually estranged following the Civil War due to theistic evolution, higher critical theories, centralization of church-wide activities through a missionary society and addition of musical instruments.

Members of Churches of Christ believe in one God, one Lord and Savior, Jesus Christ, one Holy Spirit, one body or church of God, one baptism by immersion into Christ, one faith revealed in the Holy, inspired, inerrant scriptures and one hope of eternal life based on the grace of God in Christ and a response by each individual of faith and obedience to God's gracious instructions in scripture. The New Testament pattern is followed in terms for salvation and church membership, church organization and standards of Christian living.

HEADQUARTERS

Media Contact, Ed., Gospel Advocate, Dr. F. Furman Kearley, P.O. Box 726, Kosciusko, MO 39090

PERIODICALS

Action; Wineskins; Image; Christian Bible Teacher; The Christian Chronicle; Firm Foundation; Gospel Advocate; Guardian of Truth; Restoration Quarterly; 21st Century Christian; Upreach; Rocky Mountain Christian; The Spiritual Sword; Word and Work

Churches of Christ in Christian Union

Organized in 1909 at Washington Court House, Ohio, as the Churches of Christ in Christian Union, this body believes in the new birth and the baptism of the Holy Spirit for believers. It is Wesleyan, with an evangelistic and missionary emphasis.

The Reformed Methodist Church merged with the Churches of Christ in Christian Union in 1952.

HEADQUARTERS

1426 Lancaster Pike, Box 30, Circleville, OH 43113 Tel. (614)474-8856 Fax (614)477-7766
Media Contact, Dir. of Comm., Rev. Wes Humble

OFFICERS

Gen. Supt., Dr. Daniel Tipton
Asst. Gen. Supt., Rev. David Dean
Gen. Treas., Beverly R. Salley
Gen. Bd. of Trustees: Chpsn., Dr. Daniel Tipton; Vice-Chpsn., Rev. David Dean

District Superintendents: West Central District, Rev. Ron Reese; South Central District, Rev. Jack Norman; Northeast District, Rev. Don Seymour

PERIODICAL

The Evangelical Advocate

Churches of God, General Conference

The Churches of God, General Conference had its beginnings in Harrisburg, Pa., in 1825.

John Winebrenner, recognized founder of the Church of God movement, was an ordained minister of the German Reformed Church. His experience-centered form of Christianity, particularly the "new measures" he used to promote it, his close connection with the local Methodists, his "experience and conference meetings" in the church and his "social prayer meetings" in parishioners' homes resulted in differences of opinion and the establishment of new congregations. Extensive revivals, camp meetings and mission endeavors led to the organization of additional congregations across central Pennsylvania and westward through Ohio, Indiana, Illinois and Iowa.

In 1830 the first system of cooperation between local churches was initiated as an "eldership" in eastern Pennsylvania. The organization of other elderships followed. General Eldership was organized in 1845, and in 1974 the official name of the denomination was changed from General Eldership of the Churches of God in North America to its present name.

The Churches of God, General Conference, is composed of 16 conferences in the United States. The polity of the church is presbyterial in form. The church has mission ministries in the southwest among native Americans and is extensively involved in church planting and whole life ministries in Bangladesh, Brazil, Haiti and India.

The General Conference convenes in business session triennially. An Administrative Council composed of 16 regional representatives who are responsible for the administration and ministries of the church between sessions of the General Conference.

HEADQUARTERS

Legal Headquarters, United Church Center, Rm. 213, 900 S. Arlington Ave., Harrisburg, PA 17109 Tel. (717)652-0255
Administrative Offices, General Conf. Dir., Pastor Wayne W. Boyer, 700 E. Melrose Ave., P.O. Box 926, Findlay, OH 45839 Tel. (419)424-1961
Media Contact, Exec. Sec., Roberta G. Bakies, P.O. Box 926, Findlay, OH 45839 Tel. (419)424-1961 Fax (419)424-3343

OFFICERS

Pres., Pastor Ronald E. Dull, 12 Dogwood Ct., Shippensburg, PA 17257 Tel. (919)264-2644
Journalizing Sec., Dr. C. Darrell Prichard, 700 E. Melrose Ave., P.O. Box 1132, Findlay, OH 45839 Tel. (419)423-7694
Treas., Mr. Robert E. Stephenson, 700 E. Melrose Ave., P.O. Box 926, Findlay, OH 45839 Tel. (419)424-1961

DEPARTMENTS

Church Publications, Mrs. Linda M. Draper
Cross-Cultural Ministries, Pastor Don Dennison
Pensions, Dr. Royal P. Kear
Curriculum, Mrs. Evelyn J. Sloat

Church Renewal, Pastor Jim G. Martin
Church Planting, Pastor James W. Moss, Sr.
Youth & Family Life, Mrs. Susan L. Callaway
Fin., Mr. Robert E. Stephenson

PERIODICALS

The Church Advocate; The Workman; The Gem; The Missionary Signal

Congregational Holiness Church

This body was organized in 1921 and embraces the doctrine of Holiness and Pentecost. It carries on mission work in Mexico, Honduras, Costa Rica, Cuba, Brazil, Guatemala, India, Nicaragua, El Salvador, Belize, Venezula and Haiti.

HEADQUARTERS

3888 Fayetteville Hwy., Griffin, GA 30223 Tel. (404)228-4833 Fax (404)228-1177
Media Contact, Gen. Supt., Bishop Chet Smith

EXECUTIVE BOARD

Gen. Supt., Bishop Chet Smith
1st Asst. Gen. Supt., Rev. William L. Lewis
2nd Asst. Gen. Supt., Rev. Wayne Hicks
Gen. Sec., Rev. Dennis Phillips
Gen. Treas., Rev. Ronald Wilson

PERIODICAL

The Gospel Messenger

Conservative Baptist Association of America

The Conservative Baptist Association of America was organized May 17, 1947 at Atlantic City, N.J. The Old and New Testaments are regarded as the divinely inspired Word of God and are therefore infallible and of supreme authority. Each local church is independent, autonomous and free from ecclesiastical or political authority.

CBA provides wide-ranging support to its affiliate churches and individuals. CBA offers personnel to assist churches in areas such as growth and health conflict resolution and financial analysis. The association supports its clergy with retirement planning, referrals for new places of ministry and spiritual counseling. The Conservative Baptist Women's Ministries assists women in the church to be effective in their personal growth and leadership.

Each June or July there is a National Conference giving members an opportunity for fellowship, inspiration and motivation.

HEADQUARTERS

25W560 Geneva Rd., P.O. Box 66, Wheaton, IL 60189 Tel. (708)260-3800 Fax (708)653-5387
Media Contact, Gen. Dir., Dr. Dennis N. Baker

OTHER ORGANIZATIONS

CB International, Exec. Dir., Dr. Hans Finzel, Box 5, Wheaton, IL 60189
Mission to the Americas, Exec. Dir., Rev. Rick Miller, Box 828, Wheaton, IL 60189
Conservative Baptist Higher Ed. Council, Dr. Ed Hayes, Denver Conservative Baptist Seminary, P.O. Box 10,000, Denver, CO 80250

PERIODICALS

Spectrum; Front Line

Conservative Congregational Christian Conference

In the 1930s, evangelicals within the Congregational Christian Churches felt a definite need for fellowship and service. By 1945, this loose association crystallized into the Conservative Congregational Christian Fellowship, committed to maintaining a faithful, biblical witness.

In 1948 in Chicago, the Conservative Congregational Christian Conference was established to provide a continuing fellowship for evangelical churches and ministers on the national level. In recent years, many churches have joined the Conference from backgrounds other than Congregational. These Community or Bible Churches are truly congregational in polity and thoroughly evangelical in conviction. The CCCC welcomes all evangelical churches that are, in fact, congregational. The CCCC believes in the necessity of a regenerate membership, the authority of the Holy Scriptures, the Lordship of Jesus Christ, the autonomy of the local church and the universal fellowship of all Christians.

The Conservative Congregational Christian Conference is a member of the World Evangelical Congregational Fellowship (formed in 1986 in London, England) and the National Association of Evangelicals.

HEADQUARTERS

7582 Currell Blvd., Ste. #108, St. Paul, MN 55125 Tel. (612)739-1474 Fax (612)739-0750
Media Contact, Conf. Min., Rev. Clifford R. Christensen

OFFICERS

Pres., Rev. Donald Ehler, 620 High Ave., Hillsboro, WI 54634
Vice-Pres., Rev. Clarence Schultz, 7023 Pershing Blvd., Kenosha, WI 53142-1723
Conf. Min., Rev. Clifford R. Christensen, 457 S. Mary St., Maplewood, MN 55119
Controller, Mr. Leslie Pierce, 5220 E. 105th St. S., Tulsa, OK 74137
Treas., Mr. John D. Nygren, 579 Sterling St., Maplewood, MN 55119
Rec. Sec., Rev. Larry E. Scovil, 317 W. 40th St., Scottsbluff, NE 69361
Editor, Rev. George T. Allen, Box 881026, Steilacoom, WA 98388
Historian, Rev. Milton Reimer, P.O. Box 4456, Lynchburg, VA 24502

PERIODICAL

Foresee

Conservative Lutheran Association

The Conservative Lutheran Association (CLA) was originally named Lutheran's Alert National (LAN) when it was founded in 1965 by 10 conservative Lutheran pastors and laymen meeting in Cedar Rapids, Iowa. Its purpose was to help preserve from erosion the basic doctrines of Christian theology, including the inerrancy of Holy Scripture. The group grew to a worldwide constituency, similarly concerned with maintaining the doctrinal integrity of the Bible and the Lutheran Confessions.

HEADQUARTERS

Trinity Lutheran Church, 4101 E. Nohl Ranch Rd., Anaheim, CA 92807 Tel. (714)637-8370

Media Contact, Pres., The Rev. P. J. Moore

OFFICERS

Pres., Rev. P. J. Moore, 420 Fernhill La., Anaheim, CA 92807 Tel. (714)637-8370
Vice-Pres., Rev. Dr. R. H. Redal, 409 Tacoma Ave. N., Tacoma, WA 98403 Tel. (206)383-5528
Sec., Rev. James Sheasley, 409 Tacoma Ave. N., Tacoma, WA 98403 Tel. (206)383-5528
Faith Seminary, Dean, The Rev. Dr. Michael J. Adams, 3504 N. Pearl St., P.O. Box 7186, Tacoma, WA 98407 Tel. (800)228-4650 Fax (206)-759-1790

Coptic Orthodox Church

This body is part of the ancient Coptic Orthodox Church of Egypt which is currently headed by His Holiness Pope Shenouda III, 116th Successor to St. Mark the Apostle. Egyptian immigrants have organized many parishes in the United States. Copts exist outside Egypt in Ethiopia, Europe, Asia, Australia, Canada and the United States. The total world Coptic community is estimated at 27 million. The church is in full communion with the other members of The Oriental Orthodox Church Family, The Syrian Orthodox Church, Armenian Orthodox Church, Ethiopian Orthodox Church, the Syrian Orthodox Church in India and the Eritrean Orthodox Church.

HEADQUARTERS

427 West Side Ave., Jersey City, NJ 07304 Tel. (201)333-0004 Fax (201)333-0502
Media Contact, Fr. Abraam D. Sleman

CORRESPONDENT

Fr. Abraam D. Sleman

Cumberland Presbyterian Church

The Cumberland Presbyterian Church was organized in Dickson County, Tenn., on Feb. 4, 1810. It was an outgrowth of the Great Revival of 1800 on the Kentucky and Tennessee frontier. The founders were Finis Ewing, Samuel King and Samuel McAdow, ministers in the Presbyterian Church who rejected the doctrine of election and reprobation as taught in the Westminster Confession of Faith.

By 1813, the Cumberland Presbytery had grown to encompass three presbyteries, which constituted a synod. This synod met at the Beech Church in Sumner County, Tenn., and formulated a "Brief Statement" which set forth the points in which Cumberland Presbyterians dissented from the Westminster Confession. These points are:

1. That there are no eternal reprobates;
2. That Christ died not for some, but for all people;
3. That all those dying in infancy are saved through Christ and the sanctification of the Spirit;
4. That the Spirit of God operates on the world, or as coextensively as Christ has made atonement, in such a manner as to leave everyone inexcusable.

From its birth in 1810, the Cumberland Presbyterian Church grew to a membership of 200,000 at the turn of the century. In 1906 the church voted to merge with the then-Presbyterian Church. Those who dissented from the merger became the nucleus of the continuing Cumberland Presbyterian Church.

HEADQUARTERS

1978 Union Ave., Memphis, TN 38104 Tel. (901)-276-4572 Fax (901)272-3913
Media Contact, Stated Clk., Rev. Robert D. Prosser, Fax (901)276-4578

OFFICERS

Mod., Rev. Clinton Buck, 168 E. Parkway S., Memphis, TN 38104
Stated Clk., Rev. Robert D. Prosser, Fax (901)276-4578
General Assembly Council, Exec. Dir., Davis Gray

INSTITUTIONS

Cumberland Presbyterian Children's Home, Exec. Dir., Rev. Stan E. Rush, Drawer G, Denton, TX 76202 Tel. (817)382-5112 Fax (817)387-0821
Cumberland Presbyterian Center, Fax (901)276-4578
Memphis Theological Seminary, Pres., Dr. J. David Hester, 168 E. Parkway S., Memphis, TN 38104 Tel. (901)458-8232 Fax (901)452-4051
Bethel College, Pres., Dr. Bill Elkins, 212 Cherry St., McKenzie, TN 38201 Tel. (901)352-1000 Fax (901)352-1008

BOARDS

Bd. of Christian Education, Exec. Dir., Ms. Claudette Pickle
Bd. of Missions, Exec. Dir., Rev. Jack Barker
Bd. of Finance, Exec. Sec., Rev. Richard Magrill

PERIODICALS

The Cumberland Presbyterian; The Missionary Messenger

Cumberland Presbyterian Church in America

This church, originally known as the Colored Cumberland Presbyterian Church, was formed in May 1874. In May 1869, at the General Assembly meeting in Murfreesboro, Tenn., Moses Weir of the black delegation sucessfully appealed for help in organizing a separate African church so that: blacks could learn self-reliance and independence; they could have more financial assistance; they could minister more effectively among blacks; and they could worship close to the altar, not in the balconies. He requested that the Cumberland Presbyterian Church organize blacks into presbyteries and synods, develop schools to train black clergy, grant loans to assist blacks to secure hymnbooks, Bibles and church buildings and establish a separate General Assembly.

In 1874 the first General Assembly of the Colored Cumberland Presbyterian Church met in Nashville. The moderator was Rev. P. Price and the stated clerk was Elder John Humphrey.

The denomination's General Assembly, the national governing body, is organized around its three program boards and agencies: Finance, Publication and Christian Education, and Missions and Evangelism. Other agencies of the General Assembly are under these three program boards.

The church has four synods (Alabama, Kentucky, Tennessee and Texas), 15 presbyteries and 153 congregations. The CPC extends as far north as Cleveland, Ohio, and Chicago, as far west as Marshalltown, Iowa, and Dallas, Tex., and as far south as Selma, Ala.

HEADQUARTERS

Media Contact, Stated Clk., Rev. Dr. R. Stanley Wood, 226 Church St., Huntsville, AL 35801 Tel. (205)536-7481 Fax (205)536-7482

OFFICERS

Mod., Rev. Endia Scruggs, 1684 Carroll Rd., Harvest, AL 35749
Stated Clk., Rev. Dr. R. Stanley Wood, 226 Church St., Huntsville, AL 35801 Tel. (205)536-7481

SYNODS

Alabama, Stated Clk., Arthur Hinton, 511 10th Ave. N.W., Aliceville, AL 35442
Kentucky, Stated Clk., Mary Martha Daniels, 8548 Rhodes Ave., Chicago, IL 60619
Tennessee, Stated Clk., Elder Clarence Norman, 145 Jones St., Huntington, TN 38334
Texas, Stated Clk., Arthur King, 2435 Kristen, Dallas, TX 75216

PERIODICAL

The Cumberland Flag

Diocese of the Armenian Church of America

The Armenian Apostolic Church was founded at the foot of the biblical mountain of Ararat in the ancient land of Armenia, where two of Christ's Holy Apostles, Saints Thaddeus and Bartholomew, preached Christianity. In A.D. 303 the historic Mother Church of Etchmiadzin was founded by Saint Gregory the Illuminator, the first Catholicos of All Armenians. This cathedral still stands and serves as the center of the Armenian Church. A branch of this Church was established in North America in 1889 and the first Armenian Diocese was set up in 1898 by the then-Catholicos of All Armenians, Mgrditch Khrimian (Hairig). Armenian immigrants built the first Armenian church in the new world in Worcester, Mass., under the jurisdiction of Holy Etchmiadzin.

In 1927, the churches and the parishes in California were formed into a Western Diocese and the parishes in Canada formed their own diocese in 1984. Other centers of major significance of the Armenian Apostolic Church are the Catholicate of Cilicia, now located in Lebanon, the Armenian Patriarchate of Jerusalem and the Armenian Patriarchate of Constantinople.

HEADQUARTERS

Eastern Diocese: 630 Second Ave., New York, NY 10016-4885 Tel. (212)686-0710 Fax (212)779-3558
Western Diocese: 1201 N. Vine St., Hollywood, CA 90038 Tel. (213)466-5265
Canadian Diocese: 615 Stuart Ave., Outremont, QC H2V 3H2 Tel. (514)276-9479 Fax (514)276-9960
Media Contact, Dir., Zohrab Information Ctr., V. Rev. Fr. Krikor Maksoudian, Eastern Diocese

OFFICERS

Eastern Diocese
Primate, Archbishop Khajag Barsamian, Eastern Diocese Ofc.
Vicar Gen., V. Rev. Fr. Haigazoun Najarian, Eastern Diocese Ofc.
Chancellor, Rev. Fr. Garabed Kochakian
Diocesan Council, Chpsn., Vincent Gurahian, Macauley Rd., RFD 2, Katonah, NY 10536
Western Diocese
Primate, His Em. Archbishop Vatche Hovsepian, Western Diocese Ofc.
Diocesan Council, Chpsn., The Rev. Fr. Vartkes Barsam, St. Mary Armenian Church, P.O. Box 367, Yettem, CA 93670
Diocesan Council, Sec., Armen Hampar, 6134 Pat Ave., Woodland Hills, CA 91367
Canadian Diocese
Primate, His Em. Archbishop Hovnan Derderian

PERIODICALS

The Armenian Church; The Mother Church

Elim Fellowship

The Elim Fellowship, a Pentecostal Body established in 1947, is an outgrowth of the Elim Missionary Assemblies formed in 1933.

It is an association of churches, ministers and missionaries seeking to serve the whole Body of Christ. It is of Pentecostal conviction and charismatic orientation, providing ministerial credentials and counsel and encouraging fellowship among local churches. Elim Fellowship sponsors leadership seminars at home and abroad and serves as a transdenominational agency sending long-term, short-term and tent-making missionaries to work with national movements.

HEADQUARTERS

7245 College St., Lima, NY 14485 Tel. (716)582-2790 Fax (716)624-1229
Media Contact, Gen. Sec., Chester Gretz

OFFICERS

Gen. Overseer, L. Dayton Reynolds
Asst. Gen. Overseer, Bernard J. Evans
Gen. Sec., Chester Gretz
Gen. Treas., H. David Edwards

PERIODICAL

Elim Herald

Episcopal Church

The Episcopal Church entered the colonies with the earliest settlers at Jamestown, Va., in 1607 as the Church of England. After the American Revolution, it became autonomous in 1789 as The Protestant Episcopal Church in the United States of America. (The Episcopal Church became the official alternate name in 1967.) Samuel Seabury of Connecticut was elected the first bishop and consecrated in Aberdeen by bishops of the Scottish Episcopal Church in 1784.

In organizing as an independent body, the Episcopal Church created a bicameral legislature, the General Convention, modeled after the new U.S. Congress. It comprises a House of Bishops and a House of Deputies and meets every three years. A 38-member Executive Council, which meets three times a year, is the interim governing body. An elected presiding bishop serves as Primate and Chief Pastor.

After severe setbacks in the years immediately following the Revolution because of its association with the British Crown and the fact that a number of its clergy and members were Loyalists, the church soon established its own identity and sense of mission. It sent missionaries into the newly settled territories of the United States, establishing dioceses from coast to coast, and also undertook substantial missionary work in Africa, Latin America and the Far East. Today, the overseas dioceses are developing into independent provinces of the

Anglican Communion, the worldwide fellowship of churches in communion with the Church of England and the Archbishop of Canterbury.

The beliefs and practices of The Episcopal Church, like those of other Anglican churches, are both Catholic and Reformed, with bishops in the apostolic succession and the historic creeds of Christendom regarded as essential elements of faith and order, along with the primary authority of Holy Scripture and the two chief sacraments of Baptism and Eucharist.

EPISCOPAL CHURCH CENTER

815 Second Ave., New York, NY 10017 Tel. (212)867-8400 Fax (212)949-8059

Media Contact, Dir. of News & Info., James Solheim

OFFICERS

Presiding Bishop & Primate, The Most Rev. Edmond L. Browning
Vice-Pres., Diane Porter
Interim Treas., Mr Robert E. Brown
Sec., The Rev. Canon Donald A. Nickerson, Jr.
House of Deputies: Pres., Pamela P. Chinnis; Vice-Pres., The Ven. George Werner

OFFICE OF THE PRESIDING BISHOP

Presiding Bishop, The Most Rev. Edmond L. Browning
COO, Rt. Rev. Charlie F. McNutt, Jr.
Admn. Asst. to COO, The Rev. Canon Richard Chang
Information Officer, Barbara Braver
Exec. Dir., Office of Pastoral Dev., The Rt. Rev. Harold Hopkins
Suffragan Bishop for the Armed Forces, The Rt. Rev. Charles L. Keyser
Suffragan Bishop for American Churches in Europe, The Rt. Rev. Jeffery Rowthorn
Office of Prof. Ministry Dev., The Rev. John Docker

ADMINISTRATION AND FINANCE

Interim Treas., Mr. Robert E. Brown
Asst. Treas., ----
Controller, ----
Archivist, Mark Duffy
Human Resources, John Colon
Episcopal Parish Services, Margaret Landis

SERVICE, EDUCATION AND WITNESS

Senior Exec., Diane Porter
Congregational Ministries, The Rev. Winston Ching
Hispanic Ministries, The Rev. Herbert Arrunategui
Jubilee Centers, Ntsiki Kabane-Langford
Native American Ministries, Owanah Anderson
Peace & Justice, The Rev. Brian Grieves
Rural Workers Fellowship, The Rev. Allen Brown
Washington Ofc., The Rev. Robert Brooks
Media Services, Sonia Francis
Electronic Media, The Rev. Clement Lee
Dir. of News & Info., James Solheim
Episcopal Life, Jerrold Hames
Children's Ministry, The Rev. Howard Williams
Ministries with Young Persons, The Rev. Sheryl Kujawa
Evangelism Office, The Rev. Canon Linda Strohmeier
Liturgy & Music, The Rev. Clayton Morris
Theological Education, The Rev. Preston Kelsey
Dir. of Anglican/Global Relations, The Rev. Patrick Mauney
Ecumenical Office, The Rev. David Perry
Mission Personnel, Dorothy Gist
Dep. Dir. of Anglican/Global Relations, The Rev. Ricardo Potter
Women in Mission & Ministry, Ann Smith
Dir. of Bishops Fund for World Relief, Nancy Marvel
Planning Officer, Vernon Hazelwood
Stewardship, The Rev. Hugh Magers

BISHOPS IN THE U.S.A.

C, Coadjutor; S, Suffragan; A Assistant
Address: Right Reverend
Headquarters Staff: Chief Operating Officer, Rt. Rev. Charlie F. McNutt, Jr.; Presiding Bishop & Primate, The Most Rev. Edmond L. Browning; Pastoral Dev., Rt. Rev. Harold Hopkins; S. Bishop for Chaplaincies to Military\Prisons\Hosp., Rt. Rev. Charles L. Keyser
Alabama: Robert O. Miller, 521 N. 20th St., Birmingham, AL 35203
Alaska: ----, 1205 Denali Way, Fairbanks, AK 99701-4137
Albany: David S. Ball, 68 S. Swan St., Albany, NY 12210
Arizona: Robert Shahan, 114 W.Roosevelt, Phoenix, AZ 85003-1406
Arkansas: Larry E. Maze, P.O. Box 162668, Little Rock, AR 72216
Atlanta: Frank Kellog Allan, 2744 Peachtree Rd. N.W., Atlanta, GA 30363
Bethlehem: J. Mark Dyer, 333 Wyandotte St., Bethlehem, PA 18015
California: William E. Swing, 1055 Taylor St., San Francisco, CA 94115
Central Florida: John H. Howe, 1017 E. Robinson St., Orlando, FL 32801
Central Gulf Coast: Charles F. Duvall, P.O. Box 13330, Pensacola, FL 32591-3330
Central New York: David B. Joslin, 310 Montgomery St., Ste. 200, Syracuse, NY 13202
Central Pennsylvania: Michael Creighton, P.O. Box 11937, Harrisburg, PA 17108
Chicago: Frank T. Griswold, III, 65 E. Huron St., Chicago, IL 60611
Colorado: William J. Winterrowd, 1300 Washington St., Denver, CO 80203
Connecticut: Clarence N. Coleridge, 1335 Asylum Ave., Hartford, CT 06105
Dallas: James M. Stanton, 1630 Garrett St., Dallas, TX 75206
Delaware: Calvin Cabell Tennis, 2020 Tatnall St., Wilmington, DE 19802
East Carolina: B. Sidney Sanders, P.O. Box 1336, Kinston, NC 28501
East Tennessee: Robert Tharp, 401 Cumberland Ave., Knoxville, TN 37902-2302
Eastern Michigan: ----, 4611 Swede Ave., Midland, MI 48642
Eastern Oregon: Rustin R. Kimsey, P.O. Box 620, The Dalles, OR 97058
Easton: Martin G. Townsend, P.O. Box 1027, Easton, MD 21601
Eau Claire: William C. Wantland, 510 S. Farwell St., Eau Claire, WI 54701
El Camino Real: Richard Shimpfky, P.O. Box 1903, Monterey, CA 93940
Florida: Stephen H. Jecko, 325 Market St., Jacksonville, FL 32202
Fond du Lac: Russell E. Jacobus, P.O. Box 149, Fond du Lac, WI 54936
Fort Worth: Jack Iker, 6300 Ridgelea Pl., Ste. 1100, Fort Worth, TX 76116
Georgia: Henry Louttit, Jr., 611 East Bay St., Savannah, GA 31401

Hawaii: George Hunt, Interim, Ecclesiastical Authority, 229 Queen Emma Square, Honolulu, HI 96813

Idaho: John S. Thornton, P.O. Box 936, Boise, ID 83701

Indianapolis: Edward W. Jones, 1100 W. 42nd St., Indianapolis, IN 46208

Iowa: C. Christopher Epting, 225 37th St., Des Moines, IA 50312

Kansas: William E. Smalley, 833-35 Polk St., Topeka, KS 66612

Kentucky: Edwin F. Gulick, 600 E. Maine, Louisville, KY 40202

Lexington: Don A. Wimberly, P.O. Box 610, Lexington, KY 40586

Long Island: Orris G. Walker, 36 Cathedral Ave., Garden City, NY 11530

Los Angeles: Frederick H. Borsch; Chester Talton, (S), P.O. Box 2164, Los Angeles, CA 90051

Louisiana: James Barrow Brown, 1623 7th St., New Orleans, LA 70115-4411

Maine: Edward C. Chalfant, 143 State St., Portland, ME 04101

Maryland: Bob Ihloff, 4 East University Pkwy., Baltimore, MD 21218-2437

Massachusetts: M. Thomas Shaw, SSJE; Barbara Harris, (S), 138 Tremont St., Boston, MA 02111

Michigan: R. Stewart Wood, Jr., 4800 Woodward Ave., Detroit, MI 48201

Milwaukee: Roger J. White, 804 E. Juneau Ave., Milwaukee, WI 53202

Minnesota: James L. Jelinek; Sanford Hampton, (S), 430 Oak Grove St., #306, Minneapolis, MN 55403

Mississippi: Alfred C. Marble, P.O. Box 23107, Jackson, MS 39225-3107

Missouri: Hays Rockwell, 1210 Locust St., St. Louis, MO 63103

Montana: Charles I. Jones, 515 North Park Ave., Helena, MT 59601

Nebraska: James E. Krotz, 200 N. 62nd St., Omaha, NE 68132

Nevada: Stewart C. Zabriskie, P.O. Box 6357, Reno, NV 89513

New Hampshire: Douglas E. Theuner, 63 Green St., Concord, NH 03301

New Jersey: Joe M. Doss, 808 W. State St., Trenton, NJ 08618

New York: Richard F. Grein; Walter D. Dennis, (S), 1047 Amsterdam Ave., New York, NY 10025; Don Taylor

Newark: John Shelby Spong; Jack McKelvey, (S), 24 Rector St., Newark, NJ 07102

North Carolina: Robert C. Johnson, Jr., 201 St. Albans Dr., Raleigh, NC 27619

North Dakota: Andrew H. Fairfield, P.O. Box 10337, Fargo, ND 58106-0337

Northern California: Jerry A. Lamb, P.O. Box 161268, Sacramento, CA 95816

Northern Indiana: Francis C. Gray, 117 N. Lafayette Blvd., South Bend, IN 46601

Northern Michigan: Thomas K. Ray, 131 E. Ridge St., Marquette, MI 49855

Northwest Texas: Sam Byron Hulsey, P.O. Box 1067, Lubbock, TX 79408

Northwestern Pennsylvania: Robert D. Rowley, 145 W. 6th St., Erie, PA 16501

Ohio: J. Clark Grew; Arthur B. Williams, (S), 2230 Euclid Ave., Cleveland, OH 44115

Oklahoma: Robert M. Moody; William J. Cox, (A), 924 N. Robinson, Oklahoma City, OK 73102

Olympia: Vincent W. Warner, P.O. Box 12126, Seattle, WA 98102

Oregon: Robert Louis Ladehoff, P.O. Box 467, Portland, OR 97034

Pennsylvania: Allen L. Bartlett, 240 S. 4th St., Philadelphia, PA 19106

Pittsburgh: Alden M. Hathaway; Franklin D. Turner, (S), 325 Oliver Ave., Pittsburgh, PA 15222

Quincy: Keith Ackerman, 3601 N. North St., Peoria, IL 61604

Rhode Island: Geralyn Wolf, 275 N. Main St., Providence, RI 02903

Rio Grande: Terence Kelshaw, 4304 Carlisle St. NE, Albuquerque, NM 87107

Rochester: William G. Burrill, 935 East Ave., Rochester, NY 14607

San Diego: Gethin B. Hughes, St. Paul's Church, 2728 6th Ave., San Diego, CA 92103

San Joaquin: John-David Schofield, 4159 East Dakota Ave., Fresno, CA 93726

South Carolina: Edward L. Salmon; G. Edward Haynesworth, (A), P.O. Box 20127, Charleston, SC 29413-0127

South Dakota: Creighton Robertson, 500 S. Main St., Sioux Falls, SD 57102-0914

Southeast Florida: Calvin O. Schofield, Jr.; Calvin O. Schofield, Jr., 525 NE 15th St., Miami, FL 33132

Southern Ohio: Herbert Thompson, Jr.; Kenneth Price, (S), 412 Sycamore St., Cincinnati, OH 45202

Southern Virginia: Frank H. Vest, 600 Talbot Hall Rd., Norfolk, VA 23505

Southwest Florida: Rogers S. Harris, P.O. Box 491, St. Petersburg, FL 33731

Southwestern Virginia: A. Heath Light, P.O. Box 2279, Roanoke, VA 24009

Spokane: Frank J. Terry, 245 E. 13th Ave., Spokane, WA 99202

Springfield: Peter H. Beckwith, 821 S. 2nd St., Springfield, IL 62704

Tennessee: Bertram M. Herlong, One LaFleur Bldg., Ste. 100, 50 Vantage Way, Nashville, TN 37228

Texas: Claude E. Payne, (C), 3203 W. Alabama St., Houston, TX 77098

Upper South Carolina: Dorsey F. Henderson, Jr., P.O. Box 1789, Columbia, SC 29202

Utah: George E. Bates, 231 E. First St. S., Salt Lake City, UT 84111

Vermont: Mary Adelia McLeod, Rock Point, Burlington, VT 05401

Virginia: Peter J. Lee; Clayton Matthews, (S), 110 W. Franklin St., Richmond, VA 23220

Washington: Ronald Haines; Jane H. Dixon, (S), Episc. Church House, Mt. St. Alban, Washington, DC 20016

West Missouri: John Buchanan, P.O. Box 413216, Kansas City, MO 64141

West Tennessee: James M. Coleman, (C), 692 Poplar Ave., Memphis, TN 38105

West Texas: James E. Folts; Earl N. MacArthur, (S), P.O. Box 6885, San Antonio, TX 78209

West Virginia: John H. Smith, P.O. Box 5400, Charleston, WV 25361-0400

Western Kansas: Vernon Strickland, P.O. Box 2507, Salina, KS 67402

Western Louisiana: Robert J. Hargrove, Jr., P.O. Box 2031, Alexandria, LA 71309-2031

Western Massachusetts: ----, 37 Chestnut St., Springfield, MA 01103

Western Michigan: Edward L. Lee, 2600 Vincent Ave., Kalamazoo, MI 49008

Western New York: David C. Bowman, 1114 Delaware Ave., Buffalo, NY 14209

Western North Carolina: Robert H. Johnson, P.O. Box 369, Black Mountain, NC 28711
Wyoming: Bob Gordon Jones, 104 S. 4th St., Laramie, WY 82070
Am. Churches in Europe--Jurisdiction: Jeffery Rowthorn, The American Cathedral, 23 Avenue Georges V, 75008, Paris, France
Navajoland Area Mission: Steven Plummer, P.O. Box 720, Farmington, NM 87499

The Estonian Evangelical Lutheran Church

For information on the Estonian Evangelical Lutheran Church (EELC), please see the listing in Chapter 4, "Religious Bodies in Canada."

HEADQUARTERS

383 Jarvis St., Toronto, ON M5B 2C7

The Evangelical Church

The Evangelical Church was born June 4, 1968 in Portland, Ore., when 46 congregations and about 80 ministers, under the leadership of V. A. Ballantyne and George Millen, met in an organizing session. Within two weeks a group of about 20 churches and 30 ministers from the Evangelical United Brethren and Methodist churches in Montana and North Dakota became a part of the new church. Richard Kienitz and Robert Strutz were the superintendents.

Under the leadership of Superintendent Robert Trosen, the former Holiness Methodist Church became a part of the Evangelical Church in 1969, bringing its membership and a flourishing mission field in Bolivia. The Wesleyan Covenant Church joined in 1977, with its missionary work in Mexico, in Brownsville, Tex. and among the Navajos in New Mexico.

The Evangelical Church in Canada, where T. J. Jesske was superintendent, became an autonomous organization on June 5, 1970. In 1982, after years of discussions with the Evangelical Church of North America, a founding General Convention was held at Billings, Mont., where the two churches united. In 1993 the Canadian conference merged with the Canadian portion of the Missionary Church to form the Evangelical Missionary Church. The new group maintains close ties with their American counterparts. Currently there are nearly 150 U.S. congregations of the Evangelical Church.

The following guide the life, program and devotion of this church: faithful, biblical and sensible preaching and teaching of those truths proclaimed by scholars of the Wesleyan-Arminian viewpoint; an itinerant system which reckons with the rights of individuals and the desires of the congregation; local ownership of all church properties and assets.

The church is officially affiliated with the Christian Holiness Association, the National Association of Evangelicals, Wycliffe Bible Translators, World Gospel Mission and OMS International. The denomination has nearly 150 missionaries.

HEADQUARTERS

Media Contact, Gen. Supt., John F. Sills, 3000 Market St. NE, Ste. 528, Salem, OR 97301 Tel. (503)371-4818 Fax (503)364-5022

OFFICERS

Gen. Supt., Rev. John F. Sills
Dir. of Missions, Rev. Duane Erickson

PERIODICALS

Share; Church Leader's Newsletter

The Evangelical Church Alliance

What is known today as the Evangelical Church Alliance began in 1887 under the name "World's Faith Missionary Association. Years later, on March 28, 1928, a nonprofit organization was incorporated in the state of Missouri under the same name. In October, 1931, the name "Fundamental Ministerial Association" was chosen to reflect the organization's basis of unity.

On July 21, 1958, during the annual convention at Trinity Seminary and Bible College in Chicago, Illinois, a more comprehensive constitution was created and the name was changed to "The Evangelical Church Alliance."

The ECA licenses and ordains ministers who are qualified providing them with credentials from a recognized ecclesiastical body; provides training courses through the Bible Extension Institute for those who have not had the opportunity to attend Seminary or Bible School; provides Associate Membership for churches and Christian organizations giving opportunity for fellowship and networking with other evangelical ministers and organizations who share the same goals amd mission, while remaining autonomous; provides Regional Conventions and an Annual International Convention where members can find fellowship, encouragement and training; cooperates with churches in finding new pastors when they have openings.

ECA is an international, nonsectarian, Evangelical organization. There are currently 2,023 ordained and licensed members.

HEADQUARTERS

205 W. Broadway St., P.O. Box 9, Bradley, IL 60915 Tel. (815)937-0720 Fax (815)937-0001
Media Contact, Exec. Dir., Rev. George L. Miller

OFFICERS

Exec. Dir., Rev. George L. Miller
Pres., Dr. Sterling L. Cauble, Sunman Bible Church, P.O. Box 216, Sunman, IN 47041
1st Vice-Pres., Rev. Richard J. Sydnes, P.O. Box 355, Des Moines, IA 50302
2nd Vice-Pres., Dr. Allen A. Hammond, 1921 Ohio St., Bluefield, WV 24701

PERIODICAL

The Evangel

The Evangelical Congregational Church

This denomination had its beginning in the movement known as the Evangelical Association, organized by Jacob Albright in the early nineteenth century. A division which occurred in 1891 in the Evangelical Association resulted in the organization of the United Evangelical Church in 1894. An attempt to heal this division was made in 1922, but a portion of the United Evangelical Church was not satisfied with the plan of merger and remained apart, taking the above name in 1928. This denomination is Arminian in doctrine, evangelistic in spirit and Methodistic in church government, with congregational ownership of local church property.

Congregations are located from New Jersey to Illinois. A denominational center, a retirement village and a seminary are located in Myerstown, Pa. Three summer youth camps and four camp meetings continue evangelistic outreach. A worldwide missions movement includes conferences in North East India, Liberia, Mexico and Japan. The denomination is a member of National Association of Evangelicals.

HEADQUARTERS

Evangelical Congregational Church Center, 100 W. Park Ave., Myerstown, PA 17067 Tel. (717)-866-7581 Fax (717)866-7581

Media Contact, Bishop, Rev. Richard W. Kohl, Tel. (717)-866-7581

OFFICERS

Presiding Bishop, Rev. Richard W. Kohl

1st Vice-Chpsn., Rev. Jack Ward, 452 Jarvis Rd., Akron, OH 44319

Sec., Rev. Robert J. Stahl, RD 2, Box 1468, Schuylkill Haven, PA 17972

Asst. Sec.: Rev. Gregory Dimick, Hatfield, PA; Rev. Richard Reigle, Dixon, IL

Treas., Martha Metz

E.C.C. Retirement Village, Supt., Rev. Bruce Hill, Fax (717)866-6448

Evangelical School of Theology, Pres., Dr. Kirby N. Keller, Fax (717)866-4667

OTHER ORGANIZATIONS

Administrative Council: Chpsn., Bishop Richard W. Kohl; Vice-Chpsn., Rev. Keith Miller; Treas., Martha Metz

Div. of Evangelism & Spiritual Care, Chpsn., Bishop Richard W. Kohl

Div. of Church Ministries & Services, Chpsn., Rev. Keith R. Miller

Div. of Missions, Chpsn., Rev. John Ragsdale

Bd. of Pensions: Pres., Mr. William Kautz, New Cumberland, PA; Business Mgr., Dr. James D. Yoder, Myerstown, PA 17067

The Evangelical Covenant Church

The Evangelical Covenant Church has its roots in historic Christianity as it emerged during the Protestant Reformation, in the biblical instruction of the Lutheran State Church of Sweden and in the great spiritual awakenings of the 19th century.

The Covenant Church adheres to the affirmations of the Protestant Reformation regarding the Holy Scriptures, believing that the Old and the New Testament are the Word of God and the only perfect rule for faith, doctrine and conduct. It has traditionally valued the historic confessions of the Christian church, particularly the Apostles' Creed, while at the same time emphasizing the sovereignty of the Word over all creedal interpretations. It has especially cherished the pietistic restatement of the doctrine of justification by faith as basic to its dual task of evangelism and Christian nurture. It recognizes the New Testament emphasis upon personal faith in Jesus Christ as Savior and Lord, the reality of a fellowship of believers which acknowledges but transcends theological differences and the belief in baptism and the Lord's Supper as divinely ordained sacraments of the church.

While the denomination has traditionally practiced the baptism of infants, in conformity with its principle of freedom it has also recognized the practice of believer baptism. The principle of personal freedom, so highly esteemed by the Covenant, is to be distinguished from the individualism that disregards the centrality of the Word of God and the mutual responsibilities and disciplines of the spiritual community.

HEADQUARTERS

5101 N. Francisco Ave., Chicago, IL 60625 Tel. (312)784-3000 Fax (312)784-4366

Media Contact, Pres., Paul E. Larsen

OFFICERS

Pres., Dr. Paul E. Larsen

Vice-Pres., Rev. Timothy C. Ek

Sec., John R. Hunt

Treas., Dean A. Lundgren

ADMINISTRATIVE BOARDS

Bd. of Christian Educ. & Discipleship: Exec. Dir., Rev. Evelyn M. R. Johnson

Bd. of Church Growth & Evangelism: Exec. Dir., Dr. James E. Persson

Bd. of Covenant Women Ministries: Exec. Dir., Rev. Deirdre M. Banks

Bd. of Human Resources: Advisory Member, John R. Hunt

Bd. of the Ministry: Exec. Dir., Rev. Donald A. Njaa

Bd. of Pensions: Dir. of Pensions, John R. Hunt

Bd. of Publication: Exec. Dir., Dr. John E. Phelan, Jr.

Bd. of World Mission: Exec. Dir., Rev. Raymond L. Dahlberg

Bd. of Benevolence: Pres. of Covenant Benevolent Institutions, Rolland S. Carlson, 5145 N. California Ave., Chicago, IL 60625

North Park College & Theological Sem.: Pres., Dr. David G. Horner, 3225 W. Foster Ave., Chicago, IL 60625

SERVICE ORGANIZATIONS

National Covenant Properties: Pres., David W. Johnson, 5101 N. Francisco, Chicago, IL 60625 Tel. (312)784-3000

Covenant Trust Company: Pres., Gilman G. Robinson, 5101 N. Francisco, Chicago, IL 60625 Tel. (312)784-9911

REGIONAL CONFERENCES OF THE E.C.C.

Central Conference: Supt., Herbert M. Freedholm, 3319 W. Foster Ave., Chicago, IL 60625 Tel. (312)267-3060

East Coast Conference: Supt., George B. Elia, Missionary Rd., Cromwell, CT 06416 Tel. (203)-635-2691

Great Lakes Conference: Supt., David S. Dahlberg, 70 W. Streetsboro St., P.O. Box 728, Hudson, OH 44236 Tel. (216)655-9345

Midwest Conference: Supt., Kenneth P. Carlson, 15774 Q St., Omaha, NE 68135 Tel. (402)895-6997

North Pacific Conference: Supt., Glenn R. Palmberg, 925 116th Ave. NE, # 221, Bellevue, WA 98004 Tel. (206)451-7434

Northwest Conference: Supt., Paul Erickson, 4721 E. 31st St., Minneapolis, MN 55406 Tel. (612)-721-4893

Pacific Southwest Conference: Supt., John D. Notehelfer, 2120 Foothill Blvd., #215, LaVerne, CA 91750 Tel. (909)596-6790

Southeast Conference: Supt., Kurt A. Miericke, 11929 E. Colonial Dr., #146, Orlando, FL 32826 Tel. (407)381-5789

E.C.C. of Canada: Supt., Jerome K. Johnson, 630 Westchester Rd., Strathmore, AB T1P 1H8 Tel. (403)934-6200

Midsouth Region: Exec. Dir., Gary B. Walter, 5101 N. Francisco, Chicago, IL 60625 Tel. (312)784-3000

E.C.C. of Alaska: Field Dir., Paul W. Wilson, P.O. Box 190729, Anchorage, AK 99519 Tel. (907)-562-8624

PERIODICALS

Covenant Companion; Covenant Quarterly; Covenant Home Altar

The Evangelical Free Church of America

In October 1884, 27 representatives from Swedish churches met in Boone, Iowa, to establish the Swedish Evangelical Free Church. In the fall of that same year, two Norwegian-Danish groups began worship and fellowship (in Boston and in Tacoma) and by 1912 had established the Norwegian-Danish Evangelical Free Church Association. These two denominations, representing 275 congregations, came together at a merger conference in 1950.

The Evangelical Free Church of America is an association of local, autonomous churches across the United States and Canada, blended together by common principles, policies and practices. A 12-point statement addresses the major doctrines but also provides for differences of understanding on minor issues of faith and practice.

Overseas outreach includes 500 missionaries serving in 31 countries.

HEADQUARTERS

901 East 78th St., Minneapolis, MN 55420-1300 Tel. (612)854-1300 Fax (612)853-8488

Media Contact, Exec. Dir. of Ministry Advancement, Mr. Timothy Addington

OFFICERS

Pres., Dr. Paul Cedar

Exec. Vice-Pres., Rev. William Hamel

Moderator, Mr. Ronald Aucutt, 3417 Silver Maple Pl., Falls Church, VA 22042

Vice-Moderator, Rev. Mark J. Wold, 41827 Higgins Way, Fremont, CA 94539

Sec., Dr. Roland Peterson, 235 Craigbrook Way, NE, Fridley, MN 55432

Vice-Sec., Rev. William S. Wick, 92 South Main, Northfield, VT 05663

Chief Fin. Ofc., Mr. Robert Peterson, 901 E. 78th St., Minneapolis, MN 55420-1300

Exec. Dir., Evangelical Free Church Mission, Dr. Ben Swatsky

Exec. Dir. of Mission USA, Rev. Bill Hull

PERIODICALS

Evangelical Beacon; Pursuit

Evangelical Friends International--North America Region

The organization restructured from Evangelical Friends Alliance in 1990 to become internationalized for the benefit of its world-wide contacts. The North America Region continues to function within the United States as EFA formerly did. The organization represents one corporate step of denominational unity, brought about as a result of several movements of spiritual renewal within the Society of Friends. These movements are: (1) the general evangelical renewal within Christianity, (2) the new scholarly recognition of the evangelical nature of 17th-century Quakerism, and (3) EFA, which was formed in 1965.

The EFA is conservative in theology and makes use of local pastors. Sunday morning worship includes singing, Scripture reading, a period of open worship and a sermon by the pastor.

HEADQUARTERS

5350 Broadmoor Cr. NW, Canton, OH 44709 Tel. (216)493-1660 Fax (216)493-0852

Media Contact, Regional Dir., Dr. John P. Williams, Jr.

YEARLY MEETINGS

Evangelical Friends Church, Eastern Region, Wayne Ickes, 5350 Broadmoor Cir., N.W., Canton, OH 44709 Tel. (216)493-1660 Fax (216)-493-0852

Rocky Mountain YM, John Brawner, 3350 Reed St., Wheat Ridge, CO 80033 Tel. (303)238-5200 Fax (303)766-9609

Mid-America YM, Roscoe Townsend, 2018 Maple, Wichita, KS 67213 Tel. (316)267-0391 Fax (316)263-1092

Northwest YM, Mark Ankeny, 200 N. Meridian St., Newberg, OR 97132 Tel. (503)538-9419 Fax (503)538-7033

Alaska YM, Robert Sheldon, P.O. Box 687, Kotebue, AK 99752 Tel. (907)442-3906

PERIODICAL

Friends Voice

Evangelical Lutheran Church in America

The Evangelical Lutheran Church in America (ELCA) was organized April 30-May 3, 1987, in Columbus, Ohio, bringing together the 2.3 million-member American Lutheran Church, the 2.9 million-member Lutheran Church in America, and the 100,000-member Association of Evangelical Lutheran Churches.

The ELCA is, through its predecessors, the oldest of the major U.S. Lutheran churches. In the mid-17th century, a Dutch Lutheran congregation was formed in New Amsterdam (now New York). Other early congregations were begun by German and Scandinavian immigrants to Delaware, Pennsylvania, New York and the Carolinas.

The first Lutheran association of congregations, the Pennsylvania Ministerium, was organized in 1748 under Henry Melchior Muhlenberg. Numerous Lutheran organizations were formed as immigration continued and the United States grew.

In 1960, the American Lutheran Church (ALC) was created through a merger of an earlier American Lutheran Church, formed in 1930, the Evangelical Lutheran Church, begun in 1917, and the United Evangelical Lutheran Church in America. In 1963 the Lutheran Free Church merged with the ALC.

In 1962, the Lutheran Church in America (LCA) was formed by a merger of the United Lutheran Church, formed in 1918, with the Augustana Lutheran Church, begun in 1860, the American Evangelical Lutheran Church, founded in 1872, and the Finnish Lutheran Church or Suomi Synod, founded in 1891.

The Association of Evangelical Lutheran Churches arose in 1976 from a doctrinal split with the Lutheran Church-Missouri Synod.

The ELCA, through its predecessor church bodies, was a founding member of the Lutheran World Federation, the World Council of Churches, and the National Council of the Churches of Christ in the USA.

The church is divided into 65 geographical areas or synods. These 65 synods are grouped into nine regions for mission, joint programs and service.

HEADQUARTERS

8765 W. Higgins Rd., Chicago, IL 60631 Tel. (312)380-2700

Media Contact, Dir. for News, Ann E. Haffen, Tel. (312)380-2957 Fax (312)380-1465

OFFICERS

Bishop, The Rev. Dr. H. George Anderson
Sec., The Rev. Dr. Lowell G. Almen
Treas., Richard L. McAuliffe
Vice-Pres., Kathy J. Magnus
Exec. for Admn., Rev. Dr. Robert N. Bacher
Office of the Bishop: Exec. Asst. for Federal Chaplaincies, Rev. Lloyd W. Lyngdal; Exec. Assts., Lita B. Johnson

DIVISIONS

Div. for Congregational Min.: Co-Exec. Dir., Rev. Mark R. Moller-Gunderson; Co-Exec. Dir., Ms. M. Wyvetta Bullock; Bd. Chpsn., Richard Moe; Lutheran Youth Organization, Pres., Vance Robbins

Div. for Higher Educ. & Schools: Exec. Dir., Rev. Dr. W. Robert Sorensen; Bd. Chpsn., Ms. Mary Ann Shealy

Div. for Global Mission: Exec. Dir., Rev. Bonnie L. Jensen; Bd. Chpsn., Rev. Nancy Maeker

Div. for Ministry: Exec. Dir., Rev. Dr. Joseph M. Wagner; Bd. Chpsn., Dr. Nelvin Vos

Div. for Outreach: Exec. Dir., Rev. Dr. Malcolm L. Minnick, Jr.; Bd. Chpsn., Rev. Gary A. Marshall

Div. for Church in Society: Exec. Dir., Rev. Charles S. Miller; Chpsn., Ingrid Christiansen

COMMISSIONS

Comm. for Multicultural Ministries: Exec. Dir., Rev. Fred E.N. Rajan; Chpsn., Rev. W. Arthur Lewis

Comm. for Women: Exec. Dir., Joanne Chadwick; Chpsn., Rev. Ann Tiemeyer

CHURCHWIDE UNITS

Conference of Bishops: Asst. to the Bishop, Rev. Michael L. Cooper-White; Chpsn., Rev. Dr. Kenneth H. Sauer

ELCA Foundation: Exec. Dir., Rev. Dr. Harvey A. Stegemoeller

ELCA Publishing House: Exec. Dir., Rev. Marvin L. Roloff; Bd. Chpsn., Rev. Alan T. Seagren

ELCA Bd. of Pensions: Exec. Dir., John G. Kapanke; Bd. Chpsn, Ralph J. Eckert

Women of the ELCA: Exec. Dir., Charlotte E. Fiechter; Bd. Chpsn., Janet Peterson

DEPARTMENTS

Dept. for Communication, Dir., Rev. Eric C. Shafer

Dept. for Ecumenical Affairs, Int. Dir., Rev. Daniel F. Martensen

Dept. for Human Resources, Dr., Rev. A. C. Stein

Dept. for Research & Evaluation, Dir., Kenneth W. Inskeep

Dept. for Synodical Relations, Dir., Rev. Michael L. Cooper-White

SYNODICAL BISHOPS

Region 1

Alaska, Rev. Donald D. Parsons, 1847 W. Northern Lights Blvd., #2, Anchorage, AK 99517-3342 Tel. (907)272-8899

Northwest Washington, Rev. Donald H. Maier, 5519 Pinney Ave. N, Seattle, WA 98103-5899 Tel. (206)783-9292

Southwestern Washington, Rev. David C. Wold, 420 121st St., S., Tacoma, WA 98444-5218 Tel. (206)535-8300

Eastern Washington-Idaho, Rev. Robert M. Keller, 314 South Spruce St., Ste. A, Spokane, WA 99204-1098 Tel. (509)838-9871

Oregon, Rev. Paul R. Swanson, 2801 N. Gantenbein Ave., Portland, OR 97227-1674 Tel. (503)-413-4191

Montana, Rev. Dr. Mark R. Ramseth, 2415 13th Ave. S., Great Falls, MT 59405-5199 Tel. (406)-453-1461

Regional Coord., Ronald L. Coen, Region 1, 766-B John St., Seattle, WA 98109-5186 Tel. (206)-624-0093

Region 2

Sierra Pacific, Rev. Robert W. Mattheis, 401 Roland Way, #215, Oakland, CA 94621-2011 Tel. (510)430-0500

Southern California (West), Bishop, Rev. Paul W. Egertson, 1340 S. Bonnie Brae St., Los Angeles, CA 90006-5416 Tel. (213)387-8183

Pacifica, Rev. Robert L. Miller, 23655 Via Del Rio, Ste. B, Yorba Linda, CA 92687-2718 Tel. (714)-692-2791

Grand Canyon, Rev. Dr. Howard E. Wennes, 4423 N. 24th St., Ste. 400, Phoenix, AZ 85016-5544 Tel. (602)957-3223

Rocky Mountain, Rev. Allan C. Bjornberg, 7000 Broadway Ofc. Bldg., Ste. 401, 7000 N. Broadway, Denver, CO 80221-2907 Tel. (303)427-7553

Region 2, Admin. ELCA(part-time), Ms. Beverly Anderson, 18829 Grandview Dr., Sun City West, AZ 85375 Tel. (602)214-9779

Region 3

Western North Dakota, Rev. Robert D. Lynne, 721 Memorial Way, P.O. Box 370, Bismarck, ND 58502-3070 Tel. (701)223-5312

Eastern North Dakota, Rev. Richard J. Foss, 1703 32nd Ave., S., Fargo, ND 58103-5936 Tel. (701)232-3381

South Dakota, Rev. Andrea DeGroot-Nesdahl, Augustana College, Sioux Falls, SD 57197-0001 Tel. (605)336-4011

Northwestern Minnesota, Rev. Arlen D. Hermodson, Concordia College, Moorhead, MN 56562-0001 Tel. (218)299-3019

Northeastern Minnesota, Rev. Roger L. Munson, 3900 London Rd., Duluth, MN 55804-2241 Tel. (218)525-1947

Southwestern Minnesota, Rev. Stanley N. Olson, 175 E. Bridge St., P.O. Box 277, Redwood Falls, MN 56283-0277 Tel. (507)637-3904

Minneapolis Area, Rev. David W. Olson, 122 W. Franklin Ave., Rm. 600, Minneapolis, MN 55404-2474 Tel. (612)870-3610

Saint Paul Area, Rev. Mark S. Hanson, 105 W. University Ave., St. Paul, MN 55103-2094 Tel. (612)224-4313

Southeastern Minnesota, Rev. Glenn W. Nycklemoe, Assisi Heights, 1001-14 St. NW, P.O. Box 4900, Rochester, MN 55903-4900 Tel. (507)280-9457

Regional Coord., Rev. Craig A Boehlke, Region 3, Bockman Hall, 2481 Como Ave., W. St. Paul, MN 55108 Tel. (612)649-0454

Region 4

Nebraska, Rev. Dr. Richard N. Jessen, 4980 S. 118th St., Ste. D, Omaha, NE 68137-2220 Tel. (402)896-5311

Central States, Rev. Dr. Charles H. Maahs, 6400 Glenwood, Ste. 210, Shawnee Mission, KS 66202-4021 Tel. (913)362-0733

Arkansas-Oklahoma, Rev. Floyd M. Schoenhals, 6911 S. 66th E. Ave., Ste. 200, Tulsa, OK 74133-1748 Tel. (918)492-4288

Northern Texas-Northern Louisiana, Rev. Mark B. Herbener, 1230 Riverbend Dr., Ste. 105, P.O. Box 560587, Dallas, TX 75356-0587 Tel. (214)-637-6865

Southwestern Texas, Rev. James E. Bennet, 8918 Tesoro Dr., Ste. 109, P.O. Box 171270, San Antonio, TX 78217-8270 Tel. (210)824-0068

Texas-Louisiana Gulf Coast, Rev. Paul J. Blom, 12707 N. Freeway, #580, Houston, TX 77060-1239 Tel. (713)873-5665

Regional Coord., Rev. Richard N. Jessen, Region 4, 4980 S. 118th St., Ste. D, Omaha, NE 68137-2220 Tel. (402)896-5311

Region 5

Metropolitan Chicago, Rev. Kenneth R. Olson, 18 S. Michigan Ave., Rm. 605, Chicago, IL 60603-3283 Tel. (312)346-3150

Northern Illinois, Rev. Ronald K. Hasley, 103 W. State St., Rockford, IL 61101-1105 Tel. (815)-964-9934

Central/Southern Illinois, Rev. Alton Zenker, 524 S. Fifth St., Springfield, IL 62701-1822 Tel. (217)753-7915

Southeastern Iowa, Rev. Dr. Paul M. Werger, 2635 Northgate Dr., P.O. Box 3167, Iowa City, IA 52244-3167 Tel. (319)388-1273

Western Iowa, Rev. Curtis H. Miller, 318 E. Fifth St., P.O. Box 1145, Storm Lake, IA 50588-2312 Tel. (712)732-4968

Northeastern Iowa, Rev. Steven L. Ullestad, 201-20th St. SW, P.O. Box 804, Waverly, IA 50677-0804 Tel. (319)352-1414

Northern Great Lakes, Rev. Dale R. Skogman, 1029 N. Third St., Marquette, MI 49855-3588 Tel. (906)228-2300

Northwest Synod of Wisconsin, Rev. Robert D. Berg, 12 W. Marshall St., P.O. Box 730, Rice Lake, WI 54868-0730 Tel. (715)234-3373

East-Central Synod of Wisconsin, Rev. John C. Beem, 16 Tri-Park Way, Appleton, WI 54914-1658 Tel. (414)734-5381

Greater Milwaukee, Rev. Peter Rogness, 1212 S. Layton Blvd., Milwaukee, WI 53215-1653 Tel. (414)671-1212

South-Central Synod of Wisconsin, Rev. Dr. Jon S. Enslin, 2705 Packers Ave., Madison, WI 53704-3085 Tel. (608)249-4848

La Crosse Area, Rev. April Ulring Larson, 3462 Losey Blvd. S., La Crosse, WI 54601-7217 Tel. (608)788-5000

Regional Coord., Rev. Carl R. Evenson, Region 5, 333 Wartburg Pl., Dubuque, IA 52003-7797 Tel. (319)589-0312

Region 6

Southeast Michigan, Rev. J. Philip Wahl, 218 Fisher Bldg., 3011 W. Grand Blvd., Detroit, MI 48202-3099 Tel. (313)875-1881

North/West Lower Michigan, Rev. Gary L. Hansen, 801 S. Waverly Rd., Ste. 201, Lansing, MI 48917-4254 Tel. (517)321-5066

Indiana-Kentucky, Rev. Dr. Ralph A. Kempski, 911 E. 86th St., Ste. 200, Indianapolis, IN 46240-1840 Tel. (317)253-3522

Northwestern Ohio, Rev. James A. Rave, 621 Bright Rd., Findlay, OH 45840-6987 Tel. (419)-423-3664

Northeastern Ohio, Rev. Marcus J. Miller, 282 W. Bowery, 3rd Fl., Akron, OH 44307-2598 Tel. (216)253-1500

Southern Ohio, Rev. Dr. Kenneth H. Sauer, 57 E. Main St., Columbus, OH 43215-7102 Tel. (614)-464-3532

Regional Coord., Rev. Hermann J. Kuhlmann, 6100 Channingway Blvd., Ste. 406, Columbus, OH 43232-2910 Tel. (614)759-9090

Region 7

New Jersey, Rev. E. Leroy Riley, Jr., 1930 State Hwy. 33, Trenton, NJ 08690-1714 Tel. (609)-586-6800

New England, Rev. Robert L. Isaksen, 20 Upland St., Worcester, MA 01607-1624 Tel. (508)791-1530

Metropolitan New York, Rev. James E. Sudbrock, 390 Park Ave., S., 7th Floor, New York, NY 10016-8803 Tel. (212)532-5369

Upstate New York, Rev. Dr. Lee M. Miller, 3049 E. Genesee St., Syracuse, NY 13224-1699 Tel. (315)446-2502

Northeastern Pennsylvania, Rev. Dr. Harold S. Weiss, 4865 Hamilton Blvd., Wescosville, PA 18106-9705 Tel. (610)395-6891

Southeastern Pennsylvania, Rev. Roy G. Almquist, 4700 Wissahickon Ave., Philadelphia, PA 19144-4248 Tel. (215)438-0600

Slovak Zion, Rev. Juan Cobrda, 8340 N. Oleander, Niles, IL 60648-2552 Tel. (708)965-2475

Regional Coord., Rev. Richard H. Summy, Region 7, Hagan Hall, 7301 Germantown Ave., Philadelphia, PA 19119-1794 Tel. (215)248-4616

Region 8

Northwestern Pennsylvania, Rev. Paul E. Spring, Rte. 257, Salina Rd., P.O. Box 338, Seneca, PA 16346-0338 Tel. (814)677-5706

Southwestern Pennsylvania, Rev. Donald J. McCoid, 9625 Perry Hwy., Pittsburgh, PA 15237-5590 Tel. (412)367-8222

Allegheny, Rev. Gregory R. Pile, 701 Quail Ave., Altoona, PA 16602-3010 Tel. (814)942-1042

Lower Susquehanna, Rev. Dr. Guy S. Edmiston, Jr., 900 S. Arlington Ave., Rm. 208, Harrisburg, PA 17109-5031 Tel. (717)652-1852

Upper Susquehanna, Rev. Dr. A. Donald Main, Rt. 192 & Reitz Blvd., P.O. Box 36, Lewisburg, PA 17837-0036 Tel. (717)524-9778

Delaware-Maryland, Rev. Dr. George P. Mocko, 7604 York Rd., Baltimore, MD 21204-7570 Tel. (410)825-9520

Metropolitan Washington, D.C., Rev. Theodore F. Schneider, 224 E. Capitol St., Washington, DC 20003-1036 Tel. (202)543-8610

West Virginia-Western Maryland, Rev. L. Alexander Black, The Atrium, Ste. 100, 503 Morgantown Avenue, Fairmont, WV 26554-4374 Tel. (304)363-4030

Regional Coord., Dir., Rev. Phillip C. Huber, Lutheran Theological Sem. at Gettysburg, 61 NW Confederate Ave., Gettysburg, PA 17325-1795 Tel. (717)334-6286

Region 9

Virginia, Rev. Richard F. Bansemer, Roanoke College, Bittle Hall, P.O. Drawer 70, Salem, VA 24153-3794 Tel. (540)389-1000

North Carolina, Rev. Dr. Mark W. Menees, 1988 Lutheran Synod Dr., Salisbury, NC 28144-4480 Tel. (704)633-4861

South Carolina, Rev. Dr. James S. Aull, 1003 Richland St., P.O. Box 43, Columbia, SC 29202-0043 Tel. (803)765-0590

Southeastern, Rev. Ronald B. Warren, 756 W. Peachtree St. NW, Atlanta, GA 30308-1188 Tel. (404)873-1977

Florida-Bahamas, Rev. William B. Trexler, 3838 W. Cypress St., Tampa, FL 33607-4897 Tel. (813)876-7660

Caribbean, Rev. Calle Constitucion, Puerto Nuevo, PR 00920 Tel. (809)273-8300

Regional Coord., Dr. Dorothy L. Jeffcoat, Region 9, 4201 N. Main St., Columbia, SC 29203 Tel. (803)754-2879

PERIODICALS

The Lutheran; Currents in Theology and Mission

Evangelical Lutheran Synod

The Evangelical Lutheran Synod had its beginning among the Norwegian settlers who brought with them their Lutheran heritage. The Synod was organized in 1853. It was reorganized in 1918 by those who desired to adhere to the synod's principles not only in word but also in deed.

The Synod owns and operates Bethany Lutheran College and Bethany Lutheran Theological Seminary. It has congregations in 18 states and maintains foreign missions in Peru, Chile, the Czech Republic and Ukraine. It operates a seminary in Lima, Peru.

HEADQUARTERS

447 N. Division St., Mankato, MN 56001

Media Contact, Pres., Rev. George Orvick, Tel. (507)386-5426 Fax (507)386-5376

OFFICERS

Pres., Rev. George Orvick, 447 Division St., Mankato, MN 56001 Tel. (507)386-5356 Fax (507)386-5376

Sec., Rev. Alf Merseth, 106 13th St. S., Northwood, IA 50459

Treas., Mr. LeRoy W. Meyer, 1038 S. Lewis Ave., Lombard, IL 60148

OTHER ORGANIZATIONS

Lutheran Synod Book Co., Bethany Lutheran College, Mankato, MN 56001

PERIODICALS

Lutheran Sentinel; Lutheran Synod Quarterly

Evangelical Mennonite Church

The Evangelical Mennonite Church is an American denomination in the European free church tradition, tracing its heritage to the Reformation period of the 16th century. The Swiss Brethren of that time believed that salvation could come only by repentance for sins and faith in Jesus Christ; that baptism was only for believers; and that the church should be separate from controls of the state. Their enemies called them Anabaptists, since they insisted on rebaptizing believers who had been baptized as infants. As the Anabaptist movement spread to other countries, Menno Simons became its principal leader. In time his followers were called Mennonites.

In 1693 a Mennonite minister, Jacob Amman, insisted that the church should adopt a more conservative position on dress and style of living and should more rigidly enforce the "ban" -- the church's method of disciplining disobedient members. Amman's insistence finally resulted in a division within the South German Mennonite groups; his followers became known as the Amish.

Migrations to America, involving both Mennonites and Amish, took place in the 1700s and 1800s, for both religious and economic reasons.

The Evangelical Mennonite Church was formed in 1866 out of a spiritual awakening among the Amish in Indiana. It was first known as the Egly Amish, after its founder Bishop Henry Egly. Bishop Egly emphasized regeneration, separation and nonconformity to the world. His willingness to rebaptize anyone who had been baptized without repentance created a split in his church, prompting him to gather a new congregation in 1866. The conference, which has met annually since 1895, united a number of other congregations of like mind. This group became The Defenseless Mennonite Church in 1898 and has been known as the Evangelical Mennonite Church since 1948.

HEADQUARTERS

1420 Kerrway Ct., Fort Wayne, IN 46805 Tel. (219)423-3649 Fax (219)420-1905

Media Contact, Admn. Asst., Diane Rodocker

OFFICERS

Pres., Rev. Donald W. Roth

Chpsn., Rev. Roger Andrews, 11275 Eckel Junction Rd., Perrysburg, OH 43551

Vice-Chpsn., Rev. Scott Wagoner, Box 160, Grabill, IN 46741

Sec., Jerry Lugbill, 320 Short-Buehrer Rd., Archbold, OH 43502

Treas., Alan L. Rupp, 5724 Spring Oak Ct., Ft. Wayne, IN 46845

PERIODICAL

EMC Today

Evangelical Methodist Church

The Evangelical Methodist Church was organized in 1946 at Memphis, Tenn., largely as a movement of people who opposed modern liberalism and wished for a return to the historic Wesleyan position. In 1960, it merged with the Evangel Church (formerly Evangelistic Tabernacles) and with the People's Methodist Church in 1962.

HEADQUARTERS

P.O. Box 17070, Indianapolis, IN 46217 Tel. (317)398-0141 Fax (317)398-0143

Media Contact, Gen. Conf. Sec.-Treas., Vernon W. Perkins

OFFICERS

Gen. Supt., Rev. Jack W. Wease

Gen. Conf. Sec.-Treas., Rev. Vernon W. Perkins

Evangelical Presbyterian Church

The Evangelical Presbyterian Church (EPC), established in March 1981, is a conservative denomination of 9 geographic presbyteries -- 8 in the United States and one in Argentina. From its inception with 12 churches, the EPC has grown to 180 churches with a membership of over 56,000.

Planted firmly within the historic Reformed tradition, evangelical in spirit, the EPC places high priority on church planting and development along with world missions. Fifty-six missionaries serve the church's mission.

Based on the truth of Scripture and adhering to the Westminster Confession of Faith plus its Book of Order, the denomination is committed to the "essentials of the faith." The historic motto "In essentials, unity; in nonessentials, liberty; in all things charity" catches the irenic spirit of the EPC, along with the Ephesians theme, "truth in love."

The Evangelical Presbyterian Church is a member of the World Alliance of Reformed Churches, National Association of Evangelicals, World Evangelical Fellowship and the Evangelical Council for Financial Accountability. Observers annually attend the North American Presbyterian and Reformed Council (NAPARC).

HEADQUARTERS

Office of the General Assembly, 29140 Buckingham Ave., Ste. 5, Livonia, MI 48154 Tel. (313)-261-2001 Fax (313)261-3282

Media Contact, Stated Clk., Dr. L. Edward Davis, 29140 Buckingham Ave., Ste. 5, Livonia, MI 48154 Tel. (313)261-2001 Fax (313)261-3282

OFFICERS

Mod., Rev. Wayne Hoffman, 2700 Colby Woods Dr., Des Moines, IA 50322

Administration Committee, Chmn., Mr. William Johns, 103 Brentwood, Rome, GA 30165

Stated Clk., Dr. L. Edward Davis

PERMANENT COMMITTEES

Committee on Admn., Chmn., Mr. William Johns, 103 Brentwood, Rome, GA 30165

Committee on National Outreach, Chmn., Rev. Ed G. Davis, Christ Fellowship Church, P.O. Box 272592, Fort Collins, CO 80527

Committee on World Outreach, Chmn., Mr. Vern Porter, Faith Presbyterian Church, 11373 E. Alameda Ave., Aurora, CO 80012

Committee on Ministerial Vocation, Chmn., Dr. William Moore, Trinity Presbyterian Church, 10101 W. Ann Arbor Rd., Plymouth, MI 48170

Comm. on Christian Educ. & Publ., Chmn., Rev. Mark Hudson, Knox Presbyterian Church, 25700 Crocker Blvd., Harrison Township, MI 48045

Committee on Women's Ministries, Chmn., Ms. Susan Nash, Second Presbyterian Church, 4055 Poplar Ave., Memphis, TN 38111

Committee on Theology, Chmn., Dr. James Russell, 3228 Franklin Ave., Laurel, MI 39441

Committee on Youth Ministries, Chmn., Rev. Richard Stauffer, Perrow Presbyterian Church, 5345 Big Tyler Rd., Cross Lanes, WV 25313

PRESBYTERIES

Central South, Stated Clk., Rev. Dennis Flach

East, Stated Clk., Mr. Gerald Moser, 20660 Plum Creek Ct., Gaithersburg, MD 20882

Florida, Stated Clk., Rev. Robert Garment, Trinity EPC, 5150 Oleander, Ft. Pierce, FL 34982

Mid-America, Stated Clk., Mr. Kenneth Breckner, 7500 Wydown Blvd., St. Louis, MO 64105

Mid-Atlantic, Stated Clk., Mr. Lew Fischer, 3164 Golf Colony Dr., Salem, VA 24153

Fellowship of Evangelical Bible Churches

Formerly known as Evangelical Mennonite Brethren, this body emanates from the Russian immigration of Mennonites into the United States, 1873-74. Established with the emphasis on true repentance, conversion and a committed life to Jesus as Savior and Lord, the conference was founded in 1889 under the leadership of Isaac Peters and Aaron Wall. The founding churches were located in Mountain Lake, Minn., and in Henderson and Janzen, Neb. The conference has since grown to a fellowship of 40 churches with approximately 4,400 members in Argentina, Canada, Paraguay and the United States.

Foreign missions have been a vital ingredient of the total ministry. Today missions constitute about 35 percent of the total annual budget, with one missionary for every 30 members in the home churches. The conference does not develop and administer foreign mission fields of its own, but actively participates with existing evangelical "faith" mission societies. The conference has representation on several mission boards and has missionaries serving under approximately 41 different agencies around the world.

The church is holding fast to the inerrancy of Scripture, the Deity of Christ and the need for spiritual regeneration of man from his sinful natural state by faith in the death, burial and resurrection of Jesus Christ as payment for sin. Members look forward to the imminent return of Jesus Christ and retain a sense of urgency to share the gospel with those who have never heard of God's redeeming love.

HEADQUARTERS

5800 S. 14th St., Omaha, NE 68107 Tel. (402)731-4780 Fax (402)731-1173

Admn., Robert L. Frey, 5800 S. 14th St., Omaha, NE 68107 Tel. (402)731-4780 Fax (402)731-1173

OFFICERS

Pres., Rev. Melvin Epp, 322 Laurier Dr., Swift Current, SK S9H 1L4 Tel. (306)773-6845

Vice-Pres., Rev. C. Dwain Holsppple, 3006 Eastview St., Abbotsford, BC V2S 6W3

Rec. Sec., Rev. Al Tschiegg, 10655 Orrs Corner Rd., Rickreall, OR 97371

Admn., Robert L. Frey, 5800 S. 14th, Omaha, NE 68107

Commission on Churches, Chpsn., Rev. Bob Vogt, Box 339, Waldheim, SK S0K 4R0

Commission on Missions, Chpsn., Rev. Paul Boeker, 22018 22 Rd., Meade, KS 67864-9506

Commission of Trustees, Chpsn., Mr. Larry Mierau, 2666 Cottonwood St., Abbotsford, BC V4X 1K5

Commission on Educ. & Publ., Chpsn., Rev. Ben Watson, 5800 S. 14th St., Apt. 3, Omaha, NE 68107

Commission on Church Planting, Chpsn., Mr. Dennis Goertzen, R R 1, Box 157, Henderson, NE 68371

Ministries Coord., Chpsn., Rev. Harvey Schultz, P.O. Box 8, Waldheim, SK S0K 4R0

PERIODICAL

Gospel Tidings

Fellowship of Fundamental Bible Churches

This body was called the Bible Protestant Church until 1985. The FFBC is a fellowship of fundamental Bible-believing local autonomous churches which believe in an inerrant and infallible Bible. The FFBC is dispensational as related to the study of the Scriptures, espouses the pre-Tribulation Rapture and is premillenial. It is evangelistic and missions-oriented. It regards itself as separatistic in areas of personal life and ecclesiastical association and believes that baptism by immersion most adequately symbolizes the truth of death and resurrection with Christ.

The Fellowship of Fundamental Bible Churches relates historically to the Eastern Conference of the Methodist Protestant Church, which changed its name to Bible Protestant Church at the 2nd Annual Session, held in Westville, N.J., Sept. 26-30, 1940.

HEADQUARTERS

P.O. Box 43, Glassboro, NJ 08028

Media Contact, Natl. Rep., Rev. Harold E. Haines, Tel. (609)881-5516

OFFICERS

Pres., Rev. Gary Myers, P.O. Box 191, Meshoppen, PA 18630 Tel. (717)833-2294

Vice-Pres., Rev. Edmund Cotton, P.O. Box 31, Cassville, PA 16623 Tel. (814)448-3394

Sec., Rev. Ron Whitehead, P.O. Box 151, Penns Grove, NJ 08069 Tel. (609)299-3307

Treas., Mr. William Rainey, RR 1, Box 302, Monroeville, NJ 08343 Tel. (609)881-4790

Natl. Rep., Rev. Harold Haines, Tel. (609)881-5516

Fellowship of Grace Brethren Churches

A division occurred in the Church of the Brethren in 1882 on the question of the legislative authority of the annual meeting. It resulted in the establishment of the Brethren Church under a legal charter requiring congregational government. This body divided in 1939 with the Grace Brethren establishing headquarters at Winona Lake, Ind., and the Brethren Church at Ashland, Ohio.

HEADQUARTERS

Media Contact, Fellowship Coord., Rev. Charles Ashman, P.O. Box 386, Winona Lake, IN 46590 Tel. (219)269-1269

OFFICERS

Mod., Steve Peters, 600 S. Main St., West Milton, OH 45383

Mod.-Elect, Wayne Hannah, 2519 Lochness Rd., Richmond, VA 23235

2nd Mod.-Elect, H. Don Rough, R.R.3 Box 135, Holsopple, PA 15935

Fellowship Coord., Charles Ashman, P.O. Box 386, Winona Lake, IN 46590 Tel. (219)267-5566

Sec., Greg Howell, 129 NW Second St., Goldendale, WA 98620

Treas., Steve Poppenfoose, R. 1, Box 425A, Warsaw, IN 46580

OTHER BOARDS

Grace Missions Intl., Exec. Dir., Rev. Tom Julien, P.O. Box 588, Winona Lake, IN 46590

Grace Brethren Home Missions, Exec. Dir., Larry Chamberlain, P.O. Box 587, Winona Lake, IN 46590

Grace Schools, Pres., Ronald E. Manahan, 200 Seminary Dr., Winona Lake, IN 46590 Tel. (210)372-5100

Brethren Missionary Herald Co., Pub. & Gen. Mgr., Jeffry Carroll, P.O. Box 544, Winona Lake, IN 46590

Women's Missionary Council, Pres., Mrs. Geneva Inman, 2244 Fernwood Dr., Colorado Springs, CO 80910

CE National, Exec. Dir., Rev. Ed Lewis, P.O. Box 365, Winona Lake, IN 46590

Natl. Fellowship of Grace Brethren Min., Pres., John Teevan, 1200 Kings Hwy., Winona Lake, IN 46590

Grace Brethren Navajo Ministries, Dir., Steve Galegor, Counselor, NM 87018

Grace Village Retirement Community, Exec. Dir., ----, P.O. Box 337, Winona Lake, IN 46590

PERIODICAL

Brethren Missionary Herald

Free Christian Zion Church of Christ

This church was organized in 1905 at Redemption, Ark., by a company of African-American ministers associated with various denominations. Its polity is in general accord with that of Methodist bodies.

HEADQUARTERS

1315 S. Hutchinson St., Nashville, AR 71852 Tel. (501)845-4933

Media Contact, Gen. Sec., Shirlie Cheatham

OFFICER

Chief Pastor, Willie Benson, Jr.

Free Methodist Church of North America

The Free Methodist Church was organized in 1860 in Western New York by ministers and laymen who had called the Methodist Episcopal Church to return to what they considered the original doctrines and lifestyle of Methodism. The issues included human freedom (anti-slavery), freedom and simplicity in worship, free seats so that the poor would not be discriminated against and freedom from secret oaths (societies) so the truth might be spoken freely at all times. The founders emphasized the teaching of the entire sanctification of life by means of grace through faith.

The denomination continues to be true to its founding principles. It communicates the gospel and its power to all people without discrimination through strong missionary, evangelistic and educational programs. Six colleges, a Bible college and numerous overseas schools train the youth of the church to serve in lay and ministerial roles.

Its members covenant to maintain simplicity in life, worship, daily devotion to Christ, responsible stewardship of time, talent and finance.

HEADQUARTERS

World Ministries Center: 770 N. High School Rd., Indianapolis, IN 46214 Tel. (317)244-3660 Fax (317)244-1247

Mailing Address, P.O. Box 535002, Indianapolis, IN 46253 Tel. (800)342-5531

Media Contact, Yearbook Ed., P.O. Box 535002, Indianapolis, IN 46253

OFFICERS

Bishops: Gerald E. Bates; David M. Foster; Robert Nxumalo; Noah Nzeyimana; Daniel Ward; Richard D. Snyder; Luis Uanela Nhaphale; Jim Tuan

Gen. Conf. Sec., Melvin J. Spencer

Admn. & Finance, Gen. Dir., Gary M. Kilgore

Christian Educ., Gen. Dir., Daniel L. Riemenschneider

Evangelism & Church Growth, Gen. Dir., Raymond W. Ellis

Free Methodist Publishing House, Gen. Dir., John E. Van Valin

Higher Education, Gen. Sec., Timothy M. Beuthin

Light & Life Magazine, Ed., Robert B. Haslam
Light & Life Men Intl., Exec. Dir., Lucien E. Behar
Free Methodist Foundation, Stanley B. Thompson
Women's Ministries Intl., Pres., Mrs. Carollyn Ellis
World Missions, Gen. Dir., M. Doane Bonney

PERIODICALS

Light and Life Magazine; Free Methodist World Mission People

Friends General Conference

Friends General Conference is an association of yearly meetings within the Religious Society of Friends, open to all Friends meetings which wish to be actively associated with its programs and services. It was organized in 1900, bringing together four associations, including the First-day School Conference (1868) and the Friends Union for Philanthropic Labor (1882).

Friends General Conference is primarily a service organization and has no authority over its constituent meetings. Its purpose is to nurture the Religious Society of Friends by developing and providing resources and opportunities for spiritual growth. A Central Committee, to which constituent yearly meetings name appointees approximately in proportion to membership, or its Executive Committee, is responsible for the direction of FGC's year-round services.

There are seven standing program committees: Advancement & Outreach, Christian & Interfaith Relations, Long Range Conference Planning, Ministry & Nurture, Publications & Distribution, Religious Education and Friends Meeting House Fund.

HEADQUARTERS

1216 Arch St., 2B, Philadelphia, PA 19107 Tel. (215)561-1700
Media Contact, Gen. Sec., Bruce Birchard

OFFICERS

Gen. Sec., Bruce Birchard
Clerk, Tyla Ann Burger
Treas., David Miller

YEARLY MEETINGS

Philadelphia, Martha Bryans, 1515 Cherry St., Philadelphia, PA 19102
Lake Erie, Damon Hickey, 208 W. University St., Wooster, OH 44691
*New England, Elizabeth Cazden, 901 Pleasant St., Worchester, MA 01602
*New York, George Rubin, 15 Rutherford Pl., New York, NY 10003
*Baltimore, Miriam Green, 17100 Quaker Ln., Sandy Spring, MD 20860
*Canadian, Elaine Bishop, 91A Fourth Ave., Ottawa, ON K1S 2L1
Illinois, Patricia Wixom, 359 Crown Pt., Columbia, MO 65203 Tel. (219)232-5729
Ohio Valley, Mike Fallahay, 4240 Cornelius Ave., Indianapolis, IN 46208
South Central, Marian Lockard, R.R. 3 Box 666, Hope, AR 71801
*Southeastern, Gay Howard, 1210 Powhattan Ave., Tampa, FL 33604
Northern, Jim Greenley, 1909 Vilas Ave., Madison, WI 53711 Tel. (608)251-0372
Piedmont FF, Ralph McCracken, 913 Ridgecrest Dr., Greensboro, NC 27410-3237 Tel. (919)292-8631
Southern Appalachian YM & Assoc., Janet Minshall, 701 E. Howard Ave., Decatur, GA 30030
Central Alaska, Jan Pohl, P.O. Box 22316, Juneau, AK 99802
* also affiliated with Friends United Meeting

Friends United Meeting

Friends United Meeting was organized in 1902 (the name was changed in 1963 from the Five Years Meeting of Friends) as a loose confederation of North American yearly meetings to facilitate a united Quaker witness in missions, peace work and Christian education.

Today Friends United Meeting is comprised of 16 member yearly meetings (10 North American plus Cuba, East Africa, East Africa Yearly Meeting (South), Elgon Religious Society of Friends, Nairobi, Jamaica and Canadian yearly meetings) representing about half the Friends in the world. FUM's current work includes programs of mission and service and congregational renewal. FUM publishes Christian education curriculum, books of Quaker history and religious thought and a magazine, Quaker Life.

HEADQUARTERS

101 Quaker Hill Dr., Richmond, IN 47374-1980 Tel. (317)962-7573 Fax (317)966-1293
Media Contact, Gen. Sec., Johan Maurer

OFFICERS

Presiding Clk., Miriam Brush
Treas., Ann Kendall
Gen. Sec., Johan Maurer

DEPARTMENTS

World Ministries Commission, Assoc. Sec., Bill Wagoner
Meeting Ministries Commission, Assoc. Sec., Mary Glenn Hadley
Quaker Hill Bookstore, Mgr., Dick Talbot
Friends United Press, Ed., Ardith Talbot

YEARLY MEETINGS

Nebraska, Allyson Bowen, R. R. 1, Box 88, Kingman, KS 67068
*New England, Margaret Wentworth, 281 Rabbit Rd., Durham, ME 04222 Tel. (203)928-6356
*New York, Steven Ross, 400 Sairs Ave. No. 1, Long Branch, NJ 07740
*Baltimore, Miriam Green, 316 Rossiter Ave., Baltimore, MD 21212
Iowa, Stan Bauer, 52473 Norwegian Church Rd., Lavalle, WI 53941
Western, Charles Heavilin, 7040 S. County Rd., 1050 E., Camby, IN 46113
North Carolina, Clifford Winslow, Rt.1, Box 324A, Belvidere, NC 27919
Indiana, Don Garner, 471 W 1125 S, Fairmont, IN 46928
Wilmington, Neil Snarr, 171 College St., Wilmington, OH 45177
*Canadian, Elaine Bishop, Box 5333, Peace River, AB T8S 1R9
*Southeastern, Gay Howard, 2705 Neuchatel, Tallahassee, FL 32303
* also affiliated with Friends Gen. Conference

PERIODICAL

Quaker Life

Full Gospel Assemblies International

The Full Gospel Assemblies International was founded in 1962 under the leadership of Dr. Charles Elwood Strauser. The roots of Full Gospel

Assemblies may be traced to 1947 with the beginning of the Full Gospel Church of Coatesville, Pennsylvania. As an Assemblies of God Pentecostal church, the Full Gospel Church of Coatesville was active in evangelization and educational ministries to the community. In service to the ministers and students of the Full Gospel Church ministries, the Full Gospel Trinity Ministerial Fellowship was formed in 1962, later changing name to Full Gospel Assemblies International.

Retaining its original doctrine and faith, Full Gospel Assemblies is trinitarian and believes in the Bible as God's infallible Word to all people, in baptism in the Holy Spirit according to Acts 2, in divine healing made possible by the sufferings of our Lord Jesus Christ and in the imminent return of Christ for those who love him.

The body of Full Gospel Assemblies is an evangelical missionary fellowship sponsoring ministry at home and abroad, composed of self governing ministries and churches. Congregations, affiliate ministries and clerical bodies are located throughout the United States and over 30 countries of the world.

HEADQUARTERS

P.O. Box 1230, Coatesville, PA 19320 Tel. (610)-857-2357

Media Contact, Simeon Strauser

OFFICERS

Pres., Dr. AnnaMae Strauser

Exec. Dir of Admn., Simeon Strauser

Exec. Dir. of Ministry, J. Victor Fisk

Exec. Dir. of Comm., Shirley Carozzolo

Exec. Sec., Betty Stewart

National Ministers Council & Trustees: Chpsn., Simeon Strauser, Sadsburyville, PA; Marilyn Allen, Colorado Springs, CO; Donald Campbell, Mt. Morris, PA; David Treat, Bloomington, IN; Carol Strauser, Parkesburg, PA; Paul Bryson, Gordonville, PA

PERIODICAL

Full Gospel Ministries Outreach Report

Full Gospel Fellowship of Churches and Ministers International

In the early 1960s a conviction grew in the hearts of many ministers that there should be closer fellowship between the people of God who believed in the apostolic ministry. At the same time, many independent churches were experiencing serious difficulties in receiving authority from the IRS to give governmentally accepted tax-exempt receipts for donations.

In September 1962 a group of ministers met in Dallas, Tex., to form a Fellowship to give expression to the essential unity of the Body of Christ under the leadership of the Holy Spirit--a unity that goes beyond individuals, churches or organizations. This was not a movement to build another denomination, but rather an effort to join ministers, churches and ministry organizations of like mind across denominational lines.

To provide opportunities for fellowship and to support the objectives and goals of local and national ministries: regional conventions and an annual international convention are held.

HEADQUARTERS

4325 W. Ledbetter Dr., Dallas, TX 75233 Tel. (214)339-1200 Fax (214)339-8790

Media Contact, Exec. Sec., Dr. Chester P. Jenkins

PERIODICAL

Fellowship Tidings

Fundamental Methodist Church, Inc.

This group traces its origin through the Methodist Protestant Church. It withdrew from The Methodist Church and organized on Aug. 27, 1942.

HEADQUARTERS

1034 N. Broadway, Springfield, MO 65802

Media Contact, Dist. Supt., Rev. Ronnie Howerton, 1952 Highway H, Monett, MO 65708 Tel. (417)235-3849

OFFICERS

Treas., Mr. Everett Etheridge, 3844 W. Dover, Springfield, MO 65802 Tel. (417)865-4438

Sec., Mrs. Betty Nicholson, Rt. 2, Box 397, Ash Grove, MO 65604 Tel. (417)672-2268

Dist. Supt., Rev. Ronnie Howerton, 1952 Highway H, Monett, MO 65708 Tel. (417)235-3849

General Assembly of the Korean Presbyterian Church in America

This body came into official existence in the United States in 1976 and is currently an ethnic church, using the Korean language.

HEADQUARTERS

P.O. Box 457, Morganville, NJ 07951 Tel. (908)-591-2771 Fax (908)591-2260

Media Contact, Gen. Sec., Rev. John Woo

General Association of General Baptists

Similar in doctrine to those General Baptists organized in England in the 17th century, the first General Baptist churches were organized on the Midwest frontier following the Second Great Awakening. The first church was established by the Rev. Benoni Stinson, in 1823 at Evansville, Ind.

Stinson's major theological emphasis was general atonement -- "Christ tasted death for every man." The group also allows for the possibility of apostasy. It practices open communion and believer's baptism by immersion.

Called "liberal" Baptists because of their emphasis on the freedom of man, General Baptists organized a General Association in 1870 and invited other "liberal" Baptists (e.g., "free will" and Separate Baptists) to participate.

The policy-setting body is composed of delegates from local General Baptist churches and associations. Each local church is autonomous but belongs to an association. The group currently consists of more than 60 associations in 16 states, as well as several associations in the Philippines, Guam, Saipan, Jamaica and India. Ministers and deacons are ordained by a presbytery.

A number of boards continue a variety of missions, schools and other support ministries. General Baptists belong to the Baptist World Alliance, the North American Baptist Fellowship and the National Association of Evangelicals.

HEADQUARTERS

100 Stinson Dr., Poplar Bluff, MO 63901 Tel. (314)785-7746 Fax (314)785-0564
Media Contact, Exec. Dir., Rev. Dwight Chapman

OFFICERS

Mod., Rev. Ron Austin, 1552 Enlow Ave., Evansville, IN 47711-4158
Clk., Rev. Franklin Dumond, 1717 N. Main, Mt. Vernon, IN 47620
Exec. Dir., Rev. Dwight Chapman

OTHER ORGANIZATIONS

Gen. Bd., Sec., Rev. Franklin Dumond, 1717 N. Main, Mt. Vernon, IN 47620
Foreign Missions Bd., Exec. Dir., Rev. Charles Carr
Bd. of Christian Educ. & Publication, Exec. Dir., Rev. Samuel S. Ramdial
Home Mission Bd., Exec. Dir., Dr. Leland Duncan
Brotherhood Bd., Pres., Mr. Eithal Davis, 2731 Apache, Bowling Green, KY 42101
Women's Mission Bd., Exec. Dir., Mrs. Sandra Trivitt
Stewardship Dir., Rev. Ron D. Black
Nursing Home Admn., Ms. Wanda Britt, Rt. #2, Box 230, Campbell, MO 63933
College Bd., Pres., Dr. James Murray, Oakland City College, P.O. Box 235, Oakland City, IN 47660

PERIODICALS

General Baptist Messenger; Capsule; Voice; The Wave

General Association of Regular Baptist Churches

This association was founded in May, 1932, in Chicago by a group of churches which had withdrawn from the Northern Baptist Convention (now the American Baptist Churches in the U.S.A.) because of doctrinal differences. Its Confession of Faith, which it requires all churches to subscribe to, is essentially the old, historic New Hampshire Confession of Faith with a premillennial ending applied to the last article.

HEADQUARTERS

1300 N. Meacham Rd., Schaumburg, IL 60173 Tel. (708)843-1600 Fax (708)843-3757
Media Contact, (Interim), Dr. Mark Jackson

OFFICERS

Chpsn., Rev. John Greening
Vice-Chpsn., Rev. David Graham
Treas., Vernon Miller
Sec., Rev. Bryce Augsburger
Natl. Rep. (Interim), Dr. Mark Jackson

PERIODICAL

Baptist Bulletin

General Church of the New Jerusalem

The General Church of the New Jerusalem is the result of a reorganization in 1897 of the General Church of The Advent of the Lord. It stresses the full acceptance of the doctrines contained in the theological writings of Emanuel Swedenborg.

HEADQUARTERS

Bryn Athyn, PA 19009 Tel. (215)947-4200
Media Contact, Ed., Church Journal, Donald L. Rose, Tel. (215)947-6225 Fax (215)947-3078

OFFICERS

Presiding Bishop, Rt. Rev. P. M. Buss
Sec., Mr. Donald Fitzpatrick
Treas., Neil M. Buss

PERIODICAL

New Church Life

General Conference of Mennonite Brethren Churches

A small group, requesting that closer attention be given to prayer, Bible study and a consistent lifestyle, withdrew from the larger Mennonite Church in the Ukraine in 1860. Anabaptist in origin, the group was influenced by Lutheran pietists and Baptist teachings and adopted a quasi-congregational form of church government. In 1874 and years following, small groups of these German-speaking Mennonites left Russia, settled in Kansas and then spread to the Midwest west of the Mississippi and into Canada. Some years later the movement spread to California and the West Coast. In 1960, the Krimmer Mennonite Brethren Conference merged with this body.

Today the General Conference of Mennonite Brethren Churches conducts services in many European languages as well as in Vietnamese, Mandarin and Hindi. It works with other denominations in missionary and development projects in 25 countries outside North America.

HEADQUARTERS

4824 E. Butler Ave., Fresno, CA 93727 Tel. (209)-452-1713 Fax (209)251-7212
Media Contact, Exec. Sec., Marvin Hein

OFFICERS

Mod., Ed Boschman, 439 Highway 33 W., Kelowna, BC V1X 1T2
Asst. Mod., Larry Martens, 5724 N. Fresno St., Fresno, CA 93710
Sec., Valerie Rempel, 3401 Granny White Pike, M233, Nashville, TN 37204
Exec. Sec., Marvin Hein, 4812 E. Butler Ave., Fresno, CA 93727

Grace Gospel Fellowship

The Grace Gospel Fellowship was organized in 1944 by a group of pastors who held to a dispensational interpretation of Scripture. Most had ministries in the Midwest. Two prominent leaders were J. C. O'Hair of Chicago and Charles Baker of Milwaukee. Subsequent to 1945, a Bible Institute was founded (now Grace Bible College of Grand Rapids, Mich.), and a previously organized foreign mission (now Grace Ministries International of Grand Rapids) was affiliated with the group. Churches have now been established in most sections of the country.

The body has remained a fellowship, each church being autonomous in polity. All support for its college, mission and headquarters is on a contributory basis.

The binding force of the Fellowship has been the members' doctrinal position. They believe in the Deity and Saviorship of Jesus Christ and subscribe to the inerrant authority of Scripture. Their method of biblical interpretation is dispensational, with emphasis on the distinctive revelation to and the ministry of the apostle Paul.

HEADQUARTERS

Media Contact, Pres., Roger G. Anderson, 2125 Martindale SW, P.O. Box 9432, Grand Rapids, MI 49509 Tel. (616)245-0100 Fax (616)241-2542

OFFICER

Pres., Roger G. Anderson

OTHER ORGANIZATIONS

Grace Bible College, Pres., Rev. Bruce Kemper, 1011 Aldon St. SW, Grand Rapids, MI 49509

Grace Ministries Intl., Exec. Dir., Dr. Samuel Vinton, 2125 Martindale Ave. SW, Grand Rapids, MI 49509

Prison Mission Association, Gen. Dir., Mr. Vern Bigelow, P.O. Box 1587, Port Orchard, WA 98366-0140

Grace Publications Inc., Exec. Dir., Roger G. Anderson, 2125 Martindale Ave. SW, Grand Rapids, MI 49509

Bible Doctrines to Live By, Exec. Dir., Lee Homoki, P.O. Box 2351, Grand Rapids, MI 49501

PERIODICAL

Truth

Greek Orthodox Archdiocese of North and South America

The Greek Orthodox Archdiocese of North and South America is under the jurisdiction of the Ecumenical Patriarchate of Constantinople in Istanbul. It was chartered in 1922 by the State of New York and has parishes in the United States, Canada and Central and South America. The first Greek Orthodox Church was founded in New Orleans in 1864.

HEADQUARTERS

8-10 E. 79th St., New York, NY 10021 Tel. (212)-570-3500 Fax (212)861-2183

Media Contact, News Media Liaison, Jim Golding, Tel. (212)628-2590 Fax (212)570-4005

ARCHDIOCESAN COUNCIL

Chpsn., Archbishop Iakovos
Vice-Chpsn., Metropolitan Silas, New Jersey
Pres., Demitrios Moschos, Worchester, MA
1st Vice-Pres., Anthony Stefanis, Atlanta, GA
2nd Vice-Pres., Dr. John Collis, Cleveland, OH
Sec., Bert W. Moyar, Cleveland, OH
Treas., Helen Bender, New York, NY

SYNOD OF BISHOPS

Chpsn., Archbishop Iakovos

New Jersey, His Excellency Metropolitan Silas, 8 East 79th St., New York, NY 10021

Chicago, His Grace Bishop Iakovos, Forty East Burton Pl., Chicago, IL 60610

Toronto, His Grace Bishop Sotirios, 40 Donlands Ave., Toronto, ON M4J 3N6

San Francisco, His Grace Bishop Anthony, 372 Santa Clara Ave., San Francisco, CA 94127

Pittsburgh, His Grace Bishop Maximos, 5201 Ellsworth Ave., Pittsburgh, PA 15232

Buenos Aires, His Grace Bishop Gennadios, Avenida Figueroa Alcorta 3187, Buenos Aires, Argentina

Boston, His Grace Bishop Methodios, 162 Goddard Ave., Brookline, MA 02146

Atlanta, His Grace Bishop Philip, 6 W. Druid Hills, Ste. 620, Atlanta, GA 30329

Denver, His Grace Bishop Isaiah, 10225 E. Gill Pl., Denver, CO 80231

Assistant Bishops: His Grace Bishop Philotheos, of Meloa

Assistant Bishops to Archbishop Iakovos: His Grace Bishop Alexios, of Troas, Chorepiscopos of Astoria, 27-09 Crescent St., Astoria, NY 11102

ARCHDIOCESAN DEPARTMENTS

Rel. Educ., 50 Goddard Ave., Brookline, MA 02146

Go Telecom, 27-09 Crescent St., Astoria, NY 11102

Mission Center, P.O. Box 4319, St. Augustine, FL 32085

Youth Ministry & Camping
Economic Development
Church & Society
Ecumenical Ofc.
Stewardship
Registry
Ionian Village
Communications

ORGANIZATIONS

Ladies Philoptochos Society, 345 E. 74th St., New York, NY 10021

Greek Orthodox Young Adult League (GOYAL)
Order of St. Andrew the Apostle
Archdiocesan Presbyters' Council
National Sisterhood of Presbyteres

Natl. Forum of Greek Orthodox Church Musicians, 1700 N. Walnut St., Bloomington, IN 47401

PERIODICAL

The Orthodox Observer

Holy Ukrainian Autocephalic Orthodox Church in Exile

This church was organized in a parish in New York in 1951 by Ukrainian laymen and clergy who settled in the Western Hemisphere after World War II. In 1954 two bishops, immigrants from Europe, met with clergy and laymen and formally organized the religious body.

HEADQUARTERS

103 Evergreen St., W. Babylon, NY 11704

OFFICER

Admn., Rt. Rev. Serhij K. Pastukhiv, Tel. (516)-669-7402

House of God, Which is the Church of the Living God, the Pillar and Ground of the Truth, Inc.

This body, founded by Mary L. Tate in 1919, is episcopally organized.

HEADQUARTERS

58 Thompson St., Philadelphia, PA 19131

Media Contact, Sec., Rose Canon, 515 S. 57th St., Philadelphia, PA 19143 Tel. (215)474-8913

OFFICER

Bishop, Raymond W. White, 6107 Cobbs Creek Pkwy., Philadelphia, PA 19143 Tel. (215)748-6338

Hungarian Reformed Church in America

A Hungarian Reformed Church was organized in New York in 1904 in connection with the Reformed Church of Hungary. In 1922, the Church in Hungary transferred most of its congregations in the United States to the Reformed Church in the U.S. Some, however, preferred to continue as an autonomous, self-supporting American denomination, and these formed the Free Magyar Reformed Church in America. This group changed its name in 1958 to Hungarian Reformed Church in America.

This church is a member of the World Alliance of Reformed Churches, Presbyterian and Congregational, the World Council of Churches and the National Council of Churches of Christ.

HEADQUARTERS

Bishop's Office, 13 Grove St., Poughkeepsie, NY 12601 Tel. (914)454-5735

Media Contact, Bishop, Dr. Andrew Harsanyi, P.O. Box D, Hopatcong, NJ 07843 Tel. (201)-398-2764

OFFICERS

Bishop, Rt. Rev. Alexander Forro

Chief Lay-Curator, Prof. Stephen Szabo, 464 Forest Ave., Paramus, NJ 07652

Gen. Sec. (Clergy), Rt. Rev. Stefan Torok, 331 Kirkland Pl., Perth Amboy, NJ 08861 Tel. (908)-442-7799

Gen Sec. (Lay), Zoltan Ambrus, 3358 Maple Dr., Melvindale, MI 48122

Eastern Classis, Dean (Senior of the Deans, Chair in Bishop's absence), The Rt. Rev. Stefan M. Torok, 331 Kirkland Pl., Perth Amboy, NJ 08861

Lay-Curator, Balint Balogh, 519 N. Muhlenberg St., Allentown, PA 18104

New York Classis, Dean pro tem., The Rev. August J. Molnar, 300 Somerset St., P.O. Box 1084, New Brunswick, NJ 08903

Lay-Curator, Laszlo B. Vanyi, 229 E 82nd St., New York, NY 10028

Western Classis, Dean, The V. Rev. Andor Demeter, 3921 W. Christy Dr., Phoenix, AZ 85029

Lay-Curator, Zolton Kun, 2604 Saybrook Dr., Pittsburgh, PA 15235

Synod Treas., Ms. Priscilla Hunyady, 50 N. Washington Ave., Colonia, NJ 07067

PERIODICAL

Magyar Egyhaz

Hutterian Brethren

Small groups of Hutterites derive their names from Jacob Hutter, a 16th-century Anabaptist who taught true discipleship after accepting Jesus and advocated communal ownership of property and was burned as a heretic in Austria in 1536.

Many believers are of German descent and still use their native tongue at home and in church. Much of the denominational literature is produced in German and English. "Colonies" share property, practice non-resistance, dress differently, refuse to participate in politics and operate their own schools. There are 375 colonies with 40,000 members in North America.

Each congregation conducts its own youth work through Sunday school. Until age 15, children attend German school after attending public school. All youth ages 15 to 20 must attend Sunday school. They are baptized upon confession of faith, around age 20.

HEADQUARTERS

Media Contact, Paul S. Gross, Rt. 1, Box 6E, Reardon, WA 99029 Tel. (509)299-5400 Fax (509)299-3099

OFFICERS

Smiedleut Chmn., No. 1, Jacob Wipf, Spring Creek Colony, R. R. 3, Box 111, Forbes, ND 58439 Tel. (605)358-8621

Smiedleut Chmn., No. 2, Jacob Waldner Blumengart, Box 384, Plum Coulee, MB R0G 1R0 Tel. (204)829-3527

Dariusleut, Chmn., Mike Stahl, Box 66, Byemoor, AB T0J 0L0 Tel. (403)579-2180

Lehrerleut, Bishop, Rev. John Wipf, P.O. Box 1509, Rosetown, SK S0L 2V0 Tel. (306)882-3112

Independent Fundamental Churches of America

This group of churches was organized in 1930 at Cicero, Ill., by representatives of the American Council of Undenominational Churches and representatives of various independent churches. The founding churches and members had separated themselves from various denominational affiliations.

The IFCA provides a way for independent churches and ministers to unite in close fellowship and cooperation, in defense of the fundamental teachings of Scripture and in the proclamation of the gospel of God's grace.

HEADQUARTERS

3520 Fairlanes, Grandville, MI 49468 Tel. (616)-531-1840 Fax (616)531-1814

Mailing Address, P.O. Box 810, Grandville, MI 49418

Media Contact, Natl. Exec. Dir., Dr. Richard Gregory, Tel. (513)531-1840

OFFICERS

Natl. Exec. Dir., Dr. Richard Gregory, 2684 Meadow Ridge Dr., Byron Center, MI 49315 Tel. (616)878-1285

Pres., Dr. David L. Meschke, 6763 S. High St., Littleton, CO 80122 Tel. (303)794-0095

1st Vice-Pres., Dr. Elwood Chipchase, 3645 S. 57th Ct., Cicero, IL 60650 Tel. (708)656-6857

2nd Vice-Pres., Rev. Noel Olson, 90 Bertsch Cir., Naches, WA 98937-9622 Tel. (509)965-1256

PERIODICAL

The Voice

International Church of the Foursquare Gospel

Founded by Aimee Semple McPherson in 1927, the International Church of the Foursquare Gospel proclaims the message of Jesus Christ the Savior, Healer, Baptizer with the Holy Spirit and Sooncoming King. Headquartered in Los Angeles, this evangelistic missionary body of believers consists of nearly 1,691 churches in the United States and Canada.

The International Church of the Foursquare Gospel is incorporated in the state of California and governed by a Board of Directors who direct its corporate affairs. A Foursquare Cabinet, consisting of the Corporate Officers, Board of Directors and District Supervisors of the various districts of the Foursquare Church in the United States and other elected or appointed members, serves in an advisory capacity to the President and the Board of Directors.

Each local Foursquare Church is a subordinate unit of the International Church of the Foursquare Gospel. The pastor of the church is appointed by the Board of Directors and is responsible for the spiritual and physical welfare of the church. To assist and advise the pastor, a church council is elected by the local church members.

Foursquare Churches seek to build strong believers through Christian education, Christian day schools, youth camping and ministry, Foursquare Women International who support and encourage Foursquare missionaries abroad, radio and television ministries, the Foursquare World Advance Magazine and 248 Bible Colleges worldwide.

Worldwide missions remains the focus of the Foursquare Gospel Church with over 17,000 churches and meeting places, 21,224 national Foursquare pastors/leaders and 1,965,942 members and adherents in 72 countries around the globe. The Church is affiliated with the Pentecostal Fellowship of North America, National Association of Evangelicals and the World Pentecostal Fellowship.

HEADQUARTERS

1910 W. Sunset Blvd., Ste. 200, P.O. Box 26902, Los Angeles, CA 90026-0176 Tel. (213)484-2400 Fax (213)413-3824

Media Contact, Editor, Dr. Ron Williams

CORPORATE OFFICERS

Pres., Dr. John R. Holland
Pres. Emeritus, Dr. Rolf K. McPherson
Vice-Pres., Dr. Harold E. Helms
Gen. Supvr., Rev. Donald D. Long
Dir. of Missions Intl., Dr. Don McGregor
Sec., Dr. John W. Bowers
Treas., Rev. Virginia Cravens
Exec. Sec., Rev. James Rogers
Bd. of Directors: Dr. John R. Holland; Dr. Don McGregor; Dr. Paul Risser; Rev. Ralph Torres; Rev. Naomi Beard; Dr. John W. Bowers; Dr. Harold E. Helms; Rev. Donald D. Long; Dr. Ron Williams; Rev. Kenneth Hart; Mr. Mark Simon
District Supervisors: Eastern, Rev. Dewey Morrow; Great Lakes, Rev. Fred Parker; Midwest, Dr. Glenn Metzler; Northwest, Dr. Tom Ferguson; South Central, Dr. Sidney Westbrook; Southeast, Rev. Glenn Burris, Jr.; Southern California, Rev. Jim Tolle; Southwest, Rev. John Watson; Western, Rev. Robert Booth
Foursquare Cabinet: Composed of Corp. Officers; Board of Directors; District Supervisors, Rev. Sharon Pummel; Rev. James Scott, Jr.; Rev. Doug Murren; Rev. Ken Wold, Jr.; Dr. Daniel Brown

SUPPORT MINISTRIES

Natl. Dept. of Youth, Natl. Youth Minister, Rev. Jerry Dirmann
Natl. Dept. of Chr. Educ. & Publications, Dir., Rev. Rick Wulfestieg
Foursquare Women International, Dir., Rev. Beverly Brafford

PERIODICAL

Foursquare World Advance

International Council of Community Churches

This body is a fellowship of locally autonomous, ecumenically minded, congregationally governed, non-creedal Churches. The Council came into being in 1950 as the union of two former councils of community churches, one formed of black churches known as the Biennial Council of Community Churches and the other of white churches known as the National Council of Community Churches.

HEADQUARTERS

21116 Washington Pky., Frankfort, IL 60423-1253 Tel. (815)464-5690 Fax (815)464-5692

Media Contact, Exec. Dir., Dr. Jeffrey R. Newhall

OFFICERS

Pres., J. Ronald Miller
Vice-Pres., Rev. Dr. Gregory Smith
Vice-Pres., Rev. Judson Souers
Sec., Abraham Wright
Treas., Martha Nolan
Exec. Dir., Dr. Jeffrey R. Newhall

OTHER ORGANIZATIONS

Commission on Church Relations, Rev. Martin Singley
Commission on Ecumenical Relations, Rev. Gerald Brown
Commission on Clergy Relations, Rev. Dr. Robert Puckett
Commission on Laity Relations, Miss Winifred West
Commission on Faith & Order, Rev. Dr. Mike Owens
Commission on Social Concerns, Rev. B. Herbert Martin
Commission on Missions, Susan A. Miller
Commission on Informational Services, Margaret House
Commission on Informational Services, Vermille Barnes
Women's Christian Fellowship, Pres., Lorene Albergottie
Samaritans (Men's Fellowship), Pres., Rodney Young
Young Adult Fellowship, Pres., Sendra Woodard
Youth Fellowship, Pres., Daniel Nelson

PERIODICAL

The Christian Community

The International Pentecostal Church of Christ

At a General Conference held at London, Ohio, Aug. 10, 1976, the International Pentecostal Assemblies and the Pentecostal Church of Christ consolidated into one body, taking the name International Pentecostal Church of Christ.

The International Pentecostal Assemblies was the successor of the Association of Pentecostal Assemblies and the International Pentecostal Missionary Union. The Pentecostal Church of Christ was founded by John Stroup of Flatwoods, Ky., on May 10, 1917 and was incorporated at Portsmouth, Ohio, in 1927. The International Pentecostal Church of Christ is an active member of the Pentecostal Fellowship of North America, as well as a member of the National Association of Evangelicals.

The priorities of the International Pentecostal Church of Christ are to be an agency of God for evangelizing the world, to be a corporate body in which people may worship God and to be a channel of God's purpose to build a body of saints being perfected in the image of His Son.

The Annual Conference is held each year during the first full week of August in London, Ohio.

HEADQUARTERS

2245 St. Rt. 42 SW, P.O. Box 439, London, OH 43140 Tel. (614)852-0348 Fax Same

Media Contact, Gen. Overseer, Clyde M. Hughes

EXECUTIVE COMMITTEE

Gen. Overseer, Clyde M. Hughes, P.O. Box 439, London, OH 43140 Tel. (614)852-0348

Asst. Gen. Overseer, Wells T. Bloomfield, P.O. Box 439, London, OH 43140 Tel. (614)852-0448

Gen. Sec., Rev. Thomas Dooley, 3200 Dueber Ave. S.W., Canton, OH 44706 Tel. (216)484-6053

Gen. Treas., Rev. Clifford A. Edwards, P.O. Box 18145, Atlanta, GA 30316 Tel. (404)627-2681

Dir. of Global Missions, Dr. James B. Keiller, P.O. Box 18145, Atlanta, GA 30316 Tel. (404)627-2681

DISTRICT OVERSEERS

Blue Ridge District, Wells Bloomfield, Box 439, London, OH 43140 Tel. (614)852-0448 Fax (614)852-0348

Central District, Ervin Hargrave, 2279 Seminole Ave., Springfield, OH 45506 Tel. (513)323-6433

Mid-Eastern District, H. Gene Boyce, 705 W. Grubb St., Hertford, NC 27944 Tel. (919)426-5403

Mountain District, Jerry L. Castle, Rt. 276, Box 377, Paintsville, KY 41240 Tel. (606)789-5598

New River District, Calvin Weikel, Rt. 2, Box 300, Ronceverte, WV 24970 Tel. (304)647-4301

North Central District, David West, 9977 M-46, Lakeview, MI 48850 Tel. (517)352-8161

North Eastern District, Franklin Myers, Rt. 3, Box 175, Harpers Ferry, WV 25425 Tel. (304)535-6355

South Eastern District, Scott Combs, 110 Trace Dr., Stockbridge, GA 30281 Tel. (404)255-7290

Tri-State District, Cline McCallister, 5210 Wilson St., Portsmouth, OH 45662 Tel. (614)776-6357

OTHER ORGANIZATIONS

Beulah Heights Bible College, Pres., Samuel R. Chand, 892 Berne St., Atlanta, GA 31306 Tel. (404)627-2681

Ladies Auxiliary, Gen. Pres., Janice Boyce, 121 W. Hunters Tr., Elizabeth City, NC 27909 Tel. (919)338-3003

Locust Grove Rest Home, Dir., Frank Myers, Rt. 3, Box 175, Harpers Ferry, WV 25425 Tel. (304)-535-6355

Pentecostal Ambassadors, Gen. Pres., Richard Chesney, National Youth Dir., Box 439, London, OH 43140 Tel. (614)852-0448

Sunday School Dept., P.O. Box 439, London, OH 43140 Tel. (614)852-0348

PERIODICALS

The Bridegroom's Messenger; Pentecostal Leader

International Pentecostal Holiness Church

This body grew out of the National Holiness Association movement of the last century, with roots in Methodism. Beginning in the South and Midwest, the church represents the merger of the Fire-Baptized Holiness Church founded by B. H. Irwin in Iowa in 1895; the Pentecostal Holiness Church founded by A. B. Crumpler in Goldsboro, N.C., in 1898; and the Tabernacle Pentecostal Church founded by N. J. Holmes in 1898.

All three bodies joined the ranks of the pentecostal movement as a result of the Azusa Street revival in Los Angeles in 1906 and a 1907 pentecostal revival in Dunn, N.C., conducted by G. B. Cashwell, who had visited Azusa Street. In 1911 the Fire-Baptized and Pentecostal Holiness bodies merged in Falcon, N.C., to form the present church; the Tabernacle Pentecostal Church was added in 1915 in Canon, Ga.

The church stresses the new birth, the Wesleyan experience of entire sanctification, the pentecostal baptism in the Holy Spirit, evidenced by speaking in tongues, divine healing and the premillennial second coming of Christ.

HEADQUARTERS

P.O. Box 12609, Oklahoma City, OK 73157 Tel. (405)787-7110 Fax (405)789-3957

Media Contact, Admn. Asst.

OFFICERS

Gen. Supt., Bishop B. E. Underwood

Vice Chpsn./Asst. Gen. Supt., Rev. James Leggett

Asst. Gen. Supt., Rev. Jesse Simmons

Asst. Gen. Supt., Rev. Paul Howell

Gen. Sec.-Treas., Rev. Donald Duncan

OTHER ORGANIZATIONS

The Publishing House (Life Springs), Gen. Admn., Greg Hearn, Franklin Springs, GA 30639

Gen. Woman's Ministries, Pres., Mrs. Doris Moore

Gen. Men's Ministries, Natl. Dir., Col. Jack Kelley, P.O. Box 53307, Fayetteville, NC 28305

PERIODICALS

The International Pentecostal Holiness Life Springs; Helping Hand; Evangelism USA; Worldorama

Jehovah's Witnesses

Modern-day Jehovah's Witnesses began in the early 1870s when Charles Taze Russell was the leader of a Bible study group in Allegheny City, Pa. In July 1879, the first issue of Zion's Watch Tower and Herald of Christ's Presence (now called *The Watchtower*) appeared. In 1884 Zion's Watch Tower Tract Society was incorporated, later changed to Watch Tower Bible and Tract Society. Congregations spread into other states and followers witnessed from house to house.

By 1913, printed sermons were in four languages in 3,000 newspapers in the United States, Canada and Europe. Books, booklets and tracts had been distributed by the hundreds of millions. In 1931 the name Jehovah's Witnesses, based on Isaiah 43:10-12, was adopted.

During the 1930s and 1940s Jehovah's Witnesses fought many court cases in the interest of preserving freedom of speech, press, assembly and worship. They have won a total of 43 cases before the Supreme Court.

The Watchtower Bible School of Gilead was established in 1943 for training missionaries. Since then the Witnesses have grown to 4.9 million in 232 countries (1994).

Jehovah's Witnesses believe in one almighty God, Jehovah; that Christ is God's Son, the first of God's creations and subject to Jehovah; that Christ's human life was paid as a ransom for obedient humans; and that Jehovah has assigned Christ a heavenly Kingdom to rule in righteousness over the earth. 144,000 individuals will rule with

Christ over an unnumbered great crowd who will receive salvation into an earth cleansed of evil. (Rev. 7:9,10; 14:1-5). These, along with the resurrected dead, will transform the earth into a global Edenic paradise.

HEADQUARTERS

25 Columbia Heights, Brooklyn, NY 11201 Tel. (718)625-3600

Media Contact, Information Desk, Robert P. Johnson

OFFICER

Pres., Milton G. Henschel

The Latvian Evangelical Lutheran Church in America

This body was organized into a denomination on Aug. 22, 1975 after having existed as the Federation of Latvian Evangelical Lutheran Churches in America since 1955. This church is a regional constituent part of the Lutheran Church of Latvia in Exile, a member of the Lutheran World Federation and the World Council of Churches.

The Latvian Evangelical Lutheran Church in America works to foster religious life, traditions and customs in its congregations in harmony with the Holy Scriptures, the Apostles', Nicean and Athanasian Creeds, the unaltered Augsburg Confession, Martin Luther's Small and Large Catechisms and other documents of the Book of Concord.

The LELCA is ordered by its Synod (General Assembly), executive board, auditing committee and district conferences.

HEADQUARTERS

2140 Okla Dr., Golden Valley, MN 55427 Tel. (612)722-0174

Media Contact, Juris Pulins, 9531 Knoll Top Rd., Union, IL 60180 Tel. (815)923-5919

OFFICERS

Pres., Rev. Uldis Cepure, Tel. (612)546-3712

Vice-Pres., Rev. Maris Kirsons, 171 Erskin Ave. #1101, Toronto, ON M4P 1Y8 Tel. (416)486-3910

2nd Vice-Pres., Aivrs Ronis, 449 S. 40th St., Lincoln, NE 68510 Tel. (402)489-2776

Sec., Ansis Abele, 25182 Northrup Dr., Laguna Beach, CA 92653 Tel. (714)830-9712

Treas., Mr. Alfreds Trautmanis, 103 Rose St., Freeport, NY 11520 Tel. (516)623-2646

PERIODICAL

Cela Biedrs

The Liberal Catholic Church—Province of the United States of America

The Liberal Catholic Church was founded Feb. 13, 1916 as a reorganization of the Old Catholic Church in Great Britain with the Rt. Rev. James I. Wedgwood as the first Presiding Bishop. The first ordination of a priest in the United States was Fr. Charles Hampton, later a Bishop. The first Regionary Bishop for the American Province was the Rt. Rev. Irving S. Cooper (1919-1935).

HEADQUARTERS

Pres., Rt. Rev. Lawrence J. Smith, 9740 S. Avers Ave., Evergreen Park, IL 60642 Tel. (708)424-6548 Fax (708)423-8053

Media Contact, Regionary Bishop, The Rt. Rev. Lawrence J. Smith

OFFICERS

Pres. & Regionary Bishop, The Rt. Rev. Lawrence J. Smith

Vice-Pres., Rev. L. Marshall Heminway, P.O. Box 19957 Hampden Sta., Baltimore, MD 21211-0957

Sec. (Provincial), Rev. Lloyd Worley, 1232 24th Avenue Ct., Greeley, CO 80631 Tel. (303)356-3002

Provost, The V. Rev. Wm. Holme, P.O. Box 7042, Rochester, MN 55903

Treas., Rev. Lloyd Worley

BISHOPS

Regionary Bishop for the American Province, The Rt. Rev. Lawrence J. Smith

Aux. Bishops of the American Province: Rt. Rev. Dr. Robert S. McGinnis, Jr., 2204 Armond Blvd., Destrehan, LA 70065; Rt. Rev. Joseph L. Tisch, P.O. Box 1117, Melbourne, FL 32901; Rt. Rev. Dr. Hein VanBeusekom, 12 Krotona Hill, Ojai, CA 93023; Rt. Rev. Ruben Cabigting, P.O. Box 270, Wheaton, IL 60189

PERIODICAL

Ubique

Liberty Baptist Fellowship

The Liberty Baptist Fellowship consists of independent Baptist churches and pastors organized for the purpose of planting indigenous local New Testament churches in North America. The Fellowship is in general accord with the doctrines and philosophy of the Independent Baptist movement.

HEADQUARTERS

Candler's Mountain Rd., Lynchburg, VA 24506 Tel. (804)582-2410

Media Contact, Pres., Rev. Gary Roy, P.O. Box 368, Madison Heights, VA 24572 Tel. (804)582-2410

OFFICERS

Natl. Chmn.: Jerry Falwell

Pres., Rev. Gary Roy

Vice-Pres., Allen McFarland

Exec. Sec., Danny Lovett

Treas., Brian Metzger

LBF Endorsing Agent, Rev. Lew A. Weider

Natl. Comm.: Pres., Rev. Gary Roy; John Cartwright; Johnny Basham; Herb Fitzpatrick; Ken Hankins; Frank Lacey; Elmer Towns; Steve Reynolds; David Rhodenhizer; Daren Ritchey; Harold Willmington; George Sweet

The Lutheran Church—Missouri Synod

The Lutheran Church--Missouri Synod, which began in the state of Missouri in 1847, has more than 6,000 congregations in the United States and works in 54 other countries. It has 2.6 million members worldwide and is the second-largest Lutheran denomination in North America.

Christian education is offered for all ages. The North American congregations operate the largest elementary and secondary school systems of any Protestant denomination in the nation, and 13,737 students are enrolled in 12 LCMS institutions of higher learning.

Traditional beliefs concerning the authority and interpretation of Scripture are important. The synod is known for mass-media outreach through "The Lutheran Hour" on radio, "This Is The Life" dramas on television, and the products of Concordia Publishing House, the third-largest Protestant publisher, whose Arch Books children's series has sold more than 55 million copies.

An extensive Braille volunteer network of more than 1,000 volunteers in 50 work centers makes devotional materials for the blind; 59 of the 85 deaf congregations affiliated with U.S. denominations are LCMS; and many denominations use the Bible lessons prepared for developmentally disabled persons.

The involvement of women is high, although they do not occupy clergy positions. Serving as teachers, deaconesses and social workers, women comprise approximately 48 percent of total professional workers.

The members' responsibility for congregational leadership is a distinctive characteristic of the synod. Power is vested in voters' assemblies, generally comprised of adults of voting age. Synod decision making is given to the delegates at national and regional conventions, where the franchise is equally divided between lay and pastoral representatives.

HEADQUARTERS

The Lutheran Church--Missouri Synod, International Center, 1333 S. Kirkwood Rd., St. Louis, MO 63122-7295

Media Contact, Dir., News & Information, Rev. David Mahsman, Tel. (314)965-9917 Fax (314)-965-3396

OFFICERS

Pres., Dr. A.L. Barry
1st Vice-Pres., Dr. Robert T. Kuhn
2nd Vice-Pres., Dr. Robert King
3rd Vice-Pres., Dr. Dale A. Meyer
4th Vice-Pres., Dr. Eugene Bunkowske
5th Vice-Pres., Dr. Wallace Schulz
Sec., Dr. Walter L. Rosin
Treas., Dr. Norman Sell
Admn. Officer of Bd. of Dir., Dr. John P. Schuelke
Dir. of Personnel, Ms. Barb Ryan
Bd. of Directors: Dr. Karl L. Barth, Milwaukee, WI; Rev. Richard L. Thompson, Watertown, WI; Donald Brosz, Laramie, WY; Dean Bell, Hendrum, MN; John L. Daniel, Allenton, PA; Clifford A. Dietrich, Fort Wayne, IN; Ernest E. Garbe, Dieterich, IL; Dr. Jean Garton, Benton, AR; Oscar H. Hanson, Lafayette, CA; Dr. Arnold G. Kuntz, Garden Grove, CA; Rev. Ulmer Marshall, Jr., Mobile, AL; Christian Preus, Plymouth, MN; Dr. Edwin Trapp, Jr., Dallas, TX

BOARDS AND COMMISSIONS

Communication Services, Exec. Dir., Rev. Paul Devantier
Mission Services, Exec. Dir., Dr. Glenn O'Shoney
Higher Education Services, Exec. Dir., Dr. William F. Meyer
Human Care Ministries, Exec. Dir., Rev. Richard L. Krenzke
Worker Benefit Plans, Exec. Dir., Mr. Dan A. Leeman
Lutheran Church Ext. Fund-Missouri Synod, Pres., Mr. Arthur C. Haake
Congregational Services, Exec. Dir., Rev. Lyle Muller
Black Ministries Services, Exec. Dir., Dr. Bryant Clancy

ORGANIZATIONS

Concordia Publishing House, Pres./CEO, Dr. Stephen Carter, 3558 S. Jefferson Ave., St. Louis, MO 63118-3968
Concordia Historical Institute, Dir., Rev. Daniel Preus, Concordia Seminary, 801 De Mun Ave., St. Louis, MO 63105
Intl. Lutheran Laymen's League, Exec. Dir., Mr. Laurence E. Lumpe, 2185 Hampton Ave., St. Louis, MO 63139-2983
KFUO Radio, Exec. Dir., Rev. Paul Devantier, 85 Founders Ln., St. Louis, MO 63105
Intl. Lutheran Women's Missionary League, Pres., Ms. Gloria Edwards, 3558 S. Jefferson Ave., St. Louis, MO 63118-3910

PERIODICALS

The Lutheran Witness; Reporter

Mennonite Church

The Mennonite Church in North America traces its beginnings to the Protestant Reformation. Conrad Grebel, Georg Blaurock and a small band of radical believers baptized one another in Zurich, Switzerland, on Jan. 21, 1525. First nicknamed Anabaptists (Rebaptizers) by their opponents, they preferred the term Brothers and Sisters in Christ. They later took their name from the Dutch priest Menno Simons, who joined the movement in 1536.

The Mennonites' refusal to conform to majesterial decrees, including bearing of arms and the swearing of oaths, attracted fierce animosity. Thousands were martyred for their beliefs in nearly a century of persecution. They moved to many places, including the United States and Canada, where some arrived as early as 1683.

North American Mennonites began their first home mission program in Chicago, Ill., in 1893 and their first overseas mission program in India in 1899. Since the 1920s the church has established extensive emergency relief and development services in conjunction with its mission program.

Mennonites hold that the Word of God is central and that new life in Christ is available to all who believe. Adult "Believers"baptism is practiced, symbolizing a conscious decision to follow Christ. Mennonites take seriously Christ's command to witness in word and deed. They stress that Christians need the support of a faith community for encouragement and growth. They view the teachings of Jesus as directly applicable to their lives. Mennonites generally refuse to serve in the military or to use violent resistance.

The largest body of Mennonites in North America, the Mennonite Church is a member of the Mennonite and Brethren in Christ World Conference, a worldwide fellowship, and the Mennonite Central Committee, an international relief and service agency. Individuals and program agencies participate in a variety of ecumenical activities at various levels of church life.

HEADQUARTERS

421 S. Second St., Ste. 600, Elkhart, IN 46516 Tel. (219)294-7131
Media Contact, Churchwide Communications Dir., Fax (219)293-3977

OFFICERS

Mod., Owen E. Burkholder, 1585 N. College Ave., Harrisonburg, VA 22801 Tel. (703)433-2138

OTHER ORGANIZATIONS

Gen. Bd., Int. Gen. Sec., Miriam F. Book

Historical Cmte., Dir., John E. Sharp, 1700 S. Main, Goshen, IN 46526 Tel. (219)535-7477
Council on Faith, Life & Strategy, Staff, Miriam F. Book
Bd. of Congregational Min., Exec. Sec., Everett J. Thomas, Box 1245, Elkhart, IN 46515 Tel. (219)294-7523
Bd. of Educ., Exec. Sec., Orville L. Yoder, Box 1142, Elkhart, IN 46515 Tel. (219)294-7523
Bd. of Missions, Pres., Stanley W. Green, Box 370, Elkhart, IN 46515 Tel. (219)294-7523
Mutual Aid Bd., Pres., Howard L. Brenneman, 1110 North Main, P.O. Box 483, Goshen, IN 46526 Tel. (219)533-9511
Mennonite Publication Bd., Publisher, J. Robert Ramer, 616 Walnut Ave., Scottdale, PA 15683 Tel. (412)887-8500

PERIODICALS

Gospel Herald; Christian Living; Rejoice!; Mennonite Historical Bulletin; Mennonite Quarterly Review; Purpose; Story Friends; Voice

Mennonite Church, The General Conference

The General Conference Mennonite Church was formed in 1860, uniting Mennonites throughout the United States who were interested in doing missionary work together. Today 63,000 Christians in 417 congregations try to follow the way of Jesus in their daily lives.

The conference consists of people of many ethnic backgrounds -- Swiss and German, Russian and Dutch, African-American, Hispanic, Chinese, Vietnamese and Laotian. Some native Americans in both Canada and the United States also relate to the conference.

The basic belief and practice of the conference come from the life and teachings of Jesus Christ, the early church of the New Testament and the Anabaptists of the 16th-century Reformation. Thus the conference seeks to be evangelical, guided by the Bible, led by the Holy Spirit and supported by a praying, discerning community of believers in congregations and fellowships. Peace, or shalom, is at the very heart of members, who seek to be peacemakers in everyday life.

The goals of the conference are to evangelize, teach and practice biblical principles, train and develop leaders and work for Christian unity.

The General Conference intends to merge with the Mennonite Church.

HEADQUARTERS

722 Main, Newton, KS 67114 Tel. (316)283-5100 Fax (316)283-0454
Media Contact, Communications Dir., David Linscheid

OFFICERS

Mod., Darrell Fast, 328 E. 2nd St., Newton, KS 67114
Asst. Mod., Bernie Wiebe, 46 Belair Rd., Winnipeg, MB R3T 0S2
Sec., Anita Penner, 33304 Century Cres., Abbotsford, BC V2S 5V5
Gen. Sec., Vern Preheim

OTHER ORGANIZATIONS

Commission on Home Ministries, Exec., Lois Barrett
Commission on Overseas Mission, Exec. Sec., Glendon Klaassen
Women in Mission, Coord., Susan Jantzen
Commission on Education, Exec. Sec., Norma Johnson
Div. of General Services: Bus. Mgr., Ted Stuckey; Planned Giving Dir., Gary Franz; Communications Dir., David Linscheid
Mennonite Men, Coord., Heinz Janzen
Faith & Life Press, Mgr., Norma Johnson
Committee on Ministry, Dir. of Ministerial Leadership, John A. Esau

PERIODICALS

Window to Mission; The Mennonite

The Metropolitan Church Association, Inc.

Organized after a revival movement in Chicago in 1894 as the Metropolitan Holiness Church, this organization was chartered as the Metropolitan Church Association in 1899. It has Wesleyan theology.

HEADQUARTERS

323 Broad St., Lake Geneva, WI 53147 Tel. (414)-248-6786
Media Contact, Pres., Rev. Warren W. Bitzer

OFFICERS

Pres., Rev. Warren W. Bitzer
Vice-Pres. & Sec., Elbert L. Ison
Treas., Gertrude J. Puckhaber

PERIODICAL

The Burning Bush

The Missionary Church

The Missionary Church was formed in 1969 through a merger of the United Missionary Church (organized in 1883) and the Missionary Church Association (founded in 1898). It is evangelical and conservative with a strong emphasis on missionary work and church planting.

There are three levels of church government with local, district and general conferences. There are 10 church districts in the United States. The general conference meets every two years. The denomination operates one college in the United States.

HEADQUARTERS

3811 Vanguard Dr., P.O. Box 9127, Ft. Wayne, IN 46899-9127 Tel. (219)747-2027 Fax (219)747-5331
Publishing Headquarters, Bethel Publishing Co., 1819 S. Main St., Elkhart, IN 46516 Tel. (219)-293-8585
Media Contact, Pres., Dr. John Moran

OFFICERS

Pres., Dr. John Moran
Vice-Pres., Rev. William Hossler
Sec., Rev. Dave Engbrecht
Treas., Mr. Milt Gerber
Asst. to the Pres., Rev. Bob Ransom
Overseas Ministries (World Partners): Dir., Rev. Paul DeMerchant; Dir. of Mission Ministries, Rev. David Mann
Services Dir., Mr. David von Gunten
Bethel Publishing Co., Exec. Dir., Rev. Richard Oltz
Stewardship, Dir., Rev. Ken Stucky
Youth Dir., Mr. Eric Liechty
Children's Dir., Dr. Neil McFarlane
Adult Dir., Dr. Duane Beals
Senior Adult Ministry Dir., Dr. Charles Cureton

Missionary Men Liaison, Rev. Bob Ransom
Missionary Women Intl., Pres., Mrs. Lois Bjork
Investment Foundation, Mr. Bob Henschen

PERIODICALS

Emphasis on Faith and Living; Ministry Today; World Partners; Priority

Moravian Church in America (Unitas Fratrum)

In 1735 German Moravian missionaries of the pre-Reformation faith of Jan Hus came to Georgia, in 1740 to Pennsylvania, and in 1753 to North Carolina. They established the American Moravian Church, which is broadly evangelical, ecumenical, liturgical, "conferential" in form of government and with an episcopacy as a spiritual office.

HEADQUARTERS

See Provincial addresses
Media Contact, Editor, *The Moravian*, The Rev. Hermann I. Weinlick, Tel. (610)867-7566 Fax (610)866-9223

NORTHERN PROVINCE

1021 Center St., P.O. Box 1245, Bethlehem, PA 18016-1245 Tel. (610)867-7566 Fax (610)866-9223

PROVINCIAL ELDERS' CONFERENCE

Pres., Rev. Dr. Gordon L. Sommers
Vice-Pres./Sec. (Eastern Dist.), The Rev. David L. Wickmann
Vice-Pres. (Western Dist.), Rev. R. Burke Johnson, P.O. Box 386, Sun Prairie, WI 53590 Fax (608)825-6610
Comptroller, Theresa E. Kunda, 1021 Center St., P.O. Box 1245, Bethlehem, PA 18016-1245

SOUTHERN PROVINCE

459 S. Church St., Winston-Salem, NC 27101 Tel. (910)725-5811 Fax (910)725-1029

PROVINCIAL ELDERS' CONFERENCE

Pres., Rev. Dr. Robert E. Sawyer
Vice-Pres./Asst. to Pres., The Rev. William H. McElveen
Sec., Lane A. Sapp
Treas., Richard Cartner, Drawer M, Salem Station, Winston-Salem, NC 27108

ALASKA PROVINCE

P.O. Box 545, Bethel, AK 99559

OFFICERS

Pres., The Rev. Frank Chingliak
Vice-Pres., The Rev. David Paul
Sec., Annie Kinegak
Treas., Juanita Asicksik
Dir. of Theological Ed., Rev. Dr. Kurt H. Vitt

PERIODICAL

The Moravian

National Association of Congregational Christian Churches

This association was organized in 1955 in Detroit, Mich., by delegates from Congregational Christian Churches committed to continuing the Congregational way of faith and order in church life. Participation by member churches is voluntary.

HEADQUARTERS

P.O. Box 1620, Oak Creek, WI 53154 Tel. (414)-764-1620 Fax (414)764-0319
Media Contact, Exec. Sec., Michael S. Robertson, 8473 So. Howell Ave., Oak Creek, WI 53154 Tel. (414)764-1620 Fax (414)764-0319

OFFICERS

Exec. Sec., Michael S. Robertson, 8473 South Howell Ave., Oak Creek, WI 53154
Assoc. Exec. Secs.: Rev. Dr. Michael Halcomb; Rev. Phil Jackson

PERIODICAL

The Congregationalist

National Association of Free Will Baptists

This evangelical group of Arminian Baptists was organized by Paul Palmer in 1727 at Chowan, N.C. Another movement (teaching the same doctrines of free grace, free salvation and free will) was organized June 30, 1780, in New Durham, N.H., but there was no connection with the southern organization except for a fraternal relationship.

The northern line expanded more rapidly and extended into the West and Southwest. This body merged with the Northern Baptist Convention Oct. 5, 1911, but a remnant of churches reorganized into the Cooperative General Association of Free Will Baptists Dec. 28, 1916, at Pattonsburg, Mo.

Churches in the southern line were organized into various conferences from the beginning and finally united in one General Conference in 1921.

Representatives of the Cooperative General Association and the General Conference joined Nov. 5, 1935 to form the National Association of Free Will Baptists.

HEADQUARTERS

5233 Mt. View Rd., Antioch, TN 37013-2306 Tel. (615)731-6812 Fax (615)731-0771
Mailing Address, P.O. Box 5002, Antioch, TN 37011-5002
Media Contact, Exec. Sec., Melvin Worthington

OFFICERS

Exec. Sec., Dr. Melvin Worthington
Mod., Rev. Ralph Hampton, P.O. Box 50117, Nashville, TN 37205

DENOMINATIONAL AGENCIES

Free Will Baptist Foundation, Exec. Dir., William Evans
Free Will Baptist Bible College, Pres., Dr. Tom Malone
Foreign Missions Dept., Dir., Rev. R. Eugene Waddell
Home Missions Dept., Dir., Mr. Trymon Messer
Bd. of Retirement, Dir., Rev. William Evans
Historical Commission, Chpsn., Mary Wisehart
Comm. for Theological Integrity, Chpsn., Rev. Leroy Forlines, P.O. Box 50117, Nashville, TN 37205
Music Commission, Chpsn., Vernon Whaley, P.O. Box 50117, Nashville, TN 37205
Radio & Television Comm., Chpsn., Rev. Steve Faison, Box 50117, Nashville, TN 37205
Sunday School & Church Training Dept., Dir., Dr. Alton Loveless
Women Nationally Active for Christ, Exec. Sec., Dr. Mary R. Wisehart
Master's Men Dept., Dir., Mr. James Vallance

PERIODICALS

A Magazine for Christian Men Attack; Contact; Free Will Bible College Bulletin; Co-Laborer; Free Will Baptist Gem; Heartbeat; Mission Grams

National Baptist Convention of America, Inc.

The National Baptist Convention of America, Inc., was organized in 1880. Its mission is articulated through its history, constitution, articles of incorporation and by-laws. The Convention (corporate churches) has a mission statement with fourteen (14) objectives including: fostering unity throughout its membership and the world Christian community by proclaiming the gospel of Jesus Christ; validating and propagating the Baptist doctrine of faith and practice, and its distinctive principles throughout the world; and harnassing and encouraging the scholarly and Christian creative skills of its membership for Christian writing and publications.

HEADQUARTERS

Media Contact, Liaison Officer, Dr. Richard A. Rollins, 777 S. R.L. Thornton Fwy., Ste. 205, Dallas, TX 75203 Tel. (214)946-8913 Fax (214)-946-9619

OFFICERS

Pres., Dr. E. Edward Jones, 1327 Pierre Ave., Shreveport, LA 71103 Tel. (318)221-3701 Fax (318)222-7512

Gen. Rec. Sec., Dr. Clarence C. Pennywell, 2016 Russell Rd., Shreveport, LA 71107

Corres. Sec., Rev. E. E. Stafford, 6614 South Western Ave., Los Angeles, CA 90047

Liaison Officer, Dr. Richard A. Rollins, 777 So. R.L. Thornton Frwy., Ste. 205, Dallas, TX 75203 Tel. (214)946-8913 Fax (214)946-9619

Public Rel. Dir., Rev. Joe R. Gant, 5823 Ledbetter St., Shreveport, LA 77108

Lantern Editor, Ruthie Myles, 1327 Pierre Ave., Shreveport, LA 71103

PERIODICALS

The Lantern; Communique

National Baptist Convention, U.S.A., Inc.

The older and parent convention of black Baptists, this body is to be distinguished from the National Baptist Convention of America.

HEADQUARTERS

1700 Baptist World Center Dr., Nashville, TN 37207 Tel. (615)228-6292 Fax (615)226-5935

Media Contact, Gen. Sec., Dr. Willie D. McClung, 903 S. Holt St., Montgomery, AL 36104 Tel. (334)263-0522

OFFICERS

Pres., Dr. Henry J. Lyons, 3455 26th Ave. S., St. Petersburg, FL 33711-3550 Tel. (615)228-6292

Gen. Sec., Dr. Roscoe Cooper, Jr., 300 Grace St., Richmond, VA 23220-4908 Tel. (804)643-0192

Exec. Dir., Dr. Willie D.. McClung, 1700 Baptist World Center Dr., Nashville, TN 37203 Tel. (615)228-6292

Vice-Pres.-at-Large, Dr. Stewart Cureton, 501 Mary Knob Court, Greenville, SC 29601-5242 Tel. (803)277-0364

Treas., Dr. Stacey Shields, 3001 Clifton St., Indianapolis, IN 46208 Tel. (317)925-4563

Vice-Pres.: Dr. John Chaplin, 811 K. St. NE, Washington, DC 20002; Dr. A. L. Owens, 1881 E. 71st St., Cleveland, OH 44103; Dr. Fred Crouther, 2315 N. 38th St., Milwaukee, WI 53210; Dr. Walter Brown, 931 Bellemeade Ave., Evansville, IN 47713; Dr. Acen Phillips, 195 S. Monaco Pky., Denver, CO 80224

Asst. Sec.: Dr. Ricky Woods, 522 Valley Dr., Durham, NC 27704; Dr. Harold Middlebrooks, 117 Beaman Lake Rd., Knoxville, TN; Dr. Mack Hines, 1414 Aaron Circle, Florence, SC 29506; Rev. H. P. Rachal, 9719 S. Avalon Blvd., Los Angeles, CA 90003

Stat., Dr. Willie Davis, 500 Madison Ave., Las Vegas, NV 89106-3145

Historian, Dr. Wilson Fallin, 4007 7th Ave., Bessemer, AL 35020-1172

OFFICERS OF BOARDS

Home Mission Bd., Exec. Sec., Dr. Warren H. Stewart, 1141 E. Jefferson St., Phoenix, AZ 85034 Tel. (602)259-1998

Education Bd., Exec. Sec., Dr. J. Tallefarra Campbell, P.O. Box 8861, Los Angeles, CA 90008-8861 Tel. (213)295-2796

Laymen, Exec. Dir., Jerry Gash

Women's Auxiliary, Exec. Dir., Dr. Cynthia Ray, 8702 Ave. "A", Brooklyn, NY 11236-1203

Congress of Christian Ed., Pres., Dr. Samuel Austin, 484 Washington Ave., Brooklyn, NY 11238-2304 Tel. (508)875-2215

PERIODICAL

Mission Herald

National Missionary Baptist Convention of America

The National Missionary Baptist Convention of America was organized in 1988 as a separate entity from the National Baptist Convention of America, Inc., after a dispute over control of the convention's publishing efforts. The new organization intended to remain committed to the National Baptist Sunday Church School and Baptist Training Union Congress and the National Baptist Publishing Board.

The purpose of the National Missionary Baptist Convention of America is to serve as an agency of Christian education, church extension and missionary efforts. It seeks to maintain and safeguard full religious liberty and engage in social and economic development.

HEADQUARTERS

6717 Centennial Blvd., Nashville, TN 37209 Tel. (615)350-8000

OFFICERS

Pres., Dr. W. T. Snead, Sr., 1404 E. Firestone, Los Angeles, CA 90001 Tel. (213)582-0090

Vice-Pres., At-large, ----

Vice-Pres., Ecumenical Affairs, Dr. F. Benjamin Davis, 1535 Dr. A.J. Brown Blvd. N., Indianapolis, IN 46202

Vice-Pres., Auxiliaries, Dr. Harvey Leggett, 866 Monroe St., Ypsilanti, MI 48197

Vice-Pres., Boards, Dr. O. E. Piper, 4220 W. 18th St., Chicago, IL 60623

Pres., National Baptist Publishing Bd., Dr. T. B. Boyd, III

Gen. Sec., Dr. Melvin V. Wade, 4269 S. Figueroa, Los Angeles, CA 90037

Corres. Sec., Dr. H. J. Johnson, 2429 South Blvd., Dallas, TX 75215
Treas., Dr. W. N. Daniel, 415 W. Englewood Ave., Chicago, IL 60612
Rec. Sec., Dr. Lonnie Franks, Crocker, TX

National Organization of the New Apostolic Church of North America

This body is a variant of the Catholic Apostolic Church which began in England in 1830. The New Apostolic Church distinguished itself from the parent body in 1863 by recognizing a succession of Apostles.

HEADQUARTERS

3753 N. Troy St., Chicago, IL 60618
Media Contact, Sec. & Treas., Ellen E. Eckhardt, Tel. (312)539-3652 Fax (312)478-6691

OFFICERS

Pres., Rev. Erwin Wagner, 330 Arlene Pl., Waterloo, ON N2J 2G6
First Vice-Pres., Rev. John W. Fendt, 36 Colony La., Manhasset, NY 11030
Second Vice-Pres., Rev. Leonard E Kolb, 4522 Wood St., Erie, PA 16509-1639
Treas. & Sec., Ellen E. Eckhardt, 6380 N. Indian Rd., Chicago, IL 60646
Asst. Sec., Rev. John E. Doderer, 2605 Donald Ct., Glenview, IL 60025

National Primitive Baptist Convention, Inc.

Throughout the years of slavery and the Civil War, the Negro population of the South worshipped with the white population in their various churches. At the time of emancipation, their white brethren helped them to establish their own churches, granting them letters of fellowship, ordaining their deacons and ministers and helping them in other ways.

The doctrine and polity of this body are quite similar to that of white Primitive Baptists, except that they are "opposed to all forms of church organization"; yet there are local associations and a national convention, organized in 1907.

Each church is independent and receives and controls its own membership. This body was formerly known as Colored Primitive Baptists.

HEADQUARTERS

6433 Hidden Forest Dr., Charlotte, NC 28213 Tel. (704)596-3153
Elder T. W. Samuels

OFFICERS

Natl. Convention, Pres., Elder T. W. Samuels
Natl. Convention, Vice-Pres., F. E. Livingston, Dallas, TX
Natl. Convention, Chmn. Bd. of Dirs., Elder Ernest Ferrell, Tallahassee, FL
Natl. Church School Training Union, Pres., Jonathan Yates, Mobile, AL
Natl. Ushers Congress, Pres., Bro. Carl Batts, 21213 Garden View Dr., Maple Heights, OH 44137
Publishing Bd., Chpsn., Elder E. W. Wallace, Creamridge, NJ
Women's Congress, Pres., Betty Brown, Cocoa Beach, FL
Natl. Laymen's Council, Pres., Densimore Robinson, Huntsville, AL
Natl. Youth Congress, Pres., Robert White, Trenton, NJ

National Spiritualist Association of Churches

This organization is made up of believers that Spiritualism is a science, philosophy and religion based upon the demonstrated facts of communication between this world and the next.

HEADQUARTERS

Media Contact, Publ. Rel. Dir., Mrs. Mary Lou Baumhoff, 86 End St., Salem, NH 03079 Tel. (603)898-8854

OFFICERS

Pres., Rev. Brenda Wittich, 3903 Connecticut St., St. Louis, MO 63116
Vice-Pres., Rev. Bernard Baker, 1710 E. Bell De Mar, Tempe, AZ 85283
Sec., Rev. Sharon L. Snowman, P.O. Box 217, Lily Dale, NY 14752 Tel. (716)595-2000 Fax (716)-595-2020
Treas., Rev. Lelia Cutler, 7310 Hedfield St. #1, Norfolk, VA 23505

OTHER ORGANIZATIONS

Bureau of Educ., Supt., Rev. Joseph Sax, Morris Pratt Institute, 11811 Watertown Plank Rd., Milwaukee, WI 53226
Bureau of Public Relations, Rev. Brenda Wittich, 3903 Connecticut St., St. Louis, MO 63116
The Stow Memorial Foundation, Sec., Rev. Sharon L. Snowman, P.O. Box 217, Lily Dale, NY 14752 Tel. (716)595-2000 Fax (716)595-2020
Spiritualist Benevolent Society, Inc., P.O. Box 217, Lily Dale, NY 14752

PERIODICAL

The National Spiritualist Summit

Netherlands Reformed Congregations

The Netherlands Reformed Congregations organized denominationally in 1907. In the Netherlands, the so-called Churches Under the Cross (established in 1839, after breaking away from the 1834 Secession congregations) and the so-called Ledeboerian churches (established in 1841 under the leadership of the Rev. Ledeboer, who seceded from the Reformed State Church), united in 1907 under the leadership of the then 25-year-old Rev. G. H. Kersten, to form the Netherlands Reformed Congregations. Many of the North American congregations left the Christian Reformed Church to join the Netherlands Reformed Congregations after the Kuyperian presupposed regeneration doctrine began making inroads.

All Netherlands Reformed Congregations, office-bearers and members subscribe to three Reformed Forms of Unity: The Belgic Confession of Faith (by DeBres), the Heidelberg Catechism (by Ursinus and Olevianus) and the Canons of Dort. Both the Belgic Confession and the Canons of Dort are read regularly at worship services, and the Heidelberg Catechism is preached weekly, except on church feast days.

HEADQUARTERS

Media Contact, Synodical Clk., Rev. A. M. den Boer, 730 Skyline Dr., Sunnyside, WA 98944 Tel. (509)839-4494 Fax (509)837-7622

OTHER ORGANIZATION

Netherlands Reformed Book and Publishing, 1233 Leffingwell NE, Grand Rapids, MI 49505

PERIODICAL

The Banner of Truth

North American Baptist Conference

The North American Baptist Conference was begun by immigrants from Germany. The first church was organized by the Rev. Konrad Fleischmann in Philadelphia in 1843. In 1865 delegates of the churches met in Wilmot, Ont., and organized the North American Baptist Conference. Today only a few churches still use the German language, mostly in a bilingual setting.

The Conference meets in general session once every three years for fellowship, inspiration and to conduct the business of the Conference through elected delegates from the local churches. The General Council, composed of representatives of the various Associations and Conference organizations and departments, meets annually to determine the annual budget and programs for the Conference and its departments and agencies. The General Council also makes recommendations to the Triennial Conference on policies, long-range plans and election of certain personnel, boards and committees.

Approximately 80 missionaries serve in Cameroon, Nigeria, West Africa, Japan, Brazil, Eastern Europe, Mexico and the Philippines, as well as among various ethnic groups throughout the United States and Canada.

Ten homes for the aged are affiliated with the Conference and 12 camps are operated on the association level.

HEADQUARTERS

1 S. 210 Summit Ave., Oakbrook Terrace, IL 60181 Tel. (708)495-2000 Fax (708)495-3301

Media Contact, Marilyn Schaer

OFFICERS

Mod., Rev. Ron Norman
Vice-Mod., Wayne Wegner
Exec. Dir., Dr. Philip Yntema
Treas., Mr. Jackie Loewer

OTHER ORGANIZATIONS

Missions Dept., Dir., Dr. Herman Effa
Home Missions Dept., Dir., Rev. Jim Fann
Management Services Dept., Dir., Mr. Ron Salzman
Church Extension Investors Fund, Dir., Mr. Robert Mayforth

Old German Baptist Brethren

This group separated from the Church of the Brethren (formerly German Baptist Brethren) in 1881 in order to preserve and maintain historic Brethren Doctrine.

HEADQUARTERS

Media Contact, Vindicator Ofc. Ed., Elder Keith Skiles, 701 St. Rt. 571, Union City, OH 45390 Tel. (513)968-3877

OFFICERS

Foreman, Elder Clement Skiles, Rt. 1, Box 140, Bringhurst, IN 46913 Tel. (219)967-3367
Reading Clk., Elder Donald L. Hess, 5215 Hess-Benedict Rd., Waynesboro, PA 17268 Tel. (717)762-6592
Writing Clk., Elder Carl Bowman, 4065 State Rt. 48, Covington, OH 45318 Tel. (513)473-2729

PERIODICAL

The Vindicator

Old Order Amish Church

The congregations of this Old Order Amish group have no annual conference. They worship in private homes. They adhere to the older forms of worship and attire. This body has bishops, ministers and deacons.

INFORMATION

Der Neue Amerikanische Calendar, c/o Raber's Book Store, 2467 C R 600, Baltic, OH 43804
Telephone Contact, LeRoy Beachy, Beachy Amish Mennonite Church, 4324 SR 39, Millersburg, OH 44654 Tel. (216)893-2883

Old Order (Wisler) Mennonite Church

This body arose from a separation of Mennonites dated 1872, under Jacob Wisler, in opposition to what were thought to be innovations.

The group is in the Eastern United States and Canada. Each state, or district, has its own organization and holds semi-annual conferences.

HEADQUARTERS

Media Contact, Amos B. Hoover, 376 N. Muddy Creek Rd., Denver, PA 17517 Tel. (717)484-4849 Fax (717)484-1042

Open Bible Standard Churches, Inc.

Open Bible Standard Churches originated from two revival movements: Bible Standard Conference, founded in Eugene, Ore., under the leadership of Fred L. Hornshuh in 1919, and Open Bible Evangelistic Association, founded in Des Moines, Iowa, under the leadership of John R. Richey in 1932.

Similar in doctrine and government, the two groups amalgamated on July 26, 1935 as "Open Bible Standard Churches, Inc." with headquarters in Des Moines, Iowa.

The original group of 210 ministers has enlarged to incorporate over 1,657 ministers and 1,024 churches in 30 countries. The first missionary left for India in 1926. The church now ministers in Asia, Africa, South America, Europe, Canada, Mexico and the Caribbean Islands.

Historical roots of the parent groups reach back to the outpouring of the Holy Spirit in 1906 at Azusa Street Mission in Los Angeles and to the full gospel movement in the Midwest. Both groups were organized under the impetus of pentecostal revival. Simple faith, freedom from fanaticism, emphasis on evangelism and missions and free fellowship with other groups were characteristics of the growing organizations.

The highest governing body of Open Bible Standard Churches meets biennially and is composed of all ministers and one voting delegate per 100 members from each church. A National Board of Directors, elected by the national and regional conferences, conducts the business of the organization. Official Bible College is Eugene Bible

College in Oregon.

Open Bible Standard Churches is a charter member of the National Association of Evangelicals and of the Pentecostal/Charismatic Churches of North America. It is a member of the Pentecostal World Conference.

HEADQUARTERS

2020 Bell Ave., Des Moines, IA 50315 Tel. (515)-288-6761 Fax (515)288-2510

Media Contact, Exec. Dir., Communications & Resources, Randall A. Bach, Tel. (515)288-6761 Fax (515)288-5200

OFFICERS

Pres., Jeffrey E. Farmer
Sec.-Treas., Patrick L. Bowlin
Dir. of Intl. Min., Paul V. Canfield

PERIODICALS

Message of the Open Bible; World Vision

The (Original) Church of God, Inc.

This body was organized in 1886 as the first church in the United States to take the name "The Church of God." In 1917 a difference of opinion led this particular group to include the word (Original) in its name. It is a holiness body and believes in the whole Bible, rightly divided, using the New Testament as its rule and government.

HEADQUARTERS

P.O. Box 592, Wytheville, VA 24382

Media Contact, Gen. Overseer, Rev. William Dale, Tel. (800)827-9234

OFFICERS

Gen. Overseer, Rev. William Dale
Asst. Gen. Overseer, Rev. Alton Evans

PERIODICAL

The Messenger

The Orthodox Church in America

The Russian Orthodox Greek Catholic Church of America entered Alaska in 1794 before its purchase by the United States in 1867. Its canonical status of independence (autocephaly) was granted by its Mother Church, the Russian Orthodox Church, on April 10, 1970, and it is now known as The Orthodox Church in America.

HEADQUARTERS

P.O. Box 675, Syosset, NY 11791-0675 Tel. (516)-922-0550 Fax (516) 922-0954

Media Contact, Dir. of Communications, Rev. Gregory Havrilak

OFFICERS

Primate, Archbishop of Washington, Metropolitan of All America & Canada, The Most Blessed Theodosius

Chancellor, V. Rev. Robert S. Kondratick, P.O. Box 675, Syosset, NY 11791 Tel. (516)922-0550 Fax (516)922-0954

SYNOD

Chpsn., His Beatitude Theodosius, P.O. Box 675, Syosset, NY 11791

Archbishop of New York, The Most Rev. Peter, 33 Hewitt Ave., Bronxville, NY 10708

Archbishop of Pittsburgh & Western PA, The Most Rev. Kyrill, P.O. Box R, Wexford, PA 15090

Archbishop of Dallas, Archbishop Dmitri, 4112 Throckmorton, Dallas, TX 75219

Bishop of Philadelphia, Archbishop Herman, St. Tikhon's Monastery, South Canaan, PA 18459

Aux. Bishop of Sitka, The Rt. Rev. Innotent, P.O. Box 240805, Anchorage, AK 99524-0805

Bishop of Detroit, The Rt. Rev. Nathaniel, 2522 Grey Tower Rd., Jackson, MI 49201

Bishop of Midwest, The Rt. Rev. Job, 605 Iowa St., Oak Park, IL 60302

Bishop of San Francisco, The Rt. Rev. Tikhon, 649 North Robinson St., Los Angeles, CA 90026

Bishop of Ottawa and Canada, The Rt. Rev. Seraphim, RR 5, Box 179, Spencerville, ON K0E 1X0 Tel. (613)925-5226

Auxiliary Bishop, Titular Bishop of Bethesda, The Rt. Rev. Mark, 9511 Sun Pointe Dr., Boynton Beach, FL 33437

PERIODICAL

The Orthodox Church

The Orthodox Presbyterian Church

On June 11, 1936, certain ministers, elders and lay members of the Presbyterian Church in the U.S.A. withdrew from that body to form a new denomination. Under the leadership of the late Rev. J. Gresham Machen, noted conservative New Testament scholar, the new church determined to continue to uphold the Westminster Confession of Faith as traditionally understood by Presbyterians and to engage in proclamation of the gospel at home and abroad.

The church has grown modestly over the years and suffered early defections, most notably one in 1937 that resulted in the formation of the Bible Presbyterian Church under the leadership of Dr. Carl McIntire. It now has congregations throughout the states of the continental United States.

The denomination is a member of the North American Presbyterian and Reformed Council and the International Council of Reformed Churches.

HEADQUARTERS

607 N. Easton Rd., Bldg. E, Box P, Willlow Grove, PA 19090-0920 Tel. (215)830-0920 Fax (215)-830-0350

Media Contact, Stated Clerk, The Rev. Donald J. Duff

OFFICERS

Mod., The Rev. Douglas A. Watson, 24 Hwy. 202, Ringues, NJ 08551-1819
Stated Clk., Rev. Donald J. Duff

PERIODICAL

New Horizons in the Orthodox Presbyterian Church

Patriarchal Parishes of the Russian Orthodox Church in the U.S.A.

This group of parishes is under the direct jurisdiction of the Patriarch of Moscow and All Russia, His Holiness Aleksy II, in the person of a Vicar Bishop, His Grace Paul, Bishop of Zaraisk.

HEADQUARTERS

St. Nicholas Cathedral, 15 E. 97th St., New York, NY 10029 Tel. (212)831-6294 Fax (212)427-5003

Media Contact, Sec. to the Bishop, Deacon Vladimir Tyschuk, Tel. (212)289-1915

PERIODICAL

One Church

Pentecostal Assemblies of the World, Inc.

This organization is an interracial Pentecostal holiness of the Apostolic Faith, believing in repentance, baptism in Jesus's name and being filled with the Holy Ghost, with the evidence of speaking in tongues. It originated in the early part of the century in the Middle West has spread throughout the country.

HEADQUARTERS

3939 Meadows Dr., Indianapolis, IN 46205 Tel. (317)547-9541

Media Contact, Admin., John E. Hampton, Fax (317)543-0512

OFFICERS

Presiding Bishop, Paul A. Bowers
Asst. Presiding Bishop, David Ellis
Bishops: Arthus Brazier; George Brooks; Ramsey Butler; Morris Golder; Francis L. Smith; Brooker T. Jones; C. R. Lee; Robert McMurray; Philip L. Scott; William L. Smith; Samuel A. Layne; Freeman M. Thomas; James E. Tyson; Charles Davis; Willie Burrell; Harry Herman; Jermiah Reed; Jeron Johnson; Clifton Jones; Robert Wauls; Ronald L. Young; Henry L. Johnson; Leodis Warren; Thomas J. Weeks; Eugene Redd; Thomas W. Weeks, Sr.; Willard Saunders; Davis L. Ellis; Earl Parchia; Vanuel C. Little; Norman Wagner; George Austin; Benjamin A. Pitt; Markose Thopil; John K. Cole; Peter Warkie; Norman Walters; Alphonso Scott; David Dawkins
Gen. Sec, Suffragan Bishop Richard Young
Gen. Treas., Elder James Loving
Asst. Treas., Suffragan Bishop Willie Ellis

PERIODICAL

Christian Outlook

Pentecostal Church of God

Growing out of the pentecostal revival at the turn of the century, the Pentecostal Church of God was organized in Chicago on Dec. 30, 1919, as the Pentecostal Assemblies of the U.S.A. The name was changed to Pentecostal Church of God in 1922; in 1934 it was changed again to The Pentecostal Church of God of America, Inc.; and finally the name became the Pentecostal Church of God (Inc.) in 1979.

The International Headquarters was moved from Chicago to Ottumwa, Iowa, in 1927, then to Kansas City, Mo., in 1933 and finally to Joplin, Mo., in 1951.

The denomination is evangelical and pentecostal in doctrine and practice. Active membership in the National Association of Evangelicals and the Pentecostal/Charismatic Churches North America is maintained.

The church is Trinitarian in doctrine and teaches the absolute inerrancy of the Scripture from Genesis to Revelation. Among its cardinal beliefs are the doctrines of salvation, which includes regeneration; divine healing, as provided for in the atonement; the baptism in the Holy Ghost, with the initial physical evidence of speaking in tongues; and the premillennial second coming of Christ.

HEADQUARTERS

4901 Pennsylvania, P.O. Box 850, Joplin, MO 64802 Tel. (417)624-7050 Fax (417)624-7102

Media Contact, Gen. Sec., Dr. Ronald R. Minor

OFFICERS

Gen. Supt., Dr. James D. Gee
Gen. Sec., Dr. Ronald R. Minor

OTHER GENERAL EXECUTIVES

Dir. of World Missions, Rev. Charles R. Mosier
Dir. of Indian Missions, Dr. C. Don Burke
Gen. PYPA Pres., Reggie O. Powers
Dir. of Home Missions/Evangelism, Dr. H. O. (Pat) Wilson

ASSISTANT GENERAL SUPERINTENDENTS

Northwestern Division, Rev. Robert L. McGee
Southwestern Division, Dr. Norman D. Fortenberry
North Central Division, Rev. Freddy A. Burcham
South Central Division, Rev. E. L. Redding
Northeastern Division, Rev. Thomas E. Branham
Southeastern Division, Rev. Virgil R. Kincard

OTHER DEPARTMENTAL OFFICERS

Bus. Mgr., Rev. George Gilmore
Gen. PLA Dir., Mrs. Diana L. Gee
Christian Educ., Dir., Ms. Billie Blevins

PERIODICAL

The Pentecostal Messenger

Pentecostal Fire-Baptized Holiness Church

Organized in 1918, this group consolidated with the Pentecostal Free Will Baptists in 1919. It maintains rigid discipline over members.

HEADQUARTERS

P.O. Box 261, La Grange, GA 30241-0261 Tel. (706)884-7742

Media Contact, Gen. Mod., Wallace B. Pittman, Jr.

OFFICERS

Gen. Treas., K. N. (Bill) Johnson, P.O. Box 1528, Laurinburg, NC 28352 Tel. (919)276-1295
Gen. Sec., W. H. Preskitt, Sr., Rt. 1, Box 169, Wetumpka, AL 36092 Tel. (205)567-6565
Gen. Mod., Wallace B. Pittman, Jr.
Gen. Supt. Mission Bd., Jerry Powell, Rt. 1, Box 384, Chadourn, NC 28431

PERIODICAL

Faith and Truth

The Pentecostal Free Will Baptist Church, Inc.

The Cape Fear Conference of Free Will Baptists, organized in 1855, merged in 1959 with The Wilmington Conference and The New River Conference of Free Will Baptists and was renamed the Pentecostal Free Will Baptist Church, Inc. The doctrines include regeneration, sanctification, the Pentecostal baptism of the Holy Ghost, the Second Coming of Christ and divine healing.

HEADQUARTERS

P.O. Box 1568, Dunn, NC 28335 Tel. (910)892-4161

Media Contact, Genl. Supt., Don Sauls

OFFICERS

Gen. Supt., Dr. Don Sauls
Asst. Gen. Supt., Dr. W. L. Ellis

Gen. Sec., Dr. J. T. Hammond
Gen. Treas., Dr. W. L. Ellis
World Witness Dir., Rev. David Taylor
Christian Ed. Dir., Dr. J. T. Hammond
Gen. Services Dir., Danny Blackman
Ministerial Council Dir., Rev. Reynolds Smith
Ladies' Auxiliary Dir., Mrs. Dollie Davis
Heritage Bible College, Pres., Dr. W. L. Ellis
Crusader Youth Camp, Dir., Dr. J. T. Hammond

OTHER ORGANIZATIONS

Heritage Bible College
Crusader Youth Camp
Benefit Benevolent Assoc.
Blessings Bookstore, 1006 W. Cumberland St., Dunn, NC 28334 Tel. (910)892-2401
Cape Fear Christian Academy, Rt 1 Box 139, Erwin, NC 28339 Tel. (910)897-5423

PERIODICAL

The Messenger

Pillar of Fire

The Pillar of Fire was founded by Alma Bridwell White in Denver on Dec. 29, 1901 as the Pentecostal Union. In 1917, the name was changed to Pillar of Fire. Alma White was born in Kentucky in 1862 and taught school in Montana where she met her husband, Kent White, a Methodist minister, who was a University student in Denver.

Because of Alma White's evangelistic endeavors, she was frowned upon by her superiors, which eventually necessitated her withdrawing from Methodist Church supervision. She was ordained as Bishop and her work spread to many states, to England, and since her death to Liberia, West Africa, Malawi, East Africa, Yugoslavia, Spain, India and the Philippines.

The Pillar of Fire organization has a college and two seminaries stressing Biblical studies. It operates eight separate schools for young people. The church continues to keep in mind the founder's goals and purposes.

HEADQUARTERS

P.O. Box 9159, Zarephath, NJ 08890 Tel. (908)-356-0102 Fax (908)271-1968
Western Headquarters, 1302 Sherman St., Denver, CO 80203 Tel. (303)427-5462
Media Contact, 1st Vice Pres., Robert B. Dallenbach, 3455 W. 83 Ave., Westminster, CO 80030 Tel. (303)427-5462 Fax (303)429-0910

OFFICERS

Pres. & Gen. Supt., Bishop Donald J. Wolfram
1st Vice-Pres. & Asst. Supt., Bishop Robert B. Dallenbach
2nd Vice-Pres./Sec.-Treas., Lois R. Stewart
Trustees: Kenneth Cope; Elsworth N. Bradford; S. Rea Crawford; June Blue

PERIODICAL

Pillar of Fire

Polish National Catholic Church of America

After a number of attempts to resolve differences regarding the role of the laity in parish administration in the Roman Catholic Church in Scranton, Pa., this Church was organized in 1897. With the consecration to the episcopacy of the Most Rev. F. Hodur, this Church became a member of the Old Catholic Union of Utrecht in 1907.

HEADQUARTERS

Office of the Prime Bishop, 1002 Pittston Ave., Scranton, PA 18505 Tel. (717)346-9131
Media Contact, Prime Bishop, Most Rev. John F. Swantek, Fax (717)346-2188

OFFICERS

Prime Bishop, Most Rev. John F. Swantek, 115 Lake Scranton Rd., Scranton, PA 18505
Central Diocese: Bishop, Rt. Rev. Anthony M. Rysz, 529 E. Locust St., Scranton, PA 18505
Eastern Diocese: Bishop, Rt. Rev. Thomas J. Gnat, 166 Pearl St., Manchester, NH 03104
Buffalo-Pittsburgh Diocese: Bishop, Rt. Rev. Thaddeus S. Peplowski, 5776 Broadway, Lancaster, NY 14086
Western Diocese: Rt. Rev. Robert M. Nemkovich, 920 N. Northwest Hwy., Park Ridge, IL 60068
Canadian Diocese: Bishop, Sede Vacante, 186 Cowan Ave., Toronto, ON M6K 2N6
Ecumenical Officer, V. Rev. Stanley Skrzypek, 206 Main Street, New York Mills, NY 13416 Tel. (315)736-9757

PERIODICALS

God's Field; Polka

Presbyterian Church in America

The Presbyterian Church in America has a strong commitment to evangelism, to missionary work at home and abroad and to Christian education.

Organized in December 1973, this church was first known as the National Presbyterian Church but changed its name in 1974 to Presbyterian Church in America (PCA).

The PCA made a firm commitment on the doctrinal standards which had been significant in presbyterianism since 1645, namely the Westminster Confession of Faith and Catechisms. These doctrinal standards express the distinctives of the Calvinistic or Reformed tradition.

The PCA maintains the historic polity of Presbyterian governance, namely rule by presbyters (or elders) and the graded courts which are the session governing the local church. The presbytery is responsible for regional matters and the general assembly for national matters. The PCA has taken seriously the position of the parity of elders, making a distinction between the two classes of elders, teaching and ruling.

In 1982, the Reformed Presbyterian Church, Evangelical Synod (RPCES) joined the PCA. It brought with it a tradition that had antecedents in Colonial America. It also included Covenant College in Lookout Mountain, Ga., and Covenant Theological Seminary in St. Louis, both of which are national denominational institutions of the PCA.

HEADQUARTERS

1852 Century Pl., Atlanta, GA 30345-4305 Tel. (404)320-3366 Fax (404)329-1275
Media Contact, Ed., Rev. Robert G. Sweet, Tel. (404)320-3388 Fax (404)329-1280

OFFICERS

Mod., Mr. Frank A. Brock, Lookout Mountain, GA 30750
Stated Clk., Dr. Paul R. Gilchrist, 1852 Century Pl., Ste. 190, Atlanta, GA 30345-4305 Tel. (404)320-3366

PERMANENT COMMITTEES

Admn., Dr. Paul R. Gilchrist, 1852 Century Pl., Ste. 190, Atlanta, GA 30345-4305 Tel. (404)-320-3366 Fax (404)329-1275

Christian Educ. & Publ., Dr. Charles Dunahoo, Tel. (404)320-3388

Mission to North America, Dr. Cortez Cooper, 1852 Century Pl., Ste. 205, Atlanta, GA 30345-4305 Tel. (404)320-3330

Mission to the World, Dr. Paul D. Kooistra, 1852 Century Pl., Ste. 201, Atlanta, GA 30345-4305 Tel. (404)320-3373

Presbyterian Church (U.S.A.)

The Presbyterian Church (U.S.A.) was organized June 10, 1983, when the Presbyterian Church in the United States and the United Presbyterian Church in the United States of America united in Atlanta. The union healed a major division which began with the Civil War when Presbyterians in the South withdrew from the Presbyterian Church in the United States of America to form the Presbyterian Church in the Confederate States.

The United Presbyterian Church in the United States of America had been created by the 1958 union of the Presbyterian Church in the United States of America and the United Presbyterian Church of North America. Of those two uniting bodies, the Presbyterian Church in the U.S.A. dated from the first Presbytery organized in Philadelphia, about 1706. The United Presbyterian Church of North America was formed in 1858, when the Associate Reformed Presbyterian Church and the Associate Presbyterian Church united.

Strongly ecumenical in outlook, the Presbyterian Church (U.S.A.) is the result of at least 10 different denominational mergers over the last 250 years. A restructure, adopted by the General Assembly meeting in June 1993, has been implemented. The Presbyterian Church (U.S.A.) dedicated its new national offices in Louisville, Ky. in 1988.

HEADQUARTERS

100 Witherspoon St., Louisville, KY 40202 Tel. (502)569-5000 Fax (502)569-5018

Media Contact, Assoc. Dir. for Communications, Gary W. Luhr, Tel. (502)569-5515 Fax (502)-569-8073

OFFICERS

Mod., Marj Carpenter
Vice-Mod., William F. Henning, Jr.
Stated Clk., James E. Andrews
Assoc. Stated Clk., C. Fred Jenkins
Eugene G. Turner

THE OFFICE OF THE GENERAL ASSEMBLY

Tel. (502)569-5360 Fax (502)569-8005
Stated Clk., James E. Andrews
Dept. of the Stated Clerk: Dir., Juanita H. Granady
Dept. of Administration: Dir., ----
Dept. of Constitutional & Assembly Ser.: Dir., C. Fred Jenkins
Dept. of Governing Body: Ecumenical & Agency Rel., Dir., Eugene G. Turner
Dept. of Assembly Services: Mgr. for Assembly Arrangements, Kerry S. Clements
Dept. of Hist., Philadelphia: 425 Lombard St., Philadelphia, PA 19147 Tel. (215)627-1852 Fax (215)627-0509; Dir., Frederick J. Heuser, Jr.
Deputy Dir., Michelle Francis

GENERAL ASSEMBLY COUNCIL

Office of the Exec. Dir., James D. Brown, Fax (502)569-8080
Assoc., Operations, Frank Diaz
Worldwide Ministries Division, Dir., Clifton Kirkpatrick
Congregational Ministries Division, Dir., Eunice B. Poethig
National Ministries Division, Dir., Curtis A. Kearns, Jr.
Corp. & Admn. Services, Dir., G. A. Goff

BOARD OF PENSIONS

Pres., John J. Detterick, 215 Arch St., Philadelphia, PA 19107 Tel. 215)574-5200

PRESBYTERIAN CHURCH (U.S.A.) FOUNDATION

Ofc., 200 E. Twelfth St., Jeffersonville, IN 47130 Tel. (812)288-8841 Fax (502)569-5980
Chpsn. of the Bd., Frank Deming
Pres. & CEO, Larry Carr

PRESBYTERIAN PUBLISHING CORPORATE

Pres. & CEO, Larry Carr

SYNOD EXECUTIVES

Alaska-Northwest, Rev. David C. Meekhof, 233 6th Ave. N., Ste. 100, Seattle, WA 98109-5000 Tel. (206)448-6403

Covenant, Rev. Lowell Sims, 6172 Bush Blvd., Ste. 3000, Columbus, OH 43229-2564 Tel. (614)436-3310

Lakes & Prairies, Rev. Margaret J. Thomas, 8012 Cedar Ave. S., Bloomington, MN 55425-1204 Tel. (612)854-0144

Lincoln Trails, Rev. Verne E. Sindlinger, 1100 W. 42nd St., Indianapolis, IN 46208-3381 Tel. (317)923-3681

Living Waters, Rev. J. Harold Jackson, P.O. Box 1207, Brentwood, TN 37024 Tel. (615)370-4008

Mid-America, Rev. John L. Williams, 6400 Glenwood, Ste. 111, Overland Park, KS 66202-4072 Tel. (913)384-3020

Mid-Atlantic, Rev. Carroll D. Jenkins, P.O. Box 27026, Richmond, VA 23261-7026 Tel. (804)-342-0016

Northeast, Rev. Robert Howell White, 3049 E. Genesee St., Syracuse, NY 13224-1644 Tel. (315)446-5990

Pacific, Rev. Philip H. Young, 8 Fourth St., Petaluma, CA 94952 Tel. (707)765-1772

Puerto Rico (Boriquen in Puerto Rico), Rev. Harry Fred Del Valle Irizarry, Cond. Medical Center Plaza, Ste. 216, Mayaguez, PR 00682 Tel. (809)-832-8375

Rocky Mountains, Rev. Richard O. Wyatt, 7000 N. Broadway, Suite 410, Denver, CO 80221-2475 Tel. (303)428-0523

South Atlantic, Rev. John Niles Bartholomew, 118 E. Monroe St., Jacksonville, FL 32202 Tel. (904)356-6070

Southern California, Hawaii, Rev. R. Stephen Jenks, Int., 1501 Wilshire Blvd., Los Angeles, CA 90017-2293 Tel. (213)483-3840

Southwest, Rev. Gary Skinner, 4423 N. 24th St., Ste. 800, Phoenix, AZ 85016-5544 Tel. (602)-468-3800

Sun, Rev. Roberto Delgado, 920 S. 135 E, Denton, TX 76205-7898 Tel. (817)382-9656

Trinity, Rev. Thomas M. Johnston, Jr., 3040 Market St., Camp Hill, PA 17011-4599 Tel. (717)-737-0421

PERIODICALS

American Presbyterians: Journal of Presbyterian History; Presbyterian News Service; Church & Society Magazine; Horizons; Monday Morning; Presbyterians Today; Interpretation; Presbyterian Outlook

Primitive Advent Christian Church

This body split from the Advent Christian Church. All its churches are in West Virginia. The Primitive Advent Christian Church believes that the Bible is the only rule of faith and practice and that Christian character is the only test of fellowship and communion. The church agrees with Christian fidelity and meekness; exercises mutual watch and care; counsels, admonishes, or reproves as duty may require and receives the same from each other as becomes the household of faith. Primitive Advent Christians do not believe in taking up arms.

The church believes that three ordinances are set forth by the Bible to be observed by the Christian church: (1) baptism by immersion; (2) the Lord's Supper, by partaking of unleavened bread and wine; (3) feet washing, to be observed by the saints' washing of one another's feet.

HEADQUARTERS

Media Contact, Sec. Treas., Roger Wines, 1971 Grapevine Rd., Sissonville, WV 25320 Tel. (304)988-2668

OFFICERS

Pres., Herbert Newhouse, 7632 Hughart Dr., Sissonville, WV 25320 Tel. (304)984-9277

Vice-Pres., Roger Hammons, 273 Frame Rd., Elkview, WV 25071 Tel. (304)965-6247

Sec. & Treas., Roger Wines, 1971 Grapevine Rd., Sissonville, WV 25320 Tel. (304)988-2668

Primitive Baptists

This large group of Baptists, located throughout the United States, opposes all centralization and modern missionary societies. They preach salvation by grace alone.

HEADQUARTERS

P.O. Box 38, Thornton, AR 71766 Tel. (501)352-3694

Media Contact, Elder W. Hartsel Cayce

OFFICERS

Elder W. Hartsel Cayce

Elder L. Bradley, Jr., Box 17037, Cincinnati, OH 45217 Tel. (513)821-7289

Elder S. T. Tolley, P.O. Box 68, Atwood, TN 38220 Tel. (901)662-7417

PERIODICALS

Baptist Witness; The Christian Baptist; Primitive Baptist; For the Poor

Primitive Methodist Church in the U.S.A.

Hugh Bourne and William Clowes, local preachers in the Wesleyan Church in England, organized a daylong meeting at Mow Cop in Staffordshire on May 31, 1807, after Lorenzo Dow, a Methodist preacher from America, told them of American camp meetings. Thousands attended and many were converted but the Methodist church, founded by the open-air preacher John Wesley, refused to accept the converts and reprimanded the preachers.

After waiting for two years for a favorable action by the Wesleyan Society, Bourne and Clowes established The Society of the Primitive Methodists. This was not a schism, Bourne said, for "we did not take one from them ... it now appeared to be the will of God that we fear of God." Primitive Methodist missionaries were sent to New York in 1829. An American conference was established in 1840.

Missionary efforts reach into Guatemala, Spain and other countries. The denomination joins in federation with the Evangelical Congregational Church, the United Brethren in Christ Church and the Southern Methodist Church and is a member of the National Association of Evangelicals.

The church believes the Bible is the only true rule of faith and practice, the inspired Word of God. It believes in one Triune God, the Deity of Jesus Christ, the Deity and personality of the Holy Spirit, the innocence of Adam and Eve, the Fall of the human race, the necessity of repentance, justification by faith of all who believe, regeneration witnessed by the Holy Spirit, sanctification by the Holy Spirit, the second coming of the Lord Jesus Christ, the resurrection of the dead and conscious future existence of all people and future judgments with eternal rewards and punishments.

HEADQUARTERS

Media Contact, Exec. Dir. (Elect), Rev. Wayne Yarnall, Tel. (717)472-3436 Fax (717)472-9283

OFFICERS

Pres., Rev. Eugene Martin, 503 Grant St., Newtown, PA 18940

Vice-Pres., Rev. A. Russell Masartis, Box 345, Benton, WI 53803-0345 Tel. (608)759-3232

Exec. Dir., Rev. William H. Fudge, 1045 Laurel Run Rd., Wilkes-Barre, PA 18702 Fax (717)472-9283

Treas., Mr. Raymond Baldwin, 11012 Langton Arms Ct., Oakton, VA 22124

Gen. Sec., Rev. Reginald H. Thomas, 110 Pittston Blvd., Wilkes-Barre, PA 18702 Tel. (717)823-3425

Progressive National Baptist Convention, Inc.

This body held its organizational meeting in Cincinnati in November, 1961. Subsequent regional sessions were followed by the first annual session in Philadelphia in 1962.

HEADQUARTERS

601 50th Street, N.E., Washington, DC 20019 Tel. (202)396-0558 Fax (202)398-4998

Media Contact, Gen. Sec., Rev. Tyrone S. Pitts

OFFICERS

Pres., Dr. Bennett W. Smith, Sr., St. John Baptist Church, 184 Goodell St., Buffalo, NY 14204

Gen. Sec., Rev. Tyrone S. Pitts, 601 50th St., NE, Washington, DC 20019 Tel. (202)396-0558 Fax (202)398-4998

OTHER ORGANIZATIONS

Dept. of Christian Education, Exec. Dir., Dr. C. B. Lucas, Emmanuel Baptist Church, 3815 W. Broadway, Louisville, KY 40211

Women's Dept., Mrs. Mildred Wormly, 218 Spring St., Trenton, NJ 08618

Home Mission Bd., Exec. Dir., Rev. Archie LeMone, 601 50th St., NE, Washington, DC 20019

Congress of Christian Education, Pres., Rev. Harold S. Diggs, Mayfield Memorial Baptist Church, 700 Sugar Creek Rd. W., Charlotte, NC 28213

Baptist Global Mission Bureau, Dr. Ronald K. Hill, 161-163 60th St., Philadelphia, PA 19139

PERIODICAL

Baptist Progress

Protestant Reformed Churches in America

The Protestant Reformed Churches in America were organized in 1926 as a result of doctrinal disagreement relating to such matters as world conformity, problems of higher criticism and God's grace that pervaded the Christian Reformed Church in the early 1920s.

After the passage of the formula on Three Points of Common Grace by the Synod of the Christian Reformed Church in 1924, and during the resulting storm of controversy, three clergy and those in their congregations who agreed with them were expelled from the Christian Reformed Church. These clergy were Herman Hoeksema of the Eastern Ave. Christian Reformed Church in Grand Rapids, Mich., George Ophoff, pastor of the Hope congregation in Riverbend, Mich., and Henry Danhof in Kalamazoo, Mich.

In March 1925, the consistories of these congregations signed an Act of Agreement and adopted the temporary name of "Protesting Christian Reformed Churches." The break was made final following the Synod of the Christian Reformed Church of 1926.

The Protestant Reformed Churches in America hold to the doctrinal tenets of Calvinism, the Belgic Confession, the Heidelberg Catechism and the Canons of Dordrecht.

HEADQUARTERS

16511 South Park Ave., South Holland, IL 60473 Tel. (708)333-1314

Media Contact, Stat. Clk., Rev. Don Doezma, 5111 Ivanrest Ave., Grandville, MI 49418 Tel. (616)-247-0638

OFFICER

Stat. Clk., Rev. M. Joostens

PERIODICAL

The Standard Bearer

Reformed Church in America

The Reformed Church in America was established in 1628 by the earliest settlers of New York. It is the oldest Protestant denomination with a continuous ministry in North America. Until 1867 it was known as the Reformed Protestant Dutch Church.

The first ordained minister, Domine Jonas Michaelius, arrived in New Amsterdam from The Netherlands in 1628. Throughout the colonial period, the Reformed Church lived under the authority of the Classis of Amsterdam. Its churches were clustered in New York and New Jersey. Under the leadership of Rev. John Livingston, it became a denomination independent of the authority of the Classis of Amsterdam in 1776. Its geographical base was broadened in the 19th century by the immigration of Reformed Dutch and German settlers in the midwestern United States. The Reformed Church now spans the United States and Canada.

The Reformed Church accepts as its standards of faith the Heidelberg Catechism, Belgic Confession and Canons of Dort. It has a rich heritage of world mission activity. It claims to be loyal to reformed tradition which emphasizes obedience to God in all aspects of life.

Although the Reformed Church in America has worked in close cooperation with other churches, it has never entered into merger with any other denomination. It is a member of the World Alliance of Reformed Churches, the World Council of Churches and the National Council of the Churches of Christ in the United States of America.

HEADQUARTERS

475 Riverside Dr., New York, NY 10115 Tel. (212)870-2841 Fax (212)870-2499

Media Contact, Dir., Stewardship & Communication Services, E. Wayne Antworth, Tel. (212)-870-2954

OFFICERS AND STAFF OF GENERAL SYNOD

Pres., I. John Hesselink, 475 Riverside Dr., Rm. 1814, New York, NY 10115

Gen. Sec., Wesley Granberg- Michaelson

OTHER ORGANIZATIONS

Bd. of Directors, Pres., I. John Hesselink, 475 Riverside Dr., Rm. 1814, New York, NY 10115

Bd. of Pensions: Pres., Kenneth Weller; Sec., Wesley Granberg- Michaelson

General Synod Council: Mod., Harold J. Korver, 475 Riverside Dr., Rm. 1812, New York, NY 10115

Office of Policy, Planning & Admn. Serv., Kenneth R. Bradsell

Ofc. of Ministry & Personnel Services, Dir., Alvin J. Poppen

Office of Evangelism & Church Dev. Ser., Bruce G. Laverman

Ofc. of Finance, Treas., Andrew Lee

Ofc. of Stewardship & Comm. Services, Dir., E. Wayne Antworth

Office of Congregational Ser., Dir., Jeffrey Japinga

Reformed Church Women's Ministries, Exec. Dir., Christina VanEyl

African-American Council, Exec. Dir., John David Cato

Council for Hispanic Ministries, Natl. Sec., Luis Perez

American Indian Council, Natl. Sec., Kenneth W. Mallory

Council for Pacific/Asian-American Min., Natl. Sec., Ella Campbell

PERIODICAL

The Church Herald

Reformed Church in the United States

Lacking pastors, early German Reformed immigrants to the American colonies were led in worship by "readers." One reader, schoolmaster John Philip Boehm, organized the first congregations near Philadelphia in 1725. A Swiss pastor, Michael Schlatter, was sent by the Dutch Reformed Church in 1746. Strong ties with the Netherlands existed until the formation of the Synod of the German Reformed Church in 1793.

The Eureka Classis, organized in North and South Dakota in 1910 and strongly influenced by the writings of H. Kohlbruegge, P. Geyser and J. Stark, refused to become part of the 1934 merger of the Reformed Church with the Evangelical Synod of North America, holding that it sacrificed the Reformed heritage. (The merged Evangelical and Reformed Church became part of the United Church of Christ in 1957.) Under the leadership of pastors W. Grossmann and W. J. Krieger, the Eureka Classis in 1942 incorporated as the continuing Reformed Church in the United States.

The growing Eureka Classis dissolved in 1986 to form a Synod with four regional classes. An heir to the Reformation theology of Zwingli and Calvin, the Heidelberg Catechism of 1563 is used as the confessional standard. The Bible is strictly held to be the inerrant, infallible Word of God.

The RCUS supports Dordt College and Mid-America Reformed Seminary in Iowa. The RCUS is the official sponsor to the Reformed Confessing Church of Zaire.

HEADQUARTERS

Media Contact, Rev. Steven Work, P.O. Box 280, Quinter, KS 67752 Tel. (913)754-3406

OFFICERS

Pres., Rev. Vernon Pollema, 235 James Street, Shafter, CA 93263 Tel. (805)746-6907

Vice-Pres., Rev. Paul Treick, 1515 Carlton Ave., Modesto, CA 95350 Tel. (209)526-0637

Stated Clk., Rev. Steven Work, P.O. Box 280, Quinter, KS 67752 Tel. (913)754-3406

Treas., Mr. Clayton Greiman, 2115 Hwy. 69, Garner, IA 50438 Tel. (515)923-2950

PERIODICAL

Reformed Herald

Reformed Episcopal Church

The Reformed Episcopal Church was founded Dec. 2, 1873 in New York City by Bishop George D. Cummins, an assistant bishop in the Protestant Episcopal Church from 1866 until 1873. Cummins and other evangelical Episcopalians viewed with alarm the influence of the Oxford Movement in the Protestant Episcopal Church, for the interest it stimulated in Roman Catholic ritual and doctrine and for intolerance it bred toward evangelical Protestant doctrine.

Throughout the late 1860s, evangelicals and ritualists clashed over ceremonies and vestments, exchanges of pulpits with clergy of other denominations, the meaning of critical passages in the Book of Common Prayer, interpretation of the sacraments and validity of the Apostolic Succession.

In October, 1873, other bishops publicly attacked Cummins in the church newspapers for participating in an ecumenical Communion service sponsored by the Evangelical Alliance. Cummins resigned and drafted a call to Episcopalians to organize a new Episcopal Church for the "purpose of restoring the old paths of their fathers." On Dec. 2, 1873, a Declaration of Principles was adopted and Dr. Charles E. Cheney was elected bishop to serve with Cummins. The Second General Council, meeting in May 1874 in New York City, approved a Constitution and Canons and a slightly amended version of the Book of Common Prayer. In 1875, the Third General Council adopted a set of Thirty-Five Articles.

Cummins died in 1876. The church had grown to nine jurisdictions in the United States and Canada at that time. The Reformed Episcopal Church is a member of the National Association of Evangelicals.

HEADQUARTERS

2001 Frederick Rd., Baltimore, MD 21228-5599 Tel. (410)719-8944 Fax (410)719-8945

Media Contact, Bishop Daniel G. Cox

Media Contact, Bishop Sanco K. Rembert, P.O. Box 20068, Charleston, SC 29413 Tel. (803)-873-3451

OFFICERS

Pres. & Presiding Bishop, Rev. Franklin H. Sellers, Sr., 81 Buttercup Ct., Marco Island, FL 33937-3480 Tel. (813)642-4202 Fax (813)642-4202

Vice-Pres., Bishop Sanco K. Rembert, P.O. Box 20068, Charleston, SC 29413

Sec., Rev. Willie J. Hill, Jr., 271 W. Tulpehocken St., Philadelphia, PA 19144

Treas., Mr. William B. Schimpf, 67 Westaway Lane, Warrington, PA 18976

OTHER ORGANIZATIONS

Bd. of Foreign Missions: Pres., Miss Barbara West

Bd. of Natl. Church Extension: Pres., Rt. Rev. Royal Grote, Jr., 19 Heather Ct., New Providence, NJ 07974

Publication Society: Pres., Rev. Gregory Hotchkiss

BISHOPS

William H.S. Jerdan, Jr., 414 W. 2nd South St., Summerville, SC 29483

Sanco K. Rembert, P.O. Box 20068, Charleston, SC 29413

Franklin H. Sellers, Sr., 81 Buttercup Ct., Marco Island, FL 33937-3480

Leonard W. Riches, Sr., RD 1, Box 501, Smithown Rd., Pipersville, PA 18947

Daniel G. Cox, 9 Hilltop Pl., Catonsville, MD 21228

Royal U. Grote, Jr., 19 Heather Ct., New Providence, NJ 07974

James C. West, Sr., 91 Anson St., Charleston, SC 29401

Robert H. Booth, 1222 Haworth St., Philadelphia, PA 19124

PERIODICAL

The Evangelical Episcopalian

Reformed Mennonite Church

This is a small group of believers in Pennsylvania, Ohio, Michigan, and Illinois who believe in non-resistance of evil,non-conformity to the world and practice separation from unfaithful worship. They believe that Christian unity is the effect of brotherly love and are of one mind and spirit. Their church was established in 1812 by John Herr who agreed with the teachings of Menno Simon as well as those of Jesus Christ.

HEADQUARTERS

Lancaster County only, Reformed Mennonite Church, 602 Strasburg Pike, Lancaster, PA 17602

Media Contact, Bishop, Glenn M. Gross, Tel. (717)697-4623

OFFICER

Bishop Glenn M. Gross, 906 Grantham Rd., Mechanicsburg, PA 17055

Reformed Methodist Union Episcopal Church

The Reformed Methodist Union Episcopal church was formed after a group of ministers withdrew from the African Methodist Episcopal Church following a dispute over the election of ministerial delegates to the General Conference.

These ministers organized the Reformed Methodist Union church during a four-day meeting beginning on Jan. 22, 1885 at Hills Chapel (now known as Mt. Hermon RMUE church), in Charleston, S.C. The Rev. William E. Johnson was elected president of the new church. Following the death of Rev. Johnson in 1896, it was decided that the church would conform to regular American Methodism (the Episcopacy). The first Bishop, Edward Russell Middleton, was elected, and "Episcopal" was added to the name of the church. Bishop Middleton was consecrated on Dec. 5, 1896, by Bishop P. F. Stephens of the Reformed Episcopal Church.

HEADQUARTERS

1136 Brody Ave., Charleston, SC 29407

Media Contact, Gen. Secretary, Brother Willie B. Oliver, P.O. Box 1995, Orangeburg, SC 29116 Tel. (803)536-3293

OFFICERS

Bishop, Rt. Rev. Leroy Gethers, Tel. (803) 766-3534

Asst. Bishop, Rt.Rev. Jerry M. DeVoe, Jr.

Gen. Sec., Brother Willie Oliver

Treas., Rev. Daniel Green

Sec. of Education, Rev. William Polite

Sec. of Books Concerns, Sister Ann Blanding

Sec. of Pension Fund, Rev. Joseph Powell

Sec. of Church Extension, Brother William Parker

Sec. of Sunday School Union, Sister Constance Walker

Sec. of Mission, Rev. Warren Hatcher

Reformed Presbyterian Church of North America

Also known as the Church of the Covenanters, this church's origin dates back to the Reformation days of Scotland when the Covenanters signed their "Covenants" in resistance to the king and the Roman Church in the enforcement of state church practices. The Church in America has signed two "Covenants" in particular, those of 1871 and 1954.

HEADQUARTERS

Media Contact, Stated Clk., Louis D. Hutmire, 7408 Penn Ave., Pittsburgh, PA 15208 Tel. (412)731-1177 Fax (412)731-8861

OFFICERS

Mod., Robert Copeland, PhD, 3111 5th Ave., Beaver Falls, PA 15010 Tel. (412)847-2759

Clk., J. Bruce Martin, 1328 Goodin Dr., Clay Center, KS 67432 Tel. (913)632-5861

Asst. Clk., Raymond E. Morton, 411 N. Vine St., Sparta, IL 62286 Tel. (618)443-3419

Stated Clk., Louis D. Hutmire, 7408 Penn Ave., Pittsburgh, PA 15208 Tel. (412)731-1177

PERIODICAL

The Covenanter Witness

Reformed Zion Union Apostolic Church

This group was organized in 1869 at Boydton, Va., by Elder James R. Howell of New York, a minister of the A.M.E. Zion Church, with doctrines of the Methodist Episcopal Church.

HEADQUARTERS

Rt. 1, Box 64D, Dundas, VA 23938 Tel. (804)676-8509

Media Contact, Bishop G. W. Stedvant

OFFICER

Exec. Brd., Chair, Rev. Hilman Wright, Tel. (804)-447-3988

Sec., Joseph Russell, Tel. (804)634-4520

Religious Society of Friends (Conservative)

These Friends mark their present identity from separations occurring by regions at different times from 1845 to 1904. They hold to a minimum of organizational structure. Their meetings for worship, which are unprogrammed and based on silent, expectant waiting upon the Lord, demonstrate the belief that all individuals may commune directly with God and may share equally in vocal ministry.

They continue to stress the importance of the Living Christ and the experience of the Holy Spirit working with power in the lives of individuals who obey it.

YEARLY MEETINGS

North Carolina YM, David Martin, 788 W. 52nd St., Norfolk, VA 23508 Tel. (804)489-3946

Iowa YM: Bill Deutsch, 1478 Friends End Rd., Decorah, IA 52101 Tel. (319)382-3699

Ohio YM, Edward T. Kirk, 61830 Sandy Ridge Rd., Barnesville, OH 43713 Tel. (614)425-3655

Religious Society of Friends (Unaffiliated Meetings)

Though all groups of Friends acknowledge the same historical roots, 19th-century divisions in theology and experience led to some of the current organizational groupings. Many newer yearly meetings, often marked by spontaneity, variety and experimentation and hoping for renewed Quaker unity, have chosen not to identify with past divisions by affiliating in traditional ways with the larger organizations within the Society. Some of these unaffiliated groups have begun within the past 25 years.

HEADQUARTERS

Friends World Committee for Consulation, Section of the Americas, 1506 Race St., Philadelphia, PA 19102 Tel. (215)241-7250 Fax (215)241-7285

Media Contact, Exec. Sec., Asia Bennett

YEARLY MEETINGS

Alaska Yearly Meeting (E), Supt., Roland Booth, P.O. Box 687, Kotzebue, AK 99752 Tel. (907)-442-3906

Baltimore Yearly Meeting (G & U), Gen. Sec., Frank Massey, 17100 Quaker Ln., Sandy Spring, MD 20860 Tel. (301)774-7663 Fax (301)779-7087

Central Alaska Friends Conference (G), Clerk, Art Koeninger, Box 22, Chitina, AK 99566 Tel. (907)583-2222

Central Yearly Meeting CI), Supt., Cecil Hinshaw, Rt. 2, Box 232, Winchester, IN 46394 Tel. (317)-584-1089

Evangelical Friend Church-E. Region (E), Gen. Supt., Dr. John Williams, 5350 Broadmoor Circle NW, Canton, OH 44709 Tel. (216)493-1660 Fax (216)493-0852

Friends Church SW Yearly Meeting (E), Gen. Supt., Charles Mylander, P.O. Box 1607, Whittier, CA 90609-1607 Tel. (310)947-2883 Fax (310)947-9385
Illinois Yearly Meeting (G), Clerk Coord., Mary Nurenberg, 602 Normal Ave., Normal, IL 61761 Tel. (309)888-2704
Indiana Yearly Meeting (U), Gen. Supt., David Brock, 4715 N. Wheeling Ave., Muncie, IN 47304-1222 Tel. (317)284-6900 Fax (317)284-8925
Intermountain Yearly Meeting(I), Clerk, Chuck Rostkowski, 962 26th St., Ogden, UT 84401 Tel. (801)399-9491
Iowa Yearly Meeting (C), Clerk, Bill Deutsch, 1478 Friends Rd., Decorah, IA 52101 Tel. (319)-382-3699
Iowa Yearly Meeting (U), Gen. Supt., Del Coppinger, P.O. Box 657, Oskaloosa, IA 52577 Tel. (515)673-6380 Fax (515)673-9718
Lake Erie Yearly Meeting (G), Clerk, Damon Hickey, 208 W. University, Wooster, OH 44691 Tel. (216)262-7059 Fax (216)263-2483
Mid-America Yearly Meeting (E), Int. Supt., Royce Frazier, 2018 Maple, Wichita, KS 67213 Tel. (316)267-0391 Fax (316)267-0681
Nebraska Yearly Meeting (U), Clerk, Allyson Bowen, 1126 N. Chariton, Kingman, KS 67068 Tel. (316)532-5522
New England Yearly Meeting (G & U), Admn. Sec., Katherine Clark, 9901 Pleasant St., Worcester, MA 01602-1908 Tel. (508)754-6760
New York Yearly Meeting (G & U), Clerk, Steven W. Ross, 15 Rutherford Pl., New York, NY 10003 Tel. (212)673-5750
North Carolina Yearly Meeting (C), Clerk, Deborah Shaw, 1009 W. McGee St., Greensboro, NC 27410 Tel. (910)273-2199
North Carolina Yearly Meeting (U), Int. Supt., Clifford Winslow, 5506 W. Friendly Ave., Greensboro, NC 27410 Tel. (910)292-6957
North Pacific Yearly Meeting (I), Staff Sec., Lexamme Blumm, 3311 NW Polk, Corvallis, OR 97330 Tel. (206)633-4860
Northern Yearly Meeting (G), Co-Clerk, Mary Snyder, 1915 Midway Rd., Menomonie, WI 54751-5312 Tel. (715)235-2886 Fax (612)825-2130
Northwest Yearly Meeting (E), Supt., Joseph Gerick, 200 N. Meridian St., Newberg, OR 97132-2714 Tel. (503)538-9419 Fax (503)538-9410
Ohio Yearly Meeting (C), Corr., John Brady, 61830 Sandy Ridge Rd., Barnesville, OH 43713 Tel. (614)425-1197
Ohio Valley Yearly Meeting (G), Corr., Barbarie Hillahay, 6921 Stonington Rd., Cincinnati, OH 45230 Tel. (513)232-5348
Pacific Yearly Meeting (I), Clerk, Eric Moon, 2151 Vine St., Berkeley, CA 94709 Tel. (510)841-5471
Philadelphia Yearly Meeting (G), Gen. Sec., Nancy Middleton, 1515 Cherry St., Philadelphia, PA 19102 Tel. (215)241-7210 Fax (215)-567-2096
Rocky Mountain Yearly Meeting (E), Gen. Supt., Stanley Perisho, 3350 Reed St., Wheat Ridge, CO 80033 Tel. (303)238-5200 Fax (303)238-5200
South Central Yearly Meeting (G), Clerk, Marianne Lockard, 602 N. Greening St., Hope, AR 71801 Tel. (501)777-5382
Southeastern Yearly Meeting (G & U), Sec., Nadine Mandolang, 1822 Medart Dr., Tallahassee, FL 32303 Tel. (904)422-1446 Fax (904)-385-0303
So. Appalachian Yearly Meeting (G), Corr., Sandy Mershon, 701 W. Howard Ave., Decatur, GA 30030 Tel. (404)377-2474
Western Yearly Meeting (U), Gen. Supt., Curtis Shaw, P.O. Box 70, Plainfield, IN 46168 Tel. (317)839-2789 Fax (317)839-2616
Wilmington Yearly Meeting (U), Exec. Sec., Marvin Hall, P.O. Box 1194, 251 Ludovic St., Wilmington, OH 45177 Tel. (513)382-2491 Fax (513)382-7077

Reorganized Church of Jesus Christ of Latter Day Saints

This church was founded April 6, 1830, by Joseph Smith, Jr., and reorganized under the leadership of the founder's son, Joseph Smith III, in 1860. The church, with headquarters in Independence, Mo., is established in 36 countries in addition to the United States and Canada. A biennial world conference is held in Independence, Mo. The current president is Wallace B. Smith, great-grandson of the original founder. The church has a world-wide membership of approximately 245,000.

HEADQUARTERS

World Headquarters, P.O. Box 1059, Independence, MO 64051 Tel. (816)833-1000 Fax (816)521-3096
Media Contact, Publ. Rel. Commissioner, Shirlene Flory

OFFICERS

First Presidency: Wallace B. Smith; Counselor, Howard S. Sheehy, Jr.; Counselor, W. Grant McMurray
Council of 12 Apostles, Pres., A. Alex Kahtava
Presiding Bishopric: Presiding Bishop, Norman E. Swails; Counselor, Larry R. Norris; Counselor, Dennis D. Piepergerdes
Presiding Evangelist, Everett S. Graffeo
World Church Sec., A. Bruce Lindgren
Public Relations, Shirlene Flory

PERIODICALS

Saints Herald; Restoration Witness

The Roman Catholic Church

The largest single body of Christians in the United States, the Roman Catholic Church, is under the spiritual leadership of His Holiness the Pope. Its establishment in America dates back to the priests who accompanied Columbus on his second voyage to the New World. A settlement, later discontinued, was made at St. Augustine, Fla. The continuous history of this Church in the Colonies began at St. Mary's in Maryland, in 1634.

(The following information has been furnished by the editor of The Official Catholic Directory, published by P. J. Kenedy & Sons, 3004 Glenview Rd., Wilmette, IL 60091. Reference to this complete volume will provide additional information.)

INTERNATIONAL ORGANIZATION

His Holiness the Pope, Bishop of Rome, Vicar of Jesus Christ, Supreme Pontiff of the Catholic Church.

Pope John Paul II, Karol Wojtyla (born May 18, 1920; installed Oct. 22, 1978)

APOSTOLIC PRO NUNCIO TO THE UNITED STATES

Archbishop Agostino Cacciavillan, 3339 Massachusetts Ave., N.W., Washington, DC 20008. Tel. (202)333-7121 Fax (202)337-4036

U.S. ORGANIZATION

National Conference of Catholic Bishops, 3211 Fourth St., Washington, DC 20017-1194. (202)541-3000

The National Conference of Catholic Bishops (NCCB) is a canonical entity operating in accordance with the Vatican II Decree, Christus Dominus. Its purpose is to foster the Church's mission to mankind by providing the Bishops of this country with an opportunity to exchange views and insights of prudence and experience and to exercise in a joint manner their pastoral office.

OFFICERS

Pres., William Cardinal Keeler
Vice-Pres., Archbishop Anthony M. Pilla
Treas., Archbishop Thomas J. Murphy
Sec., Bishop Joseph A. Fiorenza

NCCB GENERAL SECRETARIAT

Gen. Sec., Rev. Msgr. Robert N. Lynch
Assoc. Gen. Sec., Francis X. Doyle, Sr. Sharon A. Euart, R.S.M.
Sec. for Communication, Rev. Msgr. Francis J. Maniscalco, Interim

NCCB COMMITTEES

Administrative Committee: Chmn., William Cardinal Keeler
Executive Committee: Chmn., Archbishop William Cardinal Keeler
Committee on Budget and Finance: Chmn., Archbishop Thomas J. Murphy
Committee on Personnel: Bishop Anthony M. Pilla
Committee on Priorities and Plans: Chmn., William Cardinal Keeler
American Board of Catholic Missions: Chmn., Bishop Victor H. Balke.
American College Louvain: Chmn., Bishop Frank J. Rodimer
Bishop's Welfare Emergency Relief: Chmn., Archbishop William Cardinal. Keeler
Aid to the Church in Central and Eastern Europe: Chmn., Archbishop Theodore E. McCarrick
African American Catholics: Chmn., Archbishop Curtis J. Guillory, S.V.D.
Bishop's Life and Ministry: Chmn. Bishop William Skylstad_
Boundaries of Dioceses and Provinces: Chmn., William Cardinal . Keeler
Catholic Charismatic Renewal: Chmn., Bishop Sam G. Jacobs
Canonical Affairs: Chmn., Adam Cardinal Maida
Church in Latin America: Chmn., Bishop Raymundo J. Pena
Doctrine: Chmn., Archbishop John R. Quinn
Economic Concerns of the Holy See: Chmn. Archbishop James P. Keleher
Ecumenical and Interreligious Affairs: Chmn., Archbishop Oscar H. Lipscomb, O.S.B.
Evangelization: Chmn., Bishop John G. Vlazny
Hispanic Affairs: Chmn., Bishop Roberto O. Gonzalez, O.F.M.
Laity: Chmn. Bishop Tod D. Brown
Liaison with Catholic News Service: Chmn., Bishop Edward J. O'Donnell
Liturgy: Chmn., Bishop Donald W. Troutman
Marriage and Family Life: Chmn., Joseph J. Charron, C.P.P.S.
Migration: Chmn., Archbishop Theodore E. McCarrick
Mission and Structure of the NCCB: Chmn., Joseph Cardinal Bernardin
Missions: Chmn., Bishop Edmond Carmody
Native American Catholics: Chmn. Bishop Donald Pelotte
Nomination of Conference Offices: Chmn. Bishop Joseph A. Florenza
North American College Rome: Chmn., James Cardinal Hickey
Pastoral Practices: Chmn., Bishop Emil A. Wcela
Permanent Diaconate: Chmn., Bishop Dale J. Melczek
Priestly Formation: Chmn., Archbishop Donald W. Wuerl
Priestly Life and Ministry: Chmn., Archbishop Harry J. Flynn
Pro-Life Activities: Chmn., Roger Cardinal Mahony
Relationship Between Eastern and Latin Catholic Churches: Chmn., Bishop Basil Losten
Religious Life and Ministry: Chmn., Bishop Joseph A. Galante.
Review of Scripture Translations: Chmn., Bishop Richard J. Sklba
Science and Human Values: Chmn., Bishop Francis X. DiLorenzo
Selection of Bishops: Chmn., William Cardinal Keeler
Sexual Abuse: Chmn. Bishop John F. Kinney
Shrines: Chmn. Archbishop James P. Keleher
Stewardship: Chmn. Archbishop Thomas J. Murphy
Vocations: Chmn. Bishop Robert J. Carlson
Women in Society and in the Church: Chmn., Bishop John Snyder

United States Catholic Conference, 3211 Fourth St., Washington, DC 20017, Tel. (202)541-3000

The United States Catholic Conference (USCC) is a civil entity of the American Catholic Bishops assisting them in their service to the Church in this country by uniting the people of God where voluntary, collective action on a broad diocesan level is needed. The USCC provides an organizational structure and the resources needed to insure coordination, cooperation and assistance in the public, educational and social concerns of the church at the national, regional, state and, as appropriate, diocesan levels.

OFFICERS

Pres., Archbishop William Cardinal Keeler
Vice-Pres., Anthony M. Pilla
Treas., Archbishop Thomas J. Murphy
Sec., Bishop Joseph A. Fiorenza

GENERAL SECRETARIAT

Gen. Sec., Dennis M. Schnurr
Assoc. Gen. Sec., Mr. Francis X. Doyle, Sr. Sharon A. Euart, R.S.M.,
Sec. for Communications, Rev. Msgr. Francis J. Maniscalco Interim

USCC COMMITTEES AND DEPARTMENTS

Administrative Board: Chmn., William Cardinal Keeler
Executive Committee: Chmn., William Cardinal Keeler

Committee on Budget and Finance: Chmn., Archbishop Thomas J. Murphy

Committee on Personnel: Chmn., Bishop Anthony M. Pilla

Committee on Priorities and Plans: Chmn., William Cardinal Keeler

Campaign for Human Development: Chmn., Bishop James H. Garland

Committee on Communications: Chmn., Bishop Thomas J. Costello

Committee on Education: Chmn., Bishop Robert J. Banks

Committee of Bishops and Catholic College and University Presidents: Chmn., Bishop Robert J. Banks

Advisory Committee on Public Policy and Catholic Schools: Chmn., Bishop Robert J. Banks

Ex Corde Ecclesiae: Chmn., Bishop John J. Leibrecht

Sapientia Christiana: Chmn., Bishop John P. Boles

USCC Department of Education: Sec., Sr. Lourdes Sheehan, R.S.M.

Committee of Domestic Policy: Chmn., Bishop John H. Ricard, S.S.J.

Committee on International Policy: Chmn., Archbishop Daniel P. Reilly

Department of Social Development and World Peace: Sec., John L. Carr

Office of Domestic Social Development: Dir., Nancy Wisdo

Office of International Justice and Peace: Dir., Rev. Drew Christiansen, S.J.

U.S. Catholic Bishops' National Advisory Council: Chmn. Mrs. Jessie Shields

RELATED ORGANIZATIONS

U.S.CATHOLIC BISHOPS' NATIONAL ADVISORY COUNCIL

Chmn., Elizabeth Habergerger

NATIONAL ORGANIZATIONS

Catholic Legal Immigration Network, Inc., CEO, Mr. John Swenson , 3211 4th St. NE, Washington, D.C. 20017-1194. Tel. (202)541-3317. Fax (202)541-3055

Catholic Relief Services, Exec. Dir., Mr. Kenneth Hackett, 209 W. Fayette St., Baltimore, MD 21201. Tel. (401)625-2220. Fax (401)685-1635

CTNA Telecommunications Inc., Pres., Dr. Peter J. Dirr, 3211 4th St. N.E., Washington, D.C. 20017-1194. Tel. (202)541-3444. Fax (202)541-3138

American Catholic Correctional Chaplains Association, Pres., Bro. Peter Donohue, C.F.X., 1717 N.E. 9th St., Ste. 123, Gainesville, FL 32609

American Catholic Historical Association, Pres. Rev. Elisabeth Gregorich Gleason The Catholic University of America, Washington, D.C. 20064

The American College of the Roman Catholic Church of the United States - North American College, Chmn., Most Rev. Edward M. Egan, 238 Jewett Ave., Bridgeport, CT 06606

Association of Catholic Diocesan Archivists, Pres., John J. Treanor, 5150 Northwest Hwy., Chicago, IL 60630. Tel. (312)736-5150. Fax (312)736-0488

Catholic Association of Teachers of Homiletics, Pres. Rev. Thomas A. Kane,, Weston School of Theology, 3 Phillips Pl., Cambridge, MA 02138. Tel. (617)492-1960. Fax (617)492-5833

Catholic Campus Ministry Association, Exec. Dir., Donald R. McCrabb, 300 College Park Ave., Dayton, OH 45469-2515. Tel. (513)229-4648. Fax (513)229- 4024

Catholic Charities,-USA Episcopal Liaison., Rev. Joseph M. Sullivan, 1731 King St., Ste. 200, Alexandria, VA 22314. Tel. (703)549-1390. Fax (703)549-1656

Catholic Communications Foundation, Chmn., Most Rev. Anthony G. Bosco, P.O. Box 374, Pawling, NY 12564. Tel. (203)746-6685

Catholic Health Association of the United States, Pres. John E. Curley, 4455 Woodson Rd., St. Louis MO 63134. Tel. (314)427-2500. Fax (314)427-0029

Catholic Kolping Society of America, Sec., Joseph Cardinal Bernardin, P.O. Box 46252, Chicago, IL 60646-0252

Catholic Network of Volunteer Service, Exec. Dir. Sr. Ellen Cavanaugh, 4121 Harewood Rd. N.E., Washington, D.C. 20017. Tel. (202)529-1100. Fax (202)526-1094

Catholic Theological Society of America, Pres., Rev. Roger Haight, S.J., Creighton University, 2500 California Plaza, Omaha, NE 68178-0116. Tel. (402)280-2505. Fax (402) 280-2320.

Center For Human Development, Pres., ----

Conference of Diocesan Coordinators of Health Affairs, Chmn., Rev. Frank Godic , 1030 Superior Ave. Cleveland, OH 44114. Tel. (216)696-6525

Conference of Major Religious Superiors of Men's Institutes of the United States, Inc., Exec. Dir., Rev. Gregory Reisert, 8808 Cameron St., Silver Spring, MD 20910. Tel. (301)588-4030. Fax (301)587-4575

Confraternity of Christian Doctrine, Inc., Mgr. Richard J. Nare, 3211 4th St. N.E., Washington, D.C. 20017. Tel. (202)541-3090

Council of Major Superiors of Women Religious in the United States of America, Pres., Mother Vincent Marie Finnegan, 4200 Harewood Rd. N.E., Washington, D.C. 20017-0467. Tel. (202)832-2575. Fax (202)832-6325

Federation of Diocesan Liturgical Commissions, Exec. Sec., Rev. Michael Spillane, 401 Michigan Ave. N.E., Washington, D.C. 20017. Tel. (202)635- 6990

Diocesan Fiscal Management Conference, Exec. Dir., Rev. Robert J. Yeager, 3225 Pickle Rd., Oregon, OH 43616-4099. Tel. (419)693-0465

Instituto de Liturgia Hispana, Pres., Sr. Rosa Maria Icaza, P.O. Box 28229, San Antonio, TX 78228-0229. Tel. (512)732-2156

International Catholic Migration Commission, Pres., Michael Whiteley, 1319 F St. N.W., Washington, D.C. 20004.

Jesuit Conference Inc., Pres., Rev. Gregory F. Lucey, 1424 16th St. N.W., Ste. 300, Washington, D.C. 20036. Tel. (202)462-0400. Fax (202)328-9212

Ladies of Charity of the United States of America, Pres., Mrs. James R. Dunne, 102 Hickory Dr., Longwood, FL 32779

Leadership Conference of Women Religious, Exec. Dir., Sr. Margaret Cafferty, 8808 Cameron St., Silver Spring, MD 20910. Tel. (301)588-4955. Fax (301)587-4575

Lithuanian Roman Catholic Federation of America, Pres., Saulius V. Kuprys, 4545 W. 63rd St. Chicago, IL 60629. Tel. (312)585-9500

Mariological Society of America, Exec. Sec., Rev. Thomas A. Thompson, Marian Library, University of Dayton, Dayton, OH 45469-1390. Fax (513)229-4590

Mexican American Cultural Center, Chmn., Most Rev. Patrick F. Flores, 3019 W. French Pl., San Antonio, TX 78228. Tel. (512)732-2156

National Apostolate with People with Mental Retardation, Exec. Dir., Charles M. Luce, P.O. Box 4711, Columbia, SC 29240. Tel. (800)736-1280

National Assembly of Religious Brothers, Pres., Br. Joseph Jozwiak, 1337 W. Ohio St. Chicago, IL 60622-6490. Tel. (312)829-8529. Fax (312)829-8915

National Assembly of Religious Women, Natl. Coord., Sr. Judith Vaughan, 529 S. Wabash, Rm. 404, Chicago, IL 60605. Tel. (312)663-1980. Fax (312)663-9161

National Assoc. of African American Catholic Deacons, Inc. 2338 E. 99th St. Chicago, IL 60617. Tel. (312)375-6311. Fax (312)375-7426

National Association of Catholic Chaplains, Exec. Dir., Joseph J. Driscoll, 3501 South Lake Dr., Milwaukee, WI 53207. Tel. (414)483-4898

National Association of Catholic Family Life Ministers, Pres., Joan McGuiness Wagner, 300 College Park, Dayton, OH 45469-1445

National Association of Church Personnel Administrators, Exec. Dir., Sr. Ann White, 100 E. 8th St. Cincinnati, OH 45202. Tel. (513)421-3134. Fax (513)421-6225

National Association of Deacon Organizations, Pres., Deacon Ron Lesjak, 4410 89th St. Kenosha, WI 53142. Tel. (414)694-9143

National Association of Diocesan Directors of Campus Ministry, Pres., Rev. Frederick J. Pennett, Jr., 6 Madbury Rd., P.O. Box 620, Durham, NH 03824-0620. Tel. (603)862-1310

National Association of Diocesan Ecumenical Officers, Pres., Rev. Vincent A. Heier, 462 N. Taylor St., St. Louis, MO 63108. Tel. (314)531-9700. Fax (314)531-2269

National Association of the Holy Name Society, Mod. Most Rev. Michael A. Saltarelli, P.O. Box 26038, Baltimore, MD 21224-0738

National Association of Pastoral Musicians, Exec. Dir., Rev. Virgil C. Funk, 225 Sheridan St. N.W., Washington, D.C. 20011. Tel. (202)723-5800. Fax (202)723-2262

National Association of Permanent Diaconate Directors, Exec. Dir., Deacon John Pistone, 1337 W. Ohio St., Chicago, IL 60622. Tel. (312)226-4033. Fax (312)829-8915

National Black Catholic Clergy Caucus, Exec. Dir., Rev. Albert J. McKnight, 343 N. Walnut St., P.O. Box 1088, Opelousas, LA 70571-1088. Tel. (318)942- 2481. Fax (318)942-9201

National Catholic Cemetery Conference, Exec. Dir., Leo A. Droste, 710 N. River Rd., Des Plaines, IL 60016. Tel. (708)824-8131

National Catholic Conference of Airport Chaplains, Pres., Rev. John A. Jamnicky, Chicago O'Hare Intl. Airport, P.O. Box 66353, Chicago, IL 60666-0353. Tel. (312)686-2636. Fax (312)686-0130

National Catholic Conference for Seafarers, Pres., Rev. Sinclair Oubre, 545 Savannah Ave., Port Arthur, TX 77640. Tel. (409)985-9661. Fax (409)985-9691

National Catholic Committee on Scouting Executive Committee, Advisor, Most Rev. Robert Carlson, P.O. Box 152079, Irving, TX 75015-2079. Fax (214)580-2502

National Catholic Conference for Total Stewardship, Inc., Pres., Rev. Francis A. Novak, 1633 N. Cleveland Ave., Chicago IL 60614. Tel. (312)363-8046. Fax (312)363-2123

National Catholic Council on Alcoholism and Related Drug Problems, Treas. Rev. Msgr. Kieran Martin, 210 Noel Rd., Far Rockaway, NY 11693-1091. Tel. (718)634-5965. Fax (718)474-1538

National Catholic Development Conference, Pres., Peter A. Eltink, 86 Front St., Hempstead, NY 11550. Tel. (516)481-6000

National Catholic Educational Association, Pres., Sr. Catherine McNamee, 1077 30th St., N.W., Ste. 100, Washington, DC 20007. Tel. (202)337-6232 Fax (202)333-6706

National Catholic Office for the Deaf, Exec. Dir., Nora Letourneau, 814 Thayer Ave., Silver Spring, MD 20910. Tel. (301) 587-7992. TTY/V (301)585-5084 (TTY only)

National Catholic Office for Persons with Disabilities, Exec. Dir., Mary Jane Owen, P.O. Box 29113, Washington, D.C. 20017. Tel. (202)529-2933. (TT-voice)

National Catholic Rural Life Conference, Exec. Dir., Bro. David G. Andrews, 4625 Beaver Ave., Des Moines, IA 50310. Tel. (515)270-2634

National Catholic Stewardship Council, Inc., Nat'l. Dir. Sr. Helene Black , 1275 K St. N.W., Ste. 980 Washington, D.C. 20005. Tel. (202)289-1093. Fax (202)682- 9018

National Catholic Student Coalition, Dir., Jamie Williams, 300 College Park Ave., Dayton, OH 45469-2515. Tel.(513)229-3590. Fax (513)229-4024

National Center for Urban Ethnic Affairs, Pres., John A. Kromkowski, P.O. Box 20, Cardinal Station, Washington, D.C. 20064. Tel. (202)232-3600

National Conference of Catechetical Leadership, Exec. Dir., Neil Parent, 3021 4th St. N.E., Washington, D.C. 20017-1102. Tel. (202)636-3826. Fax (202)832-2712

National Council for Catholic Evangelization, Pres., John Simon, 905 E. 166th St., South Holland, IL. 60473-2420

National Council of Catholic Men, Pres., William Sandweg, 4712 Randolph Dr., Annandale, VA 22003

National Council of Catholic Women, Exec. Adm., Annette Kane, 1275 K. St. NW, Ste. 975, Washington, DC 20005. Tel. (202)682-0334. Fax (202)682-0338

National Federation of Catholic Physicians' Guilds, Exec. Dir., Robert H. Herzog, 850 Elm Grove Rd., Elm Grove, WI 53122. Tel. (414)784-3435. Fax (414)782-8788

National Federation for Catholic Youth Ministry, Inc. Exec. Dir., Rev. Leonard C. Wenke, 3700-A Oakview Ter. N.E., Washington, D.C.20017-2591. Tel. (202)636-3825

National Federation of Spiritual Directors, Pres., Rev. Robert M. Coerver, 127 Lake St., Brighton, MA 02135. Fax (617)787-2336

National Foundation for Catholic Youth, Exec. Dir., Rev. Leonard C. Wenke, 3700-A Oakview Ter., Washington, D.C. 20017.Tel. (202)636-3825

National Office for Black Catholics, Exec. Dir., Walter T. Hubbard, The Paulist Center, 3025 4th St., N.E., Washington, D.C. 20017. Tel. (202)635-1778

National Organization for Continuing Education of Roman Catholic Clergy, Inc., Exec. Dir., Br. Paul J. Murray, 1337 W. Ohio St., Chicago, IL 60622. Tel. (312)226-1890

National Pastoral Center for the Chinese Apostolate, Inc., Dir. Rev. Joseph Chang, 5 Monroe St. Rm. 52, New York, NY 10002-7303. Tel, (212)233-3303

National Pastoral Life Center, Dir. Rev. Philip Murnion, 299 Elizabeth St., New York, NY 10012. Tel. (212)431-7825. Fax (212)274-9786

Papal Foundation, Exec. Dir., Rev. Msgr. Thomas J. Benestad, 222 N. 17th St., Philadelphia, PA 19103. Tel. (215)587-2491

Parish Evaluation Project, Dir. Rev. Thomas P. Sweetser, O'Hare Lake Office Plaza, 2200 E. Devon, Ste. 283, Des Plaines, IL 60018. Tel. (708)297-2080. Fax (708)297-2107

Pax Christi U.S.A., National Catholic Peace Movement, Intl. Sec. Mr. Etienne De'Jonghe, 348 E. 10th St., Erie, PA 16503-1110. Tel. (814)453-4955. Fax (814)452-4784

Religious Formation Conference, Exec. Dir. Sr. Margaret Fitzer, 8820 Cameron St., Silver Spring, MD 20910. Tel. (301)588-4938. Fax (301)585-7649

Retreats International Inc., Dir., Most Rev. Thomas W. Gedeon, National Office, Box 1067, Notre Dame, IN 46556. Tel. (219)631-5320

Slovak Catholic Federation, Pres., Rev. Msgr. Thomas V. Banick, 134 S. Washington St., P. O. Box 348, Wilkes-Barre, PA 18701. Tel. (717)823-4168

UNDA-USA National Catholic Association for Communicators, Pres., William G. Halpin, National Office, 901 Irving Ave., Dayton, OH 45409-2316. Tel. (513)229-2303. Fax (513)229-2300

USCC Commission on Certification and Accreditation, Exec. Dir., Sr. Kay L. Sheskaitis, 4455 Woodson Rd., St. Louis, MO 63134. Tel. (314)428-2000. Fax (314)427-0029

United States Catholic Mission Association, Exec. Dir., Sr. Margaret F. Loftus, 3029 4th St. N.E., Washington, D.C. 20017. Tel. (202)832-3112. Fax (202)832-3688

CATHOLIC ORGANIZATIONS WITH INDIVIDUAL I.R.S. RULINGS

Apostleship of the Sea in the United States, Dir. Deacon Robert Mario Balderas, 3211 4th St. N.W., Washington, D.C. 20017. Tel.(202)541-3226. Fax (202)541-3399

The Beginning Experience, Exec. Dir., Sr. Cynthia Hruby, 305 Michigan Ave., Detroit, MI 48226. Tel. (313)965-5110. Fax (313)965-5557

Canon Law Society of America, Exec. Coord., Rev. Patrick J. Cogan, Catholic University, Washington, DC 20064. Tel. (202)269-3491. Fax (202)319-5719

Catholic Coalition on Preaching, Inc., Pres., Rev. Eugene F. Lauer, University of Notre Dame, 1201 Hesburgh Library, Notre Dame, IN 46556. Tel. (219)631-5328

Catholic Engaged Encounter, Inc., Exec. Dir. Dave Florijan, 5 Tara Dr., Pittsburgh, PA 15209. Tel. (412)487-5116

Catholic Library Association, Pres. Br. Paul J. Osterdorf, 461 W. Lancaster Ave., Haverford, PA 19041. Tel. (215)649-5250

Catholic Mutual Relief Society of America, Pres., Donald E. Ruth, 4223 Center St., Omaha, NE 68105. Tel. (402)551-8765

Catholic Relief Insurance Company of America, Pres., Donald E. Ruth, 4223 Center St., Omaha, NE 68105. Tel. (402)551-8765

Conference for Pastoral Planning and Council Development, Exec. Dir., Arthur X. Deegan II, 625 Cleveland St., Clearwater, FL 34615. Tel. (813)461-5000. Fax (813)462-6037

National Association for Lay Ministry, Chmn. Linda Perrone Rooney, 80 W. 78th St. Chanhasssen, MN 55317. Tel. (612)949-9242

National Catholic Conference for Interracial Justice, Exec. Dir. Jerome B. Ernst, 3033 4th St. N.E., Washington, D.C. 20017-1102. Tel. (202)529-6480. Fax (202)526-1262

National Catholic Risk Retention Group, Inc., Dir. Henry P. Devlin, 2333 Hillcrest Dr., Bloomfield Hills, MI 48302. Tel. (313)333-3785. Fax (313)333-2536

National Catholic Young Adult Ministry Association, Inc. Pres. James Breen, 3700 - A Oakview Ter. N.E. Washington, D.C. 20017-2591. Tel. (202)636- 3825. Fax (202)526-7544

National Conference of Diocesan Vocation Directors, Pres., Rev. Patrick Zurek, 1603 S. Michigan Ave. #400, Chicago, IL 60616. Tel. (312)663-5456

National Federation of Priests' Councils, Exec. Dir. Bro.. Bernard F. Stratman, 1337 W. Ohio, Chicago, IL 60622. Tel.(312)226-3334. Fax (312)829-8915

National Institute for the Word of God, Exec. Dir., Rev. John Burke, O. P., 487 Michigan Ave., NE, Washington, DC 20017. Tel. (202)529-0001

National Service Committee of the Catholic Charismatic Renewal of the United States Inc., Dir. Walter Matthews, P.O. Box 628, Locust Grove, VA 22508-0628

North American Forum on the Catechumenate, Exec. Dir., Thomas H. Morris,7115 Leesburg pike, Ste. 308, Fall Church, VA 22043-2301. Tel (703)534-8082

Catholic Committee for Refugees & Children, Pres. Richard Ryscavage, 3211 4th St. NE, Washington, D.C. 20017-1194. Fax (202)541-3245

Worldwide Marriage Encounter, Mod., Most Rev. Paul V. Dudley, 1908 E. Highland Ave., Ste. A, San Bernardino, CA 92404. Tel. (909)881-3456. Fax (909)881-3531

ARCHDIOCESES AND DIOCESES

There follows an alphabetical listing of Archdioceses and Dioceses of The Roman Catholic Church. Each Archdiocese or Diocese contains the following information in sequence: Name of incumbent Bishop; name of Auxiliary Bishop or Bishops, and the Chancellor or Vicar General of the Archdiocese or Diocese, or just the address and telephone number of the chancery office.

Cardinals are addressed as His Eminence and Archbishops and Bishops as Most Reverend.

Albany, Bishop Howard J. Hubbard; Chancellor, Rev. Randall P. Patterson. Chancery Office, Pastoral Center, 40 N. Main Ave., Albany, NY 12203. Tel. (518)453-6600. Fax (518)453-6795

Diocese of Alexandria, Bishop Sam G. Jacobs; Chancellor, Rev. Msgr. Joseph M. Susi. Chancery Office, 4400 Coliseum Blvd., P.O. Box 7417, Alexandria, LA 71306. Tel. (318)445-2401. Fax (318)448-6121

Allentown, Bishop Thomas J. Welsh; Chancellor, Rev. Msgr. Joseph M. Whalen. Chancery Office, 202 N. 17th St., P.O. Box F, Allentown, PA 18105. Tel. (610)437-0755. Fax (610)433-7822

Altoona-Johnstown, Bishop Joseph V. Adamec; Chancellor, Rev. Dennis P. Boggs. Chancery Office, 126 Logan Blvd., Hollidaysburg, PA 16648. Tel. (814)695-5579. Fax (814)695-8894

Amarillo, Bishop Leroy T. Matthiesen; Chancellor, Sr. Christine Jensen. Chancery Office, 1800 N. Spring St., P.O. Box 5644, Amarillo, TX 79117. Tel.(806)383-2243. Fax (806)383-8452

Archdiocese of Anchorage, Archbishop Francis T. Hurley;Chancellor-Vacant, Chancery Office, 225 Cordova St., Anchorage, AK 99501. Tel. (907)258-7898. Fax (905)279-3885

Arlington, Bishop John R. Keating; Chancellor, Rev. Robert J. Rippy. Chancery, Ste. 704, 200 N. Glebe Rd., Arlington, VA 22203. Tel. (703)841-2500. (703)524-5028

Archdiocese of Atlanta, Most Rev. John Frances Donoghue; Chancellor, Rev. Donald A. Kenny. Chancery Office, 680 W. Peachtree St., N.W., Atlanta, GA 30308. Tel. (404)888-7804. Fax (404)885-7494

Austin, Bishop John E. McCarthy; Vicar General, Rev. Msgr. Edward C. Matocha. Chancery Office, N. Congress and 16th, P.O. Box 13327 Capital Sta. Austin, TX 78711. Tel. (512)476-4888. (512)469-9537

Baker, Bishop Thomas J. Connolly; Chancellor, Mary Ann Davis. Chancery Office, 911 S.E. Armour, Bend, OR 97702, P.O. Box 5999, Bend, OR 97708. Tel. (503)388-4004. Fax (503)388-2566

Archdiocese of Baltimore, Archbishop William Cardinal Keeler; Auxiliary Bishops: John H. Ricard, P. Francis Murphy, William C. Newman. Chancery Office, 320 Cathedral St., Baltimore, MD 21201. Tel. (410)547-5446

Baton Rouge, Most Rev. Alfred C. Hughes; Chancellor, Rev. Msgr. Robert Berggreen. Chancery Office, 1800 S. Acadian Thruway, P.O. Box 2028, Baton Rouge, LA 70821-2028. Tel. (504)387-0561. Fax (504)336-8789

Beaumont, Most Rev. Joseph A. Galante; Chancellor Rev. Bennie J. Patillo. Chancery Office, 703 Archie St., P.O. Box 3948, Beaumont, TX 77704-3948. Tel. (409)838-0451. Fax (409)838-4511.

Belleville, Bishop Wilton D. Gregory; Chancellor, Rev. James E. Margason. Chancery Office, 222 S. Third St., Belleville IL 62220-1985. Tel. (618)277-8181. Fax (618)277-0387

Biloxi, Bishop Joseph L. Howze; Chancellor, Rev. Msgr. Andrew Murray. Chancery Office, 120 Reynoir St., P.O. Box 1189, Biloxi, MS 39533. Tel. (601)374-0222. Fax (601)435-7949

Birmingham, Most Rev. David E. Foley Chancellor, Sr. Mary Frances Loftin. Chancery Office, 8131 Fourth Ave. S., P.O. Box 12047, Birmingham, AL 35202-2047. Tel. (205)833-0175. Fax (205)836-1910

Bismarck, Bishop John F. Kinney, Chancellor, Sr. Joanne Graham. Chancery Office, 420 Raymond St., Box 1575, Bismarck, ND 58502-1575. Tel. (701)223-1347. Fax (701)223-3693

Boise, Bishop Tod D. Brown; Chancellor, Deacon James Bowen; Chancery Office, 303 Federal Way, Boise, ID 83705-5925. Tel. (208)342-1311. Fax (208)342-0224

Archdiocese of Boston, Archbishop Bernard Cardinal Law; Auxiliary Bishops: Lawrence J. Riley, Daniel A. Hart, Roberto O. Gonzalez, John P. Boles, John R. McNamara; Chancellor, Gerald T. Reilly. Chancery Office, 2121 Commonwealth Ave., Brighton, MA 02135. Tel. (617)254-0100. Fax (617)783-4564

Bridgeport, Bishop Edward M. Egan; Chancellor, Rev. Msgr. Thomas J. Driscoll. Chancery Office, 238 Jewett Ave., Bridgeport CT 06606-2892. Tel. (203)372-4301. Fax (203)371-8698

Brooklyn, Bishop Thomas V. Daily; Auxiliary Bishops: Joseph M. Sullivan, Rene A. Valero; Ignatius A. Catanello, Gerald M. Barbarito. Chancellor, Rev. Msgr. Otto L. Garcia. Chancery Office, 75 Greene Ave., Box C, Brooklyn, NY 11202. Tel. (718)399-5900. Fax (718)399-5934

Brooklyn, St. Maron of, Bishop Francis M. Zayek; Auxiliary Bishop Joseph M. Sullivan; Chancellor, James B. Namie. Chancery Office, 294 Howard Ave., Staten Island, NY 10301 Tel. (718)815-0436. Fax (718)815-0536

Brownsville, Bishop Raymundo J. Pena; Chancellor, Sr. Esther Dunegan. Chancery, P.O. Box 2279, Brownsville, TX 78522-2279. Tel. (210)542-2501. Fax (210)542-6751

Buffalo, Bishop Henry J. Mansell; Auxiliary Bishops Edward M. Grosz; Bernard J. McLaughlin Chancellor, Rev. Msgr. Robert J. Cunningham. Chancery Office, 795 Main St., Buffalo, NY 14203. Tel. (716)847-5500. Fax (716)847-5557

Burlington, Bishop Kenneth A. Angell; Chancellor, Rev. Jay C. Haskin. Chancery Office, 351 North Ave., Burlington, VT 05401. Tel. (802)658-6110. Fax (802)658-0436

Camden, Bishop James T. McHugh; Auxiliary Bishop James L. Schad; Chancellor, Rev. Msgr. Joseph W. Pokusa. Chancery Office, 1845 Haddon Ave., P.O. Box 709, Camden, NJ 08101-0709. Tel. (609)756-7900. Fax (609)963-2655

Canton, Romanian Diocese of, Vacant See; 1121 44th St., NE, Canton, OH 44714, Tel. (216)492-4086

Charleston, Bishop David B. Thompson; Vicar General, Rev. Msgr. Sam R. Miglarese; Chancellor for Administration, Miss Cleo C. Cantey. Chancery Office, 119 Broad St., P.O. Box 818, Charleston, SC 29402. Tel. (803)723-3488. Fax (803)724- 6387

Charlotte, Bishop William G. Curlin; Chancellor, Very Rev. Mauricio W. West. Chancery Office P.O. 1521 Dilworth Rd., Charlotte, NC 28203. Tel. (704)376-4337. Fax (704)375-7359

Cheyenne, Bishop Joseph H. Hart; Chancellor, Rev. Carl Beavers. Chancery Office, 2121 Capitol Ave., Box 426, Cheyenne, WY 82003-0426. Tel. (307)638-1530. Fax (307)637-7936

Archdiocese of Chicago, Archbishop Joseph Cardinal Bernardin; Auxiliary Bishops: Bishop Alfred L. Abramowicz, Bishop Timothy J. Lyne, Bishop Edwin M. Conway, Bishop Thad J. Jakubowski; Bishop John R. Gorman, Raymond E. Goedert; Bishop Gerald Kicanas;Bishop George Murry.Chancellor, Rev. Thomas J. Paprocki Chancery Office, P.O. Box 1979, Chicago, IL 60690. Tel. (312)751- 7999

Chicago, St. Nicholas for Ukrainians, Bishop Michael Wiwchar; Chancellor, Sonia Ann Peczeniuk. Chancery Office, 2245 W. Rice St., Chicago, IL 60622. Tel. (312)276-5080. Fax (312)276-6799

Archdiocese of Cincinnati, Archbishop Daniel E. Pilarczyk; Chancellor, Most Rev. Carl K. Moeddel. Chancery Office, 100 E. 8th St., Cincinnati, OH 45202. Tel. (513)421-3131. Fax (513)421-6225.

Cleveland, Bishop Anthony M. Pilla; Auxiliary Bishops: Bishop A. Edward Pevec, Bishop A. James Quinn; Chancellor, Rev. Ralph E. Wiatrowski. Chancery Office, 350 Chancery Bldg., Cathedral Square, 1027 Superior Ave., Cleveland, OH 44114. Tel. (216)696-6525. Fax (216)621-7332

Colorado Springs, Bishop Richard C. Hanifen; Chancellor, Rev. George V. Fagan. Chancery Office, 29 West Kiowa St., Colorado Springs, CO 80903-1498. Tel. (719)636-2345. Fax (719)636-1216

Columbus, Bishop James A. Griffin; Chancellor, Rev. Joseph M. Hendricks. Chancery Office, 198 E. Broad St., Columbus, OH 43215. Tel. (614)224-2251. Fax (614)224-6306

Corpus Christi, Bishop Roberto O. Gonzalez; Chancellor, Deacon Roy M. Grassedonio. Chancery Office, 620 Lipan St., P.O. Box 2620, Corpus Christi, TX 78403-2620. Tel. (512)882-6191. Fax (512)882-1018

Covington, Bishop William A. Hughes; Chancellor, Rev. Roger L. Kriege. Chancery Office, The Catholic Center, P. O. Box 18548, Erlanger, KY 41018-0548. Tel. (606)283-6210. Fax (606)283-6334

Crookston, Bishop Victor Balke; Chancellor, Rev. Michael H. Foltz. Chancery Office, 1200 Memorial Dr., P.O. Box 610, Crookston, MN 56716. Tel. (218) 281-4533. Fax (218)281-3328

Dallas, Bishop Charles V. Grahmann; Chancellor, Rev. Ramon Alvarez. Chancery Office, 3725 Blackburn, P.O. Box 190507, Dallas, TX 75219. Tel. (214) 528-2240. Fax (214)526-1743

Davenport, Bishop William E. Franklin; Chancellor, Rev. Msgr. Leo J. Feeney. Chancery Office, 2706 N. Gaines St., Davenport, IA 52804-1998. Tel. (319)324-1911. Fax (319)324-5842

Archdiocese of Denver, Archbishop J. Francis Stafford; Chancellor, Sr. Rosemary Wilcox. Chancery Office, 200 Josephine St., Denver, CO 80206. Tel. (303) 388-4411. Fax (303)388-0517

Des Moines, Bishop Joseph J. Charron; Chancellor, Lawrence Breheny. Chancery Office, 601 Grand Ave., P.O. Box 1816, Des Moines, IA 50306. Tel. (515)243-7653. Fax (515)237-5070

Archdiocese of Detroit, Archbishop Adam Cardinal Maida; Auxiliary Bishops: Moses B. Anderson, Thomas J. Gumbleton, Bishop Dale J. Melczek, Walter J. Schoenherr; Kevin Britt; Bernard Harrington. Chancery Office, 1234 Washington Blvd., Detroit, MI 48226. Tel. (313) 237-5800. Fax (313)237-4642

Dodge City, Bishop Stanley G. Schlarman; Chancellor, Rev. Warren L. Stecklein. Chancery Office, 910 Central Ave., P.O. Box 137, Dodge City, KS 67801-0137. Tel. (316) 227-1500. Fax (316)227-1570

Archdiocese of Dubuque, Archbishop Daniel W. Kucera; Chancellor, Rev. Joseph L. Hauer , P.O. Box 479, Dubuque IA 52004-0479. Tel. (319) 556-2580. Fax (319)556-5464

Duluth, Bishop Roger L. Schwietz; Chancellor, Rev. Dale Nau, Chancery Office, 2830 E. 4th St., Duluth, MN 55812. Tel. (218)724-9111. Fax (218)724-1056

El Paso, Bishop Raymundo J. Pena; Chancellor, Rev. Richard A. Matty . Chancery Office, 499 St. Matthews, El Paso, TX 79907. Tel. (915)595-5000. Fax (915)595-5095

Erie, Bishop Donald W. Trautman; Chancellor, Rev. Msgr. Lawrence E. Brandt. Chancery Office, P.O. Box 10397, Erie, PA 16514. Tel. (814)824-1135. Fax (814)824-1128

Evansville, Bishop Gerald A. Gettelfinger; Chancellor, Sr. Louise Bond. Chancery Office, 4200 N. Kentucky Ave., P.O. Box 4169, Evansville, IN 47724-0169. Tel. (812)424-5536. Fax (812)421-1334

Fairbanks, Bishop Michael Kaniecki; Chancellor, Sr. Marilyn Marx. Chancery Office, 1316 Peger Rd., Fairbanks, AK 99709. Tel. (907) 474-0753.

Fall River, Bishop Sean P. O'Malley; Chancellor, Rev. Msgr. John J. Oliveira. Chancery Office, 410 Highland Ave., Box 2577, Fall River, MA 02722. Tel. (508) 675-1311. Fax (508)679-9220

Fargo, Bishop James S. Sullivan; Chancellor, Rev. T. William Coyle. Chancery Office, 1310 Broadway, P.O. Box 1750, Fargo, ND 58107. Tel. (701)235-6429. (701)235-0296

Fort Wayne-South Bend, Bishop John M. D'Arcy; Auxiliary Bishop John R. Sheets. Chancellor, Rev. Msgr. J. William Lester. Chancery Office, 1103 S. Calhoun St., P.O. Box 390, Fort Wayne, IN 46801. Tel. (219)422-4611. Fax (219)423-3382

Fort Worth, Bishop Joseph P. Delaney; Chancellor, Rev. Robert W. Wilson. Chancery Office, 800 W. Loop 820 S., Fort Worth, TX 76108. Tel. (817)560-3300. Fax (817)244-8839

Fresno, Bishop John T. Steinbock; Chancellor, Rev. Perry Kavookjian. Chancery Office, 1550 N. Fresno St., Fresno, CA 93703-3788. Tel. (209)488-7400. Fax (209)488-7464

Gallup, Bishop Donald E. Pelotte; Chancellor, Br. Duane Torisky. Chancery Office, 711 S. Puerco Dr., P.O. Box 1338, Gallup, NM 87305. Tel. (505)863-4406. Fax (505)722-9131

Galveston-Houston, Bishop Joseph A. Fiorenza; Auxiliary Bishops: Bishop Curtis J. Guillory, James A. Tamayo; Chancellor, Rev. Frank H. Rossi. Chancery Office, 1700 San Jacinto St., Houston, TX 77002-8291, P.O. Box 907, Houston, TX 77001-0907. Tel. (713)659-5461. Fax (713)759-9151

Gary, Bishop Norbert F. Gaughan; Chancellor, Rev. Gerald H. Schweitzer. Chancery Office, 9292 Broadway, Merrillville, IN 46410. Tel. (219)769-9292. Fax (219)738-9034

Gaylord, Bishop Patrick R. Cooney; Vicar Gen., James L. Brucksch. Chancery Office, 1665 West M-32, Gaylord, MI 49735. Tel. (517)732-5147. Fax (517)732-1706

Grand Island, Bishop Lawrence J. McNamara; Chancellor, Rev. Richard L Pionkowski, Chancery Office, 311 W. 17th St., P.O. Box 996, Grand Island, NE 68802. Tel. (308)382-6565. Fax (308)382-6569

Grand Rapids, Bishop Robert J. Rose; Auxiliary Bishop Joseph McKinney; Chancellor, Sr. Patrice Konwinski. Chancery Office, 660 Burton St. S.E., Grand Rapids, MI 49507. Tel. (616)243-0491. Fax (616)243- 4910

Great Falls-Billings, Bishop Anthony M. Milone; Chancellor, Rev. Robert D. Grosch. Chancery Office, 121 23rd St. S., P.O. Box 1399, Great Falls, MT 59403. Tel. (406)727-6683. Fax (406)454-3480

Green Bay, Bishop Robert J. Banks; Auxiliary Bishop Robert F. Morneau; Chancellor, Sr. Ann F. Rehrauer. Chancery Office, Box 23066, Green Bay, WI 54305-3066. Tel. (414)435-4406. Fax (414)435-1330

Greensburg, Bishop Anthony G. Bosco; Chancellor, Rev. Lawrence T. Persico. Chancery Office, 723 E. Pittsburgh St., Greensburg, PA 15601. Tel. (412)837-0901. Fax (412)837-0857

Harrisburg, Bishop Nicholas C. Dattilo; Chancellor, Carol Houghton. Chancery Office, P.O. Box 2557, Harrisburg, PA 17105-2557. Tel. (717)657-4804. Fax (717)657-7673

Archdiocese of Hartford, Archbishop Daniel A. Cronin; Auxiliary Bishop Peter A. Rosazza; Chancellor, Rev. Msgr. Daniel J. Plocharaczyk. Chancery Office, 134 Farmington Ave., Hartford, CT 06105-3784. Tel. (203) 541-6491. Fax (203)541-6309

Helena, Bishop Alexander J. Brunett; Chancellor, Rev. John W. Robertson. Chancery Office, 515 N. Ewing, P.O. Box 1729, Helena, MT 59624. Tel. (406)442-5820. Fax (406)442-5191

Honolulu, Bishop Francis X. Di Lorenzo; Chancellor, Sr. Grace Dorothy Lim. Chancery Office, 1184 Bishop St., Honolulu, HI 96813. Tel. (808)533-1791. Fax (808)521-8428

Houma-Thibodaux, Bishop Michael Jarrell; Chancellor, Rev. Msgr. Albert G. Bergeron. Chancery Office, P.O. Box 9077, Houma, LA 70361. Tel. (504)868-7720. Fax (504)868-7727

Archdiocese of Indianapolis, Archbishop Daniel M. Buechlein; Chancellor, Suzanne L. Magnant. Chancery Office, 1400 N. Meridian St., P.O. Box 1410, Indianapolis, IN 46206. Tel. (317)236-1400. Fax (317)236-1406

Jackson, Bishop William R. Houck; Chancellor, Rev. Francis J. Cosgrove. Chancery Office, 237 E. Amite St., P.O. Box 2248, Jackson, MS 39225-2248. Tel. (601)969-1880. Fax (601)960-8455

Jefferson City, Bishop Michael F. McAuliffe; Chancellor, Vacant See; Chancery Office, 605 Clark Ave., P.O. Box 417, Jefferson City, MO 65101. Tel. (314)635-9127. Fax (314)635-2286

Joliet, Bishop Joseph L. Imesch; Auxiliary Bishop Roger L. Kaffer; Chancellor, Sr. Judith Davies. Chancery Office, 425 Summit St., Joliet, IL 60435. Tel. (815) 722-6606. Fax (815)722-6602

Juneau, Vacant See; Vicar General, Rev. Msgr. James F. Miller. Chancery Office, 419 6th St., #200, Juneau, AK 99801. Tel. (907)586-2227. Fax(907)463-3237

Kalamazoo, Bishop Paul V. Donovan; Chancellor, Rev. Msgr. Dell F. Stewart. Chancery Office, 238 Fallkirk, Kalamazoo, MI 49006. Tel. (616)349-8714. Fax (616)349-6440

Archdiocese of Kansas City in Kansas, Archbishop James P. Keleher; Chancellor, Rev. Msgr. William T. Curtin. Chancery Office, 12615 Parallel, Kansas City, KS 66109. Tel. (913)721-1570. Fax (913)721-1577

Kansas City-St. Joseph, Bishop Raymond J. Boland; Chancellor, Rev. Richard F. Carney. Chancery Office, P.O. Box 419037, Kansas City, MO 64141-6037. Tel. (816)756-1850. (816)756-0878

Knoxville, Bishop Anthony J. O'Connell; Chancellor, Rev. F. Xavier Mankel. Chancery Office, 417 Erin Dr., P.O. Box 11127, Knoxville, TN 37939-1127. Tel. (615)584-3307.

La Crosse, Bishop John J. Paul; Chancellor, Rev. Michael J. Gorman. Chancery Office. 3710 East Ave. S., P.O. Box 4004, La Crosse, WI 54602-4004. Tel. (608)788-7700. Fax (608)788-8413

Lafayette in Indiana, Bishop William L. Higi; Chancellor, Rev. Robert L. Sell. Chancery Office, P. O. Box 260, Lafayette, IN 47902. Tel. (317) 742-0275. Fax (317)742-7513

Lafayette, Bishop Harry J. Flynn; Chancellor, Sr. Joanna Valoni. Chancery Office, Diocesan Office Bldg., 1408 Carmel Ave., Lafayette, LA 70501. Tel. (318)261-5500. Fax (318) 261-5635

Lake Charles, Bishop Jude Speyrer; Chancellor Deacon George Stearns. Chancery Office, 414 Iris St., P.O. Box 3223, Lake Charles, LA 70602. Tel. (318)439-7400. (318)439-7413

Lansing, Bishop Kenneth J. Povish; Chancellor, Rev. James A. Murray. Chancery Office, 300 W. Ottowa, Lansing, MI 48933. Tel. (517)342-2440. Fax (517)342-2515

Las Cruces, Bishop Ricardo Ramirez; Chancellor, Sr. Mary Ellen Quinn. Chancery Office, 1280 Med Park Dr., Las Cruces, NM 88005. Tel. (505)523-7577. Fax (505)524-3874

Lexington, Bishop James K. Williams; Chancellor, Sr. Mary Kevan Seibert. Chancery Office, 1310 Leestown Rd., P.O. Box 12350, Lexington, KY 40582-2350. Tel. (606)253-1993. Fax (606)254-6284

Lincoln, Fabian W. Bruskewitz; Chancellor, Rev. Timothy J. Thorburn. Chancery Office, 3400 Sheridan Blvd., Lincoln, NE 68506, P.O. Box 80328, Lincoln, NE 68501. Tel. (402)488-0921. Fax (402)488-3569

Little Rock, Bishop Andrew J. McDonald; Chancellor, Francis I. Malone. Chancery Office, 2415 N. Tyler St., P.O. Box 7239, Little Rock, AR 72217. Tel. (501) 664-0340

Archdiocese of Los Angeles, Cardinal Roger Mahony; Auxiliary Bishops: Juan Arzube, John J. Ward, Armando Ochoa, Stephen E. Blaire, Thomas J. Curry, Joseph M. Sartoris, Gabino Zavala; Chancellor, Rev. Msgr.Terrance Fleming. Chancery Office, 1531 W. Ninth St., Los Angeles, CA 90015-1194. Tel. (213) 251-3200. Fax (213)251-2607

Bishop of Las Vegas, Bishop Daniel F. Walsh, Chancellor, Vacant See, Chancery Office 336 E. Desert Inn Rd. Las Vegas, NV 89109. Tel. (702)735-3500. Fax (702)735-8941.

Archdiocese of Louisville, Archbishop Thomas C. Kelly; Auxiliary Bishop Charles G. Maloney; Chancellor, Rev. Robert Dale Cieslik. Chancery Office, 212 E. College St., P.O. Box 1073, Louisville, KY 40201. Tel. (502)585-3291

Lubbock, Bishop Pacido Rodriguez; Chancellor, Sr. Antonio Gonzalez. Chancery Office. 4620 4th St., Lubbock, TX 79416, P.O. Box 98700, Lubbock, TX 79499- 8700. Tel. (806)792-3943. Fax (806)792-8109

Madison, Bishop William H. Bullock; Auxiliary Bishop George O. Wirz; Chancellor, Rev. Joseph P. Higgins. Chancery Office, 15 E. Wilson St., Box 111, Madison, WI 53701. Tel. (608)256-2677. Fax (608)256-1006

Manchester, Bishop Leo E. O'Neil; Chancellor Rev. Msgr. Francis J. Christian. Chancery Office, 153 Ash St., P.O. Box 310, Manchester, NH 03105. Tel. (603)669-3100. Fax (603)669-0377

Marquette, Bishop James H. Garland; Chancellor, Rev. Peter Oberto. Chancery Office, 444 S. Fourth St., P.O. Box 550, Marquette, MI 49855. Tel. (906)225-1141. Fax (906)225-0437

Memphis, Bishop J. Terry Steib; Chancellor, Rev. Robert D. Ponticello. Chancery Office, 1325 Jefferson Ave., P.O. Box 41679, Memphis, TN 38174-1679. Tel. (901)722- 4700. Fax (901)722-4769

Metuchen, Bishop Edward T. Hughes; Chancellor, Sr. M. Michaelita Wiechetek. Chancery Office, P.O. Box 191, Metuchen, NJ 08840. Tel. (908)283-3800. Fax (908)283-2012

Archdiocese of Miami, Archbishop John C. Favalora; Auxiliary Bishop Agustin A. Roman; Chancellor, Very Rev. Tomas M. Mabin. Chancery Office, 9401 Biscayne Blvd., Miami Shores, FL 33138. Tel. (305)757-6241. Fax (305)754-1797.

Archdiocese for the Military Services, Bishop Joseph T. Dimino; Auxiliary Bishops: Francis X. Roque, John G. Nolan, Joseph J. Madera, John J. Glynn; Chancellor, Bishop John J. Glynn. Chancery Office, P.O. Box 4469, Washington, D.C. 20017-0469. Tel. (301)853-0400. Fax (301)853-2246

Archdiocese of Milwaukee, Archbishop Rembert G. Weakland, Auxiliary Bishop Richard J. Sklba; Chancellor, Ms. Barbara Anne Cusack, J.C.D. Chancery Office, 3501 S. Lake Dr., P.O. Box 07912, Milwaukee, WI 53207-0912. (414)769-3340. Fax (414)769-3408

Archdiocese of Mobile, Archbishop Oscar H. Lipscomb; Chancellor, Very Rev. G. Warren Wall. Chancery Office, 400 Government St., P.O. Box 1966, Mobile, AL 36633. Tel. (205)434-1585. Fax (205) 434-1588

Monterey, Bishop Sylvester D. Ryan; Chancellor, Rev. Charles G. Fatooh. Chancery Office, 580 Fremont St., P.O. Box 2048, Monterey, CA 93942-2048. (408)373-4345. Fax (408)373-1175

Nashville, Bishop Edward U. Kmiec, Chancellor, Rev. J. Patrick Connor. Chancery Office, 2400 21st Ave., S., Nashville, TN 37212. Tel. (615)383-6393. Fax (615)292-8411

Archdiocese of Newark, Archbishop Theodore E. McCarrick; Chancellor, Sr. Thomas Mary Salerno, P.O. Box 726, Newark, NJ 07101-0726. Tel. (201)497-4009. Fax (201)497-4033

Archdiocese of New Orleans, Archbishop Francis B. Schulte; Auxiliary Bishops: Robert W. Muench; Dominic Carmon; Chancellor, Rev. Msgr. Thomas J. Rodi. Chancery Office, 7887 Walmsley Ave., New Orleans, LA 70125. Tel. (504)861-9521. Fax (504)866-2906

Newton, Melkite Diocese of, Bishop John A. Elya; Auxiliary Bishop: Nicholas J. Samra. Chancellor, Deacon Paul F. Lawler. Chancery Office, 19 Dartmouth St., West Newton, MA 02165. Tel. (617)969-8957. Fax (617)969-4115

New Ulm, Bishop Raymond A. Lucker; Chancellor, Rev. Dennis C. Labat. Chancery Office, 1400 Sixth St. N., New Ulm, MN 56073-2099. Tel. (507)359-2966. Fax (507)354-3667

Archdiocese of New York, Archbishop John Cardinal O'Connor; Auxiliary Bishops: Patrick V. Ahern, Francis Garmendia, James P. Mahoney, Emerson J. Moore, Austin B. Vaughan, Anthony F. Mestice, William J. McCormack, Patrick J. Sheridan; Henry J. Mansell. Chancellor, Rev. Msgr. Robert A. Brucato. Chancery Office, 1011 First Ave., New York, NY 10022. Tel. (212)371-1000. Fax (212)826-6020

Norwich, Bishop Vacant See; Chancellor, Rev. Msgr. Robert L. Brown. Chancery Office, 201 Broadway, P.O. Box 587, Norwich, CT 06360. Tel. (203)887-9294. Fax (203)886-1670

Oakland, Bishop John S. Cummins; Chancellor, Sr. Barbara Flannery, C.S.J. Chancery Office, 2900 Lakeshore Ave., Oakland, CA 94610. Tel. (510)893-4711. Fax (510)893-0945

Ogdensburg, Bishop Paul S. Loverde; Chancellor, Rev. Robert H. Aucoin. Chancery Office, P.O. Box 369, 622 Washington St., Ogdensburg, NY 13669. Tel. (315)393-2920. Fax (315)394-7401.

Archdiocese of Oklahoma City, Archbishop Eusebius J. Beltran, Chancellor, Rev. John A. Steichen. Chancery Office, 7501 Northwest Expressway, P.O. Box 32180, Oklahoma City, OK 73123. Tel. (405)721-5651. Fax (405)721-5210

Archdiocese of Omaha, Archbishop Elden Francis Curtiss; Chancellor, Rev. Michael F. Gutgsell. Chancery Office, 100 N. 62nd St., Omaha, NE 68132-2795. Tel. (402)558-3100. Fax (402)551-4212

Orange, Bishop Norman F. McFarland; Auxiliary Bishop Michael P. Driscoll; Chancellor, Rev. John Urell. Chancery Office, 2811 E. Villa Real Dr., P.O. Box 14195, Orange, CA 92613-1595. Tel. (714)282-3000. Fax (714)282-3029

Orlando, Bishop Norbert M. Dorsey; Chancellor, Sr. Lucy Vazquez. Chancery Office, 421 E. Robinson, P.O. Box 1800, Orlando, FL 32802-1800. Tel. (305)425-3556. Fax (407)649-7846

Owensboro, Bishop John J. McRaith; Chancellor, Sr. Joseph Angela Boone. Chancery Office, 600 Locust St., Owensboro, KY 42301. Tel. (502)683-1545. Fax (502)683-6883

Palm Beach, Bishop J. Keith Symons; Chancellor, Rev. Charles Hawkins. Chancery Office, P.O. Box 109650, Palm Beach Gardens, FL 33410-9650. Tel. (407)775-9500. Fax (407)775-9556

Parma, Byzantine Eparchy of, Bishop Andrew Pataki; Chancellor, Vacant See. Chancery Office, 1900 Carlton Rd., Parma, OH 44134-7180. Tel. (216)741-8773. Fax (216)741-9356

Parma, Ukrainian Diocese of St. Joseph in, Bishop Robert M. Moskal; Chancellor, Rev. Msgr. Thomas A. Sayuk. Chancery Office 5720 State Rd., P.O. Box 347180, Parma, OH 44134-7180. Tel. (216)888-1522. Fax (216)888-3477

Passaic, Byzantine Diocese of, Bishop Michael J. Dudick; Chancellor, Rev. Msgr. Raymond Misulich. Chancery Office, 445 Lackawanna Ave., West Paterson, NJ 07424. Tel. (201)890-7777. Fax (201)890- 7175

Paterson, Bishop Frank J. Rodimer; Chancellor, Rev. Msgr. Herbert K. Tillyer. Chancery Office, 777 Valley Rd., Clifton, NJ 07013. Tel. (201)777-8818. Fax (201)777-8976

Pensacola-Tallahassee, Bishop John M. Smith; Chancellor, Rev. Msgr. James Amos. Chancery Office, P.O. Drawer 17329, Pensacola, FL 32522. Tel. (904)432-1515. Fax (904)436-6424

Peoria, Bishop John J. Myers; Chancellor, Rev. James F. Campbell. Chancery Office, P.O. Box 1406, 607 NE Madison Ave., Peoria, IL 61655. Tel. (309)671-1550. Fax (309)671-5079

Archdiocese of Philadelphia, Archbishop Anthony Cardinal Bevilacqua; Auxiliary Bishops: Louis A. DeSimone, Martin N. Lohmuller; Edward P. Cullen; Chancellor, Rev. Steven J. Harris. Chancery Office, 222 N. 17th St. Philadelphia, PA 19103. Tel. (215)587-4538. Fax (215)587-3907

Phoenix, Bishop Thomas J. O'Brien; Chancellor, Sr. Mary Ann Winters , Chancery Office, 400 E. Monroe St., Phoenix, AZ 85004. Tel. (602)257-0030. Fax (602)258-3425

Pittsburgh, Bishop Donald W. Wuerl; Auxiliary Bishops: John B. McDowell, William J. Winter; Thomas J. Tobin. Chancellor, Rev. Benedetto P. Voghetto. Chancery Office, 111 Blvd. of Allies, Pittsburgh, PA 15222. Tel. (412)456-3000

Archdiocese of Pittsburgh, Byzantine, Bishop Judson M. Procyk; Chancellor. Rev. Msgr. Raymond Balta. Chancery Office, 925 Liberty Ave., Pittsburgh, PA 15222. Tel. (412)281-1000. Fax (412)281-0388

Portland, Bishop Joseph J. Gerry; Aux. Bishop, Most Rev. Michael R. Cote; Co-Chancellors, Rev. Michael J. Henchal, Sr. Rita-Mae Bissonnette. Chancery Office, 510 Ocean Ave., P.O. Box 11559, Portland, ME 04104-7559. Tel. (207)773-6471. Fax (207)773-0182

Archdiocese of Portland in Oregon, Archbishop William J. Levada; Auxiliary Bishop Kenneth Steiner; Chancellor, Mary Jo Tully. Chancery Office, 2838 E. Burnside St., Portland, OR 97214-1895. Tel. (503)234-5334. Fax(503)234-2545

Providence, Bishop Louis E. Gelineau; Chancellor, Rev. Msgr. William I. Varsanyi. Chancery Office, 1 Cathedral Sq., Providence, RI 02903-3695. Tel. (401)278-4500. Fax (401)278-4548

Pueblo, Bishop Arthur N. Tafoya; Vicar General, Rev. Edward H. Nunez. Chancery Office, 1001 N. Grand Ave., Pueblo, CO 81003. Tel. (303)544-9861. Fax (719)544-5202

Raleigh, Bishop F. Joseph Gossman; Chancellor, John P. Riedy. Chancery Office, 300 Cardinal Gibbons Dr., Raleigh, NC 27606. Tel. (919)821-9703. Fax (919)821-9705

Rapid City, Bishop Charles J. Chaput; Chancellor, Sr. M. Celine Erk. Chancery Office, 606 Cathedral Dr., P.O. Box 678, Rapid City, SD 57709. Tel. (605)343-3541. Fax (605)348-7985

Reno, Bishop Phillip F. Straling; Chancellor, Rev. Patrick Leary. Chancery Office, 336 E. Desert Inn Rd., Las Vegas, NV 89109, P.O. Box 18316, Las Vegas, NV 89114-8316. Tel. (702)735-3500. Fax (702)735-8941

Richmond, Bishop Walter F. Sullivan; Chancellor, Rev. Thomas F. Shreve. Chancery Office, 811 Cathedral Pl., Richmond, VA 23220-4898. Tel. (804)359-5661. Fax (804)358-9159

Rochester, Bishop Matthew H. Clark; Chancellor, Rev. Kevin E. McKenna. Chancery Office, 1150 Buffalo Rd., Rochester, NY 14624-1890. Tel. (716)328-3210. Fax (716)328-3149

Rockford, Bishop Thomas G. Doran; Chancellor, V. Rev. Charles W. McNamee. Chancery Office, 1245 N. Court St., Rockford, IL 61103 Tel. (815)962-3709. Fax (815)968-2824

Rockville Centre, Bishop John R. McGann; Auxiliary Bishops: James J. Daly, Emil A. Wcela, John C. Dunne; Chancellor, Rev. Msgr. John A. Alesandro. Chancery Office, 50 N. Park Ave. Rockville Centre, NY 11570. Tel. (516)678-5800. Fax (516)678-1786

Sacramento, Bishop William K. Weigand; Chancellor, Sr. Eileen Enright. Chancery Office, 2110 Broadway. Sacramento, CA 95818. Tel. (916)733-0200. Fax (916)733-0295

Saginaw, Bishop Kenneth E. Untener; Chancellor, Rev. Msgr. Thomas P. Schroeder. Chancery Office, 5800 Weiss St., Saginaw, MI 48603-2799. Tel. (517)799-7910. Fax (517)797-6670

St. Augustine, Bishop John J. Snyder; Chancellor, Rev. Keith R. Brennan. Chancery Office, 11625 Old St. Augustine Rd., Jacksonville, FL 32258, P.O. Box 24000, Jacksonville, FL 32241-3200. Tel. (904)262-3200. Fax (904)262-0698

St. Cloud, Vacant See; Chancellor, Rev. Severin Schwieters. Chancery Office, P.O. Box 1248, 214 Third Ave. S., St. Cloud, MN 56302. Tel. (612)251-2340

Archdiocese of St. Louis, Most Rev. Justin Rigali; Auxiliary Bishops: Paul A. Zipfel; Edward K. Braxton. Chancellor, Rev. Richard F. Stika. Chancery Office, 4445 Lindell Blvd., St. Louis, MO 63108-2497. Tel. (314)533-1887. Fax (314)533-1887 (Station 212)

Archdiocese of St. Paul and Minneapolis, Archbishop John R. Roach; Auxiliary Bishop: Lawrence H. Welsh; Chancellor, William S. Fallon. Chancery Office, 226 Summit Ave., St. Paul, MN 55102. Tel. (612)291-4400. Fax (612)290-1629

St. Petersburg, Bishop Vacant See; Chancellor, V. Rev. Robert C. Gibbons. Chancery Office, 6363 9th Ave. N., St. Petersburg, FL 33710, P.O. Box 40200, St. Petersburg, FL 33743-0200. Tel. (813)344-1611. Fax (813)345-2143

Salina, Bishop George K. Fitzsimons; Chancellor, Rev. Msgr. James E. Hake. Chancery Office, 103 N. 9th, P.O. Box 980, Salina, KS 67402-0980. Tel. (913)827- 8746

Salt Lake City, Bishop George H. Niederauer; Chancellor, Deacon Silvio Mayo. Chancery Office, 27 C. St., Salt Lake City, UT 84103. Tel. (801)328-8641. Fax (801)328-9680

San Angelo, Bishop Michael Pfeifer; Chancellor, Rev. Msgr. Larry J. Droll. Chancery Office, 804 Ford, Box 1829, San Angelo, TX 76902. Tel. (915)651-7500. Fax (915)651- 6688

Archdiocese of San Antonio, Archbishop Patrick F. Flores; Auxiliary Bishop; John W. Yanta; Chancellor, Rev. Msgr. Patrick J. Murray. Chancery Office, 2718 W. Woodlawn Ave., P.O. Box 28410, San Antonio, TX 78228-0410. Tel. (210)734-2620. Fax (210)734-0231

San Bernardino, Bishop Phillip F. Straling; Auxiliary Bishop, Gerald R. Barnes, Chancellor, Rev. Donald Webber. Chancery Office, 1450 North D St., San Bernardino, CA 92405 Tel. (909)384-8200. Fax (909)884-4890

San Diego, Bishop Robert Brom; Auxiliary Bishop Gilbert E. Chavez; Chancellor, Rev. Msgr. Daniel J. Dillabough. Chancery Office, P.O. Box 85728, San Diego, CA 92186-5728. Tel. (619)490-8200. Fax (619)490-8272

Archdiocese of San Francisco, Archbishop John R. Quinn; Auxiliary Bishops: Carlos A. Sevilla, Patrick J. McGrath; Chancellor, Sr. Mary B. Flaherty. Chancery Office, 445 Church St., San Francisco, CA 94114. Tel. (415)565-3600. Fax (415)565-3633

San Jose, Bishop Pierre DuMaine; Chancellor, Sr. Patricia Marie Mulpeters. Chancery Office, 900 Lafayette St., Ste. 301, Santa Clara, CA 95050-4966. Tel. (408)983-0100. Fax (408)983-0295

Archdiocese of Santa Fe, Archbishop Michael J. Sheehan; Chancellor, Rev. Richard Olona. Chancery Office, 4000 St. Joseph Pl., NW, Albuquerque, NM 87120. Tel. (505)831-8100

Santa Rosa, Bishop Patrick G. Ziemann; Chancellor, Rev. Msgr. James E. Pulskamp. Chancery Office, 547 B St., P.O. Box 1297, Santa Rosa, CA 95402. Tel. (707)545-7610. Fax (707)542-9702

Savannah, Bishop Raymond W. Lessard; Chancellor, Rev. Jeremiah J. McCarthy. Chancery Office, 601 E. Liberty St., Savannah, GA 31401-5196. Tel. (912)238-2320 (912)238-2335

Scranton, Bishop James C. Timlin; Auxiliary Bishop, Most Rev. John Dougherty.Chancellor, Rev. Msgr. Neil J. Van Loon. Chancery Office, 300 Wyoming Ave., Scranton, PA 18503. Tel. (717)346-8910

Archdiocese of Seattle, Archbishop Thomas J. Murphy; Chancellor, V. Rev. George L. Thomas. Chancery Office, 910 Marion St., Seattle, WA 98104. Tel. (206)382-4560. Fax (206)382-4840

Shreveport, Bishop William B. Friend; Chancellor, Sr. Margaret Daues. Chancery Office, 2500 Line Ave., Shreveport, LA 71104-3043. Tel. (318)222-2006. Fax (318)222-2080

Sioux City, Bishop Lawrence D. Soens; Chancellor, Rev. Kevin C. McCoy. Chancery Office, 1821 Jackson St., P.O. Box 3379, Sioux City, IA 51102-3379. Tel. (712)255-7933. Fax (712)233-7598

Sioux Falls, Bishop Robert J. Carlson; Chancellor, Rev. Jerome Klein. Chancery Office, 3100 W. 41st St., Box 5033, Sioux Falls, SD 57117. Tel. (605)334-9861. Fax (605)334-2092

Spokane, Bishop William Skylstad; Chancellor, Rev. Mark Pautler. Chancery Office, 1023 W. Riverside Ave., P.O. Box 1453, Spokane, WA 99210-1453. Tel. (509)456-7100

Springfield-Cape Girardeau, Bishop John J. Leibrecht; Chancellor, Rev. Msgr. Thomas E. Reidy. Chancery Office, 601 S. Jefferson, Springfield, MO 65806-3143. Tel. (417)866-0841. Fax (417)866-1140

Springfield in Illinois, Bishop Daniel L. Ryan; Vicar Gen., V. Rev. John Renken. Chancery Office, 1615 W. Washington, P.O. Box 3187, Springfield, IL 62708-3187. Tel. (217)698-8500. Fax (217)698-8620

Springfield in Massachusetts, Bishop Thomas L. Dupre; Chancellor, Rev. Daniel P. Liston. Chancery Office, 76 Elliot St., Springfield, MA 01105, P.O. Box 1730, Springfield, MA 01101. Tel. (413)732-3175. Fax (413)737-2337

Stamford, Ukrainian, Bishop Basil H. Losten; Chancellor, Rt. Rev. Mitred Matthew Berko. Chancery Office, 14 Peveril Rd., Stamford, CT 06902-3019. Tel. (203)324-7698. Fax (203)967-9948

Steubenville, Bishop Gilbert I. Sheldon; Chancellor, Linda A. Nichols. Chancery Office, 422 Washington St., P.O. Box 969, Steubenville, OH 43952. Tel. (614)282-3631. Fax (614)282-3327

Stockton, Bishop Donald W. Montrose; Chancellor, Rev. Richard J. Ryan. Chancery Office, 1105 N. Lincoln St., Stockton, CA 95203, P.O. Box 4237, Stockton, CA 95204-0237. Tel. (209)466-0636. Fax (209)941-9722

Superior, Bishop Raphael M. Fliss; Chancellor, Rev. James F. Tobolski. Chancery Office, 1201 Hughitt Ave., Box 969, Superior, WI 54880. Tel. (715)392-2937

Syracuse, Bishop James M. Moynihan; Auxiliary Bishop Thomas J. Costello; Chancellor, Rev. Richard M. Kopp. Chancery Office, 240 E. Onondaga St., Syracuse, NY 13202, P.O. Box 511, Syracuse, NY 13201. Tel. (315)422-7203. Fax (315)478-4619

Toledo, Bishop James R. Hoffman; Auxiliary Bishop Robert W. Donnelly. Chancery Office, 1933 Spielbush, Toledo, OH 43624, P.O. Box 985, Toledo, OH 43697-0985. Tel. (419)244-6711. Fax (419)244-4791

Trenton, Bishop John C. Reiss; Chancellor, Rev. Msgr. William F. Fitzgerald. Chancery Office, 701 Lawrenceville Rd., P.O. Box 5309, Trenton, NJ 08638. Tel. (609)882-7125. Fax (609)771-6793

Tucson, Bishop Manuel D. Moreno; Chancellor, Rev. John P. Lyons, Chancery Office, 192 S. Stone Ave., Box 31, Tucson, AZ 85702. Tel. (602)792-3410

Tulsa, Bishop Edward J. Slattery, Chancellor, Rev. Patrick J. Gaalaas. Chancery Office, 820 S. Boulder St., Tulsa, OK 74119, P.O. Box 2009, Tulsa, OK 74101. Tel. (918)587-3115

Tyler, Bishop Edmond Carmody; Chancellor, Rev. Gavin Vaverek. Chancery Office, 1015 E.S.E. Loop 323, Tyler, TX 75701-9663. Tel. (903)534-1077. Fax (903)534-1370

Van Nuys Eparchy, Byzantine Rite, Bishop George M. Kuzma; Chancellor, Rev. Wesley Izer. Chancery Office, 8131 N. 16th St., Phoenix, AZ 85020. Tel. (602)861-9778. Fax (602)861-9796

Venice, Bishop John J. Nevins; Chancellor, V. Rev. Jerome A. Carosella. Chancery Office, 1000 Pinebrook Rd., Venice, FL 34292, P.O. Box 2006, Venice, FL 34284. Tel. (813) 484-9543. Fax (813)484-1121

Victoria, Bishop David E. Fellhauer; Chancellor, Rev. Msgr. Thomas C. McLaughlin. Chancery Office, 1505 E. Mesquite Lane, P.O. Box 4070, Victoria, TX 77903. Tel. (512)573-0828. Fax (512)573-5725

Archdiocese of Washington, Archbishop James Cardinal Hickey; Auxiliary Bishops: Alvaro Corrada, Leonard J. Olivier; William C. Curlin; Chancellor, Rev. William E. Lori. Chancery Office, 5001 Eastern Ave., P.O. Box 29260, Washington, DC 20017. Tel. (301)853-3800. Fax (301)853-3246

Wheeling-Charleston, Bishop Bernard W. Schmitt; Chancellor, Rev. Robert C. Nash. Chancery Office, 1300 Byron St., P.O. Box 230, Wheeling, WV 26003. Tel. (304) 233-0880. Fax (304)233-0890

Wichita, Bishop Eugene J. Gerber; Chancellor, Rev. Robert E. Hemberger. Chancery Office, 424 N. Broadway, Wichita, KS 67202. Tel. (316)269-3900. Fax (316)269-3936

Wilmington, Vacant See; Chancellor, Rev. Msgr. Joseph F. Rebman. Chancery Office, P.O. Box 2030, 1925 Delaware Ave., Ste. 1A, Wilmington, DE 19899. Tel. (302)573-3100. Fax (302)573-3128

Winona, Bishop John G. Vlazny; Chancellor, Mr. John M. Vitek. Chancery Office, 55 W. Sanborn, P.O. Box 588, Winona, MN 55987. Tel. (507)454-4643. Fax (507)454-8106

Worcester, Bishop Daniel P. Reilly; Auxiliary Bishop George E. Rueger. Chancery Office, 49 Elm St., Worcester, MA 01609. Tel. (508)791-7171. Fax (508)753-7180

Yakima, Bishop Francis E. George; Chancellor, V. Rev. Perron J. Auve. Chancery Office, 5301-A Tieton Dr., Yakima, WA 98908. Tel. (509)965-7117

Youngstown, Bishop James W. Malone; Auxiliary Bishop Benedict C. Franzetta; Chancellor, Rev. Robert J. Siffrin. Chancery Office, 144 W. Wood St., Youngstown, OH 44503. Tel. (216)744-8451. Fax (216)744-2848

PERIODICALS

Our Sunday Visitor; The New World; The Criterion; Commonweal; Maryknoll; Columbia; Clarion Herald; The Evangelist; Catholic Universe Bulletin; The Catholic World; Catholic Worker; The Catholic Transcript; Catholic Standard and Times; Liguorian; The Catholic Review; Catholic Light; Homiletic and Pastoral Review; Catholic Herald; Extension; Catholic Digest; Catholic Chronicle; New Oxford Review; The Long Island Catholic; Pastoral Life; Columban Mission; Salt of the Earth; The Pilot; Praying; Providence Visitor; The Tidings; Worship; Saint Anthony Messenger; Review for Religious; The Tablet; Theology Digest; U.S. Catholic

The Romanian Orthodox Church in America

The Romanian Orthodox Church in America is an autonomous Archdiocese chartered under the name of "Romanian Orthodox Archdiocese in America."

The diocese was founded in 1929 and approved by the Holy Synod of the Romanian Orthodox Church in Romania in 1934. The Holy Synod of the Romanian Orthodox Church of July 12, 1950, granted it ecclesiastical autonomy in America, continuing to hold only dogmatical and canonical ties with the Holy Synod and the Romanian Orthodox Patriarchate of Romania.

In 1951, approximately 40 parishes with their clergy from the United States and Canada separated from this church. In 1960, they joined the Russian Orthodox Greek Catholic Metropolia, now called the Orthodox Church in America, which reordained for these parishes a bishop with the title "Bishop of Detroit and Michigan."

The Holy Synod of the Romanian Orthodox Church, on June 11, 1973, elevated the Bishop of Romanian Orthodox Missionary Episcopate in America to the rank of Archbishop.

HEADQUARTERS

19959 Riopelle, Detroit, MI 48203 Tel. (313)893-8390

Media Contact, Archdiocesan Dean & Secretary, V. Rev. Fr. Nicholas Apostola, 44 Midland St., Worcester, MA 01602-4217 Tel. (508)799-0040 Fax (508)756-9866

OFFICERS

Archbishop, His Eminence Victorin Ursache, 19959 Riopelle St., Detroit, MI 48203 Tel. (313)893-8390

Vicar, V. Rev. Archim. Dr. Vasile Vasilachi, 45-03 48th Ave., Woodside, Queens, NY 11377 Tel. (718)784-4453

Inter-Church Relations, Dir., Rev. Fr. Nicholas Apostola, 14 Hammond St., Worcester, MA 01610 Tel. (617)799-0040

Sec., V. Rev. Fr.Rev. Nicholas Apostola, 44 Midland St., Worchester, MA 01602 Tel. (508)756-9866 Fax (508)799-0040

PERIODICAL

Credinta--The Faith

The Romanian Orthodox Episcopate of America

This body of Eastern Orthodox Christians of Romanian descent was organized in 1929 as an autonomous Diocese under the jurisdiction of the Romanian Patriarchate. In 1951 it severed all relations with the Orthodox Church of Romania. Now under the canonical jurisdiction of the autocephalous Orthodox Church in America, it enjoys full administrative autonomy and is headed by its own Bishop.

HEADQUARTERS

P.O.Box 309, Grass Lake, MI 49240 Tel. (517)-522-4800 Fax (517)522-5907

Mailing Address, P.O. Box 309, Grass Lake, MI 49240

Media Contact, Ed./Sec., Dept. of Publications, David Oancea, P.O. Box 185, Grass Lake, MI 49240-0185 Tel. (517)522-3656 Fax (517)522-5907

OFFICERS

Ruling Bishop, His Grace Bishop Nathaniel Popp

Dean of all Canada, V. Rev. Nicolae Marioncu, Box 995, Ste. 1, 709 First St., W., Assiniboia, SK S0H 0B0

OTHER ORGANIZATIONS

The American Romanian Orthodox Youth, Pres., David Zablo, 6310 Woodmoor Ave. NW, Canton, OH 44718

Assoc. of Romanian Orthodox Ladies' Aux., Pres., Dr. Eleanor Bujea, P.O. Box 1341, Regina, SK S4P 3B8

Orthodox Brotherhood U.S.A., Pres., John Stanitz, 1908 Doncaster Ct., Wheaton, IL 60187

Orthodox Brotherhood of Canada, Pres., Robert Buchanan, 26 Mill Bay, Regina, SK S4N 1L6

PERIODICAL

Solia/The Herald

The Russian Orthodox Church Outside of Russia

This group was organized in 1920 to unite in one body of dioceses the missions and parishes of the Russian Orthodox Church outside of Russia. The governing body, set up in Constantinople, was sponsored by the Ecumenical Patriarchate. In November, 1950, it came to the United States. The Russian Orthodox Church Outside of Russia emphasizes being true to the old traditions of the Russian Church. It is not in communion with the Moscow Patriarchate.

HEADQUARTERS

75 E. 93rd St., New York, NY 10128 Tel. (212)-534-1601 Fax (212)534-1798

Media Contact, Dep. Sec., Bishop Hilarion

SYNOD OF BISHOPS

Pres., His Eminence Metropolitan Vitaly

Sec., Archbishop of Syracuse and Trinity, Laurus

Dep. Sec., Bishop of Manhattan, Hilarion, Tel. (212)722-6577

Dir. of Public & Foreign Relations Dept., Archbishop of Syracuse and Trinity, Laurus

PERIODICALS

Living Orthodoxy; Orthodox America; Orthodox Family; Orthodox Russia (Russian); Orthodox Life (English); Orthodox Voices

The Salvation Army

The Salvation Army, founded in 1865 by William Booth (1829-1912) in London, England, and introduced into America in 1880, is an international religious and charitable movement organized and operated on a paramilitary pattern and is a branch of the Christian church. To carry out its purposes, The Salvation Army has established a widely diversified program of religious and social welfare services which are designed to meet the needs of children, youth and adults in all age groups.

HEADQUARTERS

615 Slaters La., Alexandria, VA 22313 Tel. (703)-684-5500 Fax (703)684-5538

Media Contact, Natl. Commications Dir., Col. Leon R. Ferraez, Tel. (703)684-5521 Fax (703)-684-5538

OFFICERS

Natl. Commander, Commissioner Robert A. Watson

Natl. Chief Sec., Col. John M. Bate

Natl. Community Relations, Dir., Lt. Col. Clarence W. Harvey

TERRITORIAL ORGANIZATIONS

Central Territory: 10 W. Algonquin Rd., Des Plaines, IL 60016 Tel. (708)294-2000 Fax (708)-294-2299; Territorial Commander, Commissioner Harold D. Hinson

Eastern Territory: 440 W. Nyack Rd., P.O. Box C-635, West Nyack, NY 10994 Tel. (914)623-4700 Fax (914)620-7466; Territorial Commander, Commissioner Ronald G. Irwin

Southern Territory: 1424 Northeast Expressway, Atlanta, GA 30329 Tel. (404)728-1300 Fax (404)728-1331; Territorial Commander, Commissioner Kenneth Hood

Western Territory: Peter A. Chang, 30840 Hawthorne Blvd., Ranchos Palos Verdes, CA 90274 Tel. (310)541-4721 Fax (310)544-1674

PERIODICAL

The War Cry

The Schwenkfelder Church

The Schwenkfelders are the spiritual descendants of the Silesian nobleman Caspar Schwenkfeld von Ossig (1489-1561), a scholar, reformer, preacher and prolific writer who endeavored to aid in the cause of the Protestant Reformation. A contemporary of Martin Luther, John Calvin, Ulrich Zwingli and Phillip Melanchthon, Schwenkfeld sought no following, formulated no creed and did not attempt to organize a church based on his beliefs. He labored for liberty of religious belief, for a fellowship of all believers and for one united Christian church.

He and his cobelievers supported a movement known as the Reformation by the Middle Way. Persecuted by state churches, ultimately 180 Schwenkfelders exiled from Silesia emigrated to Pennsylvania. They landed at Philadelphia Sept. 22, 1734. In 1782, the Society of Schwenkfelders, the forerunner of the present Schwenkfelder Church, was formed. The church was incorporated in 1909.

The General Conference of the Schwenkfelder Church is a voluntary association for the Schwenkfelder Churches at Palm, Worcester, Lansdale, Norristown and Philadelphia, Pa.

They practice adult baptism and dedication of children, and observe the Lord's Supper regularly with open Communion. In theology, they are Christo-centric; in polity, congregational; in missions, world-minded; in ecclesiastical organization, ecumenical.

The ministry is recruited from graduates of colleges, universities and accredited theological seminaries. The churches take leadership in ecumenical concerns through ministerial associations, community service and action groups, councils of Christian education and other agencies.

HEADQUARTERS

105 Seminary St., Pennsburg, PA 18073 Tel. (215)679-3103

Media Contact, Dennis Moyer

OFFICERS

Mod., John Graham, Collegeville, PA 19426

Sec., Frances Witte, Central Schwenkfelder Church, Worcester, PA 19490

Treas., Syl Rittenhouse, 1614 Kriebel Rd., Lansdale, PA 19446

PERIODICAL

The Schwenkfeldian

Separate Baptists in Christ

The Separate Baptists in Christ are a group of Baptists found in Indiana, Ohio, Kentucky, Tennessee, Virginia, West Virginia, Florida and North Carolina dating back to an association formed in 1758 in North Carolina and Virginia.

Today this group consists of approximately 100 churches. They believe in the infallibility of the Bible, the divine ordinances of the Lord's Supper, feetwashing, baptism and that those who endureth to the end shall be saved.

The Separate Baptists are Arminian in doctrine, rejecting both the doctrines of predestination and eternal security of the believer.

At the 1991 General Association, an additional article of doctrine was adopted. "We believe that at Christ's return in the clouds of heaven all Christians will meet the Lord in the air, and time shall be no more," thus leaving no time for a literal one thousand year reign. Seven associations comprise the General Association of Separate Baptists.

HEADQUARTERS

Media Contact, Clk., Rev. Mark Polston, 787 Kitchen Rd., Mooresville, IN 46158 Tel. (317)-834-0286

OFFICERS

Mod., Rev. Jim Goff, 1020 Gagel Ave., Louisville, KY 40216

Asst. Mod., Rev. Jimmy Polston, 785 Kitchen Rd., Mooresville, IN 46158 Tel. (317)831-6745

Clk., Rev. Mark Polston

Asst. Clk., Greg Erdman, 10102 N. Hickory Ln., Columbus, IN 47201

Serbian Orthodox Church in the U.S.A. and Canada

The Serbian Orthodox Church is an organic part of the Eastern Orthodox Church. As a local church it received its autocephaly from Constantinople in 1219 A.D. The Patriarchal seat of the church today is in Belgrade, Yugoslavia.

In 1921, a Serbian Orthodox Diocese in the United States of America and Canada was organized. In 1963, it was reorganized into three dioceses, and in 1983 a fourth diocese was created for the Canadian part of the church. The Serbian Orthodox Church in the USA and Canada received its administrative autonomy in 1928. The Serbian Orthodox Church is in absolute doctrinal unity with all other local Orthodox Churches.

HEADQUARTERS

St. Sava Monastery, P.O. Box 519, Libertyville, IL 60048 Tel. (708)367-0698

BISHOPS

Metropolitan of Midwestern America, Most Rev. Metropolitan Christopher

Bishop of Canada, Georgije, 5A Stockbridge Ave., Toronto, ON M8Z 4M6 Tel. (416)231-4009

Diocese of Western America, Bishop Jovan, 2541 Crestline Terr., Alhambra, CA 91803 Tel. (818)-264-6825

Bishop of Eastern America, Rt. Rev. Bishop Mitrophan, P.O. Box 368, Sewickley, PA 15143 Tel. (412)741-5686

OTHER ORGANIZATIONS

Brotherhood of Serbian Orth. Clergy in U.S.A. & Canada, Pres., V. Rev. Lazar Kostur, Merrilville, IN
Federation of Circles of Serbian Sisters
Serbian Singing Federation

PERIODICALS

The Path of Orthodoxy; The Path of Orthodoxy

Seventh-day Adventist Church

The Seventh-day Adventist Church grew out of a worldwide religious revival in the mid-19th century. People of many religious persuasions believed Bible prophecies indicated that the second coming or advent of Christ was imminent.

When Christ did not come in the 1840s, a group of these disappointed Adventists in the United States continued their Bible studies and concluded they had misinterpreted prophetic events and that the second coming of Christ was still in the future. This same group of Adventists later accepted the teaching of the seventh-day Sabbath and became known as Seventh-day Adventists. The denomination organized formally in 1863.

The church was largely confined to North America until 1874, when its first missionary was sent to Europe. Today over 39,000 congregations meet in 208 countries. Membership exceeds 8.5 million and increases between six and seven percent each year.

In addition to a mission program, the church has the largest worldwide Protestant parochial school system with more than 5,500 schools with more than 820,000 students on elementary through college and university levels.

The Adventist Development and Relief Agency (ADRA) helps victims of war and natural disasters, and many local congregations have community service facilities to help those in need close to home.

The church also has a worldwide publishing ministry with more than 50 printing facilities producing magazines and other publications in over 200 languages and dialects. In the United States and Canada, the church sponsors a variety of radio and television programs, including "Christian Lifestyle Magazine," "It Is Written," "Breath of Life," "Ayer, Hoy, y Mañana," "Voice of Prophecy," and "La Voz de la Esperanza."

The North American Division of Seventh-day Adventist includes 58 Conferences which are grouped together into 9 organized Union Conferences. The various Conferences work under the general direction of these Union Conferences.

HEADQUARTERS

12501 Old Columbia Pike, Silver Spring, MD 20904-6600 Tel. (301)680-6000
Media Contact, Asst. Dir., Archives & Statistics, Evelyn D. Osborn

WORLD-WIDE OFFICERS

Pres., Robert S. Folkenberg
Sec., G. Ralph Thompson
Treas., Robert L. Rawson

WORLD-WIDE DEPARTMENTS

Adventist Chaplaincy Ministries, Dir., Richard O. Stenbakken
Children's Ministries, Dir., Virginia L. Smith
Education, Dir., Humberto M. Rasi
Communication, Dir., Rajmund Dabrowski
Family Ministries, Dir., Ronald M. Flowers
Health and Temperance, Dir., Albert S. Whiting
Ministerial Assoc., Dir., James A. Cress
Public Affairs & Religious Liberty, Dir., John Graz
Publishing, Dir., Ronald E. Appenzeller
Sabbath School & Personal Ministries, James W. Zackrison
Stewardship, Dir., Benjamin C. Maxson
Trust Services, G. Tom Carter
Women's Ministries, Rose M. Otis
Youth, Baraka G. Muganda

NORTH AMERICAN OFFICERS

Pres., Alfred C. McClure
Vice Pres., Clarence Hodges
Vice Pres., Cyril Miller
Vice Pres., Manuel Vasquez
Vice Pres., Richard C. Osborn
Admn. Asst. to Pres., Donald Jacobsen
Sec., Harold W. Baptiste
Assoc. Sec., Rosa T. Banks
Treas., George H. Crumley
Assoc. Treas., Donald R. Pierson
Assoc. Treas., Juan Prestol

NORTH AMERICAN ORGANIZATIONS

Atlantic Union Conf.: P.O. Box 1189, South Lancaster, MA 01561-1189; Pres., Theodore T. Jones

Canada: Seventh-day Adventist Church in Canada (see Ch. 4)

Columbia Union Conf.: 5427 Twin Knolls Rd., Columbia, MD 21045; Pres., Ralph W. Martin

Lake Union Conf.: P.O. Box C, Berrien Springs, MI 49103; Pres., Don C. Schneider

Mid-America Union Conf.: Pres., Charles Sandefur

North Pacific Union Conf.: P.O. Box 16677, Portland, OR 97216; Pres., Bruce Johnston

Pacific Union Conf.: P.O. Box 5005, Westlake Village, CA 91359; Pres., Thomas J. Mostert, Jr

Southern Union Conf.: P.O. Box 849, Decatur, GA 30031; Pres., Malcolm D. Gordon

Southwestern Union Conf.: P.O. Box 4000, Burleson, TX 76097; Pres., ----

PERIODICALS

Collegiate Quarterly; Celebration; Adventist Review; Christian Record; Cornerstone Connections; Guide; Insight; Journal of Adventist Education; Liberty; Listen; Message; Ministry; Adult, Junior-Teen, and Children's Editions Mission; Our Little Friend; Primary Treasure; Signs of the Times; Vibrant Life; Youth Ministry Accent

Seventh Day Baptist General Conference, USA and Canada

Seventh Day Baptists emerged during the English Reformation, organizing their first churches in the mid-1600s. The first Seventh Day Baptists of record in America were Stephen and Ann Mumford, who emigrated from England in 1664. Beginning in 1665 several members of the First Baptist Church at Newport, R.I. began observing the seventh day Sabbath, or Saturday. In 1671, five members, together with the Mumfords, formed the first Seventh Day Baptist Church in America at Newport.

Beginning about 1700, other Seventh Day Baptist churches were established in New Jersey and Pennsylvania. From these three centers, the denomination grew and expanded westward. They founded the Seventh Day Baptist General Conference in 1802.

The organization of the denomination reflects an interest in home and foreign missions, publications and education. Women have been encouraged to participate. From the earliest years religious freedom has been championed for all and the separation of church and state advocated.

Seventh Day Baptists are members of the Baptist World Alliance. The Seventh Day Baptist World Federation has 17 member conferences on six continents.

HEADQUARTERS

Seventh Day Baptist Center, 3120 Kennedy Rd., P.O. Box 1678, Janesville, WI 53547-1678 Tel. (608)752-5055 Fax (608)752-7711

Media Contact, Gen. Services Admn., Calvin Babcock

OTHER ORGANIZATIONS

Seventh Day Baptist Missionary Society, Exec. Dir., Mr. Kirk Looper, 119 Main St., Westerly, RI 02891

Seventh Day Bapt. Bd. of Christian Ed., Exec. Dir., Dr. Ernest K. Bee, Jr., Box 115, Alfred Station, NY 14803

Women's Soc. of the Gen. Conference, Pres., Mrs. Donna Bond, RFD 1, Box 426, Bridgeton, NJ 08302

American Sabbath Tract & Comm. Council, Dir. of Communications, Rev. Kevin J. Butler, 3120 Kennedy Rd., P.O. Box 1678, Janesville, WI 53547

Seventh Day Baptist Historical Society, Historian, Don A. Sanford, 3120 Kennedy Rd., P.O. Box 1678, Janesville, WI 53547

Seventh Day Baptist Center on Ministry, Dir. of Pastoral Services, Rev. Rodney Henry, 3120 Kennedy Rd., P.O. Box 1678, Janesville, WI 53547

PERIODICAL

Sabbath Recorder

Southern Baptist Convention

The Southern Baptist Convention was organized on May 10, 1845, in Augusta, GA.

Cooperating Baptist churches are located in all 50 states, the District of Columbia, Puerto Rico, American Samoa and the Virgin Islands. The members of the churches work together through 1,208 district associations and 39 state conventions and/or fellowships. The Southern Baptist Convention has an Executive Committee and 20 national agencies -- four boards, six seminaries, seven commissions, a foundation and two associated organizations.

The purpose of the Southern Baptist Convention is "to provide a general organization for Baptists in the United States and its territories for the promotion of Christian missions at home and abroad and any other objects such as Christian education, benevolent enterprises, and social services which it may deem proper and advisable for the furtherance of the Kingdom of God". (Constitution, Article II)

The Convention exists in order to help the churches lead people to God through Jesus Christ.

From the beginning, there has been a mission desire to share the Gospel with the peoples of the world. The Cooperative Program is the basic channel of mission support. In addition, the Lottie Moon Christmas Offering for Foreign Missions and the Annie Armstrong Easter Offering for Home Missions support Southern Baptists' world mission programs.

In 1995, there were over 4,000 foreign missionaries serving in 127 foreign countries and over 5,000 home missionaries serving within the United States.

In 1987, the Southern Baptist Convention adopted themes and goals for the major denominational emphasis of Bold Mission Thrust for 1990-2000. Bold Mission Thrust is an effort to enable every person in the world to have opportunity to hear and to respond to the Gospel of Christ by the year 2000.

HEADQUARTERS

901 Commerce St., Ste. 750, Nashville, TN 37203 Tel. (615)244-2355

Media Contact, Vice-Pres. for Convention Relations, Herb Hollinger, Int., Tel. (615)244-2355 Fax (615)742-8919

OFFICERS

Pres., Jim Henry, First Baptist Church, 3701 L.B. McLead Rd., Orlando, FL 32805

Recording Sec., David W. Atchison, P.O. Box 1543, Brentwood, TN 37027

Executive Committee: Pres., Morris M. Chapman; Exec. Vice-Pres., Ernest E. Mosley; Vice-Pres., Business & Finance, Jack Wilkerson; Vice-Pres., Convention News, Herb V. Hollinger

GENERAL BOARDS AND COMMISSIONS

Foreign Mission Board: Pres., Jerry A. Rankin, Box 6767, Richmond, VA 23230 Tel. (804)353-0151

Home Mission Board: Pres., Larry L. Lewis, 1350 Spring St., NW, Atlanta, GA 30367 Tel. (404)-898-7000

Annuity Board: Pres., Paul W. Powell, P.O. Box 2190, Dallas, TX 75221 Tel. (214)720-0511

Sunday School Board: Pres., James T. Draper, Jr., 127 Ninth Ave., N., Nashville, TN 37234 Tel. (615)251-2000

Brotherhood Commission: Pres., James D. Williams, 1548 Poplar Ave., Memphis, TN 38104 Tel. (901)272-2461

Christian Life Commission: Exec. Dir., Richard D. Land, 901 Commerce St., Nashville, TN 37203 Tel. (615)244-2495

Education Commission: Exec. Sec.-Treas., Stephen P. Carlton, 901 Commerce St., Nashville, TN 37203 Tel. (615)244-2362

Historical Commission: Exec. Dir., Treas., Lynn E. May, Jr., 901 Commerce Street, Nashville, TN 37203 Tel. (615)244-0344

The Radio & TV Commission: Pres., Jack Johnson, 6350 West Freeway, Ft. Worth, TX 76150 Tel. (817)737-4011

Stewardship Commission: Pres., A. R. Fagan, 901 Commerce St., Nashville, TN 37203 Tel. (615)-244-2303

STATE CONVENTIONS

Alabama, Troy L. Morrison, 2001 E. South Blvd., Montgomery, AL 36198 Tel. (205)288-2460

Alaska, Bill G. Duncan, 1750 O'Malley Rd., Anchorage, AK 99516 Tel. (907)344-9627

Arizona, Dan C. Stringer, 4520 N. Central Ave., Ste. 550, Phoenix, AZ 85013 Tel. (602)264-9421

Arkansas, Don Moore, P.O. Box 552, Little Rock, AR 72203 Tel. (501)376-4791

California, C. B. Hogue, 678 E. Shaw Ave., Fresno, CA 93710 Tel. (209)229-9533

Colorado, David T. Bunch, 7393 So. Alton Way, Englewood, CO 80112 Tel. (303)771-2480
District of Columbia, W. Jere Allen, 1628 16th St. NW, Washington, DC 20009 Tel. (202)265-1526
Florida, John Sullivan, 1230 Hendricks Ave., Jacksonville, FL 32207 Tel. (904)396-2351
Georgia, Dr. J. Robert White, 2930 Flowers Rd., S, Atlanta, GA 30341 Tel. (404)455-0404
Hawaii, O. W. Efurd, 2042 Vancouver Dr., Honolulu, HI 96822 Tel. (808)946-9581
Illinois, Gene Wilson, P.O. Box 19247, Springfield, IL 62794 Tel. (217)786-2600
Indiana, Charles Sullivan, 900 N. High School Rd., Indianapolis, IN 46224 Tel. (317)241-9317
Kansas-Nebraska, R. Rex Lindsay, 5410 W. Seventh St., Topeka, KS 66606 Tel. (913)273-4880
Kentucky, William W. Marshall, P.O. Box 43433, Middletown, KY 40243 Tel. (502)245-4101
Louisiana, Mark Short, Box 311, Alexandria, LA 71301 Tel. (318)448-3402
Maryland-Delaware, Charles R. Barnes, 10255 S. Columbia Rd., Columbia, MD 21064 Tel. (301)-290-5290
Michigan, ----, 15635 W. 12 Mile Rd., Southfield, MI 48076 Tel. (313)557-4200
Minnesota-Wisconsin, William C. Tinsley, 519 16th St. SE, Rochester, MN 55904 Tel. (507)-282-3636
Mississippi, William W. Causey, P.O. Box 530, Jackson, MS 39205 Tel. (601)968-3800
Missouri, Donald V. Wideman, 400 E. High, Jefferson City, MO 65101 Tel. (314)635-7931
Nevada, David Meacham, 406 California Ave., Reno, NV 89509 Tel. (702)786-0406
New England, Kenneth R. Lyle, Box 688, 5 Oak Ave., Northboro, MA 01532 Tel. (508)393-6013
New Mexico, Claude Cone, P.O. Box 485, Albuquerque, NM 87103 Tel. (505)247-0586
New York, R. Quinn Pugh, 6538 Collamer Dr., East Syracuse, NY 13057 Tel. (315)475-6173
North Carolina, Roy J. Smith, 205 Convention Dr., Cary, NC 27511 Tel. (919)467-5100
Ohio, Exec. Dir., Orville H. Griffin, 1680 E. Broad St., Columbus, OH 43203 Tel. (614)258-8491
Northwest Baptist Convention, Cecil Sims, 1033 N.E. 6th Ave., Portland, OR 97232 Tel. (503)-238-4545
Oklahoma, William G. Tanner, 3800 N. May Ave., Oklahoma City, OK 73112 Tel. (405)942-3800
Pennsylvania-South Jersey, David C. Waltz, 4620 Fritchey St., Harrisburg, PA 17109 Tel. (717)-652-5856
South Carolina, B. Carlisle Driggers, 907 Richland St., Columbia, SC 29201 Tel. (803)765-0030
Tennessee, James M. Porch, P.O. Box 728, Brentwood, TN 37024 Tel. (615)373-2255
Texas, William M. Pinson, Jr., 333 N. Washington, Dallas, TX 75246 Tel. (214)828-5100
Utah-Idaho, Sec., C. Clyde Billingsley, P.O. Box 1039, Sandy, UT 84091 Tel. (801)255-3565
Virginia, Reginald M. McDonough, P.O. Box 8568, Richmond, VA 23226 Tel. (804)672-2100
West Virginia, George Kinchen, Interim, Number One Mission Way, Scott Depot, WV 25560 Tel. (304)757-0944
Wyoming, John W. Thomason, Box 3074, Casper, WY 82602 Tel. (307)472-4087

FELLOWSHIPS

Dakota Southern Baptist Fellowship, Dewey W. Hickey, P.O. Box 7187, Bismark, ND 58502 Tel. (701)255-3765
Iowa Southern Baptist Fellowship, O. Wyndell Jones, Westview #27, 2400 86th St., Des Moines, IA 50322 Tel. (515)278-1516
Montana Southern Baptist Fellowship, ----, P.O. Box 99, Billings, MT 59103 Tel. (406)252-7537
Canadian Convention of Southern Baptists, Allen E. Schmidt, Postal Bag 300, Cochrane, AL T0L 0W0 Tel. (403)932-5688

PERIODICALS

The Commission; SBC Life; MissionsUSA; Baptist History and Heritage

Southern Methodist Church

Organized in 1939, this body is composed of congregations desirous of continuing in true Biblical Methodism and preserving the fundamental doctrines and beliefs of the Methodist Episcopal Church, South. These congregations declined to be a party to the merger of the Methodist Episcopal Church, The Methodist Episcopal Church, South and the Methodist Protestant Church into The Methodist Church.

HEADQUARTERS

P.O. Box 39, Orangeburg, SC 29116-0039 Tel. (803)536-1378 Fax (803)535-3881
Media Contact, Pres., Rev. Dr. Richard G. Blank

OFFICERS

Pres., Rev. Dr. Richard G. Blank
Admn. Asst. to Pres., Philip A. Rorabaugh
Vice-Pres.: The Carolinas-Virginia Conf., Rev. E. Legrand Adams, Rt. 2, Box 1050, Laurens, SC 29360; Alabama-Florida-Georgia Conf., Rev. John Courson, 2214 Woodland Ave., Augusta, GA 30904; Mid-South Conf., Rev. George C. Howell, 11483 Centerhill Martin Rd., Collinsville, MS 39325; South-Western Conf., Rev. John H. Price, 108 Oak Cir., Monroe, LA 71203
Gen. Conf., Treas., Rev. Philip A. Rorabaugh, P.O. Drawer A, Orangeburg, SC 29116-0039

PERIODICAL

The Southern Methodist

Sovereign Grace Baptists

The Sovereign Grace Baptists are a contemporary movement which began its stirrings in the mid-1950s when some pastors in traditional Baptist churches returned to a Calvinist-theological perspective.

The first "Sovereign Grace" conference was held in Ashland, Ky., in 1954 and since then, conferences of this sort have been sponsored by various local churches on the West Coast, Southern and Northern states and Canada. This movement is a spontaneous phenomenon concerning reformation at the local church level. Consequently, there is no interest in establishing a Reformed Baptist "Convention" or "Denomination." Each local church is to administer the keys to the kingdom.

Most Sovereign Grace Baptists formally or informally relate to the "First London" (1646), "Second London" (1689) or "Philadelphia" (1742) Confessions.

There is a wide variety of local church government in this movement. Many Calvinist Baptists have a plurality of elders in each assembly. Other Sovereign Grace Baptists, however, prefer to function with one pastor and several deacons.

Membership procedures vary from church to church but all require a profession of faith in Christ, and baptism as a basis for membership.

Calvinistic Baptists financially support gospel efforts (missionaries, pastors of small churches at home and abroad, literature publication and distribution, radio programs, etc.) in various parts of the world.

HEADQUARTERS

Media Contact, Corres., Jon Zens, P.O. Box 548, St. Croix Falls, WI 54024 Tel. (715)755-3560 Fax (612)465-5101

PERIODICALS

Reformation Today; Kindred Minds

The Swedenborgian Church

Founded in North America in 1792 as the Church of the New Jerusalem, the Swedenborgian Church was organized as a national body in 1817 and incorporated in Illinois in 1861. Its biblically-based theology is derived from the spiritual, or mystical, experiences and exhaustive biblical studies of the Swedish scientist and philosopher Emanuel Swedenborg (1688-1772).

The church centers its worship and teachings on the historical life and the risen and glorified present reality of the Lord Jesus Christ. It looks with an ecumenical vision toward the establishment of the kingdom of God in the form of a universal Church, active in the lives of all people of good will who desire and strive for freedom, peace and justice for all. It is a member of the NCCC and active in many local councils of churches.

With churches and groups throughout the United States and Canada, the denomination's central administrative offices and its seminary -- Swedenborg School of Religion -- are located in Newton, Mass. Affiliated churches are found in Africa, Asia, Australia, Canada, Europe, the United Kingdom, Japan and South America. Many philosophers and writers have acknowledged their appreciation of Swedenborg's teachings.

HEADQUARTERS

48 Sargent St., Newton, MA 02158 Tel. (617)969-4240 Fax (617)964-3258

Media Contact, Central Ofc. Mgr., Martha Bauer

OFFICERS

Pres., Rev. Edwin G. Capon, 170 Virginia St., St. Paul, MN 55102

Vice-Pres., Ms. Phyllis Bosley, 3931 Sacramento St., San Francisco, CA 94118

Rec. Sec., Mrs. Betty Yenetchi, 2601 E. Victoria St., SP65, Rancho Dominguez, CA 90220

Treas., John C. Perry, RFD 2, Box 2341A, Brunswick, ME 04011

Ofc. Mgr., Mrs. Martha Bauer

PERIODICALS

The Messenger; Our Daily Bread

Syrian Orthodox Church of Antioch (Archdiocese of the United States and Canada)

An archdiocese in North America of the Syrian Orthodox Church of Antioch, the church traces its origin to the Patriarchate established in Antioch by St. Peter the Apostle. It is under the supreme ecclesiastical jurisdiction of His Holiness the Syrian Orthodox Patriarch of Antioch and All the East, now residing in Damascus, Syria. The Syrian Orthodox Church -- composed of several archdioceses, numerous parishes, schools and seminaries - professes the faith of the first three Ecumenical Councils of Nicaea, Constantinople and Ephesus, and numbers faithful in the Middle East, India, the Americas, Europe and Australia.

The first Syrian Orthodox faithful came to North America during the late 1800s, and by 1907 the first Syrian Orthodox priest was ordained to tend to the community's spiritual needs. In 1949, His Eminence Archbishop Mar Athanasius Y. Samuel came to America and was soon appointed Patriarchal Vicar. The Archdiocese was officially established in 1957.

There are 15 official archdiocesan parishes and two mission congregations in the United States, located in California, District of Columbia, Florida, Illinois, Massachusetts, Michigan, New Jersey, New York, Oregon, Rhode Island and Texas. In Canada, there are four official parishes: two in the Province of Ontario and two in the Province of Quebec and a mission congregation in the Province of Alberta.

HEADQUARTERS

Archdiocese of the U.S. and Canada, 49 Kipp Ave., Lodi, NJ 07644 Tel. (201)778-0638 Fax (201)-773-7506

Media Contact, Archdiocesan Gen. Sec., V. Rev. Chorepiscopus John Meno, 263 Elm Ave., Teaneck, NJ 07666 Tel. (201)928-1810

OFFICERS

Primate, ----

Archdiocesan Gen. Sec., V. Rev. Chorepiscopus John Meno

Triumph the Church and Kingdom of God in Christ Inc. (International)

This church was given through the wisdom and knowledge of God to the Late Apostle Elias Dempsey Smith on Oct. 20, 1897, in Issaquena County, Miss., while he was pastor of a Methodist church.

The Triumph Church, as this body is more commonly known, was founded in 1902. Its doors opened in 1904 and it was confirmed in Birmingham, Ala., with 225 members in 1915. It was incorporated in Washington, D.C., in 1918 and currently operates in 31 states and overseas. The General Church is divided into 13 districts, including the Africa District.

Triumphant doctrine and philosophy are based on the principles of life, truth and knowledge; the understanding that God is in man and expressed through man; the belief in manifested wisdom and the hope for constant new revelations. Its concepts and methods of teaching the second coming of Christ are based on these and all other attributes of goodness.

Triumphians emphasize that God is the God of the living, not the God of the dead.

HEADQUARTERS

213 Farrington Ave. S.E., Atlanta, GA 30315

Media Contact, Bishop C. W. Drummond, 7114 Idlewild, Pittsburg, PA 15208 Tel. (412)731-2286

OFFICERS

Chief Bishop, Bishop C. W. Drummond, 7114 Idlewild, Pittsburgh, PA 15208 Tel. (412)731-2286

Gen. Bd of Trustees, Chmn., Bishop Leon Simon, 1028 59th St., Oakland, CA 94608 Tel. (415)-652-9576

Gen. Treas., Bishop Hosea Lewis, 1713 Needlewood Ln., Orlando, FL 32818 Tel. (407)295-5488

Gen. Rec. Sec., Bishop Zephaniah Swindle, Box 1927, Shelbyville, TX 75973 Tel. (409)598-3082

True Orthodox Ch. of Greece (Synod of Metropolitan Cyprian), American Exarchate

The American Exarchate of the True (Old Calendar) Orthodox Church of Greece adheres to the tenets of the Eastern Orthodox Church, which considers itself the legitimate heir of the historical Apostolic Church.

When the Orthodox Church of Greece adopted the New or Gregorian Calendar in 1924, many felt that this breach with tradition compromised the church's festal calendar, based on the Old or Julian calendar, and its unity with world Orthodoxy. In 1935, three State Church Bishops returned to the Old Calendar and established a Synod in Resistance, The True Orthodox Church of Greece. When the last of these Bishops died, the Russian Orthodox Church Abroad consecrated a new hierarchy for the Greek Old Calendarists and, in 1969, declared them a sister church.

In the face of persecution by the state church, some Old Calendarists denied the validity of the Mother Church of Greece and formed two synods, now under the direction of Archbishop Chrysostomos of Athens and Archbishop Andreas of Athens. A moderate faction under Metropolitan Cyprian of Oropos and Fili does not maintain communion with the Mother Church of Greece, but recognizes its validity and seeks a restoration of unity by a return to the Julian Calendar and traditional ecclesiastical polity by the state church. About 1.5 million Orthodox Greeks belong to the Old Calendar Church.

The first Old Calendarist communities in the United States were formed in the 1930s. The Exarchate under Metropolitan Cyprian was established in 1986. Placing emphasis on clergy education, youth programs and recognition of the Old Calendarist minority in American Orthodoxy, the Exarchate has encouraged the establishment of monastic communities and missions. Cordial contacts with the New Calendarist and other Orthodox communities are encouraged. A center for theological training and Patristic studies has been established at the Exarchate headquarters in Etna, Calif.

In July 1994, the True Orthodox Church of Greece (Synod of Metropolitan Cyprian), the True Orthodox Church of Romania, the True Orthodox Church of Bulgaria, and the Russian Orthodox Church Abroad entered into liturgical union, forming a coalition of traditionalist Orthodox bodies several million strong.

HEADQUARTERS

St. Gregory Palamas Monastery, P.O. Box 398, Etna, CA 96027 Tel. (916)467-3228 Fax (916)-467-3996

Media Contact, Exarch in America, His Eminence Archbishop Chrysostomos

OFFICERS

Synodal Exarch in America, His Eminence Archbishop Chrysostomos

Asst. to the Exarch, His Grace Bishop Auxentios

Dean of Exarchate, The Rev. James P. Thornton, P.O. Box 2833, Garden Grove, CA 92642

Ukrainian Orthodox Church of America (Ecumenical Patriarchate)

This body was organized in the United States in 1928, when the first convention was held. In 1932, Dr. Joseph Zuk was consecrated as first Bishop. His successor was the Most Rev. Bishop Bohdan, Primate, who was consecrated by the order of the Ecumenical Patriarchate of Constantinople in 1937, in New York City. He was succeeded by the Most Rev. Metropolitan Andrei Kuschak, consecrated by the blessing of Ecumenical Patriarch by Archbishop Iakovos, Metropolitan Germanos and Bishop Silas of Greek-Orthodox Church, in 1967. His successor is Bishop Vsevolod, ordained in 1987 by Archbishop Iakovos, Metropolitan Silas and Bishops Philip and Athenagoras.

HEADQUARTERS

Ukrainian Orthodox Church of America, 90-34 139th St., Jamaica, NY 11435 Tel. (718)297-2407 Fax (718)291-8308

Media Contact, Primate, Bishop Vsevolod

OFFICERS

Primate, Rt. Rev. Bishop Vsevolod

PERIODICAL

Ukrainian Orthodox Herald

Ukrainian Orthodox Church of the U.S.A.

The church was formally organized in the United States in 1919. Archbishop John Theodorovich arrived from Ukraine in 1924.

HEADQUARTERS

P.O. Box 495, South Bound Brook, NJ 08880 Tel. (908)356-0090 Fax (908)356-5556

135 Davidson Ave., Somerset, NJ 08873

Media Contact, Archbishop, Archbishop His Eminence Anthony, 4 Von Steuben Ln., South Bound Brook, NJ 08880 Tel. (908)356-0090 Fax (908)-356-5556

OFFICERS

Metropolitan, His Beatitude Constantine [Buggan], Archbishop of Chicago & Philadelphia, P.O. Box 495, South Bound Brook, NJ 08880

Archbishop, His Eminence Antony, Archbishop of New York & Washington, 4 Von Steuben La., South Bound Brook, NJ 08880

United Brethren in Christ

The Church of the United Brethren in Christ had its beginning with Philip William Otterbein and Martin Boehm, who were leaders in the revivalistic movement in Pennsylvania and Maryland from the late 1760s into the early 1800s.

On Sept. 25, 1800, they and others associated with them formed a society under the name of United Brethren in Christ. Subsequent conferences adopted a Confession of Faith in 1815 and a constitution in 1841. The Church of the United Brethren in Christ adheres to the original constitution as amended in 1957, 1961 and 1977.

HEADQUARTERS

302 Lake St., Huntington, IN 46750 Tel. (219)356-2312 Fax (219)356-4730

Media Contact, Bishop, Dr. Ray A. Seilhamer

OFFICERS

Bishop, Dr. Ray A. Seilhamer

Gen. Treas./Office Mgr., Marda J. Hoffman

Dept. of Education, Dir., Dr. G. Blair Dowden

Dept. of Church Services, Dir., Rev. Paul Hirschy

United Christian Church

The United Christian Church originated about 1864. There were some ministers and laymen in the United Brethren in Christ Church who disagreed with the position and practice of the church on infant baptism, voluntary bearing of arms and belonging to oath-bound secret combinations. This group developed into United Christian Church, organized at a conference held in Campbelltown, Pa., on May 9, 1877. The principal founders of the denomination were George Hoffman, John Stamn and Thomas Lesher. Before they were organized, they were called Hoffmanites.

The United Christian Church has district conferences, a yearly general conference, a general board of trustees, a mission board, a board of directors of the United Christian Church Home, a camp meeting board, a young peoples' board and local organized congregations.

It believes in the Holy Trinity and the inspired Holy Scriptures with the doctrines they teach. The church practices the ordinances of Baptism, Holy Communion and Foot Washing.

It welcomes all into its fold who are born again, believe in Jesus Christ as Savior and Lord and have received the Holy Spirit.

HEADQUARTERS

c/o John P. Ludwig, Jr., 523 W. Walnut St., Cleona, PA 17042 Tel. (717)273-9629

Media Contact, Presiding Elder, John P. Ludwig, Jr.

OFFICERS

Presiding Elder, Elder John P. Ludwig, Jr.

Conf. Sec., Mr. Lee Wenger, 1625 Thompson Ave., Annville, PA 17003

Conf. Moderator, Elder Gerald Brinser, RR 1, Box 225, Annville, PA 17003

OTHER ORGANIZATIONS

Mission Board: Pres., Elder John P. Ludwig, Jr.; Sec., Elder Walter Knight, Jr., Rt. #3, Box 98, Palmyra, PA 17078; Treas., Mark Copenhaver, RR 4, Box 195, Lebanon, PA 17042

United Church of Christ

The United Church of Christ was constituted on June 25, 1957 by representatives of the Congregational Christian Churches and of the Evangelical and Reformed Church, in Cleveland, Ohio.

The Preamble to the Constitution states: "The United Church of Christ acknowledges as its sole head, Jesus Christ ... It acknowledges as kindred in Christ all who share in this confession. It looks to the Word of God in the Scriptures, and to the presence and power of the Holy Spirit ... It claims ... the faith of the historic Church expressed in the ancient creeds and reclaimed in the basic insights of the Protestant Reformers. It affirms the responsibility of the Church in each generation to make this faith its own in worship, in honesty of thought and expression, and in purity of heart before God.

The creation of the United Church of Christ brought together four unique traditions:

(1) Groundwork for the Congregational Way was laid by Calvinist Puritans and Separatists during the late 16th-early 17th centuries, then achieved prominence among English Protestants during the civil war of the 1640s. Opposition to state control prompted followers to emigrate to the United States, where they helped colonize New England in the 17th century. Congregationalists have been self-consciously a denomination from the mid-19th century.

(2) The Christian Churches, an 18th-century American restorationist movement emphasized Christ as the only head of the church, the New Testament as their only rule of faith, and "Christian" as their sole name. This loosely organized denomination found in the Congregational Churches a like disposition. In 1931, the two bodies formally united as the Congregational Christian Churches.

(3) The German Reformed Church comprised an irenic aspect of the Protestant Reformation, as a second generation of Reformers drew on the insights of Zwingli, Luther and Calvin to formulate the Heidelberg Catechism of 1563. People of the German Reformed Church began immigrating to the New World early in the 18th century, the heaviest concentration in Pennsylvania. Formal organization of the American denomination was completed in 1793. The church spread across the country. In the Mercersburg Movement, a strong emphasis on evangelical catholicity and Christian unity was eveloped.

(4) In 19th-century in Germany, Enlightenment criticism and Pietist inwardness decreased long-standing conflicts between religious groups. In Prussia, a royal proclamation merged Lutheran and Reformed people into one United Evangelical Church (1817). Members of this new church way migrated to America. The Evangelicals settled in large numbers in Missouri and Illinois, emphasizing pietistic devotion and unionism; in 1840 they formed the German Evangelical Church Society in the West. After union with other Evangelical church associations, in 1877 it took the name of the German Evangelical Synod of North America.

On June 25, 1934, this Synod and the Reformed Church in the U.S. (formerly the German Reformed Church) united to form the Evangelical and Reformed Church. They blended the Reformed tradition's passion for the unity of the church and the Evangelical tradition's commitment to the liberty of conscience inherent in the gospel.

HEADQUARTERS

700 Prospect Ave., Cleveland, OH 44115 Tel. (216)736-2100 Fax (216)736-2120

Media Contact, UCC-Sec., Edith A. Guffey, Tel. (216)736-2110

OFFICERS

Pres., Rev. Paul H. Sherry

Sec., Ms. Edith A. Guffey

Dir. of Fin. & Treas., Rev. Doris R. Powell

Exec. Assoc. to Pres., Rev. Kenneth K. Iha

Asst. to Pres. for Ecumenical Concerns, Rev. John H. Thomas

Asst. to Pres., Ms. Marilyn Dubasak

Chpsn. Exec. Council, Ms. Brenda F. Allen

Vice-Chpsn., Rev. Mark R. Kuether

Mod., Rev. David J. Dean

Asst. Mod.: Ms. Margaret E. MacDonald; Mr. Frank E. Thomas

ORGANIZATIONS

United Church Board for World Min.: Tel. (216)-736-3200; 475 Riverside Dr., New York, NY 10115 Tel. (212)870-2637; 14 Beacon St., Boston, MA 02018; Exec. Vice-Pres., Rev. David Y. Hirano; Mission Program Unit, Gen. Sec., Rev. Daniel F. Romero; Support Services Unit, Treas., Mr. Bruce Foresman

United Church Board for Homeland Min.: Tel. (216)736-3800 Fax (216)736-3803; Office of Exec. Vice-Pres., Exec. Vice-Pres., Rev. Thomas E. Dipko; Gen. Sec., Rev. Robert P. Noble, Jr.; Office of the Treasurer, Treas., Matthew O'Brien; Div. of Evangelism & Local Church Dev., Gen. Sec., Rev. Robert L. Burt; Div. of Education & Publication, Gen. Sec., ----; Div. of American Missionary Association, Gen. Sec., Rev. F. Allison Phillips

Commission for Racial Justice: ; Ofc. for Urban & Natl. Racial Justice, 5113 Georgia Ave. NW, Washington, DC 20011 Tel. (202)291-1593; Ofc. for Constituency Dev./Rural Racial Justice, Franklinton Center, P.O. Box 187, Enfield, NC 27823 Tel. (919)437-1723; Ofc. for Ecumenical Racial Justice, 475 Riverside Dr., Room 1948, New York, NY 10115 Tel. (212)870-2077; Exec. Dir., Ms. Bernice Powell Jackson

Council for American Indian Ministry: 122 W. Franklin Ave., Rm. 304, Minneapolis, MN 55405 Tel. (612)870-3679; Exec. Dir., Rev. Armin L. Schmidt

Council for Health & Human Service Min.: Tel. (216)736-2250; Exec. Dir., Rev. Bryan Sickbert

Coord. Center for Women in Church & Soc.: Tel. (216)736-2150; Exec. Dir., Rev. Mary Sue Gast

Office for Church in Society: ; 110 Maryland Ave. NE, Washington, DC 20002; Exec. Dir., Ms. Valerie E. Russell; Dir., Washington Ofc., Rev. Jay E. Lintner

Office for Church Life & Leadership: ; Exec. Dir., Rev. William A. Hulteen, Jr.

Office of Communication: Tel. (216)736-2222 Fax (216)736-2223; 475 Riverside Dr., 16th Fl., New York, NY 10115 Tel. (212)870-2137; Dir., Dr. Beverly J. Chain

Stewardship Council: ; 409 Prospect St., Box 304, New Haven, CT 06511; Exec. Dir., Rev. Earl D. Miller

Commission on Development: Dir. Planned Giving, Rev. Donald G. Stoner

Historical Council: ; Office of Archivist, Phillip Schaff Library, 555 W. James St., Lancaster, PA 17603

Pension Boards: 475 Riverside Dr., New York, NY 10115; Exec. Vice-Pres., Dr. John Ordway

United Church Foundation, Inc.: 475 Riverside Dr., New York, NY 10115; Financial Vice-Pres. & Treas., Mr. Donald G. Hart

CONFERENCES

Western Region

California, Nevada, Northern, Rev. John Rogers, 20 Woodside Ave., San Francisco, CA 94127

California, Southern, Rev. Davida Foy Crabtree, 466 E. Walnut St., Pasadena, CA 91101

Hawaii, Rev. Norman Jackson, 15 Craigside Pl., Honolulu, HI 96817

Montana-Northern Wyoming, Rev. John M. Schaeffer, 2016 Alderson Ave., Billings, MT 59102

Central Pacific, Rev. Donald J. Sevetson, 0245 SW Bancroft St., Ste. E, Portland, OR 97201

Rocky Mountain, Rev. William A. Dalke, 7000 Broadway, Ste. 420, ABS Bldg., Denver, CO 80221

Southwest, Rev. Ann C. Rogers-Witte, 4423 N. 24th St., Ste. 600, Phoenix, AZ 85016

Washington-North Idaho, Rev. Lynne S. Fitch, 720 14th Ave. E., Seattle, WA 98102

Washington-North Idaho, Rev. David J. Brown, 12 N. Chelan, Wenatchee, WA 98801

West Central Region

Iowa, Rev. Susan J. Ingham, 600 42nd St., Des Moines, IA 50312

Kansas-Oklahoma, Rev. John H. Krueger, 1248 Fabrique, Wichita, KS 67218

Minnesota, Rev. William Kaseman, 122 W. Franklin Ave., Rm. 323, Minneapolis, MN 55404

Missouri, Rev. A. Gayle Engel, 461 E. Lockwood Ave., St. Louis, MO 63119

Nebraska, Rev. Daniel A. VanderPloeg, 825 M St., Lincoln, NE 68508

North Dakota, Rev. Jack J. Seville, Jr., 227 W. Broadway, Bismarck, ND 58501

South Dakota, Rev. Eugene E. Miller, 3500 S. Phillips Ave., #121, Sioux Falls, SD 57105-6864

Great Lakes Region

Illinois, Rev. Jeffrey T. Nichols, 1840 Westchester Blvd., Westchester, IL 60154

Illinois South, Rev. Ronald L. Eslinger, Box 325, 1312 Broadway, Highland, IL 62249

Indiana-Kentucky, Rev. Carla J. Bailey, 1100 W. 42nd St., Indianapolis, IN 46208

Michigan, Rev. Herman Haller, P.O. Box 1006, East Lansing, MI 48826

Ohio, Rev. Ralph C. Quellhorst, 4041 N. High St., Ste. 301, Columbus, OH 43214

Wisconsin, Rev. Frederick R. Trost, 4459 Gray Rd., Box 495, De Forest, WI 53532-0495

Southern Region

Florida, Rev. William C. Tuck, 222 E. Welbourne Ave., Winter Park, FL 32789

South Central, Rev. David K. Felton, Jr., 6633 E. Hwy. 290, #200, Austin, TX 78723-1157

Southeast, Rev. Edwin Mehlhaff, 756 W. Peachtree St., NW, Atlanta, GA 30308

Southern, Rev. Rollin O. Russell, 217 N. Main St., Box 658, Graham, NC 27253

Middle Atlantic Region

Central Atlantic, Rev. John R. Deckenback, 916 S. Rolling Rd., Baltimore, MD 21228

New York, Rev. William Briggs, The Church Center, Rm. 202, 3049 E. Genesee St., Syracuse, NY 13224

Penn Central, Rev. Lyle J. Weible, The United Church Center, Rm. 126, 900 S. Arlington Ave., Harrisburg, PA 17109

Penn Northeast, Rev. Donald E. Overlock, 431 Delaware Ave., P.O. Box 177, Palmerton, PA 18071

Penn Southeast, Rev. Franklin R. Mittman, Jr., 505 Second Ave., P.O. Box 400, Collegeville, PA 19426

Penn West, Rev. Paul L. Westcoat, Jr., 320 South Maple Ave., Greensburg, PA 15601

Puerto Rico, Rev. Osvaldo Malave-Rivera, Box 5427, Hato Rey, PR 00919

New England Region

Connecticut, Rev. Donald W. Hinze, 125 Sherman St., Hartford, CT 06105

Maine, Rev. C. Jack Richards, 68 Main St., P.O. Box 966, Yarmouth, ME 04096

Massachusetts, Rev. Bennie E. Whiten, Jr., P.O. Box 2246, Salem & Badger Rds., Framingham, MA 01701

New Hampshire: Rev. Carole C. Carlson; Rev. Benjamin C. L. Crosby; Rev. Robert D. Witham, 314 S. Main, P.O. Box 465, Concord, NH 03302
Rhode Island, Rev. H. Dahler Hayes, 56 Walcott St., Pawtucket, RI 02860
Vermont, Rev. D. Curtis Minter, 285 Maple St., Burlington, VT 05401

Nongeographic

Calvin Synod, Rev. Francis Vitez, 493 Amboy Ave., Perth Amboy, NJ 08861

PERIODICALS

United Church News; Common Lot; Courage in the Struggle for Justice and Peace

United Holy Church of America, Inc.

The United Holy Church of America, Inc. is an outgrowth of the great revival that began with the outpouring of the Holy Ghost on the Day of Pentecost. The church is built upon the foundation of the Apostles and Prophets, Jesus Christ being the cornerstone.

During a revival of repentence, regeneration and holiness of heart and life that swept through the South and West, the United Holy Church was born. The founding fathers had no desire to establish a denomination but were pushed out of organized churches because of this experience of holiness and testimony of the Spirit-filled life.

On the first Sunday in May 1886, in Method, N.C., what is today known as the United Holy Church of America, Inc. was born. The church was incorporated on Sept. 25, 1918.

Baptism by immersion, the Lord's Supper and feet washing are observed. The premillennial teaching of the Second Coming of Christ, Divine healing, justification by faith, sanctification as a second work of grace and Spirit baptism are accepted.

HEADQUARTERS

5104 Dunstan Rd., Greensboro, NC 27405 Tel. (919)621-0669
Mailing Address, Bishop Thomas E. Talley, P.O. Box 1035, Portsmouth, VA 23705
Media Contact, Gen. Rec. Sec., Mrs. Beatrice S. Faison, 224 Wenz Rd., Toledo, OH 43615 Tel. (419)531-1859

PERIODICAL

The Holiness Union

United House of Prayer

The United House of Prayer was founded and organized as a hierarchical church in the 1920s by the late Bishop C. M. Grace, who had built the first House of Prayer in 1919 in West Wareham, MA, with his own hands. The purpose of the organization is to establish, maintain and perpetuate the doctrine of Christianity and the Apostolic Faith throughout the world among all people; to erect and maintain houses of prayer and worship where all people may gather for prayer and to worship the almighty God in spirit and in truth, irrespective of denomination or creed, and to maintain the Apostolic faith of the Lord and Savior, Jesus Christ.

HEADQUARTERS

1117 7th St. NW, Washington, DC 20001 Tel. (202)289-0238 Fax (202)289-8058
Media Contact, Apostle S. Green

OFFICERS

CEO, Bishop S. C. Madison, 1665 N. Portal Dr. NW, Washington, DC 20012 Tel. (202)882-3956 Fax (202)829-4717

NATIONAL PROGRAM STAFF

The General Assembly, Presiding Officer, Bishop S. C. Madison, 1665 N. Portal Dr. NW, Washington, DC 20012 Tel. (202)882-3956 Fax (202)-829-4717
General Council Ecclesiastical Court, Clerk, Apostle R. Price, 1665 N. Portal Dr. NW, Washington, DC 20012 Tel. (202)882-3956 Fax (202)829-4717
Annual Truth & Facts Publication, Exec. Editor, Bishop S. C. Madison, 1665 N. Portal Dr. NW, Washington, DC 20012 Tel. (202)882-3956 Fax (202)829-4717
Nationwide Building Program, General Builder, Bishop S. C. Madison, 1665 N. Portal Dr. NW, Washington, DC 20012 Tel. (202)882-3956 Fax (202)829-4717
Special Projects, Dir., Apostle S. Green

The United Methodist Church

The United Methodist Church was formed April 23, 1968, in Dallas by the union of The Methodist Church and The Evangelical United Brethren Church. The two churches shared a common historical and spiritual heritage. The Methodist Church resulted in 1939 from the unification of three branches of Methodism -- the Methodist Episcopal Church, the Methodist Episcopal Church, South, and the Methodist Protestant Church.

The Methodist movement began in 18th-century England under the preaching of John Wesley, but the Christmas Conference of 1784 in Baltimore is regarded as the date on which the organized Methodist Church was founded as an ecclesiastical organization. It was there that Francis Asbury was elected the first bishop in this country.

The Evangelical United Brethren Church was formed in 1946 with the merger of the Evangelical Church and the Church of the United Brethren in Christ, both of which had their beginnings in Pennsylvania in the evangelistic movement of the 18th and early 19th centuries. Philip William Otterbein and Jacob Albright were early leaders of this movement among the German-speaking settlers of the Middle Colonies.

HEADQUARTERS

Information InfoServ, Dir., Woodley McEachern, Tel. 1-800-251-8140
Media Contact, Dir., United Methodist News Service, Thomas S. McAnally, Tel. (615)742-5470 Fax (615)742-5469

OFFICERS

Gen. Conference, Sec., Carolyn M. Marshall, 204 N. Newlin St., Veedersburg, IN 47987
Council of Bishops: Pres., Bishop Roy I. Sano, P.O. Box 6006, Pasadena, CA 91102 Tel. (818)-568-7300; Sec., Bishop Melvin G. Talbert, P.O. Box 467, San Francisco, CA 94101 Tel. (415)-474-3101

BISHOPS AND CONFERENCE COUNCIL DIRECTORS

North Central Jurisdiction

Central Illinois: Bishop David J. Lawson, Tel. (217)544-4604; Larry L. Lawler, 501 E. Capitol Ave., Springfield, IL 62701 Tel. (217)544-4604 Fax (217)544-4651

Dakotas: Bishop William B. Lewis, 815 25th St. S., Fargo, ND 58103-2303 Tel. (701)232-2241 Fax (701)232-2615; Richard W. Fisher, 1331 W. University Ave., P.O. Box 460, Mitchell, SD 57301 Tel. (605)996-6552 Fax (605)996-1766

Detroit: Bishop Donald A. Ott, Tel. (810)559-7000 Fax (810)569-4830; Cecile Adams, 21700 Northwestern Hwy., Ste. 1200, Southfield, MI 48075 Tel. (313)559-7000 Fax (313)569-4830

East Ohio: Bishop Edwin C. Boulton, Tel. (216)-499-3972 Fax (216)499-3279; Judith A. Olin, 8800 Cleveland Ave. NW, P.O. Box 2800, North Canton, OH 44720 Tel. (216)499-3972 Fax (216)499-3279

Iowa: Bishop Charles W. Jordan, Tel. (515)283-1991; Don Mendenhall, 500 E. Court Ave., Ste. C, Des Moines, IA 50309 Tel. (515)283-1991 Fax (515)288-1906

Minnesota: Bishop Sharon Brown Christopher, 122 W. Franklin Ave., Rm. 200, Tel. (612)870-4007 Fax (612)870-3587; Patricia Hinker, 122 W. Franklin Ave., Ste. 200, Minneapolis, MN 55404 Tel. (612)870-0058 Fax (612)870-1260

North Indiana: Bishop Woodie W. White, 1100 W. 42nd St., Indianapolis, IN 46208 Tel. (317)924-1321 Fax (317)924-4859; Steven Burris, P.O. Box 869, Marion, IN 46952 Tel. (317)664-5138 Fax (317)664-2307

Northern Illinois: Bishop R. Sheldon Duecker, Tel. (312)380-5060 Fax (312)380-5067; Bonnie Ogie-Kristianson, 8765 W. Higgins Rd., Ste. 650, Chicago, IL 60631 Tel. (312)380-5060 Fax (312)380-5067

South Indiana: Bishop Woodie W. White, 1100 W. 42nd St., Indianapolis, IN 46208 Tel. (317)924-1321 Fax (317)924-4859; Susan W.N. Ruach, Box 5008, Bloomington, IN 47407 Tel. (812)-336-0186 Fax (812)336-0216

Southern Illinois: Bishop David J. Lawson, 501 E. Capitol Ave., Ste. 212, Springfield, IL 62701 Tel. (217)544-4604 Fax (217)544-4651; William Frazier, 1919 Broadway, Mt. Vernon, IL 62864 Tel. (618)242-4070 Fax (618)242-9227

West Michigan: Bishop Donald A. Ott, 21700 Northwestern Hwy., Ste. 1200, Southfield, MI 48075-4917 Tel. (810)559-7000 Fax (810)569-4830; David B. Nelson, P.O. Box 6247, Grand Rapids, MI 49516 Tel. (616)459-4503 Fax (616)459-0191

West Ohio: Bishop Judith Craig, Tel. (614)228-6784 Fax (614)222-0612; Stanley T. Ling, 471 E. Broad St., Ste. 1106, Columbus, OH 43215-3889 Tel. (614)228-6784 Fax (614)222-0612

Wisconsin: Bishop Sharon Z. Rader, 750 Windsor St., Ste. 303, Sun Prairie, WI 53590 Tel. (608)-837-8526 Fax (608)837-0281; Forrest S. Clark, P.O. Box 220, Sun Prairie, WI 53590 Tel. (608)-837-7328 Fax (608)837-8547

Northeastern Jurisdiction

Baltimore-Washington: Bishop Joseph H. Yeakel, 9226 Colesville Rd., Silver Spring, MD 20910-1658 Tel. (301)587-9226 Fax (301)608-0071; Marcus Matthews, 5124 Greenwich Ave., Baltimore, MD 21229 Tel. (410)233-7300 Fax (410)-233-7308

Central Pennsylvania: Bishop Felton E. May, 900 S. Arlington Ave., #214, Tel. (717)652-6705 Fax (717)652-5109; G. Edwin Zeiders, 900 S. Arlington Ave., #112, Harrisburg, PA 17109 Tel. (717)652-0460 Fax (717)652-3499

Eastern Pennsylvania: Bishop Susan M. Morrison, Tel. (610)666-9090 Fax (610)666-9181; Robert Daughtery, P.O. Box 820, Valley Forge, PA 19482 Tel. (610)666-9090 Fax (610)666-9093

New England: Bishop F. Herbert Skeete, 566 Commonwealth Ave., Boston, MA 02215 Tel. (617)-266-3900 Fax (617)266-4619; Lornagrace Stuart, 74 State Rd., Unit 203, Kittery, ME 03904 Tel. (207)439-3836 Fax (207)439-3933

New York: Bishop James K. Mathews, Tel. (914)-684-6922; Clayton Miller, 252 Bryant Ave., White Plains, NY 10605 Tel. (914)997-1570 Fax (914)684-6874

North Central New York: Bishop Hae-Jong Kim, 1010 East Ave., Rochester, NY 14607 Tel. (716)271-3400 Fax (716)271-3404; Garrie F. Stevens, P.O. Box 1515, Cicero, NY 13039 Tel. (315)699-8715 Fax (315)699-8774

Northern New Jersey: Bishop Neil Irons, 112 W. Delaware Ave., Pennington, NJ 08534 Tel. (609)737-3940 Fax (609)737-7422; George E. Olive, III, 22 Madison, Madison, NJ 07940 Tel. (201)377-3800 Fax (201)765-9868

Peninsula-Delaware: Bishop Susan M. Morrison, P.O. Box 820, Valley Forge, PA 19482 Tel. (610)666-9090 Fax (610)666-9181; Lehman R. Tomlin, Jr., 139 N. State St., Dover, DE 19901 Tel. (302)674-2626 Fax (302)674-1573

Southern New Jersey: Bishop Neil Irons, 112 W. Delaware Ave., Pennington, NJ 08534 Tel. (609)737-3940 Fax (609)737-7422; George T. Wang, 1995 E. Marlton Pike, Cherry Hill, NJ 08003 Tel. (609)424-1700 Fax (609)424-9282

Troy: Bishop William B. Grove, 215 Lancaster St., Albany, NY 12210-1131 Tel. (518)426-0386 Fax (518)426-0347; James M. Perry, P.O. Box 560, Saratoga Springs, NY 12866 Tel. (518)584-8214 Fax (518)584-8378

West Virginia: Bishop S. Clifton Ives, 900 Washington St., East Charleston, WV 25301 Tel. (304)344-8330 Fax (304)344-8330; Thomas E. Dunlap, Sr., P.O. Box 2313, Charleston, WV 25328 Tel. (304)344-8331 Fax (304)344-8338

Western New York: Bishop Hae-Jong Kim, 1010 East Ave., Rochester, NY 14607 Tel. (716)271-3400 Fax (716)271-3404; James M. Pollard, 8499 Main St., Buffalo, NY 14221 Tel. (716)-633-8558 Fax (716)633-8581

Western Pennsylvania: Bishop George W. Bashore, Tel. (412)776-2300 Fax (412)776-1355; John Ross Thompson, 1204 Freedom Rd., Cranberry Township, PA 16066-4914 Tel. (412)776-2300 Fax (412)776-1355

Wyoming: Bishop William B. Grove, 215 Lancaster St., Albany, NY 12210-1131 Tel. (518)426-0386 Fax (518)426-0347; Penelope A. Gladwell, 1700 Monroe St., Endicott, NY 13760 Tel. (607)757-0608 Fax (607)757-0752

South Central Jurisdiction

Exec. Sec.: L. Ray Branton, 5646 Milton St., #240, Dallas, TX 75228 Tel. (214)692-9081

Central Texas: Bishop Joe A. Wilson, Tel. (817)-877-5222 Fax (817)332-4609; J. Michael Patison, 464 Bailey, Ft. Worth, TX 76107 Tel. (817)877-5222 Fax (817)338-4541

Kansas East: Bishop Albert F. Mutti, Tel. (913)-272-0587 Fax (913)272-9135; Dale L. Fooshee, P.O. Box 4187, Topeka, KS 66604 Tel. (913)-272-9111 Fax (913)272-9135

Kansas West: Bishop Albert F. Mutti, P.O. Box 4187, Topeka, KS 66604 Tel. (913)272-0587 Fax (913)272-9135; Wayne D. Findley, Sr., 9440 E. Boston, #150, Wichita, KS 67207 Tel. (316)684-0266 Fax (316)684-0044

Little Rock: Bishop Richard B. Wilke, 723 Center St., Little Rock, AR 72201-4399 Tel. (501)324-8019 Fax (501)324-8018; F. Gladwin Connell, 715 Center St., Ste. 202, Little Rock, AR 72201 Tel. (501)324-8027 Fax (501)324-8018

Louisiana: Bishop William B. Oden, Tel. (504)-346-1646 Fax (504)387-3662; Leslie Nichols Akin, 527 North Blvd., Baton Rouge, LA 70802-5700 Tel. (504)346-1646 Fax (504)383-2652

Missouri East: Bishop Ann B. Sherer, 870 Woods Mill Rd.,Ste. 100, Ballwin, MO 63011 Tel. (314)891-8001 Fax (314)891-8003; Elmer E. Revelle, 870 Woods Mill Rd., #400, Ballwin, MO 63011 Tel. (314)891-1207 Fax (314)891-1211

Missouri West: Bishop Ann B. Sherer, 870 Woods Mill Rd., Ste 100, Ballwin, MO 63011 Tel. (314)891-8001 Fax (314)891-8003; Keith T. Berry, 1512 Van Brunt Blvd., Kansas City, MO 64127 Tel. (816)241-7650 Fax (816)241-4086

Nebraska: Bishop Joel L. Martinez, Tel. (402)466-4955 Fax (402)466-7931; Richard D. Turner, P.O. Box 4553, Lincoln, NE 68504-4553 Tel. (402)464-5994 Fax (402)466-7931

New Mexico: Bishop Alfred L. Norris, Tel. (505)-255-8786 Fax (505)255-8738; Joan V. Roberts, 7920 Mountain Rd. NE, Albuquerque, NM 87110 Tel. (505)255-8786 Fax (505)255-8738

North Arkansas: Bishop Richard B. Wilke, 723 Center St., Little Rock, AR 72201-4399 Tel. (501)324-8019 Fax (501)324-8018; Jim Beal, 715 Center St., Ste. 202, Little Rock, AR 72201 Tel. (501)324-8034 Fax (501)324-8018

North Texas: Bishop Bruce Blake, 3300 Mockingbird Ln., P.O. Box 8127, Dallas, TX 75205 Tel. (214)522-6741 Fax (214)528-4435; Gary E. Mueller, P.O. Box 516069, Dallas, TX 75251 Tel. (214)490-3438 Fax (214)490-7216

Northwest Texas: Bishop Alfred L. Norris, 7920 Mountain Rd. NE, Albuquerque, NM 87110-7805 Tel. (505)255-8786 Fax (505)255-8738; Louise Schock, 1415 Ave. M, Lubbock, TX 79401 Tel. (806)762-0201 Fax (806)762-0205

Oklahoma: Bishop Dan E. Solomon, Tel. (405)-525-2252 Fax (405)525-2216; David Severe, 2420 N. Blackwelder, Oklahoma City, OK 73106 Tel. (405)525-2252 Fax (405)525-4164

Oklahoma Indian Missionary: Bishop Dan E. Solomon, 2420 N. Blackwelder Ave., Oklahoma City, OK 73106-1499 Tel. (405)525-2252 Fax (405)525-2216; Becky Thompson, 3020 S. Harvey, Oklahoma City, OK 73109 Tel. (405)-632-2006 Fax (405)632-0209

Rio Grande: Bishop Raymond Owen, P.O. Box 28509, San Antonio, TX 78284 Tel. (210)431-6400 Fax (210)431-5470; Roberto L. Gomez, P.O. Box 28098, San Antonio, TX 78284 Tel. (210)431-6410 Fax (210)431-6470

Southwest Texas: Bishop Raymond Owen, P.O. Box 28509, San Antonio, TX 78284 Tel. (210)-431-6400 Fax (210)431-5470; Harry G. Kahl, P.O. Box 28098, San Antonio, TX 78284 Tel. (210)431-6440 Fax (210)431-6470

Texas: Bishop J. Woodrow Hearn, Tel. (713)528-6881 Fax (713)521-3724; Lamar E. Smith, 5215 S. Main St., Houston, TX 77002 Tel. (713)521-9383 Fax (713)521-3724

Southeastern Jurisdiction

Exec. Dir.: Gordon C. Goodgame, P.O. Box 67, Lake Junaluska, NC 28745 Tel. (704)452-2881

Alabama-West Florida: Bishop William W. Morris, 424 Interstate Park Dr., Montgomery, AL 36109 Tel. (334)277-1787 Fax (334)277-0109; William Calhoun, P.O. Drawer 700, Andalusia, AL 36420 Tel. (334)222-3127 Fax (334)222-0469

Florida: Bishop H. Hasbrock Hughes, Jr., P.O. Box 1747, Lakeland, FL 33802 Tel. (813)688-4427 Fax (813)687-0568; David T. Brewer, P.O. Box 3767, Lakeland, FL 33802 Tel. (813)688-5563 Fax (813)680-1912

Holston: Bishop Clay F. Lee, P.O. Box 51787, Knoxville, TN 37950 Tel. (423)525-1809 Fax (423)673-4474; Peyton L. Rowlett, Jr., P.O. Box 1178, Johnson City, TN 37605 Tel. (423)928-2156 Fax (423)928-8807

Kentucky: Bishop Robert C. Morgan, Professional Tower, Ste. 264, 4010 DuPont Circle, Louisville, KY 40207 Tel. (502)893-6715 Fax (502)-893-6753; Larry B. Gardner, P.O. Box 55107, Lexington, KY 40555 Tel. (606)254-7388 Fax (606)231-8180

Louisville: Bishop Robert C. Morgan, Professional Towers, Ste. 264, 4010 Dupont Cir., Louisville, KY 40207 Tel. (502)893-6715 Fax (502)893-6753; Rhoda Peters, 1115 S. Fourth St., Louisville, KY 40203 Tel. (502)584-3838 Fax (502)584-9373

Memphis: Bishop Kenneth L. Carder, 520 Commerce St., Ste. 201, Nashville, TN 37203 Tel. (615)742-8834 Fax (615)742-3726; Benny Hopper, 575 Lambuth Blvd., Jackson, TN 38301 Tel. (901)427-8589 Fax (901)423-2419

Mississippi: Bishop M. L. Meadows, Jr., P.O. Box 931, Jackson, MS 39205-0931 Tel. (601)948-4561 Fax (601)948-5981, Jack Loflin, P.O. Box 1147, Jackson, MS 39215 Tel. (601)354-0515 Fax (601)948-5982

North Alabama: Bishop Robert E. Fannin, Tel. (205)322-8665 Fax (205)322-8938; C. Phillip Huckaby, 898 Arkadelphia Rd., Birmingham, AL 35204 Tel. (205)226-7954 Fax (205)226-7975

North Carolina: Bishop C. P. Minnick, Jr., 1307 Glenwood Ave., Raleigh, NC 27605-0955 Tel. (919)832-9560 Fax (919)834-7989; Robert L. Baldridge, P.O. Box 10955, Raleigh, NC 27605 Tel. (919)832-9560 Fax (919)834-7989

North Georgia: Bishop J. Lloyd Knox, Tel. (404)-659-0002 Fax (404)577-0068; Rudolph R. Baker, Jr., 159 Ralph McGill Blvd. NE, Rm. 106, Atlanta, GA 30308-3391 Tel. (404)659-0002 Fax (404)577-0131

Red Bird Missionary: Bishop Robert C. Morgan, Professional Towers, Ste. 264, 4010 Dupont Cir., Louisville, KY 40207 Tel. (502)893-6715 Fax (502)893-6753; Ruth Wiertzema, 6 Queendale Ctr., Box 3, Beverly, KY 40913 Tel. (606)-598-5915

South Carolina: Bishop Robert H. Spain, 4908 Colonial Dr., Ste. 108, Columbia, SC 29203 Tel. (803)786-9486 Fax (803)754-9327; Charles L. Johnson, Sr., 4908 Colonial Dr., Ste. 101, Columbia, SC 29203 Tel. (803)786-9486 Fax (803)691-0220

South Georgia: Bishop Richard C. Looney, P.O. Box 13616, Macon, GA 31208-3616 Tel. (912)-738-0048 Fax (912)738-9778; James T. Pennell, P.O. Box 20408, St. Simons Island, GA 31522 Tel. (912)638-8626 Fax (912)634-0642

Tennessee: Bishop Kenneth L. Carder, 520 Commerce St., Ste. 201, Nashville, TN 37203 Tel. (615)742-8834 Fax (615)742-3726; Charles F. Armistead, P.O. Box 120607, Nashville, TN 37212 Tel. (615)329-1177 Fax (615)329-0884

Virginia: Bishop Thomas B. Stockton, Tel. (804)-359-9451 Fax (804)358-7736; Lee B. Sheaffer, P.O. 11367, Richmond, VA 23230 Tel. (804)-359-9451 Fax (804)359-5427

Western North Carolina: Bishop L. Bevel Jones, III, P.O. Box 18750, Charlotte, NC 28218 Tel. (704)535-2260 Fax (704)567-6117; Harold K. Bales, P.O. Box 18005, PO Box 18005, Charlotte, NC 28218 Tel. (704)535-2260 Fax (704)-567-6117

Western Jurisdiction

Alaska Missionary: Bishop William W. Dew, Jr., 1505 SW 18th Ave., Portland, OR 97201-2599 Tel. (503)226-7931 Fax (503)228-3189; Chris Spencer, 3402 Wesleyan Dr., Anchorage, AK 99508 Tel. (907)333-5050 Fax (907) 333-2304

California-Nevada: Bishop Melvin G. Talbert, 1276 Halyard Dr., P.O. Box 980250, West Sacramento, CA 95798-0250 Tel. (916)374-1510 Fax (916)372-5544; James H. Corson, P.O. Box 980250, 1276 Halyard Dr., West Sacramento, CA 95798-0250 Tel. (916)374-1516 Fax (916)-372-5544

California-Pacific: Bishop Roy I. Sano, Tel. (818)-568-7300 Fax (818)796-7297; J. Delton Pickering, P.O. Box 6006, Pasadena, CA 91102 Tel. (818)568-7300 Fax (818)796-7297

Desert Southwest: Bishop Elias Galvin, Tel. (602)-266-6956 Fax (602)266-5343; Lawrence A. Hinshaw, 1515 E. Meadowbrook Ave., Ste. 200, Phoenix, AZ 85014-4040 Tel. (602)266-6956 Fax (602)266-5343

Oregon-Idaho: Bishop William W. Dew, Jr., 1505 SW 18th Ave., Portland, OR 97201-2599 Tel. (503)226-7931 Fax (503)228-3189; Thomas Rannells, 1505 SW 18th Ave., Portland, OR 97201 Tel. (503)226-7931 Fax (503)226-4158

Pacific Northwest: Bishop Calvin D. McConnell, 2112 Third Ave. Ste. 301, Seattle, WA 98121-2333 Tel. (206)728-7674 Fax (206)728-8442; Daniel P. Smith, 2112 Third Ave., Ste. 300, Seattle, WA 98121 Tel. (206)728-7462 Fax (206)728-8442

Rocky Mountain: Bishop Mary Ann Swenson, Tel. (303)733-5035 Fax (303)733-5047; Janet Forbes, 2200 S. University Blvd., Denver, CO 80210 Tel. (303)733-3736 Fax (303)733-1730

Yellowstone: Bishop Mary Ann Swenson, 2200 S. University Blvd., Denver, CO 80210 Tel. (303)-733-5035 Fax (303)733-5047; Gary Keene, 2913 2nd Ave. N., Billings, MT 59101 Tel. (406)256-1385 Fax (406)256-4948

AGENCIES

Judicial Council: Pres., Tom Matheny; Sec., Wayne Coffin, 4937 NW 62nd Terr., Oklahoma City, OK 73122 Tel. (405)721-5528

Council on Finance & Administration: Acting Pres., Bishop Edwin C. Boulton; Gen. Sec., Sandra Kelley Lackore, 1200 Davis St., Evanston, IL 60201-4193 Tel. (708)869-3345

Council on Ministries: Pres., Bishop William W. Dew, Jr.; Gen. Sec., C. David Lundquist, 601 W. Riverview Ave., Dayton, OH 45406 Tel. (513)-227-9400

Board of Church & Society: Pres., Bishop Joseph H. Yeakel; Gen. Sec., Thom White Wolf Fassett, 100 Maryland Ave. NE, Washington, DC 20002 Tel. (202)488-5600

Board of Discipleship: Pres., Bishop David J. Lawson; Gen. Sec., Ezra Earl Jones, P.O. Box 840, Nashville, TN 37202 Tel. (615)340-7200

Board of Global Ministries: Pres., Bishop F. Herbert Skeete; Gen. Sec., Randolph Nugent, 475 Riverside Dr., New York, NY 10115 Tel. (212)-870-3600

Board of Higher Education & Ministry: Pres., Bishop Calvin D. McConnell; Gen. Sec., Roger Ireson, P.O. Box 871, Nashville, TN 37202 Tel. (615)340-7000 Fax (615)340-7048

Board of Pension & Health Benefits: Pres., Bishop Clay F. Lee; Gen. Sec., Barbara Boigegrain, 1201 Davis St., Evanston, IL 60201 Tel. (708)-869-4550

Board of Publications: Chpsn., William Deel; United Methodist Publishing House, Pres. & Publisher, Robert K. Feaster, P.O. Box 801, Nashville, TN 37202 Tel. (615)749-6000

Commission on Archives & History: Pres., Bishop Emilio de Carvalho; Gen. Sec., Charles Yrigoyen, P.O. Box 127, Madison, NJ 07940 Tel. (201)408-3189 Fax (201)408-3909

Comm. Christian Unity/Interrel. Concerns: Pres., Bishop William B. Grove; Gen. Sec., Bruce Robbins, 475 Riverside Dr., Rm. 1300, New York, NY 10115 Tel. (212)749-3553

Comm. on Communication/UM Communications: Pres., Bishop L. Bevel Jones, III; Gen. Sec., Judith Weidman, P.O. Box 320, zip 37202, 810 12th Ave. S., Nashville, TN 37203 Tel. (615)-742-5400

Commission on Religion & Race: Acting Pres., Bishop Clifton Ives; Gen. Sec., Barbara R. Thompson, 100 Maryland Ave. NE, Washington, DC 20002 Tel. (202)547-4270

Commission on the Status & Role of Women: Pres., Bishop Ann B. Sherer; Gen. Secretariats, Stephanie Anna Hixon; Cecelia M. Long, 1200 Davis St., Evanston, IL 60201 Tel. (312)869-7330

PERIODICALS

Mature Years; El Intérprete; New World Outlook; Newscope; Interpreter; Methodist History; Christian Social Action; Pockets; Response; Social Questions Bulletin; United Methodist Reporter; United Methodist Review; United Methodist Record; Quarterly Review; Alive Now; Circuit Rider; El Aposento Alto; Weavings:A Journal of the Christian Spiritual Life; The Upper Room

United Pentecostal Church International

The United Pentecostal Church International came into being through the merger of two oneness Pentecostal organizations -- the Pentecostal Church, Inc., and the Pentecostal Assemblies of Jesus Christ. The first of these was known as the Pentecostal Ministerial Alliance from its inception in 1925 until 1932. The second was formed in 1931 by a merger of the Apostolic Church of Jesus Christ with the Pentecostal Assemblies of the World.

The church contends that the Bible teaches that there is one God who manifested himself as the Father in creation, in the Son in redemption and as the Holy Spirit in regeneration; that Jesus is the name of this absolute deity and that water baptism should be administered in his name, not in the titles Father, Son and Holy Ghost (Acts 2:38, 8:16, and 19:6).

The Fundamental Doctrine of the United Pentecostal Church International, as stated in its Articles of Faith, is "the Bible standard of full salvation, which is repentance, baptism in water by immersion in the name of the Lord Jesus Christ for the remission of sins, and the baptism of the Holy Ghost with the initial sign of speaking with other tongues as the Spirit gives utterance."

Further doctrinal teachings concern of a life of holiness and separation, the operation of the gifts of the Spirit within the church, the second coming of the Lord and the church's obligation to take the gospel to the whole world.

HEADQUARTERS

8855 Dunn Rd., Hazelwood, MO 63042 Tel. (314)-837-7300 Fax (314)837-4503

Media Contact, Gen. Sec.-Treas., Rev. C. M. Becton

OFFICERS

Gen. Supt., Rev. Nathaniel A. Urshan

Asst. Gen. Supts.: Rev. Kenneth Haney, 7149 E. 8 Mile Rd., Stockton, CA 95212; Jesse Williams, P.O. Box 64277, Fayetteville, NC 28306

Gen. Sec.-Treas., Rev. C. M. Becton

Dir. of Foreign Missions, Rev. Harry Scism

Gen. Dir. of Home Missions, Rev. Jack Cunningham

Editor-in-Chief, Rev. J. L. Hall

Gen. Sunday School Dir., Rev. E. J. McClintock

OTHER ORGANIZATIONS

Pentecostal Publishing House, Mgr., Rev. Marvin Curry

Youth Division (Pentecostal Conquerors), Pres., Brian Kinsey, Hazelwood, MO 63042

Ladies Auxiliary, Pres., Gwyn Oakes, P.O. Box 247, Bald Knob, AR 72010

Harvestime Radio Broadcast, Dir., Rev. J. Hugh Rose, 698 Kerr Ave., Cadiz, OH 43907

Stewardship Dept., Contact Church Division, Hazelwood, MO 63042

Education Division, Supt., Rev. Arless Glass, 4502 Aztec, Pasadena, TX 77504

Public Relations Division, Contact Church Division, Hazelwood, MO 63042

Historical Society & Archives

PERIODICALS

World Harvest Today; The North American Challenge; Homelife; Conqueror; Reflections; Forward

United Zion Church

A branch of the Brethren in Christ which settled in Lancaster County, Pa., the United Zion Church was organized under the leadership of Matthias Brinser in 1855.

HEADQUARTERS

United Zion Home, 722 Furnace Hills Pk., Lititz, PA 17543

Media Contact, Bishop, Carl Eberly, 270 Clay School Rd., Ephrata, PA 17522 Tel. (717)733-3932

OFFICERS

Gen. Conf. Mod., Bishop Carl Eberly, 270 Clay School Rd., Ephrata, PA 17522 Tel. (717)733-3932

Asst. Mod., ----

Gen. Conf. Sec., Rev. Melvin Horst, 2021 Main St., Rothsville, PA 17573 Tel. (717)626-0677

Gen. Conf. Treas., Kenneth Kleinfelter, 919 Sycamore Lane, Lebanon, PA 17042

PERIODICAL

Zion's Herald

Unity of the Brethren

Czech and Moravian immigrants in Texas (beginning about 1855) established congregations which grew into an Evangelical Union in 1903, and with the accession of other Brethren in Texas, into the Evangelical Unity of the Czech-Moravian Brethren in North America. In 1959, it shortened the name to the original name used in 1457, the Unity of the Brethren (Unitas Fratrum, or Jednota Bratrska).

HEADQUARTERS

4202 Ermine Trail, Temple, TX 76574

Media Contact, Sec. of Exec. Committee, Georgia Anderson, 2501 Daivd St., #42, Taylor, TX 76574 Tel. (512)352-3239

OFFICERS

Pres., Dr. Mark L. Labaj, 4202 Ermine Trail, Temple, TX 76504

1st Vice Pres., Rev. James D. Hejl, 309 Cherrywood Cir., Taylor, TX 76574 Tel. (512)352-6890

Sec., Georgia Anderson, 2501 David St., #42, Taylor, TX 76574 Tel. (512)352-3239

Fin. Sec., Ron Sulak, 1217 Christine, Troyn, TX 76579

Treas., Frank McKay, III, 919 Hartman, Baytown, TX 77520

OTHER ORGANIZATIONS

Bd. of Christian Educ., Chmn., Rev. Dick Stone, 403 S. Main St., Caldwell, TX 77836

Brethren Youth Fellowship, Pres., Melynda Tomasek, Route 1, Box 101A, Georgetown, TX 78626

Young Adult Fellowship, Pres., Kimberly Stewart, 3719 Thursa Ln., Friendswood, TX 77546

Christian Sisters Union, Pres., Mrs. Ruth Paul, Route 2,, Caldwell, TX 77836

Sunday School Union, Pres., Mrs. Dorothy Kocian, 107 S. Barbara, Waco, TX 76705

PERIODICAL

Brethren Journal

Universal Fellowship of Metropolitan Community Churches

The Universal Fellowship of Metropolitan Community Churches was founded Oct. 6, 1968 by the Rev. Troy D. Perry in Los Angeles, with a particular but not exclusive outreach to the gay community. Since that time, the Fellowship has grown to include congregations throughout the world.

The group is trinitarian and accepts the Bible as the divinely inspired Word of God. The Fellowship has two sacraments, baptism and holy communion, as well as a number of traditionally recognized rites such as ordination.

This Fellowship acknowledges "the Holy Scriptures interpreted by the Holy Spirit in conscience and faith, as its guide in faith, discipline, and government." The government of this Fellowship is vested in its General Council (consisting of Elders and District Coordinators), clergy and church delegates, who exert the right of control in all of its affairs, subject to the provisions of its Articles of Incorporation and By-Laws.

HEADQUARTERS

5300 Santa Monica Blvd. #304, Los Angeles, CA 90029 Tel. (213)464-5100 Fax (213)464-2123

Media Contact, PR Rep., Rev. Kittredge Cherry

OFFICERS

Mod., Rev. Elder Troy D. Perry

Vice-Mod., Rev. Elder Nancy L. Wilson

Treas., Rev. Elder Donald Eastman

Clk., Rev. Elder Darlene Garner, 7245 Lee Hwy., Falls Church, VA 22046

Rev. Elder Wilhelmina A. Hein, P.O. Box 13468, Armagh, New Zealand

Rev. Elder Hong Kia Tan, 72 Fleet Rd., Hampstead, London, NW3 2QT England

Elder Larry Rodriguez, 6245 Bristol Parkway, Box 327, Culver City, CA 90232

Dir. of Admn., Mr. Ravi Verma

DISTRICT COORDINATORS

Australian District, Rev. Greg Smith, MCC Sydney, P.O. Box 1237, Darlinghurst NSW 2012, Australia

Eastern Canadian District, Rev. Marcie Wexler, 33 Holly St. No. 1117, Toronto, ON M4S 2G8

European North Sea District, Rev. Roy Beaney, 62 Brochenhurst Way, London SW164UD England

Great Lakes District, Judy Dale, 1300 Ambridge Dr., Louisville, KY 40207 Tel. (502)897-3821

Gulf Lower Atlantic District, Rev. Jay Neely, c/o First MCC of Atlanta, 1379 Tullie Rd., Atlanta, GA 30329

Mid-Central District, Rev. L. Robert Arthur, P.O. Box 8291, Omaha, NE 68103

Mid-Atlantic District, Rev. Arlene Ackerman, P.O. Box 552, Mountville, PA 17554

Northeast District, Rev. Sheila Rawls, 340 North St., Burlington, VT 05401

Northwest District, Rev. Janet Suess-Pierce, P.O. Box 3018, Vancouver, WA 98668

South Central District, Rev. Ed Paul, P.O. Box 51147, Denton, TX 76206

Southeast District, Rev. Judy Davenport, P.O. Box 12768, St. Petersburg, FL 33733

Southwest District, Rev. Don Pederson, 3600 S. Harbor Blvd., No. 183, Oxnard, CA 93035-4136

Western Canadian District, Rev. Bev Baptiste, 3531-3rd Ave., Edmonton, AB T6L 4N6

OTHER COMMISSIONS & COMMITTEES

Bd. of World Church Extension, Field Dir., Rev. Judy Dahl

Commission on Faith, Fellowship & Order, Chpsn., Rev. Charles Bidwell

Min. of Diversity in Spiritual Comm., Exec. Dir., Bernard Barbour, 1744 Michigan, Houston, TX 77006

Commission on the Laity, Chpsn., JoNee Shelton, 7624 Kingsmill Terr., Ft. Worth, TX 76112

Clergy Credentials & Concerns, Admn., Rev. Michael Piazza

Bd. of Pensions, Admn., Hal Nesbitt, P.O. Box 362, Long Beach, CA 90801-0362

Ecumenical Witness & Ministry: Dir., Rev. Kittredge Cherry

UFMCC AIDS Ministry: Field Dir., Rev. A. Stephen Pieters

Women's Secretariat, Chpsn., Rev. Coni Staff, 254 Faxon Ave., San Francisco, CA 94112-2214

PERIODICALS

Keeping in Touch; ALERT

Volunteers of America

Volunteers of America, founded in 1896 by Ballington and Maud Booth, provides spiritual and material aid for those in need in more than 300 communities across the United States. As one of the nation's largest and most diversified human-service agencies, Volunteers of America offers more than 400 programs for the elderly, families, youth, alcoholics, drug abusers, offenders and the disabled.

HEADQUARTERS

3939 N. Causeway Blvd., Metairie, LA 70002 Tel. (504)837-2652 Fax (504)837-4200

Media Contact, Dir. of Publ. Relations, Arthur Smith

OFFICERS

Chpsn., Walter Faster

Pres., Charles W. Gould

Vice-Pres.: Alex Brodrick; Thomas Clark; Dianna Kunz; Margaret Ratcliff; John Hood

PERIODICAL

Spirit

The Wesleyan Church

The Wesleyan Church was formed on June 26, 1968, through the union of the Wesleyan Methodist Church of America (1843) and the Pilgrim Holiness Church (1897). The headquarters was established at Marion, Ind., and relocated to Indianapolis in 1987.

The Wesleyan movement centers around the beliefs, based on Scripture, that the atonement in Christ provides for the regeneration of sinners and the entire sanctification of believers. John Wesley led a revival of these beliefs in the 18th century.

When a group of New England Methodist ministers led by Orange Scott began to crusade for the abolition of slavery, the bishops and others sought to silence them. This led to a series of withdrawals from the Methodist Episcopal Church. In 1843, the Wesleyan Methodist Connection of America was organized and led by Scott, Jotham Horton, LaRoy Sunderland, Luther Lee and Lucius C. Matlack.

During the holiness revival in the last half of the 19th century, holiness replaced social reform as the major tenet of the Connection. In 1947 the name was changed from Connection to Church and a central supervisory authority was set up.

The Pilgrim Holiness Church was one of many independent holiness churches which came into existence as a result of the holiness revival. Led by Martin Wells Knapp and Seth C. Rees, the International Holiness Union and Prayer League was inaugurated in 1897 in Cincinnati. Its purpose was to promote worldwide holiness evangelism and the Union had a strong missionary emphasis from the beginning. It developed into a church by 1913.

The Wesleyan Church is now spread across most of the United States and Canada and 37 other countries. The Wesleyan World Fellowship was organized in 1972 to unite Wesleyan mission bodies developing into mature churches. The Wesleyan Church is a member of the Christian Holiness Association, the National Association of Evangelicals and the World Methodist Council.

HEADQUARTERS

P.O. Box 50434, Indianapolis, IN 46250 Tel. (317)842-0444

Media Contact, Gen. Sec., Dr. Ronald R. Brannon, Tel. (317)595-4154 Fax (317)594-8309

OFFICERS

Gen. Supts.: Dr. Earle L. Wilson; Dr. Lee M. Haines; Dr. H. C. Wilson
Gen. Sec., Dr. Ronald R. Brannon
Gen. Treas., Mr. Daniel D. Busby
Gen. Director of Communications, Dr. Norman G. Wilson
Gen. Publisher, Rev. Nathan Birky
Evangelism & Church Growth, Gen. Dir., Dr. B. Marlin Mull
World Missions, Gen. Dir., Dr. Donald L. Bray
Local Church Educ., Gen. Dir., Dr. Keith Drury
Youth, Gen. Dir., Rev. Ross DeMerchant
Education & the Ministry, Gen. Dir., Dr. Kenneth R. Heer
Estate Planning, Gen. Dir., Rev. Howard B. Castle
Wesleyan Pension Fund, Gen. Dir., Mr. Bobby L. Temple
Wesleyan Investment Foundation, Gen. Dir., Dr. John A. Dunn

PERIODICALS

Wesleyan Woman; The Wesleyan Advocate; Wesleyan World

Wesleyan Holiness Association of Churches

This body was founded Aug. 4, 1959 near Muncie, Ind. by a group of ministers and laymen who were drawn together for the purpose of spreading and conserving sweet, radical, scriptural holiness. These men came from various church bodies. This group is Wesleyan in doctrine and standards.

HEADQUARTERS

R R 2, Box 9, Winchester, IN 47394 Tel. (317)584-3199 Fax (717)966-4147
Media Contact, Gen. Sec.-Treas., Rev. Robert W. Wilson, R.D. 1, Box 98A, Mifflinburg, PA 17844

OFFICERS

Gen. Supt., Rev. John Brewer, RR 2, Box 9, Winchester, IN 47394 Tel. (317)584-3199
Asst. Gen. Supt., Rev. Jack W. Dulin, Rt. 2, Box 309, Milton, KY 40045 Tel. (502)268-5826
Gen. Sec.-Treas., Rev. Robert W. Wilson, R D 1, Box 98A, Mifflinburg, PA 17844 Tel. (717)966-4147
Gen. Youth Pres., Rev. John Brewer, 504 W. Tyrell St., St. Louis, MI 48880 Tel. (517)681-2591

PERIODICAL

Eleventh Hour Messenger

Wisconsin Evangelical Lutheran Synod

Organized in 1850 at Milwaukee, Wisc. by three pastors sent to America by a German mission society, the Wisconsin Evangelical Lutheran Synod still reflects its origins, although it now has congregations in 50 states and three Canadian provinces.

The Wisconsin Synod federated with the Michigan and Minnesota Synods in 1892 in order to more effectively carry on education and mission enterprises. A merger of these three Synods followed in 1917 to give the Wisconsin Evangelical Lutheran Synod its present form.

Although at its organization in 1850 WELS turned away from conservative Lutheran theology, today it is ranked as one of the most conservative Lutheran bodies in the United States. WELS confesses that the Bible is the verbally inspired, infallible Word of God and subscribes without reservation to the confessional writings of the Lutheran Church. Its interchurch relations are determined by a firm commitment to the principle that unity of doctrine and practice are the prerequisites of pulpit and altar fellowship and ecclesiastical cooperation. It does not hold membership in ecumenical organizations.

HEADQUARTERS

2929 N. Mayfair Rd., Milwaukee, WI 53222 Tel. (414)256-3888 Fax (414)256-3899
Dir. of Communications, Rev. Gary Baumler

OFFICERS

Pres., Rev. Karl R. Gurgel
1st Vice-Pres., Rev. Richard E. Lauersdorf, 105 Aztalan Ct., Jefferson, WI 53549
2nd Vice-Pres., Rev. Robert J. Zink, S68 W14329 Gaulke Ct., Muskego, WI 53150
Sec., Rev. Douglas L. Bode, 1005 E. Broadway, Prairie du Chien, WI 53821

OTHER ORGANIZATIONS

Bd. of Trustees, Admn., Mr. Clair V. Ochs
Bd. for Ministerial Education, Admn., Rev. Wayne Borgwardt
Bd. for Parish Services, Admn., Rev. Wayne Mueller
Bd. for Home Missions, Admn., Rev. Harold J. Hagedorn
Bd. for World Missions, Admn., Rev. Duane K. Tomhave

PERIODICALS

Wisconsin Lutheran Quarterly; Northwestern Lutheran; The Lutheran Educator

RELIGIOUS BODIES IN THE UNITED STATES ARRANGED BY FAMILIES

The following list of religious bodies appearing in the Directory Section of this yearbook shows the "families," or related clusters into which American religious bodies can be grouped. For example, there are many communions that can be grouped under the heading "Baptist" for historical and theological reasons. It is not to be assumed, however, that all denominations under one family heading are similar in belief or practice. Often, any similarity is purely coincidental. The family clusters tend to represent historical factors more often than theological or practical ones. The family categories provided one of the major pitfalls of church statistics because of the tendency to combine the statistics by "families" for analytical and comparative purposes. Such combined totals are almost meaningless, although often used as variables for sociological analysis.

Religious bodies not grouped under family headings appear alphabetically and are not indented in the following list.

Adventist Bodies

Advent Christian Church
Church of God General Conference (Oregon, IL and Morrow, GA)
Primitive Advent Christian Church
Seventh-day Adventist Church

American Evangelical Christian Churches
American Rescue Workers

Anglican

The Anglican Orthodox Church
Episcopal Church
Reformed Episcopal Church

Apostolic Christian Church (Nazarene)
Apostolic Christian Churches of America

Baptist Bodies

American Baptist Association
American Baptist Churches in the U.S.A.
Baptist Bible Fellowship International
Baptist General Conference
Baptist Missionary Association of America
Conservative Baptist Association of America
General Association of General Baptists
General Association of Regular Baptist Churches
Liberty Baptist Fellowship
National Association of Free Will Baptists
National Baptist Convention of America, Inc.
National Baptist Convention, U.S.A., Inc.
National Missionary Baptist Convention of America
National Primitive Baptist Convention, Inc.
North American Baptist Conference
Primitive Baptists
Progressive National Baptist Convention, Inc.
Separate Baptists in Christ
Seventh Day Baptist General Conference, USA and Canada
Southern Baptist Convention
Sovereign Grace Baptists

Berean Fundamental Church

Brethren (German Baptists)

Brethren Church (Ashland, Ohio)
Church of the Brethren
Fellowship of Grace Brethren Churches
Old German Baptist Brethren

Brethren, River

Brethren in Christ Church
United Zion Church

Christadelphians
The Christian and Missionary Alliance
Christian Brethren (also known as Plymouth Brethren)
Christian Catholic Church (Evangelical-Protestant)
The Christian Congregation, Inc.
Christian Union
Church of Christ, Scientist
The Church of Illumination
Church of the Living God (Motto: Christian Workers for Fellowship)
Church of the Nazarene
Churches of Christ in Christian Union

Churches of Christ—Christian Churches

Christian Church (Disciples of Christ)
Christian Churches and Churches of Christ
Churches of Christ

Churches of God

Church of God (Anderson, Ind.)
Church of God by Faith, Inc.
The Church of God (Seventh Day), Denver, Colo.,
Churches of God, General Conference

Churches of the New Jerusalem

General Church of the New Jerusalem
The Swedenborgian Church

Conservative Congregational Christian Conference

Eastern Churches

Albanian Orthodox Archdiocese in America
Albanian Orthodox Diocese of America
The American Carpatho-Russian Orthodox Greek Catholic Church
The Antiochian Orthodox Christian Archdiocese of North America
Apostolic Catholic Assyrian Church of the East, North American Dioceses

Armenian Apostolic Church of America
Coptic Orthodox Church
Diocese of the Armenian Church of America
Greek Orthodox Archdiocese of North and South America
Holy Ukrainian Autocephalic Orthodox Church in Exile
The Orthodox Church in America
Patriarchal Parishes of the Russian Orthodox Church in the U.S.A.
The Romanian Orthodox Church in America
The Romanian Orthodox Episcopate of America
The Russian Orthodox Church Outside Russia
Serbian Orthodox Church in the U.S.A. and Canada
Syrian Orthodox Church of Antioch (Archdiocese of the United States and Canada)
True Orthodox Church of Greece (Synod of Metropolitan Cyprian), American Exarchate
Ukrainian Orthodox Church of America (Ecumenical Patriarchate)
Ukrainian Orthodox Church of the U.S.A.

The Evangelical Church
The Evangelical Church Alliance
The Evangelical Congregational Church
The Evangelical Covenant Church
The Evangelical Free Church of America
Fellowship of Fundamental Bible Churches
Free Christian Zion Church of Christ

Friends

Evangelical Friends International—North America Region
Friends General Conference
Friends United Meeting
Religious Society of Friends (Conservative)
Religious Society of Friends (Unaffiliated Meetings)

Grace Gospel Fellowship
House of God, Which is the Church of the Living God, the Pillar and Ground of the Truth, Inc.
Independent Fundamental Churches of America
International Council of Community Churches
Jehovah's Witnesses

Latter Day Saints

Church of Christ
The Church of Jesus Christ (Bickertonites)
The Church of Jesus Christ of Latter-day Saints
Reorganized Church of Jesus Christ of Latter Day Saints

The Liberal Catholic Church-Province of the United States of America

Lutherans

The American Association of Lutheran Churches
Apostolic Lutheran Church of America
The Association of Free Lutheran Congregations
Church of the Lutheran Brethren of America
Church of the Lutheran Confession
Conservative Lutheran Association
The Estonian Evangelical Lutheran Church
Evangelical Lutheran Church in America
Evangelical Lutheran Synod
The Latvian Evangelical Lutheran Church in America
The Lutheran Church—Missouri Synod
Wisconsin Evangelical Lutheran Synod

Mennonite Bodies

Beachy Amish Mennonite Churches
Bible Fellowship Church
Church of God in Christ (Mennonite)
Evangelical Mennonite Church
Fellowship of Evangelical Bible Churches
General Conference of Mennonite Brethren Churches
Hutterian Brethren
Mennonite Brethren Churches
Mennonite Church, General Conference
Old Order Amish Church
Old Order (Wisler) Mennonite Church
Reformed Mennonite Church

Methodist Bodies

African Methodist Episcopal Church
African Methodist Episcopal Zion Church
Allegheny Wesleyan Methodist Connection (Original Allegheny Conference)
Bible Holiness Church
Christian Methodist Episcopal Church
Evangelical Methodist Church
Free Methodist Church of North America
Fundamental Methodist Church, Inc.
Primitive Methodist Church in the U.S.A.
Reformed Methodist Union Episcopal Church
Reformed Zion Union Apostolic Church
Southern Methodist Church
The United Methodist Church
The Wesleyan Church

The Metropolitan Church Association, Inc.
The Missionary Church

Moravian Bodies

Moravian Church in America (Unitas Fratrum)
Unity of the Brethren

National Association of Congregational Christian Churches
National Organization of the New Apostolic Church of North America
National Spiritualist Association of Churches

Old Catholic Churches

Christ Catholic Church

Pentecostal Bodies

Apostolic Faith Mission Church of God
Apostolic Faith Mission of Portland, Oregon
Apostolic Overcoming Holy Church of God, Inc.
Assemblies of God
Assemblies of God International Fellowship (Independent/Not Affiliated)
The Bible Church of Christ, Inc.
Bible Way Church of Our Lord Jesus Christ, World Wide, Inc.
Christian Church of North America, General Council
The Church of God

Church of God (Cleveland, Tenn.)
The Church of God in Christ
Church of God in Christ, International
Church of God, Mountain Assembly, Inc.
The Church of God of Prophecy
Church of Our Lord Jesus Christ of the Apostolic Faith, Inc.
Congregational Holiness Church
Elim Fellowship
Full Gospel Assemblies International
Full Gospel Fellowship of Churches and Ministers International
International Church of the Foursquare Gospel
The International Pentecostal Church of Christ
International Pentecostal Holiness Church
Open Bible Standard Churches, Inc.
The (Original) Church of God, Inc.
Pentecostal Assemblies of the World, Inc.
Pentecostal Church of God
Pentecostal Fire-Baptized Holiness Church
The Pentecostal Free Will Baptist Church, Inc.
United Holy Church of America, Inc.
United Pentecostal Church International

Pillar of Fire
Polish National Catholic Church of America

Presbyterian Bodies

Associate Reformed Presbyterian Church (General Synod)
Cumberland Presbyterian Church
Cumberland Presbyterian Church in America
Evangelical Presbyterian Church
General Assembly of the Korean Presbyterian Church in America
The Orthodox Presbyterian Church
Presbyterian Church in America
Presbyterian Church (U.S.A.)
Reformed Presbyterian Church of North America

Reformed Bodies

Christian Reformed Church in North America
Hungarian Reformed Church in America
Netherlands Reformed Congregations
Protestant Reformed Churches in America
Reformed Church in America
Reformed Church in the United States
United Church of Christ

The Roman Catholic Church
The Salvation Army
The Schwenkfelder Church
Triumph the Church and Kingdom of God in Christ Inc. (International)
United House of Prayer
Universal Fellowship of Metropolitan Community Churches

United Brethren Bodies

United Brethren in Christ
United Christian Church

Volunteers of America
Wesleyan Holiness Association of Churches

4. RELIGIOUS BODIES IN CANADA

A large number of Canadian religious bodies were organized by immigrants from Europe and elsewhere, and a smaller number sprang up originally on Canadian soil. In the case of Canada, moreover, many denominations that overlap the U.S.-Canada border have headquarters in the United States.

If you have difficulty finding a particular denomination, check the index of organizations. In some cases alternative names for denominations are listed there. A final section lists denominations according to denominational families. This can be a helpful tool in finding a particular denomination.

Complete statistics for Canadian denominations are found in the table "Canadian Current and Non-current Statistics" in the statistical section of the *Yearbook*.

Addresses for periodicals are found in the listing of Canadian Religious Periodicals. Information about finances for some of the denominations is in the Church Finance section.

American Evangelical Christian Churches of Canada

The American Evangelical Christian Churches are associated through a common doctrine that is a combination of Calvinistic and Arminian beliefs.

Each congregation is managed independently, however ordination is supervised by the national body.

HEADQUARTERS

Moderator, Rev. David Lavigne, 49D-30 Flamingo Dr., Elmira, ON N3B 1V5 Tel. (519)669-3949

The Anglican Church of Canada

Anglicanism came to Canada with the early explorers such as Martin Frobisher and Henry Hudson. Continuous services began in Newfoundland about 1700 and in Nova Scotia in 1710. The first Bishop, Charles Inglis, was appointed to Nova Scotia in 1787. The numerical strength of Anglicanism was increased by the coming of American Loyalists and by massive immigration both after the Napoleonic wars and in the later 19th and early 20th centuries.

The Anglican Church of Canada has enjoyed self-government for over a century and is an autonomous member of the worldwide Anglican Communion. The General Synod, which normally meets triennially, consists of the Archbishops, Bishops and elected clerical and lay representatives of the 30 dioceses. Each of the Ecclesiastical Provinces—Canada, Ontario, Rupert's Land and British Columbia—is organized under a Metropolitan and has its own Provincial Synod and Executive Council. Each diocese has its own Diocesan Synod.

HEADQUARTERS

Church House, 600 Jarvis St., Toronto, ON M4Y 2J6 Tel. (416)924-9192 Fax (416)968-7983

Media Contact, Dir. of Information Resources, Mr. Douglas Tindal

GENERAL SYNOD OFFICERS

Primate of the Anglican Church of Canada, Most Rev. Michael G. Peers

Prolocutor, Mrs. Rendina Hamilton, 857 Wellington Ct., Kelowna, BC V1Y 8J2

Gen. Sec., Ven. James B. Boyles

Treas., Gen. Synod, Mr. Robert G. Armstrong

Exec. Dir. of Program, Ms. Suzanne Lawson

DEPARTMENTS AND DIVISIONS

Faith, Worship & Ministry, Dir., Rev. Alyson Barnett-Cowan

Pensions, Dir., Mrs. Jenny Mason

Financial Mngt. & Devel., Dir., Mr. Robert G. Armstrong

Dir. of Inform. Resources, Mr. Douglas Tindal

Partnerships, Dir., Dr. Eleanor Johnson

Primate's World Relief Dev. Fund, Dir., Mr. Robin Gibson

METROPOLITANS (ARCHBISHOPS)

Ecclesiastical Province of: Canada, The Most Rev. Stewart S. Payne, 25 Main St., Corner Brook, NF A2H 1C2 Tel. (709)639-8712 Fax (709)639-1636; Rupert's Land, The Most Rev. J. Barry Curtis, 3015 Glencoe Rd. SW, Calgary, AB T2S 2L9 Tel. (403)243-3673 Fax (403)243-2182; British Columbia, The Most Rev. David P. Crawley, 1876 Richter St., Kelowna, BC V1Y 2M9 Tel. (604)762-3306 Fax (604)762-4150; Ontario, The Most Rev. Percy R. O'Driscoll, 4-220 Dundas St., London, ON N6A 1H3 Tel. (519)434-6893 Fax (519)673-4151

DIOCESAN BISHOPS

Algoma: The Rt. Rev. Ronald Ferris, 619 Wellington St. E, Box 1168, Sault Ste. Marie, ON P6A 5N7 Tel. (705)256-5061 Fax (705)946-1860

Arctic: The Rt. Rev. Christopher Williams, 1055 Avenue Rd., Toronto, ON M5N 2C8 Tel. (416)-481-2263 Fax (416)487-4948

Athabasca: The Right Rev. John R. Clarke, P.O. Box 6868, Peace River, AB T8S 1S6 Tel. (403)-624-2767 Fax (403)624-2365

Brandon: The Rt. Rev. Malcolm Harding, 341-13th St., Brandon, MB R7A 4P8 Tel. (204)727-7550 Fax (204)727-4135

British Columbia: The Rt. Rev. Barry Jenks, 912 Vancouver St., Victoria, BC V8V 3V7 Tel. (604)386-7781 Fax (604)386-4013

Caledonia: The Rt. Rev. John E. Hannen, Box 278, Prince Rupert, BC V8J 3P6 Tel. (604)624-6013 Fax (604)624-4299

Calgary: Archbishop, The Most Rev. J. Barry Curtis, 3015 Glencoe Rd. SW, Calgary, AB T2S 2L9 Tel. (403)243-3673 Fax (403)243-2182

Cariboo: The Right Rev. James D. Cruickshank, 5-618 Tranquille Rd., Kamloops, BC V2B 3H6 Tel. (604)376-0112 Fax (604)376-1984

Central Newfoundland: The Rt. Rev. Edward Marsh, 34 Fraser Rd., Gander, NF A1V 2E8 Tel. (709)256-2372 Fax (709)256-2396

Eastern Newfoundland and Labrador: The Rt. Rev. Donald F. Harvey, 19 King's Bridge Rd., St. John's, NF A1C 3K4 Tel. (709)576-6697 Fax (709)576-7122

Edmonton: The Rt. Rev. Kenneth Genge, 10033 - 84 Ave., Edmonton, AB T6E 2G6 Tel. (403)439-7344 Fax (403)439-6549

Fredericton: The Rt. Rev. George C. Lemmon, 115 Church St., Fredericton, NB E3B 4C8 Tel. (506)-459-1801 Fax (506)459-8475

Huron: Archbishop, The Most Rev. Percy R. O'Driscoll, 4-220 Dundas St., London, ON N6A 1H3 Tel. (519)434-6893 Fax (519)673-4151

Keewatin: The Rt. Rev. Thomas W. R. Collings, 915 Ottawa St., Keewatin, ON P0X 1C0 Tel. (807)547-3353 Fax (807)547-3356

Kootenay: Archbishop, The Most Rev. David P. Crawley, 1876 Richter St., Kelowna, BC V1Y 2M9 Tel. (604)762-3306 Fax (604)762-4150

Montreal: The Rt. Rev. Andrew S. Hutchison, 1444 Union Ave., Montreal, QC H3A 2B8 Tel. (514)-843-6577 Fax (514)843-3221

Moosonee: The Rt. Rev. Caleb J. Lawrence, Box 841, Schumacher, ON P0N 1G0 Tel. (705)360-1129 Fax (705)360-1120

New Westminster: The Rt. Rev. Michael C. Ingham, 302-814 Richards St., Vancouver, BC V6B 3A7 Tel. (604)684-6306 Fax (604)684-7017

Niagara: The Rt. Rev. Walter Asbil, 67 Victoria Ave. S, Hamilton, ON L8N 2S8 Tel. (416)527-1278 Fax (416)527-1281

Nova Scotia: The Rt. Rev. Arthur G. Peters, 5732 College St., Halifax, NS B3H 1X3 Tel. (902)-420-0717 Fax (902)425-0717

Ontario: The Rt. Rev. Peter Mason, 90 Johnson St., Kingston, ON K7L 1X7 Tel. (613)544-4774 Fax (613)547-3745

Ottawa: The Rt. Rev. John A. Baycroft, 71 Bronson Ave., Ottawa, ON K1R 6G6 Tel. (613)232-7124 Fax (613)232-7088

Qu'Appelle: The Rt. Rev. Eric Bays, 1501 College Ave., Regina, SK S4P 1B8 Tel. (306)522-1608 Fax (306)352-6808

Quebec: The Rt. Rev. Bruce Stavert, 36 rue des Jardins, Quebec, QC G1R 4L6 Tel. (418)692-3858 Fax (418)692-3876

Rupert's Land: The Rt. Rev. Patrick V. Lee, 935 Nesbitt Bay, Winnipeg, MB R3T 1W6 Tel. (204)453-6130 Fax (204)452-3915

Saskatchewan: The Rt. Rev. Anthony Burton, Box 1088, Prince Albert, SK S6V 5S6 Tel. (306)763-2455 Fax (306)764-5172

Saskatoon: The Rt. Rev. Thomas O. Morgan, Box 1965, Saskatoon, SK S7K 3S5 Tel. (306)244-5651 Fax (306)933-4606

Toronto: The Rt. Rev. Terence E. Finlay, 135 Adelaide St. East, Toronto, ON M5C 1L8 Tel. (416)363-6021 Fax (416)363-3683

Western Newfoundland: Archbishop, The Most Rev. Stewart S. Payne, 25 Main St., Corner Brook, NF A2H 1C2 Tel. (709)639-8712 Fax (709)639-1636

Yukon: The Rt. Rev. Terry Buckle, Box 4247, Whitehorse, YT Y1A 3T3 Tel. (403)667-7746 Fax (403)667-6125

PERIODICALS

Anglican Journal; Anglican Montreal Anglican; The Anglican; Caledonia Times; Huron Church News; Newfoundland Churchman; Rupert's Land News; Saskatchewan Anglican; Topic

The Antiochian Orthodox Christian Archdiocese of North America

The approximately 100,000 members of the Antiochian Orthodox community in Canada are under the jurisdiction of the Antiochian Orthodox Christian Archdiocese of North America with headquarters in Englewood, N.J. There are churches in Edmonton, Winnipeg, Halifax, London, Ottawa, Toronto, Windsor, Montreal Saskatoon, and Hamilton.

HEADQUARTERS

Metropolitan Philip Saliba, 358 Mountain Rd., Englewood, NJ 07631 Tel. (201)871-1355 Fax (201)871-7954

Media Contact, Vicar, The V. Rev. George S. Corey, 52 78th St., Brooklyn, NY 11209 Tel. (718)748-7940 Fax (718)855-3608

Apostolic Christian Church (Nazarene)

This church was formed in Canada as a result of immigration from various European countries. The body began as a movement originated by the Rev. S. H. Froehlich, a Swiss pastor, whose followers are still found in Switzerland and Central Europe.

HEADQUARTERS

Apostolic Christian Church Foundation, 1135 Sholey Rd., Richmond, VA 23231 Tel. (804)-222-1943

OFFICER

Exec. Dir., James Hodges

The Apostolic Church in Canada

The Apostolic Church in Canada is affiliated with the worldwide organization of the Apostolic Church with headquarters in Great Britain. A product of the Welsh Revival (1904 to 1908), its Canadian beginnings originated in Nova Scotia in 1927. Today its main centers are in Nova Scotia, Ontario and Quebec. This church is evangelical, fundamental and Pentecostal, with special emphasis on the ministry gifts listed in Ephesians.

HEADQUARTERS

27 Castlefield Ave., Toronto, ON M4R 1G3

Media Contact, Pres., Rev. John Kristensen, 388 Gerald St., La Salle, QC H8P 2A5 Tel. (514)366-8356

OFFICERS

Pres., Rev. John Kristensen, 388 Gerald St., LaSalle, QC H8P 2A5 Tel. (514)366-8356

Natl. Sec., Rev. J. Karl Thomas, 22 Malmute Ct., Agincourt, ON M1T 2C7 Tel. (416)298-0977

Apostolic Church of Pentecost of Canada Inc.

This body was founded in 1921 at Winnipeg, Manitoba, by Pastor Frank Small. Doctrines include belief in eternal salvation by the grace of God, baptism of the Holy Spirit with the evidence of speaking in tongues, water baptism by immersion in the name of the Lord Jesus Christ.

HEADQUARTERS

200-809 Manning Rd. NE, Calgary, AB T2E 7M9
Media Contact, Clk./Admn., Leonard K. Larsen, Tel. (403)273-5777 Fax (403)273-8102

OFFICERS

Mod., Rev. G. Killam
Clk., Leonard K. Larsen

Armenian Evangelical Church

Founded in 1960 by immigrant Armenian evangelical families from the Middle East, this body is conservative doctrinally, with an evangelical, biblical emphasis. The polity of churches within the group differ with congregationalism being dominant, but there are presbyterian Armenian Evangelical churches as well. Most of the local churches have joined main-line denominations. All of the remaining Armenian Evangelical (congregational or presbyterian) local churches in the United States and Canada have joined with the Armenian Evangelical Union of North America.

HEADQUARTERS

Armenian Evangelical Church of Toronto, 2851 John St., P.O. Box 42015, Markham, ON L3R 5R0 Tel. (905)940-7949
Media Contact, Chief Editor, Rev. Yessayi Sarmazian

A.E.U.N.A. OFFICERS

Min. to the Union, Rev. Karl Avakian, 1789 E. Frederick Ave., Fresno, CA 93720
Mod., Rev. Solomon Nuyujukian

OFFICER

Min., Rev. Yessayi Sarmazian

PERIODICAL

Canada Armenian Press

Armenian Holy Apostolic Church - Canadian Diocese

The Canadian branch of the ancient Church of Armenia founded in A.D. 301 by St. Gregory the Illuminator was established in Canada at St. Catherines, Ontario, in 1930. The diocesan organization is under the jurisdiction of the Holy See of Etchmiadzin, Armenia. The Diocese has churches in St. Catherines, Hamilton, Toronto, Ottawa, Vancouver, Mississauga, Montreal, Brossard, Laval and Windsor.

HEADQUARTERS

Diocesan Offices: Primate, Canadian Diocese, Archbishop Hovnan Derderian, 615 Stuart Ave., Outremont, QC H2V 3H2 Tel. (514)276-9479 Fax (514)276-9960
Media Contact, Exec. Dir., Arminé Keuchgerian

Associated Gospel Churches

The Associated Gospel Churches (AGC) traces its historical roots to the 1890s. To counteract the growth of liberal theology evident in many established denominations at this time, individuals and whole congregations seeking to uphold the final authority of the Scriptures in all matters of faith and conduct withdrew from those denominations and established churches with an evangelical ministry. These churches defended the belief that "all Scripture is given by inspiration of God" and also declared that the Holy Spirit gave the identical word of sacred writings of holy men of old, chosen by Him to be the channel of His revelation to man."

At first this growing group of independent churches was known as the Christian Workers' Churches of Canada, and by 1922 there was desire for forming an association for fellowship, counsel and coperation. Several churches in southern Ontario banded together under the leadership of Dr. P. W. Philpott of Hamilton and Rev. H. E. Irwin, K. C. of Toronto.

When a new Dominion Charter was obtained on March 18, 1925, the name was changed to Associated Gospel Churches. Since that time the AGC has steadily grown, spreading across Canada by invitation to other independent churches of like faith and by actively beginning new churches.

HEADQUARTERS

3430 South Service Rd., Burlington, ON L7N 3T9 Tel. (905)634-8184 Fax (905)634-6283
Media Contact, Pres., D. G. Hamilton

OFFICERS

Pres., Rev. D. G. Hamilton
Mod., Rev. S. R. Sadlier, Box 55, King City, ON L0G 1K0 Tel. (905)833-5104
Sec.-Treas., Paul Robertson

Association of Regular Baptist Churches (Canada)

The Association of Regular Baptist Churches was organized in 1957 by a group of churches for the purpose of mutual cooperation in missionary activities. The Association believes the Bible to be God's word, stands for historic Baptist principles and opposes modern ecumenism.

HEADQUARTERS

130 Gerrard St. E., Toronto, ON M5A 3T4 Tel. (416)925-3261
Media Contact, Sec., Rev. W. P. Bauman, Tel. (416)925-3263 Fax (416)925-8305

OFFICERS

Chmn., Rev. S. Kring, 67 Sovereen St., Delhi, ON N4B 1L7
Sec., Rev. W. P. Bauman

PERIODICAL

The Gospel Witness

Baptist General Conference of Canada

The Baptist General Conference was founded in Canada by missionaries from the United States. Originally a Swedish body, BGC Canada now includes people of many nationalities and is conservative and evangelical in doctrine and practice.

HEADQUARTERS

4306-97 St. NW, Edmonton, AB T6E 5R9 Tel. (403)438-9127 Fax (403)435-2478
Media Contact, Exec. Dir., Rev. Abe Funk

OFFICERS

Exec. Dir., Rev. Abe Funk, 27-308 Jackson Rd. NW, Edmonton, AB T6L 6W1 Tel. (403)466-6244
Bd. Chpsn., Rev. Wes Long, 110 Kellins Cres., Saskatoon, SK S7N 2X6

PERIODICAL

BGC Canada News

The Central Canada Baptist Conference

Central Baptist Conference, originally a Scandinavian group, is one of four districts of the Baptist General Conference of Canada. In 1907, churches from Winnipeg--Grant Memorial, Teulon, Kenora, Port Arthur, Sprague, Erickson and Midale--organized under the leadership of Fred Palmberg. Immigration from Sweden declined, and in 1947 only nine churches remained. In 1948 the group dropped the Swedish language, withdrew from the Baptist Union and city churches were started. Today the CCBC has 22 functioning churches.

An evangelical Baptist association holding to the inerrancy of the Bible, CCBC seeks to reach Central Canada for Christ by establishing local gospel-preaching churches.

CCBC offers pastoral aid to new churches and recommendations as to pastoral supply, counsel and fellowship. It encourages contributions to the CCBC and BGC of Canada budgets, support of the Conference BATT program (contributions to special needs of churches) and other projects to assist needy churches and pastors.

HEADQUARTERS

877 Wilkes Ave., Winnipeg, MB R3P 1B8 Tel. (204)989-6740

Media Contact, Exec. Min., Rev. Alf Bell

OFFICERS

Exec. Min., Rev. Alf Bell

Baptist General Conference in Alberta

HEADQUARTERS

5011 122nd A St., Edmonton, AB T6H 3S8 Tel. (403)438-9126 Fax (403)438-5258

Media Contact, District Exec. Minister, Dr. Cal Netterfield

British Columbia Baptist Conference

British Columbia Baptist Conference is a district of the Baptist General Conference of Canada, with roots in Sweden, where Christians began to read the Bible in their homes. One convert, F.O. Nilsson, saw the significance of baptism subsequent to a personal commitment to Christ; he went to Hamburg, Germany, where he was baptized in the Elbe River by Rev. John Oncken. When Nilsson returned to Sweden, five of his converts were baptized in the North Sea and, with him, formed the first Swedish Baptist Church. Nilsson was imprisoned by the local government for violation of state church regulations and later, when exiled from Sweden, went to the United States. As Swedish Baptists came to the United States to escape persecution, they formed churches in Illinois, Iowa, Minnesota and Wisconsin and carried on aggressive evangelism among other immigrating Swedes. In 1879 they formed the Swedish Baptist General Conference of America, later named The Baptist General Conference.

The Mission Statement of British Columbia Baptist Conference reads "To aggressively plant and grow worshiping, caring churches through evangelism and discipleship."

HEADQUARTERS

7600 Glover Rd., Langley, BC V2Y 1Y1 Tel. (604)888-2246 Fax (604)888-0046

Media Contact, District Exec. Min., Rev. Walter W. Wieser

OFFICER

Dist. Exec. Min., Rev. Walter W. Wieser

PERIODICAL

B.C. Conference Call

The Bible Holiness Movement

The Bible Holiness Movement, organized in 1949 as an outgrowth of the city mission work of the late Pastor William James Elijah Wakefield, an early-day Salvation Army officer, has been headed since its inception by his son, Evangelist Wesley H. Wakefield, its bishop-general.

It derives its emphasis on the original Methodist faith of salvation and scriptural holiness from the late Bishop R. C. Horner. It adheres to the common evangelical faith in the Bible, the Deity and the atonement of Christ. It stresses a personal experience of salvation for the repentant sinner, of being wholly sanctified for the believer and of the fullness of the Holy Spirit for effective witness.

Membership involves a life of Christian love and evangelistic and social activism. Members are required to totally abstain from liquor and tobacco. They may not attend popular amusements or join secret societies. Divorce and remarriage are forbidden. Similar to Wesley's Methodism, members are, under some circumstances, allowed to retain membership in other evangelical church fellowships. Interchurch affiliations are maintained with a number of Wesleyan-Arminian Holiness denominations.

Year-round evangelistic outreach is maintained through open-air meetings, visitation, literature and other media. Noninstitutional welfare work, including addiction counseling, is conducted among minorities. There is direct overseas famine relief, civil rights action, environment protection and antinuclearism. The movement sponsors a permanent committee on religious freedom and an active promotion of Christian racial equality.

The movement has a world outreach with branches in the United States, India, Nigeria, Philippines, Ghana, Liberia, Cameroon, Kenya, Zambia, South Korea, Mulawi, and Tanzania. It ministers to 89 countries in 42 languages through literature, radio and audiocassettes.

HEADQUARTERS

Box 223, Postal Stn. A, Vancouver, BC V6C 2M3 Tel. (604)498-3895

Media Contact, Bishop-General, Evangelist Wesley H. Wakefield, P.O. Box 223, Postal Station A, Vancouver, BC V6C 2M3 Tel. (604)-498-3895

DIRECTORS

Bishop-General, Evangelist Wesley H. Wakefield, (Intl. Leader)

Evangelist M. J. Wakefield, Oliver, BC

Mrs. W. Sneed, Dalhousie Rd., N.W., Calgary, AB

Pastor Vincente & Morasol Hernando, Phillipines

Pastor & Mrs. Daniel Stinnett, 1425 Mountain View W., Phoenix, AZ 85021

Evangelist I. S. Udoh, Abak, Akwalbom, Nigeria, West Africa

Pastor Richard & Laura Wesley, Monrovia, Liberia

Pastor Choe Chong Dee, Cha Pa Puk, S. Korea

Pastor S. A. Samuel, Andra, India

Laypastors Heinz and Catherine Speitelsbach, Sardis, BC V2R 3W2

Pastor and Mrs. Daniel Vandee, Ghana, W. Africa

PERIODICAL

Hallelujah

Brethren in Christ Church, Canadian Conference

The Brethren in Christ, formerly known as Tunkers in Canada, arose out of a religious awakening in Lancaster County, Pa. late in the 18th century. Representatives of the new denomination reached Ontario in 1788 and established the church in the southern part of the present province. Presently the conference has congregations in Ontario, Alberta, Quebec and Saskatchewan. In theology they have accents of the Pietist, Anabaptist, Wesleyan and Evangelical movements.

HEADQUARTERS

Brethren in Christ Church, Gen. Ofc., P.O. Box 290, Grantham, PA 17027-0290 Tel. (717)697-2634 Fax (717)697-7714

Canadian Headquarters, Bishop's Ofc., 2619 Niagara Pkwy., Ft. Erie, ON L2A 5M4 Tel. (905)-871-9991

Media Contact, Mod., Harvey R. Sider, Brethren in Christ Church Gen. Ofc.

OFFICERS

Mod., Bishop R. Dale Shaw, 2619 Niagara Pkwy., Ft. Erie, ON L2A 5M4 Tel. (905)871-9991

Sec., Betty Albrecht, RR 2, Petersburg, ON N0B 2H0

British Methodist Episcopal Church of Canada

The British Methodist Episcopal Church was organized in 1856 in Chatham, Ontario and incorporated in 1913. It has congregations across the Province of Ontario.

HEADQUARTERS

460 Shaw St., Toronto, ON M6G 3L3 Tel. (416)-534-3831

Gen. Sec., Rev. Maurice M. Hicks, 3 Boxdene Ave., Scarborough, ON M1V 3C9 Tel. (416)-298-5715 Fax (416)298-2276

OFFICERS

Gen. Supt., Rev. Dr. D. D. Rupwate, 66 Golfwood Dr., Hamilton, ON L9C 6W3 Tel. (416)383-6856

Asst. Gen. Supt., Rev. Livingston Yearwood, 16 Lynvalley Cres., Scarborough, ON M1R 2V3 Tel. (416)445-2646

Gen. Sec., Rev. Maurice M. Hicks, 3 Boxdene Ave., Scarborough, ON M1V 3C9 Tel. (416)-298-5715

Canadian and American Reformed Churches

The Canadian and American Reformed Churches accept the Bible as the infallible Word of God, as summarized in The Belgic Confession of Faith (1561), The Heidelberg Cathechism(1563) and The Canons of Dordt (1618-1619). The denomination was founded in Canada in 1950 and in the United States in 1955.

HEADQUARTERS

Synod: 607 Dynes Rd., Burlington, ON L7N 2V4

Canadian Reformed Churches: Ebenezer Canadian Reformed Church, 607 Dynes Rd., Burlington, ON L7N 2V4

American Reformed Churches: American Reformed Church, Rev. P. Kingma, 3167-68th St. S.E., Caledonia, MI 46316

Media Contact, Rev. G. Nederveen, 3089 Woodward Ave., Burlington, ON L7N 2M3 Tel. (905)-681-7055 Fax (905)681-7055

PERIODICALS

Reformed Perspective: A Magazine for the Christian Fam.; In Holy Array; Evangel: The Good News of Jesus Christ; Clarion: The Canadian Reformed Magazine

Canadian Baptist Ministries

The Canadian Baptist Ministries has four federated member bodies: (1) Baptist Convention of Ontario and Quebec, (2) Baptist Union of Western Canada, (3) the United Baptist Convention of the Atlantic Provinces, (4) Union d'Églises Baptistes Françaises au Canada (French Baptist Union). Its main purpose is to act as a coordinating agency for the four groups for mission in all five continents. Before 1995 the church was known as the Canadian Baptist Federation.

HEADQUARTERS

7185 Millcreek Dr., Mississauga, ON L5N 5R4 Tel. (905)821-3533 Fax (905)826-3441

Media Contact, Communications, Rev. David Rogelstad

OFFICERS

Pres., Dr. Bruce Milne

Gen. Sec., Rev. David Phillips

Baptist Convention of Ontario and Quebec

The Baptist Convention of Ontario and Quebec is a family of 386 churches in Ontario and Quebec, united for mutual support and encouragement and united in missions in Canada and the world.

The Convention was formally organized in 1888. It has two educational institutions--McMaster Divinty College founded in 1887, and the Baptist Leadership Education Centre at Whitby. The Convention works through the all-Canada missionary agency, Canadian Baptist Ministries. The churches also support the Sharing Way, its relief and development arm of Canadian Baptist Ministries.

HEADQUARTERS

195 The West Mall, Ste. 414, Etobicoke, ON M9C 5K1 Tel. (416)622-8600 Fax (416)622-2308

Media Contact, Exec. Min., Rev. John Wilton

OFFICERS

Pres., Mr. Vince Judge

1st Vice-Pres., Rev. Alex Moir

2nd Vice-Pres., Rev. Ralph Neil

Treas./Bus. Admn., Mrs. Nancy Bell

Exec. Min., Rev. John Wilton

Baptist Union of Western Canada

HEADQUARTERS

605-999 8th St. SW, Calgary, AB T2R 1J5

Media Contact, Gen. Sec., ----

OFFICERS

Pres., Peter Isaak

Assoc. Exec. Min., Rev. Gerald Fisher, 14 Milford Cr., Sherwood Park, AB T8A 3V4

Area Min., Alberta, Dr. Keith Churchill, 307, 10328-81 Ave., Edmonton, AB T6E 1X2

Area Min., British Columbia, Rev. Paul Pearce, 201, 20349-88th Ave., Langley, BC VlM 2K5

Area Min., Saskatchewan, Rev. Wayne Larson, 2155 Cross Pl., Regina, SK S4S 4C8

Carey Theological College, Principal, Dr. Brian Stelck, 5920 Iona Dr., Vancouver, BC V6T 1J6
Baptist Leadership Training School (Lay), Principal, Rev. Myrna Sears, 4330-16 Street SW, Calgary, AB T2T 4H9

United Baptist Convention of the Atlantic Provinces

The United Baptist Convention of the Atlantic Provinces is the largest Baptist Convention in Canada. Through the Canadian Baptist Ministries, it is a member of the Baptist World Alliance.

In 1763 two Baptist churches were organized in Atlantic Canada, one in Sackville, New Brunswick and the other in Wolfville, Nova Scotia. Although both these churches experienced crises and lost continuity, they recovered and stand today as the beginning of organized Baptist work in Canada.

Nine Baptist churches met in Lower Granville, Nova Scotia in 1800 and formed the first Baptist Association in Canada. By 1846 the Maritime Baptist Convention was organized consisting of 169 churches. Two streams of Baptist life merged in 1905 to form the United Baptist Convention. This is how the term "United Baptist" was derived. Today there are 554 churches within 21 associations across the Convention.

The Convention has two educational institutions: Atlantic Baptist College in Moncton, New Brunswick, a Christian Liberal Arts University, and Acadia Divinity College in Wolfville, Nova Scotia, a Graduate School of Theology. The Convention engages in world mission through Canadian Baptist Ministries, the all-Canada mission agency. In addition to an active program of home mission, evangelism, training, social action and stewardship, the Convention operates ten senior citizen complexes and a Christian bookstore.

HEADQUARTERS

1655 Manawagonish Rd., Saint John, NB E2M 3Y2 Tel. (506)635-1922 Fax (506)635-0366
Media Contact, Dir. of Communications, Rev. Doug Hapeman

OFFICERS

Pres., Mr. Rupert Tingley
Exec. Min., Dr. Harry G. Gardner
Dir. of Admn. & Treas., Mr. Daryl MacKenzie
Dir. of Home Missions & Church Planting, ----
Dir. of Evangelism, Dr. Malcolm Beckett
Dir. of Training, Ms. Marilyn McCormick
Dir. of Communications, Rev. Doug Hapeman

PERIODICALS

The Atlantic Baptist; Tidings

Union d'Eglises Baptistes Françaises au Canada

Baptist churches in French Canada first came into being through the labors of two missionaries from Switzerland, Rev. Louis Roussy and Mme. Henriette Feller, who arrived in Canada in 1835. The earliest church was organized in Grande Ligne (now St.-Blaise), Quebec in 1838.

By 1900 there were 7 churches in the province of Quebec and 13 French-language Baptist churches in the New England states. The leadership was totally French Canadian.

By 1960, the process of Americanization had caused the disappearance of the French Baptist churches. During the 1960s, Quebec as a society, began rapidly changing in all its facets: education, politics, social values and structures. Mission, evangelism and church growth once again flourished. In 1969, in response to the new conditions, the Grande Ligne Mission passed control of its work to the newly formed Union of French Baptist Churches in Canada, which then included 8 churches. By 1990 the French Canadian Baptist movement had grown to include 25 congregations.

The Union d'Églises Baptistes Françaises au Canada is a member body of the Canadian Baptist Ministries and thus is affiliated with the Baptist World Alliance.

HEADQUARTERS

2285 avenue Papineau, Montreal, QC H2K 4J5 Tel. (514)526-6643
Media Contact, Gen. Sec., Rev. D. Afflick

OFFICER

Sec. Gen., Rev. D. Afflick

PERIODICAL

Le Trait d'Union

Canadian Conference of Mennonite Brethren Churches

The conference was incorporated Nov. 22, 1945.

HEADQUARTERS

3-169 Riverton Ave., Winnipeg, MB R2L 2E5 Tel. (204)669-6575 Fax (204)654-1865
Media Contact, Conf. Min., Reuben Pauls

OFFICERS

Mod., Abe Konrad, 12404-40 Ave., Edmonton, AB T6J 0S5 Tel. (403)435-1074
Asst. Mod., Roland Marsch, 1420 Portage Ave., Winnipeg, MB R3G 0W2 Tel. (204)774-4414
Sec., Elizabeth Esau, 45314 Vedder Mtn. Rd., R.R.3, Sardis, BC V2R 1B2 Tel. (604)824-8941

PERIODICALS

Mennonite Brethren Herald; Mennonitische Rundschau; IdeaBank; Le Lien; Expression; Chinese Herald

Canadian Convention of Southern Baptists

The Canadian Convention of Southern Baptists was formed at the Annual Meeting, May 7-9, 1985, in Kelowna, British Columbia. It was formerly known as the Canadian Baptist Conference, founded in Kamloops, British Columbia, in 1959 by pastors of existing churches.

HEADQUARTERS

Postal Bag 300, Cochrane, AB T0L 0W0 Tel. (403)932-5688 Fax (403)932-4937
Media Contact, Exec. Dir.-Treas., Rev. Allen E. Schmidt

OFFICERS

Exec. Dir.-Treas., Allen E. Schmidt, 128 Riverview Cir., Cochrane, AB T0L 0W4
Pres., Rev. Ray Woodard, Towers Baptist Church, 10311 Albion Rd., Richmond, BC V7A 3E5

PERIODICAL

The Baptist Horizon

Canadian District of the Moravian Church in America, Northern Province

The work in Canada is under the general oversight and rules of the Moravian Church, Northern Province, general offices for which are located in Bethlehem, PA. For complete information, see "Religious Bodies in the United States" section of the *Yearbook*.

HEADQUARTERS

1021 Center St., P.O. Box 1245, Bethlehem, PA 18016-1245

Media Contact, Ed., *The Moravian*, The Rev. Hermann I. Weinlick

OFFICER

Pres., Ruth Humphreys, 25-23332 Twp. Rd. 520, Sherwood Park, AB T8B 1L5 Tel. (403)467-6745 Fax (403)467-0411

Canadian Yearly Meeting of the Religious Society of Friends

Canadian Yearly Meeting of the Religious Society of Friends was founded in Canada as an offshoot of the Quaker movement in Great Britain and colonial America. Genesee Yearly Meeting, founded 1834, Canada Yearly Meeting (Orthodox), founded in 1867, and Canada Yearly Meeting, founded in 1881, united in 1955 to form the Canadian Yearly Meeting. Canadian Yearly Meeting is affiliated with Friends United Meeting and Friends General Conference. It is also a member of Friends World Committee for Consultation.

HEADQUARTERS

91A Fourth Ave., Ottawa, ON K1S 2L1 Tel. (613)-235-8553 Fax (613)235-8553

Media Contact, Gen. Sec.-Treas., Anne Thomas

OFFICERS

Gen. Sec.-Treas., Anne Thomas

Clerks: Betty Polster; Chris Springer

Archivist, Jane Zavitz Bond

Archives, Arthur G. Dorland, Pickering College, 389 Bayview St., Newmarket, ON L3Y 4X2 Tel. (416)895-1700

PERIODICALS

The Canadian Friend; Quaker Concern

Christ Catholic Church

The Christ Catholic Church, with cathedrals, churches and missions in both Canada and the United States, is a Catholic communion established in 1968 to minister to the growing number of people seeking an experiential relationship with God. In 1992 the Christ Catholic Church merged with the Liberal Catholic Church of Ontario. It is working to bring together various branches of Old Catholicism into one united church.

HEADQUARTERS

5165 Palmer Ave., Niagara Falls, ON L2E 3T9 Tel. (905)354-2329 Fax (905)354-9934

OFFICERS

Presiding Bishop, The Most Rev. Donald W. Mullan

Auxiliary Bishops, The Rt. Rev. Karl Pruter, Box 98, Highlandville, MO 65669

Auxiliary Bishops, The Rt. Rev. John W. Brown, 1504-75 Queen St. N., Hamilton, ON L8R 3J3

PERIODICAL

St. Luke Magazine

Christian and Missionary Alliance in Canada

A Canadian movement, dedicated to the teaching of Jesus Christ the Saviour, Sanctifier, Healer and Coming King, commenced in Toronto in 1887 under the leadership of the Rev. John Salmon. Two years later, the movement united with The Christian Alliance of New York, founded by Rev. A. B. Simpson, becoming the Dominion Auxiliary of the Christian Alliance, Toronto, under the presidency of the Hon. William H. Howland. Its four founding branches were Toronto, Hamilton, Montreal, and Quebec. By Dec. 31, 1994, there were 376 churches across Canada, with 1193 official workers, including a worldwide missionary force of 230.

In 1980, the Christian and Missionary Alliance in Canada became autonomous. Its General Assembly is held every two years.

NATIONAL OFFICE

#510-105 Gordon Baker Rd., North York, ON M2H 3P8 Tel. (416)492-8775 Fax (416)492-7708

Media Contact, Dir. of Communications, Myrna McCombs

OFFICERS

Pres., Dr. Arnold Cook, Box 7900, Postal Sta. B, Willowdale, ON M2K 2R6

Vice-Pres./Personnel & Missions, Rev. Wallace C.E. Albrecht

Vice-Pres./Fin., Mr. Milton H. Quigg

Vice-Pres./Canadian Ministries, Rev. C. Stuart Lightbody

Vice-Pres./Gen. Services, Mr. Kenneth Paton

DISTRICT SUPERINTENDENTS

Canadian Pacific: Rev. Brian Thom

Western Canadian: Rev. Arnold Downey

Canadian Midwest: Rev. Bob Peters

Central Canadian: Rev. David Lewis

East Canadian District: Rev. Doug Wiebe

St. Lawrence: Rev. Yvan Fournier

Christian Brethren (also known as Plymouth Brethren)

This orthodox and evangelical movement, which began in the British Isles in the 1820s, is now worldwide. For more detail on the history and theology, see "Religious Bodies in the United States" section of this Yearbook.

In the 1840s the movement divided. The "exclusive" branch, led by John Darby, stressed the interdependence of congregations. Canadian congregations number approximately 150, with an inclusive membership estimated at 11,000. The "open" branch of the movement, stressing evangelism and foreign missions, followed the leadership of George Muller in rejecting the "exclusive" principle of binding discipline and has escaped large-scale division.

Canadian congregations number approximately 450, with an inclusive membership estimated at 41,000. There are 250 "commended" full-time ministers, not including foreign missionaries.

HEADQUARTERS

Quebec: C.B.C. in the Province of Quebec, Sec., Norman R. Buchanan, 222 Alexander St., Sherbrooke, QC J1H 4S7

North America: Interest Ministries, Pres., Jim Hislop, P.O. Box 190, Wheaton, IL 60189 Tel. (708)653-6573 Fax (708)653-6595

Media Contact, Edit., Kenneth Botton, P.O. Box 190, Wheaton, IL 60189 Tel. (708)653-6573 Fax (708)653-6595

OTHER ORGANIZATIONS

Missionary Service Comm., Administrator, William Yuille, 1562A Danforth Ave., Toronto, ON M4J 1N4 Tel. (416)469-2012

Vision Ontario, Dir., Gord Martin, P.O. Box 28032, Waterloo, ON N2L 6J8 Tel. (519)725-1212 Fax (519)725-9421

PERIODICAL

News of Quebec

Christian Church (Disciples of Christ) in Canada

Disciples have been in Canada since 1810, and were organized nationally in 1922. This national church seeks to serve the Canadian context as part of the whole Christian Church (Disciples of Christ) in the United States and Canada.

HEADQUARTERS

128 Woolwich St., #202, P.O. Box 64, Guelph, ON N1H 6J6 Tel. (519)823-5190 Fax (519)823-5766

Media Contact, Exec. Min., Robert W. Steffer

OFFICERS

Mod., Mrs. A. Elizabeth Manthorne, P.O. Box 156, Milton, NS B0T 1P0

Vice-Mod., Mr. Mervin Bailey, 1205 Jubilee Ave., Regina, SK S4S 3S7

Exec. Min., Rev. Dr. Robert W. Steffer, P.O. Box 30013, 2 Quebec St., Guelph, ON N1H 8J5

PERIODICAL

Canadian Disciple

Christian Reformed Church in North America

Canadian congregations of the Christian Reformed Church in North America have been formed since 1908. For detailed information about this denomination, please refer to the listing for the Christian Reformed Church in North America in Chapter 3, "Religious Bodies in the United States."

HEADQUARTERS

United States Office: 2850 Kalamazoo Ave., S.E., Grand Rapids, MI 49560 Tel. (616)246-0744 Fax (616)247-5895

Canadian Office: 3475 Mainway, P.O. Box 5070, Burlington, ON L7R 3Y8 Tel. (905)336-2920 Fax (905)336-8344

Media Contact, Gen. Sec., Dr. David H. Engelhard, U.S. Office

OFFICERS

Gen. Sec., Dr. David H. Engelhard, U.S. Office

Exec. Dir./Ministries, Dr. Peter Borgdorff, U.S.Office

Dir. of Fin.& Administration, Mr. Robert Van Stright, U.S. Office

Coun. of Christian Ref. Churches in Can., Exec. Sec., Rev. Arie G. Van Eek, Canadian Office

PERIODICAL

The Banner

Church of God (Anderson, Ind.)

This body is one of the largest of the groups which have taken the name "Church of God." Its headquarters are at Anderson, Ind. It originated about 1880 and emphasizes Christian unity.

HEADQUARTERS

Western Canada Assembly, Chpsn., Jack Wagner, 4717 56th St., Camrose, AB T4V 2C4 Tel. (403)672-0772 Fax (403)672-6888

Eastern Canada Assembly, Chpsn., Jim Wiebe, 38 James St., Dundas, ON L9H 2J6

Media Contact for Western Canada, Church Service/Mission Coordinator, John D. Campbell, 4717 56th St., Camrose, AB T4V 2C4 Tel. (403)672-0772 Fax (403)672-6888

PERIODICALS

College News & Updates; The Gospel Contact; The Messenger

Church of God (Cleveland, Tenn.)

This body began in the United States in 1886 as the outgrowth of the holiness revival under the name Christian Union. Reorganized in 1902 as the Holiness Church, in 1907 the church adopted the name Church of God. Its doctrine is fundamental and Pentecostal. It maintains a centralized form of government and an evangelistic and missionary program.

The first church in Canada was established in 1919 in Scotland Farm, Manitoba. Paul H. Walker became the first overseer of Canada in 1931.

HEADQUARTERS

Intl. Offices: 2490 Keith St., NW, Cleveland, TN 37311 Tel. (423)478-3361

Media Contact, Dir. of Publ. Relations, Michael L. Baker, P.O. Box 2430, Cleveland, TN 37320-2430 Tel. (423)478-7112 Fax (423)478-7066

OFFICERS

Canada-Eastern, Rev. Canute Blake, P.O. Box 2036, Brampton, ON L6T 3TO Tel. (905)793-2213

Canada-Western, Rev. Raymond W. Wall, Box 54055, 2640 52 St. NE, Calgary, AB T1Y 6S6 Tel. (403)293-8817 Fax (403)293-8832

Canada-Quebec/Maritimes, Rev. Jacques Houle, 582 St. Hubert, Granby, QC J2H 1Y5 Tel. (514)-378-4442 Fax (514)378-8646

PERIODICAL

Church of God Beacon

Church of God in Christ (Mennonite)

The Church of God in Christ, Mennonite was organized by the evangelist-reformer John Holdeman in Ohio. The church unites with the faith of the Waldenses, Anabaptists and other such groups throughout history. Emphasis is placed on obedience to the teachings of the Bible, including the doctrine of the new birth and spiritual life, noninvolvement in government or the military, a head-covering for women, beards for men and separation from the world shown by simplicity in clothing, homes, possessions and lifestyle. The church has a worldwide membership of about 15,000, largely concentrated in the United States and Canada.

HEADQUARTERS

P.O. Box 313, 420 N. Wedel Ave., Moundridge, KS 67107 Tel. (316)345-2532 Fax (316)345-2582

Media Contact, Dale Koehn, P.O.Box 230, Moundridge, KS 67107 Tel. (316)345-2532 Fax (316)-345-2582

PERIODICAL

Messenger of Truth

The Church of God of Prophecy in Canada

In the late 19th century, people seeking God's eternal plan as they followed the Reformation spirit began to delve further for scriptural light concerning Christ and his church. A small group emerged which dedicated and covenanted themselves to God and one another to be the Church of God. On June 13, 1903, A.J. Tomlinson joined them during a period of intense prayer and Bible study. Under Tomlinson's dynamic leadership, the church enjoyed tremendous growth.

In 1923 two churches emerged. Those that opposed Tomlinson's leadership are known today in Canada as the New Testament Church of God. Tomlinson's followers are called the Church of God of Prophecy.

In Canada, the first Church of God of Prophecy congregation was organized in Swan River, Manitoba, in 1937. Churches are now established in British Columbia, Manitoba, Alberta, Saskatchewan, Ontario, Quebec and all 50 states.

The church accepts the whole Bible rightly divided, with the New Testament as the rule of faith and practice, government and discipline. The membership upholds the Bible as the inspired Word of God and believes that its truths are known by the illumination of the Holy Spirit. The Trinity is recognized as one supreme God in three persons--Father, Son and Holy Ghost. It is believed that Jesus Christ, the virgin-born Son of God, lived a sinless life, fulfilled his ministry on earth, was crucified, resurrected and later ascended to the right hand of God. Believers now await Christ's return to earth and the establishment of the millenial kingdom.

HEADQUARTERS

World Headquarters: Bible Place, P.O. Box 2910, Cleveland, TN 37320-2910

Canadian Headquarters West: Bishop Vernon Van Deventer, Box 952, Strathnore, AB T0J 3H0 Tel. (403)934-4787

Canadian Headquarters East: Bishop Aston R. Morrison, P.O. Box 457, Brampton, ON L6V 2L4 Tel. (905)843-2379

Media Contact, Natl. Overseer, Bishop Vernon Van Deventer, P.O. Box 952, Strathmore, AB T0J 3H0 Tel. (403)934-4787

OFFICERS

Canada East, Natl. Overseer, Bishop Aston R. Morrison, P.O. Box 457, Brampton, ON L6V 2L4 Tel. (905)843-2379

Canada West, Natl. Overseer, Bishop Vernon Van Deventer, Box 952, Strathmore, AB T0J 3H0 Tel. (403)934-4787

BOARD OF DIRECTORS

Pres., Bishop Aston R. Morrison
Vice-Pres., Bishop Vernon Van Deventer
Sec., John Anderson
Members: Bishop Billy D. Murray; Bishop Adrian Varlack; Bishop Tony Denbok; Bishop Leroy V. Greenaway; Bishop Randy Howard

PERIODICAL

Canadian Trumpeter Canada-West

The Church of Jesus Christ of Latter-day Saints in Canada

This body has only stake and mission offices in Canada. Elders Cree-L Kofford, Vaughn J. Featherstone and W. Don Ladd of the Quorum of the Seventy oversee the church's activities in Canada. They reside in Salt Lake City, Utah. All General Authorities may be reached at the headquarters. [See U.S. Directory, "Religious Bodies in the United States" in this edition for further details.] In Canada there are 34 stakes, 7 missions, 9 districts and 391 wards/branches (congregations), with 130,000 members.

HEADQUARTERS

50 East North Temple St., Salt Lake City, UT 84150

Media Contact, Public Affairs Dir., Donald & Joan Conkey, 91 Scenic Millway, Willowdale, ON M2L 1S9 Tel. (416)441-0452 Fax (416)441-0457

PERIODICALS

Church News; The Ensign

Church of the Lutheran Brethren

The Church of the Lutheran Brethren of America was organized in December 1900. Five independent Lutheran congregations met together in Milwaukee, WI, and adopted a constitution patterned very closely to that of the Lutheran Free Church of Norway.

The spiritual awakening in the Midwest during the 1890s crystallized into convictions that led to the formation of a new church body. Chief among the concerns were church membership practices, observance of Holy Communion, confirmation practices and local church government.

The Church of the Lutheran Brethren practices a simple order of worship with the sermon as the primary part of the worship service. It believes that personal profession of faith is the primary criterion for membership in the congregation. The Communion service is reserved for those who profess faith in Christ as savior. Each congregation is autonomous and the synod serves the congregations in advisory and cooperative capacities.

The synod supports a world mission program in Cameroon, Chad, Japan and Taiwan. Approximately 40 percent of the synodical budget is earmarked for world missions. A growing home mission ministry is planting new congregations in the United States and Canada. Affiliate organizations operate several retirement/nursing homes, conference and retreat centers.

HEADQUARTERS

1007 Westside Dr., P.O. Box 655, Fergus Falls, MN 56538 Tel. (218)739-3336 Fax (218)739-5514

Media Contact, Asst. to Pres., Rev. Luther Larson

OFFICERS

Pres., Rev. Arthur Berge, 14540 6th St. SW, Calgary, AB T2Y 2E7

Vice-Pres., ----

Sec., Mr. Robert Miller, Box 1237, Martensville, SK S0K 2T0

Treas., Mr. Edwin Rundbraaten, Box 739, Birch Hills, SK S0J 0G0

Youth Coord., Rev. Harold Rust, 2617 Preston Ave. S., Saskstoon, SK S7J 2G3

PERIODICAL

Faith and Fellowship

Church of the Nazarene Canada

The first Church of the Nazarene in Canada was organized in November, 1902, by Dr. H. F. Reynolds. It was in Oxford, Nova Scotia. The Church of the Nazarene is Wesleyan Arminian in theology, representative in church government and warmly evangelistic.

HEADQUARTERS

20 Regan Rd., Unit 9, Brampton, ON L7A 1C3 Tel. (905)846-4220 Fax (905)846-1775

Media Contact, Gen. Sec., Dr. Jack Stone, 6401 The Paseo, Kansas City, MO 64131 Tel. (816)-333-7000 Fax (816)361-4983

OFFICERS

Natl. Dir., Dr. William E. Stewart, 20 Regan Rd. Unit 9, Brampton, ON L7A 1C3 Tel. (905)846-4220 Fax (905)846-1775

Exec. Asst., John T. Martin, 20 Regan Rd. Unit 9, Brampton, ON L7A 1C3 Tel. (905)846-4220 Fax (905)846-1775

Chmn., Rev. Wesley G. Campbell, #205, 1255 56th St., Delta, BC V4L 2B9

Vice-Chmn., Rev. Ronald G. Fry, 1280 Finch Ave. W. Ste. 416, North York, ON M3J 3K6

Sec., Rev. Larry Dahl, 14320 94th St., Edmonton, AL T5E 3W2

Churches of Christ in Canada

Churches of Christ are autonomous congregations, whose members appeal to the Bible alone to determine matters of faith and practice. There are no central offices or officers. Publications and institutions related to the churches are either under local congregational control or independent of any one congregation.

Churches of Christ shared a common fellowship in the 19th century with the Christian Churches/Churches of Christ and the Christian Church (Disciples of Christ). Fellowship was broken after the introduction of instrumental music in worship and centralization of church-wide activities through a missionary society. Churches of Christ began in Canada soon after 1800, largely in the middle provinces. The few pioneer congregations were greatly strengthened in the mid-1800s, growing in size and number.

Members of Churches of Christ believe in the inspiration of the Scriptures, the divinity of Jesus Christ, and immersion into Christ for the remission of sins. The New Testament pattern is followed in worship and church organization.

HEADQUARTERS

Media Contact, Man. Ed., Gospel Herald, Eugene C. Perry, 4904 King St., Beansville, ON L0R 1B6 Tel. (416)563-7503 Fax (416)563-7503

PERIODICALS

Gospel Herald; Sister Triangle; Good News West; Cross Training

Conference of Mennonites in Canada

The Conference of Mennonites in Canada began in 1902 as an organized fellowship of Mennonite immigrants from Russia clustered in southern Manitoba and around Rosthern, Saskatchewan. The first annual sessions were held in July, 1903. Its members hold to traditional Christian beliefs, believer's baptism and congregational polity. They emphasize practical Christianity: opposition to war, service to others and personal ethics. Further immigration from Russia in the 1920s and 1940s increased the group which is now located in all provinces from New Brunswick to British Columbia. In recent years a variety of other ethnic groups, including native Canadians, have joined the conference. This conference is affiliated with the General Conference Mennonite Church whose offices are at Newton, Kan.

HEADQUARTERS

600 Shaftesbury Blvd., Winnipeg, MB R3P 0M4 Tel. (204)888-6781 Fax (204)831-5675

Media Contact, Roma Quapp

OFFICERS

Chpsn., Menno Epp, 78 Oak St. E., Leamington, ON N8H 2C6

Vice-Chpsn., Gerd Bartel, 6250 49 Ave., Delta, BC V4K 4S5

Sec., Mary Anne Loeppky, Box 973, Altona, MB R0G 0B0

Gen. Sec., Helmut Harder

PERIODICALS

Mennonite Reporter; NEXUS

Congregational Christian Churches in Canada

This body originated in the early 18th century when devout Christians within several denominations in the northern and eastern United States, dissatisfied with sectarian controversy, broke away from their own denominations and took the simple title "Christians." First organized in 1821 at Keswick, Ontario, the Congregational Christian Churches in Canada was incorporated on Dec. 4, 1989, as a national organization. In doctrine the body is evangelical, being governed by the Bible as the final authority in faith and practice. It believes that Christian character must be expressed in daily living; it aims at the unity of all true believers in Christ that others may believe in Him and be saved. In church polity, the body is democratic and autonomous. It is a member of The World Evangelical Congregational Fellowship.

HEADQUARTERS

222 Fairview Dr. Ste. 202, Brantford, ON N3T 2W9 Tel. (519)751-0606 Fax (519)751-0852

Media Contact, Pres., Jim Potter, 18665 Mountainview Rd., R. R. 2, Caledon East, ON L0N 1E0 Tel. (519)927-9380

OFFICERS

Pres., Jim Potter
Exec. Dir., Rev. Walter Riegert
Sec., Mr. Len Ryder

PERIODICAL

Communications Bi Monthly

The Coptic Church in Canada

The Coptic Church in North America was begun in Canada in 1964 and was registered in the province of Ontario in 1965. The Coptic Church has spread since then to a number of locations in North America.

The governing body of each local church is an elected Board of Deacons. The Diocesan Council is the national governing body and meets at least once a year.

HEADQUARTERS

St. Mark Coptic Church, 41 Glendinning Ave., Agincourt, ON M1W 3E2 Tel. (416)494-4449
Media Contact, Fr. M. A. Marcos

OFFICER

Archpriest, Fr. M. A. Marcos, St. Mark's Coptic Orthodox Church, 41 Glendinning Ave., Agincourt, ON M1W 3E2 Tel. (416)494-4449
Officer, Fr. Ammonrius Guirguis, 41 Glendinning Ave., Agincourt, ON M1W 3E2 Tel. (416)494-4449

Elim Fellowship of Evangelical Churches and Ministers

The Elim Fellowship of Evangelical Churches and Ministers, a Pentecostal body, was established in 1984 as a sister organization of Elim Fellowship in the United States.

This is an association of churches, ministers and missionaries seeking to serve the whole body of Christ. It is Pentecostal and has a charismatic orientation.

HEADQUARTERS

30 Amelia St., Paris, ON N3L 3V5 Tel. (519)442-3288 Fax (519)442-1487
Ofc. Mgr., Larry Jones
Sec., Debbie Jones

OFFICERS

Pres., Errol Alchin
Vice-Pres., Winston Nunes, 4 Palamino Cres., Willowdale, ON M2K 1W1
Sec., Paul Heidt, 123 Woodlawn Ave., Brantford, ON N3V 1B4
Treas., Aubrey Phillips, 267 Steeple Chase Dr., Exton, PA 19341
President Emeritus, Carlton Spencer

COUNCIL OF ELDERS

Errol Alchin, Tel. (519)442-1310
Paul Heidt, Tel. (519)758-1335
Howard Ellis, Tel. (519)579-9844
Winston Nunes, Tel. (416)225-4824
Aubrey Phillips, Tel. (706)745-3304
L. Dayton Reynolds, Tel. (716)624-2253

The Estonian Evangelical Lutheran Church

The Estonian Evangelical Lutheran Church (EELC) was founded in 1917 in Estonia and reorganized in Sweden in 1944. The teachings of the EELC are based on the Old and New Testaments, explained through the Apostolic, Nicean and Athanasian confessions, the unaltered Confession of Augsburg and other teachings found in the Book of Concord.

HEADQUARTERS

383 Jarvis St., Toronto, ON M5B 2C7 Tel. (416)-925-5465 Fax (416)925-5688
Media Contact, Archbishop, Rev. Udo Petersoo

OFFICERS

Archbishop, The Rev. Udo Petersoo
Gen. Sec., Dean Edgar Heinsoo

PERIODICAL

Eesti Kirik

The Evangelical Covenant Church of Canada

A Canadian denomination organized in Canada at Winnipeg in 1904 which is affiliated with the Evangelical Covenant Church of America and with the International Federation of Free Evangelical Churches, which includes churches in 11 European countries.

This body believes in the one triune God as confessed in the Apostles' Creed, that salvation is received through faith in Christ as Saviour, that the Bible is the authoritative guide in all matters of faith and practice. Christian Baptism and the Lord's Supper are accepted as divinely ordained sacraments of the church. As descendants of the 19th century northern European pietistic awakening, the group believes in the need of a personal experience of commitment to Christ, the development of a virtuous life and the urgency of spreading the gospel to the "ends of the world."

HEADQUARTERS

630 Westchester Rd., Strathmore, AB T1P 1H8 Tel. (403)934-5845 Fax (403)934-5847
Media Contact, Supt., Rev. Jerome Johnson

OFFICERS

Supt., Rev. Jerome Johnson
Chpsn., Les Doell, RR 2, Wefaskiwin, AB T9A 1W9
Sec., Lori Koop, 6568 Claytonwood Pl., Surrey, BC V3S 7T5
Treas., Rod Johnson, Box 196, Norquay, SK S0A 2V0

PERIODICAL

The Covenant Messenger

Evangelical Free Church of Canada

The Evangelical Free Church of Canada traces its beginning back to 1917 when the church in Enchant, Alberta opened its doors. Today the denomination has nearly 140 churches from the West Coast to Quebec. Approximately 45 missionaries are sponsored by the EFCC in 10 countries. The Evangelical Free Church is the founding denomination of Trinity Western University in Langley, British Columbia. Church membership is 6,930, average attendance is 14,139.

HEADQUARTERS

Mailing Address, Box 56109, Valley Centre P.O., Langley, BC V3A 8B3 Tel. (604)888-8668 Fax (604)888-3108
Location, 7600 Glover Rd., Langley, BC
Media Contact, Admn. Asst., Tracy Morris, Box 56109, Valley Centre P.O., Langley, BC V3A 8B3 Tel. (604)888-8668 Fax (604)888-3108

OFFICERS

Pres., Dr. Richard J. Penner
Mod., Rev. Tim Seim, S.S. 1-3-131, Lethbridge, AB T1J 4B3

PERIODICAL

The Pulse

Evangelical Lutheran Church in Canada

The Evangelical Lutheran Church in Canada was organized in 1985 through a merger of The Evangelical Lutheran Church of Canada (ELCC) and the Lutheran Church in America--Canada Section.

The merger is a result of an invitation issued in 1972 by the ELCC to the Lutheran Church in America--Canada Section and the Lutheran Church--Canada. Three-way merger discussions took place until 1978 when it was decided that only a two-way merger was possible. The ELCC was the Canada District of the ALC until autonomy in 1967.

The Lutheran Church in Canada traces its history back more than 200 years. Congregations were organized by German Lutherans in Halifax and Lunenburg County in Nova Scotia in 1749. German Lutherans, including many United Empire Loyalists, also settled in large numbers along the St. Lawrence and in Upper Canada. In the late 19th century, immigrants arrived from Scandinavia, Germany and central European countries, many via the United States. The Lutheran synods in the United States have provided the pastoral support and help for the Canadian church.

HEADQUARTERS

1512 St. James St., Winnipeg, MB R3H 0L2 Tel. (204)786-6707 Fax (204)783-7548
Media Contact, Bishop, Rev. Telmor G. Sartison

OFFICERS

Bishop, Rev. Telmor G. Sartison
Vice-Pres., Janet Morley
Sec., Rev. Leon C. Gilbertson
Treas., William C. Risto

ASSISTANTS TO THE BISHOPS

Rev. James A. Chell
Rev. Dr. Lawrence Denef
Rev. Peter Mathiasen
Ms. Eleanor Sander

DIVISIONS AND OFFICES

Evangelical Lutheran Women, Pres., Marquise Sopher
Exec. Dir., Diane Doth

SYNODS

Alberta and the Territories: Bishop, Rev. Stephen P. Kristenson, 10014-81 Ave., Edmonton, AB T6E 1W8 Tel. (403)439-2636 Fax (403)433-6623
Eastern: Bishop, Rev. Dr. William D. Huras, 50 Queen St. N., Kitchener, ON N2H 6P4 Tel. (519)743-1461 Fax (519)743-4291
British Columbia: Bishop, Rev. Dr. Marlin Aadland, 80-10th Ave., E., New Westminster, BC V3L 4R5 Tel. (604)524-1318 Fax (604)524-9255
Manitoba/Northwestern Ontario: Bishop, Rev. Richard M. Smith, 201-3657 Roblin Blvd., Winnipeg, MB R3G 0E2 Tel. (204)889-3760 Fax (204)869-0272
Saskatchewan: Bishop, Rev. Allan A. Grundahl, Bessborough Towers, Rm. 707, 601 Spadina Cres. E., Saskatoon, SK S7K 3G8 Tel. (306)244-2474 Fax (306)664-8677

PERIODICAL

Canada Lutheran

The Evangelical Mennonite Conference of Canada

The Evangelical Mennonite Conference came about as the result of a renewal movement among a small group of Mennonites in Southern Russia in 1812. Klaas Reimer, a Mennonite minister, had become concerned about the apparent decline of spiritual life in the church, lack of discipline and the church's backing of the Russian government in the Napoleonic War. Around 1812, Reimer and several others began separate worship services, emphasizing a more strict discipline and separation from the world. By 1814, they were organized as a separate group, called the Kleine Gemeinde (small church).

Increasing pressure from the Russian government, particularly in the area of military conscription, finally led to a migration (1874 to 1875) of the entire group to North America. Fifty families settled in Manitoba and 36 families settled in Nebraska. Ties between the two segments gradually weakened, and eventually the U.S. group gave up its EMC identity.

The conference has passed through numerous difficult times and survived several schisms and migrations. Beginning in the 1940s, a growing vision for missions and concern for others fostered a new vitality and growth, reaching people from a variety of cultural backgrounds. Thirty-two of the 49 congregations are in Manitoba with two in British Columbia, five in Alberta, six in Saskatchewan and four in Ontario. In 1995 its membership passed 6,400. The conference has some 132 mission workers in 20 countries of the world.

HEADQUARTERS

Box 1268, 440 Main St., Steinbach, MB R0A 2A0 Tel. (204)326-6401 Fax (204)326-1613
Media Contact, Conf. Sec., Don Thiessen

OFFICERS

Conf. Mod., Ralph Unger, 271 Hamilton Ave., Winnipeg, MB R2Y 0H3
Bd. of Missions, Exec. Sec., Henry Klassen

PERIODICAL

The Messenger

Evangelical Mennonite Mission Conference

This group was founded in 1936 as the Rudnerweider Mennonite Church in Southern Manitoba and organized as the Evangelical Mennonite Mission Conference in 1959. It was incorporated in 1962. The Annual Conference meeting is held in July.

HEADQUARTERS

Box 52059, Niakwa P.O., Winnipeg, MB R2M 5P9 Tel. (204)253-7929 Fax (204)256-7384

Media Contact, David Penner, 906-300 Sherk St., Leamington, ON N8H 4N7 Tel. (519)322-0221

OFFICERS

Mod., Mr. David Penner, 906-300 Sherk St., Leamington, ON N8H 4N7

Vice-Mod., Dale Dueck, 991 Southview Dr., Winkler, MB R6W 1Y4

Sec., ----

Exec. Sec., Henry Dueck

OTHER ORGANIZATIONS

Missions Dir., Rev. Leonard Sawatzky

The Gospel Message: Box 1622, Saskatoon, SK S7K 3R8 Tel. (306)242-5001 Fax (306)242-6115; 210-401-33rd St. W., Saskatoon, SK S7L 0V5 Tel. (306)242-5001; Radio Pastor, Rev. Ed Martens; Radio Admn., Ernest Friessen

Aylmer Bible School: Principal, Abe Harms, Box 246, Aylmer, ON N5H 2R9 Tel. (519)773-5095

PERIODICAL

EMMC Recorder

The Evangelical Missionary Church of Canada

This denomination was formed in 1993 with the merger of The Evangelical Church of Canada and The Missionary Church of Canada. The Evangelical Missionary Church of Canada maintains fraternal relations with the worldwide body of the Missionary Church and with the Evangelical Church in the U.S. The Evangelical Church of Canada was among those North American Evangelical United Brethern Conferences which did not join the EUB in merging with the Methodist Church in 1968. The Missionary Church of Canada is Anabaptist in heritage. Its practices and theology were shaped by the Holiness Revivals of the late 1800s. The Evangelical Missionary Church consists of 145 churches in two conferences in Canada.

HEADQUARTERS

#550 1212-31st Ave. NE, Calgary, AB T2E 7S8 Tel. (403)250-2759 Fax (403)291-4720

Media Contact, Asst. to Pres., Mr John Hedegaard

OFFICERS

Pres., Rev. David Crouse, #550, 1212-31st Ave. NE, Calgary, AB T2E 7S8 Tel. (403)250-2759 Fax (403)291-4720

Canada East District, Dist. Supt., Rev. Dennis Bells, 130 Fergus Ave., Kitchener, ON N2A 2H2

Canada West District, Dist. Supt., Rev. David Crouse, #550, 1212-31st Ave. NE, Calgary, AB T2E 7S8

The Fellowship of Evangelical Baptist Churches in Canada

This organization was founded in 1953 by the merging of the Union of Regular Baptist Churches of Ontario and Quebec with the Fellowship of Independent Baptist Churches of Canada.

HEADQUARTERS

679 Southgate Dr., Guelph, ON N1G 4S2 Tel. (519)821-4830 Fax (519)821-9829

Media Contact, Pres., Rev. Terry D. Cuthbert

OFFICERS

Pres., Rev. Terry D. Cuthbert

Chmn., Dr. Donald Launstein

PERIODICALS

B.C. Fellowship Baptist; Evangelical Baptist Magazine

Foursquare Gospel Church of Canada

The Western Canada District was formed in 1964 with the Rev. Roy Hicks as supervisor. Prior to 1964 it had been a part of the Northwest District of the International Church of the Foursquare Gospel with headquarters in Portland, Oregon.

A Provincial Society, The Church of the Foursquare Gospel of Western Canada, was formed in 1976; a Federal corporation, the Foursquare Gospel Church of Canada, was incorporated in 1981 and a national church formed.

HEADQUARTERS

#100 8459 160th St., Surrey, BC V3S 3T9

Media Contact, Pres. & Gen. Supervisor, Timothy J. Peterson, 160th St., Surrey, BC V4N 1B4 Tel. (604)543-8414 Fax (604)543-8417

OFFICERS

Pres. & Gen. Supervisor, Timothy J. Peterson

Free Methodist Church in Canada

The Free Methodist Church was founded in New York in 1860 and expanded to Canada in 1880. It is Methodist in doctrine, evangelical in ministry and emphasizes the teaching of holiness of life through faith in Jesus Christ.

The Free Methodist Church in Canada was incorporated in 1927 after the establishment of a Canadian Executive Board. In 1959 the Holiness Movement Church merged with the Free Methodist Church. Full autonomy for the Canadian church was realized in 1990 with the formation of a Canadian General Conference. Mississauga, Ontario, continues to be the location of the Canadian Headquarters.

The Free Methodist Church ministers in 28 countries through its World Ministries Center in Indianapolis, Indiana. Aldersgate College in Moose Jaw, Saskatchewan, is the church's Canadian college.

HEADQUARTERS

4315 Village Centre Ct., Mississauga, ON L4Z 1S2 Tel. (905)848-2600 Fax (905)848-2603

Media Contact, Norman Bull

OFFICERS

Pres., Bishop Gary R. Walsh

Dir. of Admn. Ser., Norman Bull

Dir. of Development, Mary-Elsie Fletcher

Dir. of Pastoral Ser., Rev. Dennis Camplin

PERIODICAL

The Free Methodist Herald

Free Will Baptists

As revival fires burned throughout New England in the mid- and late 1700s, Benjamin Randall proclaimed his doctrine of Free Will to large crowds of seekers. In due time, a number of Randall's converts moved to Nova Scotia. One such believer was Asa McGray, who was to become instrumental in the establishment of several Free Baptist churches. Local congregations were organized in New Brunswick. After several years of numerical and geographic gains, disagreements surfaced over the question of music, Sunday school, church offerings, salaried clergy and other issues. Adherents of the more progressive element decided to form their own fellowship. Led by George Orser, they became known as Free Christian Baptists.

The new group faithfully adhered to the truths and doctrines which embodied the theological basis of Free Will Baptists. Largely through Archibald Hatfield, contact was made with Free Will Baptists in the United States in the 1960s. The association was officially welcomed into the Free Will Baptist family in July 1981, by the National Association.

HEADQUARTERS

RR 6, Woodstock, NB E0J 2B0 Tel. (506)325-9381

Media Contact, Oral McAffee

OFFICER

Mod., Mr. Oral McAffee

Greek Orthodox Diocese of Toronto (Canada)

Greek Orthodox Christians in Canada are under the jurisdiction of the Ecumenical Patriarchate of Constantinople (Istanbul).

HEADQUARTERS

27 Teddington Park Ave., Toronto, ON M4N 2C4 Tel. (416)322-5055

Media Contact, Sec. to the Bishop, Fr. Stavros Moschos, Tel. (416)485-5929

OFFICERS

Primate of the Archdiocese of North & South America, The Most Rev. Iakovos

Bishop of the Diocese of Toronto, The Rt. Rev. Bishop Sotirios

Independent Assemblies of God International (Canada)

This fellowship of churches has been operating in Canada for over 25 years. It is a branch of the Pentecostal Church in Sweden. Each church within the fellowship is completely independent.

HEADQUARTERS

1211 Lancaster St., London, ON N5V 2L4 Tel. (519)451-1751

Media Contact, Gen. Sec., Rev. Harry Wuerch

OFFICER

Gen. Sec., Rev. Harry Wuerch

PERIODICAL

The Mantle

Independent Holiness Church

The former Holiness Movement of Canada merged with the Free Methodist Church in 1958. Some churches remained independent of this merger and they formed the Independent Holiness Church in 1960, in Kingston, Ontario. The doctrines are Methodist and Wesleyan. The General Conference is every three years, next meeting in 1995.

HEADQUARTERS

Rev. R. E. Votary, 1564 John Quinn Rd., R.R.1, Greeley, ON K4P 1J9 Tel. (613)821-2237

Media Contact, Gen. Sec., Dwayne Reaney, 5025 River Rd. RR #1, Manotick, ON K4M 1B2 Tel. (613)692-3237

OFFICERS

Gen. Supt., Rev. R. E. Votary, 1564 John Quinn Rd., Greeley, ON K4P 1J9

Gen. Sec., Mr. Dwayne Reaney

Additional Officers: E. Brown, 104-610 Pesehudoff Cresc., Saskatoon, SK S7N 4G7; D. Wallace, RR #3, Metcalfe, ON K0A 2P0

PERIODICAL

Gospel Tidings

The Italian Pentecostal Church of Canada

This body had its beginnings in Hamilton, Ontario, in 1912 when a few people of an Italian Presbyterian Church banded themselves together for prayer and received a Pentecostal experience of the baptism in the Holy Spirit. Since 1912, there has been a close association with the teachings and practices of the Pentecostal Assemblies of Canada.

The work spread to Toronto, then to Montreal, where it also flourished. In 1959, the church was incorporated in the province of Quebec. The early leaders of this body were the Rev. Luigi Ippolito and the Rev. Ferdinand Zaffuto. The churches carry on their ministry in both the English and Italian languages.

HEADQUARTERS

6724 Fabre St., Montreal, QC H2G 2Z6 Tel. (514)-593-1944 Fax (514)593-1835

Media Contact, Gen. Sec., Rev. John DellaForesta, 12216 Pierre Baillargeon, Montreal, QC H1E 6K1 Tel. (514)494-6969

OFFICERS

Gen. Supt., Rev. Daniel Ippolito, 46 George Anderson Dr., Toronto, ON M6M 2Y8 Tel. (416)-244-4005 Fax (416)244-0381

Gen. Sec., Rev. John DellaForesta, 12216 Pierre Baillargeon, Montreal, QC H1E 6K1 Tel. (514)-494-6969

Gen. Treas., Mr. Joseph Manafò, 384 Sunnyside Ave., Toronto, ON M6R 2S1 Tel. (416)766-6692 Fax (416)766-8014

Overseer, Rev. Mario Spiridigliozz, 23 Wildwood Dr., Port Moody, BC V3H 4M4 Tel. (604)469-0788

Overseer, Rev. David Mortelliti, 6 Valade, St. Constant, QB J5A 1P3 Tel. (514)638-0644

PERIODICAL

Voce Evangelica/Evangel Voice

Jehovah's Witnesses

For details on Jehovah's Witnesses see "Religious Bodies in United States" in this edition of the Yearbook.

HEADQUARTERS

25 Columbia Heights, Brooklyn, NY 11201 Tel. (718)625-3600

Canadian Branch Office: Box 4100, Halton Hills, ON L7G 4Y4

Media Contact, Robert P. Johnson

The Latvian Evangelical Lutheran Church in America

This body was organized into a denomination on Aug. 22, 1975, after having existed as the Federation of Latvian Evangelical Lutheran Churches in America since 1955. This church is a regional constituent part of the Lutheran Church of Latvia in Exile, a member of the Lutheran World Federation and the World Council of Churches.

The Latvian Evangelical Lutheran Church in America works to foster religious life, tradition and customs in its congregations in harmony with the Holy Scriptures, the Apostles', Nicene and Athanasian Creeds, the unaltered Augsburg Confession, Martin Luther's Small and Large Catechisms and other documents of the Book of Concord.

The LELCA is ordered by its Synod, executive board, auditing committee and district conferences.

HEADQUARTERS

2140 Orkla Dr., Golden Valley, MN 55427-3432 Tel. (612)546-3712 Fax (612)546-3712
Media Contact, Pres., Uldis Cepure

Lutheran Church—Canada

Lutheran Church-Canada was established in 1959 at Edmonton, Alberta, as a federation of Canadian districts of the Lutheran Church, Missouri Synod; it was constituted in 1988 at Winnipeg, Manitoba, as an autonomous church.

The church confesses the Bible as both inspired and infallible, the only source and norm of doctrine and life and subscribes without reservation to the Lutheran Confessions as contained in the Book of Concord of 1580.

HEADQUARTERS

3074 Portage Ave., Winnipeg, MB R3K 0Y2 Tel. (204)895-3433 Fax (204)897-4319
Media Contact, Dir. of Comm., Ian Adnams

OFFICERS

Pres., Rev. Edwin Lehman
Vice-Pres., Rev. Karl Koslowsky, 871 Cavalier Dr., Winnipeg, MB R2Y 1C7
2nd Vice-Pres., Rev. Dennis Putzman, 24 Valencia Dr., St. Catharines, ON L2T 3X8
3rd Vice-Pres., Rev. Ralph Mayan, 8631 Wagner Dr., Richmond, BC V7A 4N2
Sec., Rev. William Ney, 7100 Ada Blvd., Edmonton, AB T5B 4E4
Treas., Mr. Ken Werschler

DISTRICT OFFICES

Alberta-British Columbia: Pres., Rev. H. Ruf, 7100 Ada Blvd., Edmonton, AB T5B 4E4 Tel. (403)474-0063 Fax (403)477-9829
Central: Pres., Dr. R. Holm, 1927 Grant Dr., Regina, SK S4S 4V6 Tel. (306)586-4434 Fax (306)-586-0656
East: Pres., Dr. R. Winger, 275 Lawrence Ave., Kitchener, ON N2M 1Y3 Tel. (519)578-6500 Fax (519)578-3369

PERIODICALS

Update; Canadian Lutheran

Mennonite Church (Canada)

This body has its origins in Europe in 1525 as an outgrowth of the Anabaptist movement. It was organized in North America in 1898.(See: Mennonite Church description in the section "Religious Bodies in the United States")

HEADQUARTERS

421 S. Second St., Ste. 600, Elkhart, IN 46516 Tel. (219)294-7131 Fax (219)293-3977
Media Contact, Churchwide Communications Director

OFFICERS

Mod., Owen E. Burkholder, 1585 N. College Ave., Harrisonburg, VA 22801 Tel. (703)433-2138

North American Baptist Conference

Churches belonging to this conference emanated from German Baptist immigrants of more than a century ago. Although scattered across Canada and the U.S., they are bound together by a common heritage, a strong spiritual unity, a Bible-centered faith and a deep interest in missions.

Note: The details of general organization, officers, and periodicals of this body will be found in the North American Baptist Conference directory in the "Religious Bodies in the United States" section of this *Yearbook*.

HEADQUARTERS

1 S. 210 Summit Ave., Oakbrook Terrace, IL 60181 Tel. (708)495-2000 Fax (708)495-3301
Media Contact, Marilyn Schaer

OFFICER

Exec. Dir., Dr. Philip Yntema

PERIODICALS

N.A.B. Today; Opening Doors

The Old Catholic Church of Canada

The church was founded in 1948 in Hamilton, Ontario. The first bishop was the Rt. Rev. George Davis. The Old Catholic Church of Canada accepts all the doctrines of the Eastern Orthodox Churches and, therefore, not Papal Infallibility or the Immaculate Conception. The ritual is Western (Latin Rite) and is in the vernacular language. Celibacy is optional.

HEADQUARTERS

RR #1, Midland, ON L4R 4K3 Tel. (705)835-6940
Media Contact, Bishop, The Most Rev. David Thomson

OFFICER

Bishop, The Most Rev. David Thomson

Old Order Amish Church

This is the most conservative branch of the Mennonite Church and direct descendants of Swiss Brethren (Anabaptists) who emerged from the Reformation in Switzerland in 1525. The Amish, followers of Bishop Jacob Ammann, became a distinct group in 1693. They began migrating to North America about 1720; all of them still reside in the United States or Canada. They first migrated to Ontario in 1824 directly from Bavaria, Germany and also from Pennsylvania and Alsace-Lorraine. Since 1953 some Amish have migrated to Ontario from Ohio, Indiana and Iowa.

In 1995 there were 17 congregations in Ontario, each being autonomous. No membership figures are kept by this group, and there is no central headquarters. Each congregation is served by a bishop, two ministers and a deacon, all of whom are chosen from among the male members by lot for life.

CORRESPONDENT

Pathway Publishers, David Luthy, Rt. 4, Aylmer, ON N5H 2R3

PERIODICALS

Blackboard Bulletin; The Budget; The Diary; Die Botschaft; Family Life; Herold der Wahrheit; Young Companion

The Open Bible Standard Churches of Canada

This is the Canadian branch of the Open Bible Standard Churches, Inc., USA of Des Moines, Iowa. It is an evangelical, full gospel denomination emphasizing evangelism, missions and the message of the Open Bible. The Canadian Branch was chartered Jan. 7, 1982.

HEADQUARTERS

Bramalea Christian Fellowship, Lot 17, RR #4, Bramalea Rd. N., Bramalea, ON L6T 3S1 Tel. (905)799-2400

Media Contact, Gen. Overseer, Dr. Peter Morgan

OFFICERS

Gen. Supt., Dr. Peter Morgan

Sec.-Treas., Rev. Jaime C. Buslon, 62 Overlea Blvd., Toronto, ON M4H 1N9 Tel. (416)429-3882

Prov. Supt., Rev. Harry Armoogan, 343 Albert St., Waterloo, ON N2L 3T9 Tel. (519)885-2784

Orthodox Church in America (Canada Section)

The Archdiocese of Canada of the Orthodox Churchâin America was established in 1926. First organized by St. Tikhon, martyr Patriarch of Moscow, previously Archbishop of North America, it is part of the Russian Metropolia and its successor, the autocephalous Orthodox Church in America.

The Archdiocesan Council meets twice yearly, the General Assembly of the Archdiocese takes place every three years.

HEADQUARTERS

P.O. Box 179, Spencerville, ON K0E 1X0 Tel. (613)925-5226 Fax (613)925-1521

OFFICERS

Bishop of Ottawa & Canada, The Rt. Rev. Seraphim

Chancellor, V. Rev. John Tkachuk, P.O. Box 1390, Place Bonaventure, Montreal, QC H5A 1H3 Tel. (514)481-5093 Fax (514)481-2256

Treas., Mr. Nikita Lopoukhine, 55 Clarey Ave., Ottawa, ON K1S 2R6

Eastern Sec., Olga Jurgens

Western Sec., Deacon Andrew Piasta, #3, 27004 Township Rd. 514, Spruce Grove, AB Tel. (403)-987-4833

ARCHDIOCESAN COUNCIL

Clergy Members: V. Rev. Nicolas Boldireff; V. Rev. Orest Olekshy; Rev. Andrew Morbey; Rev. Dennis Pihach; Rev. Larry Reinheimer; Protodeacon Cyprian Hutcheon

Lay Members: Audrey Ewanchuk; Nicholas Ignatieff; David Grier; John Hadjinicolaou; Rhoda Zion; Oleh Kutowy

Ex Officio: Chancellor; Treas.; Eastern Sec.; Western Sec.

REPRESENTATIVES TO METROPOLITAN COUNCIL

Rev. Andrew Morbey

Mary Ann Lopoukhine

PERIODICAL

Canadian Orthodox Messenger

Patriarchal Parishes of the Russian Orthodox Church in Canada

This is the diocese of Canada of the former Exarchate of North and South America of the Russian Orthodox Church. It was originally founded in 1897 by the Russian Orthodox Archdiocese in North America.

HEADQUARTERS

St. Barbara's Russian Orthodox Cathedral, 10105 96th St., Edmonton, AB T5H 2G3

Media Contact, Sec.-Treas., Victor Lopushinsky, #303 9566-101 Ave., Edmonton, AB T5H 0B4 Tel. (403)455-9071

OFFICER

Admn., Bishop of Kashira, Most Rev. Mark, 10812-108 St., Edmonton, AB T5H 3A6

The Pentecostal Assemblies of Canada

This body is incorporated under the Dominion Charter of 1919 and is also recognized in the Province of Quebec as an ecclesiastical corporation. Its beginnings are to be found in the revivals at the turn of the century, and most of the first Canadian Pentecostal leaders came from a religious background rooted in the Holiness movements.

The original incorporation of 1919 was implemented among churches of eastern Canada only. In the same year, a conference was called in Moose Jaw, Saskatchewan, to which the late Rev. J. M. Welch, general superintendent of the then-organized Assemblies of God in the U.S., was invited. The churches of Manitoba and Saskatchewan were organized as the Western District Council of the Assemblies of God. They were joined later by Alberta and British Columbia. In 1921, a conference was held in Montreal, to which the general chairman of the Assemblies of God was invited. Eastern Canada also became a district of the Assemblies of God, joining Eastern and Western Canada as two districts in a single organizational union.

In 1920, at Kitchener, Ontario, eastern and western churches agreed to dissolve the Canadian District of the Assemblies of God and unite under the name The Pentecostal Assemblies of Canada.

Today the Pentecostal Assemblies of Canada operates throughout the nation and in about 31 countries around the world. Religious services are conducted in more than 25 different languages in the 1,087 local churches in Canada. Members and adherents number 225,000. The number of local churches includes approximately 100 Native congregations.

HEADQUARTERS

6745 Century Ave., Mississauga, ON L5N 6P7 Tel. (905)542-7400 Fax (905)542-7313

Media Contact, Public Relations, Rev. W. A. Griffin

OFFICERS

Gen. Supt., Rev. James M. MacKnight
Gen. Sec.-Treas., Rev. Gordon Upton
Overseas Missions, Exec. Dir., Rev. Lester E. Markham
Canadian Ministries, Exec. Dir., Rev. Kenneth B. Birch

FULL GOSPEL PUBLISHING HOUSE

Mgr., Mr. Harry E. Anderson

DISTRICT SUPERINTENDENTS

British Columbia: Rev. William R. Gibson, 5641 176 A St., Surrey, BC V3S 4G8 Tel. (604)576-9421 Fax (604)576-1499
Alberta: Rev. Lorne D. McAlister, 10585-111 St., #101, Edmonton, AB T5H 3E8 Tel. (403)426-0084 Fax (403)420-1318
Saskatchewan: Rev. Samuel O. Bird, 119-C Cardinal Cres., Saskatoon, SK S7L 6H5 Tel. (306)-652-6088 Fax (306)652-0199
Manitoba: Rev. Gordon V. Peters, 187 Henlow Bay, Winnipeg, MB R3Y 1G4 Tel. (204)488-6800 Fax (204)489-0499
Western Ontario: Rev. W. D. Morrow, 3214 S. Service Rd., Burlington, ON L7M 3J2 Tel. (905)-637-5566 Fax (905)637-7558
Eastern Ontario and Quebec: Rev. E. Stewart Hunter, Box 13250, Kanata, ON K2K 1X4 Tel. (613)599-3422 Fax (613)599-7284
Maritime Provinces: Rev. David C. Slauenwhite, Box 1184, Truro, NS B2N 5H1 Tel. (902)895-4212 Fax (902)897-0705

BRANCH CONFERENCES

German Conference: Rev. Philip F. Kniesel, #310, 684 Belmont Ave., W, Kitchener, ON N2M 1N6
Slavic Conferences: Eastern District, Rev. Walter Senko, RR 1, Wilsonville, ON N0E 1Z0; Western District, Rev. Michael Brandebura, 4108-134 Ave., Edmonton, AB T5A 3M2
Finnish Conference: Rev. A. Wirkkala, 1920 Argyle Dr., Vancouver, BC V5P 2A8

PERIODICALS

Pentecostal Testimony; Resource: The National Leadership Magazine

Pentecostal Assemblies of Newfoundland

This body began in 1910 and held its first assembly at the Bethesda Pentecostal Mission at St. John's. It was incorporated in 1925 as the Bethesda Pentecostal Assemblies and changed its name in 1930 to the Pentecostal Assemblies of Newfoundland.

HEADQUARTERS

57 Thorburn Rd., St. John's, NF A1B 3N4 Tel. (709)753-6314 Fax (709)753-4945
Media Contact, Gen. Supt., Roy D. King, 50 Brownsdale, St. John's, NF A1E 4R2

OFFICERS

Gen. Supt., Roy D. King, 50 Brownsdale St., St. John's, NF A1E 4R2
First Asst. Supt., B. Q. Grimes, 14 Chamberlain St., Grand Falls, NF A2A 2G4
Second Asst. Supt., H. E. Perry, P.O. Box 449, Lewisporte, NF A0G 3A0
Gen. Sec.-Treas., Clarence Buckle, P.O. Box 8895, Stn. A, St. John's, NF A1B 3T2

DEPARTMENTS

Youth & Sunday School, Dir., Robert H. Dewling, 26 Wicklow St., St. John's, NF A1B 3H2
Literature, Gen. Mgr., Clarence Buckle, P.O. Box 8895, Stn. A, St. John's, NF A1B 3T2
Women's Ministries, Dir., Mrs. Nancy Hunter, 10 Hardy Ave., Grand Falls-Windsor, NF A2A 2J9
Men's Fellowship, Dir., Eugene Rowe, Box 9, Little Burnt Bay, NF A0G 3B0
World Missions Promotion, A. Scott Hunter, 10 Hardy Ave., Grand Falls-Windsor, NF A2A 2J9

PERIODICAL

Good Tidings

Presbyterian Church in America (Canadian Section)

Canadian congregations of the Reformed Presbyterian Church, Evangelical Synod, became a part of the Presbyterian Church in America when the RPCES joined PCA in June 1982. Some of the churches were in predecessor bodies of the RPCES, which was the product of a 1965 merger of the Reformed Presbyterian Church in North America, General Synod and the Evangelical Presbyterian Church. Others came into existence later as a part of the home missions work of RPCES. Congregations are located in six provinces, and the PCA is continuing church extension work in Canada. The denomination is committed to world evangelization and to a continuation of historic Presbyterianism. Its officers are required to subscribe to the Reformed faith as set forth in the Westminster Confession of Faith and Catechisms.

HEADQUARTERS

Media Contact, Correspondent, Doug Codling, Faith Reformed Presbyterian Church, 2581 E. 45th St., Vancouver, BC V5R 3B9 Tel. (604)-438-8755

The Presbyterian Church in Canada

This is the nonconcurring portion of the Presbyterian Church in Canada that did not become a part of The United Church of Canada in 1925.

HEADQUARTERS

50 Wynford Dr., North York, ON M3C 1J7 Tel. (416)441-1111 Fax (416)441-2825
Media Contact, Principal Clk., Rev. Thomas Gemmell

OFFICERS

Mod., Dr. Alan M. McPherson
Clks. of Assembly: Principal Clk., Rev. Thomas Gemmell; Dep. Clk., Dr. T. Plomp; Dep. Clk., Mrs. B. McLean
Assembly Council: Sec., Rev. Thomas Gemmell; Treas., Mr. Russel McKay

NATIONAL BOARDS

Life & Mission Agency: Gen. Sec., Rev. Glen Davis; Sec. for Ministry, Rev. Jean Armstrong; Sec. for Educ. & Discipleship, Rev. John Bannerman; Sec. for Educ. & Discipleship, Mrs. Joyce Hodgson; Sec. for Educ. & Discipleship, Rev. Diane Strickland; Justice Ministries, Rev. Dr. Ray Hodgson; Canada Ministries, Rev. Ian Morrison; Intl. Ministries, Dr. Marjorie Ross; Presbyterian World Service & Dev., Dir., Rev. Richard Fee

Service Agency: Sec. for Resource Production, Rev. Glenn Cooper
Presbyterian Church Building Corp.: Dir., Rev. F. R. Kendall
Service Agency: Gen. Sec., Rev. Karen A. Hincke; Comp., D. A. Taylor
Women's Missionary Society (WD): Pres., Rev. Rosemary Doran, Hamilton, ON; Exec. Dir., Mrs. Tamiko Corbett
Atlantic Missionary Society (ED): Pres., Mrs. Marlene Sinns, Chatham, NB

PERIODICALS

Channels; The Presbyterian Message; Presbyterian Record; Glad Tidings; La Vie Chrétienne

Reformed Church in Canada

The Canadian branch of the Reformed Church in America consists of 43 churches organized under the Council of the Reformed Church in Canada and within the classis of Ontario (25 churches), British Columbia (11 churches), Canadian Prairies (7 churches). The Reformed Church in America was established in 1628 by the earliest Dutch settlers in America as the Reformed Protestant Dutch Church. It is evangelical in theology and presbyterian in government.

HEADQUARTERS

Gen. Sec., Rev. Wesley Granberg- Michaelson, 475 Riverside Dr., Rm. 1812, New York, NY 10115 Tel. (212)870-2841 Fax (212)870-2499
Council of the Reformed Church in Canada, Exec. Sec., ----, Reformed Church Center, RR #4, Cambridge, ON N1R 5S5 Tel. (519)622-1777
Media Contact, Dir., Stewardship & Communication Services, Rev. E. Wayne Antworth, 475 Riverside Dr., New York, NY 10115 Tel. (212)-870-2954 Fax (212)870-2499

PERIODICAL

Pioneer Christian Monthly

The Reformed Episcopal Church of Canada

The Reformed Episcopal Church is a separate entity. It was established in Canada by an act of incorporation given royal assent on June 2, 1886. It maintains the founding principles of episcopacy (in historic succession from the apostles), Anglican liturgy and Reformed doctrine and evangelical zeal. In practice it continues to recognize the validity of certain nonepiscopal orders of evangelical ministry. The Church has reunited with the Reformed Episcopal Church and is now composed of two Dioceses in this body - the Diocese of British Columbia and the Diocese of Ontario.

HEADQUARTERS

Office of the Secretary, 7822 Langley St., Burnaby, BC V3N 3Z8 Tel. (604)521-3580 Fax (604)521-3580
Media Contact, Sec., Miss Eleanor R. MacQueen

OFFICERS

Pres., Rev. Charles W. Dorrington, 1210 Camas Ct., Victoria, BC V8X 4R1
Vice-Pres., Rt. Rev. E. A. Follows, Church of Our Lord, 626 Blanchard St., Victoria, BC V8W 3G6
Sec., Miss Eleanor R. MacQueen
Treas., Mr. Paul Collins, 307-628 Dallas Rd., Victoria, BC V8V 1B5

BISHOPS

Diocese of Ontario: Bishop Michael Fedechko, Box 2532, New Liskeard, ON P0J 1P0 Tel. (705)647-4565 Fax (705)647-5429
Diocese of Western Canada: Bishop Ted Follows, 626 Blanshard St., Victoria, BC V8W 3G6 Tel. (604)383-8915 Fax (604)383-8916

PERIODICAL

The Messenger

Reinland Mennonite Church

This group was founded in 1958 when 10 ministers and approximately 600 members separated from the Sommerfelder Mennonite Church. In 1968, four ministers and about 200 members migrated to Bolivia. The church has work in six communities in Manitoba and one in Ontario.

HEADQUARTERS

Bishop William H. Friesen, P.O. Box 96, Rosenfeld, MB R0G 1X0 Tel. (204)324-6339
Media Contact, Deacon, Henry Wiebe, Box 2587, Winkler, MB R6W 4C3 Tel. (204)325-8487

Reorganized Church of Jesus Christ of Latter Day Saints

Founded April 6, 1830, by Joseph Smith, Jr., the church was reorganized under the leadership of the founder's son, Joseph Smith III, in 1860. The Church is established in 38 countries including the United States and Canada, with nearly a quarter of a million members. A biennial world conference is held in Independence, Missouri. The current president is Wallace B. Smith, great-grandson of the founder.

HEADQUARTERS

World Headquarters Complex: P.O. Box 1059, Independence, MO 64051 Tel. (816)833-1000 Fax (816)521-3095
Ontario Regional Ofc.: 390 Speedvale Ave. E., Guelph, ON N1E 1N5
Media Contact, Public Relations Coordinator, Shirlene Flory

CANADIAN REGIONS AND DISTRICTS

North Plains & Prairie Provinces Region: Regional Admn., Kenneth Barrows, c/o Calgary Congregation, 6415 Ranchview Dr. NW, Calgary, AB T3G 1B5; Alberta District, R.A.(Ryan) Levitt, #325, 51369 Range Rd., Sherwood Park, AB T8C 1H3; Saskatchewan District, Charles J. Lester, 629 East Place, Saskatoon, SK S7J 2Z1
Pacific Northwest Region: Regional Admn., Raymond Peter, P.O. Box 18469, 4820 Morgan, Seattle, WA 98118; British Columbia District, E. Carl Bolger, 410-1005 McKenzie Ave., Victoria, BC V8X 4A9
Ontario Region: Regional Admn., Larry D. Windland, 390 Speedvale Ave. E., Guelph, ON N1E 1N5; Chatham District, David R. Wood, 127 Mount Pleasant Crescent, Wallaceburg, ON N8A 5A3; Grand River District, C. Allen Taylor, R R 2, Orangeville, ON L9W 2Y9; London District, William T. Leney, Jr., 18 Glendon Road, Stratford, ON N5A 5B3; Niagara District, Dennis Jones, 1449 Columbia Crescent, Burlington, ON L7P 4C5; Northern Ontario District, Donald Males, P.O. Box 662, New Liskeard, ON P0J 1P0; Ottawa District, Marion Smith, 70 Mayburry St., Hull, QC J9A 2E9;

Owen Sound District, Robin M. Duff, P.O. Box 52, Owen Sound, ON N1K 5P1; Toronto Metropole, Kerry J. Richards, 74 Parkside Dr., Brampton, ON L6Y 2G9

PERIODICAL

Saints Herald

The Roman Catholic Church in Canada

The largest single body of Christians in Canada, the Roman Catholic Church is under the spiritual leadership of His Holiness the Pope. Catholicism in Canada dates back to 1534, when the first Mass was celebrated on the Gaspé Peninsula on July 7, by a priest accompanying Jacques Cartier. Catholicism had been implanted earlier by fishermen and sailors from Europe. Priests came to Acadia as early as 1604. Traces of a regular colony go back to 1608 when Champlain settled in Quebec City. The Recollets (1615), followed by the Jesuits (1625) and the Sulpicians (1657), began the missions among the native population. The first official Roman document relative to the Canadian missions dates from March 20, 1618. Bishop François de Montmorency-Laval, the first bishop, arrived in Quebec in 1659. The church developed in the East, but not until 1818 did systematic missionary work begin in western Canada.

In the latter 1700s, English-speaking Roman Catholics, mainly from Ireland and Scotland, began to arrive in Canada's Atlantic provinces. After 1815 Irish Catholics settled in large numbers in what is now Ontario. The Irish potato famine of 1847 greatly increased that population in all parts of eastern Canada.

By the 1850s the Catholic Church in both English- and French-speaking Canada had begun to erect new dioceses and found many religious communities. These communities did educational, medical and charitable work among their own people as well as among Canada's native peoples. By the 1890s large numbers of non-English and non-French-speaking Catholics had settled in Canada, especially in the Western provinces. In the 20th century the pastoral horizons have continued to expand to meet the needs of what has now become a very multiracial church.

HEADQUARTERS

Media Contact, Dir. of Information(interim), Rev. Mr. William Kokesch

OFFICERS

General Secretariat of the Episcopacy
Secrétaire général (French Sector), Father Émilius Goulet
General Secretary (English Sector), Rev. V. James Weisgerber
Assistant General Secretary (English Sector), Mr. Bede Martin Hubbard
Secrétaire général adjoint (French Sector), Mr. M. J. Fernand Tanguay

CANADIAN ORGANIZATION

Canadian Conference of Catholic Bishops: (Conférence des évêques cath. du Canada), 90 Parent Ave., Ottawa, ON K1N 7B1 Tel. (613)241-9461 Fax (613)241-8117

EXECUTIVE COMMITTEE

National Level
Pres., Most Rev. Francis J. Spence, (Kingston)
Vice-Pres., m le cardinal Jean-Claude Turcotte, (Montreal)
Co-Treas.: Msgr. Henri Goudreault, (Labrador City-Schefferville); Most Rev. Gerald Wiesner, (Prince George)

EPISCOPAL COMMISSIONS

National Level
Social Affairs, Msgr. Francois Thibodeau
Canon Law, Msgr. Jean-Guy Couture
Relations with Assoc. of Priests, Religious, & Laity, Most Rev. James H. MacDonald
Missions, Most Rev. Joseph Faber MacDonald
Ecumenism, Most Rev. Brendan O'Brien
Theology, Msgr. Henri Goudreault
Sector Level
Comm. sociales, Msgr. Roger Ebacher
Social Comm., Most Rev. Fred Colli
Éducation chrétienne, Msgr. Gilles Cazabon
Christian Education, Most Rev. Anthony Tonnos
Liturgie, Msgr. Antoine Hacault
Liturgy, Most Rev. John Knight

OFFICES

Secteur français
Missions Office, Dir., Fr. Douglas Crosby, O.M.I.
Office des communications sociales, Dir. général, L'abbé Jacques Paquette, 1340 est, boul. St. Joseph, Montréal, QC H2J 1M3 Tel. (514)524-8223 Fax (514)524-8522
Office national de liturgie, coordonnateur, M. l'abbé Paul Boily, 3530, rue Adam, Montréal, QC H1W 1Y8 Tel. (514)522-4930 Fax (514)-522-1557
Service incroyance et foi, Dir., P. Georges Convert, 7400, boulevard Saint-Laurent, Montréal, QC H2R 2Y1 Tel. (514)948-3186
Centre canadien d'oecuménisme, Rev. Thomas Ryan, C.S.P., 2065 rue Sherbrooke, Ouest, Montréal, QC H3H 1G6 Tel. (514)937-9176 Fax (514)935-5497
Services des relations publiques, Dir., M. Gérald Baril
Service des Editions, Dir., Mme Claire Dubé
Affaires sociales, Dir., M. Bernard Dufresne
English Sector
Natl. Liturgical Ofc., Dir., Sr. Donna Kelly, c.n.d.
Natl. Ofc. of Religious Educ., Dir., Mrs. Bernadette Tourangeau
Ofc. for Missions, Dir., Fr. Douglas Crosby, O.M.I.
Public Information Ofc., Dir., Rev. Mr. William Kokesch
Social Affairs, Dir., Mr. Joe Gunn

REGIONAL EPISCOPAL ASSEMBLIES

Atlantic Episcopal Assembly: Pres., Bishop Joseph Faber MacDonald; Vice-Pres., Msgr. Henri Goudreault; Sec.-Treas., Daniel Deveau, c.s.c., Tel. (506)758-2589 Fax (506)758-2580
Assemblée des évêques du Que: Prés., Msrg. Maurice Couture; Vice-Pres., Msgr. André Gaumond; Sécretaire général, L'abbé Clément Vigneault; Secrétariat, 1225 Boulevard Saint Joseph est, Montréal, QC H2J 1L7 Tel. (514)-274-4323 Fax (514)274-4383
Ontario Conference of Catholic Bishops: Pres., Msgr. Eugène La Rocque; Vice-Pres., Bishop Anthony Tonnos; Sec., Thomas J. Reilly; Secretariat, Ste. 800, 10 St. Mary St., Toronto, ON M4Y 1P9 Tel. (416)923-1423 Fax (416)923-1509
Western Catholic Conference: Pres., Bishop Paul J. O'Byrne; Vice-Pres., Bishop Blaise Morand; Sec., Abbot Peter Novecosky, O.S.B., P.O. Box 10, Muenster, SK S0K 2Y0 Tel. (306)682-1788 Fax (306)682-1766

MILITARY ORDINARIATE

Ordinaire aux forces canadiennes: Msgr. André Vallée, P.M.É., National Defence Headquarters, Ottawa, ON K1A 0K2 Tel. (613)992-1261 Fax (613)991-1056

Canadian Religious Conference: Sec. Gen., Sr. Hélène Robitaille, F.D.L.S., 324 Laurier Ave. East, Ottawa, ON K1N 6P6 Tel. (613)236-0824 Fax (613)236-0825

LATIN RITE

Alexandria-Cornwall: Msgr. Eugene P. LaRocque, Centre diocésain, 220 Chemin Montréal, C. P. 1388, Cornwall, ON K6H 5V4 Tel. (613)933-1138

Amos: Evêché, Msgr. Gérard Drainville, 450, Principale Nord, Amos, QC J9T 2M1 Tel. (819)732-6515

Antigonish: Bishop Colin Campbell, Chancery Office, 155 Main St., P.O. Box 1330, Antigonish, NS B2G 2L7 Tel. (902)863-4818

Baie-Comeau: Evêché, Msgr. Pierre Morissette, 639 Rue de Bretagne, Baie-Comeau, QC G5C 1X2 Tel. (418)589-5744

Bathurst: Evêché, Msgr. André Richard, 645, avenue Murray, C.P. 460, Bathurst, NB E2A 3Z4 Tel. (506)546-3493

Calgary: Bishop Paul J. O'Byrne, Rm. 200-120, 17th Ave SW, Calgary, AB T1S 2T2 Tel. (403)-264-4501

Charlottetown: Bishop Joseph Vernon Fougere, D.D., P.O. Box 907, Charlottetown, PE C1A 7L9 Tel. (902)368-8005

Chicoutimi: Evêché, Msgr. Jean-Guy Couture, 602 est, rue Racine, C.P. 278, Chicoutimi, QC G7H 6J6 Tel. (418)543-0783

Churchill-Baie D'Hudson: Evêché, Msgr. Reynald Rouleau, O.M.I., C.P. 10, Churchill, MB R0B 0E0 Tel. (204)675-2541

Archdiocese of Edmonton: Archbishop, Joseph N. MacNeil, Archdiocesan Office, 8421-101st Ave., Edmonton, AB T6A 0L1 Tel. (403)469-1010

Edmundson: Evêché, Msgr. François Thibodeau, C.J.M., Centre diocésain, Edmundston, NB E3V 3K1 Tel. (506)735-5578

Gaspé: Evêché, Msgr. Raymond Dumais, C.P. 440, Gaspé, QC G0C 1R0 Tel. (418)368-2274

Gatineau-Hull: Archévêché, Msgr. Roger Ébacher, 180, boulevard Mont-Bleu, Hull, QC J8Z 3J5 Tel. (819)771-8391

Grand Falls: Bishop, Joseph Faber MacDonald, Chancery Office, P.O. Box 397, Grand Falls-Windsor, NF A2A 2J8 Tel. (709)489-4019

Gravelbourg: Secrétariat, Msgr. Raymond Roussin, s.m., C.P. 690, Gravelbourg, SK S0H 1X0 Tel. (306)648-2615

Archidiocèse de Grouard-McLennan: Archévêché, Msgr. Henri Légaré, C.P. 388, McLennan, AB T0H 2L0 Tel. (403)324-3002

Archdiocese of Halifax: Archbishop, Austin E. Burke, Archbishop's Residence, 6541 Coburg Rd., P.O. Box 1527, Halifax, NS B3J 2Y3 Tel. (902)429-9388

Hamilton: Bishop, Bishop Anthony Tonnos, 700 King St. W., Hamilton, ON L8P 1C7 Tel. (416)-528-7988

Hearst: Evêché, Msgr. Pierre Fisette, P.M.E., 76, 7 rue C.P. 1330, Hearst, ON P0L 1N0 Tel. (705)-362-4903

Joliette: Evêché, Msgr. Gilles Lussier, 2 rue St.-Charles Borromée, Nord. C.P. 470, Joliette, QC J6E 6H6 Tel. (514)753-7596

Kamloops: Bishop, Lawrence Sabatini, Bishop's Residence, 635A Tranquille Rd., Kamloops, BC V2B 3H5 Tel. (604)376-3351

Archidiocèse de Keewatin-LePas: Archbishop, Peter-Alfred Sutton, Résidence, 108 1st St. W., C.P. 270, Le Pas, MB R9A 1K4 Tel. (204)623-3529

Archdiocese of Kingston: Archbishop, Francis J. Spence, 390 Palace Rd., Kingston, ON K7L 4X3 Tel. (613)548-4461

Labrador City-Schefferville: Evêché, Msgr. Henri Goudreault, 318 Ave. Elizabeth, Labrador City, Labrador, NF A2V 2K7 Tel. (709)944-2046

London: Bishop, John M. Sherlock, Chancery Office, 1070 Waterloo St., London, ON N6A 3Y2 Tel. (519)433-0658

Mackenzie-Fort Smith (T.No.O.): Evêché, Msgr. Denis Croteau, 5117, 52 rue, Yellowknife, T.N.O., X1A 1T7 Tel. (403)920-2129

Archidiocèse de Moncton: Archévêché, ----, C.P. 248, Moncton, NB E1C 8K9 Tel. (506)857-9531

Mont-Laurier: Evêché, Msgr. Jean Gratton, 435 rue de la Madone, C.P. 1290, Mont Laurier, QC J9L 1S1 Tel. (819)623-5530

Archidiocèse de Montréal: Archévêché, Monsieur le cardinal Jean-Claude Turcotte, 2000 ouest rue Sherbrooke, Montréal, QC H3H 1G4 Tel. (514)-931-7311

Monsonee: Msgr. Vincent Cadieux, Résidence, C.P. 40, Moosonee, ON P0L 1Y0 Tel. (705)336-2908

Abbatia Mullius of Muenster: Rt. Rev. Peter Novecosky, OSB, Abbot's Residence, St. Peter's Abbey, Muenster, SK S0K 2Y0 Tel. (306)682-1788

Nelson: Diocesan Admn., Rev. Wayne Phliger, Chancery Office, 813 Ward St., Nelson, BC V1L 1T4 Tel. (604)352-6921

Nicolet: Evêché, Msgr. Raymond Saint Gelais, 49 rue Brunault, Nicolet, QC J3T 1X7 Tel. (819)-293-4234

Archidiocèse D'Ottawa: Chancellerie, Msgr. Marcel A.J. Gervais, 1247, avenue Kilborn, Ottawa, ON K1H 6K9 Tel. (613)738-5025

Pembroke: Bishop, Brendan M. O'Brien, Bishop's Residence, 188 Renfrew St., P.O. Box 7, Pembroke, ON K8A 6X1 Tel. (613)732-3895

Peterborough: Bishop, James L. Doyle, Bishop's Residence, 350 Hunter St. W., Peterborough, ON K9J 6Y8 Tel. (705)745-5123

Prince-Albert: Evêché, Msgr. Blaise Morand, 1415-ouest, 4e Ave. West, Prince-Albert, SK S6V 5H1 Tel. (306)922-4747

Prince-George: Bishop Gerald Wisner, Chancery Office, 2935 Highway 16 West, P.O. Box 7000, Prince George, BC V2N 3Z2 Tel. (604)964-4424

Archidiocèse de Québec: Archévêché, Msgr. Maurice Couture, 2 rue Port Dauphin, C.P. 459, Québec, QC G1R 4R6 Tel. (418)692-3935

Archdiocese of Regina: Archbishop, Peter Mallon, D.D., Chancery Office, 455 Broad St. North, Regina, SK S4R 2X8 Tel. (306)352-1651

Archidiocèse de Rimouski: Archévêché, Msgr. Bertrand Blanchet, 34 ouest, rue de L'évêché, ouest C.P. 730, Rimouski, QC G5L 7C7 Tel. (418)723-3320

Rouyn-Noranda: Evêché, Msgr. Jean-Guy Hamelin, 515 avenue Cuddihy, C.P. 1060, Rouyn-Noranda, QC J9X 5W9 Tel. (819)764-4660

Ste-Anne de la Pocatière: Diocesan Admn., M. Le chanoine Roland Picard, C.P. 430 La Pocatière, Pocatière, QC G0R 1Z0 Tel. (418)856-1811

Archidiocèse de Saint-Boniface: Archevêché, Msgr. Antoine Hacault, 151 ave de la Cathédrale, St-Boniface, MB R2H 0H6 Tel. (204)237-9851

St. Catharine's: Bishop, John A. O'mara, Bishop's Residence, 122 Riverdale Ave., St. Catharines, ON L2R 4C2 Tel. (416)684-0154

St. George's: Bishop, Raymond J. Lahey, Bishop's Residence, 16 Hammond Dr., Corner Brook, NF A2H 2W2 Tel. (709)639-7073

Saint Hyacinthe: Evêché, Msgr. Louis-de-Gonzaque Langevin, 1900 ouest Girouard, C. P. 190, Saint-Hyacinthe, QC J2S 7B4 Tel. (514)773-8581

Saint-Jean-de-Longueuil: Evêché, Msgr. Bernard Hubert, 740 boul. Ste-Foy, C.P. 40, Longueuil, QC J4K 4X8 Tel. (514)679-1100

Saint-Jérome: Evêché, Msgr. Charles Valois, 355 rue St-Georges, C.P. 580, Saint-Jérome, QC J7Z 5V3 Tel. (514)432-9741

Saint John: Bishop, J. Edward Troy, Chancery Office, 1 Bayard Dr., Saint John, NB E2L 3L5 Tel. (506)632-9222

Archdiocese of St. John's: Archbishop, James H. MacDonald, Archbishop's Residence, P.O. Box 37, Basilica Residence, St. John's, NF A1C 5H5 Tel. (709)726-3660

Saint-Paul: Evêché, Msgr. Raymond Roy, 4410 51e Ave., St-Paul, AB T0A 3A2 Tel. (403)645-3277

Saskatoon: Diocesan Admn., Rev. Leonard Morand, Chancery Office, 106 - 5th Ave. N., Saskatoon, SK S7K 2N7 Tel. (306)242-1500

Sault Ste. Marie: Bishop, Jean-Louis Plouffe, Bishop's Residence, 480 McIntyre St., W., P.O. Box 510, North Bay, ON P1B 8J1 Tel. (705)476-1300

Archidiocèse de Sherbrooke: Archévêché, Msgr. Jean-Marie Fortier, 130 rue de la Cathedrale, C.P. 430, Sherbrooke, QC J1H 5K1 Tel. (819)-563-9934

Thunder Bay: Diocesan Admn., Rev. Edward T. Kennedy, Bishop's Residence, P.O. Box 756, Thunder Bay, ON P7C 4W6 Tel. (807)622-8144

Timmins: Msgr. Gilles Cazabon, O.M.I., 65, avenue Jubilee est, Timmins, ON P4N 5W4 Tel. (705)267-6224

Archdiocese of Toronto: Archbishop, Aloysius M. Ambrozic, Chancery Office, 355 Church St., Toronto, ON M5B 1Z8 Tel. (416)977-1500

Trois-Rivières: Evêché, Msgr. Laurent Noel, 362 rue Bonaventure, C.P. 879, Trois-Rivièrès, QC G9A 5J9 Tel. (819)374-9847

Valleyfield: Evêché, Msgr. Robert Lebel, 11 rue de l'Eglise, Valleyfield, QC J6T 1J5 Tel. (514)373-8122

Archdiocese of Vancouver: Archbishop, Adam Exner, Chancery Office, 150 Robson St., Vancouver, BC V6B 2A7 Tel. (604)683-0281

Victoria: Bishop, Remi J. De Roo, Bishop's Office, 1 - 4044 Nelthorpe St., Victoria, BC V8X 2A1 Tel. (604)479-1331

Whitehorse (Yukon): Bishop, Thomas Lobsinger, O.M.I. Bishop's Residence, 5119 5th Ave., Whitehorse, YT Y1A 1L5 Tel. (403)667-2052

Archdiocese of Winnipeg: Archbishop, Leonard J. Wall, 1495 Pembina Hwy, Winnipeg, ON R3T 2C6 Tel. (204)452-2227

Yarmouth: Bishop James Wingle, 53 rue Park, Yarmouth, NS B5A 4B2 Tel. (902)742-7163

EASTERN RITES

Eparchy of Edmonton Eparch: Most Rev. Myron Daciuk, V Eparch's Residence, 6240 Ada Blvd., Edmonton, AB T5W 4P1 Tel. (403)479-0381

Eparchy of New Westminster: Eparch, Severian S. Yakymyshyn, O.S.B.M., Eparch's Residence, 502 5th Ave., New Westminster, BC V3L 1S2 Tel. (604)521-8015

Eparchy of Saskatoon: Eparch, Most Rev. Cornelius Ivan Pasichny, Eparch's Residence, 866 Saskatchewan. Crescent East, Saskatoon, SK S7N 0L4 Tel. (306)653-0138

Ukrainian Eparchy of Toronto: Eparch, Most Rev. Isidore Borecky, Eparch's Residence, 61 Glen Edyth Dr., Toronto, ON M4V 2V8 Tel. (416)-924-2381

Toronto, Ontario Eparchy: For Slovaks, Eparch, Most Rev. Michael Rusnak, Chancery Office, 223 Carlton Rd., Unionville, ON L3R 3M2 Tel. (416)477-4867

Ukrainian Archeparchy of Winnipeg: Most Rev. Michael Bzdel, Archeparch's Residence, 235 Scotia St., Winnipeg, MB R2V 1V7 Tel. (204)-339-7457

Montréal (Qué) Archéparchie: Pour Les Grecs-Melkites, Archéparque, Msgr. Michel Hakim, Chancelerie: 34 Maplewood, Montréal, QC H2V 2M1 Tel. (514)272-6430

Archéparchie de Montréal: Pour les Maronites, Éparque, Msgr. Georges Abi-Saber, 12475, rue Grenet, Montréal, QC H4J 2K4 Tel. (514)331-2807

Canada/États-Unis, Msgr. Hovhannes Tersakian

PERIODICALS

Cahiers de Spiritualité Ignatienne; The Catholic Register; The Catholic Times (Montreal); Companion Magazine; Global Village Voice; Discover the Bible; L'Église Canadienne; Missions Today; The Monitor; National Bulletin on Liturgy; The New Freeman; Messenger (of the Sacred Heart); Foi et Culture (Bulletin natl. de liturgie) Liturgie; Prairie Messenger; La Vie des Communautés religieuses; Relations; Insight: A Resource for Adult Religious Education; Présence; The Communicator; Scarboro Missions

Romanian Orthodox Church in America (Canadian Parishes)

The first Romanian Orthodox immigrants in Canada called for Orthodox priests from their native country of Romania. Between 1902 and 1914, they organized the first Romanian parish communities and built Orthodox churches in different cities and farming regions of western Canada (Alberta, Saskatchewan, Manitoba) as well as in the eastern part (Ontario and Quebec).

In 1929, the Romanian Orthodox parishes from Canada joined with those of the United States in a Congress held in Detroit, Michigan, and asked the Holy Synod of the Romanian Orthodox Church of Romania to establish a Romanian Orthodox Missionary Episcopate in America. The first Bishop, Policarp (Morushca), was elected and consecrated by the Holy Synod of the Romanian Orthodox Church and came to the United States in 1935. He established his headquarters in Detroit with jurisdiction over all the Romanian Orthodox parishes in the United States and Canada.

In 1950, the Romanian Orthodox Church in America (i.e. the Romanian Orthodox Missionary Episcopate in America) was granted administrative autonomy by the Holy Synod of the Romanian Orthodox Church of Romania, and only doctrinal and canonical ties remain with this latter body.

In 1974 the Holy Synod of the Romanian Orthodox Church of Romania approved the elevation of the Episcopate to the rank of the Romanian Orthodox Archdiocese in America and Canada.

HEADQUARTERS

Canadian Office: Descent of the Holy Ghost, Romanian Orthodox Church, 2895 Seminole St., Windsor, ON N8Y 1Y1

Media Contact, Most Rev. Archbishop Victorin, 19959 Riopelle St., Detroit, MI 48203 Tel. (313)893-8390

OFFICERS

Archbishop, Most Rev. Archbishop Victorin, 19959 Riopelle St., Detroit, MI 48203 Tel. (313)893-8390

Vicar, V. Rev. Archim., Dr. Vasile Vasilachi, 45-03 48th Ave., Woodside, Queens, NY 11377 Tel. (718)784-4453

Cultural Councilor, Very Rev. Fr. Nicolae Ciurea, 19 Murray St. W., Hamilton, ON L8L 1B1 Tel. (416)523-8268

Admn. Councilor, V. Rev. Fr. Mircea Panciuk, 11024-165th Ave., Edmonton, AB T5X 1X9

Sec., Rev. Fr. Simion John Catau, 31227 Roan Dr., Warren, MI 48093 Tel. (810)264-1924

The Romanian Orthodox Episcopate of America (Jackson, MI)

This body of Eastern Orthodox Christians of Romanian descent is fully autonomous. For complete description and listing of officers, please see chapter 3, "Religious Bodies in the United States."

HEADQUARTERS

2522 Grey Tower Rd., Jackson, MI 49201 Tel. (517)522-4800 Fax (517)522-5907

Mailing Address, P.O. Box 309, Grass Lake, MI 49240

Media Contact, Ed./Sec., David Oancea, P.O. Box 185, Grass Lake, MI 49240-0185 Tel. (517)522-4800 Fax (517)522-5907

OFFICERS

Ruling Bishop, Rt. Rev. Nathaniel Popp

Dean of all Canada, Very Rev. Nicolae Marioncu, G.D. 2071, Qu'Appelle, SK S0G 1S0

PERIODICAL

Solia - The Herald

The Salvation Army in Canada

The Salvation Army, an evangelical branch of the Christian Church, is an international movement founded in 1865 in London, England. The ministry of Salvationists, consisting of clergy (officers) and laity, comes from a commitment to Jesus Christ and is revealed in practical service, regardless of race, color, creed, sex or age.

The goals of The Salvation Army are to preach the gospel, disseminate Christian truths, instill Christian values, enrich family life and improve the quality of all life.

To attain these goals, The Salvation Army operates local congregations, provides counseling, supplies basic human needs and undertakes spiritual and moral rehabilitation of any needy people who come within its influence.

A quasi-military system of government was set up in 1878, by General William Booth, founder (1829-1912). Converts from England started Salvation Army work in London, Ontario, in 1882. Two years later, Canada was recognized as a Territorial Command, and since 1933 it has included Bermuda. An act to incorporate the Governing Council of The Salvation Army in Canada received royal assent on May 19, 1909.

HEADQUARTERS

2 Overlea Blvd., Toronto, ON M4H 1P4 Tel. (416)425-2111

Media Contact, Asst. Public Rel. Sec. for Comm. & Spec. Events, Major Renaud J. Bowles, Tel. (416)425-6156 Fax (416)425-6157

OFFICERS

Territorial Commander, Commissioner Donald Kerr

Territorial Pres., Women's Organizations, Commissioner Joyce Kerr

Chief Sec., Col. John Busby

Sec. for Personnel, Lt.Col. John Carew

Bus. Adm. Sec., Lt. Col. Clyde Moore

Fin. Sec., Major Glen Shepherd

Public Rel. Sec., Lt. Col. Mel W. Bond

Property Sec., Major Boyde Goulding

Program Sec., Lt. Col. Ralph Stanley

PERIODICALS

The War Cry; En Avant!; The Young Soldier; The Edge; Sally Ann; Horizons

Serbian Orthodox Church in the U.S.A. and Canada, Diocese of Canada

The Serbian Orthodox Church is an organic part of the Eastern Orthodox Church. As a local church it received its autocephaly from Constantinople in A.D. 1219. The Patriarchal seat of the church today is in Belgrade, Yugoslavia. In 1921, a Serbian Orthodox Diocese in the United States of America and Canada was organized. In 1963, it was reorganized into three dioceses, and in 1983 a fourth diocese was created for the Canadian part of the church. The Serbian Orthodox Church is in absolute doctrinal unity with all other local Orthodox Churches.

HEADQUARTERS

7470 McNiven Rd., RR 3, Campbellville, ON L0P 1B0 Tel. (905)878-0043 Fax (905)878-1909

Media Contact, Rev. Branko Dopalovic

OFFICERS

Serbian Orthodox Bishop of Canada, Rt. Rev. Georgije

Dean of Western Deanery, V. Rev. Mirko Malinovic, 924 12th Ave., Regina, SK S4N 0K7 Tel. (306)352-2917

Dean of Eastern Deanery, Rev. Stevo Stojsavljevich, 143 Nash Rd. S., Hamilton, ON L8K 4J9 Tel. (416)560-9424

PERIODICAL

Stocnmik

Seventh-day Adventist Church in Canada

The Seventh-day Adventist Church in Canada is part of the worldwide Seventh-day Adventist Church with headquarters in Washington, D.C. (See "Religious Bodies in the United States" section of this *Yearbook* for a fuller description.) The Seventh-day Adventist Church in Canada was organized in 1901 and reorganized in 1932.

HEADQUARTERS

1148 King St., E., Oshawa, ON L1H 1H8 Tel. (905)433-0011 Fax (905)433-0982

Media Contact, Orville Parchment

OFFICERS

Pres., Orville Parchment
Sec., Claude Sabot
Treas., Donald Upson

DEPARTMENTS

Under Treas., Brian Christenson
Asst. Treas., Clareleen Ivany
Computer Services, Brian Ford
Coord. of Ministries, ----
Education, Jan Saliba
Public Affairs/Religious Liberty Trust, Karnik Doukmetzian

PERIODICAL

Canadian Adventist Messenger

The Swedenborgian Church

The Swedenborgian Church is a Christian Church founded on the Bible and the Writings of Emanuel Swedenborg (1688-1772). These Writings were first brought to Ontario in 1835 by Christian Enslin.

HEADQUARTERS

c/o Olivet Church, 279 Burnhamthorpe Rd., Etobicoke, ON M9B 1Z6 Tel. (416)239-3054
Media Contact, Exec. Vice-Pres., Rev. Michael D. Gladish

OFFICERS

Pres., Rt. Rev. P. M. Buss, Bryn Athyn, PA 19009
Exec. Vice-Pres., Rev. Michael D. Gladish
Sec., Penny Orr, 1286 Islington Ave.,#206, Etobicoke, ON M9A 3K1
Treas., James Bellinger, 182 Martin Grove Rd., Etobicoke, ON M9B 4L1

PERIODICAL

New Church Canadian

Syrian Orthodox Church of Antioch (Archdiocese of the United States and Canada)

An archdiocese of the Syrian Orthodox Church of Antioch in North America, the Syrian Orthodox Church professes the faith of the first three ecumenical councils of Nicaea, Constantinople and Ephesus and numbers faithful in the Middle East, India, the Americas, Europe and Australia. It traces its origin to the Patriarchate established in Antioch by St. Peter the Apostle and is under the supreme ecclesiastical jurisdiction of His Holiness the Syrian Orthodox Patriarch of Antioch and All the East, now residing in Damascus, Syria.

The Archdiocese of the Syrian Orthodox Church in the U.S. and Canada was formally established in 1957. The first Syrian Orthodox faithful came to Canada in the 1890s and formed the first Canadian parish in Sherbrooke, Quebec. Today four official parishes of the Archdiocese exist in Canada--two in Quebec and two in Ontario. There is also an official mission congregation in Calgary, Alberta.

HEADQUARTERS

Archdiocese of the U.S. & Canada, 49 Kipp Ave., Lodi, NJ 07644 Tel. (201)778-0638 Fax (201)-773-7506
Media Contact, Archdiocesan Gen. Sec., Very Rev. Chorepiscopus John Meno, 263 Elm Ave., Teaneck, NJ 07666 Tel. (201)928-1810 Fax (201)773-7506

OFFICERS

Primate, ----
Archdiocesan Gen. Sec., Very Rev. Chorepiscopus John Meno, 263 Elm Ave., Teaneck, NJ 07666 Tel. (201)928-1810

Ukrainian Orthodox Church of Canada

Toward the end of the 19th century many Ukrainian immigrants settled in Canada--1991 marked the centenary of this immigration. In 1918, these pioneers established the Ukrainian Orthodox Church of Canada, today the largest Ukrainian Orthodox Church beyond the borders of Ukraine.

HEADQUARTERS

Consistory of the Ukrainian Orthodox Church of Canada, 9 St. John's Ave., Winnipeg, MB R2W 1G8 Tel. (204)586-3093 Fax (204)582-5241
Media Contact, V. Rev. Dr. Ihor Kutash, 6270-12th Ave., Montreal, QC H1X 3A5 Tel. (514)727-2236 Fax (514)728-9834

OFFICERS

Presidium, Chpsn., Very Rev. Oleg Krawchenvo
Primate, Most Rev. Metropolitan Wasyly, 174 Seven Oaks Ave., Winnipeg, MB R2V 0K8

PERIODICAL

Visnyk: The Herald

Union of Spiritual Communities of Christ (Orthodox Doukhobors in Canada)

The Doukhobors are groups of Canadians of Russian origin living in the western provinces of Canada, but their beginnings in Russia are unknown. The name "Doukhobors," or "Spirit Wrestlers," was given in derision by the Russian Orthodox clergy in Russia as far back as 1785. Victims of decades of persecution in Russia, about 7,500 Doukhobors arrived in Canada in 1899.

The teaching of the Doukhobors is penetrated with the Gospel spirit of love. Worshiping God in the spirit they affirm that the outward church and all that is performed in it and concerns it has no importance for them; the church is where two or three are gathered together, united in the name of Christ. Their teaching is founded on tradition, which they call the "Book of Life," because it lives in their memory and hearts. In this book are sacred songs or chants, partly composed independently, partly formed out of the contents of the Bible, and these are committed to memory by each succeeding generation. Doukhobors observe complete pacifism and non-violence.

The Doukhobors were reorganized in 1938 by their leader, Peter P. Verigin, shortly before his death, into the Union of Spiritual Communities of Christ, commonly called Orthodox Doukhobors. It is headed by a democratically elected Executive Committee which executes the will and protects the interests of the people.

At least 99 percent of the Doukhobors are law-abiding, pay taxes, and "do not burn or bomb or parade in the nude" as they say a fanatical offshoot called the "Sons of Freedom" does.

HEADQUARTERS

USCC Central Office, Box 760, Grand Forks, BC V0H 1H0 Tel. (604)442-8252 Fax (604)442-3433

Media Contact, John J. Verigin, Sr.

OFFICERS

Hon. Chpsn. of the Exec. Comm., John J. Verigin, Sr.

Chpsn., Andrew Evin

Admn., S. W. Babakaiff

PERIODICAL

ISKRA

United Brethren Church in Canada

Founded in 1767 in Lancaster County, Pa., missionaries came to Canada about 1850. The first class was held in Kitchener in 1855, and the first building was erected in Port Elgin in 1867.

The Church of the United Brethren in Christ had its beginning with Philip William Otterbein and Martin Boehm, who were leaders in the revivalistic movement in Pennsylvania and Maryland during the late 1760s.

HEADQUARTERS

302 Lake St., Huntington, IN 46750 Tel. (219)356-2312 Fax (219)356-4730

GENERAL OFFICERS

Pres., Rev. Brian Magnus, 120 Fife Rd., Guelph, ON N1H 6Y2 Tel. (519)836-0180

Treas., Mr. Brian Winger, 2233 Hurontario St., Apt. 916, Mississauga, ON L5A 2E9

The United Church of Canada

The United Church of Canada was formed on June 10, 1925, through the union of the Methodist Church, Canada, the Congregational Union of Canada, the Council of Local Union Churches and 70 percent of the Presbyterian Church in Canada. The union culminated years of negotiation between the churches, all of which had integral associations with the development and history of the nation.

In fulfillment of its mandate to be a uniting as well as a United Church, the denomination has been enriched by other unions during its history. The Wesleyan Methodist Church of Bermuda joined in 1930. On January 1, 1968, the Canada Conference of the Evangelical United Brethren became part of The United Church of Canada. At various times, congregations of other Christian communions have also become congregations of the United Church.

The United Church of Canada is a full member of the World Methodist Council, the World Alliance of Reformed Churches (Presbyterian and Congregational), and the Canadian and World Councils of Churches.

The United Church is the largest Protestant denomination in Canada.

NATIONAL OFFICES

The United Church House, 3250 Bloor St. W., Etobicoke, ON M8X 2Y4 Tel. (416)231-5931 Fax (416)231-3103

Media Contact, Publicist, Mary-Frances Denis

GENERAL COUNCIL

Mod., Marion S. Best

Gen. Sec., K. Virginia Coleman

Management & Personnel, Sec., Anne Shirley Sutherland

Theology, Faith & Ecumenism, Sec., Rev. S. Peter Wyatt

Personnel Dir., Margaret C. Scriven

Archivist, Jean E. Dryden, 73 Queen's Park Cr., E., Toronto, ON M5C 1K7 Tel. (416)585-4563 Fax (416)585-4584

ADMINISTRATIVE DIVISIONS

Communication: Gen. Sec., ----

Finance: Int. Gen. Sec., Albion R. Wright

Ministry Personnel & Education: Int. Gen. Sec., Ann Naylor

Mission in Canada: Gen. Sec., Rev. David Iverson

World Outreach: Gen. Sec., Rhea Whitehead

CONFERENCE EXECUTIVE SECRETARIES

Alberta and Northwest: Rev. George H. Rodgers, 9911-48 Ave., Edmonton, AB T6E 5V6 Tel. (403)435-3995 Fax (403)434-0597

All Native Circle: Int. Speaker, Rev. William J. Hickerson, 18-399 Berry St., Winnipeg, MB R3J 1N6 Tel. (204)831-0740 Fax (204)837-9703

Bay of Quinte: Int., Rev. Carolyn A. Hudson, 218 Barrie St., Kingston, ON K7L 3K3 Tel. (613)-549-2503 Fax (613)549-1050

British Columbia: Rev. Brian D. Thorpe, 1955 W. 4th Ave., Vancouver, BC V6J 1M7 Tel. (604)-734-0434 Fax (604)734-7024

Hamilton: Rev. Roslyn A. Campbell, Box 100, Carlisle, ON L0R 1H0 Tel. (905)659-3343 Fax (905)659-7766

London: Rev. W. Peter Scott, 359 Windermere Rd., London, ON N6G 2K3 Tel. (519)672-1930 Fax (519)439-2800

Manitoba and Northwestern Ontario: Rev. Roger A. Coll, 120 Maryland St., Winnipeg, MB R3G 1L1 Tel. (204)786-8911 Fax (204)774-0159

Manitou: Rev. J. Stewart Bell, 1402 Regina St., North Bay, ON P1B 2L5 Tel. (705)474-3350 Fax (705)497-3597

Maritime: Rev. Catherine H. Craw, Box 1560, Sackville, NS E0A 3C0 Tel. (506)536-1334 Fax (506)536-2900

Montreal and Ottawa: Int., Dr. Charles Knight, 225-50 Ave., Lachine, QC H8T 2T7 Tel. (514)-634-7015 Fax (514)634-2489

Newfoundland and Labrador: Rev. Clarence R. Sellars, 320 Elizabeth Ave., St. John's, NF A1B 1T9 Tel. (709)754-0386 Fax (709)754-8336

Saskatchewan: Rev. Wilbert R. Wall, 418 A. McDonald St., Regina, SK S4N 6E1 Tel. (306)-721-3311 Fax (306)721-3171

Toronto: Rev. David W. Allen, 65 Mayall Ave., Downsview, ON M3L 1E7 Tel. (416)241-2677 Fax (416)241-2689

PERIODICALS

Fellowship Magazine; United Church Observer; Mandate

United Pentacostal Church in Canada

This body, which is affiliated with the United Pentecostal Church, International, with headquarters in Hazelwood, Mo., accepts the Bible standard of full salvation, which is repentance, baptism by immersion in the name of the Lord Jesus Christ for the remission of sins and the baptism of the Holy Ghost, with the initial signs of speaking in tongues as the Spirit gives utterance. Other tenets of faith include the Oneness of God in Christ, holiness, divine healing and the second coming of Jesus Christ.

HEADQUARTERS

United Pentecostal Church Intl., 8855 Dunn Rd., Hazelwood, MO 63042 Tel. (314)837-7300 Fax (314)837-4503

Media Contact, Gen. Sec.-Treas., Rev. C. M. Becton

DISTRICT SUPERINTENDENTS

Atlantic: Rev. Harry Lewis, P.O. Box 1046, Perth Andover, NB E0J 1V0

British Columbia: Rev. Paul V. Reynolds, 13447-112th Ave., Surrey, BC V3R 2E7

Canadian Plains: Rev. Johnny King, 615 North-mount Dr., NW, Calgary, AB T2K 3J6

Central Canadian: Rev. Clifford Heaslip, 4215 Roblin Blvd., Winnipeg, MB R3R 0E8

Newfoundland: Jack Cunningham

Nova Scotia: Superintendent, Rev. Jack D. Mean, P.O. Box 2183, D.E.P.S., Dartmouth, NS B2W 3Y2

Ontario: Rev. Carl H. Stephenson, 63 Castlegrove Blvd., Don Mills, ON M3A 1L3

Universal Fellowship of Metropolitan Community Churches

The Universal Fellowship of Metropolitan Community Churches is a Christian church which directs a special ministry within, and on behalf of, the gay and lesbian community. Involvement, however, is not exclusively limited to gays and lesbians; U.F.M.C.C. tries to stress its openness to all people and does not call itself a "gay church."

Founded in 1968 in Los Angeles by the Rev. Troy Perry, the U.F.M.C.C. has over 250 member congregations worldwide. Eleven congregations are in Canada; Vancouver, Edmonton, Windsor, London, Toronto, Ottawa, Winnipeg, Halifax, Barrie and Belleville.

Theologically, the Metropolitan Community Churches stand within the mainstream of Christian doctrine, being "ecumenical" or "interdenominational" in stance (albeit a "denomination" in their own right).

The Metropolitan Community Churches are characterized by their belief that the love of God is a gift, freely offered to all people, regardless of sexual orientation and that no incompatibility exists between human sexuality and the Christian faith.

The Metropolitan Community Churches in Canada were founded in Toronto in 1973 by the Rev. Robert Wolfe.

HEADQUARTERS

Media Contact, Marcie Wexler, 33 Holly St., #1117, Toronto, ON M4S 2G8 Tel. (416)487-8429 Fax (416)932-1836

OFFICERS

Western Canada District: Rev. Bev Baptiste, 3531 33rd Ave., Edmonton, AB T6L 4N6 Tel. (403)-490-0478

Eastern Canada District: Rev. Marcie Wexler, 33 Holly St., #1117, Toronto, ON M4S 2G8 Tel. (416)487-8429

The Wesleyan Church of Canada

This group is the Canadian portion of The Wesleyan Church which consists of the Atlantic and Central Canada districts. The Central Canada District of the former Wesleyan Methodist Church of America was organized at Winchester, Ontario, in 1889 and the Atlantic District was founded in 1888 as the Alliance of the Reformed Baptist Church, which merged with the Wesleyan Methodist Church in July, 1966.

The Wesleyan Methodist Church and the Pilgrim Holiness Church merged in June, 1968, to become The Wesleyan Church. The doctrine is evangelical and Arminian and stresses holiness beliefs. For more details, consult the U.S. listing under The Wesleyan Church.

HEADQUARTERS

The Wesleyan Church Intl. Center, P.O. Box 50434, Indianapolis, IN 46250-0434

Media Contact, Dist. Supt., Central Canada, Rev. S. Allan Summers, 3 Applewood Dr., Ste. 102, Belleville, ON K8P 4E3 Tel. (613)966-7527 Fax (613)968-6190

DISTRICT SUPERINTENDENTS

Central Canada: Rev. Donald E. Hodgins, 3 Applewood Dr., Ste.101, Belleville, ON K8P 4E3

Atlantic: Rev. Ray E. Barnwell, P.O. Box 20, 41 Summit Ave., Sussex, NB E0E 1P0 Tel. (506)-433-1007

PERIODICAL

Central Canada Clarion

RELIGIOUS BODIES IN CANADA ARRANGED BY FAMILIES

The following list of religious bodies appearing in the preceding directory, "Religious Bodies in Canada," shows the "families" or related clusters into which Canadian religious bodies can be grouped. For example, there are many bodies that can be grouped under the heading "Baptist" for historical and theological reasons. It is not to be assumed, however, that all denominations under one family heading are necessarily similar in belief or practice. Often any similarity is purely coincidental since ethnicity, theological divergence and even political and personality factors have shaped the directions denominational groups have taken.

Family categories provide one of the major pitfalls of church statistics because of the tendency to combine statistics by "families" for analytical and comparative purposes. Such combined totals are almost meaningless, although often used as variables for sociological analysis.

Religious bodies not grouped under family headings appear alphabetically and are not indented in the following list.

American Evangelical Christian Churches of Canada
The Anglican Church of Canada
Apostolic Christian Church (Nazarene)
Armenian Evangelical Church
Associated Gospel Churches

Baptist Bodies

- *Association of Regular Baptist Churches (Canada)*
- *Baptist General Conference of Canada*
  - The Central Canada Baptist Conference
  - Baptist General Conference in Alberta
  - British Columbia Baptist Conference
- *Canadian Baptist Ministries*
  - Baptist Convention of Ontario and Québec
  - Baptist Union of Western Canada
  - Union d'Églises Baptistes Françaises au Canada
  - United Baptist Convention of the Atlantic Provinces
- *Canadian Convention of Southern Baptists*
- *The Fellowship of Evangelical Baptist Churches in Canada*
- *Free Will Baptists*
- *North American Baptist Conference*

The Bible Holiness Movement
Brethren in Christ Church, Canadian Conference
Canadian District of the Moravian Church in America, Northern Province
Canadian Yearly Meeting of the Religious Society of Friends
Christ Catholic Church
Christian and Missionary Alliance in Canada
Christian Brethren (aka Plymouth Brethren)
Church of God (Anderson, Ind.)
Church of the Nazarene Canada

Churches of Christ—Christian Churches

- *Christian Church (Disciples of Christ) in Canada*
- *Churches of Christ in Canada*

Congregational Christian Churches in Canada

Doukhobors

- *Union of Spiritual Communities of Christ (Orthodox Doukhobors in Canada)*

Eastern Churches

- *The Antiochian Orthodox Christian Archdiocese of North America*
- *Armenian Holy Apostolic Church--Canadian Diocese*
- *The Coptic Church in Canada*
- *Greek Orthodox Diocese of Toronto (Canada)*
- *Orthodox Church in America (Canada Section)*
- *Patriarchal Parishes of the Russian Orthodox Church in Canada*
- *Romanian Orthodox Church in America (Canadian Parishes)*
- *The Romanian Orthodox Episcopate of America (Jackson, MI)*
- *Serbian Orthodox Church in the U.S.A. and Canada, Diocese of Canada*
- *Syrian Orthodox Church of Antioch (Archdiocese of the United States and Canada)*
- *Ukrainian Orthodox Church of Canada*

The Evangelical Covenant Church of Canada
The Evangelical Missionary Church of Canada
Evangelical Free Church of Canada
Independent Holiness Church
Jehovah's Witnesses

Latter-Day Saints

- *The Church of Jesus Christ of Latter-day Saints in Canada*
- *Reorganized Church of Jesus Christ of Latter Day Saints*

Lutherans

- *Church of the Lutheran Brethren*
- *The Estonian Evangelical Lutheran Church*
- *Evangelical Lutheran Church in Canada*
- *The Latvian Evangelical Lutheran Church in America*
- *Lutheran Church—Canada*

Mennonite Bodies

- *Church of God in Christ (Mennonite)*
- *Canadian Conference of Mennonite Brethren Churches*
- *Conference of Mennonites in Canada*
- *The Evangelical Mennonite Conference of Canada*
- *Evangelical Mennonite Mission Conference*
- *Mennonite Church (Canada)*
- *Old Order Amish Church*
- *Reinland Mennonite Church*

Methodist Bodies

British Methodist Episcopal Church of Canada
Free Methodist Church in Canada
The Wesleyan Church of Canada

The Old Catholic Church of Canada

Pentecostal Bodies

The Apostolic Church in Canada
Apostolic Church of Pentecost of Canada Inc.
Church of God (Cleveland, Tenn.)
The Church of God of Prophecy in Canada
Elim Fellowship of Evangelical Churches and Ministers
Foursquare Gospel Church of Canada
Independent Assemblies of God International (Canada)
The Italian Pentecostal Church of Canada
The Open Bible Standard Churches of Canada
The Pentecostal Assemblies of Canada
Pentecostal Assemblies of Newfoundland
United Pentecostal Church of Canada

Presbyterian Bodies

Presbyterian Church in America (Canadian Section)
The Presbyterian Church in Canada

Reformed Bodies

Canadian and American Reformed Churches
Christian Reformed Church in North America
Reformed Church in Canada
The United Church of Canada

The Reformed Episcopal Church of Canada

The Roman Catholic Church in Canada

The Salvation Army in Canada

Seventh-day Adventist Church in Canada

The Swedenborgian Church

United Brethren Church in Canada

Universal Fellowship of Metropolitan Community Churches

5. OTHER RELIGIONS IN CANADA AND THE UNITED STATES

People in Canada and the United States participate in a wide variety of religious organizations. Some of those that do not claim to be Christian are listed below.

OTHER RELIGIONS

Bahá'í Faith

The Bahá'í Faith, the most widespread religion after Christianity, is an independent world religion whose teachings are the oneness of God, the oneness of religion, and the oneness of humanity. Bahá'is promote the unity of mankind and the establishment of world peace by advancing such principles as the cause of universal education, the eradication of all prejudices, the emanicipation of women, the agreement of science and religion, the elimination of the extremes of wealth and poverty, the adoption of a universal auxiliary language and the establishment of a world federal system.

U.S. HEADQUARTERS

National Spiritual Assembly, 536 Sheridan Rd., Wilmette, IL 60091 Tel. (708)869-9039 Fax (708)869-0247

Media Contact, Dir. of Public Information, Trish Swanson Blaine, 866 U.N. Plaza, Ste. 120, New York, NY 10017 Tel. (212)803-2500 Fax (212)-803-2573

CANADIAN HEADQUARTERS

Bahá'í National Centre of Canada, 7200 Leslie St., Thornhill, ON L3T 6L8 Tel. (416)889-8168 Fax (416)889-8184

Media Contact, Dir., Dept. of Public Affairs, Dr. Gerald Filson, 7200 Leslie St., Thornhill, ON L3T 6L8 Tel. (416)889-8168 Fax (416)889-8184

Buddhist Churches

Founded in 1899, organized in 1914 as the Buddhist Mission of North America, this body was incorporated in 1944 under the present name and represents the Jodo Shinshu Sect of Buddhism affiliated with the Hongwanji-ha Hongwanji denomination in the continental United States. It is a school of Buddhism which believes in becoming aware of the ignorant self and relying upon the infinite wisdom and compassion of Amida Buddha, which is expressed in sincere gratitude through the recitation of the Nembutsu, Namu Amida Butsu.

In Canada, the Buddhist Churches were first established in 1904. This body is the Mahayana division of Buddhism, and its sectarian belief is the Pure Land School based on the Three Canonical Scriptures with emphasis on pure faith.

U.S. HEADQUARTERS

1710 Octavia St., San Francisco, CA 94109 Tel. (415)776-5600 Fax (415)771-6293

Media Contact, Admn. Ofc., Henry N. Shibata

CANADIAN HEADQUARTERS

4860 Garry St., Richmond, BC V7E 2V2 Tel. (604)272-3330 Fax (604)272-6865

Media Contact, Bishop Yoshihide Matsubayashi, Ed.D.

Ethical Culture Movement

The American Ethical Union is a federation of Ethical Culture/Ethical Humanist Societies. Ethical Culture, founded in 1876 in New York by Felix Adler, is a humanistic religious and educational movement, based on the primacy of ethics, the belief in intrinsic worth of every human being and the faith in the capacity of human beings to act in their personal relationships and in the larger community to help create a better world.

HEADQUARTERS

2 West 64th St., New York, NY 10023 Tel. (212)-873-6500

Media Contact, Margaretha E. Jones

Jewish Organizations

There are organized Jewish communities throughout Canada and the United States. Jews arrived in the colonies before 1650. The first congregation, the Shearith Israel (Remnant of Israel), is recorded in New York City in 1654.

A few Jews came north to Halifax from the Atlantic Colonies as early as 1752. The Colony of Lower Canada (now Quebec) had the first considerable settlement and it was there that, in 1768, a synagogue was organized.

US HEADQUARTERS

Orthodox Judaism: Union of Orthodox Jewish Congregations in America, Dr. Mandell Ganchrow, 333 Seventh Ave., New York, NY 10001 Tel. (212)563-4000 Fax (212)564-9058

Conservative Judaism: United Synagogue of Conservative Judaism, Alan Ades, 155 Fifth Ave., New York, NY 10010 Tel. (212)533-7800 Fax (212)353-9439

Reconstructionist Judaism: Federation of Reconstructionist Congregations, Church Rd. and Greenwood Ave., Wyncote, PA 19095 Tel. (215)887-1988 Fax (215)576-6143

CANADIAN HEADQUARTERS

3101 Bathurst St. #400, Toronto, ON M6A 2A6 Tel. (416)789-3351 Fax (416)789-9436

U.S. PERIODICALS

Tradition: A Journal of Orthodox Jewish Thought; Conservative Judaism; American Jewish History; Jewish Action; CCAR Journal: A Reform Jewish Quarterly; Reconstructionism Today; Judaism

CANADIAN PERIODICALS

Canadian Jewish News; Canadian Jewish Outlook; Jewish Standard

Muslims

Islam claims several million adherents in the United States and Canada. Some are Muslims who have immigrated from many parts of the world.

Others are Americans and Canadians who converted to Islam. In addition to the citizens who are Muslims, there are many who come to America temporarily as Muslim diplomats, students and those who work in international institutions such as the World Bank, the International Monetary Fund and the United Nations.

Many Islamic organizations exist under such titles as Islamic Society, Islamic Center or Muslim Mosque. The aim is to provide a group in a locality with a place of worship and of meeting for other religious, social and educational purposes. These societies and organizations are not regarded as religious sects or divisions. All the groups hold the same beliefs and aspire to practice the same rituals: prayers, fasting, alms giving and pilgrimage to Makkah.

REGIONAL AND NATIONAL GROUPS

The Islamic Center of Washington, 2551 Massachusetts Ave., Washington, DC 20008 Tel. (202)332-8343

Federation of Islamic Associations in the US and Can., 25351 Five Mile Rd., Redford Twp., MI 48239 Tel. (313)534-3295 Fax (313)534-1474

Council of Muslim Communities of Canada, Dir. Dr. Mir Iqbal Ali, 1250 Ramsey View Ct., Ste. 504, Sudbury, ON P3E 2E7 Tel. (705)522-2948

U.S. PERIODICALS

Islamic Horizons

Sikh

Sikhs are found in all major cities of the United States and Canada.

Sikhism was born in the northwestern part of the Indo-Pakistan sub-continent in Punjab province about 500 years ago. Guru Nanak, founder of the religion, was born in 1469. He was followed by nine successor Gurus. The Guruship was then bestowed on the Sikh Holy Book, popularly known as the Guru Granth.

The Granth contains writings of the Sikh Gurus and some Hindu and Muslim saints and was compiled by the fifth Guru, Arjan Dev. For the Sikhs, the Granth is the only object of worship. It contains hymns of praise of God, the Formless One.

Another Sikh group is the Sikh Dharma, founded in 1968 by Yogi Bhajah in Los Angeles. This group is the primary Sikh community operating among non-Punjabis in the western hemisphere. They are found, among other places, in New Mexico and California.

HEADQUARTERS

Sikh Council of North America, 95-30 118th Street, Richmond Hill, NY 11419

Sikh Dharma International, Head Minister, Siri Singh Sahib Harbhjan Singh Khalsa Yogiji, Rte 3 Box 132D, Espenola, NM 87532 Tel. (310)-552-3416 Fax (505)557-8414

Unitarian Universalist Association

The Unitarian Universalist Association is the consolidated body of the former American Unitarian Association and the Universalist Church of America.

The Unitarian movement arose in congregationalism in the 18th century, producing the American Unitarian Association in 1825. In 1865 a national conference was organized. The philosophy of Universalism originated with the doctrine of universal salvation in the first century and was brought to America in the 18th century. Universalists were first formally organized in 1793.

In May, 1961, the Unitarian and Universalist bodies were consolidated to become the Unitarian Universalist Association. The movement is noncreedal. The UUA has observer status with the National Council of Churches.

HEADQUARTERS

25 Beacon St., Boston, MA 02108 Tel. (617)742-2100 Fax (617)367-3237

Media Contact, Dir. of Publ. Info., Deborah Weiner

Vedanta Societies

These societies are followers of the Vedas, the scriptures of the Indo-Aryans, doctrines expounded by Swami Vivekananda at the Parliament of Religions, Chicago, 1893. There are 13 such Centers in the United States and one in Canada. All are under the spiritual guidance of the Ramakrishna Mission, organized by Swami Vivekananda in India.

HEADQUARTERS

34 W. 71st St., New York, NY 10023 Tel. (212)-877-9197 Fax (212)769-4280

Media Contact, John Schlenck

6. UNITED STATES REGIONAL AND LOCAL ECUMENICAL AGENCIES

One of the many ways Christians and Christian churches relate to one another locally and regionally is through ecumenical agencies. The membership in these ecumenical organizations is diverse. Historically, councils of churches were formed primarily by Protestants, but many local and regional organizations now include Orthodox and Roman Catholics. Many are made up of congregations or judicatory units of churches. Some have a membership-base of individuals. Others foster cooperation between ministerial groups, community ministries, coalitions or church agencies. While Councils of Churches is a term still commonly used to describe this form of cooperation, other terms such as "conference of churches," "ecumenical councils," "churches united," "metropolitan ministries," are coming into use.

Ecumenical organizations that are national in scope are listed in section 1, "Cooperative Organizations."

An increasing number of ecumenical agencies have been exploring ways to strengthen the interreligious aspect of life in the context of religious pluralism in the U.S. today. Some organizations in this listing are interfaith agencies primarily through the inclusion of Jewish congregations in their membership. Other organizations nurture partnerships with a broader base of religious groups in their communities, especially in the areas of public policy and interreligious dialogue.

This list does not include all local and regional ecumenical and interfaith organizations in existence today. For information about other groups contact the Ecumenical Networks Working Group of the National Council of the Churches of Christ in the U.S.A., Director, Dr. Kathleen S. Hurty, Room 868, New York, NY 10115-0050. Tel. (212)870-2155. Fax (212)870-2158.

The terms regional and local are relative, making identification somewhat ambiguous. Regional councils may cover sections of large states or cross state borders. Local councils may be made up of several counties, towns or clusters of congregations. State councils or state-level ecumenical contacts exist in 47 of the 50 states. These state-level or multi-state organizations are marked with a "*" and are the first listing for each state. Other listings are in alphabetical order under the state. Consult the index to find organizations if the state is not known.

ALABAMA

Greater Birmingham Ministries

2304 12th Ave. N, Birmingham, AL 35234-3111 Tel. (205)326-6821 Fax (205)252-8458

Media Contact, Scott Douglas

Exec. Dir., Scott Douglas

Economic Justice, Co-Chpsn.: Helen Holdefer; Karnie Smith

Direct Services, Chpsn., Benjamin Greene

Finance & Fund-Raising, Chpsn., Dick Sales

Pres., Hattie Belle Lester

Sec., Carolyn Crawford

Treas., Chris Hamlin

Major activities: Direct Service Ministries (Food, Utilities, Rent and Nutrition Education, Shelter); Alabama Arise (Statewide legislative network focusing on low income issues); Economic Justice Issues (Low Income Housing and Advocacy, Health Care, Community Development, Jobs Creation, Public Transportation); Faith in Community Ministries (Interchurch Forum, Interpreting and Organizing, Bible Study)

Interfaith Mission Service

411-B Holmes Ave. NE, Huntsville, AL 35801 Tel. (205)536-2401 Fax (205)536-2402

Exec. Min., Rev. Robert Loshuertos, 411-B Holmes Ave. NE, Huntsville, AL 35801 Tel. (205)-536-2401 Fax (205)536-2402

Exec. Min., Rev. Robert Loshuertos

Pres., Rev. John Bush

Major activities: Foodline & Food Pantry; Emergency Funds; Local FEMA Committee; Ministry Development; Clergy Luncheon; Workshops; Evaluation of Member Ministries; Response to Community Needs; Information and Referral; Police Department Chaplains; Interfaith Understanding; Christian Unity; Gang, Violence & Drug Taskforce; Homeless Needs

ALASKA

*Alaska Christian Conference

First Presbyterian Church, 1375 E. Bogard Rd., Wasilla, AK 99687 Tel. (907)376-5053

Media Contact, Pres., Dr. Gene Straatmeyer

Pres., Dr. Gene Straatmeyer

Vice-Pres., Barbara Block, 3840 O'Malley Rd., Anchorage, AK 99516

Sec., Phyllis Sullivan, 1725 Tillicum Ave., Wasilla, AK 99654

Treas., Mary Kron, 9650 Arlene Dr., Anchorage, AK 99515

Major activities: Legislative & Social Concerns; Resources and Continuing Education; New Ecumenical Ministries; Communication; Alcoholism (Education & Prevention); Family Violence (Education & Prevention); Native Issues; Ecumenical/Theological Dialogue; HIV/AIDS Education and Ministry; Criminal Justice

ARIZONA

*Arizona Ecumenical Council

4423 N. 24th St., Ste. 750, Phoenix, AZ 85016 Tel. (602)468-3818 Fax (602)468-3839

Media Contact, Pres., Mr. Bernard Barkman, 2431 W. Tierra Buena Ln., Phoenix, AZ 85023 Tel. (602)967-6040 Fax (602)468-3839

Exec. Dir., Dr. Paul Eppinger

Pres., Bishop Howard E. Wennes, 4423 N. 24th St. Ste. 400, Phoenix, AZ 85016

Major activities: Donohoe Ecumenical Forum Series; Political Action Team; Legislative Workshop; Arizona Ecumenical Indian Concerns Committee; Mexican/American Border Issues; VISN-TV; Disaster Relief; Break Violence-Build Community; Truckin' for Kids; "Souper Bowl"; Gun Info. and Safety Program

ARKANSAS

*Arkansas Interfaith Conference

P.O. Box 151, Scott, AR 72142 Tel. (501)961-2626
Media Contact, Conf. Exec., Mimi Dortch, Tel. (501)961-2626
Conf. Exec., Mimi Dortch
Pres., Rev. Jesse Yarborough, Christ Episcopal Church, 501 S. Scott St., Little Rock, AR 72201
Sec., Rabbi Eugene Levy, Temple Binai Israel, 3700 Rodney Pauhan Rd., Little Rock, AR 72212
Treas., Mr. Jim Davis, Box 7239, Little Rock, AR 72217
Major activities: Task Force on Hunger; Task Force on Violence; Institutional Ministry; Interfaith Executives' Advisory Council; Drug Abuse, Interfaith Relations; Church Women United; IMPACT; AIDS Task Force; Our House-Shelter; Governor's Task Force on Education; Statewide Fair Trial Committee Legislation; Ecumenical Choir Camp; Interreligious Health Care

CALIFORNIA

*California Council of Churches/California Church Impact

1300 N. St., Sacramento, CA 95814 Tel. (916)442-5447 Fax (916)442-3036
Media Contact, Exec. Dir., Patricia Whitney-Wise
Exec. Dir., Patricia Whitney-Wise
Assoc. Dir., Scott Anderson
Major activities: Monitoring State Legislation; Calif. IMPACT Network; Legislative Principles; Food Policy Advocacy; Family Welfare Issues; Health; Church/State Issues; Violence Prevention

*Northern California Ecumenical Council

942 Market St., No. 301, San Francisco, CA 94102 Tel. (415)434-0670 Fax (415)434-3110
Media Contact, Juliet Twomey
Exec. Dir., ----
Pres., Nancy Nielsen
Vice-Pres., ----
Sec., Allan Solomonow
Treas., James Faulk
Program Dir., Juliet Twomey
Major activities: Peace with Justice; Faith and Witness; Unlearning Racism Training; Public Policy Advocacy

*Southern California Ecumenical Council

54 N. Oakland Ave., Pasadena, CA 91101 Tel. (818)578-6371 Fax (818)578-6358
Pres., The Rev. Barb Mudge
Ecology Task Force, Dir., Rev. Al Cohen
Faith & Order Commission, Dir., Rev. Rod Parrott
Faith & Values Cable TV Regional Comm., Dir., Ms. Nyla LaDuke
Hope Publishing, Dir., Ms. Faith Sand
Interfaith Taskforce of S. Africa, Dir., Rev. Hans Holborn
Major activities: Consultation with the regional religious sector concerning the well being and spiritual vitality of this most diverse and challenging area

Council of Churches of Contra Costa County

1543 Sunnyvale Ave., Walnut Creek, CA 94596 Tel. (510)933-6030
Media Contact, Dir., Rev. Machrina L. Blasdell
Dir., Rev. Machrina L. Blasdell
Chaplains: Rev. Charles Tinsley; Rev. Duane Woida; Rev. Harold Wright
Pres., Ms. Vernita Kenner
Treas., Mr. Bertram Sturm
Major activities: Institutional Chaplaincies, Community Education

Ecumenical Ministries of Northern California

1449 Creekside Dr., No. 1055, Walnut Creek, CA 94596 Tel. (415)923-9595
Media Contact, Neil Housewright
Exec. Dir., Neil Housewright
Major activities: Ecumenical Dialogue; Peace and Justice; Human Services

Fresno Metropolitan Ministry

1055 N. Van Ness, Ste. H, Fresno, CA 93728 Tel. (209)485-1416 Fax (209)485-9109
Media Contact, Exec. Dir., Rev. Walter P. Parry
Exec. Dir., Rev. Walter P. Parry
Admn. Asst., Sandy Sheldon
Pres., Rev. Gail McDougle-Roy
Major activities: Hunger Relief Advocacy; Homelessness, Human Relations and Anti-Racism; Cross Cultural Mental Health; Health Care Advocacy; Public Education Concerns; Children's Needs; Biblical and Theological Education For Laity; Refugee Advocacy; Ecumenical & Interfaith Celebrations & Cooperation; Youth Needs; Community Network Building

Interfaith Service Bureau

3720 Folsom Blvd., Sacramento, CA 95816 Tel. (916)456-3815
Media Contact, Interim Dir., Dexter McNamara
Interim Dir., Dexter McNamara
Pres.: Lloyd Hanson
Vice-Pres.: Fenton Williams
Major activities: Food Bank Program (Interfaith Foodlink); Clergy Concerns Committee; Religious Cable Television; Brown Bag Network (ages 60 & up); Faith in Crisis; Refugee Support; Sacramento Area Interfaith Flood Relief

Marin Interfaith Council

35 Mitchell Blvd., Ste. 13, San Rafael, CA 94903 Tel. (415)492-1052
Media Contact, Rev. Linda Compton, 35 Mitchell Blvd. # 13, San Rafael, CA 94903 Tel. (415)492-1052 Fax (415)492-8907
Exec. Dir., Rev. Linda Compton
Major activities: Interfaith Dialogue; Education; Advocacy; Convening; Interfaith Worship Services & Commemorations; Three Commissions: Basic Human Needs; Values & the Public Good; Religious Leadership Development for Lay & Clergy

Pacific and Asian American Center for Theology and Strategies (PACTS)

Graduate Theological Union, 2400 Ridge Rd., Berkeley, CA 94709 Tel. (510)849-0653
Media Contacts: Deborah Lee; Ron Nakasone
Dir., Deborah Lee

Pres., Rosadia Escueta
Major activities: Collect and Disseminate Resource Materials; Training Conferences; Public Seminars; Women in Ministry; Racial and Ethnic Minority Concerns; Journal and Newsletter; Hawaii & Greater Pacific Programme; Sale of Sadao Watanabe Calendars; Informational Forums on Peace & Social Justice in Asian Pacific American Community and Asia/Pacific Internationally

Pomona Inland Valley Council of Churches

1753 N. Park Ave., Pomona, CA 91768 Tel. (909)-622-3806 Fax (909)622-0484
Media Contact, Dir. of Development, Don Hafner
Pres., Lynn Jackson
Exec. Dir., Ms. Joyce Ewen
Sec., Ken Coates
Treas., T. J. Liggett
Major activities: Advocacy and Education for Social Justice; Ecumenical Celebrations; Hunger Advocacy; Emergency Food and Shelter Assistance; Farmer's Market; Affordable Housing; Transitional Housing

San Diego County Ecumenical Conference

4075 Park Bldg., San Diego, CA 92103
Media Contact, Exec. Dir., Rev. Glenn S. Allison, P.O. Box 3628, San Diego, CA 92163 Tel. (619)-296-4557
Exec. Dir., Rev. Glenn S. Allison
Admn., Patricia R. Munley
Pres., Rev. Nancy R. McMaster
Treas., Joseph Ramsey
Major activities: Interfaith Shelter Network/Transitional Housing for the Homeless; Emerging Issues; Faith Order & Witness; Worship & Celebration; Ecumenical Tribute Dinner; Advent Prayer Breakfast; AIDS Chaplaincy Program; Third World Opportunies; Vigil Against Violence Events; Seminars and Workshops; Called to Dance Assn.; S.D. Names Project *Quilt*

San Fernando Valley Interfaith Council

10824 Topanga Canyon Blvd., No. 7, Chatsworth, CA 91311 Tel. (818)718-6460 Fax (818)718-8694
Media Contact, Dir., Public Relations, Arlene C. Landon
Exec. Dir., Barry Smedberg
Pres., Rev. Dr. Dudley Chatman
Major activities: Seniors Multi-Purpose Centers; Nutrition & Services; Meals to Homebound; Meals on Wheels; Interfaith Reporter; Interfaith Relations; Interfaith AIDS Committee; Social Adult Day Care; Hunger/Homelessness; Volunteer Care-Givers; Clergy Gatherings; Food Pantries and Outreach; Social Concerns; Aging; Hunger; Human Relations; Child Abuse Program; Medical Service; Homeless Program; Earthquake Response Preparedness

South Coast Ecumenical Council

3326 Magnolia Ave., Long Beach, CA 90806 Tel. (310)595-0268 Fax (310)595-0268
Media Contact, Exec. Dir., Rev. Ginny Wagener
Exec. Dir., Rev. Ginny Wagener
Interfaith Action for the Aging, Cathy Trott
Good Samaritan Counseling Ctr.: Dr. Lester Kim; Dr. William Scar
Farmers' Markets, Rev. Dale Whitney
Sage House, Rev. Charles Kothe
Pres., Joel Hummel
Major activities: Homeless Support Services; Interfaith Action for Aging; Farmers' Markets; Hunger Projects; Lay Academy of Religion; Church Athletic Leagues; Community Action; Hunger Walks; Christian Unity Worships; Interreligious Dialogue; Justice Advocacy; Martin Luther King, Jr. Celebration; Violence Prevention

The Council of Churches of Santa Clara County

1229 Naglee Ave., San Jose, CA 95126 Tel. (408)-297-2660 Fax (408)297-2661
Media Contact, Assoc. Dir., Nina Klepac
Exec. Dir., Rev. Hugh Wire
Pres., Rev. John L. Freesemann
Assoc. Dir., Nina Klepac
Major activities: Social Education/Action; Ecumenical and Interfaith Witness; Affordable Housing; Environmental Ministry; Family/Children

The Ecumenical Council of the Pasadena Area Churches

P.O. Box 41125, Pasadena, CA 91114-8125 Tel. (818)797-2402
Media Contact, Exec. Dir., Rev. Dr. Donald R. Locher
Exec. Dir., Rev. Dr. Donald R. Locher
Pres., Rev. Dr. Byron Light
Major activities: Christian Education; Community Worship; Community Concerns; Christian Unity; Ethnic Ministries; Hunger; Peace; Food, Clothing Assistance for the Poor; Emergency Shelter Line

Westside Interfaith Council

P.O. Box 1402, Santa Monica, CA 90406 Tel. (310)394-1518 Fax (310)576-1895
Media Contact, Rev. Janet A. Bregar
Exec. Dir., Rev. Janet A. Bregar
Major activities: Meals on Wheels; Community Religious Services; Convalescent Hospital Chaplaincy; Homeless Partnership; Hunger & Shelter Coalition

COLORADO

*Colorado Council of Churches

1234 Bannock St., Denver, CO 80204-3631 Tel. (303)825-4910 Fax (303)534-1266
Media Contact, Exec. Dir., Rev. Lucia Guzman
Pres., Rev. Leonard Jepson
Staff Assoc, Heather Thomas
Staff Assoc., Meggie Roe
Major activities: Institutional Ministries; Human Needs and Economic Issues (Includes Homelessness, Migrant Ministry, Justice in the Workplace); World Peace and Global Affairs; Religion in the Media; Interreligious Dialogue

Interfaith Council of Boulder

3700 Baseline Rd., Boulder, CO 80303 Tel. (303)-494-8094
Media Contact, Pres., Stan Adamson
Pres., Stan Adamson

Major activities: Interfaith Dialogue and Programs; Thanksgiving Worship Services; Food for the Hungry; Share-A-Gift; Monthly Newsletter

CONNECTICUT

*Christian Conference of Connecticut (CHRISCON)

60 Lorraine St., Hartford, CT 06105 Tel. (203)236-4281 Fax (203)236-9977
Media Contact, Exec. Dir., Rev. Stephen J. Sidorak, Jr.
Exec. Dir., Rev. Stephen J. Sidorak, Jr.
Exec. Asst., Sharon Anderson
Admn. Asst., Mildred Robertson
Pres., Mrs. Elisabeth C. Miller
Vice-Pres., The Most Rev. Daniel A. Cronin
Sec., The Rev. George B. Elia
Treas., Mr. Thomas F. Sarubbi
Major activities: Communications; Institutional Ministries; Conn. Bible Society; Conn. Council on Alcohol Problems; Ecumenical Forum; Faith & Order; Social Concerns; Public Policy

Association of Religious Communities

213 Main St., Danbury, CT 06810 Tel. (203)792-9450
Media Contact, Exec. Dir., Samuel E. Deibler, Jr.
Exec. Dir., Samuel E. Deibler, Jr.
Pres., The Rev. Michael Coburn
Major activities: Refugee Resettlement, Family Counseling; Family Violence Prevention; Affordable Housing

Center City Churches

170 Main St., Hartford, CT 06106-1817 Tel. (860)-728-3201 Fax (860)724-1777
Media Contact, Exec. Dir., Paul C. Christie
Exec. Dir., Paul C. Christie
Pres., David Hetzel, Esq.
Sec., Tim Cole
Treas., Ann Morrissey
Major activities: Senior Services; Family Support Center; Energy Bank; Crisis Intervention; After School Tutoring; Summer Day Camp; Housing for Persons with AIDS; Mental Health Residence; Community Soup Kitchen; Job Training for Homeless

Christian Community Action

98 S. Main St., South Norwalk, CT 06854 Tel. (203)854-1811
Dir., Jacquelyn P. Miller
Major activities: Emergency Food Program; Used Furniture; Loans for Emergencies; Loans for Rent, Security and Fuel

Christian Community Action

168 Davenport Ave., New Haven, CT 06519 Tel. (203)777-7848 Fax (203)777-7923
Exec. Dir., The Rev. Bonita Grubbs
Major activities: Emergency Food Program; Used Furniture & Clothing; Loans for Rent, Security and Fuel; Emergency Housing for Families; Advocacy

Council of Churches and Synagogues of Southwestern Connecticut

628 Main St., Stamford, CT 06901 Tel. (203)348-2800 Fax (203)358-0627
Media Contact, Communications Ofc., Doreen LeMoult
Major activities: Partnership Against Hunger; The Food Bank of Lower Fairfield County; HARVEST; Table to Table; Interfaith Caregivers, Friendly Visitors and Friendly Shoppers; Senior Neighborhood Support Services; Christmas in April; Adopt A House; Interfaith; Programming; Prison Visitation; Friendship House

Council of Churches of Greater Bridgeport, Inc.

943-961 Main St., Bridgeport, CT 06604 Tel. (203)334-1121 Fax (203)367-8113
Media Contact, Exec. Dir., Rev. John S. Kidd
Exec. Dir., Rev. John S. Kidd
Pres., Rev. Richard Yerrington
Sec., Mrs. Dorothy Allsop
Treas., Christine Watkins
Major activities: Youth in Crisis; Youth Shelter; Criminal Justice; Hospital, Nursing Home and Jail Ministries; Local Hunger; Ecumenical Relations, Prayer and Celebration; Covenantal Ministries; Homework Help; Summer Programs; Race/Relations/Bridge Building

Manchester Area Conference of Churches

P.O. Box 773, Manchester, CT 06045-0773 Tel. (203)649-2093
Media Contact, Exec. Dir., Denise Cabana
Exec. Dir., Denise Cabana
Dir. of Human Ministries, Joseph Piescik
Dept. of Human Needs, Dir., Karen Bergin
Pres., Rev. Charles Ericson
Vice-Pres., Theresa Ghabrial
Sec., Jean Richert
Treas., Clive Perrin
Major activities: Provision of Basic Needs (Food, Fuel, Clothing, Furniture); Emergency Aid Assistance; Emergency Shelter; Soup Kitchen; Reentry Assistance to Ex-Offenders; Pastoral Care in Local Institutions; Interfaith Day Camp; Advocacy for the Poor; Ecumenical Education and Worship

New Britain Area Conference of Churches (NEWBRACC)

830 Corbin Ave., New Britain, CT 06052 Tel. (860)229-3751
Media Contact, Exec. Dir., Michael Gorzoch
Exec. Dir., Michael Gorzoch
Pastoral Care/Chaplaincy: Rev. Ron Smith; Rev. Will Baumgartner; Diane Cardinal
Pres., Ernie Groth
Treas., Jakob Koch
Major activities: Worship; Social Concerns; Emergency Food Bank Support; Communications-Mass Media; Hospital and Nursing Home Chaplaincy; Elderly Programming; Homelessness and Hunger Programs; Telephone Ministry; Urban Sisters Center; Thanksgiving Vouchers

The Capital Region Conference of Churches

30 Arbor St., Hartford, CT 06106 Tel. (860)236-1295

Media Contact, Exec. Dir., Rev. Roger W. Floyd
Exec. Dir., Rev. Roger W. Floyd
Pastoral Care & Training, Dir., Rev. Susan Lyon
Aging Project, Dir., Barbara Malcolm
Community Organizer, Mr. Joseph Wasserman
Broadcast Ministry Consultant, Ivor T. Hugh
Pres., John Kidwell
Major activities: Organizing for Peace and Justice; Aging; Legislative Action; Cooperative Broadcast Ministry; Ecumenical Cooperation; Interfaith Reconciliation; Chaplaincies; Low-Income Senior Empowerment; Anti-Racism Education

The Downtown Cooperative Ministry Greater New Haven

57 Olive St., New Haven, CT 06511 Tel. (203)776-9526
Media Contact, Coord., Rev. K. Dexter Cheney
Coord., Rev. K. Dexter Cheney
Pres., Ms. Patricia Anderson, Interfaith Volunteer Caregivers, 30 Gillies Rd., Hamden, CT 06517
Treas., Murray Harrison, 264 Curtis St., Meriden, CT 06450
Major activities: Mission to Poor and Dispossessed; Criminal Justice; Elderly; Sheltering Homeless; Soup Kitchen; Low Income Housing; AIDS Residence; Summer Children's Program; Pastoral Counseling Center

Waterbury Area Council of Churches

24 Central Ave., Waterbury, CT 06702 Tel. (203)-756-7831
Media Contact, Coord., Susan Girdwood
Coord., Susan Girdwood
Pres., Rev. Robert Louis
Major activities: Emergency Food Program; Emergency Fuel Program; Soup Kitchen; Ecumenical Worship; Christmas Toy Sale

DELAWARE

*The Christian Council of Delaware and Maryland's Eastern Shore

E-62 Omega Dr., Newark, DE 19713-2061 Tel. (302)366-0595 Fax (302)366-0714
Media Contact, Rev. Patricia McClurg
Pres., Rev. Patricia McClurg
Vice-pres., Rt. Rev. Martin G. Townsend
Sec., Rev. Elizabeth I. Doty
Treas., Rt. Rev. Calvin Cabell Tennis
Major activities: Exploring common theological, Ecclesiastical and Community Concerns; Racism

DISTRICT OF COLUMBIA

Interfaith Conference of Metropolitan Washington

1419 V St. NW, Washington, DC 20009 Tel. (202)234-6300
Media Contact, Exec. Dir., Rev. Dr. Clark Lobenstine, Fax (202)234-6303
Exec. Dir., Rev. Dr. Clark Lobenstine
Admn. Sec., Najla Robinson
Pres., Dr. Rajwant Singh
1st Vice-Pres., Dr. Siva Subramanian
Chpsn., Bishop E. Harold Jansen
Sec., Mr. Jack Serber
Treas., Mrs. Jacqueline Wilson, Esq.
Major activities: Interfaith Dialogue; Interfaith Concert; Racial and Ethnic Polarization; Hunger; Homelessness; Church-State Zoning Issues

The Council of Churches of Greater Washington

5 Thomas Circle NW, Washington, DC 20005 Tel. (202)722-9240
Media Contact, Exec. Dir., Dr. Arnold F. Keller
Pres., Dr. Rena Karefa-Smart
Interim Dir., Dr. Arnold F. Keller
Program Officer, Mr. Daniel M. Thompson
Major activities: Promotion of Christian Unity/Ecumenical Prayer & Worship; Coordination of Community Ministries; Summer Youth Employment; Summer Camping/Inner City Youth; Supports wide variety of social justice concerns

FLORIDA

*Florida Council of Churches

924 N. Magnolia Ave., Ste. 236, Orlando, FL 32803 Tel. (407)839-3454 Fax (407)246-0019
Media Contact, Pres., Dr. James Armstrong, 225 S. Interlachen Ave., Winterpark, FL 32789 Tel. (407)647-2416 Fax (407)647-5921
Exec. Dir., Walter F. Horlander
Admn. Asst., ----
Refugee Services, Orlando Ofc., Staff Assoc., H. Basil Nichols
Disaster Response, Staff Assoc., William Nix
AmeriCorp, Thelma J. Dudley
Major activities: Justice and Peace; Refugee Resettlement; Disaster Response; Legislation & Public Policy; Local Ecumenism; Farmworker Ministry

Christian Service Center for Central Florida, Inc.

808 W. Central Blvd., Orlando, FL 32805-1809 Tel. (407)425-2523
Media Contact, Exec. Dir., Rev. Arthur Dasher, Tel. (407)425-2524 Fax (407)849-1495
Exec. Dir., Rev. Arthur Dasher
Family Emergency Services, Dir., Andrea Evans
Marriage & Family Therapy Center, Dir., Dr. Gloria Lobnitz
Alzheimers Respite, Dir., Mary Ellen Ort-Marvin
Fresh Start, Dir., Rev. Homer Marigna
Dir. of Mktg., Margaret Ruffier-Farris
Pres., ----
Treas., David Steinmetz
Sec., ----
Pres. Elect, ----
Major activities: Provision of Basic Needs (food, clothing, shelter); Emergency Assistance; Professional Counseling. Noon-time Meals; Sunday Church Services at Walt Disney World; Collection and Distribution of Used Clothing; Shelter & Training for Homeless; Respite for caregivers of Alzheimers

GEORGIA

*Georgia Christian Council

P.O. Box 7193, Macon, GA 31209-7193 Tel. (912)743-2085
Media Contact, Exec. Dir., Rev. Leland C. Callins, Fax (912)743-2085
Exec. Dir., Rev. Leland C. Collins

Pres., Rev. Anne Sayre, 1455 Tullie Rd. NE, Ste. 10, Atlanta, GA 30329-2137
Pres.-Elect, Bishop Othal C. Lakey, 2001 MLK Jr. Dr., Atlanta, GA 30310
Treas., Rev. William K. Bagwell, P.O. Box 61, Ocilla, GA 31774
Sec., Fr. Michael Kavanaugh, 1420 Monte Sano Ave., Augusta, GA 30904
Major activities: Local Ecumenical Support and Resourcing; Legislation; Rural Development; Racial Justice; Networking for Migrant Coalition; Aging Coalition; GA To GA With Love; Medical Care; Prison Chaplaincy; Training for Church Development

Christian Council of Metropolitan Atlanta

465 Boulevard, S.E., Atlanta, GA 30312 Tel. (404)622-2235 Fax (404)627-6626
Media Contact, Exec. Dir., Rev. Robert W. Younts
Exec. Dir., Rev. Robert W. Younts
Assoc. Dir., Rev. Bernard McLendon
Pres., Rev. John Rabb
Major activities: Refugee Services; Seminary Course on Ecumenism; Task Force on Year of the Child; Homeless; Ecumenical and Interreligious Events; Persons with Handicapping Conditions; Women's Concerns; Task Force on Prison Ministry; Quarterly Forums on Ecumenical Issues; Faith and Order Concerns

HAWAII

*Hawaii Council of Churches

116 S. Hotel St., Ste. 201, Honolulu, HI 96813 Tel. (808)538-0068 Fax (808)538-0126
Media Contact, The Rev. Donna Faith Eldredge, 1300 Kailua Rd. B-1, Kailua, HI 96734 Tel. (808)263-9788 Fax (808)262-8915
Exec. Dir., The Rev. Donna Faith Eldredge
Major activities: Laity and Clergy Education; Legislative Advocacy; Media and Broadcast Commission; AIDS Education; Ecumenical and Interfaith Worship; Advocacy for Peace with Justice; Hawaiian Sovereignty Issues; Anti-gambling Coalition; Building Partnerships and Collaborative Efforts with Community Groups/ Agencies

IDAHO

The Regional Council for Christian Ministry, Inc.

237 N. Water, Idaho Falls, ID 83403 Tel. (208)524-9935
Exec. Sec., Wendy Schoonmaker
Major activities: Island Park Ministry; Community Food Bank; Community Observances; Community Information and Referral Service; F.I.S.H.

ILLINOIS

*Illinois Conference of Churches

615 S. 5th St., Springfield, IL 62703 Tel. (217)544-3423
Media Contact, Exec. Dir., Rev. Dr. Carol M. Worthing, Fax (217)544-9307
Exec. Dir., Rev. Dr. Carol M. Worthing
Impact, Dir., Rev. Dr. Carol M. Worthing
Farm Worker Min., Dir., Nancy Tegtmeier
Domestic Violence Prog., Dir., Nancy Tegtmeier
Human Services Min., Dir., Nancy Tegtmeier
Unity & Relationships, Dir., Rev. Dr. Carol M. Worthing
Pres., Rev. Thomas Baima, 155 E. Superior, Chicago, IL 60611 Tel. (312)751-5325
Treas., Rev, Nars Palomar, 2100 Bates Ave., Springfield, IL 62704 Tel. (217)546-7170
Disaster Relief Coord., Nancy Tegtmeier
Major activities: Migrant & Farm Worker Ministry; Disaster Relief; Governmental Concerns and Illinois Impact; Ecumenical Courier;; Domestic Violence; Semi-annual Assemblies on Ecumenical/Ecclesial Themes

Churches United of the Quad City Area

630 - 9th St., Rock Island, IL 61201 Tel. (309)786-6494 Fax (309)786-5916
Media Contact, Exec. Dir., Charles R. Landon, Jr, 630 9th St., Rock Island, IL 61201 Tel. (309)786-6494
Exec. Dir., Charles R. Landon, Jr.
Program Admn., Juanita S. Scriven
Pres., Rev. David L. Bultemeier
Treas., Rev. Dr. Neal Lloyd
Major activities: Jail Ministry; Hunger Projects; Minority Enablement; Criminal Justice; Radio-TV; Peace; Local Church Development

Contact Ministries of Springfield

1100 E. Adams, Springfield, IL 62703 Tel. (217)-753-3939
Media Contact, Exec. Dir., Ethel Butchek
Exec. Dir., Ethel Butchek
Major activities: Information; Referral and Advocacy; Ecumenical Coordination; Low Income Housing Referral; Food Pantry Coordination; Low Income Budget Counseling; 24 hours on call; Emergency On-site Overnight Shelter

Evanston Ecumenical Action Council

P.O. Box 1414, Evanston, IL 60204 Tel. (708)475-1150
Media Contact, Comm. Chpsn., Rev. Steve Durham, 2523 Central Park, Evanston, IL 60201 Tel. (708)869-9210
Dir. Hospitality Cntr. for the Homeless, Patricia Johnson
Co-Pres., Rev. Mary Anderson
Co-Pres., Rev. Robert Oldershaw
Treas., Horton Kellogg
Admn. Dir., Barbara O'Neill
Major activities: Interchurch Communication and Education; Peace and Justice Ministries; Coordinated Social Action; Soup Kitchens; Multi-Purpose Hospitality Center for the Homeless; Worship and Renewal; Interfaith Dialogue

Greater Chicago Broadcast Ministries

112 E. Chestnut St., Chicago, IL 60611-2014 Tel. (312)988-9001
Media Contact, Exec. Dir., Lydia Talbot
Pres., Bd. of Dir., John M. Buchanan
Exec. Dir., Lydia Talbot
Admn. Asst., Margaret Early
Major activities: Television, Cable, Interfaith/Ecumenical Development; Social/Justice Concerns

Oak Park-River Forest Community of Congregations

P.O. Box 3365, Oak Park, IL 60303-3365 Tel. (708)386-8802
Media Contact, Patricia C. Koko
Admn. Sec., Patricia C. Koko
Pres., Rabbi Gary Gerson
Treas., Paul Curatolo
Major activities: Community Affairs; Ecumenical/Interfaith Affairs; Youth Education; Food Pantry; Senior Citizens Worship Services; Interfaith Thanksgiving Services; Good Friday Services; UNICEF Children's Fund Drive; ASSIST (Network); Blood Drive; Literacy Training; Christian Unity Week Pulpit Exchange; CROP/CWS Hunger Walkathon; Austin Community Table (feeding hungry); Work with Homeless Commission; Unemployed Task Force; Economic & Health Bridgemaking to Chicago Westside; PADS (Public Action to Deliver Shelter)

Peoria Friendship House of Christian Service

800 N.E. Madison Ave., Peoria, IL 61603 Tel. (309)671-5200 Fax (309)671-5206
Media Contact, Int. Exec. Dir., James McCormick
Int. Exec. Dir., James McCormick
Community Outreach, Dir., Ms. Diana Schleuter
Prog. & Spiritual Nurture, Dir., Rev. Alicia Crooks
Pres. of Bd., Lynn Pearson
Major activities: Children's After-School; Teen Programs; Parenting Groups; Recreational Leagues; Senior Citizens Activities; Emergency Food/Clothing Distribution; Emergency Payments for Prescriptions, Rent, Utilities, Transportation; Community Outreach/Housing Advocacy; Economic Development; Grassroots Community Organizing; Crime Prevention; Neighborhood Empowerment; GED Classes

The Hyde Park & Kenwood Interfaith Council

1448 East 53rd St., Chicago, IL 60615 Tel. (312)-752-1911
Media Contact, Exec. Dir., Mr. Werner H. Heymann, 1448 E. 53rd St., Chicago, IL 60615 Tel. (312)752-1911
Exec. Dir., Mr. Werner H. Heymann
Pres., Rev. David D. Stanford
Treas., Ms. Barbara Krell
Major activities: Interfaith Work; Hunger Projects; Community Development

INDIANA

*Indiana Council of Churches

Bishop Ralph Kempski, 911 E. 86th St., No. 200, Indianapolis, IN 46240 Tel. (317)923-3674 Fax (317)924-4859

Christian Ministries of Delaware County

401 E. Main St., Muncie, IN 47305 Tel. (317)288-0601
Media Contact, Exec. Dir., Susan Hughes
Exec. Dir., Susan Hughes
Pres., Rev. Stan Peterson
Treas., Dr. J. B. Black
Major activities: Feed-the-Baby Program; Youth Ministry at Detention Center; Community Church Festivals; Community Pantry; Community Assistance Fund; CROP Walk; Social Justice; Family Life Education; Combined Clergy

Church Community Services

1703 Benham Ave., Elkhart, IN 46516 Tel. (219)-295-3673
Media Contact, Dir., Rosalie J. Day
Exec. Dir., Rosalie J. Day
Major activities: Advocacy for Low Income Persons; Financial Assistance for Emergencies; Food Pantry; Used Furniture; Information and Referral

Evansville Area Council of Churches, Inc.

414 N.W. Sixth St., Evansville, IN 47708-1332 Tel. (812)425-3524 Fax (812)425-3524
Media Contact, Dir. of Programs, Barbara G. Gaisser
Dir. of Programs, Barbara G. Gaisser
Weekday Supervisor, Ms. Linda M. Schenk
Office Mgr., Rev. Barbara G. Gaisser
Pres., C. "Swede" Erickson
Sec., Rev. Shane O'Neill
Fin. Chpsn., Mr. Steve Worthington
Major activities: Christian Education; Community Responsibility & Service; Public Relations; Interpretation; Church Women United; Institutional Ministries; Interfaith Dialogue; Earth Care Ethics; Public Education Support; Disaster Preparedness; Job Loss Networking Support Group

Indiana Interreligious Commission on Human Equality

1100 W. 42nd St., Ste. 365, Indianapolis, IN 46208 Tel. (317)924-4226 Fax (317)923-3658
Media Contact, Exec. Dir., Cathy J. Cox
Exec. Dir., Cathy J. Cox
Pres., Rt. Rev. Edward W. Jones
Treas., Rev. Duane Grady
Major activities: Human Rights; Racial and Cultural Diversity Workshops; Racism/Sexism Inventory; Cultural and Religious Intolerance; Interfaith Dialogue; Conflict Management Workshops; Issues pertaining to Human Equality

Interfaith Community Council, Inc.

702 E. Market St., New Albany, IN 47150 Tel. (812)948-9248
Media Contact, Fin. Dir., Jane Alcorn
Exec. Dir., Rev. Dr. David Bos
Child Dev. Center, Dir., Carol Welsh
Programs/Emergency Assistance, Jane Alcorn
Hedden House, Dir., Stephanie Al-Uqdah
RSVP, Dir., Matie Watts
Major activities: Child Development Center; Emergency Assistance; Hedden House (Transitional Shelter for Recovering Substance Abuse Women);Retired Senior Volunteer Program; New Clothing and Toy Drives; Convalescent Sitter & Mother's Aides; Senior Day College; Emergency Food Distribution; Homeless Prevention

Lafayette Urban Ministry

525 N. 4th St., Lafayette, IN 47901 Tel. (317)423-2691 Fax (317)423-2693

Media Contact, Exec. Dir., Joseph Micon
Exec. Dir., Joseph Micon
Advocate Coord., Rebecca Smith
Public Policy Coord., Harry Brown
Pres., John Wilson
Major activities: Social Justice Ministries with and among the Poor

The Associated Churches of Fort Wayne & Allen County, Inc.

602 E. Wayne St., Fort Wayne, IN 46802 Tel. (219)422-3528 Fax (219)422-6721
Media Contact, Exec. Dir., Rev. Vernon R. Graham
Exec. Dir., Rev. Vernon R. Graham
Sec., Geoff Parker
Foodbank: Ellen Graham; Ed Pease
Foodbank, Marv Phillips
Prog. Development, Ellen Graham
WRE Coord., Maxine Bandemer
Pres., Deanna Wilkirson, 5515 Old Mill Rd., Fort Wayne, IN 46807
Treas., Jean Streicher, 436 Downing Ave., Fort Wayne, IN 46807
Major activities: Weekday Religious Ed.; Radio & TV; Church Clusters; Church and Society Commission; Overcoming Racism; A Baby's Closet; Faith and Order Commission; Christian Ed.; Widowed-to-Widowed; CROP; Campus Ministry; Feeding the Babies; Food Bank System; Peace & Justice Commission; Welfare Reform; Endowment Devel.; Habitat for Humanity; Child Care Advocacy; Project 25; Ecumenical Dialogue; Feeding Children; Vincent House (Homeless); A Learning Journey (Literacy); Reaching Out in Love

The Church Federation of Greater Indianapolis, Inc.

1100 W. 42nd St., Ste. 345, Indianapolis, IN 46208 Tel. (317)926-5371 Fax (317)926-5373
Media Contact, Comm. Consultant, Julie Foster, 1100 W. 42nd. St., Ste. 345, Indianapolis, IN 46208 Tel. (317)926-5371
Exec. Dir., Rev. Dr. Angelique Walker-Smith
Pres., Rev. Dr. James B. Lemler
Treas., R. Wayne Reynolds
Major activities: "Sacred Spaces" (A Christian Partnership of Neighborhood Action) Reclaiming Our Neighborhoods through Community Formation, Community Resourcing, Community Education, and Communications; Church Sanctuary Movement; "Loving Our Children": An Education; Partnership Between Church and Public Schools for "at risk" Children

United Religious Community of St. Joseph County

2015 Western Ave., South Bend, IN 46629 Tel. (219)282-2397
Media Contact, Exec. Dir., Dr. James J. Fisko
Exec. Dir., Dr. James J. Fisko
Pres., Mary S. Rooney
Victim Offender Reconciliation Prog., Coord., Martha Sallows
Volunteer Advocacy Project: Coord., Sara Goetz; Coord., Linda Jung-Zimmerman
Major activities: Religious Understanding; Social, Pastoral and Congregational Ministries

West Central Neighborhood Ministry, Inc.

1210 Broadway, Fort Wayne, IN 46802-3304 Tel. (219)422-9319
Media Contact, Exec. Dir., Andrea S. Thomas
Exec. Dir., Andrea S. Thomas
Ofc. Mgr., Kelly Mayer
Food Bank Coord., Carol Salge
Neighborhood Services Dir., Linnea Bartling
Neighborhood Services Coord., Carol Salge
Senior Citizens Dir., Gayle Mann
Youth Director, Sharon Gerig
Major activities: After-school Programs; Teen Drop-In Center; Summer Day Camp; Summer Overnight Camp; Information and Referral Services; Food Pantry; Nutrition Program for Senior Citizens; Senior Citizens Activities; Tutoring; Developmental Services for Families & Senior Citizens; Parent Club

IOWA

*Ecumenical Ministries of Iowa (EMI)

3816 - 36th St., Ste. 202, Des Moines, IA 50310-4722 Tel. (515)255-5905 Fax (515)255-1421
Media Contact, Exec. Dir., Dr. James R. Ryan, 3816-36th St., Ste. 202, Des Moines, IA 50310-4722
Exec. Dir., Dr. James R. Ryan
Admn. Asst., Martha E. Jungck
Major activities: Facilitating the denominations'cooperative agenda of resourcing local expression of the church; Assess needs & develop responses through Justice and Unity Commissions

*Iowa Religious Media Services

3816 36th St., Des Moines, IA 50310 Tel. (515)-277-2920
Media Contact, Dir., Sue Sonner
Educ. Consultant, Joanne Talarico, CHM
Production Mgr., Dr. Richard Harbart
Major activities: Media Library: Video and Audio-visual Production: Video Teleconferencing

Churches United, Inc.

866 4th Ave. SE, Cedar Rapids, IA 52403 Tel. (319)366-7163
Media Contact, Admn. Sec., Marcey Luxa
Admn. Sec., Mrs. Marcey Luxa
Pres., Ellen Bruckner
Treas., Joseph Luxa, 450 19th St. NW, Cedar Rapids, IA 52405
Major activities: Community Food Bank; LEAF (Local Emergency Assistance Fund; CROP; Community Information and Referral; Jail Chaplaincy; World Hunger; Nursing Home Ministry; Radio and TV Ministry; Ecumenical City-Wide Celebrations

Des Moines Area Religious Council

3816 - 36th St., Des Moines, IA 50310 Tel. (515)-277-6969 Fax (515)255-1421
Media Contact, Exec. Dir., Forrest Harms
Exec. Dir., Forrest Harms
Pres., Linda Cohen
Treas., Bill Corwin
Major activities: Outreach and Nurture; Educa-

tion; Social Concerns; Mission; Worship; Emergency Food Pantry; Ministry to Widowed; Child Care Assistance

KANSAS

*Kansas Ecumenical Ministries

5942 SW 29th St., Ste. D, Topeka, KS 66614-2539 Tel. (913)272-9531 Fax (913)272-9533
Media Contact, Exec. Dir., Rev. Alden Hickman
Exec. Dir., Rev. Alden Hickman
Pres., Rev. Kathy Timpany
Vice-Pres., Mrs. Winnie Crapson
Sec., Tom McGraw
Major activities: State Council of Churches; Legislative Activities; Program Facilitation and Coordination; World Hunger; Higher Education Concerns; Interfaith Rural Life Committee; Education; Mother-to-Mother Program; Peacemaking; Rural Development; Housing;; Health Care

Cross-Lines Cooperative Council

736 Shawnee Ave., Kansas City, KS 66105 Tel. (913)281-3388
Media Contact, Dir. of Dev., Michael Greene, Tel. (913)281-3388
Exec. Dir., Marilynn Rudell
Dir. of Programs, Rev. Robert L. Moore
Major activities: Emergency Assistance; Family Support Advocacy; Crisis Heating/Plumbing Repair; Thrift Store; Workcamp Experiences; Adult Education (GED and Basic English Literacy Skills); School Supplies; Christmas Store; Institute for Poverty and Empowerment Studies (Education on poverty for the non-poor)

Inter-Faith Ministries--Wichita

334 N. Topeka, Wichita, KS 67202-2410 Tel. (316)264-9303 Fax (316)264-2233
Media Contact, Dev./Communications Dir., Tina Lott
Exec. Dir., Rev. Sam Muyskens
Ofc. Mgr., Patricia Chebultz
Care Coordination Team: Dir., Cody Patton
Inter-Faith Inn (Homeless Shelter), Dir., Sandy Swank
Operation Holiday, Dir., Sally Dewey
Dev./Communications, Dir., Tina Lott
Major activities: Communications; Urban Education; Inter-religious Understanding; Community Needs and Issues; Theology and Worship; Hunger; Ministry for AIDS Persons

KENTUCKY

*Kentucky Council of Churches

412 Rose St., Lexington, KY 40508 Tel. (606)253-3027 Fax (606)231-5028
Media Contact, Exec. Dir., Nancy Jo Kemper
Exec. Dir., Rev. Nancy Jo Kemper
Disaster Recovery Prog., Coord., Rev. John Kays
Ed., *Intercom*, Dr. David Berg
Pres., Mr. Charles Coyle, 412 Rose Street, Lexington, KY 40508
Major activities: Christian Unity; Hunger; Church and Government; Disaster Response; Peace Issues; Racism; Health Care Issues; Local Ecumenism; Rural Land/Farm Issues

Fern Creek/Highview United Ministries

7502 Tangelo Dr., Louisvlle, KY 40228 Tel. (502)-239-7407
Exec. Dir., Kay Sanders, 7502 Tangelo Dr., Louisville, KY 40228 Tel. (502)239-7407
Exec. Dir., Kay Sanders
Pres., David Beard
Major activities: Ecumenically supported social service agency providing services to the community, including Emergency Financial Assistance, Food/Clothes Closet, Health Aid Equipment Loans, Information/Referral, Advocacy, Monthly Blood-Pressure Checks; Holiday Programs, Adult Day-Care Program, Life Skills Training and Intensive Care Management

Hazard-Perry County Community Ministries, Inc.

P.O. Box 1506, Hazard, KY 41702 Tel. (606)436-0051
Media Contact, Ms. Gerry Feamster-Roll
Exec. Dir., Ms. Gerry Feamster-Roll
Chpsn., Loyd Ketferle
Treas., Susan Duff
Major activities: Food Pantry/Crisis Aid Program; Day Care; Summer Day Camp; After-school Program; Christmas Tree; Family Support Center; Adult Day Care; Transitional Housing

Highlands Community Ministries

1140 Cherokee Rd., Louisville, KY 40204 Tel. (502)451-3695
Media Contact, Exec. Dir., Stan Esterle
Exec. Dir., Stan Esterle
Major activities: Welfare Assistance; Day Care; Counseling with Youth, Parents and Adults; Adult Day Care; Social Services for Elderly; Housing for Elderly and Handicapped; Ecumenical Programs; Community Classes; Activities for Children; Neighborhood and Business Organization

Kentuckiana Interfaith Community

1115 South 4th St., Louisville, KY 40203 Tel. (502)587-6265
Media Contact, Exec. Dir., Rev. Dr. Gregory C. Wingenbach, 1115 S. 4th St., Louisville, KY 40203 Tel. (502)587-6265
Exec. Dir., Rev. Dr. Gregory C. Wingenbach
Pres., Rev. Dr. Jim Holladay
Vice-Pres., Ms. Annette Turner
Sec., Rev. Dr. David Bos
Treas., Rev. Dr. Wallace Garner
Assoc. Dir./Justice Min., Rev. Ron Loughry
Admn. Sec., Mrs. Sue Weatherford
Major activities: Christian/Jewish Ministries in KY, Southern IN; Consensus Advocacy; Interfaith Dialogue; InterChurch Family Ministries; Community Hunger Walk; Racial Justice Forums; Network for Neighborhood-based Ministries; Community Winterhelp; IN; LUAH/ Hunger & Racial Justice Commission; *The Faith Channel-* Cable TV, *Horizon* and *Ark* Newspapers; Police/Comm. Relations Task Force; Ecumenical Strategic Planning; Networking with Seminaries & Religious-Affiliated Colleges

Northern Kentucky Interfaith Commission, Inc.

601 Greenup St., Covington, KY 41011 Tel. (606)-581-2237
Media Contact, Admin. Asst., Karen Yates
Exec. Dir., Rev. William C. Neuroth
Major activities: Understanding Faiths; Meeting Spiritual and Human Needs; Enabling Churches to Greater Ministry

Paducah Cooperative Ministry

1359 S. 6th St., Paducah, KY 42003 Tel. (502)442-6795
Media Contact, Dir., Jo Ann Ross
Dir., Jo Ann Ross
Chpsn., Rev. Michael Morris
Vice-Chpsn., Rev. Jamie Broome
Major activities: Programs for: Hungry, Elderly, Poor, Homeless, Handicapped, Undereducated

South East Associated Ministries (SEAM)

6500 Six Mile Ln., Ste.A, Louisville, KY 40218 Tel. (502)499-9350
Media Contact, Mary Beth Helton
Exec. Dir., Mary Beth Helton
Life Skills Center, Dir., Linda Leeser
Youth Services, Dir., Tracey Frazier
Pres., Bud McCord
Treas., Joe Hays
Major activities: Emergency Food and Financial Assistance; Life Skills Center (Programs of Prevention and Self-Sufficiency Through Education, Empowerment, Support Groups, etc.); Juvenile Court Diversion Program; Bloodmobile; Ecumenical Education and Worship; Family Counseling

South Louisville Community Ministries

Peterson Social Services Center, 204 Seneca Trail, Louisville, KY 40214 Tel. (502)367-6445
Media Contact, Exec. Dir., J. Michael Jupin
Exec. Dir., J. Michael Jupin
Bd. Chair., Rev. Lloyd Spencer
Bd. Vice-Chair., ----
Bd. Treas., Eugene Wells
Major activities: Food, Clothing & Financial Assistance; Home Delivered Meals, Transportation, Refugee Resettlement; Ecumenical Worship; Juvenile Diversion Program; Affordable Housing; Adult Day Care

St. Matthews Area Ministries

319 Browns Ln., Louisville, KY 40207 Tel. (502)-893-0205 Fax (502)893-0206
Media Contact, Dan G. Lane
Exec. Dir., Dan G. Lane
Child Care, Dir., Janet Hennessey
Youth Services, Dir., Tamara Davis
Admn. Asst., Jennifer Freadreacea
Dir. Assoc., Eileen Bartlett
Major activities: Child Care; Emergency Assistance; Youth Services; Interchurch Worship and Education; Housing Development; Counseling; Information & Referral; Mentor Program; Develop Mentally Disabled

LOUISIANA

*Louisiana Interchurch Conference

660 N. Foster Dr., Ste. A-225, Baton Rouge, LA 70806 Tel. (504)924-0213 Fax (504)927-7860
Media Contact, Exec. Dir., Rev. C. Dana Krutz
Exec. Dir., Rev. C. Dana Krutz
Pres., The Most Rev. Alfred C. Hughes, Jr.
Major activities: Ministries to Aging; Prison Reform; Liason with State Agencies; Ecumenical Dialogue; Institutional Chaplains; Racism

Greater Baton Rouge Federation of Churches and Synagogues

P.O. Box 626, Baton Rouge, LA 70821 Tel. (504)-925-3414 Fax (504)925-3065
Media Contact, Exec. Dir., Rev. Jeff Day
Exec. Dir., Rev. Jeff Day
Admn. Asst., Mrs. Marion Zachary
Pres., Rev. Ralph Howe, Jr.
Pres.-Elect, Ms. Bette Lavine
Treas., Rev. Isaiah Webster
Major activities: Combating Hunger; Housing (Helpers for Housing); Lay Academy of Religion (training); Interfaith Relations; Interfaith Concert; Race Relations

Greater New Orleans Federation of Churches

4545 Magnolia St., #206, New Orleans, LA 70115 Tel. (504)897-4488 Fax (504)897-4208
Exec. Dir., Rev. J. Richard Randels
Major activities: REACH (Religious Ecumenical Access Channel); Information and Referral; Food Distribution(FEMA); Forward Together TV Program; Sponsors seminars for pastors (ie church growth clergy taxes,etc.); Police Chaplaincy; Fire Chaplaincy

MAINE

*Maine Council of Churches

15 Pleasant Ave., Portland, ME 04103 Tel. (207)-772-1918 Fax (207)772-2947
Media Contact, Communications Director, Thomas C. Ewell
Pres., Edna Smith
Exec. Dir., Thomas C. Ewell
Major activities: Legislative Issues; Criminal Justice; Adult Education; Environmental Issues

MARYLAND

*Central Maryland Ecumenical Council

Cathedral House, 4 E. University Pkwy., Baltimore, MD 21218 Tel. (410)467-6194 Fax (410)-554-6387
Media Contact, Admn., Martha Young
Pres., Rev. Fr. Raymond Velencia
Major activities: Interchurch Communications and Collaboration; Information Systems; Ecumenical Relations; Urban Mission and Advocacy; Staff for Judicatory Leadership Council; Commission on Dialogue; Commission on Church & Society; Commission on Admin. & Dev.; Ecumenical Choral Concerts; Ecumenical Worship Services

Community Ministries of Rockville

114 West Montgomery Ave., Rockville, MD 20850 Tel. (301)762-8682 Fax (301)762-2939
Media Contact, Christine Tetrault
Exec. Dir. & Comm. Min., Mansfield M. Kaseman
Managing Dir., Christine Tetrault
Major activities: Shelter Care; Emergency Assistance; Elderly Home Care; Affordable Housing; Political Advocacy; Community Education

Community Ministry of Montgomery County

114 West Montgomery Ave., Rockville, MD 20850 Tel. (301)762-8682 Fax (301)762-2939
Media Contact, Exec. Dir., Lincoln S. Dring, Jr.
Exec. Dir., Lincoln S. Dring, Jr.
Major activities: Interfaith Clothing Center; Emergency Assistance Coalition; Manna Food Center; The Advocacy Function; Information and Referral Services; Friends in Action; The Thanksgiving Hunger Drive; Montgomery Habitat for Humanity; Thanksgiving in February; Congregation Based Shelters

MASSACHUSETTS

*Massachusetts Council of Churches

14 Beacon St., Rm. 416, Boston, MA 02108 Tel. (617)523-2771
Media Contact, Exec. Dir., Rev. Diane C. Kessler, Fax (617)523-2771
Exec. Dir., Rev. Diane C. Kessler
Public Policy, Assoc. Dir., Dr. Ruy Costa
Ecumenical Dev., Assoc. Dir., Rev. David A. Anderson
Children & Minority Affairs, Adjunct Assoc., Agnes Young
Major activities: Christian Unity; Education and Evangelism; Defend Social Justice & Individual Rights; Ecumenical Worship; Services and Resources for Individuals and Churches

Attleboro Area Council of Churches, Inc.

505 N. Main St., Attleboro, MA 02703 Tel. (508)-222-2933
Media Contact, Executive Director, Carolyn L. Bronkar
Exec. Dir., Carolyn L. Bronkar
Admn. Sec., Joan H. Lindstrom
Ofc. Asst., Roberta Kohler
Hosp. Chpln., Rev. Dr. William B. Udall
Pres., Sally Barton, 15 Sheridan Cir., Attleboro, MA 02703
Treas., David Quinlan, 20 Everett St., Plainville, MA 02762
Major activities: Hospital Chaplaincy; Personal Growth/Skill Workshops; Ecumenical Worship; Media Resource Center; Referral Center; Communications/Publications; Community Social Action; Food'n Friends Kitchens; Emergency Food and Shelter Fund; Nursing Home Volunteer Visitation Program

Cooperative Metropolitan Ministries

474 Centre St., Newton, MA 02158 Tel. (617)244-3650
Media Contact, Exec. Dir., Claire Kashuck, 474 Centre S., Newton, MA 01258 Tel. (617)244-3650
Exec. Dir., Claire Kashuck
Bd. Pres., Carolyn Panasevich
Treas., Bronwyn Mellquist
Clk., Shirley Taylor
Major activities: Low Income, Legislative Advocacy; Networking; Volunteerism; Publications & Workshops on Elder Housing Options; Suburban/Urban Bridges; Racial Justice

Council of Churches of Greater Springfield

32 Ridgewood Pl., Springfield, MA 01105 Tel. (413)733-2149
Media Contact, Asst. to Dir., Sr. John Bridgid, Fax (413)733-9817
Exec. Dir., Rev. Ann Geer
Community Min., Dir., Rev. L. Edgar Depaz
Pres., The Rev. Dr. Ledyard Baxter
Treas., Mr. John Pearson, Esq
Major activities: Christian Education Resource Center; Advocacy; Emergency Fuel Fund; Peace and Justice Division; Community Ministry; Task Force on Aging; Hospital and Jail Chaplaincies; Pastoral Service; Crisis Counseling; Christian Social Relations; Relief Collections; Ecumenical and Interfaith Relations; Ecumenical Dialogue with Roman Catholic Diocese; Mass Media; Church/Community Projects and Dialogue

Greater Lawrence Council of Churches

117A S. Broadway, Lawrence, MA 01843 Tel. (508)686-4012
Media Contact, Exec. Dir., David Edwards
Exec. Dir., David Edwards
Pres., Rev. Sylvia Robinson
Vice-Pres., Carol Rabs
Admn. Asst., Marianne Allatt
Major activities: Ecumenical Worship; Radio Ministry; Hospital and Nursing Home Chaplaincy; Church Women United; Afterschool Children's Program; Vacation Bible School

Inter-Church Council of Greater New Bedford

412 County St., New Bedford, MA 02740-5096 Tel. (508)993-6242 Fax (508)991-3158
Media Contact, Exec. Min., Rev. Dr. John Douhan
Exec. Min., Rev. Dr. John Douhan
Pres., Rev. Nehemiah Boynton, III
Treas., Ms. Adra Cook
Major activities: Pastoral Counseling; Chaplaincy; Housing for Elderly; Urban Affairs; Community Development

Massachusetts Commission on Christian Unity

82 Luce St., Lowell, MA 01852 Tel. (508)453-5423
Media Contact, Exec. Dir., Rev. K. Gordon White
Exec. Sec., Rev. K. Gordon White
Major activities: Faith and Order Dialogue with Church Judicatories

The Cape Cod Council of Churches, Inc.

320 Main St., P.O. Box 758, Hyannis, MA 02601 Tel. (508)775-5073

Media Contact, Exec. Dir., Rev. Ellen C. Chahey
Exec. Dir., Rev. Ellen C. Chahey
Pres., Rev. Kimball D. Cartwright, Sr.
Chaplain, Cape Cod Hospital, Rev. William Wilcox
Chaplain, Falmouth Hospital, Rev. Allen Page
Chaplain, House of Correction & Jail, Rev. Thomas Shepherd
Service Center & Thrift Shop: Dir., Linnea Snow, P.O. Box 125, Dennisport, MA 02639 Tel. (508)-394-6361; Asst. to Dir., Merilyn Lansing
Major activities: Pastoral Care; Social Concerns; Religious Education; Emergency Distribution of Food, Clothing, Furniture; Referral and Information; Church World Service; Interfaith Relations; Media Presence; Hospital & Jail Chaplaincy

Worcester County Ecumenical Council

4 Caroline St., Worcester, MA 01604 Tel. (508)-757-8385
Media Contact, Sec., Eleanor G. Bird
Interim Dir., Rev. Dr. Robert W. Johnson
Program Mgrs., Rev. Mary Jane O'Connor
Program Mgrs., Ms. Maggie Cahill
Pres., Rev. Dr. Jonathan Wright-Gray
Major activities: Clusters of Churches; Electronic Media; Youth Ministries; Ecumenical Worship and Dialogue; Interfaith Activities; Resource Connection for Churches;; Hunger Ministries; Interfaith Volunteer Caregivers Program; Group Purchasing Consortium; Alcohol & Other Drug Abuse Prevention

MICHIGAN

*Michigan Ecumenical Forum

809 Center St., Ste. 7-B, Lansing, MI 48906 Tel. (517)485-4395
Media Contact, Coord./Exec. Dir., Rev. Steven L. Johns-Boehme, 809 Centre St., Ste. 7-B, Lansing, MI 48906 Tel. (517)485-4395
Coord./Exec. Dir., Rev. Steven L. Johns-Boehme
Major activities: Communication and Coordination; Support and Development of Regional Ecumenical Fora; Ecumenical Studies; Fellowship and Celebration; Church and Society Issues; Continuing Education

ACCORD--Area Churches Together. . .Serving

312 Capital Ave., NE, Battle Creek, MI 49017 Tel. (616)966-2500
Media Contact, Exec. Dir., Patricia A. Staib
Exec. Dir., Patricia A. Staib
Pres., Rev. Ron Keller
Vice-Pres./Church, Sally Goss
Vice-Pres./Admn., David Brophy
Vice-Pres./Community, Jeanette Britton
Major activities: CROP Walk; Food Closet; Christian Sports; Week of Prayer for Christian Unity; Nursing Home Vesper Services; Ecumenical Worship

Bay Area Ecumenical Forum

103 E. Midland St., Bay City, MI 48706 Tel. (517)686-1360
Media Contact, Rev. Karen Banaszak
Chpsn., Mary Krzyzaniak
Major activities: Ecumenical Worship; Community Issues; Christian Unity; CROP Walk

Berrien County Association of Churches

275 Pipestone, Benton Harbor, MI 49022 Tel. (616)926-0030
Media Contact, Sec., Michelle Johnson
Pres., Evelyn Maki
Dir., Street Ministry, Rev. James Atterberry
Major activities: Street Ministry; CROP Walk; Community Issues; Fellowship; Christian Unity; Camp Warren; Hospital Chaplaincy Program, Publish Annual County Church Directory and Monthly Newsletter; Resource Guide for Helping Needy; Distribution of Worship Opportunity; Brochure for Tourists

Christian Communication Council of Metropolitan Detroit Churches

1300 Mutual Building, 28 W. Adams, Detroit, MI 48226 Tel. (313)962-0340
Media Contact, Rev. Edward Willingham, Jr., 28 W. Adams, Detroit, MI 48226 Tel. (313)962-0340 Fax (313)962-9044
Exec. Dir., Rev. Edward Willingham, Jr.
Assoc. Dir., Mrs. Angie Willingham
Meals for Shut-ins, Prog. Dir., Mr. John Simpson
Summer Feeding Prog., Coord., Ms. Dawn Lee
Major activities: Theological and Social Concerns; Ecumenical Worship; Educational Services; Electronic Media; Print Media; Meals for Shut-Ins; Summer Feeding Program

Grand Rapids Area Center for Ecumenism (GRACE)

38 Fulton West, Grand Rapids, MI 49503-2628 Tel. (616)774-2042 Fax (616)774-2883
Media Contact, Exec. Dir., Rev. David P. Baak
Exec. Dir., Rev. David P. Baak
Prog. Dir., Ms. Lisa H. Mitchell
Major activities: AIDS Pastoral Care Network (Client services education); Hunger Walk (also November Hunger/Shelter Emphasis); Education/Resources(Ecumenical lecture, Christian Unity Worship/Events, Interfaith Dialogue Conference, Prayer Against Violence; Congregation and Community Relations (Affiliates: ACCESS-All County Churches Emergency Support System, FISH for My People-transportation); Publications (Religious Community Directory,*Grace Notes*); Racial Justice Institute

Greater Flint Council of Churches

308 W. Third Ave., Flint, MI 48502 Tel. (810)238-3691
Media Contact, Pres., Rev. Ron Chappell
Pres., Rev. Ron Chappell
Major activities: Christian Education; Christian Unity; Christian Missions; Hospital and Nursing Home Visitors; Church in Society; American Bible Society Materials; Interfaith Dialogue; Church Teacher Exchange Sunday; Directory of Area Faiths and Clergy; Operation Brush-up; Thanksgiving & Easter Sunrise Services

Muskegon County Cooperating Churches

1218 Jefferson St., Muskegon, MI 49441 Tel. (616)727-6000
Media Contact, Clerk, Tom Wagner
Pres., Judy Clark-Ochs
Major activities: Dispute Resolution; Habitat for

Humanity; Prison Ministry; CROP Walk; Ecumenical Worship; Education; Jewish-Christian Dialogue; AIDS Ministry; Community Issues

The Jackson County Interfaith Council

425 Oakwood, P.O. Box 156, Clarklake, MI 49234-0156
Media Contact, Exec. Dir., Rev. Loyal H. Wiemer, Box 156, Clarklake, MI 49234 Tel. (517)529-9721
Exec. Dir., Rev. Loyal H. Wiemer
Major activities: Chaplaincy at Institutions and Senior Citizens Residences; Martin L. King, Jr. Day Celebrations; Ecumenical Council Representation; Radio and TV Programs; Food Pantry; Interreligious Events; Clergy Directory

MINNESOTA

*Minnesota Council of Churches

122 W. Franklin Ave., Rm. 100, Minneapolis, MN 55404 Tel. (612)870-3600 Fax (612)870-3622
Media Contact, Exec. Dir., Rev. Peg Chemberlin
Exec. Dir., Rev. Peg Chemberlin
Life & Work, Dir., Louis S. Schoen
Unity & Relationships, Dir., Molly M. Cox
Case Manager/Sponsor Developer, Evelyn Lennon
Refugee Services, Dir., Tatiana Pigoreva
Indian Ministry, Dir., Mary Ann Walt
Facilities, Dir., Cynthia Darrington-Ottinger
Tri-Council Coordinating Commission: Co-Dirs., James and Nadine Addington
Research Dir. & Admn. Asst., James Casebolt
Joint Religious Legislative Coalition, Dir., Brian A. Rusche
Pres., Rev. Robert E. Lucas
Major activities: Minnesota Church Center; Local Ecumenism; Life & Work: Anti-Racism; Hispanic Ministries, Indian Ministry; Legislative Advocacy; Refugee Services; Service to Newly Legalized/Undocumented Persons; Sexual Exploitation within the Religious Community; Unity & Relationships: Chaplaincy; Clergy Support; Consultation on Church Union; Ecumenical Study & Dialogue; Jewish-Christian Relations; Muslim-Christian Relations; State Fair Ministry

Arrowhead Interfaith Council

230 E. Skyline Pkwy., Duluth, MN 55811 Tel. (218)727-5020 Fax (218)727-5022
Media Contact, Pres., John H. Kemp
Pres., John H. Kemp
Vice-Pres., Helen Hanten
Treas., Richard Braun
Exec. Dir., ----
Major activities: InterFaith Dialogue; Joint Religious Legislative Coalition; Downtown Ecumenical Good Friday Service; Corrections Chaplaincy; Human Justice and Community Concerns; Community Seminars; Children's Concerns

Community Emergency Assistance Program (CEAP)

7231 Brooklyn Blvd., Brooklyn Center, MN 55429 Tel. (612)566-9600 Fax (612)566-9604
Media Contact, Exec. Dir., Todd Paulson
Exec. Dir., Todd Paulson
Major activities: Provision of Basic Needs (Food, Clothing, Furniture); Emergency Financial Assistance for Shelter; Home Delivered Meals; Chore Services and Homemaking Assistance; Family Loan Program; Volunteer Services

Greater Minneapolis Council of Churches

122 W. Franklin Ave., Ste. 218, Minneapolis, MN 55404 Tel. (612)870-3660 Fax (612)870-3663
Media Contact, Dir. of Communications, Robert Frame
Exec. Dir., Rev. Dr. Gary B. Reierson
Pres., Rev. Ian D. Bethel, Sr.
Treas., Dorothy Bridges
Indian Work, Assoc. Exec. Dir., Mary Ellen Dumas
Meals on Wheels, Dir., Barbara Green
Minnesota FoodShare, Dir., ----
Correctional Chaplains: Rev. Alfred Harris; Rev. Susan Allers Hatlie; Rev. Thomas Van Leer; Rev. Tyrone Partee; Imam Charles El-Amin; Eleanor Favell; Rev. Virgil Galvin-Foote
Congregations Concerned for Children, Dir., ----
Shared Ministries Tutorial Program, Dir., Rev. Belinda Green
Metro Paint-A-Thon, Dir., Peter Reis
HandyWorks, Dir., Peter Reis
Div. of Indian Work: Emerg. Asst. Prog., Dir., ----; Family Violence Prog., Dir., Barbara Dudley; Teen Parents Prog., Dir., Noya Woodrich; Youth Leadership Dev. Prog., Dir., Joseph Geary
Finance & Admn., Dir., ----
Advancement Dir., Kathy Cullen
Major activities: Indian Work (Emergency Assistance, Youth Leadership, Teen Indian Parents Program, and Family Violence Program); Minnesota FoodShare; Metro Paint-A-Thon; Meals on Wheels; Shared Ministries Tutorial Program; Congregations Concerned for Children; Correctional Chaplaincy Program; HandyWorks; Education and Celebration

St. Paul Area Council of Churches

1671 Summit Ave., St. Paul, MN 55105 Tel. (612)-646-8805 Fax (612)646-6866
Media Contact, Dir. of Development, Elaine Weber Nelson
Exec. Dir., Rev. Thomas A. Duke
Chaplaincy, Larry Mens
Congregations Concerned for Children, Ms. Peg Wangensteen
Project Spirit, Gloria Roach Thomas
Dept. of Indian Work, Ms. Sheila WhiteEagle
Pres., Bruce Thorpe
Treas., Bert Neinaber
Sec., Ms. Kay Tellekson
Major activities: Chaplaincy at Detention and Corrections Authority Institutions; Police Chaplaincy; Education and Advocacy Regarding Children and Poverty; Assistance to Churches Developing Children's/Parenting Care Services; Ecumenical Encounters and Activities; Indian Ministries; Leadership in Forming Cooperative Ministries for Children and Youth; Project Spirit

The Joint Religious Legislative Coalition

122 West Franklin Ave., Rm. 315, Minneapolis, MN 55404 Tel. (612)870-3670

Media Contact, Executive Director, Brian A. Rusche, 122 W. Franklin, Rm. 315, Minneapolis, MN 55404 Tel. (612)870-3670
Exec. Dir., Brian A. Rusche
Research Dir., James Casebolt
Major activities: Lobbying at State Legislature; Researching Social Justice Issues and Preparing Position Statements; Organizing Grassroots Citizen's Lobby

Tri-Council Coordinating Commission

122 W. Franklin, Rm. 100, Minneapolis, MN 55404 Tel. (612)871-0229 Fax (612)870-3622
Media Contact, Co-Dir., Nadine R. Addington
Co-Dir., R. James Addington
Pres., Rev. Thomas Duke, 1671 Summit Ave., St. Paul, MN 55105
Major activities: Anti-Racism; Anti-Sexism; Education; Interfaith Choral Festival

MISSISSIPPI

*Mississippi Religious Leadership Conference

P.O. Box 68123, Jackson, MS 39286-8123 Tel. (601)948-5954 Fax (601)354-3401
Media Contact, Exec. Dir., Rev. Canon Thomas E. Tiller, Jr.
Exec. Dir., Rev. Canon Thomas E. Tiller, Jr.
Chair, The Most Rev. William R. Houck
Treas., Rev. Tom Clark
Major activities: Cooperation among Religious Leaders; Lay/Clergy Retreats; Social Concerns Seminars; Disaster Task Force; Advocacy for Disadvantaged

MISSOURI

Council of Churches of the Ozarks

P.O. Box 3947, Springfield, MO 65808-3947 Tel. (417)862-3586 Fax (417)862-2129
Media Contact, Comm. Dir., Jeanne Rudloff
Exec. Dir., Dr. Dorsey E. Levell
Dev. Officer, Joyce Head
Operations Dir., Noel Chase
Major activities: Ministerial Alliance; Retired Sr. Volunteer Prog.; Treatment Center for Alcohol and Drug Abuse; Helping Elderly Live More Productively; Daybreak Adult Day Care Services; Ombundsman for Nursing Homes; Homesharing; Family Day Care Homes; USDA Food Program; Youth Ministry; Disaster Aid and Counseling; Homebound Shoppers; Food and Clothing Pantry; Ozarks Food Harvest

Ecumenical Ministries

#2 St. Louis Ave., Fulton, MO 65251 Tel. (314)-642-6065
Media Contact, Ofc. Mgr., Karen Luebbert
Exec. Dir., Andrea Langton
Pres., William Jessop
Major activities: Kingdom Hospice; CROP Hunger Walk; Little Brother and Sister; Christmas Bookmobile; Unity Service; Family Ministry; Senior Center Bible Study; Fellowship of Interdenominational Senior Highs; County Jail Ministry; Fulton High School Baccalaureate Service

Interfaith Community Services

200 Cherokee St., P.O. Box 4038, St. Joseph, MO 64504-0038 Tel. (816)238-4511
Media Contact, Exec. Dir., David G. Berger, P.O. Box 4038, St. Joseph, MO 64504-0038 Tel. (816)238-4511
Exec. Dir., David G. Berger
Major activities: Child Development; Neighborhood Family Services; Group Home for Girls; Retired Senior Volunteer Program; Nutrition Program; Mobile Meals; Southside Youth Program; Church and Community; Housing Development; Homemaker Services to Elderly;; Emergency Food, Rent, Utilities; AIDS Assistance; Family Respite; Family and Individual Casework

MONTANA

*Montana Association of Churches

Andrew Square, Ste. G, 100 24th St. W., Billings, MT 59102 Tel. (406)656-9779
Media Contact, Exec. Dir., Margaret McDonald, Andrew Square, Ste. G., 100 24th St. W., Billings, MT 59102 Tel. (406)656-9779
Exec. Dir., Margaret E. MacDonald
Admn. Asst., Larry D. Drane
Pres., Catherine D. Day, 3013 8th Ave., S., Great Falls, MT 59405
Treas., Don Patterson, East Lake Shore Rd., Big Fork, MT 59911
Christian Witness for Humanity, Susan DeComp, Andrew Square Ste. G, 100 24th St. W, Billings, MT 59102
Campus Ministries Program Assoc., Rev. Kent Elliot, P.O. Box 389, Boulder, MT 59632
Major activities: Christian Education; Montana Religious Legislative Coalition; Christian Unity; Junior Citizen Camp; Public Information; Ministries Development; Social Ministry

NEBRASKA

*Interchurch Ministries of Nebraska

215 Centennial Mall S., Rm. 411, Lincoln, NE 68508-1888 Tel. (402)476-3391 Fax (402)476-9310
Media Contact, Exec. Sec., Rev. Daniel J. Davis, Sr.
Exec. Sec., Rev. Daniel J. Davis, Sr.
Admin. Asst., Sharon K. Kalcik
Pres., Rev. Richard D. Turner
Treas., Bishop James E. Krotz
Major activities: Interchurch Planning and Development; Comity; Indian Ministry; Rural Church Strategy; Hunger; Refugee Resettlement Coordination; United Ministries in Higher Education; Disaster Response; Christian in Society Forum; Clergy Consultations; Farm Families Crisis Response Network; Interim Ministry Network; Pantry Network; Farm Mediation Services; Hispanic Ministry; the Church & Mental Illness Program; Conflict Management; Rural Health

Lincoln Interfaith Council

140 S. 27th St., Ste. B, Lincoln, NE 68510-1301 Tel. (402)474-3017 Fax (402)475-3262
Media Contact, Mr. David Hancock
Exec. Dir., Rev. Dr. Norman E. Leach
Pres., Yale Gotsdiner

Vice-Pres., The Rev. John Smeltzer
Sec., Mrs. Amrita Mahapatra
Treas., Mrs. Mary Owens
Media Specialist, Mr. David Hancock
Urban Ministries, Rev. Dr. Norman E. Leach
Admn. Asst., Ms. Jean Smith
Fiscal Mgr., Ms. Jean Smith
Asian Community & Cultural Center, Ms. Paula Reed
Banking Liaison to Asian Community, Ms. Maria Vu
Major activities: Asian Community & Cultural Center; Emergency Food Pantries System; MLK, Jr. Observance; Interfaith Passover Seder; Week of Prayer Christian Unity; Center for Spiritual Growth; Festival of Faith & Culture; Holocaust Memorial Observance; Citizens; Against Racism & Prejudice; HIV/AIDS Healing Worship Services; Community Organization; Anti-Drug & Anti-Alcohol Abuse Projects

NEW HAMPSHIRE

*New Hampshire Council of Churches

24 Warren St., P.O. Box 1087, Concord, NH 03302 Tel. (603)224-1352 Fax (603)224-9161
Media Contact, Exec. Sec., Mr. David Lamarre-Vincent
Exec. Sec., Mr. David Lamarre-Vincent
Pres., Dr. Louis George, P.O. Box 2403, Concord, NH 03302
Treas., Richard Edmunds, P.O. Box 136, Concord, NH 03302
Major activities: Ecumenical Work

NEW JERSEY

*New Jersey Council of Churches

116 N. Oraton Pkwy., East Orange, NJ 07017 Tel. (201)675-8600 Fax (201)675-0620
176 W. State St., Trenton, NJ 08608 Tel. (609)396-9546
Media Contact, Exec. Dir., Rev. Alice Downs
Pres., Rev. Denison D. Harrield, Jr.
Vice-Pres., Rev. Jack Johnson
Sec., Ms. Beverly McNally
Treas., Ms. Marge Christie
Major activities: Racial Justice; Children's Issues; Theological Unity; Ethics Public Forums; Advocacy; Economic Justice

Bergen County Council of Churches

165 Burton Ave., Hasbrouck Hts., NJ 07604 Tel. (201)288-3784
Media Contact, Pres., Rev. Stephen Giordano, Clinton Avenue Reformed Church, Clinton Ave. & James St., Bergenfield, NJ 07621 Tel. (201)-384-2454 Fax (201)384-2585
Exec. Sec., Anne Annunziato
Major activities: Ecumenical and Religious Institute; Brotherhood/Sisterhood Breakfast; Center for Food Action; Homeless Aid; Operation Santa Claus; Aging Services; Boy & Girl Scouts; Easter Dawn Services; Music; Youth; Ecumenical Representation; Support of Chaplains in Jails & Hospitals

Council of Churches of Greater Camden

P.O. Box 1208, Merchantville, NJ 08109 Tel. (609)985-5162
Media Contact, Exec. Sec., Rev. Dr. Samuel A. Jeanes, Braddock Bldg., 205 Tuckerton Road, Medford, NJ 08055 Tel. (609)985-7724
Exec. Sec., Rev. Dr. Samuel A. Jeanes
Pres., Rev. Lawrence L. Dunn
Treas., Mr. William G. Mason
Major activities: Radio & T.V.; Hospital Chaplaincy; United Services; Good Friday Breakfast; Mayors' Prayer Breakfast; Public Affairs; Easter Sunrise Service

Metropolitan Ecumenical Ministry

525 Orange St., Newark, NJ 07107 Tel. (201)481-6650 Fax (201)481-7883
Media Contact, Jacqueline Jones
Exec. Dir., C. Stephen Jones
Major activities: Community Advocacy (education, housing, environment); Church Mission Assistance; Community and Clergy Leadership Development; Economic Development; Community Revitalization

Trenton Ecumenical Area Ministry (TEAM)

1001 Pennington Rd., Trenton, NJ 08618-2629 Tel. (609)882-5942
Media Contact, Rev. Dr. John R. Norwood, Jr.
Exec. Dir., Rev. Dr. John R. Norwood, Jr.
Pres., Rev. Joanne B. Bullock
Campus Chaplains: Rev. Nancy Schulter; Rev. Joanne B. Bullock
Sec., Ms. Tina Swan
Major activities: Racial Justice; Children & Youth Ministries; Advocacy; CROP Walk; Ecumenical Worship; Hospital Chaplaincy; Church Women United; Campus Chaplaincy; Congregational Empowerment; Prison Chaplaincy; Substance Abuse Ministry Training

NEW MEXICO

*New Mexico Conference of Churches

124 Hermosa SE, Albuquerque, NM 87108-2610 Tel. (505)255-1509 Fax (505)256-0071
Media Contact, Exec. Sec., Dr. Wallace Ford
Pres., The Rev. Dr. Rodney Roberts, 501 Carlisle NE, Albuquerque, NM 87106-1322
Treas., Mr. Stan Hamamoto
Exec. Sec., Dr. Wallace Ford
Major activities: State Task Forces: Peace With Justice, Poverty, Disability Concerns, Legislative Concerns/Impact, Faith and Order, AIDS, Correctional Ministries, Public Education, Eco-Justice, Ecumenical Continuing Education Church's Solidarity with Women;; Regional Task Forces: Aging, Ecumenical Worship, Refugees, Emergency Care, Alcoholism

Inter-Faith Council of Santa Fe, New Mexico

818 Camino Sierra Vista #6, Santa Fe, NM 87501 Tel. (505)983-2892
Media Contact, Barbara A. Robinson, Fax (505)-473-5637
Pres., Mark Malachi
Treas., Barbara A. Robinson

Peace with Justice Task Force, Chpsn., Marjorie Schuckman
Major activities: Faith Community Assistance Center; Hunger Walk, Interfaith Dialogues/Celebrations/Visitations; Peace Projects; Understanding Hispanic Heritage; Newsletter

NEW YORK

*New York State Council of Churches, Inc.

Program Ofc.: 362 State St., Albany, NY 12210 Tel. (518)436-9319 Fax (518)427-6705
Center Printing: 3049 E. Genesee St., Syracuse, NY 13224 Tel. (315)446-6126
Media Contact, Rev. Dr. Arleon L. Kelley
Exec. Dir., Rev. Dr. Arleon L. Kelley
Mod., The Rev. Dr. Hazel Roper
1st Vice-Mod., Bishop Lee M. Miller
2nd Vice-Mod., The Ven. Michael S. Kendall
Sec., Isabel Morrison
Treas., The Rev. Robert L. Graham
New York State Interfaith IMPACT, Edward J. Bloch
Dir. of Chaplaincy Services, Rev. Frank Snow
Consultant for Resource Dev., Mary Lu Bowen
Dir. of Public Policy, Sheryl Sheraw
Admn. Asst., Sylvenia Cochran
Major activities: Public Policy and Ecumenical Ministries; Chaplaincy in State Institutions; Rural Poor and Migrants; Homeless; AIDS; Universal Health Care; Life and Law; U.S.-Canadian Border Concerns; Single Parent Families; Faith and Order; Environmental Issues; The Family, Education, Violence; Covenanting Congregations; Casino Gambling

Brooklyn Council of Churches

125 Ft. Greene Pl, Brooklyn, NY 11217 Tel. (718)-625-5851
Media Contact, Dir., Charles Henze
Program Dir., Mr. Charles Henze
Pres., Rev. Dan Ramm
Treas., Rev. Albert J. Berube
Major activities: Education Workshops; Food Pantries; Welfare Advocacy; Hospital and Nursing Home Chaplaincy; Church Women United; Legislative Concerns

Broome County Council of Churches, Inc.

81 Main St., Binghamton, NY 13905 Tel. (607)-724-9130
Media Contact, Exec. Dir., Mr. William H. Stanton, Fax (607)724-9148
Exec. Dir., Mr. William H. Stanton
Dir. of Development, Ms. Billie L. Briggs
Hospital Chaplains: Rev. LeRoy Flohr; Mrs. Betty Pomeroy
Jail Chaplain, Rev. Philip Singer
Aging Ministry Coord., Mrs. Dorothy Myers
CHOW Prog. Coord., Mrs. Dee Jester
Pres., Rev. Mark Ridley
Treas., Mrs. Rachel Light
Office Mgr., Ms. Joyce M. Besemer
Major activities: Hospital and Jail Chaplains; Youth and Aging Ministries; CHOW (Emergency Hunger Program); Christian Education; Ecumenical Worship and Fellowship; Media; Community Affairs; Peace; Day by Day Marriage; Prep Program; Interfaith Coalition Against Hate

Buffalo Area Council of Churches

1272 Delaware Ave., Buffalo, NY 14209-2401 Tel. (716)882-4793 Fax (716)882-7671
Media Contact, Exec. Dir., Rev. Dr. G. Stanford Bratton
Exec. Dir., Rev. Dr. G. Stanford Bratton
Pres., Rev. Dr. Robert L. Graham
1st Vice-Pres., Ms. Carol Wolf
2nd Vice-Pres., Rev. Donald Garrett
Sec., Ms. Dolores Gibbs
Treas., Ms. Eula Hooker
Chpsn. of Trustees, Ms. Elloeen Oughterson
Church Women United: Coord., Ms. Sally Giordano; Pres., Ms. Norma Roscover
Community Witness & Ministry, Chpsn., Dr. Timothy Dzierba
Spirituality & Community Bldg., Chpsn., Rev. Alice McDermott
Public Policy, Chpsn., The Rev. Simon P. Bouie
Radio & TV: Coord., Ms. Linda Velazquez; Chpsn., Rev. Robert Hutchinson
Major activities: Radio-TV; Social Services; Chaplains; Church Women United; Ecumenical Relations; Refugees; Public Policy; Community Development; Lay/Clergy Education; Interracial Dialogue; Police/Community Relations; Buffalo Coalition for Common Ground

Buffalo Area Metropolitan Ministries, Inc.

775 Main St., Ste. 203, Buffalo, NY 14203-1310 Tel. (716)854-0822 Fax (716)854-0822
Media Contact, Interim Exec. Dir., Rev. Francis X. Mazur
Interim Exec. Dir., Rev. Francis X. Mazur
Pres., Rev. John Long
Vice-Pres. for Plng. & Prog., Rev. Tom Doyle
Vice-Pres. for Admn. & Fin., Tom Dibble
Sec., Mrs. Nancee Kaufman-Gross
Treas., Rev. Amos Acree
Chair, Food for All Prog., Rev. Richard McFail
Major activities: An association of religious communities in Western New York with Bahai, Jewish, Muslim, Christian, Unitarian-Univeralist, Hindu, and Jain membership providing a united religious witness through these major activities: Hunger; Economic Issue; Interreligious Dialogue; Interfaith AIDS Network; Multifaith Forums; Fair Housing; Interfaith Holocaust Commemoration; Children's Sabbath; Resource for Hospital Chaplains

Capital Area Council of Churches, Inc.

646 State St., Albany, NY 12203 Tel. (518)462-5450
Media Contact, Admn. Asst., Renee Kemp
Exec. Dir., Rev. Dr. Robert C. Lamar
Admn. Asst., Renee Kemp
Pres., Rev. Allan Janssen
Treas., Mr. Alan Spencer
Major activities: Hospital Chaplaincy; Food Pantries; CROP Walk; Jail and Nursing Home Ministries; Martin Luther King Memorial Service and Scholarship Fund; Emergency Shelter for the Homeless; Campus Ministry; Ecumenical Dialogue; Forums on Social Concerns; Peace and Justice Education; Inter-Faith Programs; Legislative Concerns; Comm. Thanksgiving Day and Good Friday Services; Annual Ecumenical Musical Celebration

Chautaugua County Rural Ministry

127 Central Ave., P.O. Box 362, Dunkirk, NY 14048 Tel. (716)366-1787
Media Contact, Exec. Dir., Kathleen Peterson
Exec. Dir., Kathleen Peterson
Major activities: Chautaugua County Food Bank; Collection/Distribution of Furniture, Clothing, & Appliances; Homeless Services; Advocacy for the Poor; Soup Kitchen; Emergency Food Pantry; Thrift Store

Christians United in Mission, Inc.

Box 2199, Scotia, NY 12302 Tel. (518)382-7505
Media Contact, Coord., Jim Murphy
Coord., Jim Murphy
Major activities: Promote Cooperation/Coordination Among Member Judicatories in Urban Ministries, Social Action

Concerned Ecumenical Ministry to the Upper West Side

286 LaFayette Ave., Buffalo, NY 14213 Tel. (716)882-2442
Media Contact, Exec. Dir., Joseph Schuster
Exec. Dir., Mr. Joseph Schuster
Pres., Rev. Bruce McKay, Jr.
Major activities: Community center serving youth, young families, seniors and the hungry

Cortland County Council of Churches, Inc.

7 Calvert St., Cortland, NY 13045 Tel. (607)753-1002
Media Contact, Office Mgr., Joy Niswender
Exec. Dir., Rev. Donald M. Wilcox
Major activities: College Campus Ministry; Hospital Chaplaincy; Nursing Home Ministry; Newspaper Column; Interfaith Relationships; Hunger Relief; CWS; Crop Walk; Leadership Education; Community Issues; Mental Health Chaplaincy, Grief Support

Council of Churches of Chemung County, Inc.

330 W. Church St., Elmira, NY 14901 Tel. (607)-734-2294
Media Contact, Exec. Dir., Joan Geldmacher, Tel. (607)734-7622
Exec. Dir., Mrs. Joan Geldmacher
Pres., Rev. Howard Hunt
Chaplain, Rev. Nancy Lane, Tel. (607)732-0027
Major activities: CWS Clothing Collection; CROP Walk; UNICEF; Institutional Chaplaincies; Radio, Easter Dawn Service; Communications Network; Representation on Community Boards and Agencies; Campus Ministry; Ecumenical Services

Council of Churches of the City of New York

475 Riverside Dr., Rm. 1950, New York, NY 10015 Tel. (212)870-2120 Fax (212)870-3433
Media Contact, Exec. Dir., Dr. John E. Hiemstra
Exec. Dir., Dr. John E. Hiemstra
Pres., Dr. Spencer C. Gibbs
1st Vice-Pres., Rev. James O. Stallings
2nd Vice-Pres., Rev. Arlee Griffern
Sec., Rev. N. J. L'Heureux, Jr.
Treas., Dr. John Blackwell
Major activities: Radio & TV; Pastoral Care; Protestant Chapel, Kennedy International Airport; Coordination and Strategic Planning; Religious Conferences; Referral & Advocacy; Youth Development; Building Great Minds Tutoring Program

Dutchess Interfaith Council, Inc.

9 Vassar St., Poughkeepsie, NY 12601 Tel. (914)-471-7333
Media Contact, Exec. Dir., Rev. Gail A. Burger
Exec. Dir., Rev. Gail A. Burger
Pres., John McPhee
Treas., Elizabeth M. DiStefano
Major activities: CROP Hunger Walk; Interfaith Music Festival; Public Worship Events; Interfaith Dialog; Christian Unity; Interfaith Youth Evening; Oil Purchase Group; Interfaith HIV/AIDS Chaplaincy Program; County Jail Chaplaincy; Radio

Genesee County Churches United, Inc.

P.O. Box 547, Batavia, NY 14021 Tel. (716)343-6763
Media Contact, Pres., James Woodruff, 8215 Lewiston Rd., Batavia, NY 14020 Tel. (716)343-2963
Pres., James Woodruff
Exec. Sec., Helen H. Mullen
Chaplain, Rev. Bert G. Tidlund
Major activities: Jail Ministry.; Food Pantries; Serve Needy Families; Radio Ministry; Pulpit Exchange; Community Thanksgiving; Ecumenical Services at County Fair

Genesee-Orleans Ministry of Concern

118 S. Main St., Box 245, Albion, NY 14411-0245
Media Contact, Exec. Dir., Marian M. Adrian, GNSH, Tel. (716)589-9210
Exec. Dir., Marian M. Adrian, G.N.S.H., P.O. Box 245, Albion, NY 14411 Tel. (716)589-9210
Advocates: Jamie Salisbury; Margaret Grauerholz, Esq.
Pres., Susan Locke
Chaplains: Orleans County Jail, Rev. Wilford Moss; Orleans Albion Correctional Facility, Sr. Dolores O'Dowd
Major activities: Advocacy Services for the Disadvantaged, Homeless, Ill, Incarcerated and Victims of Family Violence; Emergency Food, Shelter, Utilities, Medicines

Greater Rochester Community of Churches

2 Riverside St., Rochester, NY 14613-1222 Tel. (716)254-2570
Media Contact, Coord., Marie E. Gibson
Major activities: Christian Education & Worship; Refugee Resettlement; Chaplaincy Services; Christian Unity; Interfaith Cooperation; Community Economic Development; Crossroads Program; Rochester's Religious Community Directory; Religious Information/Resources

InterReligious Council of Central New York

3049 E. Genesee St., Syracuse, NY 13224 Tel. (315)449-3552

Media Contact, Marianne Valone
Exec. Dir., Dorothy F. Rose
Pres., Rev. Ronald . Dewberry
Exec. Asst., Development Assoc., Pamela Blom
Refugee Resettlement, Dir., Nona Stewart
Senior Companion Prog., Dir., Virginia Frey
Covenant Housing, Dir., Kimberlee Dupcak
Bus. Mgr., Arthur A. West
Major activities: Pastoral Ministries; Community Ministries; Interreligious and Ecumenical Relations; Diversity Education; Worship; Community Advocacy and Planning

Livingston County Coalition of Churches

P.O. Box 676, 5 Washington St., Livonia, NY 14487 Tel. (716)346-4310
Exec. Dir., ----
Ofc. Mgr., Lynn Moran
Major activities: Hospice Program; Jail Ministry; Visitors' Center at Groveland Correctional Facility; Food Pantries; Gateways Family Service; Alternative Sentencing Program; Coordinate Services for Aging and Rural Poor; Christian Education Learning Fair; Lecture Series and Chaplain at SUNY Geneseo

The Long Island Council of Churches

1644 Denton Green, Hempstead, NY 11550 Tel. (516)565-0290 Fax call for inst
Eastern Office, 235 Sweezy Ave., Riverhead, NY 11901
Media Contact, Admn. Asst., Ms. Barbara McLaughlin
Exec. Dir., Rev. Robert L. Pierce
Admn. Asst., Ms. Barbara McLaughlin
Pastoral Care, Dir., Rev. Dr. Kai Borner
Clinical Pastoral Educ., Dir., Rev. Dr. Kai Borner
Social Services, Dir., Mrs. Lillian Sharik, Tel. (516)565-0390
Project REAL, Dir., Mr. Stephen Gervais
Nassau County Ofc., Social Services Sec., Ms. Mildred McMahon
Blood Prog. Coord.: Ms. Leila Truman; Ms. Audry Wolf
Dev. Dir.., Mr. Anthony Childs
Major activities: Pastoral Care in Hospitals and Jails; Clinical Pastoral Education; Emergency Food; Family Support & Advocacy; Advocacy for Domestic and International Peace & Justice; Blood Donor Coordination; Church World Service; Multifaith Cooperation; Clergy/Laity Training; Newsletter; Church Directory; Community Residences for Adults with Psychiatric Disabilities (Project REAL); HIV Education Projects; Special Projects

The Niagara Council of Churches Inc.

St. Paul UMC, Niagara Falls, NY 14301 Tel. (716)285-7505
Media Contact, Pres., Nessie S. Bloomquist, 7120 Laur Rd., Niagara Falls, NY 14304 Tel. (716)-297-0698 Fax (716)298-1193
Exec. Dir., Ruby Babb
Pres., Nessie S. Bloomquist, 7120 Laur Rd., Niagara Falls, NY 14304
Treas., Shirley Bathurst
Trustees Chpsn., Rev. Robert Bellingham, 1889 Pierce Ave., Niagara Falls, NY 14301
Major activities: Ecumenical Worship; Bible Study; Christian Ed. & Social Concerns; Church Women United; Evangelism & Mission; Institutional Min. Youth Activities; Hymn Festival; Week of Prayer for Christian Unity; CWS Projects; Audio-Visual Library; UNICEF; Food Pantries and Kitchens; Community Missions, Inc.; Political Refugees; Eco-Justice Task Force; Migrant/Rural Ministries; Interfaith Coalition on Energy

Niagara County Migrant Rural Ministry

5465 Upper Mountain Rd., Lockport, NY 14094 Tel. (716)434-4405
Media Contact, Exec. Dir., Ms. Grayce M. Dietz, 5465 Upper Mountain Road, Lockport, NY 14094 Tel. (716)439-0477
Chpsn., Lois Farley
Vice-Chpsn., Beverly Farnham
Sec., Anne Eifert
Treas., Rev. Patricia Ludwig
Major activities: Migrant Farm Worker Program; Primary Health Clinic; Assist with immigration problems and application process for social services; Monitor Housing Conditions; Assist Rural Poor; Referrals to appropriate service agencies; Children's Daily Enrichment Program

Queens Federation of Churches

86-17 105th St., Richmond Hill, NY 11418-1597 Tel. (718)847-6764 Fax (718)847-7392
Media Contact, Rev. N. J. L'Heureux, Jr.
Exec. Dir., Rev. N. J. L'Heureux, Jr.
York College Chaplain, Rev. Dr. Hortense Merritt
Pres., Rev. Fannye B. Walker
Treas., Lloyd W. Patterson, Jr.
Major activities: Emergency Food Service; York College Campus Ministry; Blood Bank; Scouting; Christian Education Workshops; Planning and Strategy; Church Women United; Community Consultations; Seminars for Church Leaders; Directory of Churches and Synagogues; Christian Relations (Prot/RC); Chaplaincies; Public Policy Issues; N.Y.S. Interfaith Commission on Landmarking of Religious Property; Queens Interfaith Hunger Network

Rural Migrant Ministry

P.O. Box 4757, Poughkeepsie, NY 12601 Tel. (914)485-8627 Fax (914)485-1963
Media Contact, Exec. Dir., Rev. Richard Witt
Exec. Dir., Rev. Richard Witt
Pres., Fred Wibiralske
Major activities: Serving the rural poor and migrants through a ministry of advocacy & empowerment; Women's Support Group; Youth Program; Latino Committee; Organization and Advocacy with and for Rural Poor and Migrant Farm Workers

Schenectady Inner City Ministry

5 Catherine St., Schenectady, NY 12307 Tel. (518)374-2683
Media Contact, Urban Agent, Rev. Phillip N. Grigsby
Urban Agent, Rev. Phillip N. Grigsby
Admn. Asst., Ms. Elaine MacKinnon
Emergency Food Liaison, Ms. Patricia Obrecht
Nutrition Dir., Ms. Patricia Stringfellow
Project SAFE/Safehouse Dir., Ms. Delores Edmonds-McIntosh
Church/Community Worker, Jim Murphy

Pres., Ms. Connie Clark
Bethesda House, John T. Davis
Save and Share, Ms. Donna Durkee
Demien Center, Ms. Laurie Bacheldor
Major activities: Emergency Food; Advocacy; Housing; Alternatives to Prostitution for Runaway and At-Risk Youth; Shelter for Runaway/Homeless Youth; Neighborhood and Economic Issues; Ecumenical Worship and Fellowship; Community Research; Education in Churches on Faith Responses to Social Concerns; Legislative Advocacy; Nutrition Outreach Program; Hispanic Community Ministry; Food Buying Coop; Day Shelter; CROP Walk; HIV/AIDS Ministry; Improvisation Teen Theatre

Southeast Ecumenical Ministries

25 Westminster Rd., Rochester, NY 14607 Tel. (716)271-5350
Dir., ----
Pres., Rev. Pamela Hunter
Major activities: Transportation of Elderly; Emergency Food Cupboard; Supplemental Nutrition Program

Staten Island Council of Churches

2187 Victory Blvd., Staten Island, NY 10314 Tel. (718)761-6782
Media Contact, Exec. Sec., Mrs. Mildred J. Saderholm, 94 Russell St., Staten Island, NY 10308 Tel. (718)761-6782
Troy Area United Ministries
17 First St., #2, Troy, NY 12180 Tel. (518)274-5920
Media Contact, Exec. Dir., Margaret T. Stoner
Exec. Dir., Mrs. Margaret T. Stoner
Pres., Brian O'Shaughnessy
Chaplain, R.P.I., Rev. Paul Fraser
Chaplain, Russell Sage College, Rev. Paul Fraser
Major activities: Community Dispute Settlement (mediation) Program; College Ministry; Nursing Home Ministry; CROP Walk; Homeless and Housing Concerns; Weekend Meals Program at Homeless Shelter; Community Worship Celebrations; Racial Relations; Furniture Program; Damien Center of Troy Hospitality for Persons with HIV/AIDS

Wainwright House

260 Stuyvesant Ave., Rye, NY 10580 Tel. (914)-967-6080 Fax (914)967-6114
Media Contact, Gen. Mgr., James Wall
Gen. Mgr., James Wall
Major activities: Educational Program and Conference Center; Intellectual, Psychological, Physical and Spiritual Growth; Healing and Health

NORTH CAROLINA

*North Carolina Council of Churches

Methodist Bldg., 1307 Glenwood Ave., Ste. 162, Raleigh, NC 27605-3258 Tel. (919)828-6501
Media Contact, Exec. Dir., Rev. S. Collins Kilburn
Exec. Dir., Rev. S. Collins Kilburn
Program Assoc., Jimmy Creech
Pres., Rev. W. Joseph Mann, P.O. Box 51307, Durham, NC 27717-1307
Treas., Dr. James W. Ferree, 5108 Huntcliff Tr., Winston-Salem, NC 27104
Major activities: Children and Families; Health Care Justice; Christian Unity; Equal Rights; Legislative Program; Criminal Justice; Farmworker Ministry; Rural Crisis; Racial Justice; Disaster Response; Caring Program for Children; AIDS Ministry; Death Penalty

Asheville-Buncombe Community Christian Ministry (ABCCM)

24 Cumberland Ave., Asheville, NC 28801 Tel. (704)259-5300 Fax (704)259-5316
Media Contact, Exec. Dir., Rev. Scott Rogers, Fax (704)259-5323
Exec. Dir., Rev. Scott Rogers
Pres., Dr. John Gran
Major activities: Crisis Ministry; Jail/Prison Ministry; Shelter Ministry; Medical Ministry

Greensboro Urban Ministry

305 West Lee St., Greensboro, NC 27406 Tel. (910)271-5959 Fax (910)271-5920
Media Contact, Exec. Dir., Rev. Mike Aiken
Exec. Dir., Rev. Mike Aiken
Major activities: Emergency Financial Assistance; Emergency Housing; Hunger Relief; Inter-Faith and Inter-Racial Understanding; Justice Ministry; Chaplaincy with the Poor

NORTH DAKOTA

*North Dakota Conference of Churches

227 W. Broadway, Bismarck, ND 58501 Tel. (701)255-0604 Fax (701)222-8543
Media Contact, Office Mgr., Eunice Brinckerhoff
Pres., Dr. Jack J. Seville, PBVM
Treas., Rev. L. Kaye Beau Lac
Ofc. Mgr., Eunice Brinckerhoff
Major activities: Prison Chaplaincy; Rural Life Ministry; Interfaith Dialogue; Faith and Order; North Dakota 101

OHIO

*Ohio Council of Churches

89 E. Wilson Bridge Rd., Columbus, OH 43085-2391 Tel. (614)885-9590 Fax (614)885-6097
Exec. Dir., Bishop Robert Kelley, Int.
Public Policy & Social Advocacy
Agriculture & Rural Concerns, Dir., Craig McGuire
Pres., Charles Loveless
Vice Pres., Joyce Slaughter
Sec., Rev. Barry Wolf
Treas., Jack Davis
Major activities: Agricultural Issues; Economic & Social Justice; Ecumenical Relations; Health Care Reform; Public Policy Issues; Criminal Justice Issues; Welfare Reform; Native American Concerns; African American Males; Theological Dialogue

Akron Area Association of Churches

350 S. Portage Path, Akron, OH 44320 Tel. (216)-535-3112
Media Contact, Admin. Asst., Chloe Ann Kriska
Exec. Dir., Ms. Elsbeth Fritz

Bd. of Trustees, Pres., Rev. Harry Eberts
Vice-Pres.: Rev. David Frees; William H. Fisher
Sec., Rev. Curtis Walker
Treas., Dr. Stephen Laning
Program Dir., Elsbeth Fritz
Christian Ed., Dir., Chloe Ann Kriska
Major activities: Messiah Sing; Interfaith Council; Newsletters; Resource Center; Community Worship; Training of Local Church Leadership; Radio Programs; Clergy and Lay Fellowship Breakfasts; Cable TV; Interfaith Caregivers; Neighborhood Development; Community Outreach

Alliance of Churches

470 E. Broadway, Alliance, OH 44601 Tel. (216)-821-6648
Media Contact, Dir., Lisa A. Miller
Dir., Lisa A. Miller
Pres., Rev. Robert C. Stewart, Jr.
Treas., Betty Rush
Major activities: Christian Education; Community Relations & Service; Ecumenical Worship; Community Ministry; Peacemaking; Medical Transportation for Anyone Needing It; Emergency Financial Assistance

Churchpeople for Change and Reconciliation

326 W. McKibben, Box 488, Lima, OH 45802 Tel. (419)229-6949
Media Contact, Exec. Dir., Richard Keller
Major activities: Developing Agencies for Minorities, Poor, Alienated and Despairing; Community Kitchens

Council of Christian Communions of Greater Cincinnati

42 Calhoun St., Cincinnati, OH 45219-1525 Tel. (513)559-3151
Media Contact, Exec. Dir., Joellen W. Grady
Exec. Dir., Joellen W. Grady
Justice Chaplaincy, Assoc. Dir., Rev. Jack Marsh
Educ., Assoc., Sharon D. Jones
Communication, Asst. Dir., John H. Gassett
Pres., Rev. Randall Hyvonen
Major activities: Christian Unity & Interfaith Cooperation; Justice Chaplaincies; Police-Clergy Team; Adult and Juvenile Jail Chaplains; Religious Education; Broadcasting and Communications; Information Service; Social Concerns

Ecumenical Communications Commission of Northwestern Ohio, Inc.

1011 Sandusky, Ste. M, P.O. Box 351, Perrysburg, OH 43552-0351 Tel. (419)874-3932
Media Contact, Dir., Margaret Hoepfl
Dir., Ms. Margaret Hoepfl
Major activities: Electronic Media Production; Media Education

Greater Dayton Christian Connection

601 W. Riverview Ave., Dayton, OH 45406 Tel. (513)227-9485 Fax (513)227-9486
Media Contact, James S. Burton
Acting Exec. Dir., James S. Burton
Jail Ministry, Dir., Nancy Haas
Reconciliation Ministry, Dir., James Burton
Co-Pres., Rev. Robert Thornton
Co-Pres., Sr. Alice Schottelkotte
Major activities: Communications: Service to Churches and Community; Housing Advocacy; Race Relations Advocacy; Jail Chaplaincy; Youth Task Force; Project Turnaround; CROP Walk; The Gleaning Project; Saturday Meals for Seniors; Newsletter

Inner City Renewal Society

2230 Euclid Ave., Cleveland, OH 44115 Tel. (216)781-3913
Media Contact, Exec. Dir., Myrtle L. Mitchell
Exec. Dir., Myrtle L. Mitchell
Major activities: Friendly Town; Urban Ministries Training and Community Development Center; Drug and Alcohol Education; Project Chore; Scholarship; Burial Aid

Interchurch Council of Greater Cleveland

2230 Euclid Ave., Cleveland, OH 44115 Tel. (216)621-5925 Fax (216)621-0588
Media Contact, Janice Giering
Exec. Dir., Rev. Thomas Olcott, Tel. (216)621-5925
Church & Society, Dir., Rev. Mylion Waite
Communications, Dir., Ms. Janice Giering
Pres., Rev. Gary Walling
Chmn. of the Assembly, Rev. Jeremiah Pryce
Major activities: Church and Society; Communications; Hunger; Christian Education; Legislation; Faith and Order; Public Education; Interchurch News; Tutoring; Parent-Child First Teachers Program; Shelter for Homeless Women and Children; Radio & T.V.; Interracial Cooperation; Interfaith Cooperation; Adopt-A-School; Women of Hope; Leadership Development; Religious Education; Center for Peace & Reconciliation--Youth and the Courts

Mahoning Valley Association of Churches

25 W. Rayen Ave., Youngstown, OH 44503 Tel. (216)744-8946
Media Contact, Exec. Dir., Elsie L. Dursi
Exec. Dir., Elsie L. Dursi
Pres., Rev. Barrie Bodden
Treas., Mr. Paul Fryman
Major activities: Communications; Christian Education; Ecumenism; Social Action; Advocacy

Metropolitan Area Church Council

760 E. Broad St., Columbus, OH 43205 Tel. (614)-461-7103
Media Contact, Exec. Dir., Rev. Burton Cantrell
Exec. Dir., Rev. Burton Cantrell
Chpsn. of Bd., Rev. Karen Shepler
Sec., Alvin Hadley
Treas., Alvin Hadley
Major activities: Newspaper; Liaison with Community Organizations; Assembly; Week of Prayer for Christian Unity; Support for Ministerial Associations and Church Councils; Seminars for Church Leaders; Prayer Groups; CROP Walk; Social Concerns Hearings

Metropolitan Area Religious Coalition of Cincinnati

Ste. 1035, 617 Vine St., Cincinnati, OH 45202-2423 Tel. (513)721-4843 Fax (513)721-4891

Media Contact, Dir., Rev. Duane Holm, Fax (513)-721-4844 .
Dir., Rev. Duane Holm
Pres., Ms. Alice Skirtz
Major activities: Children-At-Risk; Housing; Public Education

Pike County Outreach Council

122 E. Second St., Waverly, OH 45690 Tel. (614)-947-7151
Dir., Judy Dixon
Major activities: Emergency Service Program; Self Help Groups; Homeless Shelter; Summer Bible School

Toledo Ecumenical Area Ministries

444 Floyd St., Toledo, OH 43620 Tel. (419)242-7401 Fax (419)242-7404
Media Contact, Admn., Nancy Lee Atkins
Metro-Toledo Churches United, Admn., Nancy Lee Atkins
Toledo Campus Ministry, Exec. Dir., Rev. Dee Baker, Jr.
Toledo Metropolitan Mission, Exec. Dir., Nancy Lee Atkins
Major activities: Ecumenical Relations; Interfaith Relations; Food Program; Campus Ministry; Social Action (Public Education; Health Care; Urban Ministry; Employment; Welfare Rights; Housing; Mental Retardation; Voter Registration/Education)

Tuscarawas County Council for Church and Community

107 West High , Ste. B, New Philadelphia, OH 44663 Tel. (216)343-6012
Exec. Dir., Barbara E. Lauer
Pres., Zoe Ann Kelley, 201 E. 12th St., Dover, OH 44622
Treas., Mr. James Barnhouse, 120 N. Broadway, New Philadelphia, OH 44663
Major activities: Human Services; Health; Family Life; Child Abuse; Housing; Educational Programs; Emergency Assistance; Legislative Concerns; Juvenile Prevention Program; Teen Pregnancy Prevention Program; Prevention Program for High Risk Children; Bimonthly newsletter The Pilot

West Side Ecumenical Ministry

4315 Bridge Ave, Cleveland, OH 44113 Tel. (216)-651-2037 Fax (216)651-4145
Media Contact, Exec. Dir., Elving F. Otero
Exec. Dir., Elving F. Otero
Assoc. Dir., Kathleen O'Brien
Major activities: Emergency Food Centers; Senior Meals Programs; Youth Services; Advocacy, Empowerment Programs; Church Clusters; Employment Assistance Program; Head Start Centers; Theatre

OKLAHOMA

*Oklahoma Conference of Churches

P.O. Box 60288, 2200 Classen Blvd., Ste. 1300, 0klahoma City, OK 73146-0288 Tel. (405)525-2928 Fax (405)524-8331
Media Contact, Int. Exec. Dir., The Rev. Dr. Rita K. Cowan
Int. Exec. Dir., The Rev. Dr. Rita K. Cowan
Pres., The Rev. David Wasserman, 3304 E. 4th St., Tulsa, OK 74112-2612
Treas., Mrs. Ann Fent
Major activities: Christian Unity Issues; COCU Covenanting; Community Building Among Members; Rural Communty Care; Ecumenical Decade with Women; Children's Advocacy; Day at the Legislature; Interfaith Relations; Public Education; Impact

Tulsa Metropolitan Ministry

221 S. Nogales, Tulsa, OK 74127 Tel. (918)582-3147 Fax (918)582-3159
Exec. Dir., Sr. Sylvia Schmidt, S.F.C.C.
Assoc. Dir., James Robinson
Day Center for the Homeless, Dir., Marcia Sharp
Housing Outreach Services of Tulsa, Dir., Rev. Charles Boyle
Advocacy Program Dir., Rev. Larry Cowan
Pres., Maynard Ungerman
Vice-Pres., Rev. David Wasserman
Sec., Nancy Wirth
Treas., Rev. Ross Jones
Major activities: Corrections Ministry; Jewish-Christian Understanding; Police-Community Relations; Shelter for the Homeless; Women's Issues; Shelter for Mentally Ill; Outreach and Advocacy for Public Housing; Spirituality and Aging; Legislative Issues; Interfaith Dialogue TV Series; Christian Issues/Justice and Peace Issues; Immigration Concerns; Environmental Concerns; Communications; Racism Task Force

OREGON

*Ecumenical Ministries of Oregon

0245 S.W. Bancroft St., Ste. B, Portland, OR 97201 Tel. (503)221-1054 Fax (503)223-7007
Media Contact, Exec. Dir., Rev. Rodney I. Page
Exec. Dir., Rev. Rodney I. Page
Dep. Dir., Barbara J. George
Fin. Services Mgr., Kyler Kenney
Center for Urban Education, Dir., Rodney I. Page
Legis. & Govt. Ofc., Dir., Ellen C. Lowe
Grants & Contracts Specialist, Gary B. Logsdon
Personnel Admn., Lori L. Rimbey
Med. Dir., Neal Rendleman, M.D.
Hopewell House Dir., Colleen Lyman
Hemophilia NW, Dir.: Co-Dir., Barry Kurath; Co-Dir., Dave Tody
Drug Educ. Proj., Nigel Wrangham
Alcohol & Drug Min., Nancy Anderson
Police Chaplain, Rev. Greg Kammann
Sponsors Organized to Assist Refugees, Penny Strauss
Emergency Food, Dir., Jack Kennedy
Folk-Time (Soc. Prog. for Mentally Ill), Dir., Kristine Britton
HIV Day Center, Co-Dir., Tina Tommaso-Jennings
HIV Day Center, Co-Dir., Gary McInnis
Odyssey, Jay Atwood
Cult Resource Center, Kent Burtner
Common Ground, Jane Harper
Shared Housing, Kent Burtner
Assoc. Dir. for Admn., Stephanie C. Howell
Dir. of Nursing Ser., Judith Kenning
Patton Home, Elaine Jenks
Pres., Bonny Groshong
Pres. Elect, Bishop William W. Dew
Treas., Ron Means

Major activities: Educational Ministries; Legislation; Urban Ministries; Refugees; Chaplaincy; Social Concerns; Jewish-Christian Relations; Farm\Rural Ministry; Alcohol\Drug Ministry; Welfare Advocacy; Faith & Order; Peace Ministries; IMPACT; Diversity Training; Communications; AIDS Ministry; HIV Day Center; Prostitution Ministry; Racism; Religious Education; Health & Human Ministries; Medical Clinic; Cult Resource Center; Emergency Food; Mental Illness Support

PENNSYLVANIA

*Pennsylvania Conference on Interchurch Cooperation

P.O. Box 2835, 223 North St., Harrisburg, PA 17105 Tel. (717)545-4761 Fax (717)238-1473
900 S. Arlington Ave., Harrisburg, PA 17109
Media Contact, Dr. Howard Fetterhoff
Co-Staff: Dr. Howard Fetterhoff; Rev. Albert E. Myers
Co-Chpsns.: Bishop Nicholas C. Dattilo; Bishop Robert Rowley, Jr.
Major activities: Theological Consultation; Social Concerns; Inter-Church Planning; Conferences and Seminars; Disaster Response Preparedness

*The Pennsylvania Council of Churches

900 S. Arlington Ave., Ste. 100, Harrisburg, PA 17109-5089 Tel. (717)545-4761
Media Contact, Exec. Dir., Rev. Albert E. Myers, Fax (717)545-4765
Exec. Dir., Rev. Albert E. Myers
Public Policy, Asst. Exec. Dir., Rev. Paul D. Gehris
Coord. for Contract Chaplaincy, Rev. Charles R. Meile, Jr.
Coord. for Leisure Ministries, Rev. Gail Mogel Tillotson
Coord. For Farmworker Ministries, Rev. Ray L. Kauffman
Consultant for Trucker/Travel Ministries, Rev. John A. Rodgers
Pres., Rev. Thomas M. Johnston, Jr., 3040 Market St., Camp Hill, PA 17011-4539
Vice-Pres., Mrs. Pattee Miller
Sec., Rev. Jack Rothenberger
Treas., Barry R. Herr
Bus. Mgr., Janet Gollick
Major activities: Institutional Ministry; Migrant Ministry; Truck Stop Chaplaincy; Social Ministry; Leisure Ministry; Inter-Church Planning and Dialog; Conferences; Disaster Response; Trade Association Activities; Church Education; Ethnic Cooperation

Allegheny Valley Association of Churches

1333 Freeport Rd., Natrona Heights, PA 15065 Tel. (412)226-0606
Media Contact, Exec. Dir., Luella H. Barrage
Exec. Dir., Luella H. Barrage
Pres., Rev. Dr. W. James Legge, 232 Tarentum-Culmerville Rd., Tarentum, PA 15084
Treas., Mrs. Libby Grimm, 312 Butternut Ln., Tarentum, PA 15084
Major activities: Education Evangelism Workshops; Ecumenical Services; Dial-a-Devotion; Youth Activities; CROP Walk; Food Bank; Super Cupboard; Emergency Aid; Cross-on-the-Hill; AVAC Hospitality Network for Homeless Families; AVAC Volunteer Caregivers

Christian Associates of Southwest Pennsylvania

239 Fourth Ave., #1817, Pittsburgh, PA 15222-1769 Tel. (412)288-4020 Fax (412)288-4023
Media Contact, Exec. Dir., Rev. Dr. Robert D. Forsythe
Exec. Dir., Rev. Dr. Robert D. Forsythe
Communications Coord., Bruce J. Randolph
Cable TV Coord., Mr. Earl C. Hartman, Jr.
Admn. Asst., Mrs. Barbara Irwin
Pres., Dr. Andrew C. Harvey
Treas., Major Donald Hostetler
AIDS Care Teams, Project Dir., Mrs. Patricia Zerega
Major activities: Communications; AIDS Care Teams; Church and Community; Leadership Development; Theological Dialogue; Racism

Christian Churches United of the Tri-County Area

P.O. Box 60750, Harrisburg, PA 17106-0750 Tel. (717)230-9550 Fax (717)230-9554
Media Contact, Exec. Dir., Rev. Kirsten E. Lunde
Exec. Dir., Rev. Kirsten E. Lunde
Pres., John Carroll
Treas., Rev. Harry Skilton
Vice-Pres., Linda Hicks
Sec., Rev. Willamae Williams
HELP & LaCasa Ministries, Dir., Jacqueline Rucker, 201 Locust St., Harrisburg, PA 17101 Tel. (717)238-2851 Fax (717)238-1916
Major activities: Volunteer Ministries to Prisons; Hospitals; Mental Health; Aging; Christian Education; HELP (Housing, Rent, Food, Medication, Transportation, Home Heating, Clothing); La Casa de Amistad (The House of Friendship) Social Services; AIDS Outreach; Prison Chaplaincy; Lend-A-Hand (Disaster Rebuilding)

Christians United in Beaver County

1098 Third St., Beaver, PA 15009 Tel. (412)774-1446
Media Contact, Exec. Sec., Mrs. Lois L. Smith
Exec. Sec., Mrs. Lois L. Smith
Chaplains: Rev. Samuel Ward; Mrs. Erika Bruner; Rev. Anthony Massey; Rev. Frank Churchill; Mr. Jack Kirkpatrick
Pres., Rev. Dr. George W. Carson, 144 Rama Rd., Beaver Falls, PA 15010
Treas., Mrs. Jane Mine, 2601-19th St., Beaver Falls, PA 15010
Major activities: Christian Education; Evangelism; Radio; Social Action; Church Women United; United Church Men; Ecumenism; Hospital, Detention Home and Jail Ministry

East End Cooperative Ministry

250 N. Highland Ave., Pittsburgh, PA 15206 Tel. (412)361-5549 Fax (412)361-0151
Media Contact, Nancy Paul
Exec. Dir., Mrs. Judith Marker
Major activities: Food Pantry; Soup Kitchen; Men's Emergency Shelter; Drop-In Shelter for Homeless; Meals on Wheels; Casework and Supportive Services for Elderly; Information and Referral; Program for Children and Youth; Bridge Housing Program for Men and Women in Recovery and Their Children

Ecumenical Conference of Greater Altoona

1208 - 13th St., P.O. Box 305, Altoona, PA 16603 Tel. (814)942-0512
Media Contact, Exec. Dir., Mrs. Eileen Becker
Exec. Dir., Mrs. Eileen Becker
Major activities: Religious Education; Workshops; Ecumenical Activities; Religious Christmas Parade; Campus Ministry; Community Concerns; Peace Forum; Religious Education for Mentally Handicapped; Inter-faith Committee; Prison Ministry

Greater Bethlehem Area Council of Churches

520 E. Broad St., Bethlehem, PA 18018 Tel. (610)-867-8671
Media Contact, Exec. Dir., Rev. Dr. Catherine A. Ziel
Exec. Dir., Rev. Dr. Catherine A. Ziel
Pres., Mr. Charles Shoemaker, 2148 Grove Rd., Bethlehem, PA 18018
Treas., Mr. Robert Gerst, 900 Wedgewood Rd., Bethlehem, PA 18017
Major activities: Support Ministry; Institutional Ministry to Elderly and Infirm; Family Concerns; Scripture Center; Social Concerns; World Local Hunger Projects; Elderly Ministry

Hanover Area Council of Churches

120 York St., Hanover, PA 17331-3126 Tel. (717)-633-6353
Media Contact, Exec. Dir., Rev. Nancy M. Hewitt
Exec. Dir., Rev. Nancy M. Hewitt
Major activities: Meals on Wheels, Provide a Lunch Program, Fresh Air Program, Clothing Bank, Hospital Chaplaincy Services; Congregational & Interfaith Relations, Public Ecumenical Programs and Services, State Park Chaplaincy Services & Children's Program

Inter-Church Ministries of Erie County

252 W. 7th St., Erie, PA 16501 Tel. (814)454-2411
Media Contact, Exec. Dir., The Rev. Frederick D. Thompson
Exec. Dir., Rev. Frederick D. Thompson
Adjunct Staff: Aging Prog., Ms. Carolyn A. DiMattio
Voucher Program, Mary Stewart
Pres., The Rev. J. Kenneth Laber, P.O. Box 268, North East, PA 16428
Treas., The Rev. S. James Schmittle, 1036 E. 35th St., Erie, PA 16504
Major activities: Local Ecumenism; Ministry with Aging; Social Ministry; Continuing Education; N.W. Pa. Conf. of Bishops and Judicatory Execs.; Institute of Pastoral Care; Theological Dialogue; Coats for Kids; Voucher Program for Emergency Assistance

Lancaster County Council of Churches

447 E. King St., Lancaster, PA 17602 Tel. (717)-291-2261
Media Contact, Publ. Chpsn., Rev. Dr. J. Jeffrey Zetto, 909 Larchmont La., Lancaster, PA 17601 Tel. (717)397-4841
Pres., Rev. Robert Bailey
Exec. Dir., Rev. Dr. J. Jeffrey Zetto
Prescott House, Dir., Casey Jones
Asst. Admn., Kim Y. Wittel
Child Abuse, Dir., Louise Schiraldi
CONTACT, Dir., Lois Gascho
Service Ministry, Dir., Adela Dohner
Major activities: Social Ministry; Residential Ministry to Youthful Offenders; CONTACT; Advocacy; Child Abuse Prevention

Lebanon County Christian Ministries

818 Water St., P.O. Box 654, Lebanon, PA 17046 Tel. (717)274-2601
Media Contact, Exec. Dir., P. Richard Forney
Exec. Dir., P. Richard Forney
Food & Clothing Bank Dir., Lillian Morales
H.O.P.E. Services, P. Richard Forney
Noon Meals Coord., Mrs. Glenda Wenger
Major activities: H.O.P.E. (Helping Our People in Emergencies); Food & Clothing Bank; Free Meal Program; Commodity Distribution Program; Ecumenical Events; Chaplaincy and Support Services

Lehigh County Conference of Churches

534 Chew St., Allentown, PA 18102 Tel. (610)-433-6421 Fax (610)439-8039
Media Contact, Exec. Dir., Rev. William A. Seaman
Exec. Dir., Rev. William A. Seaman
Pres., Rev. Richard Guhl
1st Vice-Pres., Msgr. John Murphy
Sec., Mrs.. Geraldine K. Moyer
Treas., Mr. George Q. Nichols
Major activities: Chaplaincy Program; Migrant Ministry; Social Concerns and Action; Clergy Dialogues; Drop-In-Center for De-Institutionalized Adults; Ecumenical Food Kitchen; Housing Advocacy Program; Pathways (Reference to Social Services), Street Contact

Metropolitan Christian Council of Philadelphia

1501 Cherry St., Philadelphia, PA 19102 Tel. (215)563-7854 Fax (215)563-6849
Media Contact, Assoc. Communications, Ms. Nancy L. Nolde
Exec. Dir., Rev. C. Edward Geiger
Assoc. Communications, Ms. Nancy L. Nolde
Office Mgr., Mrs. Joan G. Shipman
Pres., Rt. Rev. Allen L. Bartlett, Jr.
Vice-Pres., Rev. Janet K. Hess
Treas., A. Louis Denton, Esq.
Major activities: Congregational Clusters; Public Policy Advocacy; Communication; Interfaith Dialogue

North Hills Youth Ministry (Counseling Youth and Families)

802 McKnight Park Dr., Pittsburgh, PA 15237 Tel. (412)366-1300
Media Contact, Exec. Dir., Rev. Ronald B. Barnes
Exec. Dir., Ronald B. Barnes
Major activities: Elementary, Junior and Senior High School Individual and Family Counseling; Elementary Age Youth Early Intervention Counseling; Educational Programming for Churches and Schools; Youth Advocacy; Parent Education

Northside Common Ministries

P.O. Box 99861, Pittsburgh, PA 15233 Tel. (412)-323-1163
Media Contact, Exec. Dir., Roy J. Banner
Exec. Dir., Roy J. Banner
Pres., Rev. James C. Raymond, Jr.
Major activities: Pleasant Valley Shelter for Homeless Men; Advocacy around Hunger, Housing, Poverty, and Racial Issues; Community Food Pantry and Service Center; Permanent Supportive Housing

Northwest Interfaith Movement

6757 Greene St., Philadelphia, PA 19119 Tel. (215)843-5600 Fax (215)843-2755
Media Contact, Exec. Dir., Rev. Richard R. Fernandez
Exec. Dir., Rev. Richard R. Fernandez
Chpsn., Hugh Blair
Long Term Care Connection, Dir., Valerie Pogozelski
Neighborhood Child Care Resource Prog., Dir, Amy Gendall
Major activities: Community Development & Community Reinvestment; Older Adult Concerns; Nursing Home Program; Unemployment; Economic Issues; Public Education; Peace; Racism; Poverty Issues

ProJeCt of Easton, Inc.

330 Ferry St., Easton, PA 18042 Tel. (215)258-4361
Pres., Dr. John H. Updegrove
Vice-Pres., Rev. Charles E. Staples
Sec., Rosemary Reese
Treas., Dr. George G. Sause
Exec. Dir., Maryellen Shuman
Major activities: Food Bank; Adult Literacy Program; English as a Second Language; Children's Programs; Parents as Student Support; CROP Walk; Interfaith Council; Family Literacy; Emergency Assistance; Even Start Family Literacy

Reading Berks Conference of Churches

54 N. 8th St., Reading, PA 19601 Tel. (610)375-6108
Media Contact, Exec. Dir., Rev. Calvin Kurtz
Exec. Dir., Rev. Calvin Kurtz
Pres., Rev. Thomas Pappalas
Treas., Mr. Lee M. LeVan
Major activities: Institutional Ministry; Social Action; Migrant Ministry; CWS; CROP Walk for Hunger; Emergency Assistance; Prison Chaplaincy; AIDS Hospice Development; Hospital Chaplaincy; Interchurch/Intercultural Services; Children & Youth Ministry

Reading Urban Ministry

134 N. Fifth St., Reading, PA 19601 Tel. (610)374-6917
Media Contact, Beth Bitler
Exec. Dir., Beth Bitler
Pres., Mark C. Potts
Vice-Pres., Jill Braun
Sec., Fianna Holt
Treas., Raymond Drain
Major activities: Community Clothing Center; Friendly Visitor Program to Elderly; Summer Youth Program; Family Action Support Team (Child Abuse Prevention)

South Hills Interfaith Ministries

5311 Progress Blvd., Bethel Park, PA 15102 Tel. (412)854-9120 Fax (412)854-9123
Media Contact, Publ. Rel. Dir., James Craig Yearsley
Prog. Dir., James Craig Yearsley
Psychological Services, Mr. Don Zandier
Community Services, Sherry Kotz
Business Mgr., Jeff Walley
Chpsn., Jack Kelly
Treas., James McKeen, Jr.
Major activities: Basic Human Needs; Community Organization and Development; Inter-Faith Cooperation; Personal Growth; At-Risk Youth Development

United Churches of Williamsport and Lycoming County

202 E. Third St., Williamsport, PA 17701 Tel. (717)322-1110
Media Contact, Exec. Dir., Mrs. Gwen Nelson Bernstine
Exec. Dir., Mrs. Gwen Nelson Bernstine
Ofc. Sec., Mrs. Linda Winter
Pres., Fr. Daniel C. Kovalak, 1725 Blair St., Williamsport, PA 17701
Treas., Mr. Russell E. Tingue, 1987 Yale Ave., Williamsport, PA 17701
Shepherd of the Streets, Rev. Wilbur L. Scranton, III, 130 E. 3rd St., Williamsport, PA 17701
Ecumenism, Dir., Rev. Jan L. Elsasser, R R 2, Box 105, Cogan Station, PA 17728
Educ. Ministries, Dir., Dr. Timothy A. Bryant, Jr., 1205 Grampian Blvd., Williamsport, PA 17701
Institutional Ministry, Dir., Mrs. Ruth Doran, 122 S. Main St., Hughesville, PA 17737
Radio-TV, Dir., Rev. Louis Gatti, 3200 Lycoming Creek Rd., Williamsport, PA 17701
Prison Ministry, Dir., Mrs. Jane Russell
Christian Social Concerns, Dir., Rev. H. Frank Showers, 522 N. Grier St., Williamsport, PA 17701
Major activities: Ecumenism; Educational Ministries; Church Women United; Church World Service and CROP; Prison Ministry; Radio-TV; Nursing Homes; Fuel Bank; Food Pantry; Family Life; Shepherd of the Streets Urban Ministry; Peace Concerns; Housing Initiative; Interfaith Dialogue

Wilkinsburg Community Ministry

710 Mulberry St., Pittsburgh, PA 15221 Tel. (412)-241-8072 Fax (412)241-8315
Media Contact, Dir., Rev. Vivian Lovingood
Dir., Rev. Vivian Lovingood
Pres. of Bd., Mr. Jack Peffer
Major activities: Hunger Ministry; After School Youth Programs; Summer Bible School; Teen-Moms Infant Care; Meals on Wheels; Tape Ministry

Wyoming Valley Council of Churches

35 S. Franklin St., Wilkes-Barre, PA 18701 Tel. (717)825-8543
Media Contact, Exec. Dir., Susan Grine Harper
Exec. Dir., Susan Grine Harper
Ofc. Sec., Mrs. Sandra Karrott
Pres., Marguerite Ritz
Treas., H. Merritt Hughes

Major activities: Nursing Home Chaplaincy; Martin Luther King, Jr. fuel drive in association with local agencies; Hospital Referral Service; Choral Festival of Faith; Migrant Ministry; Ecumenical Pulpit Exchange; Int; CROP Hunger Walk; Pastoral Care Ministries; Clergy Retreats and Seminars

York County Council of Churches

104 Lafayette St., P.O. Box 1865, York, PA 17405-1865 Tel. (717)854-9504 Fax (717)843-5295
Media Contact, Exec. Dir., Rev. Patrick B. Walker
Pres., Dr. Samuel Deisher
Exec. Dir., Rev. Patrick B. Walker
Major activities: Educational Development; Spiritual Growth and Renewal; Worship and Witness; Congregational Resourcing; Outreach and Mission

RHODE ISLAND

*The Rhode Island State Council of Churches

734 Hope St., Providence, RI 02906 Tel. (401)861-1700 Fax (401)331-3080
Media Contact, Exec. Minister, Rev. James C. Miller
Exec. Minister, Rev. James C. Miller
Admn. Asst., Ms. Peggy MacNie
Pres., Very Rev. Timothy Ferguson
Treas., Mr. George Weavill
Major activities: Urban Ministries; TV; Institutional Chaplaincy; Advocacy/Justice & Service: Legislative Liaison; Faith & Order; Leadership Development; Campus Ministries

SOUTH CAROLINA

*South Carolina Christian Action Council, Inc.

P.O. Box 3663, Columbia, SC 29230 Tel. (803)-786-7115 Fax (803)786-7116
Media Contact, Exec. Minister, Dr. L. Wayne Bryan
Exec. Minister, Dr. L. Wayne Bryan
Pres., Ms. Betty Park
Major activities: Advocacy and Ecumenism; Continuing Education; Interfaith Dialogue; Citizenship and Public Affairs; Publications

United Ministries

606 Pendleton St., Greenville, SC 29601 Tel. (803)232-6463 Fax (803)370-3518
Media Contact, Exec. Dir., Rev. Beth Templeton
Exec. Dir., Rev. Beth Templeton
Pres., Rev. Vic Greene
Vice-Pres., Ms. Claire Geddie
Sec., Ms. Rosemund Korybski
Treas., Mr. Joel Brockman
Major activities: Volunteer Programs; Adopt-A-House; Spend a Day; Building Wheelchair Ramps; Emergency Assistance with Rent, Utilities, Medication, Heating, Food, Shelter Referrals; Homeless Programs: Place of Hope Day Shelter for Homeless; Employment Readiness; Travelers Aid; Magdalene Project; Case Management; Life Skills Training; Transitions for Public Assistance

SOUTH DAKOTA

*Association of Christian Churches

1320 S. Minnesota Ave., Ste. 210, Sioux Falls, SD 57105 Tel. (605)334-1980
Media Contact, Pres., Rev. Charles Allen, 2412 S. Cliff Ave., Sioux Falls, SD 57105 Tel. (605)334-2802
Pres., Rev. Charles Allen
Ofc. Mgr., Pat Willard
Major activities: Ecumenical Forums; Continuing Education for Clergy; Legislative Information; Resourcing Local Ecumenism; Native American Issues; Ecumenical Fields Ministries; Rural Economic Development

TENNESSEE

*Tennessee Association of Churches

103 Oak St., Ashland City, TN 37015 Tel. (615)-792-4631
Media Contact, Ecumenical Admn., Dr. David Davis
Ecumenical Admn., Dr. David Davis
Major activities: Faith and Order; Christian Unity; Social Concern Ministries; Governmental Concerns; Governor's Prayer Breakfast; Clergy/Funeral Directors Group; Bicentennial Program

Metropolitan Inter Faith Association (MIFA)

P.O. Box 3130, Memphis, TN 38173-0130 Tel. (901)527-0208 Fax (901)527-3202
Media Contact, Dir., Media Relations, Kim Gaskill
Exec. Dir., Mr. Allie Prescott
Urban Ministries, Dir., Sara Holmes
Major activities: Emergency Housing; Emergency Services (Rent, Utility, Food, Clothing Assistance); Home-Delivered Meals and Senior Support Services; Youth Services

Volunteer Ministry Center

113 South Gay St., Knoxville, TN 37902 Tel. (423)524-3926
Exec. Dir., Angelia Moon, 103 S. Gay St., Knoxville, TN 37902 Tel. (423)524-3926
Exec. Dir., Angelia Moon
Pres., David Leech
Vice-Pres., John Moxham
Treas., Doug Thompson
Major activities: Homeless Program; Food Line; Crisis Referral Program; Subsidized Apartment Program; Counselling Program

TEXAS

*Texas Conference of Churches

6633 Hwy. 290 East, Ste. 200, Austin, TX 78723-1157 Tel. (512)451-0991 Fax (512)451-2904
Media Contact, Exec. Dir., Mary Weathers
Interim Exec. Dir., Mary Weathers
Church & Society Asst., Ms. Mary Berwick
Dir., Addictions Min., Ms. Trish Merrill
Pres., Bishop Mark Herbener
Major activities: Faith & Order; Related Ecumenism; Christian-Jewish Relations; Children's Issues; Peace; Disaster Response; Border Concerns; Criminal Justice

Austin Metropolitan Ministries

2026 Guadalupe, Ste. 226, Austin, TX 78705 Tel. (512)472-7627
Media Contact, Exec. Dir., Patrick Flood, Fax (512)472-5274
Exec. Dir., Patrick Flood
Pres., Rev. J. Charles Merrill
Treas., Rev. T. James Bethell
Program Staff: Rev. Don Bobb; David Smith; Antonia Hernandez-Salazar
Chaplain: Gardner-Betts Juvenile Center, Rev. Floyd Vick
Office Admn., Carole Hatfield
Major activities: Broadcast Ministry; Older Persons Task Force; Housing Task Force; Peace and Justice Commission; Youth at Risk; AIDS Service; Commission on Racism; Interfaith Dialogues; Economy and Jobs Issues

Border Association for Refugees from Central America (BARCA), Inc.

P.O. Box 715, Edinburg, TX 78540 Tel. (512)631-7447 Fax (512)687-9266
Media Contact, Exec. Dir., Ninfa Ochoa-Krueger
Exec. Dir, Ninfa Ochoa-Krueger
Refugee Children Serv., Dir., Bertha de la Rosa
Major activities: Food, Shelter, Clothing to Central Americans; Medical and Other Emergency Aid; Legal Services; Special Services to Children; Speakers on Refugee and Immigrant Concerns for Church Groups; Orientation and Advocacy and Legal Services for Immigrants and Refugees

Corpus Christi Metro Ministries

1919 Leopard St., P.O. Box 4899, Corpus Christi, TX 78469-4899 Tel. (512)887-0151
Media Contact, Exec. Dir., Rev. Edward B. Seeger, P.O. Box 4899, Corpus Christi, TX 78469-4899 Tel. (512)887-0151 Fax (512)887-7900
Exec. Dir., Rev. Edward B. Seeger
Admn. Dir., Daniel D. Scott
Volunteer Dir., Ann Schiro
Fin. Coord., Sue McCown
Loaves & Fishes Dir., Ray Gomez
Counseling Dir., Amie Harrell
Rustic House Dir., Amie Harrell
Employment Dir., Curtis Blevins
Bethany House Dir., Michael White
Rainbow House Dir., Alicia DeLeon Williams
Adopt A Caseworker Dir., Jo Flindt
Health Clinic Dir., Ann Schiro
Major activities: Free Cafeteria;Transitional Shelters; Counseling; Job Readiness; Job Placement; Abuse Prevention and Intervention; Primary Health Care; Community Service Restitution; Emergency Clothing;I&R

East Dallas Cooperative Parish

P.O. Box 720305, Dallas, TX 75372-0305 Tel. (214)823-9149 Fax (214)823-2015
Media Contact, Admn., Elizabeth Blessing
Pres., Jo Ann Biggs
Sec., Mary Catherine Sweet
Major activities: Emergency Food, Clothing, Job Bank; Medical Clinic; Legal Clinic, Tutorial Education; Home Companion Service; Pre-School Education; Developmental Learning Center; Asian and Hispanic Ministry; Activity Center--Low Income Older Adults; Counseling

Greater Dallas Community of Churches

2800 Swiss Ave., Dallas, TX 75204 Tel. (214)824-8680 Fax (214)824-8726
Dir. of Communcations, Colleen Townsley Hager, 2800 Swiss Ave., Dallas, TX 75204 Tel. (214)-824-8680 Fax (214)824-8726
Exec. Dir., ----
Assoc. Dirs.: Rev. Holsey Hickman
Church & Community, Assoc. Dirs.: John Stoesz
Community College Min., Dir., Dr. Philip del Rosario
Development Dir., Carole Rylander
Pres., Frank Jackson
Treas., Shirley Latham
Child Advocacy, Program Assoc., Rev. Carolyn Bullard-Zerweck
Major activities: Hospital Chaplaincy; Community College Ministry; Hunger; Peacemaking; Faith and Life; Jewish-Christian Relations; Racial Ethnic Justice; Child Advocacy; Americorps Project

Interfaith Ministries for Greater Houston

3217 Montrose Blvd., Houston, TX 77006 Tel. (713)522-3955 Fax (713)520-4663
Media Contact, Exec. Dir., David A. Leslie
Exec. Dir., David A. Leslie
Pres., Rev. John T. King
First, Vice. Pres., Rabbi Roy Walter
Second, Vice. Pres., Collyn A. Peddie
Development, Dir., Sharon Ervine
Assoc. Exec. Dir., Larry Norton
Treas., Lea Fastow
Sec., Alice Rains
Major activities: Community Concerns: Hunger; Older Adults; Families; Youth; Child Abuse; Refugee Services; Congregational Relations and Development; Social Service Programs: Refugee Services; Hunger Coalition; Youth Victim Witness; Family Connection, Meals on Wheels,; Senior Health; RSVP; Foster Grandparents

North Dallas Shared Ministries

2530 Glenda Ln., #500, Dallas, TX 75229 Tel. (214)620-8696 Fax (214)620-0433
Media Contact, Exec. Dir., J. Dwayne Martin
Exec. Dir., J. Dwayne Martin
Pres., Edward St. John
Major activities: Emergency Assistance; Job Counseling; ESL

Northside Inter-Church Agency (NICA)

506 N.W. 15th St., Fort Worth, TX 76106 Tel. (817)626-1102 Fax (817)626-1229
Media Contact, Exec. Dir., Francine Esposito Pratt
Dir., Francine Esposito Pratt
Major activities: Food; Clothing; Counseling; Information and Referral; Furniture and Household Items; Nutrition Education and Teen Program; Employment Services; Thanksgiving Basket Program; "Last Resort" Christmas Program; Community Networking; Ecumenical Worship Services; Volunteer Training; Newsletter

San Antonio Community of Churches

1101 W. Woodlawn, San Antonio, TX 78201 Tel. (210)733-9159
Media Contact, Exec. Dir., Dr. Kenneth Thompson
Exec. Dir., Dr. Kenneth Thompson
Pres., Dr. Michael Beaugh
Major activities: Christian Educ.; Missions; Infant Formula and Medical Prescriptions for Children of Indigent Families; Continuing Education For Clergy; Media Resource Center; Social Issues; Aging Concerns; Youth Concerns; Family, Congregation and Community Life Resource Center

San Antonio Urban Ministries

2002 W. Olmos Dr., San Antonio, TX 78201 Tel. (210)733-5080 Fax (210)733-5408
Media Contact, Sue Kelly
Exec. Dir., Sue Kelly
Pres., ----
Major activities: Homes for Discharged Mental Patients; After School Care for Latch Key Children; Christian Based Community Ministry

Southeast Area Churches (SEARCH)

P.O. Box 51256, Fort Worth, TX 76105 Tel. (817)-531-2211
Media Contact, Exec. Dir., Ms. Dorothy Anderson-Develrow
Dir., Ms. Dorothy Anderson-Develrow
Major activities: Emergency Assistance; Advocacy; Information and Referral; Community Worship; School Supplies; Direct Aid to Low Income and Elderly

Southside Area Ministries, Inc. (SAM)

305 W. Broadway, Fort Worth, TX 76104 Tel. (817)332-3778
Media Contact, Linda Freeto
Exec. Dir., Linda Freeto
Major activities: Assisting children for whom English is a second language; Tutoring grades K-5; Mentoring Grades 6-8; Programs for Senior Citizens

Tarrant Area Community of Churches

801 Texas St., Fort Worth, TX 76102 Tel. (817)-335-9341
Media Contact, Pres., Henry N. Smith
Pres., Dr. Douglas A. Newsom
Treas., Mr. Buzz Parkhill
Exec. Dir., Dr. Henry N. Smith
Major activities: Adopt-A-Nursing-Home Project; Eldercare Program; Collaborative Jail Ministry; Children's Sabbath Sponsorship; Interfaith Activities; Sister Church Relationships; Week of Prayer for Christian Unity; CROP Walk for Hunger Relief; Community Issues Forums

United Board of Missions

1701 Bluebonnet Ave., P.O. Box 3856, Port Arthur, TX 77643-3856 Tel. (409)982-9412 Fax (409)985-3668
Media Contact, Admn. Asst., Carolyn Schwarr, P.O.Box 3856, Port Arthur, TX 77643 Tel. (409)982-9412 Fax (409)985-3668
Exec. Dir., Clark Moore
Pres., Charlie Harris
Major activities: Emergency Assistance (Food and Clothing, Rent and Utility, Medical, Dental, Transportation); Share a Toy at Christmas; Counseling; Back to School Clothing Assistance; Information and Referral; Hearing Aid Bank; Meals on Wheels; Super Pantry; Energy Conservation Programs; Job Bank Assistance to Local Residents Only

VERMONT

*Vermont Ecumenical Council and Bible Society

285 Maple St., Burlington, VT 05401 Tel. (802)-864-7723
Media Contact, Admn. Asst., Carolyn Carpenter
Exec. Sec., Rev. John E. Nutting
Pres., Ruah Sweenerfelt
Vice-Pres., Rev. Dr. Louis A. George
Treas., Rev. Louis Drew
Major activities: Christian Unity; Bible Distribution; Social Justice; Committee on Faith and Order

VIRGINIA

*Virginia Council of Churches, Inc.

1214 W. Graham Rd., Richmond, VA 23220-1409 Tel. (804)321-3300 Fax (804)329-5066
Media Contact, Gen. Min., Rev. James F. McDonald
Gen. Min., Rev. James F. McDonald
Assoc. Gen. Min., Rev. Judith Fa Galde Bennett
Migrant Head Start, Dir., Richard D. Cagnan
Refugee Resettlement, Dir., Rev. Joseph S. Roberson
Weekday Rel. Educ., Coord., Ms. Evelyn W. Simmons, P.O. Box 245, Clifton Forge, VA 24422
Campus Ministry Forum, Coord., Rev. Robert Thomason, 5000 Echols Ave., Alexandria, VA 22304
Major activities: Faith and Order; Network Building & Coordination; Ecumenical Communications; Justice and Legislative Concerns; Educational Development; Rural Concerns, Refugee Resettlement; Migrant Ministries and Migrant Day Care; Disaster Coordination

Community Ministry of Fairfax County

10530 Rosehaven St., Ste. 350, Fairfax, VA 22030 Tel. (703)352-3434
Media Contact, Exec. Dir., John Wells, 10530 Rosehaven St. Ste. 350, Fairfax, VA 22030 Tel. (703)352-3434
Exec. Dir., John Wells
Newsletter Ed., John Wells
Chpsn., Phil True
Treas., Robert Hunt
Major activities: Ecumenical Social Ministry; Elderly; Criminal Justice; Housing; Public Education

WASHINGTON

*Washington Association of Churches

419 Occidental Ave. S., Ste. 201, Seattle, WA 98104 Tel. (206)625-9790 Fax (206)625-9791
Media Contact, John C. Boonstra
Exec. Min., Rev. John C. Boonstra

Legislative, Dir., Kathleen Russell
Pres., Rev. Laurie Rudel
Treas., Kathy Johnson
Major activities: Faith and Order; Justice Advocacy; Hunger Action; Legislation; Denominational Ecumenical Coordination; Theological Formation; Leadership Development; Refugee Advocacy; Racial Justice Advocacy; International Solidarity

Associated Ministries of Tacoma-Pierce County

1224 South "I" St., Tacoma, WA 98405 Tel. (206)-383-3056 Fax (206)383-2672
Media Contact, Exec. Dir., Rev. David T. Alger
Exec. Dir., Rev. David T. Alger, 4510 Defiance, Tacoma, WA 98407
Assoc. Dir., Janet Leng, 1809 N. Lexington, Tacoma, WA 98406
Pres., Sr. Barbara Collier
Sec., Dorothy Diers
Treas., Mr. Jack Conlin
Vice-Pres., Mary Johnson
Major activities: FISH/Food Banks; Hunger Awareness; Economic Justice; Christian Education; Shalom (Peacemaking) Resource Center; Social Service Program Advocacy; Communication and Networking of Churches; Housing; Paint Tacoma/Pierce Beautiful; Interfaith Task Force on Safe Streets; Mental Health Chaplaincy; Interfaith Hospitality Network; Theological Dialogue

Associated Ministries of Thurston County

P.O. Box 895, Olympia, WA 98507 Tel. (206)357-7224
Media Contact, Exec. Dir., Cheri Gonyaw
Exec. Dir., Cheri Gonyaw
Pres., Richard S. Smith
Treas., Pat LaViollette
Major activities: Church Information and Referral; Interfaith Relations; Social and Health Concerns; Community Action

Center for the Prevention of Sexual and Domestic Violence

936 N. 34th St., Ste. 200, Seattle, WA 98103 Tel. (206)634-1903 Fax (206)634-0115
Media Contact, Exec. Dir., Rev. Dr. Marie M. Fortune, 1914 N. 34th St., Ste. 105, Seattle, WA 98103 Tel. (206)634-1903 Fax (206)634-0115
Exec. Dir., Rev. Marie M. Fortune
Assoc. Dir., Nan Stoops
Program Staff: Jean Anton; Rev. Thelma B. Burgonio-Watson; Sandra Barone; Ellen Johanson; Elizabeth Stellas Tippins, M.Div.
Admn. Staff: Carolyn Eastman; Kata Issari
Major activities: Educational Ministry; Clergy and Lay Training; Social Action.

Church Council of Greater Seattle

4759 - 15th Ave., NE, Seattle, WA 98105 Tel. (206)525-1213 Fax (206)525-1218
Media Contact, Assoc. Dir., Alice M. Woldt, 4759 15th Ave. NE, Seattle, WA 98105 Tel. (206)525-1213 Fax (206)525-1218
Pres./Dir., Rev. Thomas H. Quigley
Urban Min., Assoc. Dir., Rev. David C. Bloom
Admn., Assoc. Dir., Alice M. Woldt
Exec. Asst., Angela W. Ford
Emergency Feeding Prog., Dir., Arthur Lee
Friend-to-Friend, Dir., Marilyn Soderquist
Youth Service Chaplaincy, Dir., Rev. Vera Diggins-Murphy
Mental Health Chaplaincy, Dir., Rev. Craig Rennebohm
Native American Task Force, Dir., Shelley Means
The Sharehouse, Dir., Shane Rock
Homelessness Project, Dir., Nancy Dorman
Mission for Music & Healing, Dir., Esther "Little Dove" John
Ecumenical Program for Urban Service, Dir., Paula Wolfe
Task Force on Aging, Dir., Mary Liz Chaffee
Interfaith Relations, Coord., Rev. Joyce Manson
Task Force on Housing & Homelessness, Dir., Josephine Archuleta
Academy of Religious Broadcasting, Dir., Rev. J. Graley Taylor
Vice-Pres., Rev. Joan Merritt
Treas., Dorothy Eley
Ed., The Source: Marge Lueders; Joan Reed
Seattle Displacement Coalition, Dir., John Fox
SW King County Mental Health Ministry, Dir., Rev. Richard Lutz
Virtues Project, Dir., Marian Bock
Taskforce on Children, Youth, & Families, Dir., Mary Cameron
Homestead Organizing Project Dir, Drew Kerr
Major activities: Pastoral Ministry; Hunger; Housing; Mental Health; Gay Rights; Aging; Latin America; Asia Pacific; South Africa; Native Americans; Jewish-Christian Relations; Ecology/Theology; Homelessness; Labor & Economic Justice; Children, Youth & Families; Race Relations; International Relations; Palestinian Concerns; Farm Workers; Racial Justice; Homestead Organizing Project

North Snohomish County Association of Churches

2301 Hoyt, P.O. Box 7101, Everett, WA 98201 Tel. (206)252-6672
Media Contact, Int. Exec. Dir., Robert L. Perry, P.O. Box 7101, Everett, WA 98201 Tel. (206)-252-6672
Int. Exec. Dir., Robert L. Perry
Pres., Ralph H. Quaas
Major activities: Housing and Shelter; Economic Justice; Hunger; Family Life; Interfaith Worship

Northwest Harvest/E. M. M.

P.O. Box 12272, Seattle, WA 98102 Tel. (206)625-0755 Fax (206)625-7518
Media Contact, Comm. Affairs Dir., Ellen Hansen
Exec. Dir., Ruth M. Velozo
Chpsn., The Rev. Ken C. Miller
Major activities: Northwest Harvest (Statewide Hunger Response); Cherry Street Food Bank (Community Hunger Response); Northwest Infants Corner (Special Nutritional Products for Infants and Babies); E.M.M. (Advocacy, Education, Communications Relative to Programs and Economic Justice); Northwest Caring Ministry (Individuals and Family Crisis Intervention and Advocacy)

Spokane Council of Ecumenical Ministries

E. 245-13th Ave., Spokane, WA 99202 Tel. (509)-624-5156
Media Contact, Editor & Comm. Dir., Mary Stamp, Tel. (509)535-1813
Exec. Dir., Rev. John Olson

Pres., Rev. Ann Price
Vice-Chair, Amy Carter
Treas., Rev. Samuel Vaughn
Sec., Mary Singer
Major activities: Greater Spokane Coalition Against Poverty; Multi-Cultural Human Relations Camp for High School Youth; Night Walk Ministry; Clergy Families in Crisis Project; Fig Tree Newspaper; Solidarity with Women Dir. of Churches & Community Age; Interfaith Thanksgiving Worship; Community Easter Sunrise Service; Forums on Issues; Friend to Friend Visitation with Nursing Home Patients; CROP Walk; Eastern Washington Legislative Conference; Children's Sabbath

WEST VIRGINIA

*West Virginia Council of Churches

1608 Virginia St. E., Charleston, WV 25311 Tel. (304)344-3141
Media Contact, Exec. Dir., Rev. James M. Kerr, 1608 Virginia St., E., Charleston, WV 25311 Tel. (304)344-3141 Fax (304)343-3295
Exec. Dir., Rev. James M. Kerr
Pres., Mrs. Mary Virginia DeRoo, 2006 Northwood Rd., Charleston, WV 25314
Vice-Pres., Dr. William B. Allen, Rt. 5, Box 167, Parkersburg, WV 26101
Sec., Rev. Gerald Dotson, 2626 Pennsylvania Ave., Charleston, WV 25302
Treas., Mrs. Patricia Trader, 114 Chestnut St., Clarksburg, WV 26301
Major activities: Leisure Ministry; Disaster Response; Faith and Order; Family Concerns; Inter-Faith Relations; Peace and Justice; Government Concerns; Support Sevices Network

Greater Fairmont Council of Churches

P.O. Box 108, Fairmont, WV 26554 Tel. (304)366-8126
Media Contact, Exec. Sec., Nancy Hoffman
Exec. Sec., Nancy Hoffman
Major activities: Community Ecumenical Services; Youth and Adult Sports Leagues; CROP Walk Sponsor; Weekly Radio Broadcasts

The Greater Wheeling Council of Churches

110 Methodist Bldg., Wheeling, WV 26003 Tel. (304)232-5315
Exec. Dir., Kathy J. Burley, 110 Methodist Bldg., Wheeling, WV 26003 Tel. (304)232-5315
Exec. Dir., Kathy J. Burley
Hospital Notification Sec., Mrs. Ruth Fletcher
Pres., Rev. Robert J. Romick
Treas., Mrs. Naoma Boram
Major activities: Christian Education; Evangelism; Christian Heritage Week Celebration; Institutional Ministry; Regional Jail Chaplaincy; Church Women United; Volunteer Chaplaincy Care at OVMC Hospital; School of Religion; Hospital Notification; Hymn Sing in the Park; Anti-Gambling Crusade; Pentecost Celebration; Clergy Council; Easter Sunrise Service; Community Seder; Church Secretaries Fellowship; Natl. Day of Prayer Service; Videotape Library/Audiotape Library

WISCONSIN

*Wisconsin Conference of Churches

750 Windsor St. Ste. 301, Sun Prairie, WI 53590 Tel. (608)837-3108 Fax (608)837-3038
Media Contact, Comm. Coord., Ms. Linda Spilde
Exec. Dir., Rev. Jerry Folk
Ofc. Mgr., Ms. Linda Spilde
Assoc. Dir., Ms. Bonnee Lauridsen Voss
Broadcasting, Assoc. Dir., Rev. Robert P. Seater, 2717 E. Hampshire, Milwaukee, WI 53211 Tel. (414)332-2133
Peace & Justice Ecumenical Partnership: Dir., ----
Chaplaincy Coord., Rev. M. Charles Davis, 1221 Jackson St., Oshkosh, WI 54901
Commission on Aging, Coord., Mr. A. Rowland Todd
Pres., The Rev. John R. Wineman
Treas., Mr. Chester Spangler, 625 Crandall, Madison, WI 53711
Major activities: Social Witness; Migrant Ministry; Broadcasting Ministry; Aging; IMPACT; Institutional Chaplaincy; Peace and Justice; Faith and Order; Rural Concerns Forum; American Indian Ministries Council; Park Ministry

Center for Community Concerns

1501 Villa St., Racine, WI 53403 Tel. (414)637-9176 Fax (414)637-9265
Media Contact, Exec. Dir., Sr. Michelle Olley
Exec. Dir., Sr. Michelle Olley
Skillbank Coord., Eleanor Sorenson
RSVP (Retired Senior Volunteer Program), Chris Udell-Sorberg
Volunteer Today (55 and under), Marilyn Ladwig
Major activities: Advocacy; Direct Services; Research; Community Consultant; Criminal Justice; Volunteerism; Senior Citizen Services

Christian Youth Council

1715-52nd St., Kenosha, WI 53140 Tel. (414)652-9543 Fax (414)652-4461
Media Contact, Exec. Dir., Steven L. Nelson
Exec. Dir., Steven L. Nelson
Sports Dir., Kris Jensen
Outreach Dir., Linda Osborne
Class Dir., Debbie Cutts
Jill Cox
Pres., Lon Knoedler
Major activities: Leisure Time Ministry; Institutional Ministries; Ecumenical Committee; Social Concerns; Outreach Sports(with a Christian Philosophy)

Interfaith Conference of Greater Milwaukee

1442 N. Farwell Ave., Ste. 200, Milwaukee, WI 53202 Tel. (414)276-9050 Fax (414)276-8442
Media Contact, Exec. Dir., Jack Murtaugh
Exec. Dir., Mr. Jack Murtaugh
First Vice-Chair, Archbishop Rembert G. Weakland
Second Vice-Chair, Rev. Fred L. Crouther
Sec., Rev. Paul Bodine, Jr.
Treas., Rev. Mary Ann Neevel
Poverty Issues, Program Coord., Mr. Marcus White
Ofc. Admn., Ms. Patricia Miller
Beyond Racism, Dir., Mrs. Charlotte Holloman

Consultant in Communications, Rev. Robert P. Seater
Chpsn., Rev. Quentin Meracle
Outreach Coord., Muhammad Abdullah
Major activities: Economic Issues; Racism; CROP Walk; Public Policy; Religion and Labor Committee; TV Programming; Peace and International Issues Committee; Annual Membership Luncheon; Substance Abuse, Violence Prevention

Madison Urban Ministry

1127 University Ave., Madison, WI 53715 Tel. (608)256-0906 Fax (608)256-4387
Media Contact, Office/Program Mgr., Shirley Manion
Exec. Dir., Charles Pfeifer
Ofc./Program Mgrs.: Shirley Manion; Dale Johnson
Major activities: Community Projects; Race Relations; Affordable Housing Coalition; Tutoring/Mentoring Network; Prayer at the Heart of Social Action; Making Diversity Work

WYOMING

*Wyoming Church Coalition

P.O. Box 990, Laramie, WY 82070 Tel. (307)745-6000
Media Contact, Chair, Rev. Doug Goodwin, 102 S. Connor, Sheridan, WY 82801 Tel. (307)674-6795
Office Mgr., Joy Hall
Chair, Rev. Doug Goodwin
Penitentiary Chaplain, Rev. Lynn Schumacher, P.O. Box 400, Rawlins, WY 82301
Major activities: Death Penalty; Empowering the Poor and Oppressed; Peace and Justice; Prison Ministry; Malicious Harassment

7. CANADIAN REGIONAL AND LOCAL ECUMENICAL AGENCIES

Most of the organizations listed below are councils of churches in which churches participate officially, whether at the parish or judicatory level. They operate at either the city, metropolitan area, or county level. Parish clusters within urban areas are not included.

Canadian local ecumenical bodies operate without paid staff, with the exception of a few which have part-time staff. In most cases the name and address of the president or chairperson is listed. As these offices change from year to year, some of this information may be out of date by the time the *Yearbook of American and Canadian Churches* is published. Up-to-date information may be secured from the Canadian Council of Churches.

ALBERTA

Calgary Council of Churches
Treas., Stephen Kendall, 1009-15 Ave. SW, Calgary, AB T2R 0S5 Tel. (403)249-2599

Edmonton Council of Churches
Ruth Hyndman, 6903-98A Ave., Edmonton, AB T6A 0B9

Edmonton District Council of Churches
Dir., Rev. Tom Wert, c/o Garneau United Church 1148 - 84 Ave., Edmonton, AB T6G 0W6

Eparchy of Edmonton
9645 108 Ave., Edmonton, AB T5H 1A3

The Micah Institute of Southern Alberta
Dir., Caroline Brown, 240-15 Ave. SW, Calgary, AB T2R 0P7 Tel. (403)262-5111 Fax (403)264-8366

Southwest Edmonton Ministerial Association
Dir., Jeff Challoner, c/o St. Anthony's Parish, 10661-82 Avenue, Edmonton, AB T6E 2A6

BRITISH COLUMBIA

Canadian Ecumenical Action
2040 West 12th Ave., Vancouver, BC V6J 2J2 Tel. (604)736-1613 Fax (604)875-1433

Central Okanagan Ministerial
Rev. Dr. Lorna Hillian, 504 Sutherland Ave., Kelowna, BC V1Y 5X1

MANITOBA

Association of Christian Churches in Manitoba
Pres., Ted Chell, 484 Maryland St., Winnipeg, MB R3G 1M5

Ecumenical Fellowship Windsor Park Southdale
Greg Anderson, 930 Winakwa Rd., Winnipeg, MB R2J 1E7. Tel. (204)256 8712

NEW BRUNSWICK

Atlantic Ecumenical Council
Pres. Rev. David Luker, 211 Peck Drive, Riverview, NB E1B 1M9

Moncton Area Council of Churches
Pres., Mrs. Chris Harper, 28 Balmoral St., Riverview, NB E1B 2P6

NEWFOUNDLAND

Labrador West Ministerial Association
Salvation Army, P.O. Box 369, Labrador City, NF A2V 2K6

Port Aux Basques Ministerial Association
Box 361, Port Aux Basques, NF A0M 1C0

NOVA SCOTIA

Amherst and Area Council of Churches
Treas., Shirley MacTavish, 8 Lorne Cres., Amherst, NS B4H 4B7 Tel. (902)667-3128

Annapolis Royal Council of Churches
Rev. Derrick Marshall, Riverview Dr., Annapolis Royal, NS B0S 1A0

Bridgewater Inter-Church Council
Pres., Wilson Jones, 39 Parkdale Ave., Bridgewater, NS B4V 1L8

Halifax-Dartmouth Council of Churches
Rep., Mr. Lorne White, 18 Winon Cres., Halifax, NS B3M 1Z1

Halifax West Ministerial Association
c/o Our Lady of Perpetual Help Parish, 2 Melody Drive, Halifax, NS B3M 1P7. Tel. (902)443-0725

Industrial Cape Breton Council of Churches
Valerie Hunt, 76 Lynch Dr., Sydney, NS B1S 1V2 Tel. (902)564-6992

Kentville Council of Churches
Rev. Canon S.J.P. Davies, 325-325 Main St., Kentville, NS B4N 1C5

Mahone Bay Council of Churches
Rev. Dale Rose, Box 902, Mahone Bay, NS B0J 2E0

Pictou Council of Churches
Sec., Rev. D. J. Murphy, c/o Stella Maris Parish P.O. Box 70, Pictou, NS B0K 1H0

Queen's County Association of Churches
Rev. Bruce Ward, Box 1369, Liverpool, NS B0T 1K0

Wolfville Area Council of Churches
Dr. R. Forsman, Box 574, RR#2, Wolfville, NS B0P 1X0

Wolfville Area Interchurch Council
Sheila Vaillancourt, Box 924, Wolfville, NS B0P 1X0

Wolfville Interchurch Council
Rev. Roger Prentice, Office of the Chaplain, Acadia Univ., Wolfville, NS B0P 1X0

ONTARIO

Ajax Pickering Ministerial Association
Glenn R. Brown, 1066 Dunbarton Rd., Pickering, ON L1V 1G8

Bothwell Ministerial Association
Harold Wilson, Bothwell, ON N0P 1CO

Christian Council of the Capital Area
Pres., Donald Friesen, 1830 Kilborn Ave., Ottawa, ON K1H 6N4

Christian Leadership Council of Downtown Toronto
Chair, Ken Bhagan, 40 Homewood Ave. #509, Toronto, ON M4Y 2K2

Cochrane Ministerial Association
Box 915, Cochrane, ON P0L 1C0. Tel. (705)272-5842

Current River Clergy Association
c/o St. Stephen the Martyr, 494 Leslie Ave., Thunder Bay, ON P7A 5E8

Danforth Ecumenical Ministerial
c/o Eastminister United Church, 310 Danforth Ave., Toronto, ON M4K 1N6

Don Mills Ministerial
Anne Howes, Donminster U.C., 40 Underhill Drive, Toronto, ON M3A 2J5. Tel. (416)447-6846

Dundas Ministerial Association
Gary Caldwell, Dundas Baptist Church, 104 Paris St. W., Dundas, ON L9H 1X4. Tel. (905)627-4231

Ecumenical Committee
Rev. William B. Kidd, 76 Eastern Ave., Sault Ste. Marie, ON P6A 4R2

Glengarry-Prescott-Russell Christian Council
Pres., Rev. Gerald Labrosse, St. Eugene's Parish, C.P. 70 St. Eugene's, Prescott, ON K0B 1P0

Goderich Ministerial Association
56 North Street, Goderich, ON N7A 2T4

Greater Windsor Ministerial Association
Sec.-Tres., Gerald Doran, 2320 Wyandotte St. West, Windsor, ON N9B 2K4. Tel. (519)253-8741

Hamilton & District Council of Churches
Rev. Dr. John Johnston, 147 Chedoke Ave., Hamilton, ON L8P 4P2 Tel. (905)529-6896 Fax (905)521-2539

Hemmingford Ecumenical Committee
Sec.-Treas., Catherine Priest, 434 Route 202, P.O. Box 213, Hemmingford, ON J0L 1H0

Ignace Council of Churches
Box 5, 205 Pine St., St. Ignace, ON P0T 1H0

Inter Church Council of Burlington
Michael Biggle, Box 62120, Burlington Mall RPO, Burlington, ON L7R 4K2 Tel. (905)526-1523

Kenora Keewatin Ministerial Association
P.O. Box 2901, Kenora, ON P9N 3X8

Kitchener-Waterloo Council of Churches
Rev. Heidi Sievert, 124 Keatsway Pl., Waterloo, ON N2L 5H3

Lakeshore Clergy Fellowship
Treas., R.C. Taylor, 119 Mimico Ave., Etobicoke, ON M8V 1R6

Lay Ecumenical Council of Aurora
c/o 53 Cambridge Cres., Bradford, ON L3Z 1E2

Listowel and Area Ministerial Association
John Makey, RR #1, Gowanstown, ON N0G 1YO

London Inter-Faith Team
Chair, David Carouthers, United Church, 711 Colbourne St., London, ON N6A 3Z4

Lucknow Ministerial Association
South Kinloss Presbyterian Church, Box 219, Lucknow, ON N0G 2H0

Massey Inter-Church Committee
Sec., Eva Fraser, Box 238, Massey, ON P0P 1P0

Prescott Ministerial Association
Box 501, Prescott, ON K0E 1TO

Smith Falls Ministerial
Rev. Dr. L. E. Siverns, 11 Church St., Smith Falls, ON K7A 1P6

Spadina-Bloor Interchurch Council
Chair, Fr. Peter Shea, 659 Markhan St, Toronto, ON M6G 2M1. Tel. (416)534-4219

St. Mary's Ministerial
Rev. Fred Rupert, Box 814, Church Street, St. Mary, ON N4X 1B5

Stratford & District Council of Churches
Chair, Rev. Ted Heinze, 202 Erie St., Stratford, ON N5A 2M8

Thorold Inter-Faith Council
1 Dunn St., St. Catharines, ON L2T 1P3

Thunder Bay Council of Churches
Rev. Richard Darling, 1800 Moodie St. E, Thunder Bay, ON P7E 4Z2

Unionville Ministerial Association
Peter Vanker, Bethseda Lutheran Church, 20 Union St., Unionville, ON L3R 2H5

Wallaceburg Ministerial Association
Lt., Mark Guiler, 17 Gillard St., Wallaceburg, ON N8A 1M8. Tel. (519)627-4491

PRINCE EDWARD ISLAND

Charlottetown Christian Council
Ms. Eunice D. Wonnacott, 45 Roper Dr., Charlottetown, PE C1A 6J1 Tel. (902)894-4363

QUEBEC

The Ecumenical Group
Mrs. C. Haten, 1185 Ste. Foy St., Bruno, QC J3V 3C3

Montreal Council of Churches
Rev. Ralph Watson, 3500 Connough Ave., Montreal, QC H4B 1X3

Canadian Centre for Ecumenism
2065 Sherbrooke St. W., Montreal, QC H3H 1G6. Tel. (514)937-9176 Fax (514)931-3432

SASKATCHEWAN

Assiniboia and District Ministerial Association
c/o United Church Manse Box 475, Mossbank, SK S0H 3G0. Tel. (306)354-2400

Humboldt Clergy Council
Fr. Leo Hinz, OSB, Box 1989, Humboldt, SK S0K 2A0

Melville Association of Churches
Catherine Gaw, Box 878, Melville, SK S0A 2P0

Saskatoon Centre for Ecumenism
1006 Broadway Ave., Saskatoon, SK S7N 1B9

Saskatoon Council of Churches
816 Spadina Cres. E, Saskatoon, SK S7K 3H4 Tel. (306)242-5146

8. THEOLOGICAL SEMINARIES AND BIBLE SCHOOLS IN THE UNITED STATES

The following list includes theological seminaries and departments in colleges and universities in which ministerial training is given. Many denominations have additional programs. The lists of Religious Bodies in the United States should be consulted for the address of denominational headquarters.

Inclusion in or exclusion from this list implies no judgment about the quality or accreditation of any institution. Those schools that are members (both accredited and affiliated) of the Association of Theological Schools are marked with a "*." Additional information about enrollment in ATS member schools can be found in the statistical section.

The listing includes the institution name, denominational sponsor when appropriate, location, head, telephone number and fax number when known.

Abilene Christian University, (Churches of Christ), ACU Station, Box 7000, Abilene, TX 79699. Royce Money. Tel. (915)674-2412. Fax (915)674-2958

Academy of the New Church (Theology School), (General Church of the New Jerusalem), 2895 College Dr., Box 717, Bryn Athyn, PA 19009. Brian W. Keith. Tel. (215)938-2525. Fax (215)938-2616

Alaska Bible College, (Nondenominational), P.O. Box 289, Glennallen, AK 99588. Gary J. Ridley. Tel. (907)822-3201. Fax (907)822-5027

Alliance Theological Seminary,* (The Christian and Missionary Alliance), 350 N. Highland Ave., Nyack, NY 10960-1416. Paul F. Bubna. Tel. (914)353-2020. Fax (914)358-2651

American Baptist College, (Interdenominational Baptist), 1800 Baptist World Center Dr., Nashville, TN 37207. Bernard Lafayette, Jr. Tel. (615)262-1369

American Baptist Seminary of the West,* (American Baptist Churches in the U.S.A.), 2606 Dwight Way, Berkeley, CA 94704. Theodore Keaton. Tel. (510)841-1905. Fax (510)841-2446

Anderson University School of Theology,* (Church of God (Anderson, Ind.)), Anderson University, Anderson, IN 46012-3495. David Sebastian. Tel. (317)641-4032. Fax (317)641-3851

Andover Newton Theological School,* (American Bapt.; United Church of Christ), 210 Herrick Rd., Newton Centre, MA 02159. Benjamin Griffin. Tel. (617)964-1100. Fax (617)965-9756

Appalachian Bible College, (Nondenominational), P.O. Box ABC, Bradley, WV 25818. Daniel L. Anderson. Tel. (304)877-6428. Fax (304)877-5082

Aquinas Institute of Theology,* (The Roman Catholic Church), 3642 Lindell Blvd., St. Louis, MO 63108. Charles E. Bouchard. Tel. (314)977-3882. Fax (314)977-7225

Arizona College of the Bible, (Interdenominational), 2045 W. Northern Ave., Phoenix, AZ 85021-5197. Robert W. Benton. Tel. (602)995-2670. Fax (602)864-8183

Arlington Baptist College, 3001 W. Division, Arlington, TX 76012-3425. David Bryant. Tel. (817)461-8741. Fax (817)274-1138

Asbury Theological Seminary,* (Interdenominational), 204 N. Lexington Ave., Wilmore, KY 40390-1199. Maxie D. Dunnam. Tel. (606)858-3581

Ashland Theological Seminary,* (Brethren Church (Ashland, Ohio)), 910 Center St., Ashland, OH 44805. Frederick J. Finks. Tel. (419)289-5161. Fax (419)289-5969

Assemblies of God Theological Seminary,* (Assemblies of God), 1445 Boonville Ave., Springfield, MO 65802. Del H. Tarr, Jr. Tel. (417)862-3344. Fax (417)862-3214

Associated Mennonite Biblical Seminary,* (Mennonite Church; General Conference Mennonite Church), 3003 Benham Ave., Elkhart, IN 46517-1999. Gerald Gerbrandt. Tel. (219)295-3726. Fax (219)295-0092

Athenaeum of Ohio,* (The Roman Catholic Church), 6616 Beechmont Ave., Cincinnati, OH 45230-2091. Robert J. Mooney. Tel. (513)231-2223. Fax (513)231-3254

Atlanta Christian College, (Christian Churches and Churches of Christ), 2605 Ben Hill Rd., East Point, GA 30344. R. Edwin Groover. Tel. (404)761-8861. Fax (404)669-2024

US SEMINARIES

Austin Presbyterian Theological Seminary,* (Presbyterian Church (U.S.A.)), 100 E. 27th St., Austin, TX 78705. Jack L. Stotts. Tel. (512)472-6736. Fax (512)479-0738

Azusa Pacific University,* (Interdenominational), 901 E. Alosta, P.O. Box APU, Azusa, CA 91702. Richard Felix. Tel. (818)969-3434. Fax (818)969-7180

Bangor Theological Seminary,* (United Church of Christ), 300 Union St., Bangor, ME 04401. Ansley Coe Throckmorton. Tel. (207)942-6781. Fax (207)942-4914

Baptist Bible College, (Baptist Bible Fellowship International), 628 E. Kearney, Springfield, MO 65803. Leland Kennedy. Tel. (417)869-9811. Fax (417)831-8029

Baptist Bible College and Seminary, (Baptist), 538 Venard Rd., Clarks Summit, PA 18411. Milo Thompson. Tel. (717)586-2400. Fax (717)586-1753

Baptist Missionary Association Theological Seminary, (Baptist Missionary Association of America), 1530 E. Pine St., Jacksonville, TX 75766. Philip R. Bryan. Tel. (903)586-2501. Fax (903)586-0378

Barclay College, (Evangelical Friends International--North America Region), P.O. Box 288, Haviland, KS 67059. ----. Tel. (316)862-5252. Fax (316)862-5403

Bay Ridge Christian College, (Church of God (Anderson, Ind.)), P.O. Box 726, Kendleton, TX 77451. Sethard Beverly. Tel. (409)532-3982. Fax (409)532-4352

Berkeley Divinity School at Yale,* (Episcopal Church), 363 St. Ronan St., New Haven, CT 06511. Dean Philip Turner. Tel. (203)764-9300. Fax (203)764-9301

Bethany College, (Assemblies of God), 800 Bethany Dr., Scotts Valley, CA 95066. Tom Duncan. Tel. (408)438-3800. Fax (408)438-4517

Bethany Lutheran Theological Seminary, (Evangelical Lutheran Synod), 447 N. Division St., Mankato, MN 56001. W. W. Petersen. Tel. (507)386-5354. Fax (507)386-5426

Bethany Theological Seminary,* (Church of the Brethren), 615 National Rd. West, Richmond, IN 47374. Eugene F. Roop. Tel. (317)983-1800. Fax (317)983-1840

Bethel Theological Seminary,* (Baptist General Conference), 3949 Bethel Dr., St. Paul, MN 55112. George K. Brushaber. Tel. (612)638-6230. Fax (612)638-6002

Beulah Heights Bible College, (The International Pentecostal Church of Christ), 892 Berne St. SE, Atlanta, GA 30316. Samuel R. Chand. Tel. (404)627-2681. Fax (404)627-0702

Biblical Theological Seminary, (Interdenominational), 200 N. Main St., Hatfield, PA 19440. David G. Dunbar. Tel. (215)368-5000. Fax (215)368-7002

Boise Bible College, (Nondenominational), 8695 Marigold St., Boise, ID 83714. Charles A. Crane. Tel. (208)376-7731. Fax (208)376-7743

Boston University (School of Theology),* (The United Methodist Church), 745 Commonwealth Ave., Boston, MA 02215. Robert C. Neville. Tel. (617)353-3050. Fax (617)353-3061

Brite Divinity School, Texas Christian University,* (Christian Church (Disciples of Christ)), P.O. Box 32923, TCU, Ft. Worth, TX 76129. Leo G. Perdue. Tel. (817)921-7575. Fax (817)921-7305

Calvary Bible College and Theological Seminary, (Independent Fundamental Churches of America), 15800 Calvary Rd., Kansas City, MO 64147-1341. Warren E. Bathke. Tel. (800)326-3960. Fax (816)331-4474

Calvin Theological Seminary,* (Christian Reformed Church in North America), 3233 Burton St. SE, Grand Rapids, MI 49546. James A. DeJong. Tel. (616)957-6036. Fax (616)957-8621

Candler School of Theology, Emory University,* (The United Methodist Church), Bishops Hall 202, Emory University, Atlanta, GA 30322. R. Kevin LaGree. Tel. (404)727-6324. Fax (404)727-2915

Catholic Theological Union at Chicago,* (The Roman Catholic Church), 5401 S. Cornell Ave., Chicago, IL 60615. Norman Bevan. Tel. (312)324-8000. Fax (312)324-8490

The Catholic University of America,* (The Roman Catholic Church), 113 Caldwell Hall, Cardinal Sta., Washington, DC 20064. Raymond F. Collins. Tel. (202)319-5683. Fax (202)319-4967

Central Baptist College, (Baptist Missionary Association of America), 1501 College Ave., Conway, AR 72032. Charles Attebery. Tel. (501)329-6872. Fax (501)329-2941

Central Baptist Theological Seminary,* (American Baptist Churches in the U.S.A.), 741 N. 31st St., Kansas City, KS 66102-3964. Thomas E. Clifton. Tel. (913)371-5313. Fax (913)371-8110

Central Baptist Theological Seminary in Indiana, (National Baptist Convention, U.S.A., Inc.), 1535 Dr. A. J. Brown Ave. N, Indianapolis, IN 46202. F. Benjamin Davis. Tel. (317)636-6622

Central Bible College, (Assemblies of God), 3000 N. Grant Ave., Springfield, MO 65803. H. Maurice Lednicky. Tel. (417)833-2551. Fax (417)833-5141

Central Christian College of the Bible, (Christian Churches and Churches of Christ), 911 E. Urbandale, Moberly, MO 65270. Lloyd M. Pelfrey. Tel. (816)263-3900. Fax (816)263-3936

Central Indian Bible College, (Assemblies of God), P.O. Box 550, Mobridge, SD 57601. M. George Kallappa. Tel. (605)845-7801. Fax (605)845-7744

Chicago Theological Seminary,* (United Church of Christ), 5757 South University Ave., Chicago, IL 60637. Kenneth B. Smith. Tel. (312)752-5757. Fax (312)752-5925

Christ the King Seminary,* (The Roman Catholic Church), 711 Knox Rd., P.O. Box 607, East Aurora, NY 14052. Frederick D. Leising. Tel. (716)652-8900. Fax (716)652-8903

Christ the Savior Seminary, (The American Carpatho-Russian Orthodox Greek Catholic Church), 225 Chandler Ave., Johnstown, PA 15906. Nicholas Smisko. Tel. (814)539-8086. Fax (814)536-4699

Christian Theological Seminary,* (Christian Church (Disciples of Christ)), 1000 W. 42nd St., Indianapolis, IN 46208. Richard D. N. Dickinson. Tel. (317)924-1331. Fax (317)923-1961

Church Divinity School of the Pacific,* (Episcopal Church), 2451 Ridge Rd., Berkeley, CA 94709. Donn F. Morgan. Tel. (510)204-0700. Fax (510)644-0712

Church of God School of Theology,* (Church of God (Cleveland, Tenn.)), P.O. Box 3330, Cleveland, TN 37320-3330. Cecil B. Knight. Tel. (615)478-1131. Fax (615)478-7711

Cincinnati Bible College and Seminary, (Christian Churches and Churches of Christ), 2700 Glenway Ave., Cincinnati, OH 45204. David A. Grubbs. Tel. (513)244-8100. Fax (513)244-8140

Circleville Bible College, (Churches of Christ in Christian Union), P.O. Box 458, Circleville, OH 43113. John Conley. Tel. (614)474-8896. Fax (614)477-7755

Clear Creek Baptist Bible College, (Southern Baptist Convention), 300 Clear Creek Rd., Pineville, KY 40977. Bill Whittaker. Tel. (606)337-3196. Fax (606)337-2372

Colegio Biblico Pentecostal de Puerto Rico, (Church of God (Cleveland, Tenn.)), P.O. Box 901, Saint Just, PR 00978. Ismael López-Borrero. Tel. (809)761-0640. Fax (809)748-9220

Colgate Rochester/Bexley Hall/Crozer,* (American Baptist Churches in the USA, Episcopal Church), 1100 S. Goodman St., Rochester, NY 14620. James H. Evans. Tel. (716)271-1320. Fax (716)271-8013

Colorado Christian University, (Nondenominational), 180 S. Garrison St., Lakewood, CO 80226. Ronald R. Schmidt. Tel. (303)202-0100. Fax (303)233-2735

Columbia Biblical Seminary & Graduate School of Missions,* (Interdenominational), P.O. Box 3122, Columbia, SC 29230-3122. Johnny V. Miller. Tel. (803)754-4100. Fax (803)786-4209

Columbia Theological Seminary,* (Presbyterian Church (U.S.A.)), 701 Columbia Dr., P.O. Box 520, Decatur, GA 30031. Douglas Oldenburg. Tel. (404)378-8821. Fax (404)377-9696

Concordia Seminary,* (The Lutheran Church--Missouri Synod), 801 De Mun Ave., St. Louis, MO 63105. John F. Johnson. Tel. (314)721-5934. Fax (314)721-5902

Concordia Theological Seminary,* (The Lutheran Church--Missouri Synod), 6600 N. Clinton St., Ft. Wayne, IN 46825. David G. Schmiel. Tel. (219)452-2100. Fax (219)452-2121

Covenant Theological Seminary,* (Presbyterian Church in America), 12330 Conway Rd., St. Louis, MO 63141. Bryan Chapell. Tel. (314)434-4044. Fax (314)434-4819

Cranmer Seminary, (The Anglican Orthodox Church), P.O. Box 329, 323 Walnut St., Statesville, NC 28687. Robert J. Godfrey. Tel. (704)873-8365. Fax (704)873-8948

Criswell Center for Biblical Studies, (Southern Baptist Convention), 4010 Gaston Ave., Dallas, TX 75246. Richard R. Melick. Tel. (214)818-1300. Fax (214)818-1320

Crown College, (The Christian and Missionary Alliance), 6425 County Rd. 30, St. Bonifacius, MN 55375. Bill W. Lanpher. Tel. (612)446-4100. Fax (612)446-4149

Dallas Christian College, (Christian Churches and Churches of Christ), 2700 Christian Pky., Dallas, TX 75234. Keith Ray. Tel. (214)241-3371. Fax (214)241-8021

Dallas Theological Seminary,* (Interdenominational), 3909 Swiss Ave., Dallas, TX 75204. Charles R. Swindoll. Tel. (214)824-3094. Fax (214)841-3625

De Sales School of Theology,* (The Roman Catholic Church), 721 Lawrence St. NE, Washington, DC 20017. John W. Crossin. Tel. (202)269-9412. Fax (202)526-2720

Denver Conservative Baptist Seminary,* (Conservative Baptist Association of America), Box 10,000, Denver, CO 80250-0100. Edward L. Hayes. Tel. (303)761-2482. Fax (303)761-8060

Disciples Divinity House, University of Chicago, (Christian Church (Disciples of Christ)), 1156 E. 57th St., Chicago, IL 60637. Kristine A. Culp. Tel. (312)643-4411

Divinity School Yale University,* (Nondenominational), 409 Prospect St., New Haven, CT 06511-2167. Thomas W. Ogletree. Tel. (203)432-5303. Fax (203)432-5356

Dominican House of Studies,* (The Roman Catholic Church), 487 Michigan Ave. NE, Washington, DC 20017-1585. Thomas McCreesh. Tel. (202)529-5300. Fax (202)636-4460

Dominican School of Philosophy and Theology,* (The Roman Catholic Church), 2401 Ridge Road, Berkeley, CA 94709. Gregory Rocca. Tel. (510)849-2030. Fax (510)849-1372

Drew University (Theological School),* (The United Methodist Church), 36 Madison Ave., Madison, NJ 07940-4010. Leonard I. Sweet. Tel. (201)408-3258. Fax (201)408-3808

Duke University (Divinity School),* (The United Methodist Church), Duke U. Divinity School, Box 90968, Durham, NC 27708-0968. Dennis M. Campbell. Tel. (919)660-3400. Fax (919)660-3473

Earlham School of Religion,* (Interdenominational-Friends), 228 College Ave., Richmond, IN 47374. Andrew P. Grannell. Tel. (800)432-1377. Fax (317)983-1688

East Coast Bible College, (Church of God (Cleveland, Tenn.)), 6900 Wilkinson Blvd., Charlotte, NC 28214. Lawrence Leonhardt. Tel. (704)394-2307. Fax (704)393-3689

Eastern Baptist Theological Seminary,* (American Baptist Churches in the U.S.A.), 6 Lancaster Ave., Wynnewood, PA 19096. Manfred T. Brauch. Tel. (800)220-EBTS. Fax (610)649-3834

Eastern Mennonite Seminary,* (Mennonite Church), Eastern Mennonite Seminary, Harrisonburg, VA 22801. George R. Brunk. Tel. (540)432-4260. Fax (540)432-4444

Eden Theological Seminary,* (United Church of Christ), 475 E. Lockwood Ave., St. Louis, MO 63119. Charles R. Kniker. Tel. (314)961-3627. Fax (314)961-9063

Emmanuel School of Religion,* (Christian Churches and Churches of Christ), One Walker Dr., Johnson City, TN 37601. C. Robert Wetzel. Tel. (423)926-1186. Fax (423)461-1556

Emmaus Bible College, (Nondenominational), 2570 Asbury Rd., Dubuque, IA 52001. Daniel Smith. Tel. (319)588-8000. Fax (319)588-1216

Episcopal Divinity School,* (Episcopal Church), 99 Brattle St., Cambridge, MA 02138. William Rankin. Tel. (617)868-3450. Fax (617)864-5385

Episcopal Theological Seminary of the Southwest,* (Episcopal Church), P.O. Box 2247, Austin, TX 78768-2247. Durstan R. McDonald. Tel. (512)472-4133. Fax (512)472-3098

Erskine Theological Seminary,* (Associate Reformed Presbyterian Church (General Synod)), Drawer 668, Due West, SC 29639. R. T. Ruble. Tel. (803)379-8885. Fax (803)379-2171

Eugene Bible College, (Open Bible Standard Churches, Inc.), 2155 Bailey Hill Rd., Eugene, OR 97405. Jeffrey E. Farmer. Tel. (503)485-1780. Fax (503)343-5801

Evangelical School of Theology,* (The Evangelical Congregational Church), 121 S. College St., Myerstown, PA 17067. Kirby N. Keller. Tel. (717)866-5775. Fax (717)866-4667

Faith Baptist Bible College and Theological Seminary, (General Association of Regular Baptist Churches), 1900 NW 4th St., Ankeny, IA 50021-2152. Richard W. Houg. Tel. (515)964-0601. Fax (515)964-1638

Faith Evangelical Lutheran Seminary, (Conservative Lutheran Association), 3504 N. Pearl St., Tacoma, WA 98407. R. H. Redal. Tel. (206)752-2020

Florida Bible College, (Independent Fundamental Churches of America), 9300 Pembroke Rd., Miramar, FL 33023. Jim Sheffield. Tel. (954)704-0799. Fax (954)437-9941

Florida Christian College, (Christian Churches and Churches of Christ), 1011 Bill Beck Blvd., Kissimmee, FL 34744. A. Wayne Lowen. Tel. (407)847-8966. Fax (407)847-3925

Franciscan School of Theology,* (The Roman Catholic Church), 1712 Euclid Ave., Berkeley, CA 94709. William M. Cieslak. Tel. (510)848-5232. Fax (510)549-9466

Free Will Baptist Bible College, (National Association of Free Will Baptists), 3606 West End Ave., Nashville, TN 37205. Tom Malone. Tel. (615)383-1340. Fax (615)269-6028

Fuller Theological Seminary,* (Interdenominational), 135 N. Oakland Ave., Pasadena, CA 91182. Richard J. Mouw. Tel. (818)584-5200. Fax (818)795-8767

Garrett-Evangelical Theological Seminary,* (The United Methodist Church), 2121 Sheridan Rd., Evanston, IL 60201. Neal F. Fisher. Tel. (847)866-3900. Fax (847)866-3957

General Theological Seminary, The,* (Episcopal Church), 175 Ninth Ave., New York, NY 10011-4977. Craig B. Anderson. Tel. (212)243-5150. Fax (212)727-3907

George Mercer, Jr. Memorial School of Theology, (Episcopal Church), 65 Fourth St., Garden City, NY 11530. Lloyd A. Lewis. Tel. (516)248-4800. Fax (516)248-4883

God's Bible School and College, (Nondenominational), 1810 Young St., Cincinnati, OH 45210. Michael Avery. Tel. (513)721-7944. Fax (513)721-3971

Golden Gate Baptist Theological Seminary,* (Southern Baptist Convention), 201 Seminary Dr., Mill Valley, CA 94941. William O. Crews. Tel. (415)388-8080. Fax (415)383-0723

Gordon-Conwell Theological Seminary,* (Interdenominational), 130 Essex St., South Hamilton, MA 01982. Robert E. Cooley. Tel. (508)468-7111. Fax (508)468-6691

Grace Bible College, (Grace Gospel Fellowship), P.O. Box 910, Grand Rapids, MI 49509. Bruce Kemper. Tel. (616)538-2330. Fax (616)538-0599

Grace Theological Seminary, (Fellowship of Grace Brethren Churches), 200 Seminary Dr., Winona Lake, IN 46590. Ronald E. Manahan. Tel. (219)372-5100. Fax (219)372-5265

Grace University, (Independent), Ninth and William, Omaha, NE 68108. Neal F. McBride. Tel. (402)449-2809. Fax (402)341-9587

Graduate Theological Union,* (Nondenominational), 2400 Ridge Rd., Berkeley, CA 94709. Glenn R. Bucher. Tel. (510)649-2410. Fax (510)649-1417

Great Lakes Christian College, (Christian Churches and Churches of Christ), 6211 W. Willow Hwy., Lansing, MI 48917. Jerry M. Paul. Tel. (517)321-0242. Fax (517)321-5902

Greenville College, (Free Methodist Church of North America), 315 E. College Ave., P.O. Box 159, Greenville, IL 62246. Robert E. Smith. Tel. (618)664-1840. Fax (618)664-1748

Hartford Seminary,* (Interdenominational), 77 Sherman St., Hartford, CT 06105. Barbara Brown Zikmund. Tel. (860)509-9502. Fax (860)509-9509

Harvard Divinity School,* (Nondenominational), 45 Francis Ave., Cambridge, MA 02138. Ronald F. Thiemann. Tel. (617)495-5761. Fax (617)495-9489

Hebrew Union College--Jewish Inst. of Religion, (Jewish), 1 W. 4th St., New York, NY 10012. Alfred Gottschalk. Tel. (212)674-5300. Fax (212)533-0129

Hebrew Union College--Jewish Inst. of Religion, (Jewish), 3077 University, Los Angeles, CA 90007. Sheldon Zimmerman. Tel. (213)749-3424. Fax (213)747-6128

Hebrew Union College--Jewish Institute of Religion, (Jewish), 3101 Clifton Ave., Cincinnati, OH 45215. Alfred Gottschalk. Tel. (513)221-1875. Fax (513)221-2810

Hobe Sound Bible College, (Nondenominational), P.O. Box 1065, Hobe Sound, FL 33475. P. Daniel Stetler. Tel. (407)546-5534. Fax (407)545-1422

Holy Cross Greek Orthodox School of Theology,* (Greek Orthodox Archdiocese of North and South America), 50 Goddard Ave., Brookline, MA 02146. George D. Dragas. Tel. (617)731-3500. Fax (617)232-7819

Holy Trinity Orthodox Seminary, (The Russian Orthodox Church Outside of Russia), P.O. Box 36, Jordanville, NY 13361. Archbishop Laurus. Tel. (315)858-0940. Fax (315)858-0505

Hood Theological Seminary, (African Methodist Episcopal Zion Church), 800 W. Thomas St., Salisbury, NC 28144. Albert J.D. Aymer. Tel. (704)638-5643. Fax (704)638-5736

Howard University School of Divinity,* (Interdenominational), 1400 Shepherd St. NE, Washington, DC 20017. Clarence G. Newsome. Tel. (202)806-0500. Fax (202)806-0711

Huntington College, Graduate School of Christian Ministries, (United Brethren in Christ), 2303 College Ave., Huntington, IN 46750. Paul R. Fetters. Tel. (219)356-6000. Fax (219)356-9448

Iliff School of Theology,* (The United Methodist Church), 2201 S. University Blvd., Denver, CO 80210. Donald E. Messer. Tel. (303)744-1287. Fax (303)744-3387

Immaculate Conception Seminary School of Theology,* (The Roman Catholic Church), 400 S. Orange Ave., South Orange, NJ 07079. John Flesey. Tel. (201)761-9575. Fax (201)761-9577

Indiana Wesleyan University, (The Wesleyan Church), 4201 S. Washington, Marion, IN 46953. James Barnes. Tel. (317)674-6901. Fax (317)677-2499

Interdenominational Theological Center,* (Interdenominational), 671 Beckwith St. SW, Atlanta, GA 30314. James H. Costen. Tel. (404)527-7702. Fax (404)527-0901

Jesuit School of Theology at Berkeley,* (The Roman Catholic Church), 1735 LeRoy Ave., Berkeley, CA 94709. T. Howland Sanks. Tel. (510)841-8804. Fax (510)841-8536

Jewish Theological Seminary of America, (Jewish), 3080 Broadway, New York, NY 10027-4649. Ismar Schorsch. Tel. (212)678-8000. Fax (212)678-8947

John Wesley College, (Interdenominational), 2314 N. Centennial St., High Point, NC 27265. Brian C. Donley. Tel. (919)889-2262. Fax (919)889-2261

Johnson Bible College, (Christian Churches and Churches of Christ), 7900 Johnson Dr., Knoxville, TN 37998. David L. Eubanks. Tel. (615)573-4517. Fax (615)579-2336

Kansas City College and Bible School, (Church of God (Holiness)), 7401 Metcalf Ave., Overland Park, KS 66204. Gayle Woods. Tel. (913)722-0272. Fax (913)722-0351

Kenrick-Glennon Seminary,* (The Roman Catholic Church), 5200 Glennon Dr., St. Louis, MO 63119. George Lucas. Tel. (314)644-0266. Fax (314)644-3079

Kentucky Christian College, (Christian Churches and Churches of Christ), 100 Academic Parkway, Grayson, KY 41143-2205. Keith P. Keeran. Tel. (606)474-3000. Fax (606)474-3155

Kentucky Mountain Bible College, (Interdenominational), Box 10, Vancleve, KY 41385. Philip Speas. Tel. (606)666-5000. Fax (606)666-7744

L.I.F.E. Bible College, (International Church of the Foursquare Gospel), 1100 Covina Blvd., San Dimas, CA 91773. Dick Scott. Tel. (909)599-5433. Fax (909)599-6690

La Sierra University, (Seventh-day Adventist Church), 4700 Pierce St., Riverside, CA 92515-8247. Lawrence T. Geraty. Tel. (709)785-2000. Fax (709)785-2901

Lancaster Bible College, (Nondenominational), 901 Eden Rd., Lancaster, PA 17601. Gilbert A. Peterson. Tel. (717)569-7071. Fax (717)560-8213

Lancaster Theological Sem. of the United Church of Christ,* (United Church of Christ), 555 W. James St., Lancaster, PA 17603-2897. Peter Schmiechen. Tel. (717)393-0654. Fax (717)393-4254

Lexington Theological Seminary,* (Christian Church (Disciples of Christ)), 631 S. Limestone St., Lexington, KY 40508. Richard L. Harrison, Jr.. Tel. (606)252-0361. Fax (606)281-6042

Lincoln Christian College and Seminary,* (Christian Churches and Churches of Christ), 100 Campus View Dr., Lincoln, IL 62656. Charles A. McNeely. Tel. (217)732-3168. Fax (217)732-5914

Louisville Presbyterian Theological Seminary,* (Presbyterian Church (U.S.A.)), 1044 Alta Vista Rd., Louisville, KY 40205. John M. Mulder. Tel. (502)895-3411. Fax (502)895-1096

Luther Seminary,* (Evangelical Lutheran Church in America), 2481 Como Ave., St. Paul, MN 55108. David L. Tiede. Tel. (612)641-3456. Fax (612)641-3425

Lutheran Bible Institute in California, (Interdenominational Lutheran), 5321 University Dr. Ste.H, Irvine, CA 92715-2938. Clifton Pederson. Tel. (714)262-9222. Fax (714)262-0283

Lutheran Bible Institute of Seattle, (Interdenominational Lutheran), 4221 - 228th Ave. SE, Issaquah, WA 98027. James A. Bergquist. Tel. (206)392-0400. Fax (206)392-0404

Lutheran Brethren Seminary, (Church of the Lutheran Brethren of America), 815 W. Vernon, Fergus Falls, MN 56537. John C. Kilde. Tel. (218)739-3375. Fax (218)739-3372

Lutheran Center for Christian Learning, (Church of the Lutheran Brethren of America), 815 W. Vernon Ave., Fergus Falls, MN 56537-2699. Joel Egge. Tel. (218)739-3375. Fax (218)739-3372

Lutheran School of Theology at Chicago,* (Evangelical Lutheran Church in America), 1100 E. 55th St., Chicago, IL 60615-5199. William E. Lesher. Tel. (312)256-0700. Fax (312)256-0782

Lutheran Theological Seminary,* (Evangelical Lutheran Church in America), 61 NW Confederate Ave., Gettysburg, PA 17325-1795. Darold H. Beekmann. Tel. (717)334-6286. Fax (717)334-3469

Lutheran Theological Seminary at Philadelphia,* (Evangelical Lutheran Church in America), 7301 Germantown Ave., Philadelphia, PA 19119. Robert G. Hughes. Tel. (215)248-4616. Fax (215)248-4577

Lutheran Theological Southern Seminary,* (Evangelical Lutheran Church in America), 4201 North Main St., Columbia, SC 29203. H. Frederick Reisz. Tel. (803)786-5150. Fax (803)786-6499

Magnolia Bible College, (Churches of Christ), P.O. Box 1109, Kosciusko, MS 39090. Cecil May. Tel. (601)289-2896. Fax (601)289-1850

Manhattan Christian College, (Christian Churches and Churches of Christ), 1415 Anderson Ave., Manhattan, KS 66502. Kenneth Cable. Tel. (913)539-3571. Fax (913)539-0832

Manna Bible Institute, (Nondenominational), 700 E. Church La., Philadelphia, PA 19144. Tel. (215)843-3600

McCormick Theological Seminary, * (Presbyterian Church (U.S.A.)), 5555 S. Woodlawn Ave., Chicago, IL 60637. Cynthia M. Campbell. Tel. (312)947-6300. Fax (312)947-0376

Meadville/Lombard Theol. School, * (Unitarian Universalist Association), 5701 S. Woodlawn Ave., Chicago, IL 60637. Spencer Lavan. Tel. (312)753-3195. Fax (312)753-1323

Memphis Theol. Sem. of the Cumberland Presbyterian Church,* (Cumberland Presbyterian Church), 168 E. Parkway S at Union, Memphis, TN 38104-4395. J. David Hester. Tel. (901)458-8232. Fax (901)452-4051

Mennonite Brethren Biblical Seminary,* (General Conference of Mennonite Brethren Churches), 4824 E. Butler Ave. (at Chestnut Ave.), Fresno, CA 93727. Henry J. Schmidt. Tel. (209)251-8628. Fax (209)251-7212

Methodist Theological School in Ohio,* (The United Methodist Church), 3081 Columbus Pike, Box 1204, Delaware, OH 43015-0931. Norman E. Dewire. Tel. (614)363-1146. Fax (614)362-3135

Mid-America Bible College, (The Church of God), 3500 SW 119th St., Oklahoma City, OK 73170. Forrest R. Robinson. Tel. (405)691-3800. Fax (405)692-3165

Midwestern Baptist Theological Seminary,* (Southern Baptist Convention), 5001 N. Oak St. Trafficway, Kansas City, MO 64118. Mark Coppenger. Tel. (816)453-4600. Fax (816)455-3528

Minnesota Bible College, (Christian Churches and Churches of Christ), 920 Mayowood Rd. SW, Rochester, MN 55902. Robert W. Cash. Tel. (507)288-4563. Fax (507)288-9046

Moody Bible Institute, (Interdenominational), 820 N. La Salle Blvd., Chicago, IL 60610. Joseph M. Stowell. Tel. (312)329-4000. Fax (312)329-4109

Moravian Theological Seminary,* (Moravian Church in America (Unitas Fratrum)), 1200 Main St., Bethlehem, PA 18018. David A. Schattschneider. Tel. (610)861-1516. Fax (610)861-1569

Moreau Seminary (Congregation of Holy Cross), (The Roman Catholic Church), Moreau Seminary, Notre Dame, IN 46556. Thomas K. Zurcher. Tel. (219)631-7735. Fax (219)631-9233

Morehouse School of Religion, (Interdenominational Baptist), 645 Beckwith St. SW, Atlanta, GA 30314. William T. Perkins. Tel. (404)527-7777. Fax (404)681-1005

Mount Angel Seminary,* (The Roman Catholic Church), St. Benedict, OR 97373. Patrick S. Brennan. Tel. (503)845-3951. Fax (503)845-3126

Mt. St. Mary's Seminary,* (The Roman Catholic Church), Emmitsburg, MD 21727-7797. Kenneth W. Roeltgen. Tel. (301)447-5295. Fax (301)447-5636

Mt. St. Mary's Seminary of the West, (The Roman Catholic Church), 6616 Beechmont Ave., Cincinnati, OH 45230. Robert J. Mooney. Tel. (513)231-2223. Fax (513)231-3254

Multnomah Bible College and Biblical Seminary,* (Interdenominational), 8435 NE Glisan St., Portland, OR 97220. Joseph C. Aldrich. Tel. (503)255-0332. Fax (503)251-5351

Mundelein Seminary of the Univ. of St. Mary-of-the-Lake,* (The Roman Catholic Church), 1000 E. Maple, Mundelein, IL 60060-1174. John Canary. Tel. (708)566-6401. Fax (708)566-7330

Nashotah House (Theological Seminary),* (Episcopal Church), 2777 Mission Rd., Nashotah, WI 53058-9793. Gary W. Kriss. Tel. (414)646-3371. Fax (414)646-2215

Nazarene Bible College, (Church of the Nazarene), 1111 Chapman Dr., Box 15749, Colorado Springs, CO 80916. Hiram Sanders. Tel. (719)596-5110. Fax (719)550-9437

Nazarene Theological Seminary,* (Church of the Nazarene), 1700 E. Meyer Blvd., Kansas City, MO 64131. A. Gordon Wetmore. Tel. (816)333-6254. Fax (816)333-6271

Nebraska Christian College, (Christian Churches and Churches of Christ), 1800 Syracuse Ave., Norfolk, NE 68701. Ray D. Stites. Tel. (402)371-5960. Fax (402)371-5967

New Brunswick Theological Seminary,* (Reformed Church in America), 17 Seminary Pl., New Brunswick, NJ 08901-1107. Norman J. Kansfield. Tel. (908)247-5241. Fax (908)249-5412

New Orleans Baptist Theological Seminary,* (Southern Baptist Convention), 3939 Gentilly Blvd., New Orleans, LA 70126. Landrum P. Leavell. Tel. (504)282-4455. Fax (504)944-4455

New York Theological Seminary,* (Interdenominational), Five W. 29th St., 9th Floor, New York, NY 10001. M. William Howard. Tel. (212)532-4012. Fax (212)684-0757

North American Baptist Seminary,* (North American Baptist Conference), 1525 S. Grange Ave., Sioux Falls, SD 57105. Charles M. Hiatt. Tel. (605)336-6588. Fax (605)335-9090

North Central Bible College, (Assemblies of God), 910 Elliot Ave. S, Minneapolis, MN 55404. Gordon L. Anderson. Tel. (612)332-3491. Fax (612)343-4778

North Park Theological Seminary,* (The Evangelical Covenant Church), 3225 W. Foster Ave., Chicago, IL 60625. David G. Horner. Tel. (312)244-5710. Fax (312)244-4953

Northern Baptist Theological Seminary,* (American Baptist Churches in the U.S.A.), 660 E. Butterfield Rd., Lombard, IL 60148. Ian M. Chapman. Tel. (708)620-2100. Fax (708)620-2194

Northwest College of the Assembies of God, (Assemblies of God), 5520 108th Ave. NE, P.O. Box 579, Kirkland, WA 98083-0579. Dennis A. Davis. Tel. (206)822-8266. Fax (206)827-0148

Notre Dame Seminary,* (The Roman Catholic Church), 2901 S. Carrollton Ave., New Orleans, LA 70118-4391. Gregory M. Aymond. Tel. (504)866-7426. Fax (504)866-3119

Oak Hills Bible College, (Interdenominational), 1600 Oak Hills Rd. SW, Bemidji, MN 56601. Mark Hovestol. Tel. (218)751-8670. Fax (218)751-8825

Oblate College,* (The Roman Catholic Church), 391 Michigan Ave. NE, Washington, DC 20017. George F. Kirwin. Tel. (202)529-6544. Fax (202)636-9444

Oblate School of Theology,* (The Roman Catholic Church), 285 Oblate Dr., San Antonio, TX 78216-6693. J. William Morell. Tel. (210)341-1366. Fax (210)341-4519

Oral Roberts University School of Theology and Missions,* (Interdenominational), 7777 South Lewis Ave., Tulsa, OK 74171. Paul G. Chappell. Tel. (918)495-6096. Fax (918)495-6033

Ozark Christian College, (Christian Churches and Churches of Christ), 1111 N. Main St., Joplin, MO 64801. Ken Idleman. Tel. (417)624-2518. Fax (417)624-0090

Pacific Christian College, (Christian Churches and Churches of Christ), 2500 E. Nutwood Ave., Fullerton, CA 92631. E. Leroy Lawson. Tel. (714)879-3901. Fax (714)526-0231

Pacific Lutheran Theological Seminary,* (Evangelical Lutheran Church in America), 2770 Marin Ave., Berkeley, CA 94708. Jerry L. Schmalenberger. Tel. (510)524-5264. Fax (510)524-2408

Pacific School of Religion,* (United Church of Christ), 1798 Scenic Ave., Berkeley, CA 94709. Thomas J. Henderson. Tel. (510)848-0528. Fax (510)845-8948

Payne Theological Seminary,* (African Methodist Episcopal Church), Box 474, 1230 Wilberforce-Clifton Rd., Wilberforce, OH 45384-0474. Louis-Charles Harvey. Tel. (513)376-2946. Fax (513)376-3330

Pepperdine University, (Churches of Christ), Religion Division, Malibu, CA 90263. Thomas H. Olbricht. Tel. (310)456-4352. Fax (310)456-4314

Perkins School of Theology (Southern Methodist University),* (The United Methodist Church), Kirby Hall, Dallas, TX 75275-0133. Robin W. Lovin. Tel. (214)768-2138. Fax (214)768-2117

Philadelphia College of Bible, (Nondenominational), 200 Manor Ave., Langhorne, PA 19047-2990. W. Sherrill Babb. Tel. (215)752-5800. Fax (215)702-4341

Philadelphia Theological Seminary, (Reformed Episcopal Church), 7372 Henry Ave., Philadelphia, PA 19128. Leonard W. Riches. Tel. (215)483-2480. Fax (215)483-2484

Phillips Theological Seminary,* (Christian Church (Disciples of Christ)), Box 2335, Enid, OK 73702. William Tabbernee. Tel. (405)548-2238. Fax (405)237-7686

Piedmont Bible College, (Baptist (independent)), 716 Franklin St., Winston-Salem, NC 27101. Howard L. Wilburn. Tel. (910)725-8344. Fax (910)725-5522

Pittsburgh Theological Seminary,* (Presbyterian Church (U.S.A.)), 616 N. Highland Ave., Pittsburgh, PA 15206. Carnegie Samuel Calian. Tel. (412)362-5610. Fax (412)363-3260

Point Loma Nazarene College, (Church of the Nazarene), 3900 Lomaland Dr., San Diego, CA 92106. Jim Bond. Tel. (619)221-2200. Fax (619)221-2579

Pontifical College Josephinum,* (The Roman Catholic Church), 7625 N. High St., Columbus, OH 43235. Blase J. Cupich. Tel. (614)885-5585. Fax (614)885-2307

Pope John XXIII National Seminary,* (The Roman Catholic Church), 558 South Ave., Weston, MA 02193. Francis D. Kelly. Tel. (617)899-5500. Fax (617)899-9057

Practical Bible College, (Independent Baptist), Box 601, Bible School Park, NY 13737. Dale E. Linebaugh. Tel. (607)729-1581. Fax (607)729-2962

Presbyterian School of Christian Education,* (Presbyterian Church (U.S.A.)), 1205 Palmyra Ave., Richmond, VA 23227. Wayne G. Boulton. Tel. (804)359-5031. Fax (804)254-8060

Princeton Theological Seminary,* (Presbyterian Church (U.S.A.)), P.O. Box 821, Princeton, NJ 08542-0803. Thomas W. Gillespie. Tel. (609)921-8300. Fax (609)924-2973

Protestant Episcopal Theological Seminary in Virginia,* (Episcopal Church), 3737 Seminary Rd., Alexandria, VA 22304. Martha J. Horne. Tel. (703)370-6600. Fax (703)370-6234

Puget Sound Christian College, (Christian Churches and Churches of Christ), 410 Fourth Ave. N, Edmonds, WA 98020-3171. R. Allan Dunbar. Tel. (206)775-8686. Fax (206)775-8688

Rabbi Isaac Elchanan Theological Seminary, (Jewish), 2540 Amsterdam Ave., New York, NY 10033. Zevulun Charlop. Tel. (212)960-5344. Fax (212)960-0061

Reconstructionist Rabbinical College, (Jewish), Church Rd. and Greenwood Ave., Wyncote, PA 19095. David A. Teutsch. Tel. (215)576-0800. Fax (215)576-6143

Reformed Bible College, (Interdenominational), 3333 East Beltline NE, Grand Rapids, MI 49505. Nicholas Kroeze. Tel. (616)363-2050. Fax (616)363-9771

Reformed Presbyterian Theological Seminary,* (Reformed Presbyterian Church of North America), 7418 Penn Ave., Pittsburgh, PA 15208. Jerry F. O'Neill. Tel. (412)731-8690. Fax (412)731-4834

Reformed Theological Seminary,* (Nondenominational), 5422 Clinton Blvd., Jackson, MS 39209. Luder G. Whitlock. Tel. (601)922-4988. Fax (601)922-1153

Regent University School of Theology,* (Interdenominational), 1000 Regent University Dr., Virginia Beach, VA 23464-5041. Terry Lindvall. Tel. (804)579-4000. Fax (804)579-4037

Roanoke Bible College, (Christian Churches and Churches of Christ), 714 First St., Elizabeth City, NC 27909. William A. Griffin. Tel. (919)338-5191. Fax (919)338-0801

Sacred Heart Major Seminary,* (The Roman Catholic Church), 2701 Chicago Blvd., Detroit, MI 48206. Allen H. Vigneron. Tel. (313)883-8500. Fax (313)868-6440

Sacred Heart School of Theology,* (The Roman Catholic Church), P.O. Box 429, Hales Corners, WI 53130-0429. James D. Brackin. Tel. (414)425-8300. Fax (414)529-6999

Saint Bernard's Institute,* (The Roman Catholic Church), 1100 S. Goodman St., Rochester, NY 14620. Patricia A. Schoelles. Tel. (716)271-3657. Fax (716)271-2045

Saint Paul School of Theology,* (The United Methodist Church), 5123 Truman Rd., Kansas City, MO 64127. Lovett H. Weems. Tel. (816)483-9600. Fax (816)483-9605

St. Charles Borromeo Seminary,* (The Roman Catholic Church), 1000 East Wynnewood Rd., Wynnewood, PA 19096-3002. James E. Molloy. Tel. (610)667-3394. Fax (610)667-7635

St. Francis Seminary,* (The Roman Catholic Church), 3257 S. Lake Dr., St. Francis, WI 53235. Andrew L. Nelson. Tel. (414)747-6400. Fax (414)747-6442

US SEMINARIES

St. John's Seminary,* (The Roman Catholic Church), 127 Lake St., Brighton, MA 02135. Timothy Moran. Tel. (617)254-2610. Fax (617)787-2336

St. John's Seminary College,* (The Roman Catholic Church), 5118 Seminary Rd., Camarillo, CA 93012-2599. Edward Wm. Clark. Tel. (805)482-2755. Fax (805)987-5097

St. John's University, School of Theology,* (The Roman Catholic Church), Box 7288, Collegeville, MN 56321. Dale Launderville. Tel. (612)363-2100. Fax (612)363-2504

St. Joseph's Seminary,* (The Roman Catholic Church), 201 Seminary Ave., (Dunwoodie) Yonkers, NY 10704. Edwin F. O'Brien. Tel. (914)968-6200. Fax (914)968-7912

St. Louis Christian College, (Christian Churches and Churches of Christ), 1360 Grandview Dr., Florissant, MO 63033. Kenneth L. Beck. Tel. (314)837-6777. Fax (314)837-8291

St. Mary Seminary,* (The Roman Catholic Church), 28700 Euclid Ave., Wickliffe, OH 44092. Donald B. Cozzens. Tel. (216)943-7565. Fax (216)585-3528

St. Mary's Seminary, (The Roman Catholic Church), 9845 Memorial Dr., Houston, TX 77024-3498. Chester L. Borski. Tel. (713)686-4345. Fax (713)681-7550

St. Mary's Seminary and University,* (The Roman Catholic Church), 5400 Roland Ave., Baltimore, MD 21210. Robert F. Leavitt. Tel. (301)323-3200. Fax (301)323-3554

St. Meinrad School of Theology,* (The Roman Catholic Church), St. Meinrad, IN 47577. Eugene Hensell. Tel. (812)357-6611. Fax (812)357-6964

St. Patrick's Seminary,* (The Roman Catholic Church), 320 Middlefield Rd., Menlo Park, CA 94025. Gerald D. Coleman. Tel. (415)325-5621. Fax (415)322-0997

St. Paul Seminary School of Divinity,* (The Roman Catholic Church), 2260 Summit Ave., St. Paul, MN 55105. Phillip J. Rask. Tel. (612)962-5050. Fax (612)962-5790

St. Tikhon's Orthodox Theological Seminary, (The Orthodox Church in America), Box 130, South Canaan, PA 18459-0121. Archbishop Herman. Tel. (717)937-4411. Fax (717)937-3100

St. Vincent Seminary,* (The Roman Catholic Church), 300 Fraser Rudchase Rd., Latrobe, PA 15650. Thomas Acklin. Tel. (412)537-4592. Fax (412)537-4554

St. Vincent de Paul Regional Seminary,* (The Roman Catholic Church), 10701 S. Military Trail, Boynton Beach, FL 33436-4899. Pablo A. Navarro. Tel. (407)732-4424. Fax (407)737-2205

St. Vladimir's Orthodox Theological Seminary,* (The Orthodox Church in America), 575 Scarsdale Rd., Crestwood, NY 10707. Thomas Hopko. Tel. (914)961-8313. Fax (914)961-4507

SS. Cyril and Methodius Seminary, (The Roman Catholic Church), 3535 Indian Trail, Orchard Lake, MI 48324. Francis B. Koper. Tel. (810)683-0311. Fax (810)683-0402

San Francisco Theological Seminary,* (Presbyterian Church (U.S.A.)), 2 Kensington Rd., San Anselmo, CA 94960. Donald W. McCullough. Tel. (415)258-6500. Fax (415)258-1608

San Jose Christian College, (Christian Churches and Churches of Christ), 790 S. 12th St., P.O. Box 1090, San Jose, CA 95108. Bryce L. Jessup. Tel. (408)293-9058. Fax (408)293-7352

Savonarola Theological Seminary, (Polish National Catholic Church of America), 1031 Cedar Ave., Scranton, PA 18505. John F. Swantek. Tel. (717)343-0100

School of Theology at Claremont,* (The United Methodist Church), 1325 N. College Ave., Claremont, CA 91711. Robert W. Edgar. Tel. (800)626-7821. Fax (909)626-7062

Seabury-Western Theological Seminary,* (Episcopal Church), 2122 Sheridan Rd., Evanston, IL 60201. Mark S. Sisk. Tel. (708)328-9300. Fax (708)328-9624

Seattle University Institute for Theological Studies,* (The Roman Catholic Church), Broadway & Madison, Seattle, WA 98122. Loretta Jancoski. Tel. (206)296-5330. Fax (206)296-5329

Seminario Evangelico de Puerto Rico,* (Interdenominational), 776 Ponce de Leon Ave., San Juan, PR 00925. Luis Fidel Mercado. Tel. (809)751-6483. Fax (809)751-0847

Seminary of the Immaculate Conception,* (The Roman Catholic Church), 440 West Neck Rd., Huntington, NY 11743. Vincent F. Fullam. Tel. (516)423-0483. Fax (516)423-2346

Seventh Day Baptist School of Ministry, (Seventh Day Baptist General Conference, USA and Canada), 3120 Kennedy Rd., P.O. Box 1678, Janesville, WI 53547. Rodney Henry. Tel. (608)752-5055. Fax (608)752-7711

Seventh-day Adventist Theological Seminary,* (Seventh-day Adventist Church), Andrews University, Berrien Springs, MI 49104. Werner Vyhmeister. Tel. (616)471-3537. Fax (616)471-6202

Shaw Divinity School, (Baptist), P.O. Box 2090, Raleigh, NC 27102. Talbert O. Shaw. Tel. (919)832-1701. Fax (919)832-6082

Simpson College, (The Christian and Missionary Alliance), 2211 College View Dr., Redding, CA 96003. James M. Grant. Tel. (916)224-5600. Fax (916)224-5608

Southeastern Baptist College, (Baptist Missionary Association of America), 4229 Highway 15N, Laurel, MS 39440. Gerald D. Kellar. Tel. (601)426-6346. Fax (601)426-6346

Southeastern Baptist Theological Seminary,* (Southern Baptist Convention), 222 N. Wingate, P.O. Box 1889, Wake Forest, NC 27588-1889. Paige Patterson. Tel. (919)556-3101. Fax (919)556-0998

Southeastern Bible College, (Interdenominational), 3001 Highway 280 E, Birmingham, AL 35243. John D. Talley. Tel. (205)969-0880. Fax (205)970-9207

Southeastern College of the Assemblies of God, (Assemblies of God), 1000 Longfellow Blvd., Lakeland, FL 33801. James L. Hennesy. Tel. (941)665-4404. Fax (941)666-8103

Southern Baptist Theological Seminary,* (Southern Baptist Convention), 2825 Lexington Rd., Louisville, KY 40280. R. Albert Mohler. Tel. (502)897-4011. Fax (502)899-1770

Southern Christian University, (Churches of Christ), 1200 Taylor Rd., P.O. Box 240240, Montgomery, AL 36124-0240. Rex A. Turner. Tel. (205)277-2277. Fax (205)271-0002

Southern Wesleyan University, (The Wesleyan Church), 907 Wesleyan Dr., P.O. Box 1020, Central, SC 29630-1020. David J. Spittal. Tel. (803)639-2453. Fax (803)639-0826

Southwestern Assemblies of God University, (Assemblies of God), 1200 Sycamore St., Waxahachie, TX 75165. Delmer R. Guynes. Tel. (214)937-4010. Fax (214)923-0488

Southwestern Baptist Theological Seminary,* (Southern Baptist Convention), P.O. Box 22000, Fort Worth, TX 76122. Kenneth S. Hemphill. Tel. (817)923-1921. Fax (817)923-0610

Southwestern College, (Conservative Baptist Association of America), 2625 E. Cactus Rd., Phoenix, AZ 85032. Brent D. Garrison. Tel. (602)992-6101. Fax (602)404-2159

Starr King School for the Ministry,* (Unitarian Universalist Association), 2441 LeConte Ave., Berkeley, CA 94709. Rebecca Parker. Tel. (510)845-6232. Fax (510)845-6273

Swedenborg School of Religion, (The Swedenborgian Church), 48 Sargent St., Newton, MA 02158. Mary Kay Klein. Tel. (617)244-0504. Fax (617)964-3258

Talbot School of Theology,* (Nondenominational), 13800 Biola Ave., La Mirada, CA 90639. Dennis H. Dirks. Tel. (310)903-4816. Fax (310)903-4759

Temple Baptist Seminary, (Independent Baptist), 1815 Union Ave., Chattanooga, TN 37404. Barkev Trachian. Tel. (423)493-4221. Fax (423)493-4221

Theological School of the Protestant Reformed Churches, (Protestant Reformed Churches in America), 4949 Ivanrest Ave., Grandville, MI 49418. David J. Engelsma. Tel. (616)531-1490. Fax (616)531-3033

Toccoa Falls College, (The Christian and Missionary Alliance), P.O. Box 800777, Toccoa Falls, GA 30598. Paul L. Alford. Tel. (706)886-6831. Fax (706)886-0210

Trevecca Nazarene College, (Church of the Nazarene), 333 Murfreesboro Rd., Nashville, TN 37210. Millard Reed. Tel. (615)248-1200. Fax (615)248-7728

Trinity Bible College, (Assemblies of God), 50 S. 6th Ave., Ellendale, ND 58436. Howard Young. Tel. (701)349-3621. Fax (701)349-5443

Trinity College of Florida/Tampa Bay Seminary, (Nondenominational), 2430 Trinity Oaks Blvd., New Port Richey, FL 34655. Glenn Speed. Tel. (813)376-6911. Fax (813)376-0781

Trinity Episcopal School for Ministry,* (Episcopal Church), 311 Eleventh St., Ambridge, PA 15003. Peter C. Moore. Tel. (412)266-3838. Fax (412)266-4617

Trinity Evangelical Divinity School,* (The Evangelical Free Church of America), 2065 Half Day Rd., Deerfield, IL 60015. Gregory L. Waybright. Tel. (708)945-8800. Fax (708)317-8090

Trinity Lutheran Seminary,* (Evangelical Lutheran Church in America), 2199 E. Main St., Columbus, OH 43209-2334. Dennis A. Anderson. Tel. (614)235-4136. Fax (614)238-0263

Union Theological Seminary,* (Interdenominational), 3041 Broadway, New York, NY 10027. Holland L. Hendrix. Tel. (212)662-7100. Fax (212)280-1416

Union Theological Seminary in Virginia,* (Presbyterian Church (U.S.A.)), 3401 Brook Rd., Richmond, VA 23227. Louis B. Weeks. Tel. (804)355-0671. Fax (804)355-3919

United Theological Seminary,* (The United Methodist Church), 1810 Harvard Blvd., Dayton, OH 45406. Emerson Colaw. Tel. (513)278-5817. Fax (513)278-1218

United Theological Seminary of the Twin Cities,* (United Church of Christ), 3000 Fifth St. NW, New Brighton, MN 55112. Jonathan Morgan. Tel. (612)633-4311. Fax (612)633-4315

University of Chicago (Divinity School),* (Interdenominational), 1025 E. 58th St., Chicago, IL 60637. W. Clark Gilpin. Tel. (312)702-8221. Fax (312)702-6048

University of Dubuque Theological Seminary,* (Presbyterian Church (U.S.A.)), 2000 University Ave., Dubuque, IA 52001. C. Howard Wallace. Tel. (319)589-3122. Fax (319)589-3110

University of Notre Dame, Dept. of Theology,* (The Roman Catholic Church), Notre Dame, IN 46556. Lawrence S. Cunningham. Tel. (219)631-7811. Fax (219)631-4268

University of St. Thomas School of Theology,* (The Roman Catholic Church), 9845 Memorial Drive, Houston, TX 77024. Louis T. Brusatti. Tel. (713)686-4345. Fax (713)683-8673

University of the South School of Theology,* (Episcopal Church), 335 Tennessee Ave., Sewanee, TN 37383-1000. Guy Fitch Lytle. Tel. (615)598-1288. Fax (615)598-1165

Valley Forge Christian College, (Assemblies of God), 1401 Charlestown Rd., Phoenixville, PA 19460. Wesley W. Smith. Tel. (610)935-0450. Fax (610)935-9353

Vanderbilt University Divinity School,* (Interdenominational), Nashville, TN 37240. Joseph C. Hough. Tel. (615)322-2776. Fax (615)343-9957

Vennard College, (Interdenominational), Box 29, University Park, IA 52595. Blake J. Neff. Tel. (515)673-8391. Fax (515)673-8365

Virginia Union University (School of Theology),* (Interdenominational), 1500 N. Lombardy St., Richmond, VA 23220. John W. Kinney. Tel. (804)257-5715. Fax (804)257-5785

Walla Walla College (School of Theology), (Seventh-day Adventist Church), 204 S. College Ave., College Place, WA 99324. Douglas Clark. Tel. (509)527-2194. Fax (509)527-2253

Wartburg Theological Seminary,* (Evangelical Lutheran Church in America), 333 Wartburg Pl., Dubuque, IA 52003-7797. Roger Fjeld. Tel. (319)589-0200. Fax (319)589-0333

Washington Bible College/Capital Bible Seminary, (Nondenominational), 6511 Princess Garden Pkwy., Lanham, MD 20706. Homer Heater. Tel. (301)552-1400. Fax (301)552-2775

Washington Theological Consortium, (Nondenominational), 487 Michigan Ave. NE, Washington, DC 20017. Richard G. Abbott. Tel. (202)832-2675. Fax (202)526-0818

Washington Theological Union,* (The Roman Catholic Church), 6896 Laurel St. NW, Washington, DC 20012. Vincent D. Cushing

Wesley Biblical Seminary,* (Interdenominational), P.O. Box 9938, Jackson, MS 39286-0938. Robert R. Lawrence. Tel. (601)957-1314. Fax (601)957-1314

Wesley Theological Seminary,* (The United Methodist Church), 4500 Massachusetts Ave. NW, Washington, DC 20016. G. Douglass Lewis. Tel. (202)885-8601. Fax (202)885-8605

Western Evangelical Seminary,* (Interdenominational), P.O. Box 23939, Portland, OR 97281. David Le Shana. Tel. (503)639-0559. Fax (503)598-4338

Western Seminary, (Conservative Baptist Association of America), 5511 SE Hawthorne Blvd., Portland, OR 97215. Ronald E. Hawkins. Tel. (503)233-8561. Fax (503)239-4216

Western Theological Seminary,* (Reformed Church in America), 101 E. 13th St., Holland, MI 49423. Dennis N. Voskuil. Tel. (616)392-8555. Fax (616)392-7717

Westminster Theological Seminary,* (Nondenominational), Chestnut Hill, P.O. Box 27009, Philadelphia, PA 19118. Samuel T. Logan. Tel. (215)887-5511. Fax (215)887-5404

Weston Jesuit School of Theology,* (The Roman Catholic Church), 3 Phillips Pl., Cambridge, MA 02138. Robert Wild. Tel. (617)492-1960. Fax (617)492-5833

William Tyndale College, (Interdenominational), 35700 W. Twelve Mile Rd., Farmington Hills, MI 48331. James C. McHann. Tel. (810)553-7200. Fax (810)553-5963

Winebrenner Theological Seminary,* (Churches of God, General Conference), 701 E. Melrose Ave., Box 478, Findlay, OH 45839. David E. Draper. Tel. (419)422-4824. Fax (419)424-3433

Wisconsin Lutheran Seminary, (Wisconsin Evangelical Lutheran Synod), 11831 N. Seminary Dr., 65W, Mequon, WI 53092. Armin Panning. Tel. (414)242-7200. Fax (414)242-7255

9. THEOLOGICAL SEMINARIES AND BIBLE SCHOOLS IN CANADA

The following list includes theological seminaries and departments in colleges and universities in which ministerial training is given. Many denominations have additional programs. The lists of Religious Bodies in Canada should be consulted for the address of denominational headquarters.

The list has been developed from direct correspondence with the institutions. Inclusion in or exclusion from this list implies no judgment about the quality or accreditation of any institution. A "*" after the name of the institution indicates that it is either an accredited or affiliated member of the Association of Theological Schools. Information about total enrollment in ATS schools can be found in the statistical section.

The listing includes the institution name, denominational sponsor when appropriate, location, head, telephone number and fax number when known.

Acadia Divinity College,* (United Baptist Convention of the Atlantic Provinces), Acadia University, Wolfville, NS B0P 1X0. Andrew D. MacRae. Tel. (902)542-2285. Fax (902)542-7527

Alberta Bible College, (Christian Churches and Churches of Christ in Canada), 599 Northmount Dr. N.W., Calgary, AB T2K 3J6. Ronald A. Fraser. Tel. (403)282-2994. Fax (403)282-3084

Arthur Turner Training School, (The Anglican Church of Canada), Box 378, Pangnirtung, NT X0A 0R0. Roy Bowkett. Tel. (819)473-8375. Fax (819)473-8383

Associated Can. Theological Schools of Trinity Western Univ.,* (Baptist General Conference of Canada, Evangelical Free Church of Canada, The Fellowship of Evangelical Baptist Churches in Canada), 7600 Glover Rd., Langley, BC V3A 6H4. Guy Saffold. Tel. (604)888-6158. Fax (604)888-5729

Atlantic Baptist College, (United Baptist Convention of the Atlantic Provinces), Box 6004, Moncton, NB E1C 9L7. W. Ralph Richardson. Tel. (506)858-8970. Fax (506)858-9694

Atlantic School of Theology,* (Interdenominational), 640 Francklyn St., Halifax, NS B3H 3B5. Gordon Mac Dermid. Tel. (902)423-6801. Fax (902)492-4048

Baptist Leadership Training School, (Canadian Baptist Ministries), 4330 16th St. S.W., Calgary, AB T2T 4H9. Myrna Sears. Tel. (403)243-3770. Fax (403)287-1930

Bethany Bible College--Canada, (The Wesleyan Church of Canada), 26 Western St., Sussex, NB E0E 1P0. David S. Medders. Tel. (506)432-4400. Fax (506)432-4425

Bethany Bible Institute, (Canadian Conference of Mennonite Brethren Churches), Box 160, Hepburn, SK S0K 1Z0. Doug Berg. Tel. (306)947-2175. Fax (306)947-4229

Briercrest Schools (Briercrest Biblical College), (Interdenominational), 510 College Dr., Caronport, SK S0H 0S0. John Barkman. Tel. (306)756-3200. Fax (306)756-3366

Canadian Bible College, (Christian and Missionary Alliance in Canada), 4400-4th Ave., Regina, SK S4T 0H8. Robert A. Rose. Tel. (306)545-1515. Fax (306)545-0210

Canadian Lutheran Bible Institute, (Lutheran Church--Canada), 4837 52A St., Camrose, AB T4V 1W5. Ronald B. Mayan. Tel. (403)672-4454. Fax (403)672-4455

Canadian Nazarene College, (Church of the Nazarene Canada), 610, 833 4th Ave. SW, Calgary, AB T2P 3T5. Riley Coulter. Tel. (403)571-2550. Fax (403)571-2556

Canadian Reformed Churches, Theol. College of the, (Canadian and American Reformed Churches), 110 West 27th St., Hamilton, ON L9C 5A1. J. Geertsema. Tel. (416)575-3688. Fax (416)575-0799

Canadian Theological Seminary,* (Christian and Missionary Alliance in Canada), 4400-4th Ave., Regina, SK S4T 0H8. Robert A. Rose. Tel. (306)545-1515. Fax (306)545-0210

Central Pentecostal College, University of Saskatchewan, (The Pentecostal Assemblies of Canada), 1303 Jackson Ave., Saskatoon, SK S7H 2M9. R. Kadyschuk. Tel. (306)374-6655. Fax (306)373-6968

Centre for Christian Studies, (The Anglican Church of Canada, The United Church of Canada), 77 Charles St. W., Ste. 400, Toronto, ON M5S 1K5. ----. Tel. (416)923-1168. Fax (416)923-5496

Church Army College of Evangelism, (The Anglican Church of Canada), 397 Brunswick Ave., Toronto, ON M5R 2Z2. Roy E. Dickson. Tel. (416)924-9279. Fax (416)924-2931

Collège Dominicain de Philosophie et de Théologie, (The Roman Catholic Church in Canada), 96 avenue Empress, Ottawa, ON K1R 7G3. Michel Gourgues. Tel. (613)233-5696. Fax (613)233-6064

College Biblique Québec, (The Pentecostal Assemblies of Canada), 740 Le-Boureneus, Ste. 100, Ancienne Lorette, QC G2J 1E2. Pierre Bergeron. Tel. (418)622-7552. Fax (418)622-1470

College of Emmanuel and St. Chad, (The Anglican Church of Canada), 1337 College Dr., Saskatoon, SK S7N 0W6. William Niels Christensen. Tel. (306)975-3753. Fax (306)934-2683

Columbia Bible College, (Interdenominational Mennonite), 2940 Clearbrook Rd., Abbotsford, BC V2T 2Z8. Walter Unger. Tel. (604)853-3358. Fax (604)853-3063

Concord College, (Canadian Conference of Mennonite Brethren Churches), 169 Riverton Ave., Winnipeg, MB R2L 2E5. James N. Pankratz. Tel. (204)669-6583. Fax (204)663-2468

Concordia Lutheran Seminary,* (Lutheran Church--Canada), 7040 Ada Blvd., Edmonton, AB T5B 4E3. L. Dean Hempelmann. Tel. (403)474-1468. Fax (403)479-3067

Concordia Lutheran Theological Seminary,* (Lutheran Church--Canada), 470 Glenridge Ave., St. Catharines, ON L2T 4C3. Jonathan Grothe. Tel. (905)688-2362. Fax (905)688-9744

Covenant Bible College, (The Evangelical Covenant Church of Canada), 630 Westchester Rd., Strathmore, AB T1P 1H8. Neil R. Josephson. Tel. (403)934-6200. Fax (403)934-6220

Eastern Pentecostal Bible College, (The Pentecostal Assemblies of Canada), 780 Argyle St., Peterborough, ON K9H 5T2. Carl F. Verge. Tel. (705)748-9111. Fax (705)748-3931

Edmonton Baptist Seminary,* (North American Baptist Conference), 11525-23 Ave., Edmonton, AB T6J 4T3. Paul H. Siewert. Tel. (403)437-1960. Fax (403)436-9416

Emmanuel Bible College, (The Evangelical Missionary Church of Canada), 100 Fergus Ave., Kitchener, ON N2A 2H2. Thomas E. Dow. Tel. (519)894-8900. Fax (519)894-5331

Emmanuel College,* (The United Church of Canada), 75 Queen's Park Crescent, Toronto, ON M5S 1K7. John C. Hoffman. Tel. (416)585-4539. Fax (416)585-4516

Faculté De Théologie Évangélique, (Union d'Eglises Baptistes Francaises au Canada), 2285, avenue Papineau, Montréal, QC H2K 4J5. Amar Djaballah. Tel. (514)526-6643. Fax (514)526-9269

Faith Alive Bible College, (Nondenominational), 637 University Dr., Saskatoon, SK S7N 0H8. David Pierce. Tel. (306)652-2230. Fax (306)665-1125

Full Gospel Bible Institute, (Apostolic Church of Pentecost of Canada Inc.), Box 579, Eston, SK S0L 1A0. Alan B. Mortensen. Tel. (306)962-3621. Fax (306)962-3810

Gardner College, A Centre for Christian Studies, (Church of God (Anderson, Ind.)), 4704 55th St., Camrose, AB T4V 2B6. Bruce Kelly. Tel. (403)672-0171. Fax (403)672-6888

Great Lakes Bible College, (Churches of Christ in Canada), 4875 King St., Beamsville, ON L0R 1B0. Lawrence Whitfield. Tel. (905)563-5374. Fax (905)563-0818

Heritage Baptist College/Heritage Theological Seminary, (The Fellowship of Evangelical Baptist Churches in Canada), 175 Holiday Inn Dr., Cambridge, ON N3C 3T2. Marvin Brubacher. Tel. (519)651-2869. Fax (519)651-2870

Huron College,* (The Anglican Church of Canada), 1349 Western Rd., London, ON N6G 1H3. Trish Fulton. Tel. (519)438-7224. Fax (519)438-3938

Institut Biblique Beree, (The Pentecostal Assemblies of Canada), 1711 Henri-Bourassa Est, Montréal, QC H2C 1J5. André L. Gagnon. Tel. (514)385-4238. Fax (514)462-1789

Institut Biblique Laval, (Canadian Conference of Mennonite Brethren Churches), 1775, boul. Édouard-Laurin, Ville Saint-Laurent, QC H4L 2B9. Jean Théorêt. Tel. (514)331-0878. Fax (514)331-0879

Institute for Christian Studies, (Nondenominational), 229 College St., Toronto, ON M5T 1R4. Harry Fernhout. Tel. (416)979-2331. Fax (416)979-2332

International Bible College, (Church of God (Cleveland, Tenn.)), 401 Trinity La., Moose Jaw, SK S6H 0E3. Alex Allan. Tel. (306)692-4041. Fax (306)692-7968

Key-Way-Tin Bible Institute, (Interdenominational), Box 540, Lac La Biche, AB T0A 2C0. Leigh Wolverton. Tel. (403)623-4565. Fax (403)623-1788

Knox College,* (The Presbyterian Church in Canada), 59 St. George St., Toronto, ON M5S 2E6. Arthur Van Seters. Tel. (416)978-4500. Fax (416)971-2133

Living Faith Bible College, (Independent Assemblies of God International (Canada)), Box 100, Caroline, AB T0M 0M0. Cliff A. Stalwick. Tel. (403)722-2225. Fax (403)722-2459

Lutheran Theological Seminary,* (Evangelical Lutheran Church in Canada), 114 Seminary Crescent, Saskatoon, SK S7N 0X3. Roger Nostbakken. Tel. (306)975-7004. Fax (306)975-0084

CANADIAN SEMINARIES

Maritime Christian College, (Christian Churches and Churches of Christ in Canada), 503 University Ave., Charlottetown, PE C1A 7Z4. Stewart J. Lewis. Tel. (902)628-8887. Fax (902)892-3959

Marpeck School of Discipleship, (Conference of Mennonites in Canada), Box 1268, Swift Current, SK S9H 3X4. Ray Friesen. Tel. (306)773-0604. Fax (306)773-9250

McGill University Faculty of Religious Studies,* (The Anglican Church of Canada, The Presbyterian Church in Canada, The United Church of Canada), 3520 University St., Montreal, QC H3A 2A7. Donna R. Runnalls. Tel. (514)398-4121. Fax (514)398-6665

McMaster Divinity College,* (Baptist Convention of Ontario and Quebec), McMaster Divinity College, Hamilton, ON L8S 4K1. William H. Brackney. Tel. (905)525-9140. Fax (905)577-4782

Millar College of the Bible, (Interdenominational), Box 25, Pambrun, SK S0N 1W0. A. Brian Atmore. Tel. (306)582-2033. Fax (306)582-2027

Montreal Diocesan Theological College,* (The Anglican Church of Canada), 3473 University St., Montreal, QC H3A 2A8. John Simons. Tel. (514)849-3004. Fax (514)849-4113

Mount Carmel Bible School, (Christian Brethren (also known as Plymouth Brethren)), 4725 106 Ave., Edmonton, AB T6A 1E7. Jay Gurnett. Tel. (403)465-3015. Fax (403)466-2485

National Native Bible College, (Interdenominational), Box 478, Deseronto, ON K0K 1X0. Adrian Jacobs. Tel. (613)396-2311. Fax (613)396-2555

Newman Theological College,* (The Roman Catholic Church in Canada), 15611 St. Albert Trail, Edmonton, AB T5L 4H8. Kevin J. Carr. Tel. (403)447-2993. Fax (403)447-2685

Nipawin Bible Institute, (Interdenominational), Box 1986, Nipawin, SK S0E 1E0. Mark Leppington. Tel. (306)862-5095. Fax (306)862-3651

Northwest Baptist Theological College and Seminary, (The Fellowship of Evangelical Baptist Churches in Canada), 22606 76A Ave., P.O. Box 790, Langley, BC V3A 8B8. Donald Launstein. Tel. (604)888-3310. Fax (604)888-3354

Northwest Bible College, (The Pentecostal Assemblies of Canada), 11617-106 Ave., Edmonton, AB T5H 0S1. G. Johnson. Tel. (403)452-0808. Fax (403)452-5803

Ontario Christian Seminary, (Christian Churches and Churches of Christ in Canada), P.O. Box 324, Stn. D; 260 High Park Ave., Toronto, ON M6P 3J9. James R. Cormode. Tel. (416)769-7115. Fax (416)769-7047

Ontario Theological Seminary,* (Interdenominational), 25 Ballyconnor Ct., North York, ON M2M 4B3. Brian C. Stiller. Tel. (416)226-6380. Fax (416)226-6746

Pacific Bible College, (Interdenominational), 15100 66 A Ave., Surrey, BC V3S 2A6. Dennis L. Hixson. Tel. (604)597-9331. Fax (604)597-9090

Parole de Vie Bethel/Word of Life Bethel, (Nondenominational), 1175 Chemin Woodward Hill, RR1, Lennoxville, QC J1M 2A2. Ken Beach. Tel. (819)823-8435. Fax (819)823-2468

Peace River Bible Institute, (Interdenominational), Box 99, Sexsmith, AB T0H 3C0. Reuben Kvill. Tel. (403)568-3962. Fax (403)568-4431

Prairie Graduate School, (Interdenominational), 1011 Glenmore Trail SW, Calgary, AB T2V 4R6. Paul W. Ferris, Jr. Tel. (403)777-0150. Fax (403)253-8862

The Presbyterian College, Montreal, (The Presbyterian Church in Canada), 3495 University St., Montreal, QC H3A 2A8. W. J. Klempa. Tel. (514)288-5256. Fax (514)398-6665

Providence College and Theological Seminary,* (Interdenominational), General Delivery, Otterburne, MB R0A 1G0. Larry J. McKinney. Tel. (204)433-7488. Fax (204)433-7158

Queen's College,* (The Anglican Church of Canada), 210 Prince Phillip Dr., St. John's, NF A1B 3R6. Frank Cluett. Tel. (709)753-0640. Fax (709)753-1214

Queen's Theological College,* (The United Church of Canada), Queen's Theological College, Kingston, ON K7L 3N6. Hallett E. Llewellyn. Tel. (613)545-2110. Fax (613)545-6879

Regent College,* (Interdenominational), 5800 University Blvd., Vancouver, BC V6T 2E4. Walter C. Wright. Tel. (800)663-8664. Fax (604)224-3097

Regis College,* (The Roman Catholic Church in Canada), 15 St. Mary St., Toronto, ON M4Y 2R5. John E. Costello. Tel. (416)922-5474. Fax (416)922-2898

Rocky Mountain College: Centre for Biblical Studies, (The Evangelical Missionary Church of Canada), 4039 Brentwood Rd. NW, Calgary, AB T2L 1L1. Randy L. Steinwand. Tel. (403)284-5100. Fax (403)220-9567

Saint Paul University, Faculty of Theology, (The Roman Catholic Church in Canada), 223 Main St., Ottawa, ON K1S 1C4. James R. Pambrun. Tel. (613)236-1393. Fax (613)236-4108

The Salvation Army Catherine Booth Bible College, (The Salvation Army in Canada), 447 Webb Pl., Winnipeg, MB R3B 2P2. Lloyd Hetherington. Tel. (204)947-6701. Fax (204)942-3856

Salvation Army College for Officer Training, (The Salvation Army in Canada), 2130 Bayview Ave., Toronto, ON M4N 3K6. K. Douglas Moore. Tel. (416)481-6131. Fax (416)481-6810

St. Andrew's Theological College,* (The United Church of Canada), 1121 College Dr., Saskatoon, SK S7N 0W3. Charlotte Caron and Michael Baugeois. Tel. (306)966-8970. Fax (306)966-6575

St. Augustine's Seminary of Toronto,* (The Roman Catholic Church in Canada), 2661 Kingston Rd., Scarborough, ON M1M 1M3. John A. Boissonneau. Tel. (416)261-7207. Fax (416)261-2529

St. John's College, Univ. of Manitoba, Faculty of Theology, (The Anglican Church of Canada), 92 Dysart Rd., Winnipeg, MB R3T 2M5. B. Hudson McLean. Tel. (204)474-6852. Fax (204)261-1215

St. Peter's Seminary,* (The Roman Catholic Church in Canada), 1040 Waterloo St., London, ON N6A 3Y1. Thomas C. Collins. Tel. (519)432-1824. Fax (519)432-0964

St. Stephen's College, Grad. & Continuing Theological Educ.,* (The United Church of Canada), 8810 112th St., Edmonton, AB T6G 2J6. Christopher V. Levan. Tel. (403)439-7311. Fax (403)433-8875

Steinbach Bible College, (The Evangelical Mennonite Conference, Evangelical Mennonite Mission Conference), Box 1420, Steinbach, MB R0A 2A0. Stan Plett. Tel. (204)326-6451. Fax (204)326-6908

Toronto Baptist Seminary and Bible College, (Association of Regular Baptist Churches (Canada)), 130 Gerrard St., E., Toronto, ON M5A 3T4. Andrew M. Fountain. Tel. (416)925-3263. Fax (416)925-8305

Toronto School of Theology,* (Interdenominational), 47 Queens Park Crescent E., Toronto, ON M5S 2C3. Jean-Marc Laporte. Tel. (416)978-4039. Fax (416)978-7821

Trinity College, Faculty of Divinity,* (The Anglican Church of Canada), 6 Hoskin Ave., Toronto, ON M5S 1H8. D. Wiebe. Tel. (416)978-7750. Fax (416)978-4949

United Theological College/Le Séminaire Uni, (The United Church of Canada), 3521 rue Université, Montréal, QC H3A 2A9. Pierre Goldberger. Tel. (514)849-2042. Fax (514)398-6665

Université Laval, Faculté de théologie, (The Roman Catholic Church in Canada), Cité Universitaire Ste-Foy, Ste-Foy, QC G1K 7P4. René Michael Roberge. Tel. (418)656-7823. Fax (418)656-3273

Université de Montréal, Faculté de théologie, (The Roman Catholic Church in Canada), C. P. 6128 Succ. Centre Ville, Montréal, QC H3C 3J7. Laval Letourneau. Tel. (514)343-7160. Fax (514)343-5738

Université de Sherbrooke, Faculté de théologie,, (The Roman Catholic Church in Canada), 2500 boul. Université, Sherbrooke, QC J1K 2R1. Jean-François Malherbe. Tel. (819)821-7600. Fax (819)821-7677

University of St. Michael's College, Faculty of Theology,* (The Roman Catholic Church in Canada), 81 St. Mary St., Toronto, ON M5S 1J4. Michael A. Fahey. Tel. (416)926-7140. Fax (416)926-7276

University of Winnipeg, Faculty of Theology,* (Interdenominational), 515 Portage Ave., Winnipeg, MB R3B 2E9. Harold J. King. Tel. (204)786-9390. Fax (204)775-1942

Vancouver School of Theology,* (Interdenominational), 6000 Iona Dr., Vancouver, BC V6T 1L4. W. J. Phillips. Tel. (604)228-9031. Fax (604)228-0189

Victory Bible College, (Nondenominational), Box 1780, Lethbridge, AB T1J 4K4. Kirbey Lockhart. Tel. (403)320-1565. Fax (403)327-9013

Waterloo Lutheran Seminary,* (Evangelical Lutheran Church in Canada), 75 University Ave. W., Waterloo, ON N2L 3C5. Richard C. Crossman. Tel. (519)884-1970. Fax (519)725-2434

Western Christian College, (Churches of Christ in Canada), Box 5000, 220 Whitmore Ave. W., Dauphin, MB R7N 2V5. L. John McMillan. Tel. (204)638-8801. Fax (204)638-7054

Western Pentecostal Bible College, (The Pentecostal Assemblies of Canada), Box 1700, Abbotsford, BC V2S 7E7. James G. Richards. Tel. (604)853-7491. Fax (604)853-8951

Winkler Bible Institute, (Canadian Conference of Mennonite Brethren Churches), 121 7 St. S., Winkler, MB R6W 2N4. Paul Kroeker. Tel. (204)325-4242. Fax (204)325-9028

Wycliffe College,* (The Anglican Church of Canada), 5 Hoskin Ave., Toronto, ON M5S 1H7. Michael Pountney. Tel. (416)979-2870. Fax (416)979-0471

10. RELIGIOUS PERIODICALS IN THE UNITED STATES

This list focuses on publications of the organizations listed in section 3, however, there are also some independent publications listed. Regional publications and newsletters are not included.

Probably the most inclusive list of religious periodicals published in the United States can be found in *Gale Directory of Publications and Broadcast Media*, (Gale Research, Inc., P.O. Box 33477, Detroit MI 48232-5477).

Each entry lists the title of the periodical, frequency of publication, religious affiliation, editor's name, address, telephone number and fax number when known.

21st Century Christian, (m) Churches of Christ, M. Norvel Young and Prentice A. Meador, Jr., P.O. Box 40309, Nashville, TN 37204. Tel. (800)331-5991

A.M.E. Review, (q) African Methodist Episcopal Church, Paulette Coleman, PhD, 500 Eighth Ave. S, Ste. 211, Nashville, TN 37203-4181. Tel. (615)256-7020. Fax (615)256-7092

ALERT, (q) Universal Fellowship of Metropolitan Community Churches, A. Stephen Pieters, 5300 Santa Monica Blvd., Ste. 304, Los Angeles, CA 90029. Tel. (213)464-5100. Fax (213)464-2123

Action, (10/yr) Churches of Christ, Tex Williams, Box 9346, Austin, TX 78766. Tel. (512)345-8191. Fax (512)345-6634

Adult Quarterly, The, (q) Associate Reformed Presbyterian Church (General Synod), W. H. F. Kuykendall, PhD., One Cleveland St., Greenville, SC 29601. Tel. (864)232-8297

Advent Christian News, (m) Advent Christian Church, Robert Mayer, P.O. Box 23152, Charlotte, NC 28227. Tel. (704)-545-6161. Fax (704)573-0712

Advent Christian Witness, The, (m) Advent Christian Church, Robert Mayer, P.O. Box 23152, Charlotte, NC 28227. Tel. (704)545-6161. Fax (704)573-0712

Adventist Review, (w) Seventh-day Adventist Church, W. G. Johnsson, 12501 Old Columbia Pike, Silver Spring, MD 20904-6600. Tel. (301)680-6560. Fax (301)680-6638

Again Magazine, (q) The Antiochian Orthodox Christian Archdiocese of North America, John W. Hardenbrook, P.O. Box 76, Ben Lomond, CA 95005-0076. Tel. (408)336-5118. Fax (408)336-8882

Alive Now, (6/yr) The United Methodist Church, George Graham, P.O. Box 189, Nashville, TN 37202. Tel. (615)340-7218

Allegheny Wesleyan Methodist, The, (m) Allegheny Wesleyan Methodist Connection (Original Allegheny Conference), John Englant, 1827 Allen Dr., Salem, OH 44460. Tel. (216)337-9376. Fax (216)337-9700

Alliance Life, (bi-w) The Christian and Missionary Alliance, Maurice Irvin, P.O. Box 35000, Colorado Springs, CO 80935. Tel. (719)599-5999. Fax (719)-593-8692

American Baptist Quarterly, (q) American Baptist Churches in the U.S.A., William R. Millar, P.O. Box 851, Valley Forge, PA 19482-0851. Tel. (610)768-2269

American Baptists In Mission, (6/yr) American Baptist Churches in the U.S.A., Richard W. Schramm, P.O. Box 851, Valley Forge, PA 19482-0851. Tel. (610)768-2077. Fax (610)768-2320

American Bible Society Record, (10/yr) Nondenominational, James Genovese, 1865 Broadway, New York, NY 10023. Tel. (212)408-1480. Fax (212)408-1456

American Jewish History, (q) Jewish, Marc Lee Raphael, 2 Thornton Rd., Waltham, MA 02154. Tel. (617)891-8110. Fax (617)899-9208

American Presbyterians: Journal of Presbyterian History, (q) Presbyterian Church (U.S.A.), James H. Smylie, 425 Lombard St., Philadelphia, PA 19147. Tel. (215)627-1852. Fax (215)627-0509

Armenian Church, The, (10/yr) Diocese of the Armenian Church of America, Michael A. Zeytoonian, 630 Second Ave., New York, NY 10016. Tel. (212)-686-0710. Fax (212)779-3558

Associate Reformed Presbyterian, The, (m) Associate Reformed Presbyterian Church (General Synod), Ben Johnston, One Cleveland St., Greenville, SC 29601. Tel. (864)232-8297

At Ease, (bi-m) Assemblies of God, Lemuel D. McElyea, 1445 Boonville Ave,, Springfield, MO 65802. Tel. (417)862-2781. Fax (417)863-7276

Attack, A Magazine for Christian Men, (q) National Association of Free Will Baptists, James E. Vallance, P.O. Box 5002, Antioch, TN 37011-5002. Tel. (615)731-6812. Fax (615)793-7179

Banner of Truth, The, (m) Netherlands Reformed Congregations, A. M. den Boer, 730 Skyline Dr., Sunnyside, WA 98944. Tel. (509)839-4494. Fax (509)-837-7622

Banner, The, (w) Christian Reformed Church in North America, John A. Suk, 2850 Kalamazoo Ave., SE, Grand Rapids, MI 49560. Tel. (616)246-0732. Fax (616)246-0834

Baptist Bible Tribune, The, (m) Baptist Bible Fellowship International, Mike Randall, P.O. Box 309 HSJ, Springfield, MO 65801. Tel. (417)831-3996. Fax (417)831-1470

Baptist Bulletin, (m) General Association of Regular Baptist Churches, Vernon Miller, 1300 N. Meacham Rd., Schaumburg, IL 60173-4888. Tel. (847)843-1600. Fax (847)843-3757

Baptist History and Heritage, (q) Southern Baptist Convention, Slayden A. Yarbrough, 901 Commerce St., Ste. 400, Nashville, TN 37203-3630. Tel. (615)-244-0344. Fax (615)242-2153

Baptist Leader, (q) American Baptist Churches in the U.S.A., Donald Ng, P.O. Box 851, Valley Forge, PA 19842-0851. Tel. (610)768-2143. Fax (610)768-2056

Baptist Progress, (q) Progressive National Baptist Convention, Inc., Archie D. Logan, 601 50th St. NE, Washington, DC 20019. Tel. (919)848-4673. Fax (919)870-7426

Baptist Witness, (m) Primitive Baptists, Lasserre Bradley, Jr., Box 17037, Cincinnati, OH 45217. Tel. (513)821-7289. Fax (513)821-7303

Bible Advocate, The, (m) The Church of God (Seventh Day), Denver, Colo., Roy Marrs, P.O. Box 33677, Denver, CO 80233. Tel. (303)452-7973. Fax (303)-452-0657

Brethren Evangelist, The, (m) Brethren Church (Ashland, Ohio), Richard C. Winfield, 524 College Ave., Ashland, OH 44805. Tel. (419)289-1708. Fax (419)281-0450

Brethren Journal, (10/yr) Unity of the Brethren, Milton Maly, Rte. 3, Box 558N, Brenham, TX 77833. Tel. (409)-830-8762

Brethren Missionary Herald, (bi-m) Fellowship of Grace Brethren Churches, Jeffry Carroll, P.O. Box 544, Winona Lake, IN 46590. Tel. (219)267-7158. Fax (219)267-4745

Bridegroom's Messenger, The, (bi-m) The International Pentecostal Church of Christ, Janice Boyce, 121 W. Hunters Tr., Elizabeth City, NC 27909. Tel. (919)338-3003. Fax (919)338-3003

Builder, (m) General Conference of the Mennonite Church, David R. Hiebert, 616 Walnut Ave., Scottdale, PA 15683. Tel. (412)887-8500. Fax (412)887-3111

Burning Bush, The, (bi-m) The Metropolitan Church Association, Inc., E. L. Adams, The Metropolitan Church Association, 323 Broad St., Lake Geneva, WI 53147. Tel. (414)248-6786

CCAR Journal: A Reform Jewish Quarterly, (q) Jewish, Henry Bamberger, 192 Lexington Ave., New York, NY 10016. Tel. (212)684-4990. Fax (212)689-1649

Calvary Messenger, The, (m) Beachy Amish Mennonite Churches, Ervin N. Hershberger, Rt. 1, Box 176, Meyersdale, PA 15552. Tel. (814)662-2483

Campus Life, (10/yr) Nondenominational, Harold B. Smith, 465 Gunderson Dr., Carol Stream, IL 60188. Tel. (708)260-6200. Fax (708)260-0114

Capsule, (m) General Association of General Baptists, Charles Carr, 100 Stinson Dr., Poplar Bluff, MO 63901. Tel. (314)-785-7746. Fax (314)785-0564

Caring, (9/yr) Assemblies of God, Owen Wilkie, 1445 Boonville Ave., Springfield, MO 65802. Tel. (417)862-2781. Fax (417)862-4832

Catholic Chronicle, (bi-w) The Roman Catholic Church, Patricia Lynn Morrison, 2130 Madison Ave., P.O. Box 1866, Toledo, OH 43603-1866. Tel. (419)243-4178. Fax (419)243-4235

Catholic Digest, (m) The Roman Catholic Church, Richard Reece, P. O. Box 64090, St. Paul, MN 55164. Tel. (612)-962-6725. Fax (612)962-6755

Catholic Light, (bi-w) The Roman Catholic Church, James B. Earley, 300 Wyoming Ave., Scranton, PA 18503. Tel. (717)-346-8915. Fax (717)346-8917

Catholic Review, The, (w) The Roman Catholic Church, Daniel L. Medinger, P.O. Box 777, Baltimore, MD 21203. Tel. (410)625-8477. Fax (410)385-0113

Catholic Standard and Times, (w) The Roman Catholic Church, Paul S. Quinter, 222 N. 17th St., Philadelphia, PA 19103. Tel. (215)587-3660. Fax (215)-587-3979

Catholic Transcript, The, (w) The Roman Catholic Church, Anne Marie Monteiro, 785 Asylum Ave., Hartford, CT 06105-2886. Tel. (203)527-1175. Fax (203)-947-6397

Catholic Universe Bulletin, (bi-w) The Roman Catholic Church, Patrick Hyland, 1027 Superior Ave., Cleveland, OH 44114-2556. Tel. (216)696-6525. Fax (216)696-6519

Catholic Worker, (7/yr) The Roman Catholic Church, Jennifer Belisle, 36 E. First St., New York, NY 10003. Tel. (212)777-9617

Catholic World, The, (bi-m) The Roman Catholic Church, Laurie Felknor, 997 Macarthur Blvd., Mahwah, NJ 07430. Tel. (201)825-7300. Fax (201)825-8345

Cela Biedrs, (10/yr) The Latvian Evangelical Lutheran Church in America, Eduards Putnins, 1468 Hemlock St., Napa, CA 94559. Tel. (707)252-1809

Celebration, (m) Seventh-day Adventist Church, Faith Crumbly, 55 W. Oak Ridge Dr., Hagerstown, MD 21740. Tel. (301)791-7000. Fax (301)790-9734

Celebration: An Ecumenical Worship Resource, (m) Interdenominational, William Freburger, P.O. Box 419493, Kansas City, MO 64141-6493. Tel. (816)531-0538. Fax (816)968-2280

Cerkovnyj Vistnik--The Church Messenger, (bi-m) The American Carpatho-Russian Orthodox Greek Catholic Church, James S. Dutko, 280 Clinton St., Binghamton, NY 13905. Tel. (607)797-4471. Fax (607)797-1090

Challenge, The, (q) The Bible Church of Christ, Inc., Alice M. Jones, 1358 Morris Ave., Bronx, NY 10456. Tel. (718)588-2284

Charisma, (m) Nondenominational, Lee Grady, 600 Rinehart Rd., Lake Mary, FL 32746. Tel. (407)333-0600. Fax (407)-333-9753

Childlife, (q) Nondenominational, Terry Madison, P.O. Box 9716, Federal Way, WA 98063-9716. Tel. (206)815-1000. Fax (206)815-3445

Christadelphian Advocate, (m) Christadelphians, Edward W. Farrar, 4 Mountain Park Ave., Hamilton, ON L9A 1A2. Tel. (905)383-1817

Christadelphian Tidings, (m) Christadelphians, Donald H. Styles, 42076 Hartford Dr., Canton, MI 48187. Tel. (313)844-2426. Fax (313)844-8304

Christadelphian Watchman, (m) Christadelphians, George Booker, 2500 Berwyn Cir., Austin, TX 78745. Tel. (512)447-8882

Christian Baptist, The, (m) Primitive Baptists, S. T. Tolley, P.O. Box 68, Atwood, TN 38220. Tel. (901)662-7417

Christian Bible Teacher, (m) Churches of Christ, J. J. Turner, Box 1060, Abilene, TX 79604. Tel. (915)677-6262. Fax (915)677-1511

Christian Century, The, (38/yr) Nondenominational, James M. Wall, 407 S. Dearborn St., Chicago, IL 60605. Tel. (312)427-5380. Fax (312)427-1302

Christian Chronicle, The, (m) Churches of Christ, Howard W. Norton, Box 11000, Oklahoma City, OK 73136-1100. Tel. (405)425-5070. Fax (405)425-5076

Christian Community, The, (8/yr) International Council of Community Churches, Jeffrey R. Newhall, 21116 Washington Pky., Frankfort, IL 60423. Tel. (815)464-5690. Fax (815)464-5692

Christian Education Counselor, (m) Assemblies of God, Sylvia Lee, Sunday School Promotion and Training, 1445 Boonville Ave., Springfield, MO 65802-1894. Tel. (417)862-2781. Fax (417)862-0503

Christian Endeavor World, The, (q) Nondenominational, David G. Jackson, 3575 Valley Rd., P.O. Box 820, Liberty Corner, NJ 07938-0820. Tel. (908)604-9440. Fax (908)604-6075

Christian Index, The, (m) Christian Methodist Episcopal Church, Lawrence L. Reddick, III, P.O. Box 665, Memphis, TN 38101-0665. Tel. (901)345-1173. Fax (901)345-4108

Christian Leader, (m) Mennonite, Don Ratzlaff, Box V, Hillsboro, KS 67063. Tel. (316)947-5543. Fax (316)947-3266

Christian Living, (8/yr) Mennonite Church, Steve Kriss, 616 Walnut Ave., Scottdale, PA 15683. Tel. (412)887-8500. Fax (412)887-3111

Christian Ministry, The, (37/yr) Nondenominational, James M. Wall, 407 S. Dearborn St., Chicago, IL 60605. Tel. (312)427-5380. Fax (312)427-1302

Christian Monthly, (m) Apostolic Lutheran Church of America, Alvin Holmgren, 1327 9th Ave. N., Edmonds, WA 98020. Tel. (360)687-4416

Christian Outlook, (m) Pentecostal Assemblies of the World, Inc., Johnna E. Hampton, 3939 Meadows Dr., Indianapolis, IN 46205. Tel. (317)547-9541. Fax (317)543-0512

Christian Reader, The, (bi-m) Nondenominational, Bonne Steffen, 465 Gundersen Dr., Carol Stream, IL 60188. Tel. (708)260-6200. Fax (708)260-0114

Christian Record, (q) Seventh-day Adventist Church, R. J. Kaiser, P.O. Box 6097, Lincoln, NE 68506. Tel. (402)-488-0981. Fax (402)488-7582

Christian Recorder, The, (bi-w) African Methodist Episcopal Church, Robert H. Reid, Jr., 500 8th Ave., S., Nashville, TN 37203. Tel. (615)256-8548

Christian Science Journal, The, (m) Church of Christ, Scientist, William E. Moody, One Norway St., Boston, MA 02115. Tel. (617)450-2000. Fax (617)-450-2707

Christian Science Monitor, The, (d & w) Church of Christ, Scientist, David T. Cook, One Norway St., Boston, MA 02115. Tel. (617)450-2000. Fax (617)-450-2071

Christian Science Quarterly, (q) Church of Christ, Scientist, Pamela Lishin Jones, One Norway St. P-980, Boston, MA 02115. Tel. (617)450-2000. Fax (617)450-2930

Christian Science Sentinel, (w) Church of Christ, Scientist, William E. Moody, One Norway St., Boston, MA 02115. Tel. (617)450-2000. Fax (617)450-2707

Christian Social Action, (m) The United Methodist Church, Lee Ranck, 100 Maryland Ave. NE, Washington, DC 20002. Tel. (202)488-5621. Fax (202)-488-5619

Christian Standard, (w) Christian Churches and Churches of Christ, Sam E. Stone, 8121 Hamilton Ave., Cincinnati, OH 45231. Tel. (513)931-4050. Fax (513)931-0904

Church & Society Magazine, (bi-m) Presbyterian Church (U.S.A.), Kathy Lancaster, 100 Witherspoon St., Louisville, KY 40202-1396. Tel. (502)569-5810. Fax (502)569-8116

Church Advocate, The, (q) Churches of God, General Conference, Linda M. Draper, P.O. Box 926, 700 E. Melrose Ave., Findlay, OH 45839. Tel. (419)-424-1961. Fax (419)424-3433

Church Herald, The, (11/yr) Reformed Church in America, ----, 4500 60th St. SE, Grand Rapids, MI 49512. Tel. (616)-698-7071

Church History, (q) Nondenominational, Martin E. Marty and Jerald C. Brauer, The Univ. of Chicago, 1025 E. 58th St., Chicago, IL 60637. Tel. (312)702-4805. Fax (312)702-6048

Church Leader's Newsletter, (m) The Evangelical Church, John F. Sills, 3000 Market St., NE, Ste. 528, Salem, OR 97301. Tel. (503)371-4818. Fax (503)-364-5022

Church School Herald, (q) African Methodist Episcopal Zion Church, Mary A. Love, P.O. Box 32305, Charlotte, NC 28232-2305. Tel. (704)332-9873. Fax (704)333-1769

Church of God Evangel, (m) Church of God (Cleveland, Tenn.), Homer G. Rhea, P.O. Box 2250, Cleveland, TN 37320. Tel. (423)478-7592. Fax (423)-478-7521

Church of God Missions, (bi-m) Church of God (Anderson, Ind.), E. Raymond Chin, Box 2498, Anderson, IN 46018-2498. Tel. (317)642-0256. Fax (317)-642-4279

Church of God Progress Journal, (bi-m) Church of God General Conference (Oregon, IL and Morrow, GA), David Krogh, Box 100,000, Morrow, GA 30260. Tel. (404)362-0052. Fax (404)-362-9307

Church of God Quarterly; COG Newsletter, The, (q) The Church of God, Voy M. Bullen, Box 13036, 1207 Willow Brook, Apt. #2, Huntsville, AL 35802. Tel. (205)881-9629

Churchman's Human Quest, The, (bi-m) Nondenominational, Edna Ruth Johnson, 1074 23rd Ave. N., St. Petersburg, FL 33704. Tel. (813)894-0097

Churchwoman, (q) Interdenominational, Martha M. Cruz, 475 Riverside Dr., Rm. 812, New York, NY 10115. Tel. (212)-870-2344. Fax (212)870-2338

Circuit Rider, (m) The United Methodist Church, Sheila W. McGee, 201 Eighth Ave. S., Nashville, TN 37203. Tel. (615)749-6488. Fax (615)749-6079

Clarion Herald, (bi-w) The Roman Catholic Church, Peter P. Finney, Jr., P. O. Box 53247, 1000 Howard Ave., Suite 400, New Orleans, LA 70153. Tel. (504)596-3035. Fax (504)596-3020

Clergy Journal, The, (10/yr) Nondenominational, Sharilyn Figueroa and Clyde Steckel, P.O. Box 240, South St. Paul, MN 55075. Tel. (800)328-0200. Fax (612)457-4617

Co-Laborer, (bi-m) National Association of Free Will Baptists, Suzanne Franks, Women Nationally Active for Christ, P.O. Box 5002, Antioch, TN 37011-5002. Tel. (615)731-6812. Fax (615)-731-0771

Collegiate Quarterly, (q) Seventh-day Adventist Church, Gary B. Swanson, 12501 Old Columbia Pike, Silver Spring, MD 20904. Tel. (301)680-6160. Fax (301)-680-6155

Columban Mission, (8/yr) The Roman Catholic Church, Richard Steinhilber, St. Columbans, NE 68056. Tel. (402)-291-1920. Fax (402)291-8693

Columbia, (m) The Roman Catholic Church, Richard McMunn, One Columbus Plaza, New Haven, CT 06510. Tel. (203)772-2130. Fax (203)777-0114

Commission, The, (12/yr) Southern Baptist Convention, Mary Jane Welch, Box 6767, Richmond, VA 23230-0767. Tel. (804)219-1526. Fax (804)254-9410

Common Lot, (4/yr) United Church of Christ, Martha J. Hunter, 700 Prospect Ave., Cleveland, OH 44115. Tel. (216)-736-2150

Commonweal, (bi-w) The Roman Catholic Church, Margaret O'Brien Steinfels, 15 Dutch St., Rm. 502, New York, NY 10038-3760. Tel. (212)732-0800

Communique, (m) National Baptist Convention of America, Inc., Ruthie Myles, 1327 Oierre Ave., Shreveport, LA 71103. Tel. (318)221-3701. Fax (318)-222-7512

Congregationalist, The, (5/yr) National Association of Congregational Christian Churches, Joe Polhemus, 1105 Briarwood Rd., Mansfield, OH 44907. Tel. (419)756-5526. Fax (419)524-2621

Conqueror, (bi-m) United Pentecostal Church International, Nathan Reever, 8855 Dunn Rd., Hazelwood, MO 63042. Tel. (314)837-7300. Fax (314)837-4503

Conservative Judaism, (q) Jewish, Lisa Stein, 3080 Broadway, New York, NY 10027. Tel. (212)678-8060. Fax (212)-749-9166

Contact, (m) National Association of Free Will Baptists, Jack Williams, P.O. Box 5002, Antioch, TN 37011-5002. Tel. (615)731-6812. Fax (615)731-0771

Cornerstone Connections, (q) Seventh-day Adventist Church, Gary B. Swanson, 12501 Old Columbia Pike, Silver Spring, MD 20904. Tel. (301)680-6160. Fax (301)680-6155

Courage in the Struggle for Justice and Peace, (10/yr) United Church of Christ, Rubin Tendai, 110 Maryland Ave., NE, Washington, DC 20002. Tel. (202)543-1517. Fax (202)543-5994

Covenant Companion, (m) The Evangelical Covenant Church, John E. Phelan, Jr., 5101 N. Francisco Ave., Chicago, IL 60625. Tel. (312)784-3000. Fax (312)-784-1540

Covenant Home Altar, (q) The Evangelical Covenant Church, John E. Phelan, Jr., 5101 N. Francisco Ave., Chicago, IL 60625. Tel. (312)784-3000. Fax (312)-784-1540

Covenant Quarterly, (q) The Evangelical Covenant Church, Wayne C. Weld, 3225 W. Foster Ave., Chicago, IL 60625-4895. Tel. (312)244-6230. Fax (312)-244-6244

Covenanter Witness, The, (m) Reformed Presbyterian Church of North America, Drew Gordon and Lynne Gordon, 7408 Penn Ave., Pittsburgh, PA 15208. Tel. (412)241-0436. Fax (412)731-8861

Credinta--The Faith, (q) The Romanian Orthodox Church in America, Vasile Vasilachi, 45-03 48th Ave., Woodside, Queens, NY 11377. Tel. (313)893-8390

Criterion, The, (w) The Roman Catholic Church, John F. Fink, P.O. Box 1717, 1400 N. Meridian, Indianapolis, IN 46206. Tel. (317)236-1570

Crosswalk, (w) Church of the Nazarene, Becki Privett, Word Action Publishing, Box 419527, Kansas City, MO 64141. Tel. (816)333-7000. Fax (816)333-4315

Cumberland Flag, The, (m) Cumberland Presbyterian Church in America, Robert Stanley Wood, 226 Church St., Huntsville, AL 35801. Tel. (205)536-7481. Fax (205)536-7482

Cumberland Presbyterian, The, (11/yr) Cumberland Presbyterian Church, M. Jacqueline DeBerry Warren, 1978 Union Ave., Memphis, TN 38104. Tel. (901)276-4572. Fax (901)276-4578

Currents in Theology and Mission, (6/yr) Evangelical Lutheran Church in America, Ralph W. Klein, 1100 E. 55th St., Chicago, IL 60615. Tel. (312)256-0751. Fax (312)256-0782

Decision, (12/yr) Nondenominational, Roger C. Palms, 1300 Harmon Pl., Minneapolis, MN 55403. Tel. (612)338-0500. Fax (612)335-1299

Disciple, The, (m) Christian Church (Disciples of Christ), Robert L. Friedly, 130 E. Washington St., P.O. Box 1986, Indianapolis, IN 46206-1986. Tel. (317)635-3100. Fax (317)635-3700

EMC Today, (bi-m) Evangelical Mennonite Church, Donald W. Roth, 1420 Kerrway Ct., Fort Wayne, IN 46805. Tel. (219)423-3649. Fax (219)420-1905

Ecumenical Trends, (m) Nondenominational, Kevin McMurrow, P.O. Box 300, Garrison, NY 10524. Tel. (914)424-3671

El Aposento Alto, (6/yr) The United Methodist Church, Carmen Gaud, P.O. Box 189, Nashville, TN 37202. Tel. (615)-340-7246. Fax (615)340-7006

El Intérprete, (6/yr) The United Methodist Church, Edith LaFontaine, P.O. Box 320, Nashville, TN 37202-0320. Tel. (615)742-5115. Fax (615)742-5460

Eleventh Hour Messenger, (bi-m) Wesleyan Holiness Association of Churches, John Brewer, R R 2, Box 9, Winchester, IN 47394. Tel. (317)584-3199

Elim Herald, (q) Elim Fellowship, L. Dayton Reynolds, 7245 College St., Lima, NY 14485. Tel. (716)582-2790. Fax (716)624-1229

Emphasis on Faith and Living, (bi-m) The Missionary Church, Robert Ransom, P.O. Box 9127, Ft. Wayne, IN 46899. Tel. (219)747-2027. Fax (219)747-5331

Enrichment: A Journal for Pentecostal Ministry, (q) Assemblies of God, Wayde Goodall, 1445 Boonville Ave., Springfield, MO 65802. Tel. (417)862-2781. Fax (417)862-0416

Ensign, The, (m) The Church of Jesus Christ of Latter-day Saints, Jay M. Todd, 50 E. North Temple St., Salt Lake City, UT 84105. Tel. (801)240-2950. Fax (801)240-5997

Evangel, The, (10/yr) The American Association of Lutheran Churches, Charles D. Eidum, 10800 Lyndale Ave. S., #120, Minneapolis, MN 55420-5614. Tel. (612)884-7784. Fax (612)884-7784

Evangel, The, (q) The Evangelical Church Alliance, Charles Eidum, 205 W. Broadway, Bradley, IL 60915. Tel. (815)937-0720. Fax (815)937-0001

Evangelical Advocate, The, (m) Churches of Christ in Christian Union, Wes Humble, P.O. Box 30, Circleville, OH 43113. Tel. (614)474-8856. Fax (614)477-7766

Evangelical Beacon, (7/yr) The Evangelical Free Church of America, Carol Madison, 901 East 78th St., Minneapolis, MN 55420-1300. Tel. (612)854-1300

Evangelical Episcopalian, The, (q) Reformed Episcopal Church, Barton L. Craig, 3240 Adams Ct. N., Bensalem, PA 19020. Tel. (215)757-3844

Evangelical Visitor, (m) Brethren in Christ Church, Glen A. Pierce, P.O. Box 166, Nappanee, IN 46550. Tel. (219)773-3164. Fax (219)773-5934

Evangelism USA, (m) International Pentecostal Holiness Church, James D. Leggett, P.O. Box 12609, Oklahoma City, OK 73157. Tel. (405)787-7110. Fax (405)789-3957

Evangelist, The, (w) The Roman Catholic Church, James Breig, 40 N. Main Ave., Albany, NY 12203. Tel. (518)453-6688. Fax (518)453-6793

Extension, (m) The Roman Catholic Church, Bradley Collins, 35 East Wacker Dr., Rm. 400, Chicago, IL 60601-2105. Tel. (312)236-7240. Fax (312)236-5276

Faith & Fellowship, (17/yr) Church of the Lutheran Brethren of America, David Rinden, P.O. Box 655, Fergus Falls, MN 56538. Tel. (218)736-7357. Fax (218)-736-2200

Faith and Truth, (m) Pentecostal Fire-Baptized Holiness Church, Edgar Vollrath, 593 Harris-Lord Rd., Commerce, GA 30529. Tel. (706)335-5796

Faith-Life, (bi-m) Lutheran, Marcus Albrecht, 2107 N. Alexander St., Appleton, WI 54911. Tel. (414)733-1839

Fellowship Magazine, The, (6/yr) Assemblies of God International Fellowship (Independent/Not affiliated), T. A. Lanes, 5284 Eastgate Mall, San Diego, CA 92121. Tel. (619)677-9701. Fax (619)677-0038

Fellowship News, (m) Bible Fellowship Church, Jim Neher, 1136 Marion St., Reading, PA 19604. Tel. (610)478-8940

Fellowship Tidings, (q) Full Gospel Fellowship of Churches and Ministers International, Chester P. Jenkins, 4325 W. Ledbetter Dr., Dallas, TX 75233. Tel. (214)339-1200. Fax (214)339-8790

Firm Foundation, (m) Churches of Christ, H. A. Dobbs, P.O. Box 690192, Houston, TX 77269-0192. Tel. (713)469-3102. Fax (713)469-7115

First Things: A Monthly Journal of Religion and Public, (m) Interdenominational, Richard J. Neuhaus, 156 Fifth Ave., Ste. 400, New York, NY 10010. Tel. (212)627-2288. Fax (212)627-2184

Flaming Sword, The, (m) Bible Holiness Church, Susan Davolt, 10th St. & College Ave., Independence, KS 67301. Tel. (316)331-2580. Fax (316)331-2580

For the Poor, (bi-m) Primitive Baptists, W. H. Cayce, P.O. Box 38, Thornton, AR 71766. Tel. (501)352-3694

Foresee, (bi-m) Conservative Congregational Christian Conference, George T. Allen, 7582 Currell Blvd., #108, St. Paul, MN 55125. Tel. (612)739-1474. Fax (612)739-0750

Forum Letter, (m) Interdenominational Lutheran, Russell E. Saltzman, P.O. Box 549, Stover, MO 65078-0549. Tel. (314)377-2819

Forward, (q) United Pentecostal Church International, J. L. Hall, 8855 Dunn Rd., Hazelwood, MO 63042. Tel. (314)837-7300. Fax (314)837-4503

Foursquare World Advance, (6/yr) International Church of the Foursquare Gospel, Ron Williams, P.O. Box 26902, 1910 W. Sunset Blvd., Ste. 200, Los Angeles, CA 90026-0176. Tel. (213)-484-2400. Fax (213)413-3824

Free Methodist World Mission People, (6/yr) Free Methodist Church of North America, Dan Runyon, P.O. Box 535002, Indianapolis, IN 46253-5002. Tel. (317)244-3660. Fax (317)244-1247

Free Will Baptist Gem, (m) National Association of Free Will Baptists, Nathan Ruble, P.O. Box 991, Lebanon, MO 65536. Tel. (417)532-6537

Free Will Baptist, The, (m) Original Free Will Baptist Church, Tracy A. McCoy, P.O. Box 159, 811 N. Lee St., Ayden, NC 28513. Tel. (919)746-6128. Fax (919)-746-9248

Free Will Bible College Bulletin, (6/yr) National Association of Free Will Baptists, Bert Tippett, 3606 West End Ave., Nashville, TN 37205. Tel. (615)383-1340. Fax (615)269-6028

Friend Magazine, (m) The Church of Jesus Christ of Latter-day Saints, Vivian Paulsen, 50 E. South Temple St., 23rd Floor, Salt Lake City, UT 84105. Tel. (801)-240-2210. Fax (801)240-5732

Friends Journal, (m) Nondenominational, Vinton Deming, 1501 Cherry St., Philadelphia, PA 19102-1497. Tel. (215)241-7277. Fax (215)568-1377

Friends Voice, (4/yr) Evangelical Friends International--North America Region, Becky Towne, 2748 E. Pikes Peak Ave., Colorado Springs, CO 80909. Tel. (719)635-4011

Front Line, (q) Conservative Baptist Association of America, Al Russell and Robert Rummell, P.O. Box 66, Wheaton, IL 60189. Tel. (708)260-3800. Fax (708)653-5387

Full Gospel Ministries Outreach Report, (q) Full Gospel, Simeon Strauser, P.O. Box 1230, Coatesville, PA 19320. Tel. (610)857-2357

Full Gospel Ministries Outreach Report, (q) Full Gospel Assemblies International, Simeon Strauser, P.O. Box 1230, Coatsville, PA 19320. Tel. (610)857-2357

Gem, The, (w) Churches of God, General Conference, Evelyn J. Sloat, P.O. Box 926, Findlay, OH 45839.

General Baptist Messenger, (m) General Association of General Baptists, Samuel S. Ramdial, 400 Stinson Dr., Poplar Bluff, MO 63901. Tel. (314)686-9051. Fax (314)686-5198

Gleaner, The, (m) Baptist Missionary Association of America, F. Donald Collins, P.O. Box 193920, Little Rock, AR 72219-3920.

God's Field, (bi-w) Polish National Catholic Church of America, Anthony M. Rysz, 1002 Pittston Ave., Scranton, PA 18505. Tel. (717)346-9131. Fax (717)-346-2188

Gospel Advocate, (m) Churches of Christ, F. Furman Kearley, Box 150, Nashville, TN 37202. Tel. (615)254-8781. Fax (615)254-7411

Gospel Herald, (w) Mennonite Church, J. Lorne Peachey, 616 Walnut Ave., Scottdale, PA 15683. Tel. (412)887-8500. Fax (412)887-3111

Gospel Herald, The, (m) Church of God, Mountain Assembly, Inc., Dennis McClanahan, P.O. Box 157, Jellico, TN 37762. Tel. (423)784-8260. Fax (423)-784-3258

Gospel Light, The, (m) The Bible Church of Christ, Inc., Carol Crenshaw, 1358 Morris Ave., Bronx, NY 10456. Tel. (718)588-2284

Gospel Messenger, The, (m) Congregational Holiness Church, Cullen L. Hicks, P.O. Box 643, Lincolnton, GA 30817. Tel. (706)359-4000

Gospel News, The, (m) The Church of Jesus Christ (Bickertonites), Donald Ross, 16 Trumbull Ct., Princeton, NJ 08540. Tel. (313)429-5080. Fax (313)429-4714

Gospel Tidings, (bi-m) Fellowship of Evangelical Bible Churches, Robert L. Frey, 5800 S. 14th St., Omaha, NE 68107. Tel. (402)731-4780. Fax (402)-731-1173

Gospel Truth, The, (bi-m) Church of the Living God (Motto: Christian Workers for Fellowship), W. E. Crumes, 430 Forest Ave., Cincinnati, OH 45229. Tel. (513)569-5660. Fax (513)569-5661

Grow Magazine, (4/yr) Church of the Nazarene, Neil Wiseman, 6401 The Paseo, Kansas City, MO 64131. Tel. (816)333-7000. Fax (816)361-5202

Guardian of Truth, (b-w) Churches of Christ, Mike Willis, Box 9670, Bowling Green, KY 42102. Tel. (800)428-0121. Fax (317)745-4708

Guide, (w) Seventh-day Adventist Church, Carolyn L. Rathbun, 55 W. Oak Ridge Dr., Hagerstown, MD 21740. Tel. (301)-791-7000. Fax (301)790-9734

Heartbeat, (bi-m) National Association of Free Will Baptists, Don Robirds, Foreign Missions Office, P.O. Box 5002, Antioch, TN 37011-5002. Tel. (615)-731-6812. Fax (615)731-5345

Helping Hand, (bi-m) International Pentecostal Holiness Church, Doris Moore, P.O. Box 12609, Oklahoma City, OK 73157. Tel. (405)787-7110

Herald of Christian Science, The, (m) Church of Christ, Scientist, William E. Moody, One Norway St., Boston, MA 02115. Tel. (617)450-2000. Fax (617)-450-2707

Herald of Holiness, (m) Church of the Nazarene, Wesley D. Tracy, 6401 The Paseo, Kansas City, MO 64131. Tel. (816)333-7000. Fax (816)333-1748

Heritage, (q) Assemblies of God, Wayne E. Warner, 1445 Boonville Ave., Springfield, MO 65802. Tel. (417)862-1447. Fax (417)862-8558

High Adventure, (q) Assemblies of God, Marshall Bruner, 1445 Boonville Ave., Springfield, MO 65802-1894. Tel. (417)862-2781. Fax (417)862-0416

Higher Way, (bi-m) Apostolic Faith Mission of Portland, Oregon, Dwight L. Baltzell, 6615 S.E. 52nd Ave., Portland, OR 97206. Tel. (503)777-1741. Fax (503)777-1743

Holiness Union, The, (m) United Holy Church of America, Inc., Joseph T. Durham, 13102 Morningside La., Silver Spring, MD 20904. Tel. (301)989-9093. Fax (410)319-3871

Homelife, (6/yr) United Pentecostal Church International, Brian Kinsey, 8855 Dunn Rd., Hazelwood, MO 63042. Tel. (314)-837-7300. Fax (314)837-4503

Homiletic and Pastoral Review, (m) The Roman Catholic Church, Kenneth Baker, 86 Riverside Dr., New York, NY 10024. Tel. (212)799-2600. Fax (212)-787-0351

Horizons, (bi-m) Presbyterian Church (U.S.A.), Barbara A. Roche, Presbyterian Women, 100 Witherspoon St., Louisville, KY 40202. Tel. (502)569-5367. Fax (502)569-8085

Horizons, (m) Christian Churches and Churches of Christ, Norman L. Weaver, Box 2427, Knoxville, TN 37901. Tel. (423)577-9740. Fax (423)577-9743

Image, (bi-m) Churches of Christ, Denny Boultinghouse, 3117 N. 7th St., West Monroe, LA 71291-2227. Tel. (318)-396-4366

Insight, (w) Seventh-day Adventist Church, Lori L. Peckham, 55 W. Oak Ridge Dr., Hagerstown, MD 21740. Tel. (301)791-7000. Fax (301)790-9734

Insight, (q) Advent Christian Church, Millie Griswold, P.O. Box 23152, Charlotte, NC 28227. Tel. (704)545-6161. Fax (704)573-0712

Interest, (m) Christian Brethren (also known as Plymouth Brethren), Kenneth Botton, P.O. Box 190, Wheaton, IL 60189. Tel. (708)653-6573. Fax (708)-653-6595

International Bulletin of Missionary Research, (q) Nondenominational, Gerald H. Anderson, Overseas Ministries Study Ctr., 490 Prospect St., New Haven, CT 06511. Tel. (203)624-6672. Fax (203)-865-2857

International Pentecostal Holiness Life Springs, The, (m) International Pentecostal Holiness Church, Shirley Spencer, P.O. Box 12609, Oklahoma City, OK 73157. Tel. (405)787-7110. Fax (405)789-3957

Interpretation, (q) Presbyterian Church (U.S.A.), Jack D. Kingsbury, 3401 Brook Rd., Richmond, VA 23227. Tel. (804)355-0671. Fax (804)355-3919

Interpreter, (8/yr) The United Methodist Church, M. Garlinda Burton, P.O. Box 320, Nashville, TN 37202-0320. Tel. (615)742-5107. Fax (615)742-5460

Islamic Horizons, (6/yr) Muslim, Omer Bin Abdullah, P.O. Box 38, Plainfield, IN 46168. Tel. (317)839-8157. Fax (317)839-1840

Jewish Action, (q) Jewish, Charlotte Friedland, 333 Seventh Ave., New York, NY 10001. Tel. (212)563-4000. Fax (212)-564-9058

John Three Sixteen, (q) Bible Holiness Church, Mary Cunningham, 10th St. & College Ave., Independence, KS 67301. Tel. (316)331-2580. Fax (316)331-2580

Journal From the Radical Reformation, A, (q) Church of God General Conference (Oregon, IL and Morrow, GA), Kent Ross, Box 100,000, Morrow, GA 30260-7000. Tel. (404)362-0052. Fax (404)362-9307

Journal of Adventist Education, (5/yr) Seventh-day Adventist Church, Beverly Rumble, 12501 Old Columbia Pike, Silver Spring, MD 20904-6600. Tel. (301)-680-5075. Fax (301)622-9627

Journal of Christian Education, (q) African Methodist Episcopal Church, Kenneth H. Hill, 500 Eighth Ave., S., Nashville, TN 37203. Tel. (615)242-1420. Fax (615)726-1866

Journal of Ecumenical Studies, (q) Interdenominational, Leonard Swidler, Temple Univ. (022-38), Philadelphia, PA 19122. Tel. (215)204-7714. Fax (215)-204-4569

Journal of Pastoral Care, The, (q) Nondenominational, Orlo Strunk, Jr., 1068 Harbor Dr. SW, Calabash, NC 28467. Tel. (910)579-5084. Fax (910)579-5084

Journal of Theology, (4/yr) Church of the Lutheran Confession, John Lau, Immanuel Lutheran College, 501 Grover Road, Eau Claire, WI 54701-7199. Tel. (715)836-6621. Fax (715)836-6634

Journal of the American Academy of Religion, (q) Nondenominational, Glenn Yocum, Whittier College, P.O. Box 634, Whittier, CA 90608-0634. Tel. (310)-907-4200

Judaism, (q) Jewish, Murray Baumgatter, 15 E. 84th St., New York, NY 10028. Tel. (212)879-4500. Fax (212)249-3672

Keeping in Touch, (m) Universal Fellowship of Metropolitan Community Churches, Kittredge Cherry, 5300 Santa Monica Blvd, #304, Los Angeles, CA 90029. Tel. (213)464-5100. Fax (213)-464-2123

Kindred Minds, (q) Sovereign Grace Baptists, Larry Scouten, P.O. Box 10, Wellsburg, NY 14894. Tel. (607)734-6985

Lantern, The, (bi-m) National Baptist Convention of America, Inc., Robert Jeffrey and Ruthie W. Myles, 1327 Oierre Ave., Shreveport, LA 71103. Tel. (318)221-3701. Fax (318)222-7512

Leadership: A Practical Journal for Church Leaders, (q) Nondenominational, Kevin Miller, 465 Gundersen Dr., Carol Stream, IL 60188. Tel. (708)260-6200. Fax (708)260-0114

Leaves of Healing, (q) Christian Catholic Church (Evangelical-Protestant), Earl Minton, 2500 Dowie Memorial Dr., Zion, IL 60099. Tel. (708)746-1411. Fax (708)746-1452

Liahona Magazine, The Church of Jesus Christ of Latter-day Saints, Marvin K. Gardner, 50 East South Temple St., Salt Lake City, UT 84105. Tel. (801)240-2490. Fax (801)240-5732

Liberty, (bi-m) Seventh-day Adventist Church, Clifford R. Goldstein, 12501 Old Columbia Pike, Silver Spring, MD 20904. Tel. (301)680-6691. Fax (301)-680-6695

Light and Life Magazine, (m) Free Methodist Church of North America, Robert B. Haslam, P.O. Box 535002, Indianapolis, IN 46253-5002. Tel. (317)244-3660. Fax (317)244-1247

Liguorian, (m) The Roman Catholic Church, Allan J. Weinert, C.SS.R., 1 Liguori Dr., Liguori, MO 63057. Tel. (314)464-2500. Fax (314)464-8449

Listen, (m) Seventh-day Adventist Church, Lincoln E. Steed, 55 W. Oak Ridge Dr., Hagerstown, MD 21740. Tel. (301)745-3888. Fax (301)790-9734

Living Orthodoxy, (bi-m) The Russian Orthodox Church Outside of Russia, Gregory Williams, 1180 Orthodox Way, Liberty, TN 37095. Tel. (615)536-5239. Fax (615)536-5945

Long Island Catholic, The, (w) The Roman Catholic Church, Elizabeth O'Connor, P. O. Box 9009, 99 North Village Ave., Rockville Centre, NY 11571-9119. Tel. (516)594-1000. Fax (516)594-1092

Lookout, The, (w) Christian Churches and Churches of Christ, Simon J. Dahlman, 8121 Hamilton Ave., Cincinnati, OH 45231. Tel. (513)931-4050. Fax (513)-931-0904

Lutheran Ambassador, The, (16/yr) The Association of Free Lutheran Congregations, Craig Johnson, 86286 Pine Grove Rd., Eugene, OR 97402. Tel. (541)687-8643. Fax (541)683-8496

Lutheran Educator, The, (q) Wisconsin Evangelical Lutheran Synod, John R. Isch, Martin Luther College, 1995 Luther Ct., New Ulm, MN 56073. Tel. (507)354-8221. Fax (507)354-8225

Lutheran Forum, (q) Interdenominational Lutheran, Leonard R. Klein, 29 S. George St., York, PA 17401. Tel. (717)-854-5589

Lutheran Sentinel, (m) Evangelical Lutheran Synod, Theodore Gullixson, 1451 Pearl Pl., Escondido, CA 92027. Tel. (619)745-0583

Lutheran Spokesman, The, (m) Church of the Lutheran Confession, Paul Fleischer, 710 4th Ave., SW, Sleepy Eye, MN 56085. Tel. (507)794-7793

Lutheran Synod Quarterly, (q) Evangelical Lutheran Synod, W. W. Petersen, Bethany Lutheran Theological Seminary, 447 N. Division St., Mankato, MN 56001. Tel. (507)386-5359. Fax (507)-386-5426

Lutheran Witness, The, (m) The Lutheran Church--Missouri Synod, David Mahsman, 1333 S. Kirkwood Rd., St. Louis, MO 63122-7295. Tel. (314)965-9917. Fax (314)965-3396

Lutheran, The, (m) Evangelical Lutheran Church in America, Edgar R. Trexler, 8765 W. Higgins Rd., Chicago, IL 60631-4183. Tel. (312)380-2540. Fax (312)380-2751

Magyar Egyhaz, (q) Hungarian Reformed Church in America, Stephen Szabo, 464 Forest Ave., Paramus, NJ 07652. Tel. (201)262-2338. Fax (908)442-7799

Maranatha, (q) Advent Christian Church, Robert Mayer, P.O. Box 23152, Charlotte, NC 28227. Tel. (704)545-6161. Fax (704)573-0712

Marriage Partnership, (q) Nondenominational, Ron R. Lee, 465 Gundersen Dr., Carol Stream, IL 60188. Tel. (708)260-6200. Fax (708)260-0114

Maryknoll, (11/yr) The Roman Catholic Church, Joseph R. Veneroso, M.M., Maryknoll Fathers and Brothers, P.O. Box 308, Maryknoll, NY 10545-0308. Tel. (914)941-7590. Fax (914)945-0670

Mature Years, (q) The United Methodist Church, Marvin W. Cropsey, 201 Eighth Ave. S, Nashville, TN 37202. Tel. (615)-749-6292. Fax (615)749-6512

Memos: A Magazine for Missionettes Leaders, (q) Assemblies of God, Linda Upton, 1445 Boonville Ave., Springfield, MO 65802. Tel. (417)862-2781. Fax (417)862-8558

Mennonite Historical Bulletin, (q) Mennonite Church, John E. Sharp, 1700 S. Main St., Goshen, IN 46526. Tel. (219)-535-7477. Fax (219)535-7293

Mennonite Quarterly Review, (q) Mennonite Church, John D. Roth, 1700 S. Main St., Goshen, IN 46526. Tel. (219)-535-7433. Fax (219)535-7438

Mennonite, The, (semi-m) General Conference of the Mennonite Church, Gordon Houser, P.O. Box 347, 722 Main St., Newton, KS 67114. Tel. (316)283-5100. Fax (316)283-0454

Message, (bi-m) Seventh-day Adventist Church, Stephen P. Ruff, 55 West Oak Ridge Dr., Hagerstown, MD 21740. Tel. (301)791-7000. Fax (301)714-1753

Message of the Open Bible, (bi-m) Open Bible Standard Churches, Inc., Delores A. Winegar, 2020 Bell Ave., Des Moines, IA 50315-1096. Tel. (515)288-6761. Fax (515)288-2510

Messenger, (11/yr) Church of the Brethren, Kermon Thomasson, 1451 Dundee Ave., Elgin, IL 60120. Tel. (708)742-5100. Fax (708)742-6103

Messenger of Truth, (bi-w) Church of God in Christ, Mennonite, Gladwin Koehn, P.O. Box 230, Moundridge, KS 67107. Tel. (316)345-2532. Fax (316)345-2582

Messenger, The, (m) The (Original) Church of God, Inc., Wayne Jolley and William Dale, P.O. Box 3086, Chattanooga, TN 37404-0086. Tel. (800)-827-9234

Messenger, The, (m) The Swedenborgian Church, Patte LeVan, P.O. Box 985, Julian, CA 92036. Tel. (619)765-2915. Fax (619)765-0218

Messenger, The, (m) The Pentecostal Free Will Baptist Church, Inc., Don Sauls and George Thomas, P.O. Box 1568, Dunn, NC 28335. Tel. (910)892-0297. Fax (910)892-6876

Messenger, The, (m) The Bible Church of Christ, Inc., Gwendolyn Harris, 1358 Morris Ave., Bronx, NY 10456. Tel. (718)588-2284

Methodist History, (q) The United Methodist Church, Charles Yrigoyen, Jr., P.O. Box 127, Madison, NJ 07940. Tel. (201)408-3189. Fax (201)408-3909

Mid-Stream: An Ecumenical Journal, (q) Christian Church (Disciples of Christ), Paul A. Crow, Jr., 130 E. Washington St., P.O. Box 1986, Indianapolis, IN 46206-1986. Tel. (317)635-3110. Fax (317)635-3700

Ministry, (m) Seventh-day Adventist Church, Willmore D. Eva, 12501 Old Columbia Pike, Silver Spring, MD 21029-6600. Tel. (301)680-6510. Fax (301)680-6502

Ministry Today, (bi-m) The Missionary Church, Robert Ransom, P.O. Box 9127, Ft. Wayne, IN 46899. Tel. (219)747-2027. Fax (219)747-5331

Mission Grams, (bi-m) National Association of Free Will Baptists, Roy Thomas, Home Missions Office, P.O. Box 5002, Antioch, TN 37011-5002. Tel. (615)-731-6812. Fax (615)731-7655

Mission Herald, (bi-m) National Baptist Convention, U.S.A., Inc., William J. Harvey, III, 701 S. 19th St., Philadelphia, PA 19146. Tel. (215)735-7868. Fax (215)735-1721

Mission, Adult, Junior-Teen, and Children's Editions, (q) Seventh-day Adventist Church, Charlotte Ishkanian, 12501 Old Columbia Pike, Silver Spring, MD 20904. Tel. (301)680-6167. Fax (301)680-6155

Missionary Messenger, The, (m) Christian Methodist Episcopal Church, P. Ann Pegues, 2309 Bonnie Ave., Bastrop, LA 71220. Tel. (318)281-3044

Missionary Messenger, The, (6/yr) Cumberland Presbyterian Church, Mark Brown, 1978 Union Ave., Memphis, TN 38104. Tel. (901)276-4572. Fax (901)-276-4578

Missionary Seer, (bi-m) African Methodist Episcopal Zion Church, Kermit J. DeGraffenreidt, 475 Riverside Dr., Rm. 1935, New York, NY 10115. Tel. (212)-870-2952. Fax (212)870-2055

Missionary Signal, The, (bi-m) Churches of God, General Conference, Kathy Rodabaugh, P.O. Box 926, Findley, OH 45839.

MissionsUSA, (bi-m) Southern Baptist Convention, Wayne Grinstead, 1350 Spring St. NW, At'anta, GA 30367. Tel. (770)410-6251. Fax (770)410-6006

Monday Morning, (21/yr) Presbyterian Church (U.S.A.), Stephen V. Moulton, 100 Witherspoon St., Louisville, KY 40202. Tel. (502)569-5502. Fax (502)-569-8073

Moody Magazine, (6/yr) Nondenominational, Bruce Anderson, 820 N. LaSalle Dr., Chicago, IL 60610. Tel. (312)329-2163. Fax (312)329-2149

Moravian, The, (10/yr) Moravian Church in America (Unitas Fratrum), Hermann I. Weinlick, 1021 Center St., P.O. Box 1245, Bethlehem, PA 18016. Tel. (610)-867-0594. Fax (610)866-9223

Mother Church, The, (m) Diocese of the Armenian Church of America, Sipan Mekhsian, 2215 E. Colorado Blvd., Pasadena, CA 91107. Tel. (818)683-1197. Fax (818)683-1199

Mountain Movers, (m) Assemblies of God, Joyce Wells Booze, 1445 Boonville Ave., Springfield, MO 65802. Tel. (417)862-2781. Fax (417)862-0085

Muslim World, Nondenominational, Ibrahim Abu-Rabi and David Kerr and Ibrahim Rabi, Hartford Seminary, 77 Sherman St., Hartford, CT 06105. Tel. (860)509-9534. Fax (860)509-9539

National Catholic Reporter, (44/yr) Independent, Thomas C. Fox, P.O. Box 419281, Kansas City, MO 64141. Tel. (816)531-0538. Fax (816)968-2280

National Christian Reporter, The, (w) Nondenominational, John A. Lovelace, P.O. Box 222198, Dallas, TX 75222. Tel. (214)630-6495. Fax (214)630-0079

National Spiritualist Summit, The, (m) National Spiritualist Association of Churches, Sandra Pfortmiller, 3521 W. Topeka Dr., Glendale, AZ 85308. Tel. (602)581-6686. Fax (602)581-5544

New Church Life, (m) General Church of the New Jerusalem, Donald L. Rose, Box 277, Bryn Athyn, PA 19009. Tel. (215)-947-6225. Fax (215)947-3078

New Era, The, (m) The Church of Jesus Christ of Latter-day Saints, Richard Romney, 50 E. South Temple St., Salt Lake City, UT 84105. Tel. (801)240-2951. Fax (801)240-5732

New Horizons in the Orthodox Presbyterian Church, (11/yr) The Orthodox Presbyterian Church, Thomas E. Tyson, 607 N. Easton Rd., Bldg. E, P.O. Box P, Willow Grove, PA 19090-0920. Tel. (215)830-0900. Fax (215)830-0350

New Oxford Review, (10/yr) The Roman Catholic Church, Dale Vree, 1069 Kains Ave., Berkeley, CA 94706. Tel. (510)-526-5374

New World Outlook, (bi-m) The United Methodist Church, Alma Graham, 475 Riverside Dr., Rm. 1333, New York, NY 10115. Tel. (212)870-3765. Fax (212)-870-3940

New World, The, (w) The Roman Catholic Church, Mary Claire Gart, 1144 W. Jackson Blvd., Chicago, IL 60607. Tel. (312)243-1300. Fax (312)243-1526

News, The, (m) The Anglican Orthodox Church, Margaret D. Lane, Anglican Orthodox Church, P.O. Box 128, Statesville, NC 28687. Tel. (704)873-8365. Fax (704)873-8948

Newscope, (w) The United Methodist Church, J. Richard Peck, P.O. Box 801, Nashville, TN 37202. Tel. (615)749-6007. Fax (615)749-6079

North American Catholic, The, (m) North American Old Roman Catholic Church, Theodore J. Remalt, 4200 N. Kedvale Ave., Chicago, IL 60641. Tel. (312)685-0461. Fax (312)286-5783

North American Challenge, The, (m) United Pentecostal Church International, J. L. Fiorino, 8855 Dunn Rd., Hazelwood, MO 63042. Tel. (314)837-7300. Fax (314)837-2387

Northwestern Lutheran, (m) Wisconsin Evangelical Lutheran Synod, Gary Baumler, 2929 N. Mayfair Rd., Milwaukee, WI 53222. Tel. (414)256-3888. Fax (414)256-3899

On Course, (q) Assemblies of God, Melinda Booze, 1445 Boonville Ave., Springfield, MO 65802-1894. Tel. (417)862-2781. Fax (417)866-1146

On the Line, (w) General Conference of the Mennonite Church, Mary C. Meyer, 616 Walnut Ave., Scottdale, PA 15683. Tel. (412)887-8500. Fax (412)887-3111

One Church, (bi-m) Patriarchal Parishes of the Russian Orthodox Church in the U.S.A., Feodor Kovalchuk, 727 Miller Ave., Youngstown, OH 44502-2326. Tel. (216)788-0151. Fax (216)788-9361

Orthodox America, (8/yr) The Russian Orthodox Church Outside of Russia, Mary Mansur and Katherine Mansur, P.O. Box 383, Richfield Springs, NY 13439-0383.

Orthodox Church, The, (m) The Orthodox Church in America, Leonid Kishkovsky, P.O. Box 675, Syosset, NY 11791.

Orthodox Family, (q) The Russian Orthodox Church Outside of Russia, George Johnson and Deborah Johnson, P.O. Box 45, Beltsville, MD 20705. Tel. (301)-890-3552

Orthodox Life (English), (bi-m) The Russian Orthodox Church Outside of Russia, Fr. Luke, Holy Trinity Monastery, P.O. Box 36, Jordanville, NY 13361-0036. Tel. (315)858-0940

Orthodox Observer, The, (m) Greek Orthodox Archdiocese of North and South America, Jim Golding, 8 E. 79th St., New York, NY 10021. Tel. (212)628-2590

Orthodox Russia (Russian), (26/yr) The Russian Orthodox Church Outside of Russia, Archbishop Laurus, Holy Trinity Monastery, P.O. Box 36, Jordanville, NY 13361. Tel. (315)858-0940. Fax (315)858-0505

Orthodox Voices, (q) The Russian Orthodox Church Outside of Russia, Thomas Webb and Ellen Webb, P.O. Box 23644, Lexington, KY 40523. Tel. (606)271-3877

Our Daily Bread, (m) The Swedenborgian Church, Richard H. Tafel, Jr., 8065 Lagoon Rd., Ft. Myers Beach, FL 33931. Tel. (813)463-5030

Our Little Friend, (w) Seventh-day Adventist Church, Aileen Andres Sox, P.O. Box 5353, Nampa, ID 83653-5353. Tel. (208)465-2500. Fax (208)465-2531

Our Sunday Visitor, (w) The Roman Catholic Church, David Scott, 200 Noll Plaza, Huntington, IN 46750. Tel. (219)-356-8400. Fax (219)356-8472

Outreach, (10/yr) Armenian Apostolic Church of America, Iris Papazian, 138 E. 39th St., New York, NY 10016. Tel. (212)689-7810. Fax (212)689-7168

Pastoral Life, (m) The Roman Catholic Church, Anthony Chenevey, Box 595, Canfield, OH 44406-0595. Tel. (216)-533-5503. Fax (216)533-1076

Path of Orthodoxy, The, (m) Serbian Orthodox Church in the U.S.A. and Canada, Rade Merick and Mirko Dobrijevich and Nedeljko Lunich, P.O. Box 36, Leetsdale, PA 15056. Tel. (412)741-8660. Fax (614)282-0313

Path of Orthodoxy, The, (Serbian, m) Serbian Orthodox Church in the U.S.A. and Canada, Nedeljko Lunich, 300 Striker Ave., Joliet, IL 60436. Tel. (815)741-1023. Fax (815)741-1023

Pentecostal Evangel, (w) Assemblies of God, Hal Donaldson, 1445 Boonville Ave., Springfield, MO 65802-1894. Tel. (417)862-2781. Fax (417)862-0416

Pentecostal Herald, The, (m) United Pentecostal Church International, United Pentecostal Church of Canada, J. L. Hall, 8855 Dunn Rd., Hazelwood, MO 63042. Tel. (314)837-7300. Fax (314)-837-4503

Pentecostal Leader, (q) The International Pentecostal Church of Christ, Lorraine Roberts, P.O. Box 439, London, OH 43140. Tel. (614)852-4722. Fax (614)-852-0348

Pentecostal Messenger, The, (m) Pentecostal Church of God, Donald K. Allen, P.O. Box 850, Joplin, MO 64802. Tel. (417)624-7050. Fax (417)624-7102

People's Mouthpiece, The, (q) Apostolic Overcoming Holy Church of God, Inc., Juanita R. Arrington, PhD, 1120 North 24th St., Birmingham, AL 35234. Tel. (205)324-2202

Perspectives on Science & Christian Faith, (q) Nondenominational, J. W. Haas, Jr., P.O. Box 668, Ipswich, MA 01938. Tel. (508)356-5656. Fax (508)-356-4375

Pillar of Fire, (11/yr) Pillar of Fire, Donald J. Wolfram and Mark Tomlin, P.O. Box 9045, Zarephath, NJ 08890. Tel. (908)-356-0561. Fax (908)271-1968

Pilot, The, (w) The Roman Catholic Church, Peter V. Conley, 49 Franklin St., Boston, MA 02110. Tel. (617)482-4316. Fax (617)482-5647

Pockets, (11/yr) The United Methodist Church, Janet R. Knight, P.O. Box 189, Nashville, TN 37202. Tel. (615)340-7333. Fax (615)340-7006

Polka, (q) Polish National Catholic Church of America, Cecelia Lallo, 1127 Frieda St., Dickson City, PA 18519.

Praying, (bi-m) The Roman Catholic Church, Art Winter, P.O. Box 419335, 115 E. Armour Blvd., Kansas City, MO 64141. Tel. (816)968-2258. Fax (816)-968-2280

Preacher's Magazine, (q) Church of the Nazarene, Randal Denny, 10814 E. Broadway, Spokane, WA 99206. Tel. (509)926-1545

Preacher, The, (bi-m) Baptist Bible Fellowship International, Michael Randall, P.O. Box 309 HSJ, Springfield, MO 65801. Tel. (417)831-3996. Fax (417)-831-1470

Presbyterian News Service, (m) Presbyterian Church (U.S.A.), Jerry L. VanMarter, 100 Witherspoon St., Rm. 5418, Louisville, KY 40202. Tel. (502)569-5502. Fax (502)569-8073

Presbyterian Outlook, (w) Presbyterian Church (U.S.A.), Robert H. Bullock, Jr., Box 85623, Richmond, VA 23285-5623. Tel. (804)359-8442. Fax (804)353-6369

Presbyterians Today, (m) Presbyterian Church (U.S.A.), Catherine Cottingham and Eva Stimson, 100 Witherspoon St., Louisville, KY 40202-1396. Tel. (502)-569-5637. Fax (502)569-5018

Primary Treasure, (w) Seventh-day Adventist Church, Aileen Andres Sox, P.O. Box 5353, Nampa, ID 83653-5353. Tel. (208)465-2500. Fax (208)465-2531

Primitive Baptist, The, (bi-m) Primitive Baptists, W. H. Cayce, P.O. Box 38, Thornton, AR 71766. Tel. (501)352-3694

Priority, (m) The Missionary Church, Ken Stucky, P.O. Box 9127, Ft. Wayne, IN 46899. Tel. (219)747-2027. Fax (219)-747-5331

Providence Visitor, (w) The Roman Catholic Church, Michael Brown, 184 Broad St., Providence, RI 02903. Tel. (401)-272-1010. Fax (401)421-8418

Purpose, (w) Mennonite Church, James E. Horsch, 616 Walnut Ave., Scottdale, PA 15683. Tel. (412)887-8500. Fax (412)-887-3111

Pursuit, (q) The Evangelical Free Church of America, Carol Madison, 901 East 78th St., Minneapolis, MN 55420-1300. Tel. (612)853-1763. Fax (612)853-8488

Qala min M'Dinkha (Voice from the East), (q) Apostolic Catholic Assyrian Church of the East, North American Dioceses, Shlemon Heseqial, Diocesan Offices, 7201 N. Ashland, Chicago, IL 60626. Tel. (312)465-4777. Fax (312)-465-0776

Quaker Life, (10/yr) Friends United Meeting, Johan Maurer, 101 Quaker Hill Dr., Richmond, IN 47374-1980. Tel. (317)-962-7573. Fax (317)966-1293

Quarterly Review, (q) The United Methodist Church, Sharon Hels, Box 871, Nashville, TN 37202. Tel. (615)340-7334. Fax (615)340-7048

Quarterly Review, (q) African Methodist Episcopal Zion Church, James D. Armstrong, P.O. Box 31005, Charlotte, NC 28231. Tel. (704)334-0728. Fax (704)-333-1769

Reconstructionism Today, (q) Jewish, Lawrence Bush, Church Rd. & Greedwood Ave., Wycote, PA 19095. Tel. (215)887-1988. Fax (215)887-5348

Reflections, (bi-m) United Pentecostal Church International, Melissa Anderson, P.O. Box 3, Collinsville, OK 74021. Tel. (918)371-2659

Reformation Today, (bi-m) Sovereign Grace Baptists, Erroll Hulse, c/o Tom Lutz, 3743 Nichol Ave., Anderson, IN 46011-3008. Tel. (317)644-0994. Fax (317)644-0994

Reformed Herald, (m) Reformed Church in the United States, David Dawn, Box 345, Ashley, ND 58413. Tel. (701)288-3682

Rejoice!, Philip Wiebe, 1218 Franklin St. NW, Salem, OR 97304. Tel. (503)581-5793. Fax (503)581-5793

Religious Broadcasting, (11/yr) Nondenominational, Ron Kopczick, National Religious Broadcasters, 7839 Ashton Ave., Manassas, VA 22110. Tel. (703)-330-7000. Fax (703)330-6996

Reporter, (m) The Lutheran Church--Missouri Synod, David Mahsman, 1333 S. Kirkwood Rd., St. Louis, MO 63122-7295. Tel. (314)965-9917. Fax (314)-965-3396

Rescue Herald, The, (q) American Rescue Workers, Robert N. Coles, Sr., 1209 Hamilton Blvd., Hagerstown, MD 21742. Tel. (301)797-0061. Fax (301)-797-1480

Response, (m) The United Methodist Church, Dana Jones, 475 Riverside Dr., Room 1363, New York, NY 10115. Tel. (212)870-3755. Fax (212)870-3940

Restitution Herald, The, (bi-m) Church of God General Conference (Oregon, IL and Morrow, GA), Kent Ross, Box 100,000, Morrow, GA 30260-7000. Tel. (404)362-0052. Fax (404)362-9307

Restoration Herald, (m) Christian Churches and Churches of Christ, H. Lee Mason, 5664 Cheviot Rd., Cincinnati, OH 45247-7071. Tel. (513)385-0461. Fax (513)385-0660

Restoration Quarterly, (q) Churches of Christ, James W. Thompson, Box 8227, Abilene, TX 79699-8227. Tel. (915)-674-3781. Fax (915)674-3776

Restoration Witness, (bi-m) Reorganized Church of Jesus Christ of Latter Day Saints, Lorrie Serig, P.O. Box 1770, Independence, MO 64055. Tel. (816)-252-5010. Fax (816)252-3976

Review for Religious, (bi-m) The Roman Catholic Church, David L. Fleming, S.J., 3601 Lindell Blvd., St. Louis, MO 63108. Tel. (314)977-7363. Fax (314)-977-7362

Review of Religious Research, (4/yr) Nondenominational, D. Paul Johnson, Texas Tech. Univ., Dept. of Sociology, Anthropology, & SW, Lubbock, TX 79409-1012. Tel. (806)742-2400. Fax (806)742-1088

Rocky Mountain Christian, (m) Churches of Christ, Ron L. Carter, 2247 Highway 86 E., Castlerock, CO 80104. Tel. (719)-598-4197. Fax (719)528-1549

SBC Life, (10/yr) Southern Baptist Convention, Jon Walker, Int., 901 Commerce St., Nashville, TN 37203. Tel. (615)244-2355. Fax (615)742-8919

Sabbath Recorder, (m) Seventh Day Baptist General Conference, USA and Canada, Kevin J. Butler, 3120 Kennedy Rd., P.O. Box 1678, Janesville, WI 53547. Tel. (608)752-5055. Fax (608)752-7711

Saint Anthony Messenger, (m) The Roman Catholic Church, Norman Perry, 1615 Republic St., Cincinnati, OH 45210. Tel. (513)241-5616. Fax (513)241-0399

Saints Herald, (m) Reorganized Church of Jesus Christ of Latter Day Saints, Roger Yarrington, P.O. Box 1770, Independence, MO 64055. Tel. (816)252-5010. Fax (816)252-3976

Salt of the Earth, (bi-m) The Roman Catholic Church, Mark J. Brummel, 205 W. Monroe St., Chicago, IL 60606. Tel. (312)236-7782. Fax (312)236-7230

Schwenkfeldian, The, (q) The Schwenkfelder Church, Andrew C. Anders, 1 Seminary St., Pennsburg, PA 18073. Tel. (215)679-3103

Secret Chamber, (q) African Methodist Episcopal Church, George L. Champion, Sr., 5728 Major Blvd., Orlando, FL 82819. Tel. (407)352-8797. Fax (407)-352-6097

Secret Place, The, (q) American Baptist Churches in the U.S.A., Kathleen Hayes, P.O. Box 851, Valley Forge, PA 19482-0851. Tel. (610)768-2240. Fax (610)768-2056

Share, (bi-m) The Evangelical Church, James Lanz, Evangelical Church Board of Missions, 7733 West River Rd., Minneapolis, MN 55444-2190. Tel. (612)-561-0174. Fax (612)561-2899

Sharing, (q) Interdenominational Mennonite, Judy Godshalk, P.O. Box 438, Goshen, IN 46527. Tel. (219)533-9511. Fax (219)533-5264

Shiloh's Messenger of Wisdom, (m) Israelite House of David, William Robertson, P.O. Box 1067, Benton Harbor, MI 49023.

Shining Light, The, (m) Church of God (Anderson, Ind.), Wilfred Jordan, Box 1235, Anderson, IN 46015. Tel. (317)-644-1593

Signs of the Times, (m) Seventh-day Adventist Church, Marvin Moore, P.O. Box 5353, Nampa, ID 83653-5353. Tel. (208)465-2577. Fax (208)465-2531

Silver Lining, The, (m) Apostolic Christian Churches of America, Bruce Leman, R.R. 2 Box 50, Roanoke, IL 61561-9625. Tel. (309)923-7777. Fax (309)-923-7359

Social Questions Bulletin, (bi-m) The United Methodist Church, George McClain, 76 Clinton Ave., Shalom House, Staten Island, NY 10301. Tel. (718)273-6372. Fax (718)273-6372

Sojourners, (6/yr) Nondenominational, Jim Wallis, 2401 15th St. NW, Washington, DC 20009. Tel. (202)328-8842. Fax (202)328-8757

Solia-The Herald, (m) The Romanian Orthodox Episcopate of America, David Oancea, P.O. Box 185, Grass Lake, MI 49240-0185. Tel. (517)522-3656. Fax (517)522-5907

Southern Methodist, The, (m) Southern Methodist Church, Thomas M. Owens, Sr., P.O. Box 39, Orangeburg, SC 29116-0039. Tel. (803)534-9853. Fax (803)535-3881

Spectrum, (bi-m) Conservative Baptist Association of America, Arlene Flurry and Dennis N. Baker, P.O. Box 66, Wheaton, IL 60189. Tel. (708)260-3800. Fax (708)653-5387

Spirit, (q) Volunteers of America, Arthur Smith, 3939 N. Causeway Blvd., Metairie, LA 70002. Tel. (504)837-2652. Fax (504)837-4200

Spiritual Sword, The, (q) Churches of Christ, Alan E. Highers, 1511 Getwell Rd., Memphis, TN 38111. Tel. (901)-743-0464. Fax (901)743-2197

St. Willibrord Journal, Christ Catholic Church, Charles E. Harrison, P.O. Box 271751, Houston, TX 77277-1751. Tel. (417)587-3951

Standard Bearer, The, (21/yr) Protestant Reformed Churches in America, David J. Engelsma, 4949 Ivanrest Ave., Grandville, MI 49418. Tel. (616)531-1490. Fax (616)531-3033

Standard, The, (m) Baptist General Conference, Gary D. Marsh, 2002 S. Arlington Heights Rd., Arlington Heights, IL 60005. Tel. (708)228-0200. Fax (708)228-5376

Star of Zion, (w) African Methodist Episcopal Zion Church, Morgan W. Tann, P.O. Box 31005, Charlotte, NC 28231. Tel. (704)377-4329. Fax (704)333-1769

Stewardship USA, (q) Nondenominational, Raymond Barnett Knudsen II, P.O. Box 9, Bloomfield Hills, MI 48303-0009. Tel. (313)737-0895. Fax (313)-737-0895

Story Friends, (w) Mennonite Church, Rose Mary Stutzman, 616 Walnut Ave., Scottdale, PA 15683. Tel. (412)887-8500. Fax (412)887-3111

Sunday, (q) Interdenominational, Jack P. Lowndes, 2930 Flowers Rd., S., #16, Atlanta, GA 30341-5532. Tel. (404)-936-5376. Fax (404)451-6081

Tablet, The, (w) The Roman Catholic Church, Ed Wilkinson, 653 Hicks St., Brooklyn, NY 11231. Tel. (718)858-3838. Fax (718)858-2112

The Mennonite, (24/yr) Mennonite Church, The General Conference, Gordon Houser, Box 347, Newton, KS 67114. Tel. (316)283-5100. Fax (316)-283-0454

The Vineyard/Update, (q) Albanian Orthodox Archdiocese in America, Diana M. Prift, So. Huntington Ave., Jamaica Plain, MA 02130.

Theology Digest, (q) The Roman Catholic Church, Bernhard A. Asen and Rosemary Jermann, 3634 Lindell Blvd., St. Louis, MO 63108. Tel. (314)658-2857

Theology Today, (q) Nondenominational, Thomas G. Long and Patrick D. Miller, P.O. Box 29, Princeton, NJ 08542. Tel. (609)497-7714. Fax (609)924-2973

These Days, (bi-m) Interdenominational, Vic Jameson, 100 Witherspoon St., Louisville, KY 40202-1396. Tel. (502)569-5472. Fax (502)569-5018

Tidings, The, (w) The Roman Catholic Church, Tod M. Tamberg, 1530 W. Ninth St., Los Angeles, CA 90015. Tel. (213)251-3360. Fax (213)386-8667

Today's Christian Woman, (6/yr) Nondenominational, Ramona Cramer Tucker, 465 Gunderson Dr., Carol Stream, IL 60188. Tel. (708)260-6200. Fax (708)-260-0114

Tradition: A Journal of Orthodox Jewish Thought, (q) Jewish, Emanuel Feldman, Rabbinical Council of America, 305 Seventh Ave., New York, NY 10001. Tel. (212)807-7888

Truth, (bi-m) Grace Gospel Fellowship, Roger G. Anderson, 2125 Martindale SW, Grand Rapids, MI 49509. Tel. (616)247-1999. Fax (616)247-2542

U.S. Catholic, (m) The Roman Catholic Church, Mark J. Brummel, 205 W. Monroe St., Chicago, IL 60606. Tel. (312)-236-7782. Fax (312)236-7230

Ubique, (q) The Liberal Catholic Church--Province of the United States of America, Joseph L. Tisch, P.O. Box 1117, Melbourne, FL 32902. Tel. (407)254-0499

Ukrainian Orthodox Herald, Ukrainian Orthodox Church of America (Ecumenical Patriarchate), Anthony Ugolnik, P.O. Box 774, Allentown, PA 18105.

Unique Ladies Ministries, (bi-m) Church of God (Cleveland, Tenn.), Rebecca Jenkins, P.O. Box 2430, Cleveland, TN 37320. Tel. (423)478-7170. Fax (423)-478-7891

United Church News, (10/yr) United Church of Christ, W. Evan Golder, 700 Prospect Ave., Cleveland, OH 44115. Tel. (216)736-2218. Fax (216)736-2223

United Evangelical ACTION, (bi-m) Interdenominational, David L. Melvin, 450 E. Gundersen Dr., Carol Stream, IL 60188. Tel. (708)665-0500. Fax (708)-665-8575

United Methodist Record, (m) The United Methodist Church, John A. Lovelace, P.O. Box 660275, Dallas, TX 75266-0275. Tel. (214)630-6495. Fax (214)-630-0079

United Methodist Reporter,, (w) The United Methodist Church, John A. Lovelace, P.O. Box 660275, Dallas, TX 75266-0275. Tel. (214)630-6495. Fax (214)630-0079

United Methodist Review, (26/yr) The United Methodist Church, John A. Lovelace, P.O. Box 660275, Dallas, TX 75266-0275. Tel. (214)630-6495. Fax (214)630-0079

Upper Room, The, (6/yr) The United Methodist Church, Janice Grana, P.O. Box 189, Nashville, TN 37202. Tel. (615)-340-7200. Fax (615)340-7006

Upreach, (bi-m) Churches of Christ, Randy Becton, Box 2001, Abilene, TX 79604. Tel. (915)698-4370. Fax (915)691-5736

Vanguard, (q) Christian Church (Disciples of Christ), Ann Updegraff Spleth, 130 E. Washington St., P.O. Box 1986, Indianapolis, IN 46206-1986. Tel. (317)635-3113. Fax (317)635-4426

Vibrant Life, (bi-m) Seventh-day Adventist Church, Larry Becker, 55 W. Oak Ridge Dr., Hagerstown, MD 21740. Tel. (301)791-7000. Fax (301)790-9734

Victory (Youth Magazine), (m) Church of God of Prophecy, H. E. Cardin, P.O. Box 2910, Cleveland, TN 37320-2910. Tel. (423)479-8511. Fax (423)559-5202

Vindicator, The, (m) Old German Baptist Brethren, Keith Skiles, 701 St. Rt. 571, Union City, OH 45390. Tel. (513)968-3877

Vista, (bi-m) Christian Church of North America, General Council, Gregory Mi-heli, 1294 Rutledge Rd., Transfer, PA 16154. Tel. (412)962-3501

Vital Christianity, (m) Church of God (Anderson, Ind.), David C. Shultz, Box 2499, Anderson, IN 46018. Tel. (317)-644-7721. Fax (317)622-9511

Voice, (q) General Association of General Baptists, Gene Koker, 100 Stinson Dr., Poplar Bluff, MO 63901. Tel. (314)785-7746. Fax (314)785-0564

Voice, (11/yr) Mennonite Church, Eve MacMaster, 423 Ridge Rd., Elizabethtown, PA 17022. Tel. (717)361-8088

Voice of Missions, (q) African Methodist Episcopal Church, Anne R. Elliott, 475 Riverside Dr., Rm. 1926, New York, NY 10115. Tel. (212)870-2258. Fax (212)-870-2242

Voice of Missions, The, (q) The Church Of God In Christ, Floyd Mayfield, 1932 Dewey Ave., Evanston, IL 60201. Tel. (901)578-3816. Fax (708)328-3925

Voice, The, (6/yr) Independent Fundamental Churches of America, Richard I. Gregory, P.O. Box 810, Grandville, MI 49468-0810. Tel. (616)531-1840. Fax (616)531-1814

Voice, The, (q) The Bible Church of Christ, Inc., Montrose Bushrod, 1358 Morris Ave., Bronx, NY 10456. Tel. (718)588-2284

War Cry, The, (bi-w) The Salvation Army, Marlene Chase, 615 Slaters Ln., Alexandria, VA 22313. Tel. (703)684-5500. Fax (703)684-5539

Wave, The, (q) General Association of General Baptists, Sandra Trivitt, 100 Stinson Dr., Poplar Bluff, MO 63901. Tel. (314)785-7746. Fax (314)785-0564

Weavings:A Journal of the Christian Spiritual Life, (6/yr) The United Methodist Church, John S. Mogabgab, P.O. Box 189, Nashville, TN 37202. Tel. (615)340-7254. Fax (615)340-7006

Wesleyan Advocate, The, (m) The Wesleyan Church, Norman Wilson, P.O. Box 50434, Indianapolis, IN 46250-0434. Tel. (317)595-4204. Fax (317)842-1649

Wesleyan Woman, (q) The Wesleyan Church, Martha Blackburn, P.O. Box 50434, Indianapolis, IN 46250. Tel. (317)595-4164. Fax (317)594-8309

Wesleyan World, (q) The Wesleyan Church, Wayne MacBeth, P.O. Box 50434, Indianapolis, IN 46250. Tel. (317)595-4172. Fax (317)841-1125

White Wing Messenger, (bi-w) Church of God of Prophecy, Billy D. Murray, P.O. Box 2910, Cleveland, TN 37320-2910. Tel. (423)559-5131. Fax (423)559-5133

Whole Truth, (m) The Church Of God In Christ, Larry Britton, P.O. Box 2017, Memphis, TN 38101. Tel. (901)578-3841. Fax (901)527-6807

Window to Mission, (q) Mennonite Church, The General Conference, Bek Linsenmeyer, Box 347, Newton, KS 67114. Tel. (316)283-5100. Fax (316)-283-0454

Wineskins, (m) Churches of Christ, Mike Cope and Rubel Shelly and Phillip Morrison, Box 129004, Nashville, TN 37212-9004. Tel. (615)373-5004. Fax (615)373-5006

Winner, The, (9/yr.) Nondenominational, Gerald Wheeler, The Health Connection, P.O. Box 859, Hagerstown, MD 21741. Tel. (301)790-9735. Fax (301)-790-9733

Wisconsin Lutheran Quarterly, (q) Wisconsin Evangelical Lutheran Synod, John F. Brug, 11831 N. Seminary Dr., Mequon, WI 53092. Tel. (414)242-0967. Fax (414)242-7255

With: The Magazine for Radical Christian Youth, (8/yr) Interdenominational, Eddy Hall and Carol Duerksen, P.O. Box 347, Newton, KS 67114. Tel. (316)283-5100. Fax (316)283-0454

Woman's Touch, (bi-m) Assemblies of God, Peggy Musgrove, 1445 Boonville Ave., Springfield, MO 65802-1894. Tel. (417)862-2781. Fax (417)862-0503

Women's Missionary Magazine, (9/yr) African Methodist Episcopal Church, Bettye J. Allen, 1901 E. 169th Place, S. Holland, IL 60473. Tel. (708)895-0703

Word and Work, (11/yr) Churches of Christ, Alex V. Wilson, 2518 Portland Ave., Louisville, KY 40212. Tel. (502)-897-2831

Word, The, (10/yr) The Antiochian Orthodox Christian Archdiocese of North America, George S. Corey, 52 78th St., Brooklyn, NY 11209. Tel. (718)748-7940. Fax (718)855-3608

Workman, The, (q) Churches of God, General Conference, Evelyn J. Sloat, P.O. Box 926, Findlay, OH 45839.

World Harvest Today, (q) United Pentecostal Church International, J. S. Leaman, 8855 Dunn Rd., Hazelwood, MO 63042. Tel. (314)837-7300. Fax (314)837-2387

World Mission, (m) Church of the Nazarene, Roy Stults, World Mission Division, 6401 The Paseo, Kansas City, MO 64131. Tel. (816)333-7000. Fax (816)-363-3100

World Parish: Intl. Organ of the World Meth. Council, (s-m) Interdenominational Methodist, Joe Hale, P.O. Box 518, Lake Junaluska, NC 28745. Tel. (704)456-9432. Fax (704)456-9433

World Partners, (bi-m) The Missionary Church, Michael Reynolds, P.O. Box 9127, Ft. Wayne, IN 46899-9127. Tel. (219)747-2027. Fax (219)747-5331

World Vision, (bi-m) Open Bible Standard Churches, Inc., Paul V. Canfield, 2020 Bell Ave., Des Moines, IA 50315-1096. Tel. (515)288-6761. Fax (515)288-2510

World Vision, (bi-m) Nondenominational, Terry Madison, P.O. Box 9716, Federal Way, WA 98063-9716. Tel. (206)815-2300. Fax (206)815-3445

Worldorama, (m) International Pentecostal Holiness Church, Jesse Simmons, P.O. Box 12609, Oklahoma City, OK 73157. Tel. (405)787-7110. Fax (405)-787-7729

Worship, (6/yr) The Roman Catholic Church, R. Kevin Seasoltz, St. John's Abbey, Collegeville, MN 56321. Tel. (612)363-3883. Fax (612)363-2504

Youth Ministry Accent, (q) Seventh-day Adventist Church, David S.F. Wong, 12501 Old Columbia Pike, Silver Spring, MD 20904-6600. Tel. (301)680-6180. Fax (301)680-6155

Zion's Advocate, (m) Church of Christ, Mike McGhee, 18907 E. 6th St. N, Independence, MO 64056. Tel. (816)796-6255

Zion's Herald, (m) United Zion Church, Kathy Long, R D 3, Box 701, Annville, PA 17003. Tel. (717)867-1201

11. RELIGIOUS PERIODICALS IN CANADA

The religious periodicals below constitute a basic core of important journals and periodicals circulated in Canada. Consult the religious bodies in Canada listing (section 4) for the names of periodicals published by each denomination.

Each entry gives the title of the periodical, frequency of publication, religious affiliation, editor's name, address, telephone number and fax number when known.

Anglican Journal, (10/yr) The Anglican Church of Canada, 600 Jarvis St., Toronto, ON M4Y 2J6. Tel. (416)924-9199. Fax (416)921-4452

Anglican Montreal Anglican, (10/yr) The Anglican Church of Canada, Joan Shanks, 1444 Union Ave., Montreal, QC H3A 2B8. Tel. (514)843-6344. Fax (514)843-6344

Anglican, The, (10/yr) The Anglican Church of Canada, Stuart Mann, 135 Adelaide St. E., Toronto, ON M5C 1L8. Tel. (416)363-6021. Fax (416)363-7678

Atlantic Baptist, The, (m) United Baptist Convention of the Atlantic Provinces, Michael Lipe, Box 756, Kentville, NS B4N 3X9. Tel. (902)681-6868. Fax (902)681-0315

Aujourd'hui Credo, (10/yr) The United Church of Canada, Comite de redaction, 132 Victoria, Greenfield Park, QC J4V 1L8. Tel. (514)466-7733. Fax (514)466-2664

B.C. Conference Call, (q) British Columbia Baptist Conference, Walter W. Wieser, 7600 Glover Rd., Langley, BC V2Y 1Y1. Tel. (604)888-2246. Fax (604)-888-0046

B.C. Fellowship Baptist, (m) The Fellowship of Evangelical Baptist Churches in Canada, Bruce Christensen, Box 800, Langley, BC V3A 8C9. Tel. (604)888-3616. Fax (604)888-3601

BGC Canada News, (4/yr) Baptist General Conference of Canada, Abe Funk, 4306 97th St. NW, Edmonton, AB T6E 5R9. Tel. (403)438-9127. Fax (403)435-2478

Banner, The, (w) Christian Reformed Church in North America, John A. Suk, 2850 Kalamazoo Ave. SE, Grand Rapids, MI 49560. Tel. (616)246-0791. Fax (616)246-0834

Baptist Horizon, The, (m) Canadian Convention of Southern Baptists, Nancy McGough, Postal Bag 300, Cochrane, AB T0L 0W0. Tel. (403)932-5688. Fax (403)932-4937

Blackboard Bulletin, (m) Old Order Amish Church, Delbert Farmwald, Rt. 4, Aylmer, ON N5H 2R3.

Budget, The, (w) Old Order Amish Church, George R. Smith, P.O. Box 249, Sugarcreek, OH 44681. Tel. (216)852-4634. Fax (216)852-4421

CLBI-Cross Roads, (bi-m) Lutheran, Felicitas Ackermann, 4837-52A St., Camrose, AB T4V 1W5. Tel. (403)672-4454. Fax (403)672-4455

Cahiers de Spiritualité Ignatienne, (q) The Roman Catholic Church in Canada, Jean-Guy Saint-Arnaud, SJ, Centre de Spiritualité Manrése, 2370 Rue Nicolas-Pinel, Ste. Foy, QC G1V 4L6. Tel. (418)-653-6353. Fax (418)653-1208

Caledonia Times, (10/yr) The Anglican Church of Canada, Avis Hopkins, Diocese of Caledonia, Box 278, Prince Rupert, BC V8J 3P6. Tel. (604)624-6013. Fax (604)624-4299

Canada Armenian Press, (q) Armenian Evangelical Church, Y. Sarmazian, P.O. Box 42015, 2851 John St., Markham, ON L3R 5R0. Tel. (905)305-8144. Fax (905)305-8125

Canada Lutheran, (9/yr) Evangelical Lutheran Church in Canada, Kenn Ward, 1512 St. James St., Winnipeg, MB R3H 0L2. Tel. (204)786-6707. Fax (204)783-7548

Canadian Adventist Messenger, (12/yr) Seventh-day Adventist Church in Canada, June Polishuk, Maracle Press, 1156 King St. E, Oshawa, ON L1H 7N4. Tel. (905)723-3438. Fax (905)428-6024

Canadian Baptist, The, (10/yr) Canadian Baptist Ministries, Baptist Convention of Ontario and Quebec, Larry Matthews, 195 The West Mall, Ste.414, Etobicoke, ON M9C 5K1. Tel. (416)622-8600. Fax (416)622-0780

Canadian Disciple, (4/yr) Christian Church (Disciples of Christ) in Canada, Stanley Laurel Litke, 255 Midvalley Dr. SE, Calgary, AB T2X 1K8.

Canadian Friend, The, (bi-m) Canadian Yearly Meeting of the Religious Society of Friends, Anne Marie Zilliacus, 91A Fourth Ave., Ottawa, ON K1S 2L1. Tel. (613)567-8628. Fax (613)567-1078

Canadian Jewish News, (50/yr) Jewish, ----, 10 Gateway Blvd., Ste. 420, Don Mills, ON M3C 3A1. Tel. (416)422-2331. Fax (416)422-3790

Canadian Jewish Outlook, (8/yr) Jewish, Henry M. Rosenthal, 6184 Ash St., #3, Vancouver, BC V5Z 3G9. Tel. (604)-324-5101. Fax (604)325-2470

Canadian Lutheran, (10/yr) Lutheran Church--Canada, Ian Adnams, 3074 Portage Ave., Winnipeg, MB R3K 0Y2.

Canadian Orthodox Messenger, (q) Orthodox Church in America (Canada Section), Rhoda Zion, P.O. Box 179, Spencerville, ON K0E 1X0. Tel. (613)-925-5226. Fax (613)925-1521

Canadian Trumpeter Canada-West, (q) The Church of God of Prophecy in Canada, Vernon VanDeventer, 130 Centre St., Strathmore, AB T1P 1G9. Tel. (403)934-4787. Fax (403)934-4787

Catalyst, The, (10/yr) Nondenominational, Andrew Brouwer, 229 College St. #311, Toronto, ON M5T 1R4. Tel. (416)979-2443. Fax (416)979-2458

Catholic Register, The, (w) The Roman Catholic Church in Canada, Joseph Sinasac, 67 Bond St., Ste. 303, Toronto, ON M5B 1X6. Tel. (416)362-6822. Fax (416)362-8652

Catholic Times (Montreal), The, (10/yr) The Roman Catholic Church in Canada, Eric Durocher, 2005 St. Marc St., Montreal, QC H3H 2G8. Tel. (514)937-2301. Fax (514)937-3051

Central Canada Clarion, (q) The Wesleyan Church of Canada, Donald E. Hodeins, 3 Applewood Dr., Ste. 102, Belleville, ON K8P 4E3. Tel. (613)966-7527. Fax (613)968-6190

Channels, (q) The Presbyterian Church in Canada, J. H. Kouwenberg, 5800 University Blvd., Vancouver, BC V6T 2E4. Tel. (604)224-3245. Fax (604)224-3097

China and Ourselves, (q) Interdenominational, Cynthia K. McLean, 129 St. Clair Ave. W., Toronto, ON M4V 1N5. Tel. (416)921-1923. Fax (416)921-3843

Chinese Herald, (q) Canadian Conference of Mennonite Brethren Churches, Keynes Kan, 340 Ellesmere St., Vancouver, BC V5B 3S9. Tel. (604)298-8277

Christian Contender, The, (m) Mennonite, Mervin J. Baer, Box 459, McBride, BC V0J 2E0. Tel. (604)569-2780. Fax (604)569-3256

Christian Courier, (w) Nondenominational, Bert Witvoet, 261 Martindale Rd., Unit 4, St. Catharines, ON L2W 1A1. Tel. (905)682-8311. Fax (905)-682-8313

Church News, (w) The Church of Jesus Christ of Latter-day Saints in Canada, Dell Van Orden, 30 E. 100 S., Salt Lake City, UT 84110.

Church of God Beacon, (q) Church of God (Cleveland, Tenn.), Canute Blake, P.O. Box 2036, Brampton Commercial Service Center, Brampton, ON L6T 3T0. Tel. (905)793-2213. Fax (905)793-2213

Clarion: The Canadian Reformed Magazine, (bi-w) Canadian and American Reformed Churches, J. Geertsema, One Beghin Ave., Winnipeg, MB R2J 3X5. Tel. (204)663-9000. Fax (204)663-9202

College News & Updates, (6/yr) Church of God (Anderson, Ind.), Bruce Kelly, 4704 - 55 St., Camrose, AB T4V 2B6. Tel. (403)672-0171. Fax (403)672-6888

Communications Bi Monthly, (6/yr) Congregational Christian Churches in Canada, Don Bernard, 5 Townsville Ct., Brantford, ON N3S 7H8. Tel. (519)751-0421. Fax (519)751-0852

Communicator, The, (4/yr) The Roman Catholic Church in Canada, Anne K. McLaughlin, GSIC, 290 St. Patrick St., Ottawa, ON K1N 5K5. Tel. (613)789-7925. Fax (613)789-7925

Companion Magazine, (m) The Roman Catholic Church in Canada, Richard Riccioli, OFM, Station F, Box 535, Toronto, ON M4Y 2L8. Tel. (416)690-5611. Fax (416)690-3320

Connexions, (4/yr) Interdenominational, Ulli Diemer, P.O. Box 158, Stn. D, Toronto, ON M6P 3J8. Tel. (416)537-3949

Covenant Messenger, The, (m) The Evangelical Covenant Church of Canada, Marc Evinger, RR 2, Wetaskiwin, AB T9A 1W9. Tel. (403)352-2721. Fax (403)352-6839

Cross Training, (q) Churches of Christ in Canada, Curtis Parker, 2402 Ewart Ave., Saskatoon, SK S7J 1Y6. Tel. (306)343-7884. Fax (306)343-1589

Crux, (q) Nondenominational, Donald M. Lewis, Regent College, 5800 University Blvd., Vancouver, BC V6T 2E4. Tel. (604)224-3245. Fax (604)224-3097

Diary, The, (m) Old Order Amish Church, Don Carpenter, P.O. Box 98, Gordonville, PA 17529. Tel. (717)768-7262

Die Botschaft, (w) Old Order Amish Church, James Weaver, Brookshire Publishing, Inc., 200 Hazel St., Lancaster, PA 17603. Tel. (717)392-1321. Fax (717)392-2078

Discover the Bible, (w) The Roman Catholic Church in Canada, Guy Lajoie, P.O. Box 2400, London, ON N6A 4G3. Tel. (519)439-7211. Fax (519)439-0207

EMMC Recorder, (m) Evangelical Mennonite Mission Conference, Henry Dueck, Box 52059 Niakwa P.O., Winnipeg, MB R2M 5P9. Tel. (204)253-7929. Fax (204)256-7384

Ecumenism/Oecuménisme, (q) Interdenominational, Philippe Thibodeau, 2065 Sherbrooke St. W, Montreal, QC H3H 1G6. Tel. (514)937-9176. Fax (514)937-2684

Edge, The, (m) The Salvation Army in Canada, Sharon Stinka, 2 Overlea Blvd., Toronto, ON M4H 1P4. Tel. (416)422-6110. Fax (416)422-6120

Eesti Kirik, (q) The Estonian Evangelical Lutheran Church, Edgar Heinsoo, 383 Jarvis St., Toronto, ON M5B 2C7. Tel. (416)925-5465. Fax (416)925-5688

En Avant!, (w) The Salvation Army in Canada, Betty Lessard, 2050,rue Stanley, bureau 602, Montreal, QB H3A 3G3. Tel. (514)288-2848. Fax (514)-849-7600

Ensign, The, (m) The Church of Jesus Christ of Latter-day Saints in Canada, Jay M. Todd, 50 E. South Temple St., 23rd Floor, Salt Lake City, UT 84105. Tel. (801)240-2950. Fax (801)240-5732

Enterprise, (q) Canadian Baptist Ministries, Donna Lee Pancorvo, 7185 Millcreek Dr., Mississauga, ON L5N 5R4. Tel. (905)821-3533. Fax (905)826-3441

Evangel: The Good News of Jesus Christ, (4/yr) Canadian and American Reformed Churches, D. Moes, 21804 52nd Ave., Langley, BC V3A 4R1. Tel. (604)-576-2124. Fax (604)576-2101

Evangelical Baptist, The, (m) The Fellowship of Evangelical Baptist Churches in Canada, Terry D. Cuthbert, 679 Southgate Dr., Guelph, ON N1G 4S2. Tel. (519)821-4830. Fax (519)821-9829

Expression, (q) Canadian Conference of Mennonite Brethren Churches, Burton Buller, 225 Riverton Ave., Winnipeg, MB R2L 0N1. Tel. (204)667-9576. Fax (204)669-6079

Faith Today, (bi-m) Interdenominational, Brian C. Stiller, Box 8800, Sta. B, Willowdale, ON M2K 2R6. Tel. (905)479-5885. Fax (905)479-4742

Faith and Fellowship, (17/yr) Church of the Lutheran Brethren, David Rinden, P.O. Box 655, Fergus Falls, MN 56538. Tel. (218)739-3336. Fax (218)739-5514

Family Life, (11/yr) Old Order Amish Church, Joseph Stoll, David Luthy, Elizabeth Wengerd, Delbert Farmwald, Martha Helmuth and David Wagler, Rt. 4, Aylmer, ON N5H 2R3.

Fellowship Magazine, (5/yr) The United Church of Canada, Gail Reid, Box 237, Barrie, ON L4M 4T2. Tel. (705)737-0114. Fax (705)726-7160

Free Methodist Herald, The, (m) Free Methodist Church in Canada, Donna Elford, 3719-44 St. SW, Calgary, AB T3E 3S1. Tel. (403)246-6838. Fax (403)686-3787

Glad Tidings, (6/yr) The Presbyterian Church in Canada, L. June Stevenson, Women's Missionary Society, 50 Wynford Dr., North York, ON M3C 1J7. Tel. (416)441-1111. Fax (416)441-2825

Global Village Voice, (q) The Roman Catholic Church in Canada, Jack J. Panozzo, 3028 Danforth Ave., Toronto, ON M4C 1N2. Tel. (416)698-7770. Fax (416)698-8269

Good News West, (bi-m) Churches of Christ in Canada, Jim Hawkins, 3460 Shelbourne St., Victoria, BC V8P 4G5. Tel. (604)592-4914. Fax (604)592-4945

Good Tidings, (m) Pentecostal Assemblies of Newfoundland, Roy D. King, P.O. Box 8895, Sta. A, St. John's, NF A1B 3T2. Tel. (709)753-6314. Fax (709)753-4945

Gospel Contact, The, (4/yr) Church of God (Anderson, Ind.), John D. Campbell, 4717 56th St., Camrose, AB T4V 2C4. Tel. (403)672-0772. Fax (403)672-6888

Gospel Herald, (m) Churches of Christ in Canada, Wayne Turner and Wayne Turner, 4904 King St., Beamsville, ON L0R 1B6. Tel. (905)563-7503. Fax (905)563-7503

Gospel Standard, The, (m) Nondenominational, Perry F. Rockwood, Box 1660, Halifax, NS B3J 3A1. Tel. (902)423-5540

Gospel Tidings, (m) Independent Holiness Church, R. E. Votary, 1564 John Quinn Rd., Greely, ON K4P 1J9. Tel. (613)-821-2237. Fax (613)821-4663

Gospel Witness, The, (18/yr) Association of Regular Baptist Churches (Canada), Daniel Lundy, 130 Gerrard St. E, Toronto, ON M5A 3T4. Tel. (416)925-3261. Fax (416)925-8305

Hallelujah, (bi-m) The Bible Holiness Movement, Wesley H. Wakefield, Box 223, Postal Stn. A, Vancouver, BC V6C 2M3. Tel. (604)498-3895

Herold der Wahrheit, (m) Old Order Amish Church, Cephas Kauffman, 1829 110th St., Kalona, IA 52247.

Horizons, (bi-m) The Salvation Army in Canada, Fred Ash, 2 Overlea Blvd., Toronto, ON M4H 1P4. Tel. (416)425-6118. Fax (416)422-6120

Huron Church News, (10/yr) The Anglican Church of Canada, Kevin Dixon, 220 Dundas St., 4th Fl., London, ON N6A 1H3. Tel. (519)434-6893. Fax (519)-673-4151

ISKRA, (22/yr) Union of Spiritual Communities of Christ (Orthodox Doukhobors in Canada), Elizabeth Semenoff, Box 760, Grand Forks, BC V0H 1H0. Tel. (604)442-8252. Fax (604)442-3433

IdeaBank, (q) Canadian Conference of Mennonite Brethren Churches, David Wiebe, Christian Ed. Office, 3-169 Riverton Ave., Winnipeg, MB R2L 2E5. Tel. (204)669-6575. Fax (204)654-1865

In Holy Array, (9/yr) Canadian and American Reformed Churches, E. Kampen, Canadian Ref. Young Peoples' Societies, 7949-202A St., Langley, BC V2Y 1W8. Tel. (604)888-1087

Insight Into, (bi-m) Netherlands Ref. Cong. of North America & Canada, H. Hofman, 46660 Ramona Dr., Chilliwack, BC V2P 7W6. Tel. (604)792-3755

Insight*Insound*In Touch, Interdenominational, J. V. Miller, 40 St. Clair Ave. E., Ste. 202, Toronto, ON M4T 1M9. Tel. (416)960-3953

Jewish Standard, (semi-m) Jewish, Julius Hayman, 77 Mowat Ave., Ste. 016, Toronto, ON M6K 3E3. Tel. (416)537-2696. Fax (416)789-3872

Journal of Psychology and Judaism, (q) Jewish, Reuven P. Bulka, 1747 Featherston Dr., Ottawa, ON K1H 6P4. Tel. (613)731-9119. Fax (613)521-0067

L'Église Canadienne, (11/yr) The Roman Catholic Church in Canada, Michael Maille, C.P. 990, Outremont, QC H2V 4S7. Tel. (514)278-3020. Fax (514)278-3030

Lien, Le, (11/yr) Canadian Conference of Mennonite Brethren Churches, Annie Brosseau, 1775 Édouard-Laurin, St. Laurent, QC H4L 2B9. Tel. (514)331-0878. Fax (514)331-0879

Liturgie, Foi et Culture (Bulletin natl. de liturgie), (4/yr) The Roman Catholic Church in Canada, Service des Éditions de la CECC, Office national de liturgie, 3530 rue Adam, Montréal, QC H1W 1Y8. Tel. (514)522-4930. Fax (514)-522-1557

Mandate, (4/yr) The United Church of Canada, Rebekah Chevalier, Div. of Communication, 3250 Bloor St W., Etobicoke, ON M8X 2Y4. Tel. (416)-231-5931. Fax (416)232-6004

Mantle, The, (m) Independent Assemblies of God International (Canada), A. W. Rassmussen, M.Div., P.O. Box 2130, Laguna Hills, CA 92654-9901. Tel. (714)859-0946. Fax (714)859-0683

Marketplace, The: A Magazine for Christians in Business, (bi-m) Interdenominational Mennonite, Wally Kroeker, 302-280 Smith St., Winnipeg, MB R3C 1K2. Tel. (204)956-6430. Fax (204)-942-4001

Mennonite Brethren Herald, (bi-w) Canadian Conference of Mennonite Brethren Churches, Jim Coggins, 3-169 Riverton Ave., Winnipeg, MB R2L 2E5. Tel. (204)669-6575. Fax (204)654-1865

Mennonite Historian, (q) Canadian Conference of Mennonite Brethren Churches, Conference of Mennonites in Canada, Abe Dueck and Lawrence Klippenstein, Ctr. for Menn. Brethren Studies, 169 Riverton Ave., Winnipeg, MB R2L 2E5. Tel. (204)669-6575. Fax (204)654-1865

Mennonite Reporter, (bi-w) Conference of Mennonites in Canada, Ron Rempel, 3-312 Marsland Dr., Waterloo, ON N2J 3Z1. Tel. (519)884-3810. Fax (519)884-3331

Mennonitische Post, Die, (bi-m) Interdenominational Mennonite, Abe Warkentin, Box 1120, 383 Main St., Steinbach, MB R0A 2A0. Tel. (204)326-6790. Fax (204)326-6302

Mennonitische Rundschau, (m) Canadian Conference of Mennonite Brethren Churches, Lorina Marsch, 3-169 Riverton Ave., Winnipeg, MB R2L 2E5. Tel. (204)669-6575. Fax (204)654-1865

Messenger (of the Sacred Heart), (m) The Roman Catholic Church in Canada, F. J. Power, Apostleship of Prayer, 661 Greenwood Ave., Toronto, ON M4J 4B3. Tel. (416)466-1195

Messenger of Truth, (bi-w) Church of God in Christ (Mennonite), Gladwin Koehn, P.O. Box 230, Moundridge, KS 67107. Tel. (316)345-2532. Fax (316)345-2582

Messenger, The, (bi-w) The Evangelical Mennonite Conference of Canada, Menno Hamm, Bd. of Church Ministries, Box 1268, Steinbach, MB R0A 2A0. Tel. (204)326-6401. Fax (204)-326-1613

Messenger, The, (6/yr) Church of God (Anderson, Ind.), C. Paul Kilburn, 65 Albacore Cres., Scarborough, ON M1H 2L2. Tel. (416)431-9800

Messenger, The, (q) The Reformed Episcopal Church of Canada, Michael Fedechko, P.O. Box 2532, New Liskeard, ON P0J 1P0. Tel. (705)647-4565. Fax (705)647-5429

Missions Today, (bi-m) The Roman Catholic Church in Canada, Leona Spencer, 3329 Danforth Ave., Scarborough, ON M1L 4T3. Tel. (416)699-7077. Fax (416)699-9019

Monitor, The, (m) The Roman Catholic Church in Canada, Patrick J. Kennedy, P.O. Box 986, St. John's, NF A1C 5M3. Tel. (709)739-6553. Fax (709)739-6458

N.A.B. Today, (6/yr) North American Baptist Conference, Barbara J. Binder, 1 S. 210 Summit Ave., Oakbrook Terrace, IL 60181. Tel. (708)495-2000. Fax (708)-495-3301

NEXUS, (9/yr) Conference of Mennonites in Canada, Roma Quapp, 600 Shaftesbury Blvd., Winnipeg, MB R3P 0M4. Tel. (204)888-6781. Fax (204)831-5675

National Bulletin on Liturgy, (4/yr) The Roman Catholic Church in Canada, J. Frank Henderson, 90 Parent Ave., Otttawa, ON K1N 7B1. Tel. (613)241-9461

New Church Canadian, (q) General Church of the New Jerusalem, Barry C. Halterman, 279 Burnhamthorpe Rd., Etobicoke, ON M9B 1Z6. Tel. (416)-239-3054. Fax (416)239-4935

New Freeman, The, (w) The Roman Catholic Church in Canada, Bill Donovan, One Bayard Dr., Saint John, NB E2L 3L5. Tel. (506)653-6806. Fax (506)653-6812

Newfoundland Churchman, (m) The Anglican Church of Canada, William Abraham, 28 Woodwynd St., St. John's, NF A1A 3C9. Tel. (709)754-7627. Fax (709)576-7122

News of Quebec, (q) Christian Brethren (also known as Plymouth Brethren), Richard Strout, 222 Alexander St., P.O. Box 1054, Sherbrooke, QC J1H 5L3. Tel. (819)820-1693. Fax (819)821-9287

Opening Doors, (6/yr) North American Baptist Conference, Marilyn Schaer, 1S. 210 Summit Ave., Oakbrook Terr., IL 60181. Tel. (708)495-2000. Fax (708)-495-3301

PMC: The Practice of Ministry in Canada, (4-5/yr) Interdenominational, Jim Taylor, 10162 Newene Rd., Winfield, BC V4V 1R2. Tel. (604)766-2778. Fax (604)766-2736

Passport, (q) Interdenominational, Larry Hamm, Briercrest Family of Schools, 510 College Dr., Caronport, SK S0H 0S0. Tel. (306)756-3200. Fax (306)756-3366

Pentecostal Testimony, (m) The Pentecostal Assemblies of Canada, Richard P. Hiebert, 6745 Century Ave., Mississauga, ON L5N 6P7. Tel. (905)542-7400. Fax (905)542-7313

Peoples Magazine, The, (q) Nondenominational, John David Hull, 374 Sheppard Ave. E, Willowdale, ON M2N 3B6. Tel. (416)222-3341. Fax (416)222-3344

Pioneer Christian Monthly, (m) Reformed Church in Canada, Jeff Kingswood, Reformed Church Center, RR #4, Cambridge, ON N1R 5S5. Tel. (519)622-1777. Fax (519)622-1993

Pourastan, (bi-m) The Canadian Diocese of the Armenian Holy Apostolic Church, W. Ouzounian, 615 Stuart Ave., Outremont, QC H2V 3H2. Tel. (514)279-3066. Fax (514)276-9960

Présence, (8/yr) The Roman Catholic Church in Canada, Jean-Claude Breton, Pères Dominicains, 2715 chemin de la Côte St. Catherine, Montréal, QC H3T 1B6. Tel. (514)739-9797. Fax (514)739-1664

Prairie Messenger, (w) The Roman Catholic Church in Canada, Andrew M. Britz, Box 190, Muenster, SK S0K 2Y0. Tel. (306)682-1772. Fax (306)682-5285

Presbyterian Message, The, (10/yr) The Presbyterian Church in Canada, Janice Carter, Kouchibouguac, NB E0A 2A0. Tel. (506)876-4379

Presbyterian Record, (m) The Presbyterian Church in Canada, John Congram, 50 Wynford Dr., North York, ON M3C 1J7. Tel. (416)441-1111. Fax (416)441-2825

Pulse, The, (4/yr) Evangelical Free Church of Canada, Rick Penner, EFCC Box 56109, Valley Ctr. P.O., Langley, BC V3A 8B3.

Quaker Concern, (q) Canadian Yearly Meeting of the Religious Society of Friends, Peter Chapman, 60 Lowther Ave., Toronto, ON M5R 1C7. Tel. (416)-920-5213. Fax (416)920-5214

Reformed Perspective: A Magazine for the Christian Family, (m) Canadian and American Reformed Churches, Allard Gunnink, 34 Parkwater Crescent, Winnipeg, MB R2C 4W7. Tel. (204)-224-9206. Fax (204)669-7013

Relations, (m) The Roman Catholic Church in Canada, Carolyn Sharp, 25 ouest, Jarry, Montreal, QC H2P 1S6. Tel. (514)387-2541. Fax (514)387-0206

Resource: The National Leadership Magazine, (5/yr) The Pentecostal Assemblies of Canada, Michael P. Horban, 6745 Century Ave., Mississauga, ON L5N 6P7. Tel. (905)542-7400. Fax (905)542-7313

Revival Fellowship News, (q) Interdenominational, Harold Lutzer, Canadian Revival Fellowship, Box 584, Regina, SK S4P 3A3. Tel. (306)522-3685. Fax (306)522-3686

Rupert's Land News, (10/yr) The Anglican Church of Canada, J. D. Caird, 935 Nesbitt Bay, Winnipeg, MB R3T 1W6. Tel. (214)453-6130

SR: Studies in Religion: Sciences religieuses, (q) Nondenominational, Peter Richardson, University College, University of Toronto, Toronto, ON M5S 1A1. Tel. (416)978-7149. Fax (416)-971-2027

Saints Herald, (m) Reorganized Church of Jesus Christ of Latter Day Saints, Roger Yarrington, The Herald Publishing House, P.O. Box 1770, Independence, MO 64055-0770. Tel. (816)252-5010. Fax (816)252-3976

Sally Ann, (m) The Salvation Army in Canada, Shirley Pavey, 2 Overlea Blvd., Toronto, ON M4H 1P4. Tel. (416)422-6113. Fax (416)422-6120

Saskatchewan Anglican, (10/yr) The Anglican Church of Canada, W. Patrick Tomalin, 1501 College Ave., Regina, SK S4P 1B8. Tel. (306)522-1608. Fax (306)352-6808

Scarboro Missions, (9/yr) The Roman Catholic Church in Canada, G. Curry, 2685 Kingston Rd., Scarborough, ON M1M 1M4. Tel. (416)261-7135. Fax (416)261-0820

Servant Magazine, (4/yr) Interdenominational, Phil Callaway, Prairie Bible Institute, Box 4000, Three Hills, AB T0M 2N0. Tel. (403)443-5511. Fax (403)-443-5540

Shantyman, The, (bi-m) Nondenominational, Arthur C. Dixon, 2476 Argentia Rd., Ste. 213, Mississauga, ON L5N 6M1. Tel. (905)821-6310. Fax (905)-821-6311

Sister Triangle, (q) Churches of Christ in Canada, Marge Roberts, Box 948, Dauphin, MB R7N 3J5. Tel. (204)638-8156. Fax (204)638-6025

Solia - The Herald, (m) The Romanian Orthodox Episcopate of America (Jackson, MI), David Oancea, P.O. Box 185, Grass Lake, MI 49240-0185. Tel. (517)-522-3656. Fax (517)522-5907

St. Luke Magazine, (m) Christ Catholic Church, Donald W. Mullan, 5165 Palmer Ave., Niagara Falls, ON L2E 3T9. Tel. (905)354-2329. Fax (905)354-9934

Stocnmik, Serbian Orthodox Church in the U.S.A. and Canada, Diocese of Canada, Vasilije Tomic and Milena Protich, 7470 McNiven Rd., RR 3, Campbellville, ON L0P 1B0. Tel. (905)878-0043. Fax (905)878-1909

Tidings, (10/yr) United Baptist Convention of the Atlantic Provinces, Margaret Ryan, 100 Arlington Dr., Moncton, NB E1E 3J1. Tel. (506)382-5654

Topic, (m) The Anglican Church of Canada, Lorie Chortyk, #302-814 Richards St., Vancouver, BC V6B 3A7. Tel. (604)-684-6306. Fax (604)684-7017

Trait d'Union, Le, (4-5/yr) Union d'Eglises Baptistes Françaises au Canada, Fritz Obas, 2285 Ave. Papineau, Montréal, QC H2K 4J5. Tel. (514)526-6643. Fax (514)526-9269

United Church Observer, (m) The United Church of Canada, Muriel Duncan, 478 Huron St., Toronto, ON M5R 2R3. Tel. (416)960-8500. Fax (416)960-8477

Update, (m) Lutheran Church--Canada, Ian Adnams, 3074 Portage Ave., Winnipeg, MB R3K 0Y2. . Fax (204)897-4319

VIP Communique, Timothy Peterson, 8459-160th St., Ste. 110, Surrey, BC V3S 3T9. Tel. (604)543-8414

Vie Chrétienne, La, (French, m) The Presbyterian Church in Canada, Jean Porret, 2302 Goyer, Montréal, QC H3S 1G9. Tel. (514)737-4168

Vie des Communautés religieuses, La, (5/yr) The Roman Catholic Church in Canada, Hélène Bruneau, 251 St-Jean-Baptiste, Nicolet, QC J3T 1X9. Tel. (819)293-8736. Fax (819)293-2419

Vie Liturgigue, (10/yr) The Roman Catholic Church in Canada, NOVALIS, 6255 rue Hutchinson, Bureau 103, Montreal, QC H2V 4C7. Tel. (800)668-2547

Visnyk: The Herald, (m) Ukrainian Orthodox Church of Canada, Stephan Jarmus, 9 St. John's Ave., Winnipeg, MB R2W 1G8. Tel. (204)582-0996. Fax (204)-582-5241

Voce Evangelica/Evangel Voice, (bi-m) Italian Pentecostal Church of Canada, Joseph Manafo and Daniel Ippolito, 384 Sunnyside Ave., Toronto, ON M6R 2S1. Tel. (416)766-6692. Fax (416)766-8014

War Cry, The, (bi-w) The Salvation Army in Canada, Edward Forster, 2 Overlea Blvd., Toronto, ON M4H 1P4. Tel. (416)425-2111. Fax (416)422-6120

Word Alive, (5/yr) Nondenominational, Dwayne Janke, Wycliffe Bible Translators of Canada, Box 3068, Stn. B, Calgary, AB T2M 4L6. Tel. (403)250-5411.

World:Journal of Unitarian Universalist Assoc., (bi-m) Unitarian Universalist, Linda Beyer McHugh, 25 Beacon St., Boston, MA 02108. Tel. (617)742-2100. Fax (617)367-3237

Young Companion, (11/yr) The Old Order Amish Church, Joseph Stoll and Christian Stoll, Rt. 4, Aylmer, ON N5H 2R3.

Young Soldier, The, (w) The Salvation Army in Canada, Sharon Stinka, 2 Overlea Blvd., Toronto, ON M4H 1P4. Tel. (416)422-6110. Fax (416)422-6120

12. INTERNATIONAL CONGREGATIONS

This directory lists International Congregations seeking to serve an international and ecumencial constituency using the English language.

The churches are listed within global regions and then alphabetically by country.

This list was provided by INTERNATIONAL CONGREGATIONS/Christians Abroad, 475 Riverside Dr., 6th Floor, New York, NY 10115-0050. Tel. (212)870-2463. Fax (212)870-3112.

EUROPE

Albania

International Protestant Assembly of Tirana, P.K. 1538, Tirana, Albania. Tel. [355] (042) 24549 Fax [355] (042) 34708

Austria

United Methodist Church, Sechshauser Strasse 56/2/6, A-1150 Vienna. Tel. [43] (01) 893-6989

Vienna Community Church, Schelleingasse #2/6, A-1040 Vienna. Tel. [43] (01) 50 55 233

Belgium

American Protestant Church, Veltwijklaan 297 B-2180 Ekeren, Antwerp. Tel./Fax [32] (03) 664 20 46

International Protestant Church, Kattenberg, 19 (campus of Int'l School), B-1170 Brussels. Tel. [32] (02) 673 05 81 or 660 27 10

Czechia Republic

International Church of Prague, Czech Brethren Church, Vrazova 4, 150 00 Praha 5, Smi'chov. Tel. [42] (02) 398 648

Denmark

International Church, Gjorlingsvej 10 DK-2900 Hellerup. Tel. [45] (031) 62 47 8

England

American Church in London, Whitefield Memorial Church, Tottenham Court Road, 79A London WIP 9HB. Tel. [44] (0171) 580 2791 or 722 58 46 Fax [44] (0171) 580 5013

International Community Church, Clive House, The Chase Knott Park, Oxshott, Surrey KT22 OH5. Tel. [44] (0932) 868 283 or 222 781 Fax [44] (0932) 868 927

St. Anne & St. Agnes Church, 8 Collingham Gardens, London SW5 OHW. Tel. [44] (0171) 373 5566 or 606 4986 Fax [44] (0171) 370-0299

Estonia

International Christian Fellowship, Meeting at Puhavaium Church, Tallinn. Tel. [358] (090) 446 776

Finland

International Evangelical Church, Runeberginkatu 39 A 56 SF-00100 Helsinki. Tel. [358] (0) 406 091 or 684 8051

France

Holy Trinity Episcopal Church, 11 rue de la Buffa, F-06000 Nice. Tel. [33] (093) 87 19 83

American Cathedral of the Holy Trinity, 23 Avenue George V, F-75008 Paris. Tel. [33] (01) 47 20 17 92

American Church in Paris, 65 Quai d'Orsay, F-75007 Paris. Tel. [33] (01) 47 05 07 99 or 45 55 98 48

Germany

American Church in Berlin, Onkel Tom Strasse 93 D-14169 Berlin. Tel. [49] (030) 813 2021

Berlin Methodist Church, Charlottenburg EmK, Berlin-Charlottenburg. Tel. [49] (030) 342-2462

American Protestant Church, PSC 117, Box 270, APO AE 09080. Tel. [49] (0228) 374 193 or 373 393 Fax [49] (0228) 374 723

Church of Christ the King (Episcopal), Sebastian Rinzstrasse 22, D-6000 Frankfurt am Main 1. Tel. (069) 550 184

Trinity Lutheran Church, Am Schwalbenschwanz 34, 60431 Frankfort am Main. Tel. [49] (069) 599 478, 512 552 or 598 602. Fax [49] (069) 599 845

Methodist English Language Ministry, Kirchenkanzlei, Wilhelm-Leuschner 8, D-60329 Frankfurt (M) 1. Tel. [49] (069) 236 117 or (06192) 62 497. Fax [49] (069) 239 375

Kaiserslautern Lutheran Church, Bruchstrasse 10, D-6750 Kaiserslautern. Tel. [49] (0631) 92 210

Methodist Church, Fuhlsbüttel EmK, Röntgenstrasse 1, Hamburg-Fuhlsbüttel. Tel. [49] (040) 523-3387

Church of the Ascension (Episcopal), Seyboth Strasse 4, D-8000 Munich 90. Tel. [49] (089) 648 185

Peace United Methodist Church, Frauenlobstrasse 5, D-80337 Munich. Tel. [49] (089) 231 1583 or 300 6100 Fax [49] (089) 231 1584

Greece

St. Andrew's Protestant Church, Xenopoulou 5, GR-15451 Neo Psychiko, Athens. Tel. [30] (01) 671 2368 Fax [30] (01) 277 0964

Hungary

International Church, Box 44, Budapest 1525. Tel./Fax [36] (01) 176 4518

Italy

St. James Episcopal Church, Via Bernardo Rucellai 13, Florence, I-50123. Tel. [39] (055) 294 417

All Saints Anglican Church, Via del Babuino 153B, Rome I-00187. Tel. [39] (06) 679 4357

Ponte Sant'Angelo Methodist Church, Via del Banco di Santo Spirito, 3, Rome I-00186. Tel. [39] (06) 686 8314

Rome Baptist Church, Piazza San Lorenzo in Lucina, 35, Rome I-00186. Tel. [39] (06) 892 6487 or 687 6652

St. Andrew's Church, Via XX Settembre 7, Rome I-00187. Tel. [39] (06) 482 7627

INTERNATIONAL CONGREGATIONS

St. Paul's Within the Walls (Episcopal), Via Napoli 58, Rome I-00184. Tel. [39] (06) 474 3569 or 463 339

Protestant English Church, Chiesa Evanglica Valdese, Corso Vittorio Emanuele 23, Turin I-10125. Tel [39] (011) 669 28 38 or 650 26 01 Fax [39] (011) 65 75 42

The Netherlands

Holland Methodist Church at Immanuel Kerk, Amsterdam de Der Kinderestraat or Avenue Concordia 111 Kraliengen, Rotterdam. Tel. [31] (072) 623 156

Trinity Church Eindhoven, Pensionaat Eikenburg Chapel, c/o Prof. van der Grintenlann, 18 NL-5652 NB Eindhoven. Tel. [31] (040) 512 580

American Protestant Church, Esther de Boer Van Rijklaan, 20, NL-2597 TJ The Hague. Tel. [31] (070) 324 44 90 Fax [31] (070) 326 21 11

Norway

American Lutheran Congregation, Fritznersgate 15, Postboks 3012, Elisenberg N-0207, Oslo 2. Tel. [47] (02) 22 44 35 84 Fax [47] (02) 22 44 30 15.

Stavanger International Church, Vaisenhusgt 41, 4012 Stavanger. Tel. [47] 51 56 48 43 or 51 52 21 21 Fax [47] 51 52 72 80

Poland

Warsaw International Church, ul. Zawojska 9, 02-927 Warsaw. Tel. [48] (22) 42 23 51

Portugal

International Evangelical Church, Apartado 109, 8100 Loule. Tel. [351] (089) 414 435

Russia

Moscow Protestant Chaplaincy, UPDK Hall, Ulitsa Ulofa Palme 5 Korpous 2 (behind the Swedish Embassy). Tel. [7] (095) 143-3562, 432-1532 or 252-2451 ext. 5426

Slovakia

English International Church/Bratislava, Palisady 46, #18, 811 06 Bratislava. Tel. [42] (07) 533 32 63

Spain

Community Church of Madrid, Parque Azul, P. 1, AC, E-28270 Colmenarejo (Madrid). Tel. [34] (01)858 9753

Sweden

Immanuel International Church, Kungstensgatan 17, S-113 57 Stockholm. Tel. [46] (08) 674 1307 or Fax [46] (08) 674 1330

International Church of Stockholm, Santa Clara Church, Box 2122, S-103 13 Stockholm. Tel. [46] (08) 726 30 00 Fax [46] (08) 10 70 71

Switzerland

Emmanuel Episcopal/American Church, 3 rue de Monthoux, CH-1201 Geneva. Tel. [41] (022) 732 8078

Evangelical Lutheran Church, 20 rue Verdaine, CH- 1204 Geneva. Tel./Fax [41] (022) 310 50 89 or 348 75 95

International Church, Swiss Methodist Church, Luzernerstr. 76, CH-6030 Ebikon Tel./Fax [41] (041) 36 42 28

International Protestant Ch./Zurich, French Reformed Church, Haringstrasse 20, CH-8001 Zurich. Tel. [41] (01) 262 5525 or 825 6483

MIDDLE EAST

Bahrain

National Evangelical Church, P.O. Box 1, Manama, Bahrain. Tel.[973] 254 508

Egypt

Alexandria Community Church, P.O. Box 258, Saraya, Alexandria E-21411. Tel. [20] (03) 857 525

St. Andrew's United Church, P.O. Box 367, Dokki, Cairo. Tel. [20] (02) 759 451 or 360 3527

Heliopolis Community Church, 27 Hassan Saddig St., Flat 9, Heliopolis 11341, Cairo. Tel. [20] (02) 291 4627 or 418 6828

Maadi Community Church, Box 218 Maadi, Cairo. Tel. [20] (02) 351 2755 or 353 2118

Jerusalem

Church of the Redeemer (Lutheran), P.O. Box 14076, Old City, Jerusalem, Israel. Tel. [972] (02) 281 049 or 276 111 Fax [972] (02) 281 049

Kuwait

National Evangelical Church, P.O. Box 80 Safat, 13001- Kuwait. Tel. [965] 240 7195 Fax [965] 243 1087

Libya

Union Church of Tripoli, Box 6397, Tripoli. Tel. [218] (021) 70531

Oman

Protestant Church in Oman, P.O. Box 1982 Ruwi 112. Tel. [968] 70 23 72 Fax [968]78 99 43

Salalah English-Speaking Congregation, Salalah Christian Centre, P.O. Box 19742, Salalah. Tel. [968] 23 56 77

Tunisia

Community Church, 5 rue des Protestants, 1006 Tunis, Bab Souika. Tel. [216] (01) 24 36 48

Turkey

Union Church of Istanbul, Dutch Chapel, Istiklal Caddesi 485 TR-80050 Beyoglu, Istanbul. Tel. [90] (212) 244 5212 or 244 5763 Fax [90] (212) 293-0509

United Arab Emirates

United Christian Church of Dubai, P.O. Box 8684, Dubai, U.A.E. Tel [971] (04) 442 509 or 314 969

AFRICA

Kenya

Methodist Community Church, P.O. Box 25030, Nairobi

Uhuru Hiway Lutheran Church, P.O. Box 44685, Nairobi

Mauritius

St. Columba's Presbyterian Church, 23 Palmerston Road, Pheonix, Mauritius. Tel. [230] 696-4404

South Africa

St. Peter's by the Lake Lutheran Church, P.O. Box 72023 - Parkview 2122, Johannesburg. Tel./Fax [27] (011) 646 5740

Tanzania

International English Congregation, Azania Front Lutheran Church, P.O. Box 1594, Dar es Salaam. Tel. [255] (051) 25127

Arusha Community Church, P.O. Box 117, Arusha.

NORTH AMERICA

Canada

Chalmers-Wesley United Church, 78 rue Ste-Ursule, Quebec City, Quebec, Canada G1R 4E8. Tel. (418)692-2640 or (418)692-0431 Fax (418)692-3876

Illinois

O'Hare Airport International Chapel, Mezzanine level/Terminal 2 (Central Terminal), P.O. Box 66353, Chicago, IL 60666. Tel. (708) 596-3050 or 333-0020

CENTRAL AMERICA/CARIBBEAN

Costa Rica

Escazu Christian Fellowship, Country Day School, Apartado 1462-1250, Escazu. Tel. [506] 231-5444 or 231-4159 Fax, [506] 289-7214

Union Church of San Jose, Apartado 4456, San Jose

Cuba

International Christian Community, Corner of K and 25th Streets, Vedado, Havana. Tel. [53] 32 0770 or 32 8266

Dominican Republic

Union Church of Santo Domingo with Epiphany Episcopal Church, Apartado 935, Santo Domingo. Tel. [809]689-2070 or 687-3707 Fax [809] 541-6550

El Salvador

Union Church of San Salvador, VIPSAL No. 238, P. O. Box 52-5364, Miami, FL 33152-5364. Tel. [503] 23 5505

Guatemala

Union Church of Guatemala, Apartado Postal 150-A, Guatemala City 01909. Tel. [502] 31 69 04

Haiti

Quisqueya Chapel, Rue Catalpa, P.O. Box 133438, Port-au-Prince. Tel. [509] 46-3948

Honduras

Union Christian Church, Apartado 1869, Tegucigalpa. Tel. [504] 32-3386 or 32-4454

Mexico

Union Evangelical Church, Reforma 1870-Lomas Chapultepec, Mexico City 11000 D.F. Tel. [52] (05) 520-0436 or 520-9931 Fax [52] (05) 202-8485

Union Church of Monterrey, Apartado 1317, 64000 Monterrey, N.L. Tel. [52] (08) 346-0541 or 347-1727

Panama

Balboa Union Church, APDO 3664, Balboa, Ancon. Tel. [507] 272-2295 or 228-0313 Fax [507] 228-0012

Gamboa Union Church, Apartado 44, Gamboa. Tel. [507] 56 64 70 or 56 68 30

Puerto Rico

Second Union Church of San Juan, Apolo Avenue & Mileto Street, Guaynabo 00969. Tel. (809) 720-4423 or 789-7178 Fax (809) 789-1380

Wesleyan Community Church, P.O. Box 2906, Guaynabo, PR 00970. Tel.(809)720-2595 or 790-4818

Grace Lutheran Church, Calle del Parque 150, Santurce 00911. Tel. (809) 722-5372 or 722-1137

St. John's Episcopal Cathedral, P.O. Box 9262, Santurce 00908. Tel. (809)722-3254 or 784 - 7883

Union Church of San Juan, 2310 Lauel Street, Punta Las Marias, Santurce 00913. Tel. (809)726-0280 or 726-0378

U.S. Virgin Islands

St. Croix Reformed Church, 4036 Judiths Fancy, Christiansted, 00820-4446. Tel. (809)778-0520

St. Thomas Reformed Church, PO Box 301769, St. Thomas, 00803-1769. Tel. (809) 776-8255

SOUTH AMERICA

Argentina

United Community Church, Avenida Santa Fe 839, Acassuso (1640), Buenos Aires. Tel. [54] (01) 792-1375

Bolivia

Community Church, Casilla 4718, La Paz. Tel. [591] (02) 78-6515 or 78-6525

Trinity Union Church, Santa Cruz Cooperative School, Casilla 5941, Santa Cruz. Tel. [591] (03) 32-3091 Fax (03) 36-6353

Brazil

Union Church of Brasilia, QE 30, Conj. Q, Casa 31, Guara I 71.065-170 Brasilia, DF. Tel. [55] (601)567-8602

Campinas Community Church, Caixa Postal 1114, 13.100-970, Campinas, Sao Paolo. Tel. [55] (0192) 322 722 Fax [55] (0192) 322 609

Union Church of Rio de Janiero, Caixa Postal 37530 CEP 22642-970, Rio de Janiero, RJ. Tel. [55] (021) 325-8601

Fellowship Community Church, Rua Carlos Sampaio, 107, 01333-021 Bela Vista, Sao Paulo S.P. Tel. [55] (011) 287-2294 or 844-1153

Chile

Santiago Community Church, Avenida Holanda 151, Santiago, 9

Colombia

Union Church of Bogota, Apartado Aereo 52615, Bogota, D.E. Tel. [57] (01) 248-5115

Ecuador

Advent-St. Nicholas Church, Apartado 17-03-415A, Quito. Tel. [593] (02) 507-494 or 528-533

English Christian Fellowship, Casilla 17-17-691, Quito. Tel. [593] (02) 342 447-262 or 466-808 x355. Fax [593] (02) 447-263

Peru

Union Church of Lima, Casilla 18-0298, Miraflores, Lima 18. Tel. [51] (14) 41-1472 or 41-4882

Uruguay

Christ Church, Arocena 1907, Montevideo. Tel. [598] (02) 61 03 00 or 60 27 11

Venezuela

United Christian Church, Apartado 60320, Caracas 1060-A. Tel. [58] (02) 761-3901 or 993-0546 or (031) 94 65 89 Fax [58] (02) 761-3902

Christ Church, Apartado 10160, Maracaibo. Tel. [58] (061) 977 548

Protestant Church of Puerto Ordaz, Apartado 229, Estado Bolivar, Puerto Ordaz, 8015A. Tel. [58] (86) 22 89 48

ASIA

Bangladesh

Dhaka International Christian Church, American International School, P.O. Box 6010 Gulsha, Dhaka 12

China

Beijing International Christian Fellowship in Sino-Japanese Youth Exchange Center, 40 Liange Ma Qiso Lu, Beijing

Congregation of the Good Shepherd, Western Academy of Beijing. Tel. [86] (010) 495-4912 Fax [86] (010) 467-8013.

English-Language Christian Fellowship, St. Paul's Church, c/o Amity Foundation, 17 Da Jian Tin Xiang, Nanjing, 210029 Tel. [86] (025)650-5069

Hong Kong

Kowloon Union Church, 4 Jordan Road, Kowloon. Tel. [852] 367-2585 or 369-3500 Fax [852] 723-6575.

Hong Kong Union Church, 22A Kennedy Road, Mid-Levels. Tel. [852] 2523-7247 or 2523-3027 Fax [852] 2524-0473

Church of All Nations (Lutheran), 6 South Bay Close, Repulse Bay, Hong Kong. Tel. [852] 812-0375 or 873-3585 Fax [852] 812-9508

Methodist Church, 271 Queens Road East, Wanchai. Tel. [852] 5-757 817 or 5-849 6632

India

St. Andrew's Church, (C.N.I.)15 B.B.D. Bag, Calcutta 700 001. Tel. [91] (033) 20-1994

St. Paul's Cathedral, (C.N.I.) Cathedral Road, Calcutta 700 001. Tel.[91] (033) 28-2802 or 28-5127

Centenary Methodist Church (C.N.I.), 25, Lodi Road at Flyover, New Delhi 110 003. Tel. [91] (011) 36-5396

Church of the Redemption (C.N.I.), Church Road (North Avenue), New Delhi 110 001. Tel. [91] (011) 301-4458

Free Church (C.N.I.), 10, Sansad Marg, New Delhi 110 001. Tel. [91] (011) 31-1331

Free Church Green Park (C.N.I.), A24 Green Park, New Delhi 110 016.[91] Tel. (011) 66-4574

Indonesia

Jakarta Community Church, Jalan Iskandarsyah II/176, Jakarta 12160. Tel. [62] (021) 772- 3325

Japan

Kobe Union Church, 2-4-4 Nagamindai, Nada-ku, Kobe 657. Tel. [81] (078) 871-6844 or 858-2053 Fax [81] (078) 871-3473

Nagoya Union Church, Kinjo Church UCC, Box 170, Higashi P.O., Nagoya 461-91. Tel. [81] (052) 932-1066 or 772-3043 Fax [81] (052) 931-6421

Osaka International Church, c/o Osaka Christian Centre 24-47, 2-chome Tamatsukuri, Chuo-ku, Osaka 540. Tel [81] (06) 768-4385 Fax [81] (06) 768-8085

Christ of All Nations Church, 22-1 Furuedai, 1 chome, Suita-shi, Osaka-fu 562. Tel. [81] (06) 872-3395 Fax [81] (06) 872-2197

St. Alban's Anglican/Episcopal Church, 6-25 Shiba-koen 3-chome, Minato-ku, Tokyo 105. Tel.[81] (03) 431-8534 or 432-6040 Fax [81] (03) 5472-4766

St. Paul International Lutheran Church, 1-2-32. Fujimi, 1-chome, Chiyoda-ku, Tokyo 102. Tel.[81] (03) 3261-3740 or 3262-8623

Tokyo Union Church, 7-7, Jingumae 5-chome, Shibuya-ku, Tokyo 150. Tel.[81] (03) 3400-0047 Fax [81] (03) 3400-1942

West Tokyo Union Church, c/o Claudia Genung-Yamamoto 1-14-6 Tamacho, Fuchu-shi, Tokyo 183. Tel./Fax [81] (0423) 69-1942

Yokohama Union Church, 66 Yamate-cho, Naka-ku, Yokohama 231. Tel./Fax [81] (045) 651-5177

Korea

International Lutheran Church, 726-39 Hannam-2 Dong, Yongsan-ku, Seoul 140-212. Tel.[82] (02) 794-6274 Fax [82] (02)755-4978

Onnuri Presbyterian Church, 241-96 Sobbingo-dong, Yongsan-ku, Seoul 140-240. Tel. [82] (02) 741-43543 or 336-9690 Fax [82] (02) 741-4355

Seoul Union Church, Memorial Chapel at Foreigners' Cemetery Park, 144 Hapchung-Dong, Mapo-ku, Seoul 122-220. Tel. [82] (02) 333-7393 or 333-0838 Fax [82] (02) 333-7493

Malaysia

St. Andrew's Presbyterian Church, The International Church of Kuala Lumpur, 29/31 Jalan Raja Chulan. 50200 Kuala Lumpur. Tel. [60] (03) 232-5687 or 230-5610 Fax [60] (03) 230-2567

Nepal

Kathmandu International Christian Congregation, St. Xavier's School, Jawalakhel, Box 654, Kathmandu. Tel.[977] (01) 525-176 or 522 687

Pakistan

Protestant International Congregation, P.O. Box 2301, Isalamabad. Tel[92] (051) 221 571 or 215 664 Fax [92] (051) 820 648

International Church of Karachi, P.O. Box 12251, Karachi 75500. Tel./Fax [92] (021) 585 3282 or 585 0776

International Christian Fellowship, P.O. Box 10164, Lahore 54600. Tel. [92] (042)879 955 or 305 867

Philippines

Union Church of Manila, Box 1386, MCPO, Makati, Metro Manila. Tel. [63] (02) 892-1631 or 632-3019 Fax [63] (02) 818-0362

Singapore

Lutheran Church of Our Redeemer, 28-30 Dukes Road, Singapore 1026. Tel. [65] 466-4500 or 467-5093

Orchard Road Presbyterian Church, 3 Orchard Road, Singapore 0923. Tel. [65] 337-6681

St. George's Church (Anglican), Minden Road, Tanglin, Singapore 1024. Tel. [65] 473-2783

Sri Lanka

St. Andrew's Church, Colomba, 73 Galle Road, Colomba 3. Tel. [94] (01) 323 765 Fax [94] (01) 431 657

Taiwan

Hsinchu International Church, Jyen Hwa Street - #49, 7F, Hsinchu. Tel. [886] (035) 776-852, 955-500 or 778-442

Kaohsiung Community Church, 151 Ren Yi Street, Kaohsiung 80208, R.O.C. Tel. [886] (07) 331-8131

Taipei International Church, Taipei American School, 7F, 248 Chung Shan North Road, Sec. 6, Taipei, 11135 R.O.C. Tel. [886] (02) 833-7444 Fax [886] (02) 835-2778

St. James Episcopal Church, 23, Wu-chuan West Road, Taichung. Tel.[886] (04) 372-5392 Fax [886] (04) 372-2752

Thailand

International Church of Bangkok, 61/2 Soi Saen Sabai, Sukhumvit 36 (Rama IV Road), Bangkok 10110. Tel./Fax [66] (02) 258-5821 or 260-8187

Evangelical Church of Bangkok, 42 Soi 10, Sukhumvit Road, Bangkok, 10110. Tel. [66] (02) 270-0693

Chiang Mai Community Church, P.O. Box 18, Chiang Mai 50000. Tel. [66] (053) 248 466

OCEANIA

American Samoa

Community Christian Church, Ottoville, P.O. Box 1016, Pago Pago 96799. Tel. [684] 699-1544 or 699-9184

Guam

Guam United Methodist Church, P.O. Box 20279 GMF, Barrigada 96921-0279. Tel. [671] 477-8357

Papua New Guinea

Boroko Baptist Church, P.O. Box 1689, Boroko, NCD. Tel. [675] 325-4410 Fax 325-9275

13. DEPOSITORIES OF CHURCH HISTORY MATERIAL

Kenneth E. Rowe
Drew University

Most American denominations have established central archival-manuscript depositories. In addition, many large communions have formed regional (conference, diocesan, synodical or provincial) depositories. Denominations with headquarters in the United States may also have churches in Canada. Historical material on Canadian sections of these denominations will occasionally be found at the various locations cited below. The reader is also referred to the section "In Canada," which follows.

The section for the United States was compiled by Kenneth E. Rowe. Neil Semple, Jean Dryden and Alex Thomson contributed to the Canadian section.

IN THE UNITED STATES

The most important general guide is *Directory of Archives and Manuscript Repositories* in the United States, 2nd edition, compiled by the National Historical Publications and Records Commission. New York : Oryx Press, 1988.

Major Ecumenical Collections:

American Antiquarian Society, 185 Salisbury St., Worcester, MA 01609 Tel (617)755-5221

American Bible Society Library, 1865 Broadway, New York, NY 10023-9980. Tel (212)408-1495 Fax (212)408-1512. Peter Wosh

Amistad Research Center, Old U.S.Mint Building, 400 Esplanade Ave., New Orleans, LA 70116. Tel (504)522-0432

Billy Graham Center Archives, Wheaton College, 510 College Ave., Wheaton, IL 60187-5593. Tel (708)752-5910. Robert Schuster

Boston Public Library, Copley Square, Boston, MA 02117-0286. Tel (617)536-5400 Fax (617)236-4306

Graduate Theological Union Library, 2400 Ridge Road, Berkeley, CA 94709 Tel (415)649-2540 Fax (415)649-1417. Oscar Burdick

Harvard University (Houghton Library) Cambridge, MA 02138 Tel (617)495-2440

Howard University, Moorland-Springarn Research Center, 500 Howard Place, N.W., Washington, DC 20059 Tel (202)636-7480

Huntingdon Library, 1151 Oxford Road, San Marino, CA 91108 Tel (213)792-6141.

National Council of Churches Archives, in Presbyterian Church USA Office of History Library, 425 Lombard St., Philadelphia, Pa 19147. Tel (215)627-0509. Fax (215)627-0509. Gerald W. Gillette

Newberry Library, 60 W. Walton St., Chicago, IL 60610-3394. Tel (312)943-9090.

New York Public Library, Fifth Ave. & 42nd St. New York, NY 10018. Tel (212)930-0800 Fax (212)921-2546.

Schomburg Center for Research in Black Culture, 515 Malcolm X Blvd., New York, NY 10037. Tel (212)862-4000. Howard Dodson

Union Theological Seminary (Burke Library) 3041 Broadway, New York, NY 10027. Tel (212)280-1505 Fax (212)280-1416. Richard D. Spoor. Includes Missionary Research Library

University of Chicago (Regenstein Library) 1100 E. 57th St. Chicago, IL 60637-1502. Tel (312)702-8740. Curtis Bochanyin

University of Texas Libraries, P.O. Box P, Austin, TX 78713-7330. Tel (512)471-3811 Fax (512)471-8901.

Yale Divinity School Library, 409 Prospect St. New Haven, CT 06510 Tel (203)432-5291. Includes Day Missions Library

Yale University (Sterling Memorial Library) 120 High St., P.O. Box 1603A Yale Station, New Haven, CT 06520. Tel (203)432-1775. Fax (203)432-7231 Katharine D. Morton

Adventist:

Andrews University (James White Library), Berrien Springs, MI 49104 Tel (616) 471-3264. Mr. Warren Johns.

Auroro University (Charles B. Phillips Library) 347 S. Gladstone, Aurora, IL 60506 Tel (708) 844-5437. Ken VanAndel. Advent Christian Church Archives

Berkshire Christian College (Linden J. Carter Library) Lenox, MA 01240

Seventh Day Adventists General Conference Archives, 6840 Eastern Ave. NW, Washington, DC 20012 Tel (212)722-6000

Baptist:

American Baptist Archives Center, P.O. Box 851, Valley Forge, PA 19482-0851. Tel (215)768-2000. Beverly Carlson, administrator.

American Baptist-Samuel Colgate Historical Library, 1106 S. Goodman St., Rochester, NY 14620-2532. Tel (716)473-1740. James R. Lynch.

Andover Newton Theological School, (Franklin Trask Library) 169 Herrick Road, Newton Centre, MA 02159 Tel (617) 964-1100. Ms. Sharon A. Taylor. Includes Backus Historical Library.

Bethel Theological Seminary Library, 3949 Bethel Dr., St. Paul, MN 55112 Tel (612)638-6184. Dr. Norris Magnuson. Swedish Baptist Collection.

Elon College (Iris Holt McEwen Library) P.O. Box 187, Elon, NC 27244-2010 Tel (919)584-2479. Diane Gill, archivist. Primitive Baptist Archives.

Seventh Day Baptist Historical Society Library, 3120 Kennedy Rd., P.O. Box 1678, Janesville, WI 53547 Tel (608)752-5055. Janet Thorngate.

Southern Baptist Historical Library & Archives, 901 Commerce St., Suite 400, Nashville TN 37203-3620. Tel (615)244-0344. Fax (615)242-2153. Bill Sumner, director of library and archives.

Brethren in Christ:

Messiah College (Murray Learning Resources Center) Grantham, PA 17027-9990 Tel (717)691-6042. E. Morris Sider.

Church of the Brethren:

Bethany Theological Seminary Library, Butterfield and Meyers Roads, Oak Brook, IL 60521. Tel (708) 620-2214. Dr. Helen K. Mainelli.

Brethren Historical Library and Archives, 1451 Dundee Ave., Elgin, IL 60120 Tel (708)742-5100. Kenneth M. Shaffer, Jr.

Juniata College (L. A. Beeghly Library) 18th & Moore, Huntingdon, PA 16652. Tel (814)314-6286. Peter Kupersmith.

Churches of Christ:

Abilene Christian University (Brown Library) 1700 Judge Ely Blvd., ACU Station, P.O. Box 8177, Abilene, TX 79699-8177. Tel (915)674-2344. Marsha Harper

Harding Graduate School of Religion (L.M.Graves Memorial Library) 1000 Cherry Rd., Memphis, TN 38117. Tel. (901)761-1354. Don Meredith.

Pepperdine University (Payson Library) Malibu, CA 90263. Tel (213)456-4243. Harrold Holland

Churches of God, General Conference:

University of Findlay (Shafer Library) 1000 N. Main St., Findlay, OH 45840-3695. Tel (419)424-4612. Fax (419)424-4757. Robert W. Shirmer. Archives/Museum of the Churches of God in North America.

Congregational: (See United Church of Christ)

Disciples of Christ:

Brite Divinity School Library, Texas Christian University, P.O. Box 32904, Fort Worth, TX 76219. Tel (817)921-7106. Fax (817) 921-7110. Robert Olsen, Jr.

Christian Theological Seminary Library, P.O. Box 88267, 1000 W. 42nd St., Indianapolis, IN 46208. Tel (317)924-1331. David Bundy.

Culver-Stockton College (Johnson Memorial Library) College Hill, Canton, MO 63435. Tel (314)288-5221. Fax (314)288-3984. John Sperry, Jr.

Disciples Divinity House, University of Chicago,1156 E. 57th St., Chicago, IL 60637 Tel (312)643-4411

Disciples of Christ Historical Society Library, 1101 Nineteenth Ave., S., Nashville, TN 37212-2196. Tel (615)327- 1444. Dr. James Seale.

Lexington Theological Seminary (Bosworth Memorial Library) 631 South Limestone St., Lexington, KY 40508 Tel (606)252-0361 Fax (606)281-6042. Philip N. Dare

Episcopal:

Archives of the Episcopal Church, P.O. Box 2247, 606 Rathervue Pl., Austin, TX 78768 Tel (512)472-6816. V. Nelle Bellamy

Episcopal Divinity School Library, 99 Brattle St. Cambridge, MA 02138 Tel (617)868-3450. James Dunkly

General Theological Seminary (Saint Mark's Library) 175 Ninth Ave., New York, NY 10011. Tel (212)243-5150. David Green.

Nashotah House Library, 2777 Mission Road, Nashotah, WI 53058-9793. Tel (414)646-3371 Fax (414)646-2215 Mike Tolan.

National Council, The Episcopal Church, 815 2nd Ave., New York, NY 10017. Tel (212)867-8400.

Yale Divinity School Library, 409 Prospect Street, New Haven, CT 06510 Tel (203)432-5291. Berkeley Divinity School Collection.

Evangelical and Reformed

Hartford Seminary (Educational Resources Center) 77 Sherman St., Hartford, CT 06105 Tel (203)232-4451. William Peters

Harvard Divinity Schol (Andover Harvard Theological Library) 45 Francis Ave., Cambridge, MA 02138. Tel (617)495-5770. Russell O. Pollard.

Lancaster Theological Seminary, Archives of the United Church of Christ (Philip Schaff Library) Lancaster Theological Seminary, 555 W. James St., Lancaster, PA 17603 Tel (717)393-0654. Richard R. Berg

Yale Divinity School Library, 409 Prospect Street, New Haven, CT 06510. Tel (203)432-5291

Yale University (Sterling Memorial Library) Yale University, 120 high St., Box 1603A Yale Station, New Haven, CT 06520 Tel (203)436-0907

Evangelical Congregational Church:

Evangelical School of Theology (Rostad Library), 121 S. College St., Myerstown, PA 17067. Tel (717)866-5775. Fax (717) 866-4667. Terry Heisey. Historical Society Library of the Evangelical Congregational Church

Friends:

Friends' Historical Library, Swarthmore College, 500 College Ave., Swarthmore, PA 19081. Tel (215)328-8557. Fax (215)328-8673. Mary Ellen Chijioke, curator.

Haverford College (Magill Library) Haverford, PA 19041-1392. Tel (215)-896-1175. Fax (215)896-1224. Edwin Bronner

Jewish:

American Jewish Archives, 3101 Clifton Ave., Cincinnati, OH 45220 Tel (513)221-1875. Kevin Proffit.

Friedman Memorial Library, American Jewish Historical Society, 2 Thornton Rd., Waltham, MA 02154 Tel (617)891-8110. Fax (617)899-9208. Bernard Wax, director of special projects.

YIVO Institute for Jewish Research, Library & Archives, 1048 Fifth Ave., New York, NY 10028. Tel (212)535-6700. Zachary Baker, librarian; Marek Weber, archivist.

Latter-Day Saints:

Church of Jesus Christ of the Latter-Day Saints Library-Archives, Historical Department, 50 E. North Temple St., Salt Lake City, UT 84150. Tel (801)240-2745. Steven Sorenson

Family History Library, 35 North West Temple St., Salt Lake City, UT 84150. Tel (801) 240-2331 Fax (801)240-5551 David M. Mayfield.

Lutheran:

Augustana College (Swenson Swedish Immigration History Center) Box 175, Rock Island, IL 61201. Tel (309)794-7221. Kermit Westerberg.

Evangelical Lutheran Church in American Archives, 8765 West Higgins Road, Chicago, IL 60631-4198. Tel 1-800-NET-ELCA or (312) 380-2818. Elisabeth Wittman

Region 1 (Alaska, Idaho, Montana, Oregon and Washington) Pacific Lutheran University (Mortvedt Library) Tacoma, WA 98447 Tel (206)535-7587. Kerstin Ringdahl

Region 2 (Arizona, California, Colorado, Hawaii, New Mexico, Nevada, Utah, Wyoming) Pacific Lutheran Theological Seminary, 2770 Marin Ave., Berkeley, CA, 94708; contact Ray Kibler III, 4249 N. LaJunta Drive, Claremont, CA 91711-3199.

Region 3 (Minnesota, North Dakota, South Dakota) Paul Daniels, Region 3 Archives, ELCA, 2481 Como Avenue West, Saint Paul, MN 55108-1445. Tel (612)641-3205

Region 4 (Arkansas, Kansas, Louisiana, Missouri, Nebraksa, Oklahoma, Texas) No archives established.

Region 5 (Illinois, Iowa, Wisconsin, Upper Michigan) Robert C. Wiederaenders, Region 5 Archives, ELCA, 333 Wartburg Place, Dubuque, IA 52001

Region 6 (Indiana, Kentucky, Michigan, Ohio) No archives established.

Region 7 (New York, New Jersey, Eastern Pennsylvania, New England and the non-geographic Slovak-Zion Synod) John E. Peterson, Region 7 Archives, ELCA, 7301 Germantown Ave., Philadelphioa, PA 19119 Tel (215)248-4616. For Metropolitan New York Synod : David Gaise, 32 Neptune Road, Toms River, NJ 08753

Region 8 (Delaware, Maryland, Central and Western Pennsylvania, West Virginia, Washington, DC) Paul A. Mueller, Thiel College, Greenville, PA 16125 Tel (412)588-7000; (Central Pennsylvania, Delaware, Eastern Maryland, and Washington, DC) Lutheran Theological Seminary (Wentz Library) 66 Confederate Ave., Gettysburg, PA 17325 Tel (717)334-6286. Donald Matthews

Region 9 (Alabama, North and South Carolina, Florida, Georgia, Mississippi, Tennessee, Virginia, and the Caribbean Synod) Lutheran Theological Southern Seminary, 4201 N. Main St., Columbia, SC 29203-5898. Tel (803)786-5150. Lynn A. Feider

Concordia Historical Institute (Dept. of Archives and History, Lutheran Church-Missouri Synod) 801 De Mun Ave., St. Louis, MO 63105-3199. Tel (314)721-5934, Ext 320,321. August R. Suelflow

Concordia Seminary (Fuerbringer Hall library) 801 DeMun Avenue, St. Louis, MO 63105. Tel (314) 721-5934. David O. Berger.

Finnish-American Historical Archives, Suomi College, Hancock, MI 49930. Tel (906)482-5300, ext 273.

Luther College (Preus Library) Decorah, IA 52101. Tel (319)387-1191. Fax (319)382-3717. Ted Stark.

Lutheran School of Theology at Chicago (Jesuit/Kraus/ McCormick Library) 1100 East 55th St., Chicago, IL 60615 Tel (312)753-0739. Mary R. Bischoff

Saint Olaf College (Rolvaag Memorial Library) 1510 St. Olaf Ave., Northfield, MN 55057-1097. Tel (507)663-3225 Joan Olson. Norwegian Lutheran collection.

Wisconsin Lutheran Seminary Archives, 11831 N. Seminary Drive, 65W, Mequon, WI 53092. Tel (414)272-7200. Martin Westerhaus

Mennonite:

Archives of the Mennonite Church, 1700 South Main, Goshen, IN 46526. Tel (219)533-3161, Ext 477

Associated Mennonite Biblical Seminaries, Library, 1445 Boonveille Ave, Northwest Dock, Springfield, MO 65802. Tel (417)862-3344. Joseph F. Marics, Jr.

Bethel College, Historical Library, P.O. Drawer A, North Newton, KS 67117-9998. Tel (316)283-2500, Ext 366. Fax (316)284-5286. Dale R. Schrag.

Bluffton College (Mennonite Historical Library) Bluffton, OH 45817 Tel (419)358-8015, ext 271.

Center for Mennonite-Brethren Studies, 4824 E. Butler, Fresno, CA 93727 Tel (209)251-7194, Ext 1055.

Eastern Mennonite College (Menno Simons Historical Library and Archives) Eastern Mennonite College, Harrisonburg, VA 22801 Tel (703)433-2771, ext 177

Goshen College (Mennonite Historical Library) Goshen, IN 46526 Tel (219)535-7418

Mennonite Historians of Eastern Pennsylvania Library and Archives, P.O. Box 82, 656 Yoder Road, Harleysville, PA 19438. Tel (215)256-3020. Joel D. Alderfer

Methodist:

A.M.E.Zion Church, Dept. of Records & Research, P.O. Box 32843, Charlotte, NC 28232. Tel. (704)332-3851 Fax (704)333-1769.

Asbury Theological Seminary (B. L. Fisher Library) Wilmore, KY 40390-1199. Tel (606)858-3581. David W. Faupel

Boston University School of Theology (New England Methodist Historical Society Library) 745 Commonwealth Ave., Boston, MA 02215. Tel (617)353-3034. Stephen Pentek.

Christian Methodist Episcopal Archives, Southern Center for Studies in Public Policy, Clark Atlanta University, 223 James P. Brawley Dr., Atlanta, GA 30314. Tel (404)880-8085 FAX (404)880-8090

Cincinnati Historical Society (Nippert German Methodist Collection) The Museum Center, Cincinnati Union Terminal, 1301 Western Ave., Cincinnati, OH 45403. Tel (513)287-7068. Jonathan Dembo

Drew University Library, Madison, NJ 07940. Tel (201) 408-3590, Fax 201-408-3909. E-mail: krowe@drew.edu Kenneth E. Rowe, Methodist Librarian.

Duke Divinity School Library, Duke University, Durham, NC 27708-0972. Tel (919)660-3452 Fax (919)681-7594. E-mail: rll@mail.lib.duke.edu Roger L. Loyd.

Emory University, Candler School of Theology (Pitts Theology Library) Atlanta, GA 30322. Tel (404)727-4165 Fax (404)727-2915. M. Patrick Graham

Free Methodist World Headquarters (Marston Memorial Historical Center) Winona Lake, IN 46590. Tel (219)267-7656. Frances Haslam

Garrett-Evangelical Theological Seminary (United Library) 2121 Sheridan Rd, Evanston, IL 60201. Tel (708)866-3900. David Himrod

General Commission on Archives and History, The United Methodist Church, PO Box 127, Madison, NJ 07940. Tel (201)408-3195 Fax (201)408-3909. L. Dale Patterson

Indiana United Methodist Archives, DePauw University (Roy O. West Library) Greencastle, IN 46135. Tel (317)658-4434. Fax (317)658-4789. Wesley Wilson.

Interdenominational Theological Center (Woodruff Library) 6111 James P. Brawley Drive, S.W., Atlanta, GA 30314. Tel (404)522-8980. Joseph E. Troutman. African American Methodist Collection

Livingstone College and Hood Theological Seminary (William J. Walls Heritage Center) 701 W. Monroe St., Salisbury, NC 28144 Tel (704)638-5500 A.M.E.Zion Archives

Miles College (W.A.Bell Library) 5500 Avenue G., Birmingham, AL 35208 Tel (205)923-2771. C.M.E. Collection

Mother Bethel African Methodist Episcopal Church, 419 South 6th St., Philadelphia, PA 19147 Tel (215)925-0616. Ruby Chapelle Boyd

Office of the Historiographer, African Methodist Episcopal Church, P.O. Box 301, Williamstown, MA 01267. Tel (413)597-2484 (413)458-4994. Dennis C. Dickerson, historiographer.

Paine College (Candler Library) Augusta, GA 30910 Tel (404)722-4471 C.M.E. Collection

Perkins School of Theology (Bridwell Library Center for Methodist Studies) Southern Methodist University, Dallas, TX 75275-0476. Tel. (214)768-2363. E-mail: vb7r0022@vm.cis.smu.edu Page A. Thomas.

United Methodist Historical Library, Beeghley Library, Ohio Wesleyan University, 43 University Ave., Delaware, OH 43015. Tel (614)369-4431, Ext 3245 Fax (614)363-0079.

United Methodist Publishing House Library, Room 122, 201 Eighth Ave., South, Nashville, TN 37202. Tel (615)749-6437. Rosalyn Lewis

United Theological Seminary (Center for Evangelical United Brethren Studies) 1810 Harvard Blvd., Dayton, OH 45406. Tel (513)278-5817. E-mail: uts_librarian.parti@ecunet.org Elmer J. O'Brien.

Upper Room Library, 1908 Grand Avenue, P.O. Box 189, Nashville, TN 37202-0189. Tel (615)340-7204. Fax (615)340-7006. Sarah Schaller-Linn.

Vanderbilt University, Divinity Library, 419 21st Avenue, South, Nashville, TN 37240-0007 Tel (615)322-2865. E-mail: hook@library.vanderbilt.edu William J. Hook.

Wesley Theological Seminary Library, 4500 Massachusetts Ave., NW, Washington, DC 20016 Tel (202)885-8691 Allen Mueller. Methodist Protestant Church Collection

Wesleyan Church Archives & Historical Library, International Center Wesleyan Church, P.O. Box 50434, Indianapolis, IN 46250-0434 Tel (317)842-0444. Daniel L. Burnett

Wilberforce University and Payne Theological Seminary (Rembert E. Stokes Learning Resources Center) Wilberforce, OH 45384-1003 Tel (513)376-2911 ext 628 A.M.E. Archives

World Methodist Council Library, P.O. Box 518, Lake Junaluska, NC 28745 Tel (704)456-9432.

For United Methodist annual conference depositories, see *United Methodist Church Archives and History Directory 1989-1992*. Madison, NJ : General Commission on Archives and History, UMC, 1989.

Moravian:

The Archives of the Moravian Church, 41 W. Locust St., Bethlehem, PA 18018 Tel (215)866-3255 Vernon H. Nelson

Moravian Archives, Southern Province of the Moravian Church, 4 East Bank St., Winston-Salem, NC 27101 Tel (919) 722-1742

Nazarene:

Nazarene Archives, International Headquarters, Church of the Nazarene, 6401 The Paseo, Kansas City, MO 64131. Tel (816) 333-7000, Ext 437 Stan Ingersoll

Nazarene Theological Seminary (Broadhurst Library) 1700 East Meyer Blvd., Kansas City, MO 64131. Tel (816)333-6254 William C. Miller

Pentecostal:

Assemblies of God Archives, 1445 Boonville Ave., Springfield, MO 65802.Tel (417)862-2781. Wayne Warner

Oral Roberts University Library, P.O. Box 2187,777 S. Lewis, Tulsa, OK 74171 Tel (918)495-6894. Oon-Chor Khoo

Pentecostal Research Center, Church of God (Cleveland, Tenn.), P. O. Box 3448, Cleveland, TN 37320. Tel (615)472-3361 Fax (615)478-7052. Joseph Byrd

Polish National Catholic:

Commission on History and Archives, Polish National Catholic Church, 1031 Cedar Ave., Scranton, PA 18505. Chmn., Joseph Wielczerzak

Presbyterian:

Department of History and Records Management Services, Presbyterian Church (USA) Library, 425 Lombard St., Philadelphia, PA 19147-1516 Tel (215)627-1852 Fax (215)627-0509. Frederick J. Heuser, Jr.

Department of History and Records Management Services (Montreat) Presbyterian Church (USA) P.O. Box 849, Montreat, NC 28757. Tel (704)669-7061 Fax (704)669-5369. Michelle A. Francis

Historical Center of the Presbyterian Church in America, 12330 Conway Rd., St. Louis, MO 63141. Tel 314-469-9077. Jerry Kor negay

Historical Foundation of the Cumberland Presbyterian Church, 1978 Union Ave., Memphis, TN 38104. Tel (901)276-4572 Fax (901)272-3913. Susan Knight Gore

McCormick Theological Seminary (Jesuit/Krauss/McCormick Library) 1100 East 55th St., Chicago, Il 60615 Tel (312)256-0739 Fax (312)256-0737. E-mail:kensawyer@delphi.com Mary R. Bischoff.

Princeton Seminary Libraries, Library Place and Mercer St., Princeton, NJ 08542-0803. (609)497-7940 Tel (609)497-7950. William O. Harris

Presbyterian Church in America, Historical Center,12330 Conway Rd., St. Louis, MO 63141

Reformed:

Calvin College and Seminary Library, 3207 Burton St, S.E., Grand Rapids, MI 49546 Tel (616)949-4000. Harry Boonstra (Christian Reformed)

Commission on History, Reformed Church in America, Gardner A. Sage Library, New Brunswick Theological Seminary, 21 Seminary Place, New Brunswick, NJ 08901-1159. Tel (908)247-5243 Fax (908)249-5412 Russell Gassaro

Lancaster Theological Seminary, Evangelical and Reformed Historical Society (Philip Schaff Library) 555 West James St., Lancaster, PA 17603. Tel (717)393-0654. Richard R. Berg. Reformed in the U.S., (Evangelical and Reformed)

Roman Catholic:

American Catholic Historical Society, 263 S. Fourth St., Philadelphia, PA 19106 Mrs. John T. Fisher

Archives of the American Catholic Historical Society of Philadelphia, Ryan Memorial Library, St. Charles Boromeo Seminary, 1000 E. Wynnewood Rd., Overbrook, Philadelphia, PA 19096-3012. Tel (215)667-3394. Fax (215)664-7913. Joseph S. Casino

Catholic University of America (Mullen Library) 620 Michigan Ave., NE Washington, DC 20064 Tel (202)319-5055. Carolyn T. Lee.

Georgetown University (Lauinger Library) P.O.Box 37445, Washington, DC 20013-7445. Tel (202)687-7425 Eugene Rooney

St. Louis University (Pius XII Memorial Library) 3650 Lindell Blvd., St. Louis, MO 63108 Tel (314)658-3100 Thomas Tolles

St. Mary's Seminary & University (Knott Library) 5400 Roland Ave, Baltimore, MD 21210-1994. Tel (301)323-3200, Ext 64. David P. Siemsen

University of Notre Dame Archives (Hesburg Library) Box 513, Notre Dame, IN 46556 Tel (219)239-5252. Sophia K. Jordan.

Salvation Army:

The Salvation Army Archives and Research Center, 615 Slaters Lane, Alexandria, VA 22313. Tel (703)684-5500, Ext 669. Connie Nelson

Schwenkfelder:

Schwenkfelder Library, 1 Seminary Ave., Pennsburg, PA 18073. Tel (215)679-3103. Dennis Moyer

Shaker:

Ohio Historical Society, Archives Library, 1982 Velma Ave., Columbus, OH 43211-2497. Tel (614)297-2510. Wendy Greenwood

Western Reserve Historical Society, 10825 E. Blvd. Cleveland, OH 44106-1788. Tel (216)-721-5722 Fax (216)721-0645. Kermit J. Pike

Swedenborgian:

Academy of the New Church Library, 2815 Huntingdon Pike, P.O. Box 278-68, Bryn Athyn, PA 19009. Tel (215)938-2547. Carroll C. Odhner

Unitarian and Universalist:

Harvard Divinity School (Andover-Harvard Theological Library) 45 Francis Ave., Cambridge, MA 02138 Tel (617)495-5770. Alan Seaburg

Meadville/Lombard Theological School Library, 5701 S. Woodlawn Ave., Chicago, IL 60637. Tel (312)753-3196 Neil W. Gerdes

Rhode Island Historical Society Library, 121 Hope St., Providence, RI 02906. Tel (401)331-8575. Fax (401)751-7930. Madeleine Telfeyan

Unitarian-Universalist Association Archives Library, 25 Beacon St., Boston, MA 02108 Tel (617)742-2100. Deborah Weiner

The United Church of Christ:

Chicago Theological Seminary (Hammond Library) 5757 University Ave., Chicago, IL 60637 Tel (312)752-5757. Neil W. Gerdes

Congregational Library, 14 Beacon St., Boston, MA 02108 Tel (617)523-0470. Harold Worthley

Eden Archives, 475 E. Lockwood Ave., Webster Groves, MO 63119-3192. Tel (314)961-3627. Lowell H. Zuck.

Wesleyan, see Methodist

STANDARD GUIDES TO CHURCH ARCHIVES

William Henry Allison, *Inventory of Unpublished Material for American Religious History in Protestant Church Archives and other Depositories* (Washington, DC, Carnegie Institution of Washington, 1910) 254 pp.

John Graves Barrow, *A Bibliography of Bibliographies in Religion* (Ann Arbor, Mich., 1955), pp. 185-198.

Edmund L. Binsfield, "Church Archives in the United States and Canada: a Bibliography," in *American Archivist*, V. 21, No. 3 (July 1958) pp. 311-332, 219 entries.

Nelson R. Burr, "Sources for the Study of American Church History in the Library of Congress," 1953. 13 pp. Reprinted from *Church History*, Vol. XXII, No. 3 (Sept. 1953).

Church Records Symposium, *American Archivist*, Vol. 24, October 1961, pp. 387-456.

Mable Deutrich, "Supplement to Church Archives in the United States and Canada, a Bibliography," Washington, DC: 1964.

Andrea Hinding, ed. *Women's History Sources: A Guide to Archives and Manuscript Collections in the U.S.* (New York: Bowker, 1979) 2 vols.

E. Kay Kirkham, *A Survey of American Church Records, for the Period Before The Civil War, East of the Mississippi River* (Salt Lake City, 1959-60) 2 vols. Includes the depositories and bibliographies.

Peter G. Mode, *Source Book and Bibliographical Guide for American Church History* (Menasha, Wisc., George Banta Publishing Co., 1921) 735 pp.

Society of American Archivists. *American Archivist*, 1936/37 (continuing). Has articles on church records and depositories.

A. R. Suelflow, *A Preliminary Guide to Church Records Repositories* (Society of American Archivists, Church Archives Committee, 1969) Lists more than 500 historical-archival depositories with denominational and religious history in America.

U. S. National Historical Publications and Records Commission, *Directory of Archives and Manuscript Repositories in the United States*. 2d edition. (New York : Oryx Press, 1988)

United States, Library of Congress, Division of Manuscripts, Manuscripts in Public and Private Collections in the United States (Washington, DC, 1924).

U. S. Library of Congress, Washington, DC: *The National Union Catalog of Manuscript Collections*, A59—22 vols., 1959-1986. Based on reports from American repositories of manuscripts. Contains many entries for collections of church archives. This series is continuing. Extremely valuable collection. Researchers must consult the cumulative indexes.

INTERNATIONAL CONGREGATIONS

IN CANADA

A few small Canadian religious bodies have headquarters in the United States, and therefore the reader is advised to consult "Main Depositories of Church History Material and Sources in the United States," which immediately precedes this section for possible sources of information on Canadian religious groups. Another source: *Directory of Canadian Archives*, edited by Marcel Caya.

The use of the term "main" depositories in this section implies that there are some smaller communions with archival collections not listed below and also that practically every judicatory of large religious bodies (e.g., diocese, presbytery, conference) has archives excluded from this listing. For information on these collections, write directly to the denominational headquarters or to the judicatory involved.

Most American Protestant denominational archives have important primary and secondary source material relating to missionary work in Canada during the pioneer era.

Ecumenical:

Canadian Council of Churches Archives, on deposit in National Archives of Canada, 395 Wellington, Ottawa, Ontario K1A 0N3. Some records remain at the Canadian Council of Churches office located at 40 St. Clair Ave. E., Toronto, ON M4T 1M9. The National Archives of Canada also contains a large number of records and personal papers related to the various churches.

Anglican:

General Synod Archives, 600 Jarvis St., Toronto, ON M4Y 2J6. Archivist: Mrs. Terry Thompson, Tel (416)924-9192

Baptist:

Canadian Baptist Archives, McMaster Divinity College, Hamilton, ON L8S 4K1. Librarian: Judith Colwell, Tel (416)525-9140, ext. 3511

Evangelical Baptist Historical Library, 679 Southgate Dr., Guelph, ON N1G 4S2. Tel (519)821-4830

Baptist Historical Collection, Vaughan Memorial Library, Acadia University, Wolfville, NS BOP 1XO. Archivist: Mrs. Pat Thompson. Tel (912) 542-2205

Disciples of Christ:

Canadian Disciples Archives, 39 Arkell Rd., R.R. 2, Guelph, ON N1H 6H8. Archivist: Gordon Reid, Tel (519)824-5190

Reuben Butchart Collection, E.J. Pratt Library, Victoria University, Toronto, ON M5S 1K7, Tel (416) 585-4470

Jewish:

Jewish Historical Society of Western Canada, 404-365 Hargrave St., Winnipeg, MB R3B 2K3. Archivist: Bonnie Tregobov, Tel (204) 942-4822

Canadian Jewish Congress (Central Region) Archives, 4600 Bathurst St., Toronto, ON M3T 1Y6. Archivist: Stephen A. Speisman, Tel (416)635-2883

Lutheran:

Evangelical Lutheran Church in Canada, 1512 St. James St., Winnipeg, MB R3H 0L2. Archivist: Rev. Leon C. Gilbertson (incorporating archives of the Evangelical Lutheran Church of Canada, the Lutheran Church in America—Canada Section's Central Synod Archives and those of the Western Canada Synod) Tel (204)786-6707. The Eastern Synod Archives are housed at Wilfrid Laurier University, Waterloo, ON N2L 3C5. Archivist: Rev. Erich R.W. Schultz, Tel (519)745-3505

Lutheran Church in Canada, Eastern Synod, 50 Queen St. N., ON N2H 6P4. Archivist: Rev. Roy Gross, Tel (519)743-1461

Concordia College, Edmonton, AB T5B 4E4. Archivist: Mrs. Hilda Robinson, Tel (405)479-8481

Mennonite:

Conrad Grebel College, Archives Centre, Waterloo, Ontario N2L 3G6. Archivist: Sam Steiner, Tel (519)885-0220

Mennonite Brethren Bible College, Centre for Mennonite Brethren Studies in Canada, 1-169 Riverton Ave., Winnipeg, MB R2L 2E5. Archivist: Kenneth Reddig, Tel (204)669-6575

Mennonite Heritage Centre. Archives of the General Conference of Mennonites in Canada, 600 Shaftesbury Blvd., Winnipeg, MB R3P 0M4. Tel (204)888-6781. Historian-archivist: Peter H. Rempel, Tel (204)888-6781

Free Methodist:

4315 Village Centre Ct., Mississauga, ON L4Z 1S2. Tel (416)848-2600

Pentecostal:

The Pentecostal Assemblies of Canada, 6745 Century Ave., Streetsville, ON L5N 6P7. Archivist Douglas Rudd, Tel (416) 595-1277

Presbyterian:

Presbyterian Archives, 59 St. George St., Toronto, ON M5S 2E6. Archivist: Miss Kim Arnold, Tel (416)595-1277

Roman Catholic:

For guides to many Canadian Catholic diocesan religious community and institutional archives, write: Rev. Pierre Hurtubise, O.M.I., Dir. of the Research Center in Religious History in Canada, St. Paul University, 223 Main St., Ottawa, ON K1S 1C4. Tel (613) 236-1393

Salvation Army:

The George Scott Railton Heritage Centre (Salvation Army), 2130 Bayview Ave., Toronto, ON M4N 3K6. Contact: Elayne Dobel, Tel (416)481-4441

The United Church of Canada:

Central Archives, Victoria University, Toronto, ON M5S 1K7. (Methodist, Presbyterian, Congregational, Evangelical United Brethren.) Also Regional Conference Archives. Chief Archivist Jean Dryden, Tel (416)585-4563 Fax (416)585-4584

DEPOSITORIES

III

STATISTICAL SECTION

GUIDE TO STATISTICAL TABLES

Since there are no religious questions in the U.S. census, the *Yearbook of American and Canadian Churches* is as near an "official" record of denominational statistics as is available.

Because this data represents the most complete annual compilation of church statistics, there is a temptation to expect more than is reasonable. These tables provide the answers to very simple and straight forward questions. Officials in church bodies were asked: "How many members does your organization have?" "How many clergy?" and "How much money does your organization spend?" Each respondent interprets the questions according to the policies of the organization.

Caution should, therefore, be exercised when comparing statistics across denominational lines, comparing statistics from one year to another and adding together statistics from different denominations.

1. Definitions of membership, clergy and other important characteristics differ from denomination to denomination. In this section, full or confirmed membership refers to those with full communicant, or confirmed status. Inclusive membership refers to those who are full communicants or confirmed members plus other members baptized, non-confirmed or non-communicant. Each denomination determines the age at which a young person is considered a member.

Denominations also vary in their approaches to statistics. For some, very careful counts are made of members. Other groups only make estimates.

2. Each year the data is collected with the same questions. While most denominations have consistent reporting practices from one year to the next, any change in practices is not noted in the tables. Church mergers and splits can also influence the statistics when they are compared over a number of years.

Denominations have different reporting schedules and some do not report on a regular basis. Only data that has been reported within the last 10 years is included.

3. The two problems listed above make adding figures from different denominations problematic. However, an additional complication is that individuals may be included more than once. For example, a person who attends the Church of God in Christ Wednesday evening and an AME service on Sunday morning will be included in both counts.

TABLE 1: CANADIAN CURRENT STATISTICS

Religious Body	Year Reported	No. of Churches	Full, Communicant or Confirmed Members	Inclusive Membership	No. of Pastors Serving Parishes	Total No. of Clergy	No. of Sunday or Sabbath Schools	Total Enrollment
The Anglican Church of Canada	1990	1,767	529,943	848,256		3,463	1,623	82,022
The Antiochian Orthodox Christian Archdiocese of North America	1994	16	50,000	50,000	100	110	1,000	1,100
Apostolic Christian Church (Nazarene)	1985	14		830	49	49		
The Apostolic Church in Canada	1992	14	1,200	1,600	14	19	14	350
Apostolic Church of Pentecost of Canada Inc.	1993	133		13,723	241	284	89	4,936
Associated Gospel Churches	1992	126	9,284	9,284	118	239		
Association of Regular Baptist Churches (Canada)	1994	12			8	11		
Baptist Convention of Ontario and Quebec	1991	372	33,144	44,713	315	564		
Baptist General Conference of Canada	1987	70		6,066	80	84		
Baptist Union of Western Canada	1994	161	20,006	20,006	181	273	137	7,961
The Bible Holiness Movement	1994	14	386	511	13	14	14	
Brethren in Christ Church, Canadian Conference	1994	39	3,200	3,200	30	45	39	2,152
British Columbia Baptist Conference	1994	23	2,400	2,400	40	50	23	1,318
Canadian and American Reformed Churches	1994	41	7,136	13,774	37	49		
Canadian Baptist Ministries	1994	1,150	130,000	130,000	1,225	1,600	1,150	
Canadian Conference of Mennonite Brethren Churches	1994	195	29,651	29,651	372	372	195	23,661
Canadian Convention of Southern Baptists	1993	103	6,857	6,857	84	104	103	7,806
Canadian District of the Moravian Church in America, Northern Province	1994	9	1,386	1,928	7	13	9	534
Canadian Yearly Meeting of the Religious Society of Friends	1994	22	1,125	1,893	0	0	30	185
The Central Canada Baptist Conference	1993	36			50	51		
The Christian and Missionary Alliance in Canada	1994	376	30,881	86,540	1,052	1,193	358	37,411
Christian Brethren (also known as Plymouth Brethren)	1994	60						
Christian Church (Disciples of Christ) in Canada	1994	34	1,909	3,199	24	44	34	758
Christian Reformed Church in North America	1995	244	49,105	83,848	209	290		

TABLE 1: CANADIAN CURRENT STATISTICS--Continued

Religious Body	Year Reported	No. of Churches	Full, Communicant or Confirmed Members	Inclusive Membership	No. of Pastors Serving Parishes	Total No. of Clergy	No. of Sunday or Sabbath Schools	Total Enrollment
Church of God (Anderson, Ind.)	1993	52	3,438	3,438	51	81	44	2,486
Church of God (Cleveland, Tenn.)	1994	110	7,948	7,948	90	93	82	
Church of God in Christ (Mennonite)	1993	39	3,614	3,614	127	127	39	
The Church of God of Prophecy in Canada	1994	40	3,107	3,107	99	101		
Church of Jesus Christ of Latter-day Saints in Canada	1992	391	130,000	130,000			391	
Church of the Luthern Brethren	1994	7	356	1,067	6	7	10	600
Church of the Nazarene Canada	1994	167	11,632	11,699	131	261	154	15,766
Churches of Christ in Canada	1991	147	7,181	7,181	133		108	
Conference of Mennonites in Canada	1994	149	28,075	28,075	200	383		
Congregational Christian Churches in Canada	1993	70		7,000		123		60
The Coptic Church in Canada	1992	12			20		17	
The Estonian Evangelical Lutheran Church	1993	12	5,993	6,159	11	14	4	133
The Evangelical Missionary Church of Canada	1993	145	9,923	12,217	172	367	125	7,475
The Evangelical Covenant Church of Canada	1993	22	1,245	1,245	15	26	19	1,641
Evangelical Free Church of Canada	1994	650	142,881	198,665	461	851	444	23,964
Evangelical Lutheran Church in Canada	1993	652	143,729	199,609	481	854	419	23,403
The Evangelical Mennonite Conference of Canada	1995	49	6,508	6,508	210	242	49	5,195
The Evangelical Mennonite Mission Conference of Canada	1994	27	3,587	3,587	42	60	25	3,235
Fellowship of Evangelical Baptist Churches in Canada	1994	512	65,246	85,944				
Foursquare Gospel Church of Canada	1993	53	2,531	2,531	92	109		
Free Methodist Church in Canada	1993	146	5,926	7,186		254	127	9,014
Free Will Baptists	1992	15	435	735	5	8	11	595
Greek Orthodox Diocese of Toronto (Canada)	1984	58		230,000	45	49		
Independent Assemblies of God International (Canada)	1993				260	393		
Independent Holiness Church	1994	5		150	4	10	4	118
The Italian Pentecostal Church of Canada	1995	24	2,500	2,500	20	22	20	

TABLE 1: CANADIAN CURRENT STATISTICS--Continued

Religious Body	Year Reported	No. of Churches	Full, Communicant or Confirmed Members	Inclusive Membership	No. of Pastors Serving Parishes	Total No. of Clergy	No. of Sunday or Sabbath Schools	Total Enrollment
Jehovah's Witnesses	1994	1,351	110,659	110,659				
The Latvian Evangelical Lutheran Church in America	1994	17	4,295	4,922	11	13	4	113
Lutheran Church--Canada	1994	343	63,016	84,898	265	392	311	14,727
Mennonite Church (Canada)	1994	111	14,717	14,717	139	236	108	21,657
North American Baptist Conference	1994	121	17,910	17,910	113	185	121	
The Old Catholic Church of Canada	1994	2	20	40	2	2		0
Old Order Amish Church	1992	17			61	61		
The Open Bible Standard Churches of Canada	1987	4		1,000	5	6		
Orthodox Church in America (Canada Section)	1993	606	1,000,000	1,000,000	740		502	
Patriarchal Parishes of the Russian Orthodox Church in Canada	1994	22	600	1,200	3	4	3	55
The Pentecostal Assemblies of Canada	1994	1,068		226,678		1,746	648	65,645
Pentecostal Assemblies of Newfoundland	1994	157	15,496	30,992	284	438	146	14,044
Presbyterian Church in America (Canadian Section)	1994	14	537	910	10	22		438
The Presbyterian Church in Canada	1994	999	153,928	236,822	1,211	1,211	612	34,957
Reformed Church in Canada	1994	41	4,096	6,667	35	70	41	2,030
The Reformed Episcopal Church of Canada	1992	3	284	325	3	9		
Reinland Mennonite Church	1987	7		800	10	10		
Reorganized Church of Jesus Christ of Latter Day Saints	1992	82	11,111	11,111		1,075		
The Roman Catholic Church in Canada	1993	5,844		12,584,789	4,421	6,318		
The Romanian Orthodox Episcopate of America (Jackson, MI)	1994	13	8,600	8,600	11	12	10	663
The Salvation Army in Canada	1994	370	30,330	92,338	656	2,008	366	26,227
Seventh-day Adventist Church in Canada	1994	331	43,840	43,840	169	297	361	25,758
Swedenborgians	1994	3	347	1,085	6	6	3	185
Syrian Orthodox Church of Antioch (Archdiocese of the US and Canada)	1994	5	2,500	2,500	3	4		

TABLE 1: CANADIAN CURRENT STATISTICS--Continued

Religious Body	Year Reported	No. of Churches	Full, Communicant or Confirmed Members	Inclusive Membership	No. of Pastors Serving Parishes	Total No. of Clergy	No. of Sunday or Sabbath Schools	Total Enrollment
Ukrainian Orthodox Church of Canada	1988	258		120,000	75	91		
Union d'Eglises Baptistes Francaises au Canada	1994	26	1,222	3,000	24	33	26	900
United Baptist Convention of the Atlantic Provinces	1994	546	63,625	63,625	288	545		26,475
United Brethren Church in Canada	1992	9	835	835	5	12	9	447
The United Church of Canada	1994	3,960	744,392	1,903,394	2,067	3,966	3,277	204,126
Universal Fellowship of Metropolitan Community Churches	1992	12	50	1,500	8	9	1	36
United Pentecostal Church in Canada	1993	3,724	550,000			7,561		
The Wesleyan Church of Canada	1993	82	5,024	5,256	112	155	72	
Wisconsin Evangelical Lutheran Synod	1994	17	919	1,300	15	15	16	346

TABLE 2: UNITED STATES CURRENT STATISTICS

Religious Body	Year Reported	No. of Churches	Full, Communicant or Confirmed Members	Inclusive Membership	No. of Pastors Serving Parishes	Total No. of Clergy	No. of Sunday or Sabbath Schools	Total Enrollment
Advent Christian Church	1993	328	27,300	27,300	349	487	325	15,450
African Methodist Episcopal Church	1991	8,000		3,500,000				
African Methodist Episcopal Zion Church	1994	3,098	1,020,842	1,230,842	2,571	2,767	1,672	67,320
Albanian Orthodox Diocese of America	1994	2	1,875	1,875	1	3	2	117
Allegheny Wesleyan Methodist Connection (Original Allegheny Conference)	1994	120	1,905	2,056	98	188	123	6,356
The American Association of Lutheran Churches	1993	94	16,591	22,061	99	164		
The American Baptist Association	1986	1,705		250,000	1,740	1,760		
American Baptist Churches in the U.S.A.	1994	5,686	1,507,934	1,507,934	4,359	7,670		327,442
The American Carpatho-Russian Orthodox Greek Catholic Church	1994	78	19,321	19,321	87	101	75	
American Evangelical Christian Churches	1993				72	197		
American Rescue Workers	1992	16	5,000	35,000	70	96	16	880
The Anglican Orthodox Church	1983	40		6,000	8	8		
The Antiochian Orthodox Christian Archdiocese of North America	1994	184	300,000	300,000	200	225	184	4,000
Apostolic Christian Church (Nazarene)	1993	63	3,723	3,723	217	234	55	1,665
Apostolic Christian Churches of America	1989	80		11,450	300	340		
Apostolic Faith Mission Church of God	1994	28	8,000	11,000	56	76	28	4,724
Apostolic Faith Mission of Portland, Oregon	1994	54	4,500	4,500	60	85	54	6,820
Apostolic Lutheran Church of America	1994	60	7,700	7,700	35	35	40	
Apostolic Overcoming Holy Church of God, Inc.	1994	160	12,369	12,369	160	160		
Armenian Apostolic Church of America	1992	32	30,000	150,000	20	27	20	809
Assemblies of God	1994	11,764	1,354,337	2,324,615	17,486	31,300	11,227	1,385,029
Associate Reformed Presbyterian Church (General Synod)	1994	206	33,636	38,936	164	270	177	16,631
The Association of Free Lutheran Congregations	1994	234	22,388	30,769	149	202	230	5,844

TABLE 2: UNITED STATES CURRENT STATISTICS--Continued

Religious Body	Year Reported	No. of Churches	Full, Communicant or Confirmed Members	Inclusive Membership	No. of Pastors Serving Parishes	Total No. of Clergy	No. of Sunday or Sabbath Schools	Total Enrollment
Baptist Bible Fellowship International	1994	3,600	1,500,000	1,500,000				
Baptist General Conference	1994	813	135,128	135,128	813	1,248	813	
Baptist Missionary Association of America	1994	1,360	230,171	230,171	1,225	2,745	1,358	91,577
Beachy Amish Mennonite Churches	1992	95	6,968	6,968	323	323	91	
Berean Fundamental Church	1991	51	2,768	2,768	60	60	51	4,063
The Bible Church of Christ Inc.	1993	6	4,150	6,850	11	52	6	623
Brethren Church (Ashland, Ohio), The	1994	121	13,028	13,028	88	183	109	6,406
Brethren in Christ Church	1994	198	18,152	18,152	177	290	198	13,170
Christ Catholic Church	1995	8	998	1,018	9	11	2	34
The Christian and Missionary Alliance	1993	1,943	147,367	302,414	1,610	2,407	1,726	189,935
Christian Brethren (aka Plymouth Brethren)	1984	1,150		98,000	500			
Christian Catholic Church (Evangelical-Protestant)	1994	3			2	7	3	
Christian Church (Disciples of Christ)	1994	3,933	605,996	937,644	3,938	7,150	3,933	278,493
Christian Church of North America, General Council	1985	104		13,500	107	169		
Christian Churches and Churches of Christ	1988	5,579		1,070,616	5,525	6,596		
The Christian Congregation, Inc.	1994	1,437	112,437	112,437	1,431	1,433	1,293	45,513
Christian Methodist Episcopal Church	1983	2,340		718,922	2,340	2,650		
Christian Reformed Church in North America	1995	737	138,953	211,154	666	1,171		
Christian Union, Churches of Christ in	1993	240		10,400		484	240	
Church of Christ, Scientist	1993	2,400			0		2,400	
Church of God (Anderson, Ind.)	1993	2,314	216,117	216,117	2,132	3,563	2,153	161,162
Church of God by Faith, Inc.	1991	145	6,819	8,235	155	170		
Church of God (Cleveland, Tenn.)	1994	5,918	722,541	722,541	2,400	5,493	5,202	329,224
Church of God General Conference (Oregon, IL &Morrow, GA)	1994	89	3,996	5,195	67	80	87	2,966
The Church of God in Christ	1991	15,300	5,499,875	5,499,875	28,988	33,593		

TABLE 2: UNITED STATES CURRENT STATISTICS--Continued

Religious Body	Year Reported	No. of Churches	Full, Communicant or Confirmed Members	Inclusive Membership	No. of Pastors Serving Parishes	Total No. of Clergy	No. of Sunday or Sabbath Schools	Total Enrollment
Church of God in Christ (Mennonite)	1994	90	10,742	10,742	209	390	90	
Church of God, Mountain Assembly, Inc.	1994	118	6,140	6,140	95	135	118	14,160
Church of God of Prophecy	1994	2,005	70,570	70,570	8,791	8,743	2,036	63,292
The Church of God (Seventh Day), Denver, Colo.	1994	160	5,700	5,700		125		
The Church of Illumination	1993	25	2,500	4,000	35	55	3	129
The Church of Jesus Christ (Bickertonites)	1989	63		2,707	183	262		
The Church of Jesus Christ of Latter-Day Saints	1994	10,218	4,110,000	4,613,000	30,654	34,511	10,218	3,750,600
Church of the Brethren	1994	1,127	144,282	144,282	831	1,267	1,040	
Church of the Living God (Motto: CWFF)	1985	170		42,000		170		
Church of Lutheran Brethren of America	1994	119	8,331	25,548	135	233	114	11,061
Church of the Lutheran Confession	1994	71	6,510	8,864	60	80	65	1,429
Church of the Nazarene	1994	5,156	595,303	597,841	4,474	9,628	4,916	830,370
Churches of Christ	1994	13,013	1,260,838	1,651,103	10,000	10,000	11,750	925,000
Churches of God, General Conference	1994	352	31,862	31,862	245	430	352	25,272
Congregational Holiness Church, Inc.	1993	190		2,468			190	
Conservative Baptist Association of America	1992	1,084	200,000	200,000				
Conservative Congregational Christian Conference	1993	201	36,864	36,864	307	541	189	13,163
Conservative Lutheran Association	1995	8	820	1,047	12	22		
Coptic Orthodox Church	1992	85	180,000	180,000	65	68	85	
Cumberland Presbyterian Church	1994	772	90,125	90,125		810	772	40,479
Diocese of the Armenian Church of America	1991	72	14,000	414,000	49	70		2,370
Elim Fellowship	1992	66			154	322		
Episcopal Church	1993	7,388	1,570,444	2,504,682	8,004	15,000		521,892
The Estonian Evangelical Lutheran Church	1994	23	3,989	3,989	12	18		
The Evangelical Church	1994	134	12,458	12,458		269	120	13,524
The Evangelical Congregational Church	1994	151	23,504	23,504	107	183	150	15,933

TABLE 2: UNITED STATES CURRENT STATISTICS--Continued

Religious Body	Year Reported	No. of Churches	Full, Communicant or Confirmed Members	Inclusive Membership	No. of Pastors Serving Parishes	Total No. of Clergy	No. of Sunday or Sabbath Schools	Total Enrollment
The Evangelical Covenant Church	1993	597	89,511	89,511	551	992	498	76,744
The Evangelical Free Church of America	1995	1,213	123,602	227,290	1,920	2,398		
Evangelical Lutheran Church in America	1994	10,973	3,849,692	5,199,048	9,826	17,322	9,438	1,052,570
Evangelical Lutheran Synod	1994	128	15,960	25,379	112	159	116	5,114
Evangelical Mennonite Church	1993	29	4,228	4,228	32	62	28	3,419
Evangelical Methodist Church	1992	132	8,500	8,500	137			
Evangelical Presbyterian Church	1994	177	52,241	56,499	240	380	177	32,706
Fellowship of Evangelical Bible Churches	1988	14		1,925	18	47		
Fellowship of Fundamental Bible Churches	1994	23	1,343	1,343	35	42	23	1,276
Free Methodist Church of North America	1993	1,050	59,156	74,585	923	1,859	947	91,503
Friends General Conference	1994	550	31,500	31,500				
Friends United Meeting	1991		50,803	50,803	341	637		17,566
Full Gospel Assemblies International	1994	274	13,700	13,700		675	274	
Full Gospel Fellowship of Churches and Ministers International	1995	600				2,274	557	98,738
Fundamental Methodist Church, Inc.	1993	12	682	787	17	22	12	454
General Assembly of the Korean Presbyterian Church in America	1992	203	21,788	26,988	326	381		
General Association of General Baptists	1990	876	74,156	74,156	1,384	1,384		
General Association of Regular Baptist Churches	1994	1,458	136,380	136,380				
General Church of the New Jerusalem	1994	34	3,116	6,942	37	67		
General Conference Mennonite Brethren Churches	1994	148	19,218	19,218	214	272		13,258
Grace Brethren Churches, Fellowship of	1994	273	32,229	32,229		700		23,456
Grace Gospel Fellowship	1992	128		60,000	160	196	128	
Greek Orthodox Archdiocese of North and South America	1977	535		1,950,000	610	655		
Hungarian Reformed Church in America	1989	27		9,780	29	32		

TABLE 2: UNITED STATES CURRENT STATISTICS--Continued

Religious Body	Year Reported	No. of Churches	Full, Communicant or Confirmed Members	Inclusive Membership	No. of Pastors Serving Parishes	Total No. of Clergy	No. of Sunday or Sabbath Schools	Total Enrollment
Hutterian Brethren	1994	395	35,254	41,475	780	795	395	5,830
Independent Fundamental Churches of America	1994	670	69,857	69,857	737	1,274	670	64,779
International Church of the Foursquare Gospel	1994	1,710	218,534	222,658		2,669		57,680
International Council of Community Churches	1994	423	500,000	500,000	560	619		
The International Pentecostal Church of Christ	1994	75	2,668	5,090	54	100	72	3,674
International Pentecostal Holiness Church	1994	1,645	150,133	150,133		3,250		
Jehovah's Witnesses	1994	10,307	945,990	945,990				
The Latvian Evangelical Lutheran Church in America, The	1994	55	11,322	12,446	39	65	22	600
The Liberal Catholic Church--Province of the U.S.A.	1987	34		2,800	64	127		
Liberty Baptist Fellowship	1992	100			100	110		
The Lutheran Church- Missouri Synod	1994	6,148	1,944,905	2,596,927	5,556	8,879	5,754	641,921
Mennonite Church	1994	1,099	95,591	95,591	1,364	2,468	1,077	136,076
Mennonite Church, The General Conference	1994	221	32,782	32,782	399	786	221	14,209
The Missionary Church	1994	300	28,821	28,821	462	854	289	29,563
Moravian Church in America, Northern Province	1994	95	21,448	27,713	96	168	87	6,587
Moravian Church in America, Southern Province	1991	56	17,300	21,513	63	95		8,691
National Association of Congregational Christian Churches	1994	424	70,000	70,000	400	600	400	
National Association of Free Will Baptists	1994	2,496	207,576	207,576	2,800	2,900	2,496	140,527
National Baptist Convention of America, Inc	1987	2,500		3,500,000	8,000			
National Baptist Convention, USA,Inc.	1992	33,000	8,200,000	8,200,000	32,832	32,832		
National Missionary Baptist Convention of America	1992			2,500,000				
National Organization of the New Apostolic Church of North America	1993	554	41,863	41,863	983	1,096	554	2,764
National Spiritualist Association of Churches	1994	143	2,830	3,634	97	97	40	
Netherlands Reformed Congregations	1993	15	2,252	4,374	4	5		
North American Baptist Conference	1994	263	43,236	43,236	282	451	263	

TABLE 2: UNITED STATES CURRENT STATISTICS--Continued

Religious Body	Year Reported	No. of Churches	Full, Communicant or Confirmed Members	Inclusive Membership	No. of Pastors Serving Parishes	Total No. of Clergy	No. of Sunday or Sabbath Schools	Total Enrollment
Old German Baptist Brethren	1994	58	5,622	5,622	248	248		
Old Order Amish Church	1993	898	80,820	80,820	3,592	3,617	55	
Open Bible Standard Churches, Inc.	1993	361	35,375	45,988	584	1,010	325	12,996
The Orthodox Church in America	1995	600	1,000,000	2,000,000	650	792	450	
The Orthodox Presbyterian Church	1994	181	13,970	20,151	216	341		10,096
Partiarchal Parishes, Russian Orthodox Ch. in U.S.A.	1985	38		9,780	37	45		
Pentecostal Assemblies of the World	1994	1,760	1,000,000	1,000,000	4,262	4,262	1,760	
Pentecostal Church of God, Inc.	1994	1,209	48,000	113,400		1,781		
Pentecostal Fire-Baptized Holiness Church	1993	26	200	200		26	8	
The Pentecostal Free Will Baptist Church, Inc.	1994	163	15,000	18,500	163	250		
Presbyterian Church in America	1994	1,263	204,605	257,556	1,465	2,397		110,650
Presbyterian Church (U.S.A.)	1994	11,399	2,698,262	3,698,136	9,683	20,624	9,650	1,105,645
Primitive Advent Christian Church	1993	10	345	345	11	11	10	292
Primitive Methodist Church in the U.S.A.	1994	79	5,216	7,298	81	118	75	3,977
Progressive National Baptist Convention, Inc.	1994	2,000	2,500,000	2,500,000				
Reformed Church in America	1994	915	185,242	309,459	736	1,777	915	96,159
Reformed Church in the United States	1994	36	3,160	4,172	31	40	36	832
Reformed Episcopal Church	1990	83	5,882	6,565	88	147	72	2,938
Reformed Mennonite Church	1993	10	331	346	20	20		
Reformed Presbyterian Church of North America	1993	70	4,028	5,657	60	131	70	3,073
Religious Society of Friends (Conservative)	1984	28		1,744		17		
Reorganized Church of Jesus Christ of Latter Day Saints	1992	1,001	150,143	150,143		16,742		
The Roman Catholic Church	1994	19,723		60,190,605		49,947		4,199,356
The Romanian Orthodox Episcopate of America	1994	37	65,000	65,000	37	81	30	1,800
The Russian Orthodox Church Outside of Russia	1994	177			319	319		
The Salvation Army	1994	1,222	136,309	443,246	3,642	5,238	1,238	109,797

TABLE 2: UNITED STATES CURRENT STATISTICS--Continued

Religious Body	Year Reported	No. of Churches	Full, Communicant or Confirmed Members	Inclusive Membership	No. of Pastors Serving Parishes	Total No. of Clergy	No. of Sunday or Sabbath Schools	Total Enrollment
The Schwenkfelder Church	1994	5	2,577	2,577	8	9	5	716
Separate Baptists in Christ	1992	100	8,000	8,000	95	140	100	
Serbian Orthodox Church in the U.S.A. and Canada	1986	68		67,000	60	82		
Seventh-day Adventist Church	1994	4,303	775,349	775,349	2,374	4,799	4,463	402,402
Seventh Day Baptist General Conference, USA and Canada	1994	86	4,400	4,400	57	94		
Southern Baptist Convention	1994	39,863	15,614,060	15,614,060	38,732	60,045	37,807	8,258,262
The Southern Methodist Church	1994	126	7,876	7,876		155	126	6,352
Sovereign Grace Baptists	1992	300	3,000	3,000	400	400	300	
The Swedenborgian Church	1988	50		2,423	45	54		
Syrian Orthodox Church of Antioch (Archdiocese of the United States and Canada)	1994	17	32,500	32,500	14	20		
True Orthodox Church of Greece (SOMC), American Exarchate	1993	9	1,080	1,080	18	19		
Ukrainian Orthodox Church of America (Ecumenical Patriarachate)	1986	27		5,000	36	37		
United Brethren in Christ	1994	239	24,671	24,671	297	507	239	13,265
United Christian Church	1987	12		420	8	11		
United Church of Christ	1994	6,180	1,501,310	1,501,310	4,443	10,213		379,630
The United Methodist Church	1994	36,559	8,584,125	8,584,125	19,880	38,481	34,272	3,749,942
United Pentecostal Church International	1994	3,730	550,000	550,000				
United Zion Church	1993	13	852	852	13	23	13	618
Unity of the Brethren	1993	26	2,602	2,602	21	28	21	1,194
Universal Fellowship of Metropolitan Community Churches	1992	291	14,664	30,000		296		
The Wesleyan Church	1994	1,609	109,694	116,763	1,782	2,985	1,609	
Wisconson Evangelical Lutheran Synod	1994	1,251	315,302	414,874	1,213	1,636	1,192	47,349

TABLE 3: CONSTITUENCY OF THE NATIONAL COUNCIL OF THE CHURCHES IN THE U.S.A.

A separate tabulation has been made of the constituent bodies of the National Council of Churches of Christ in the U.S.A.

Religious Body	Year	Number of Churches	Inclusive Membership	Pastors Serving Parishes
African Methodist Episcopal Church	1991	8,000	3,500,000	
African Methodist Episcopal Zion Church	1994	3,098	1,230,842	2,767
American Baptist Churches in the U.S.A.	1994	5,686	1,507,934	7,670
The Antiochian Orthodox Christian Archdiocese of North America	1994	184	300,000	225
Armenian Apostolic Church of America	1992	32	150,000	27
Christian Church (Disciples of Christ)	1994	3,933	937,644	7,150
Christian Methodist Episcopal Church	1983	2,340	718,922	2,340
Church of the Brethren	1994	1,127	144,282	1,267
Coptic Orthodox Church	1992	85	180,000	68
Episcopal Church	1993	7,388	2,504,682	15,000
Evangelical Lutheran Church in America	1994	10,973	5,199,048	17,322
Friends United Meeting	1991		50,803	637
General Assembly of the Korean Presbyterian Church in America	1992	203	26,988	381
Greek Orthodox Archdiocese of North and South America	1977	535	1,950,000	610
Hungarian Reformed Church in America	1989	27	9,780	32
International Council of Community Churches	1994	423	500,000	619
Moravian Church in America, Northern Province	1994	95	27,713	168
Moravian Church in America, Southern Province	1991	56	21,513	95
National Baptist Convention of America, Inc.	1987	2,500	3,500,000	
National Baptist Convention, USA,Inc.	1992	33,000	8,200,000	32,832
The Orthodox Church in America	1995	600	2,000,000	792
Partiarchal Parishes, Russian Orthodox Ch. in U.S.A.	1985	38	9,780	45
Philadelphia Yearly Meeting, Society of Friends	1991	105	12,627	
Polish National Catholic Church of North America	1960	162	282,411	141
Presbyterian Church (U.S.A.)	1994	11,399	3,698,136	20,624
Progressive National Baptist Convention, Inc.	1994	2,000	2,500,000	
Reformed Church in America	1994	915	309,459	1,777
Serbian Orthodox Church in the U.S.A. and Canada	1986	68	67,000	82
The Swedenborgian Church	1988	50	2,423	54
Syrian Orthodox Church of Antioch (Archdiocese of the United States and Canada)	1994	17	32,500	20
Ukrainian Orthodox Church of America (Ecumenical Patriarachate)	1986	27	5,000	37
United Church of Christ	1994	6,180	1,501,310	10,213
The United Methodist Church	1994	36,559	8,584,125	38,481
TOTALS		137,805	49,664,922	161,476

Table 4: SOME STATISTICS OF CHURCH

Communion	Year	Full or Confirmed Members	Inclusive Members	TOTAL CONTRIBUTIONS: Total Contributions	Per Capita Full or Confirmed Members	Per Capita Inclusive Members
Baptist Union of Western Canada	1994	20,006	20,006	25,581,913	1,278.71	1,278.71
The Bible Holiness Movement	1994	386	511	188,988	489.61	369.84
Brethren in Christ Church, Canadian Conference	1994	3,200	3,200	4,299,451	1,343.58	1,343.58
Canadian Conference of Mennonite Brethren Churches	1994	29,651	29,651	41,064,092	1,384.91	1,384.91
Canadian District of the Moravian Church in America, Northern Province	1994	1,386	1,928	1,287,052	928.61	667.56
The Christian and Missionary Alliance in Canada	1994	30,881	86,540	87,613,933	2,837.15	1,012.41
Christian Church (Disciples of Christ) in Canada	1994	1,909	3,199	1,406,574	736.81	439.69
Church of the Nazarene Canada	1994	11,632	11,699	8,756,244	752.77	748.46
Conference of Mennonites in Canada	1994	28,075	28,075	23,186,711	825.88	825.88
Evangelical Free Church of Canada	1994	142,881	198,665	55,851,901	390.90	281.14
The Latvian Evangelical Lutheran Church in America	1994	4,295	4,922	1,203,503	280.21	244.52
Lutheran Church--Canada	1994	63,016	84,898	28,354,000	449.95	333.98
Mennonite Church (Canada)	1994	14,717	14,717	13,218,032	898.15	898.15
North American Baptist Conference	1994	17,910	17,910	20,524,520	1,145.98	1,145.98
Presbyterian Church in America (Canadian Section)	1994	537	910	1,132,160	2,108.31	1,244.13
The Presbyterian Church in Canada	1994	153,928	236,822	83,111,244	539.94	350.94
Reformed Church in Canada	1994	4,096	6,667	4,482,378	1,094.33	672.32
Seventh-day Adventist Church in Canada	1994	43,840	43,840	39,957,579	911.44	911.44
Union d'Eglises Baptistes Francaises au Canada	1994	1,222	3,000	875,000	716.04	291.67
United Baptist Convention of the Atlantic Provinces	1994	63,625	63,625	27,684,150	435.11	435.11
The United Church of Canada	1994	744,392	1,903,394	299,350,637	402.14	157.27
Wisconsin Evangelical Lutheran Synod	1994	919	1,300	726,183	790.19	558.60

Table 5: SOME STATISTICS OF CHURCH

Communion	Year	Full or Confirmed Members	Inclusive Members	TOTAL CONTRIBUTIONS: Total Contributions	Per Capita Full or Confirmed Members	Per Capita Inclusive Members
African Methodist Episcopal Zion Church	1994	1,020,842	1,230,842	71,895,243	70.43	58.41
Albanian Orthodox Diocese of America	1994	1,875	1,875	179,100	95.52	95.52
Allegheny Wesleyan Methodist Connection (Original Allegheny Conference)	1994	1,905	2,056	4,455,144	2,338.66	2,166.90
American Baptist Churches in the U.S.A.	1994	1,507,934	1,507,934	370,230,512	245.52	245.52
Apostolic Faith Mission Church of God	1994	8,000	11,000	458,000	57.25	41.64
Associate Reformed Presbyterian Church (General Synod)	1994	33,636	38,936	27,625,383	821.30	709.51
Baptist Missionary Association of America	1994	230,171	230,171	61,565,974	267.48	267.48
Brethren in Christ Church	1994	18,152	18,152	20,466,677	1,127.52	1,127.52
Christian Church (Disciples of Christ)	1994	605,996	937,644	385,517,365	636.17	411.16
Church of God General Conference (Oregon, IL &Morrow, GA)	1994	3,996	5,195	3,410,642	853.51	656.52
Church of the Brethren	1994	144,282	144,282	81,366,277	563.94	563.94

FINANCES—CANADIAN CHURCHES

CONGREGATIONAL FINANCES			BENEVOLENCES			
Total Congregational Contributions	Per Capita Full or Confirmed Members	Per Capita Inclusive Members	Total Benevolences	Per Capita Full or Confirmed Members	PerCapita Inclusive Members	Benevolences As a Percentage of Total Contributions
21,358,787	1,067.62	1,067.62	4,223,126	211.09	211.09	17
26,219	67.92	51.31	162,769	421.68	318.53	86
3,432,496	1,072.66	1,072.66	796,955	249.05	249.05	19
30,192,574	1,018.26	1,018.26	10,871,019	366.63	366.63	26
1,156,442	834.37	599.81	130,610	94.24	67.74	10
74,660,447	2,417.68	862.73	12,953,486	419.46	149.68	15
1,244,221	651.77	388.94	162,353	85.05	50.75	12
7,157,043	615.29	611.77	1,599,201	137.48	136.70	18
13,861,452	493.73	493.73	9,325,259	332.16	332.16	40
48,866,685	342.01	245.98	6,985,216	48.89	35.16	13
1,034,815	240.93	210.24	168,688	39.28	34.27	14
23,551,000	373.73	277.40	4,803,000	76.22	56.57	17
9,752,490	662.67	662.67	3,465,542	235.48	235.48	26
15,931,260	889.52	889.52	4,593,260	256.46	256.46	22
938,596	1,747.85	1,031.42	193,564	360.45	212.71	17
71,019,043	461.38	299.88	12,092,201	78.56	51.06	15
3,727,997	910.16	559.17	754,381	184.18	113.15	17
12,286,867	280.27	280.27	27,670,712	631.18	631.18	69
800,000	654.66	266.67	75,000	61.37	25.00	9
22,369,988	351.59	351.59	5,314,162	83.52	83.52	19
256,087,609	344.02	134.54	43,263,028	58.12	22.73	14
558,922	608.18	429.94	167,261	182.00	128.66	23

FINANCES—UNITED STATES CHURCHES

CONGREGATIONAL FINANCES			BENEVOLENCES			
Total Congregational Contributions	Per Capita Full or Confirmed Members	Per Capita Inclusive Members	Total Benevolences	Per Capita Full or Confirmed Members	PerCapita Inclusive Members	Benevolences As a Percentage of Total Contributions
69,178,113	67.77	56.20	2,717,130	2.66	2.21	4
161,000	85.87	85.87	18,100	9.65	9.65	10
3,500,213	1,837.38	1,702.44	954,931	501.28	464.46	21
320,698,322	212.67	212.67	49,532,190	32.85	32.85	13
196,000	24.50	17.82	262,000	32.75	23.82	57
20,897,526	621.28	536.71	6,727,857	200.02	172.79	24
50,782,987	220.63	220.63	10,782,987	46.85	46.85	18
14,844,672	817.80	817.80	5,622,005	309.72	309.72	27
342,352,080	564.94	365.12	43,165,285	71.23	46.04	11
2,934,843	734.45	564.94	475,799	119.07	91.59	14
57,210,682	396.52	396.52	24,155,595	167.42	167.42	30

Table 5: SOME STATISTICS OF CHURCH

Communion	Year	Full or Confirmed Members	Inclusive Members	TOTAL CONTRIBUTIONS: Total Contributions	Per Capita Full or Confirmed Members	Per Capita Inclusive Members
Church of Lutheran Brethren of America	1994	8,331	25,548	9,166,074	1,100.24	358.78
Church of the Lutheran Confession	1994	6,510	8,864	3,894,989	598.31	439.42
Church of the Nazarene	1994	595,303	597,841	477,106,894	801.45	798.05
Churches of God, General Conference	1994	31,862	31,862	19,012,535	596.72	596.72
Cumberland Presbyterian Church	1994	90,125	90,125	36,596,593	406.06	406.06
The Evangelical Church	1994	12,458	12,458	11,421,392	916.79	916.79
The Evangelical Congregational Church	1994	23,504	23,504	17,201,395	731.85	731.85
Evangelical Lutheran Church in America	1994	3,849,692	5,199,048	1,689,892,487	438.97	325.04
Evangelical Lutheran Synod	1994	15,960	25,379	8,484,219	531.59	334.30
Evangelical Presbyterian Church	1994	52,241	56,499	67,990,732	1,301.48	1,203.40
General Association of Regular Baptist Churches	1994	136,380	136,380	116,463,726	853.96	853.96
General Conference Mennonite Brethren Churches	1994	19,218	19,218	32,286,743	1,680.03	1,680.03
The International Pentecostal Church of Christ	1994	2,668	5,090	3,779,665	1,416.67	742.57
International Pentecostal Holiness Church	1994	150,133	150,133	9,674,811	64.44	64.44
The Latvian Evangelical Lutheran Church in America, The	1994	11,322	12,446	3,689,092	325.83	296.41
The Lutheran Church-Missouri Synod	1994	1,944,905	2,596,927	946,937,471	486.88	364.64
Mennonite Church	1994	95,591	95,591	89,481,831	936.09	936.09
Mennonite Church, The General Conference	1994	32,782	32,782	27,198,343	829.67	829.67
The Missionary Church	1994	28,821	28,821	45,390,967	1,574.93	1,574.93
Moravian Church in America, Northern Province	1994	21,448	27,713	10,935,788	509.87	394.61
National Association of Free Will Baptists	1994	207,576	207,576	68,300,000	329.04	329.04
North American Baptist Conference	1994	43,236	43,236	40,316,267	932.47	932.47
The Orthodox Presbyterian Church	1994	13,970	20,151	17,514,334	1,253.71	869.15
Presbyterian Church in America	1994	204,605	257,556	298,318,983	1,458.02	1,158.27
Presbyterian Church (U.S.A.)	1994	2,698,262	3,698,136	2,107,167,041	780.93	569.79
Reformed Church in America	1994	185,242	309,459	181,014,238	977.18	584.94
Reformed Church in the United States	1994	3,160	4,172	2,196,009	694.94	526.37
The Schwenkfelder Church	1994	2,577	2,577	1,082,920	420.23	420.23
Seventh-day Adventist Church	1994	775,349	775,349	732,944,260	945.31	945.31
Southern Baptist Convention	1994	15,614,060	15,614,060	6,078,782,460	389.31	389.31
The Southern Methodist Church	1994	7,876	7,876	4,600,000	584.05	584.05
United Brethren in Christ	1994	24,671	24,671	18,409,757	746.21	746.21
United Church of Christ	1994	1,501,310	1,501,310	623,810,484	415.51	415.51
The United Methodist Church	1994	8,584,125	8,584,125	3,430,351,778	399.62	399.62
The Wesleyan Church	1994	109,694	116,763	142,279,911	1,297.06	1,218.54
Wisconson Evangelical Lutheran Synod	1994	315,302	414,874	166,850,854	529.18	402.17

SUMMARY STATISTICS

Nation	Number Reporting	Full or Confirmed Members	Inclusive Members	TOTAL CONTRIBUTIONS: Total Contributions	Per Capita Full or Confirmed Members	Per Capita Inclusive Members
United States (1994)	47	40,997,058	44,886,207	15,308,625,032	373.41	341.05
Canada (1994)	22	1,382,504	2,765,479	769,856,245	556.86	278.38

FINANCES—UNITED STATES CHURCHES Cont.

CONGREGATIONAL FINANCES			BENEVOLENCES			
Total Congregational Contributions	Per Capita Full or Confirmed Members	Per Capita Inclusive Members	Total Benevolences	Per Capita Full or Confirmed Members	PerCapita Inclusive Members	Benevolences As a Percentage of Total Contributions
7,275,256	873.28	284.77	1,890,818	226.96	74.01	21
3,222,816	495.06	363.58	672,173	103.25	75.83	17
387,385,034	650.74	647.97	89,721,860	150.72	150.08T19	
15,716,667	493.27	493.27	3,295,868	103.44	103.44	17
31,732,121	352.09	352.09	4,864,472	53.97	53.97	13
9,037,809	725.46	725.46	2,383,583	191.33	191.33	21
13,931,409	592.73	592.73	3,269,986	139.12	139.12	19
1,502,746,601	390.36	289.04	187,145,886	48.61	36.00	11
7,288,521	456.67	287.19	1,195,698	74.92	47.11	14
59,743,295	1,143.61	1,057.42	8,247,437	157.87	145.97	12
96,204,044	705.41	705.41	20,259,680	148.55	148.55	17
24,739,016	1,287.28	1,287.28	7,547,727	392.74	392.74	23
2,298,803	861.62	451.63	1,480,862	555.05	290.94	39
3,637,135	24.23	24.23	6,037,676	40.22	40.22	62
3,246,474	286.74	260.84	442,618	39.09	35.56	12
817,412,113	420.28	314.76	129,525,358	66.60	49.88	14
64,651,639	676.34	676.34	24,830,192	259.75	259.75	28
17,757,514	541.68	541.68	9,440,829	287.99	287.99	35
38,322,539	1,329.67	1,329.67	7,068,428	245.25	245.25	16
9,753,010	454.73	351.93	1,182,778	55.15	42.68	11
57,000,000	274.60	274.60	11,300,000	54.44	54.44	17
32,800,560	758.64	758.64	7,515,707	173.83	173.83	19
14,393,880	1,030.34	714.30	3,120,454	223.37	154.85T18	
221,172,532	1,080.97	858.74	77,146,451	377.05	299.53	26
1,800,008,292	667.10	486.73	307,158,749	113.84	83.06	15
153,107,408	826.53	494.76	27,906,830	150.65	90.18	15
1,694,176	536.13	406.08	501,833	158.81	120.29	23
898,946	348.83	348.83	183,974	71.39	71.39	17
229,596,444	296.12	296.12	503,347,816	649.19	649.19	69
5,263,421,764	337.10	337.10	815,360,696	52.22	52.22	13
3,500,000	444.39	444.39	1,100,000	139.66	139.66	24
15,422,774	625.14	625.14	2,986,983	121.07	121.07	16
556,540,722	370.70	370.70	67,269,762	44.81	44.81	11
2,698,513,430	314.36	314.36	731,838,348	85.25	85.25	21
118,843,931	1,083.41	1,017.82	23,435,980	213.65	200.71	16
142,851,919	453.06	344.33	23,998,935	76.11	57.85	14

OF CHURCH FINANCES

CONGREGATIONAL FINANCES			BENEVOLENCES			
Total Congregational Contributions	Per Capita Full or Confirmed Members	Per Capita Inclusive Members	Total Benevolences	Per Capita Full or Confirmed Members	PerCapita Inclusive Members	Benevolences As a Percentage of Total Contributions
15,308,625,032	373.41	341.05	3,259,090,326	79.50	72.61	21
620,014,953	448.47	224.20	149,770,793	108.33	54.16	19

TRENDS IN SEMINARY ENROLLMENT

Data Provided by The Association of Theological Schools (ATS) in the United States and Canada

Table 1: ATS total student enrollment figures include the number of individuals enrolled in degree programs as well as persons enrolled in continuing non-degree programs of study. The growth in total enrollment shown by the figures in this table is a function of both increased enrollment in the seminaries and the increased number of schools admitted to ATS membership.

Table 1 Enrollments in ATS Member Schools

	1988	1989	1990	1991	1992	1993	1994
Number of Schools	202	202	208	208	216	216	226
Total Enrollment	55,746	56,208	59,172	60,086	63,674	63,618	65,174
By Nation:							
Canada	3,995	4,142	4,053	4,897	4,897	5,040	5,241
United States	51,751	52,066	55,119	55,438	58,777	58,578	59,933
By Membership:							
Accredited	52,129	51,913	54,235	55,217	57,727	59,401	60,575
Non-Accredited	3,616	3,258	4,955	4,869	5,444	4,217	4,599

Table 2: ATS computes enrollment both by the total number of individuals and the equivalent of full-time students (number of credit hours divided by the amount of credits considered to be a full-time student load). If all students were enrolled full time, the number of individuals and the full-time equivalents would be the same. Most recent enrollment changes, using these two methods of computing enrollment, suggest that more students are attending seminary on a part-time basis.

Table 2 Comparisons of Total Enrollment, 1978-1994

Total Numbers of Individuals and Their Full-Time Equivalents

Year	Total Persons (HC)	% Change	FTE Enrollment	% Change	FTE % of Total Person Enrollment
1978	46,460		36,219		78.0
1979	48,433	+4.2	36,795	+1.6	76.0
1980	49,611	+2.4	37,245	+1.2	75.1
1981	50,559	+1.9	37,254	+0.02	73.7
1982	52,620	+4.1	37,705	+1.2	71.7
1983	55,112	+4.7	38,923	+3.3	70.6
1984	56,466	+2.5	39,414	+1.3	69.8
1985	56,377	-0.16	38,841	-1.5	68.9
1986	56,328	-0.09	38,286	-1.4	68.0
1987	55,766	-1.0	38,329	+0.1	68.7
1988	55,746	-0.04	41,581	+7.8	74.6
1989	56,208	+0.8	42,183	+1.5	75.1
1990	59,172	+5.3	45,018	+6.7	76.1
1991	60,086	+1.5	44,047	-2.2	73.3
1992	63,676	+6.0	48,094	+9.2	75.5
1993	63,618	-0.09	48,236	+0.3	75.8
1994	65,174	+2.74	48,560	+1.7	74.5

Table 3: ATS-related schools in the United States and Canada offer a variety of degree programs. Table 3 displays enrollment by categories of degree programs. The Master of Divinity is the general degree most associated with ordained ministry. Since 1989, M.Div. enrollment in ATS schools has grown 5.3% (from 26,208 to 27,640). By contrast, the professional masters' programs which typically lead to non-ordained congregational or parachurch employment have grown 36% over the same six-year period (from 5,080 to 6,898). Other significant enrollment gains are in the academic masters' programs (from 4,186 in 1989 to 5,330 in 1994, an increase of 27%). Thus, while enrollment in U.S. and Canadian seminaries continues to increase, the vast majority of the increase is in programs that typically do not lead to ordination.

Table 3 Total Enrollment by Degree Categories

Degree Category	1989	1990	1991	1992	1993	1994
Master of Divinity	26,208	25,925	26,110	27,318	27,549	27,640
Professional Masters	5,080	5,284	5,805	5,812	6,536	6,898
Academic Masters	5,485	6,144	6,105	6,872	7,131	7,245
Doctor of Ministry	6,462	6,741	6,934	7,274	7,610	7,423
Other Professional Doctorates	542	676	664	687	692	418
Advanced Research	4,186	5,046	5,044	5,036	5,157	5,330
Others	8,215	9,187	9,235	10,485	8,754	10,220

Table 4: In 1994, women comprised 31.6% of the total enrollment in ATS-related schools. When ATS first began counting enrollment by gender in 1972, women comprised 10.2% of enrollment. Only once in the past two decades has the number of women enrolled in theological schools decreased from one year to the next.

Table 4 Women Theological Students

Year	Number of Women	% Annual Increase	% Total Enrollment
1972	3,358		10.2
1973	4,021	+19.7	11.8
1974	5,255	+30.7	14.3
1975	6,505	+23.8	15.9
1976	7,349	+13.0	17.1
1977	8,371	+13.9	18.5
1978	8,972	+7.2	19.3
1979	10,204	+13.7	21.1
1980	10,830	+6.1	21.8
1981	11,683	+7.9	23.1
1982	12,473	+6.8	23.7
1983	13,451	+7.8	24.4
1984	14,142	+5.1	25.0
1985	14,752	+3.0	25.8
1986	14,864	+2.0	26.4
1987	15,310	+3.0	27.0
1988	16,344	+6.8	29.3
1989	16,461	+0.7	29.3
1990	17,547	+6.6	29.6
1991	18,248	+4.0	30.0
1992	19,926	+9.2	31.0
1993	19,798	-.64	31.0
1994	20,613	+4.1	31.6

Tables 5, 6, 7: ATS has also closely monitored the enrollment of racial/ethnic minority students. Since 1977, the percentage of minority seminary enrollment has increased from 6.3% of total enrollment to 17.3% of total enrollment. Tables 5, 6, and 7 show the number of African American, Hispanic, and Pacific/Asian American students enrolled by year. While progress toward a more representative enrollment of theological students is evident, the percentage of racial/ethnic minority students in ATS schools continues to be smaller than the percentage of racial/ethnic minorities in the North American population as a whole.

Table 5 African American Student Enrollment

Year	Number of Students	% Annual Increase	% Total Enrollment
1977	1,759	+15.4	3.9
1978	1,919	+9.1	4.1
1979	2,043	+6.5	4.2
1980	2,205	+7.9	4.4
1981	2,371	+7.5	4.7
1982	2,576	+8.6	4.9
1983	2,881	+11.8	5.2
1984	2,917	+1.2	5.2
1985	3,046	+4.4	5.4
1986	3,277	+7.6	5.8
1987	3,379	+3.1	6.0
1988	3,662	+8.4	6.6
1989	3,961	+8.2	7.1
1990	4,275	+7.9	7.2
1991	4,671	+9.3	7.8
1992	5,568	+19.2	8.7
1993	5,235	-6.0	8.2
1994	5,526	+5.6	8.5

Table 6 Hispanic Student Enrollment

Year	Number of Students	% Annual Increase	% Total Enrollment
1977	601	+11.1	1.3
1978	681	+13.3	1.5
1979	822	+20.7	1.7
1980	894	+8.8	1.8
1981	955	+6.8	1.9
1982	1,180	+23.6	2.2
1983	1,381	+17.0	2.5
1984	1,314	-4.9	2.3
1985	1,454	+10.6	2.6
1986	1,297	-10.8	2.3
1987	1,385	+6.8	2.5
1988	1,415	+2.2	2.5
1989	1,490	+5.3	2.7
1990	1,913	+28.0	3.2
1991	1,627	-14.9	2.7
1992	1,691	+3.9	2.6
1993	1,792	+9.8	2.8
1994	1,800	+0.4	2.8

Table 7 Pacific/Asian American Student Enrollment

Year	Students	% Annual Increase	% Total Enrollment
1977	494		1.1
1978	499	+1.0	1.1
1979	577	+15.6	1.2
1980	602	+4.3	1.2
1981	716	+18.9	1.4
1982	707	-1.3	1.3
1983	779	+10.2	1.4
1984	1,130	+45.1	2.0
1985	1,195	+5.8	2.1
1986	1,393	+16.6	2.5
1987	1,645	+18.0	2.9
1988	1,963	+19.3	3.5
1989	2,065	+5.2	3.7
1990	2,444	+18.4	4.1
1991	2,653	+8.6	4.4
1992	3,145	+18.5	4.9
1993	3,634	+15.5	5.7
1994	3,880	+6.8	6.0

IV
A CALENDAR OF RELIGIOUS DATES
1996 – 1999

This Calendar presents for a four-year period the major days of religious observance for Christians, Jews, Baha'is, Buddhists, and Muslims; and, within the Christian community, major dates observed by Roman Catholic, Orthodox, Episcopal, and Lutheran churches. Within each of these communions many other days of observance, such as saints' days, exist, but only those regarded as major are listed. Thus, for example, for the Roman Catholic Church, mainly the "solemnities" are listed. Dates of interest to many Protestant communions are also included.

In the Orthodox dates, immovable observances are listed in accordance with the Gregorian calendar. Movable dates (those depending on the date of Easter) often will differ from Western dates, since Paschal (Easter) in the Orthodox communions does not always fall on the same day as in the Western churches. For Orthodox churches that use the old Julian calendar, observances are held thirteen days later than listed here.

For Jews and Muslims, who follow differing lunar calendars, the dates of major observances are translated into Gregorian dates. Since the actual beginning of a new month in the Islamic calendar is determined by the appearance of the new moon, the corresponding dates given here on the Gregorian calendar may vary slightly. Following the lunar calendar, Muslim dates fall eleven days earlier each year on the Gregorian calendar, thus the month of Ramadan for 1998 actually begins in 1997.

Wil Krieger from the Ecumenical Book Co., 4286 Putting Green Dr., San Antonio, TX 78217 supplied information for the preparation of this calendar. The Ecumenical Book Co. supplies religious calendars.

(Note: "RC" stands for Roman Catholic, "O" for Orthodox, "E" for Episcopal, "L" for Lutheran, "ECU" for Ecumenical, "M" for Muslim, "B" for Buddhist.)

Event	1996	1997	1998	1999
New Year's Day (RC- Solemnity of Mary; O- Circumcision of Jesus Christ; E- Feast of the Holy Name; L- Name of Jesus)	Jan 01	Jan 01	Jan 01	Jan 01
New Year's Day (B)	Jan 01	Jan 01	Jan 01	Jan 01
Epiphany (Armenian Christmas)	Jan 06	Jan 06	Jan 06	Jan 06
Feast Day of St. John the Baptist (O)	Jan 07	Jan 07	Jan 07	Jan 07
First Sunday After Epiphany (Feast of the Baptism of Our Lord)	Jan 07	Jan 12	Jan 11	Jan 10
Ho-on-ko (Buddhist memorial for Shinran Shonin)	Jan 16	Jan 16	Jan 16	Jan 16
Week of Prayer for Christian Unity (ECU)	Jan 18 to Jan 25	Jan 18 to Jan 25	Jan 18 to Jan 25	Jan 18 to Jan 25
Ecumenical Sunday (ECU)	Jan 21	Jan 19	Jan 18	Jan 24
Week of Prayer for Christian Unity, Canada (ECU)	Jan 21 to Jan 28	Jan 19 to Jan 26	Jan 18 to Jan 25	Jan 24 to Jan 31
First Day of the Month of Ramadan (M)	Jan 22	Jan 10	Dec 30 '97	Dec 19 '98
Presentation of Jesus in the Temple (O- The Meeting of Our Lord and Savior Jesus Christ)	Feb 02	Feb 02	Feb 02	Feb 02
Nirvana Day (B)	Feb 15	Feb 15	Feb 15	Feb 15
Brotherhood Week (Interfaith)	Feb 18 to Feb 24	Feb 16 to Feb 22	Feb 15 to Feb 21	Feb 21 to Feb 27
Last Sunday After Epiphany (L-Transfiguration)	Feb 18	Feb 09	Feb 22	Feb 14
Id al- Fitr (M) (Festival of the End of Ramadan, celebrated on the first day of the month of Shawwal)	Feb 20	Feb 08	Jan 29	Jan 18
Ash Wednesday (Western Churches)	Feb 21	Feb 12	Feb 25	Feb 17
Easter Lent Begins (Eastern Orthodox)	Feb 26	Mar 10	Mar 02	Fe 22
World Day of Prayer (ECU)	Mar 01	Mar 07	Mar 06	Mar 05
Fasting Season begins (Baha'i, 19 days)	Mar 02	Mar 02	Mar 02	Mar 02
Purim (Jewish)	Mar 05	Mar 23	Mar 12	Mar 02
Joseph, Husband of Mary (RC, E, L)	Mar 19	Mar 19	Mar 19	Mar 19
Feast of Naw-Ruz (Baha'i New Year)	Mar 21	Mar 21	Mar 21	Mar 21
Spring Ohigan (B) (Gathering to Praise the Buddha)	Mar 21	Mar 21	Mar 21	Mar 21
The Annunciation (O) (L-Apr 01; RC, E-Apr 08)	Mar 25	Mar 25	Mar 25	Mar 25
Holy Week (Western Churches)	Mar 31 to Apr 07	Mar 23 to Mar 29	Apr 05 to Apr 11	Mar 28 to Apr 03

Event	1996	1997	1998	1999
Palm Sunday (Sunday of the Passion-Western Churches).	Mar 31	Mar 23	Apr 05	Mar 28
Holy Thursday (Western Churches)	Apr 04	Mar 27	Apr 09	Apr 01
First Day of Passover (Jewish, 8 Days)	Apr 04	Apr 22	Apr 11	Apr 01
Good Friday (Friday of the Passion of Our Lord) (Western Churches)	Apr 05	Mar 28	Apr 10	Apr 02
Easter (Western Churches)	Apr 07	Mar 30	Apr 12	Apr 04
Palm Sunday (O)	Apr 07	Apr 20	Apr 12	Apr 04
Holy Week (O)	Apr 08 to Apr 12	Apr 21 to Apr 25	Apr 13 to Apr 17	Apr 05 to Apr 09
Buddha Day/Hanamatsuri (B)	Apr 08	Apr 08	Apr 08	Apr 08
Holy Thursday (O)	Apr 11	Apr 24	Apr 16	Apr 08
Holy (Good) Friday, Burial of Jesus Christ (O)	Apr 12	Apr 25	Apr 17	Apr 09
Paschal (Orthodox Easter)	Apr 14	Apr 27	Apr 19	Apr 11
Feast of Ridvan (Baha'i) (Declaration of Baha'u'llah)	Apr 21 to May 2	Apr 21 to May 2	Apr 21 to May 2	Apr 21 to May 2
Id al-Adha (I) (Festival of Sacrifice at time of annual Pilgrimage to Mecca)	Apr 28	Apr 17	Apr 07	Mar 27
National Day of Prayer	May 02	May 01	May 07	May 06
May Fellowsip Day (ECU)	May 03	May 02	May 01	May 07
Rural Life Sunday (ECU)	May 12	May 11	May 10	May 09
Ascension Day (Western Churches)	May 16	May 08	May 21	May 13
First Day of the Month of Muharram (I) (Beginning of Muslim Liturgical Year)	May 19	May 08	Apr 27	Apr 17
Gotane/Shinran Shonin Day (B)	May 21	May 21	May 21	May 21
Ascension Day (O)	May 23	Jun 05	May 28	May 20
Declaration of the Bab (Baha'i)	May 23	May 23	May 23	May 23
First Day of Shavuot (Jewish, 2 Days)	May 24	Jun 11	May 31	May 21
Pentecost (Whitsunday) (Western Churches)	May 26	May 18	May 31	May 23
Ascension of Baha'u'llah (Baha'i)	May 29	May 29	May 29	May 29
Visitation of the Blessed Virgin Mary (RC, E, L)	May 31	May 31	May 31	May 31
Pentecost (O)	Jun 02	Jun 15	Jun 07	May 30
Holy Trinity (RC, E, L)	Jun 09	May 25	Jun 07	May 30
Corpus Christi (RC)	Jun 13	May 29	Jun 14	Jun 06
Sacred Heart of Jesus (RC)	Jun 14	Jun 05	Jun 19	Jun 11
Nativity of St. John the Bapist (RC, E, L)	Jun 24	Jun 24	Jun 24	Jun 24
Saint Peter and Saint Paul, Apostles (RC, E, L)	Jun 29	Jun 29	Jun 29	Jun 29
Feast Day of the Twelve Apostles of Christ (O)	Jun 30	Jun 30	Jun 30	Jun 30
Martyrdom of the Bab (Baha'i)	Jul 09	Jul 09	Jul 09	Jul 09
Mawlid al-Nabi (M) (Anniversary of Prophet Muhammed's Birthday)	Jul 28	Jul 17	Jul 06	Jun 26
Transfiguration of the Lord (RC, O, E)	Aug 06	Aug 06	Aug 06	Aug 06
Feast of the Blessed Virgin Mary (E) (RC-Assumption of Blessed Mary the Virgin; O- Falling Asleep (Domition) of the Blessed Virgin)	Aug 15	Aug 15	Aug 15	Aug 15
Buddhist Churches of America Founding Day	Sep 01	Sep 01	Sep 01	Sep 01
The Birth of the Blessed Virgin (RC, O)	Sep 08	Sep 08	Sep 08	Sep 08
Holy Cross Day (O- Adoration of the Holy Cross; RC- Triumph of the Cross)	Sep 14	Sep 14	Sep 14	Sep 14
First Day of Rosh Hashanah (Jewish, 2 Days)	Sep 14	Oct 02	Sep 21	Sep 11
Autumn Ohigan (B)	Sep 23	Sep 23	Sep 23	Sep 23
Yom Kippur (Jewish)	Sep 23	Oct 11	Sep 30	Sep 20
First Day of Sukkot (Jewish, 7 Days)	Sep 28	Oct 16	Oct 05	Sep 25
World Communion Sunday (ECU)	Oct 06	Oct 05	Oct 04	Oct 03
Laity Sunday (ECU)	Oct 13	Oct 12	Oct 11	Oct 10
Thanksgiving Day (Canada)	Oct 14	Oct 13	Oct 12	Oct 11
Shemini Atzeret (Jewish)	Oct 05	Oct 23	Oct 12	Oct 02
Simhat Torah (Jewish)	Oct 06	Oct 24	Oct 13	Oct 03
Birth of the Bab (Baha'i)	Oct 20	Oct 20	Oct 20	Oct 20
Reformation Sunday (L)	Oct 27	Oct 26	Oct 25	Oct 31
Reformation Day (L)	Oct 31	Oct 31	Oct 31	Oct 31
All Saints Day (RC, E, L)	Nov 01	Nov 01	Nov 01	Nov 01
World Community Day (ECU)	Nov 01	Nov 07	Nov 06	Nov 05

Event	1996	1997	1998	1999
Stewardship Day (ECU)	Nov 10	Nov 09	Nov 08	Nov 14
Birth of Baha'u'llah (Baha'i)	Nov 12	Nov 12	Nov 12	Nov 12
Bible Sunday (ECU)	Nov 17	Nov 16	Nov 15	Nov 21
Presentation of the Blessed Virgin Mary in the Temple (also Presentation of the Theotokos) (O)	Nov 21	Nov 21	Nov 21	Nov 21
Last Sunday After Pentecost (RC, L- Feast of Christ the King)	Nov 24	Nov 23	Nov 22	Nov 21
Thanksgiving Sunday (U.S.)	Nov 24	Nov 23	Nov 22	Nov 21
The Day of the Covenant (Baha'i)	Nov 26	Nov 26	Nov 26	Nov 26
Thanksgiving Day (U.S.)	Nov 28	Nov 27	Nov 26	Nov 25
Ascension of 'Abdu'l-Baha (Baha'i)	Nov 28	Nov 28	Nov 28	Nov 28
Feast Day of St. Andrew the Apostle (RC, O, E, L)	Nov 30	Nov 30	Nov 30	Nov 30
First Sunday of Advent	Dec 01	Nov 30	Nov 29	Nov 28
First Day of Hanukkah (Jewish, 8 Days)	Dec 06	Dec 24	Dec 14	Dec 04
Bodhi Day (B, Enlightenment)	Dec 08	Dec 08	Dec 08	Dec 08
Immaculate Conception of the Blessed Virgin Mary (RC)	Dec 08	Dec 08	Dec 08	Dec 08
Fourth Sunday of Advent (Sunday before Christmas)	Dec 22	Dec 21	Dec 20	Dec 19
Christmas (Except Armenian)	Dec 25	Dec 25	Dec 25	Dec 25

IV

INDEXES

ORGANIZATIONS

INDEXES

INDEXES

INDEXES

INDIVIDUALS

This list contains the names of people found in the listings of Cooperative Organizations, Religious Bodies, Regional Ecumenical Agencies, Seminaries and Bible Schools, and Periodicals.

INDEXES

INDEXES

INDEXES

LINCOLN CHRISTIAN COLLEGE AND SEMINARY